SAP® BusinessObjects™ CMS Queries and Java SDK Programming

First Edition

Copyright © 2020 by Joe Peters

ISBN: 9781679199349

www.bosdkbook.com

ii

Contents

iv

Introduction

The administration and management of a typical SAP BusinessObjects environment involve numerous kinds of content and related activities. User IDs must be created, assigned to groups, and later disabled or deleted. Permissions must be applied to objects to ensure appropriate security. Validations must be conducted regularly to ensure that these activities are performed correctly.

Traditionally, administrators use the *Central Management Console* (CMC) for this type of maintenance. As well-suited as it is to the job, it doesn't do *everything*, and it is by nature an interactive user application – little support is provided for automated execution of actions or for performing a large number of actions in batch.

The *SAP BusinessObjects Enterprise SDK* is the tool to unlock this additional functionality. With it, it is possible to create utilities to automate many of the repetitive tasks that are typically done in the CMC. It can perform many, many other functions as well, such as extracting system data, integrating SAP BusinessObjects with other applications, and enabling end-users or developers to interact with the system in different ways.

As with other application SDKs, the SAP BusinessObjects Enterprise SDK requires the creation of *programs* (Java, in our case). Thus, it is necessary to not only have knowledge of the SDK object model but also skill in the language that the program is to be written in. Naturally, this means that an investment of time and resources must be made in obtaining the knowledge and skill needed to write such a program. We believe this investment will return dividends many times over, as SDK-based programs can not only add to the value of an SAP BusinessObjects system but reduce the time and sources needed to maintain it. Without exaggeration, it would be possible for SDK utilities to perform tasks that would take literally hundreds or thousands of hours if done manually.

Structure

This book started out as *SAP BusinessObjects SDK Programming in Java*. As we began to lay out the book outline, we found that a large portion of it was consumed by CMS query topics. Although our original intent was to cover the CMS query language only as far as necessary to support SDK programming, we decided that the topics should stand on their own. Therefore, Part One is devoted entirely to the CMS query and related topics. Even if you never write a line of an SDK program, you can use the knowledge gained from Part One to write CMS queries to extract valuable information from your SAP BusinessObjects environment.

Part Two is devoted to the BI Platform Java SDK, although we begin with a quick overview of the other SDKs that are available for the SAP BusinessObjects platform. We have used Eclipse for our development environment, and so we will discuss how to set up Eclipse with the BI Platform SDK. The remainder of Part Two includes an in-depth review of commonly-used interfaces and classes and a number of tasks that benefit from the SDK.

Who This Book Is For

We developed this book with SAP BusinessObjects administrators in mind – those individuals charged with deploying, maintaining, and securing SAP BusinessObjects environments. Although the SAP BusinessObjects Enterprise SDK can be used for many, many, tasks, we are focusing primarily on tasks that pertain to administrative functions.

We are also considering Java developers who are tasked with integrating with an SAP BusinessObjects system or constructing a new application to display or manage SAP BusinessObjects content. Although we are not going in-depth into SAP BusinessObjects core functionality, we do cover some of the fundamentals as they pertain to interfacing with other applications.

What This Book Is Not

- A tutorial on using, developing content for, or administrating SAP BusinessObjects. Although we explain some SAP BusinessObjects concepts along the way, it is expected that the reader has some working knowledge of this topic.

- A Java tutorial. In order to develop programs with the SDK, the reader is expected to have a solid working knowledge of Java programming concepts.

- Comprehensive. There are many components of the SAP BusinessObjects suite, including Crystal Reports, Lumira, Data Integrator, and many more. This book focuses on SDK programming relating to the core SAP BusinessObjects BI platform – working with CMS objects and related metadata. Most notably we do not go in-depth into Web Intelligence or Crystal report programming. These two topics could consume a few books on their own.

- Authoritative. While the SAP BusinessObjects Java SDKs are fairly well documented, the CMS query syntax is not. Much of the content in this book regarding CMS queries is drawn from the authors' own observations and unofficial content from the web. As such, the material in this book is not **guaranteed** to present the CMS query syntax accurately.

Licensing

Your ability to use the various components of the SAP BusinessObjects suite, including the

SDK, may be limited by your organization's software license with SAP. It should not be assumed that since the applications and supporting files are installed that their usage falls within the scope of the license. We strongly recommend that you confirm that your license permits your intended usage of the SDK.

Companion Site

The companion site for this book is at www.bosdkbook.com. Program listings are available for download, and are freely distributable. Updates on new editions will be announced here, as well as any corrections to this book. Feedback is greatly appreciated and can be submitted from the site.

Required Software & Setup

A basic installation of the SAP BusinessObjects BI platform server software is required In order to perform most of the activities discussed in this book. The basic installation includes the core services such as the Central Management Server (CMS), Input/Output File Repository Servers, and a web/application server (Tomcat, by default).

You will need the following:

- an Enterprise user ID and password, to use any of the SAP BusinessObjects web applications (such as BI launch pad, CMC, and Query Builder), and to use in any SDK program that connects to the server.

- the URLs for the web applications. By default, they are:

    ○ BI launch pad: http://<*server*>:8080/BOE/BI

    ○ CMC: http://<*server*>:8080/BOE/CMC

    ○ Query Builder: http://<*server*>:8080/AdminTools

- the SAP BusinessObjects CMS server hostname and CMS port (default port is 6400), to connect via the SDK.

You will need a Java JDK installed on the workstation that will be compiling or executing SDK programs. The JDK must be of a version ***equal to or greater than*** the version of the SAP BusinessObjects SDK libraries that you are using. This should not be a challenge, as even the newer SDK libraries are compatible with older versions.

- For XI3, use Java JDK 1.4 or newer

- For BI4.0, use Java JDK 1.5 or newer

- For BI4.1, use Java JDK 1.6 or newer

- For BI4.2, use Java JDK 1.8 or newer

Although not required, we strongly recommend the use of a Java Integrated Development Environment ("IDE"). In this book, our samples and workflows are based on Eclipse. You may choose to use a different IDE, or none at all (and use the Java command line tools to compile, debug, and execute), but you will need to adjust the workflows accordingly.

Formatting Notes

In Part One of this book, we will be executing several CMS queries in the Query Builder application bundled with SAP BusinessObjects. The Query Builder formats query results in a vertical table, with each InfoObject in the result occupying a block of properties. An example query result is shown in Illustration 1.

SAP BusinessObjects Business Intelligence platform - Query Builder

Number of InfoObject(s) returned: **7**

1/7   top

Properties	
SI_NAME	User Folders
SI_ID	18

2/7   top

Properties	
SI_NAME	Root Folder
SI_ID	23

3/7   top

Properties	
SI_NAME	Categories
SI_ID	45

4/7   top

Properties	
SI_NAME	Personal Categories

Illustration 1: Query Builder result

In cases where it is most appropriate, we present the data in the same structure, but as text rather than a screenshot:

SI_NAME	**User Folders**
SI_ID	18

SI_NAME	**Root Folder**
SI_ID	23

SI_NAME	**Categories**
SI_ID	45

SI_NAME	**Personal Categories**
SI_ID	47

In other scenarios, we present the query result in a single table::

SI_NAME	SI_ID
User Folders	18
Root Folder	23
Categories	45
Personal Categories	47

Some query results produce objects with nested property bags, as seen below:

SAP BusinessObjects Business Intelligence platform - Query Builder

Number of InfoObject(s) returned: **107**

1/107   top

Properties			
SI_FILES	SI_NUM_FILES	1	
	SI_FILE1	aqtkbbsqn4noj3ydf.sw1ly-guid[29ae756a-b41a-4535-abcd-3b40091744955].wid	
	SI_VALUE1	55507	
	SI_PATH	frs://Input/a_130/015/000/3970/	
SI_ID	3970		

Illustration 2: Query result with property bags

Results such as this are presented as a hierarchical list:

SI_FILES

    SI_NUM_FILES

        1

    SI_FILE1

        aqtkbbsqn4noj3ydf.sw1ly-guid[29ae756a-b41a-4535-abcd-3b40091744955].wid

    SI_VALUE1

        55507

    SI_PATH

        frs://Input/a_130/015/000/3970/

SI_ID

    3970

We hope these formatting choices present the data in a more easy-to-read manner than the original screenshots.

Part One – The InfoStore

A typical SAP BusinessObjects cluster contains dozens, if not hundreds of different types of objects, including documents, users, groups, universes, connections, and many more. The primary mechanism for interacting with these objects in the SDK is the *CMS Query*, a plain text, SQL-like query language. CMS queries provide a unified, familiar syntax for accessing the various objects in a cluster. Since CMS Queries are ubiquitous in SDK programming, being proficient with them is the first step to writing efficient, effective SDK applications. For this reason, we cover CMS Queries prior to "real" SDK programming topics.

We begin this part with an overview of the CMS Query syntax; its similarities and differences from standard SQL, and the various types of data fields involved. From there, we delve into the commonly-used properties that are retrieved in CMS Queries. Finally, we cover some advanced topics, including Relationship Queries, Path Queries, and the physical repository.

Chapter 1 - CMS Query Basics

While invaluable to the SDK programmer, CMS queries can also be used for other non-programming purposes. A simple web application (*Query Builder*) packaged with BI launch pad enables users to perform CMS queries without actually having to write any code[1]. There are many use cases where this functionality can provide value; as an example, an SAP BusinessObjects administrator may want to quickly identify all reports owned by a particular user. This is a simple request with a CMS query but it would be quite challenging to obtain otherwise.

To access the Query Builder, use the following URL on XI3 or BI4:

```
http://<server>:8080/AdminTools
```

We'll start our discussion of CMS queries with a simple example of a request for the names and IDs of all top-level public folders:

```
select si_name, si_id
  from ci_infoobjects
 where si_parentid = 23
```

Due to the relationship of SAP BusinessObjects to relational databases, it is assumed that many readers of this book have familiarity with SQL and will recognize the query above as such. However, the CMS query syntax can only be best described as "SQL-ish"; only the most basic SQL functionality is supported, and even some of that functionality is quite different from standard SQL. It is essential to start from a clean slate, and not make any assumptions about the behavior (or existence) of standard SQL functionality in CMS queries.

We'll begin this section with some basic CMS query concepts, followed by a discussion about the query clauses (select.. from.. where.. order by). We finish with an in-depth examination of the more advanced query topics.

Core Concepts

CMS queries are used to extract metadata from an SAP BusinessObjects cluster. Every independent object in a cluster is associated with an *InfoObject*, a uniquely identifiable unit in the CMS repository. All InfoObjects have *properties* – such as name, ID, owner, and description. These properties make up the result set of CMS queries – they can be SELECTed, or used in WHERE or ORDER BY clauses, and are what's displayed in the query output.

---

1   The Query Builder application internally uses the Java SDK.

Applied Security

The security rights of the user running a CMS query are applied to the results. If a user has *View* rights to one root-level Public Folder but has been denied access to a second folder, that second folder will not be included in any CMS query that the user executes. This is a critical feature – it means that SDK applications consumed by SAP BusinessObjects users ensure that the same security restrictions are applied as if the users were working in BI launch pad. That is, a user's access to content in SAP BusinessObjects is applied to any custom-built SDK application as well. It is not necessary, in the SDK application, to determine whether or not a user has access to something – inherently, by executing a CMS query as that user, all appropriate security restrictions are applied.

No Write-Back

The CMS query syntax includes only a single statement: SELECT. There is no support for any form of write-back operation such as the standard INSERT, UPDATE, or DELETE statements in SQL. For this reason, CMS queries can be considered *safe*, since as a CMS query can run without risk of corrupting the CMS or changing objects in any way[2].

CMS Query Structure

CMS queries include a SELECT clause to specify the properties to be displayed, and a FROM clause to specify the tables that contain the requested objects. An optional WHERE clause may be provided to restrict the objects displayed, and an optional ORDER BY clause specifies the sort order of the result set.

We cover each of these clauses in detail below.

SELECT

As with standard SQL, the SELECT statement specifies the properties (*fields*) to return. When using the Query Builder, the SELECT clause determines the properties to display on the screen. When using a CMS query in an SDK program, the SELECT determines the properties that are available to the program.

The syntax of the SELECT clause can be described in a railroad diagram as:

---

2   We are strictly speaking of the action of running a CMS query, such as would be done in Query Builder. The Java SDK supports full manipulation of objects, and as such has a greater opportunity for inadvertent damage.

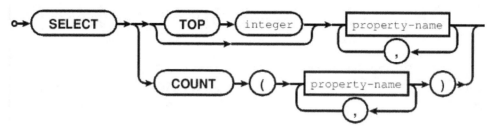

Figure 1: SELECT syntax

The word SELECT, as well as FROM, WHERE, ORDER BY, and all operators and property names, are case insensitive. In fact, the only requirement for case sensitivity in a CMS query is when using CUIDs, GUIDs, or RUIDs in a condition. Repeated white space (such as spaces and tabs) in the query is ignored. The following two queries are functionally identical:

```
select si_id from ci_infoobjects where si_name = 'report1' and si_children between 1
and 5
```

```
SELECT SI_ID
  FROM CI_infoobjects
 WHERE si_name = 'REPORT1'
       AND si_children BETWEEN 1 AND 5
```

Although the syntax appears identical to standard SQL, there are several differences:

- The order of properties in SELECT is unimportant (the order does not affect how the result is displayed).

- The only aggregate function available is COUNT(), and its use is very different from standard SQL. COUNT() is described in detail below.

- There is no DISTINCT clause, nor arithmetic or string operators.

- Table names in SELECT (CI_INFOOBJECTS.SI_NAME) are not required and produce an error if used.

- *Incorrect property names do not generate an error!* This behavior is likely to cause frustration for the new user, as you may generate a valid-looking query such as:

    ```
    select si_id,si_name,si_parent_id
    ```
    ...only to find that the result only includes SI_ID and SI_NAME. (The correct property name is SI_PARENTID).

    This behavior is due to the inherent nature of properties, in that not all objects have all properties. That is, the query parser can't know which properties are valid and which aren't until the query completes.

A TOP N statement can be used to restrict the number of results in the query. This functions similarly to standard SQL in that it limits the result to the specified number of objects after ordering as taken place. Consider the following query:

```
select top 15 si_name
from ci_infoobjects
where si_kind = 'webi'
order by si_name
```

This query sorts all objects of kind 'webi' by name, then return the first 15 objects. It is important to note that the ordering occurs *first*; the query engine does **not** extract the first 15 objects, then sort them by name.

If not specified in a query, an implied TOP 1000 is applied[3]. Thus, unless the query includes a TOP statement, at most 1,000 objects are returned . Note that the default value can be overridden with a lower **or higher** number – for example, TOP 1000000000 will display up to a billion objects. Naturally, with the more objects displayed, the more system resources are needed, and the more time the query can take.

The TOP statement is generally used in conjunction with the ORDER BY clause, which is covered below in more detail.

It is possible to retrieve a specific "page" of query results using TOP M-N. In the example above, we had retrieved the first 15 WebI reports by name. To retrieve the second page (i.e., the 16th to 30th report), we would execute the following query:

```
select top 16-30 si_name
from ci_infoobjects
where si_kind = 'webi'
order by si_name
```

There are a few special operators that can be used in the SELECT clause instead of listing specific names of properties: STATIC, DYNAMIC, RELATIONSHIPS, and *

The special character * can be used to indicate that all properties should be retrieved and functions the same as in standard SQL. For example:

```
select *
from ci_infoobjects
where si_kind = 'webi'
```

This returns all properties for each InfoObject of kind "webi". As a best practice, the * character should be avoided in queries since it can potentially cause a large amount of data to be processed by the server and client. However, it is useful for data exploration – examining which properties are available for objects. Thus, it is common to use the * character when first building queries, but then to replace it with the specific properties needed.

Object properties are either *static* (actually stored as a value in the CMS database), or dynamic (calculated on the fly when the query is executed). An example of a static property is SI_ID – this property value is stored in the CMS repository for all objects. An example of a dynamic property is SI_CHILDREN – this property is not stored, but has to be calculated by the

---

3   This default value (of 1,000) can be changed system-wide with a registry change on the CMS server machine.

query engine whenever it is selected in a query.

Most object properties are static. To select only the static properties, we use the `static` keyword:

```
select static
  from ci_infoobjects
 where si_kind = 'webi'
```

To retrieve only the dynamically-generated properties, we use the `dynamic` keyword:

```
select dynamic
  from ci_infoobjects
 where si_kind = 'webi'
```

Keywords can be combined with property names. To retrieve all dynamic properties but also include names and descriptions, we use:

```
select si_description,dynamic,si_name
  from ci_infoobjects
 where si_kind = 'webi'
```

A number of object properties are used to relate to other objects. Web Intelligence objects, for example, may contain a `SI_UNIVERSE` property which contains a list of IDs for universes associated with the report. We can retrieve all of the relationship objects with the `relationships` keyword:

```
select relationships
  from ci_infoobjects
 where si_kind = 'webi'
```

Note that the use of these keywords (`static`, `dynamic`, `relationships`, and `*`) do not change in any way in which objects are retrieved in a query – they only define which *properties* of those retrieved objects are displayed in the result.

In place of a list of properties to display, a query can alternatively use the `COUNT()` function with one or more parameters; the returns the number of objects that contain the listed properties. For example, the following query returns the number of WebI objects in a system:

```
select count(si_id)
from ci_infoobjects
where si_kind = 'webi'
```

The query may produce a result like:

```
SI_AGGREGATE_COUNT SI_ID   24612
```

SI_AGGREGATE_COUNT is a special, "virtual" property that holds the results of COUNT queries. In this case, we see that the total number of WebI objects is 24,612.

Multiple properties can be provided in the COUNT function:

```
select count(si_id,si_name,si_kind,si_description,si_path)
from ci_infoobjects
where si_kind = 'webi'
```

The result of this query is:

SI_AGGREGATE_COUNT

    SI_ID
        24612

    SI_NAME
        17288

    SI_KIND
        1

    SI_DESCRIPTION
        592

    SI_PATH
        0

The behavior of COUNT() is equivalent to COUNT(DISTINCT …) in standard SQL. That is, the result reflects the count of *distinct non-null property values*.

Consider the following CMS repository subset:

si_id	si_kind	si_name	si_description
1	WebI	Report1	
2	WebI	Report1	
3	WebI	Report2	My report

Running this query on the above system:

```
select count(si_id,si_kind,si_name,si_description,si)path)
from ci_infoobjects
```

...produces:

SI_AGGREGATE_COUNT

    SI_ID
        3

    SI_KIND
        1

    SI_NAME
        2

    SI_DESCRIPTION

2
SI_PATH
0

The result of the query reflects the fact that our cluster includes three distinct IDs, one distinct *kind*, and two distinct *names*.

Note that the count of SI_DESCRIPTION is 2, even though there is only one object with a populated description. This is because all of our objects *have an SI_DESCRIPTION property*; even though two of them are empty strings (""). Thus, we have two distinct descriptions in our system: one blank string and one of "My report".

The count of SI_PATH is zero since none of the objects in our query have that property.

> *Key point: when counting objects, the most efficient property to use in the COUNT function is SI_ID, e.g.: select count(SI_ID).*

It is not possible to mix COUNTed properties and non-COUNTed properties in the same query. As a result, there is no need for, nor support of, a GROUP BY clause in CMS query syntax. The following query is not valid and will produce a parse error:

```
select si_kind,count(si_id)
from ci_infoobjects
```

To produce the desired result of a count of objects by SI_KIND, separate queries would need to be run for each SI_KIND value:

```
select count(si_id)
from ci_infoobjects
where si_kind = 'webi'
```

or, simply select all objects and count them up in a separate process:

```
select si_id,si_kind
from ci_infoobjects
```

FROM

The FROM clause specifies the tables from which the objects are to be selected. The table (or tables) to choose are determined by the object *kinds* to be retrieved. There are only three tables that are available to be be used in a CMS query:

CI_INFOOBJECTS *(documents, folders, instances)*

CI_SYSTEMOBJECTS *(users, groups, servers)*

CI_APPOBJECTS *(universes, data connections, events)*

The syntax of the FROM clause is simply:

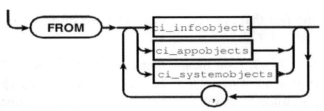

Figure 2: FROM syntax

The table (or tables) to use in your query are determined by the types ("*kinds*") of objects you wish to retrieve.   To query for WebI documents, for example, you would choose CI_INFOOBJECTS. The kinds listed above are only a small subset of what is included in each table – we will cover additional kinds later on.

The FROM clause is more straightforward as compared to standard SQL. There is no support for joins of any kind and no table aliases.

Although joins are not supported, it is possible to list more than one table in the FROM clause, in order to select objects from different tables in one query.

Consider this query:

```
select si_id
from ci_infoobjects,ci_systemobjects
where si_name = 'fred'
```

Unlike standard SQL, this query does not produce a Cartesian join, in which the result set is the product of rows from both tables. Rather, the query simply apples the WHERE conditions to each table in sequence, then produces one combined result. In this example, the result would be a list of IDs that are associated with objects having the name "fred", from CI_INFOOBJECTS and CI_SYSTEMOBJECTS.

Note that the SI_ID property in the SELECT clause does not include a table specifier of CI_INFOOBJECTS or CI_SYSTEMOBJECTS. These table names are not needed in SELECT or WHERE, and will produce an error if they are included.

Simply put, the list of tables in the FROM clause specifies the tables to be searched for results.

WHERE

The WHERE clause reduces the objects produced by the query using the specified conditions. The WHERE clause is optional – if it is not specified, then the query returns **all objects** in the repository[4].

---

4   More specifically, all objects in the tables referenced in the FROM clause.

As with the other clauses, the syntax of WHERE in CMS query syntax has a few significant differences as compared to standard SQL that may cause unexpected results:

As in SELECT, the CMS query engine does not produce an error if a property name is misspelled; it simply produces no results. Neither of these two conditions produces results[5]:

```
where foobar = 'fred'
where foobar != 'fred'
```

This behavior makes sense from the perspective of the query engine. It is checking each object for a property named "foobar"; since none exists, the comparison to "fred" never happens.

String comparison on most properties is case-insensitive! This is fortunate since the CMS query syntax includes no string conversion functions that would enable a case-insensitive search if it were case-sensitive. Thus, the following conditions produce equal results:

```
where si_name = 'fred'
where si_name = 'Fred'
where si_name = 'FrEd'
```

The one exception to this rule is alphanumeric IDs such as CUID, RUID, GUID. When used in a WHERE condition, these values must have the correct case.

It is possible to perform a case-sensitive search If so desired, by exploiting the LIKE operator. See page 22.

We will discuss datatypes in detail later in this chapter, but it is necessary to briefly talk about them with respect to specifying values in a WHERE condition.

Strings

When writing a condition that references a string property such as SI_NAME, the value should be enclosed in single quotes. For example:

```
where si_name = 'fred'
```

If the value to be specified in the condition has a double-quote, then it must be replaced with two single quotes ("). To query for a report named *Fred's Report*, use:

```
where si_name = 'fred''s report'
```

The query engine performs some amount of data conversion if necessary. If, for example, our system contained a report named "100", then the following condition would successfully return it:

```
where si_name = 100
```

---

5   *Unless* you have actually created objects custom properties named "foobar" in your system.

This is not a best practice, however; the value of 100 should be enclosed in quotes since it is technically a string.

Numerics

Conditions on properties that are of a numeric datatype should specify the value without quotes, for example:

```
where si_children = 1
```

As with strings, the query engine performs data conversion on numerics. Although not recommended, the above query could be written as:

```
where si_children = '1'
```

Booleans

Applying conditions on booleans is not **quite** as simple as it could be. Although Boolean properties display in Query Builder as "`true`" or "`false`", conditions on these properties must instead use the values 1 or 0 (respectively). For example, to retrieve document instances (where SI_INSTANCE has a value of true), use:

```
where si_instance = 1
```

Dates

Writing conditions on date properties may appear complicated at first glance, but it is fairly simple once a few key points are understood.

Generally, conditions on dates do not use the = operator since date properties contain a time component, and the specified value would have to match completely, down to the millisecond if = were to be used. Rather, date conditions usually use the < or > operators, or BETWEEN ... AND ..., for example:

```
where si_update_ts between '2015/09/20 00:00:00'
                       and '2015/09/21 00:00:00'

where si_update_ts >= '2015/09/20 00:00:00'
```

The date value in a condition must be entered in "yyyy mm dd hh mm ss sss" format (including the single quotes), but nearly any non-numeric character can be used to delimit the individual fields. The following conditions are all equivalent:

```
where si_update_ts >= '2015 08 08 00 00 00 000'
where si_update_ts >= '2015/08/08-00:00:00.000'
where si_update_ts >= '2015a08b08c00d00e00f000'
```

Date conditions can be specified with or without a time component. If time is specified, including milliseconds is optional. The following values are valid:

```
'09/12/2015 12:23:45.567'
```

```
'09/12/2015 12:23:45'
```

```
'09/12/2015'
```

These are the **only** valid formats. A query that includes a condition with `'09/12/2015 12'`, for example, does not generate an error message but returns no results[6].

All date/time properties in the system are stored in UTC, and conditional values are interpreted that way. So, if you are in the Eastern US during Daylight Saving Time, and you wish to query for objects with an update timestamp between 4:00 pm and 6:00 pm (local time) on 9/12/2015, the times would need to be adjusted by four hours:

```
select si_update_ts
where si_update_ts between '09/12/2015 20:00:00'
                       and '09/12/2015 22:00:00'
```

What is very likely to cause confusion is that the Query Builder displays dates in the **local** time zone, and without the time zone specified. Although this is generally what you ultimately want to see, it means that the input format (in the date condition) differs from the output format. The query above, which applies a date condition of 9/12/15 20:00 to 22:00 UTC, may produce the following output when run on a machine in EDT:

```
SI_UPDATE_TS    9/12/15 4:26:32 PM
SI_UPDATE_TS    9/12/15 5:12:21 PM
SI_UPDATE_TS    9/12/15 5:26:32 PM
```

Operators

Several operators can be used in WHERE conditions:

Operator	Meaning	Examples
IS NULL	Property does not exist	`where si_files is null`
IS NOT NULL	Property exists	`where si_files is not null`

=	Property exists and has specified value	`where si_id = 12345`
		`where si_name = 'report 1'`
		`where si_instance = 0`

!=	Property exists but has a value different than that specified	`where si_name != 'report 1'`
<	Property exists and has a value less than that specified	`where si_update_ts < '2015/09/01'`
>	Property exists and has a value greater than that specified	`where si_name > 'fred'` `where si_children > 0`
<=	Property exists and has a value less than	`where si_children <= 10`

---

6   Specifying a portion of a date or time like this **did** work in XI3, but not in BI4.

Operator	Meaning	Examples
	or equal to the specified value	
>=	Property exists and has a value greater than or equal to the specified value	`where si_owner >= 'fred'`

BETWEEN x AND y	Property exists and has a value greater than or equal to the first value, AND less than or equal to the second value.	`where si_children`
		`    between 2 and 5`
		
		`where si_update_ts`
		`    between '2015/08/09'`
		`        and '2015/08/12'`

IN (…)	Property exists and is one of the listed values	`where si_kind` `    in ('folder','webi')`
NOT IN (…)	Property exists but is not one of the listed values	`where si_parentid` `    not in (18,23)`

LIKE	Property exists and matches pattern	`where si_name like 'repor%'`
		`(all objects with a name starting with "report")`
		
		`where si_name like '_red%'`
		`(all objects with a name having any beginning character, followed by "red")`
		
		`where si_description like '%monthly%'`
		`(all objects with a description containing "monthly")`

NOT LIKE	Property exists but does not match pattern	`where si_name not like '%delete'` `(all objects with a name that doesn't end with "delete")`
… ANY … ALL	Property exists and matches any or all of other property	`where si_id >= all si_id`

Table 1: WHERE Operators

IS NULL / IS NOT NULL

The IS NULL and IS NOT NULL operators are used to specify if objects should be displayed based on whether or not they have a designated property. To understand this fully, we need to discuss the relationship between objects and properties in more depth.

While all objects have properties, they do not have *all possible* properties. To illustrate this, let's look at a subset of our repository containing universes and connections. The universes in our repository have the following properties:

SI_ID	SI_KIND	SI_NAME	SI_DESCRIPTION	SI_SHORTNAME
100	Universe	Sales	Universe of sales transactions	sales
101	Universe	Employee		empinfo
102	Universe	Finance	Corporate finance data	finance

Note the SI_SHORTNAME property, which is specific to universe objects. Connections in our repository do not have that property, but they do have SI_CONNECTION_DATABASE. The Connections in our repository look like this:

SI_ID	SI_KIND	SI_NAME	SI_DESCRIPTION	SI_CONNECTION_DATABASE
200	CCIS.DataC onnection	TXN DM	Connection to transactional datamart	Oracle 10
201	CCIS.DataC onnection	HR	Human resources datamart	Oracle 10
202	CCIS.DataC onnection	Finance DM		MS Access 2007

Our repository also has two folders, which do not have either of the object-specific properties mentioned above:

SI_ID	SI_KIND	SI_NAME	SI_DESCRIPTION
300	Folder	Sales	Sales universes
301	Folder	HR	

Our first test query in this repository is for objects that have an SI_NAME property. We use the IS NOT NULL operator to identify these objects:

```
select *
   from ci_appobjects
 where si_name is not null
```

The following result is generated:

SI_ID	100
SI_KIND	Universe
SI_NAME	Sales
SI_DESCRIPTION	Universe of sales transactions
SI_SHORTNAME	sales

SI_ID	101
SI_KIND	Universe
SI_NAME	Employee
SI_DESCRIPTION	
SI_SHORTNAME	empinfo

SI_ID	102
SI_KIND	Universe
SI_NAME	Finance

SI_DESCRIPTION	Corporate finance data
SI_SHORTNAME	finance

SI_ID	200
SI_KIND	CCIS.DataConnection
SI_NAME	TXN DM
SI_DESCRIPTION	Connection to transactional datamart
SI_CONNECTION_DAT ABASE	Oracle 10

SI_ID	201
SI_KIND	CCIS.DataConnection
SI_NAME	HR
SI_DESCRIPTION	Human resources datamart
SI_CONNECTION_DAT ABASE	Oracle 10

SI_ID	202
SI_KIND	CCIS.DataConnection
SI_NAME	Finance DM
SI_DESCRIPTION	
SI_CONNECTION_DAT ABASE	MS Access 2007

SI_ID	300
SI_KIND	Folder
SI_NAME	Sales
SI_DESCRIPTION	Sales universes

SI_ID	301
SI_KIND	Folder
SI_NAME	HR
SI_DESCRIPTION	

Note that, since we used the * operator in SELECT, all properties retrieved for all objects (we are only showing the properties above that we're interested in, else it would be several pages).

Next, we want to extract the objects that do not have the SI_SHORTNAME property. We use the IS NULL operator:

```
select *
  from ci_appobjects
```

```
where si_shortname is null
```

This produces all of our connections and folders.

SI_ID	200
SI_KIND	CCIS.DataConnection
SI_NAME	TXN DM
SI_DESCRIPTION	Connection to transactional datamart
SI_CONNECTION_DAT ABASE	Oracle 10

SI_ID	201
SI_KIND	CCIS.DataConnection
SI_NAME	HR
SI_DESCRIPTION	Human resources datamart
SI_CONNECTION_DAT ABASE	Oracle 10

SI_ID	202
SI_KIND	CCIS.DataConnection
SI_NAME	Finance DM
SI_DESCRIPTION	Corporate finance data
SI_CONNECTION_DAT ABASE	MS Access 2007

SI_ID	300
SI_KIND	Folder
SI_NAME	Sales
SI_DESCRIPTION	Sales universes

SI_ID	301
SI_KIND	Folder
SI_NAME	HR
SI_DESCRIPTION	

You may have noticed that the behavior of IS NOT and IS NOT NULL is similar to that of standard SQL. Thus far, that is true. However, the similarities diverge with respect to *properties with blank values*. In some relational databases, the IS NULL operator matches fields that have an empty string (""). So, the following expressions in **standard SQL** are equivalent:

```
where field_name = ''
where field_name is null
```

This is not the case with CMS queries – an object having a property with an empty string is not matched with IS NULL. In our sample repository above, several of the objects do not have a value in SI_DESCRIPTION. If we attempt to extract these objects with:

```
select *
  from ci_appobjects
 where si_description is null
```

...then we get no results. Although some of the objects' SI_DESCRIPTION properties are blank, they nonetheless exist and therefore are not null[7]. The proper way to identify these objects (those with a blank description) is to use the = operator with an empty string (")[8], as follows:

```
select *
  from ci_appobjects
 where si_description = ''
```

This produces the desired result:

SI_ID	101
SI_KIND	Universe
SI_NAME	Employee
SI_DESCRIPTION	
SI_SHORTNAME	finance

SI_ID	202
SI_KIND	CCIS.DataConnection
SI_NAME	Finance DM
SI_DESCRIPTION	
SI_CONNECTION_DATABASE	MS Access 2007

Boolean Operators

The boolean operators (= != < > =< =>) all have the same structure:

property-name **operator** (*property-name or value*)

Note that the left side of the expression **must** be a property name and not a value. While this would be proper in standard SQL:

---

7   This may be a somewhat abstract concept for anyone not familiar with SQL. It may help to think of an analogy of a row of houses with mailboxes. Some houses have mailboxes while others don't, and some of the mailboxes have mail in them while other mailboxes don't. The houses without mailboxes would have a NULL mailbox property; the houses with mailboxes that are empty would have a NOT NULL mailbox. Finally houses with mailboxes that are not empty would have a NOT NULL mailbox, and the mailbox itself would have a value.

8   That's two single quotes with no space between them.

```
where 'fred' = si_name
```

...it produces no results in a CMS query. Worse, it does not generate a syntax error. The only correct form is:

```
where si_name = 'fred'
```

This rule prevents us from using "1=1" expressions, which are sometimes used in SQL queries[9]. The following query produces no results:

```
select *
  from ci_infoobjects
 where 1=1
```

Implicit IS NOT NULL

In the listing of operators above, we stated that all of them, except for IS NULL, implicitly apply a "Property exists and..." condition. While this is intuitive when the = operator is used, it is less obvious with the other boolean operators. Using the sample repository from the previous section, we run the following query to obtain Connection objects having a SI_CONNECTION_DATABASE property of "Oracle 10":

```
select *
  from ci_appobjects
 where si_connection_database = 'oracle 10'
```

This produces the following result:

SI_ID	200
SI_KIND	CCIS.DataConnection
SI_NAME	TXN DM
SI_DESCRIPTION	Connection to transactional datamart
SI_CONNECTION_DAT ABASE	Oracle 10

SI_ID	201
SI_KIND	CCIS.DataConnection
SI_NAME	HR
SI_DESCRIPTION	Human resources datamart
SI_CONNECTION_DAT ABASE	Oracle 10

This result, of course, includes only objects that have the SI_CONNECTION_DATABSE property, **and** where it is equal to "Oracle 10".

---

9   This seemingly meaningless WHERE condition has its uses sometimes in standard SQL but is invalid in CMS query syntax.

If we change the above query to use the != operator in our condition:

```
select *
  from ci_appobjects
 where si_connection_database != 'oracle 10'
```

...then the query will *still* implicitly exclude any objects that do not have the SI_CONNECTION_DATABASE property. That is, the CMS query engine interprets this query to mean:

```
select *
  from ci_appobjects
 where si_connection_database is not null
       and si_connection_database != 'oracle 10'
```

and the following output is generated:

SI_ID	202
SI_KIND	CCIS.DataConnection
SI_NAME	Finance DM
SI_DESCRIPTION	
SI_CONNECTION_DATABASE	MS Access 2007

What if you really want to extract all objects that either don't have the SI_CONNECTION_DATABASE property or have an SI_CONNECTION_DATABASE value other than "Oracle 10"? This can be done, using exactly that logic:

```
select *
  from ci_appobjects
 where (si_connection_database is null
       or si_connection_database != 'oracle 10')
```

This returns all objects in the CI_APPOBJECTS table, except for the two connections associated with Oracle 10:

SI_ID	100
SI_KIND	Universe
SI_NAME	Sales
SI_DESCRIPTION	Universe of sales transactions
SI_SHORTNAME	sales

SI_ID	101
SI_KIND	Universe
SI_NAME	Employee
SI_DESCRIPTION	
SI_SHORTNAME	empinfo

SI_ID	102
SI_KIND	Universe
SI_NAME	Finance
SI_DESCRIPTION	Corporate finance data
SI_SHORTNAME	finance

SI_ID	202
SI_KIND	CCIS.DataConnection
SI_NAME	Finance DM
SI_DESCRIPTION	
SI_CONNECTION_DATABASE	MS Access 2007

SI_ID	300
SI_KIND	Folder
SI_NAME	Sales
SI_DESCRIPTION	Sales universes

SI_ID	301
SI_KIND	Folder
SI_NAME	HR
SI_DESCRIPTION	

It is important to note that the handling of NULLs is quite different in CMS query syntax as compared to standard SQL. In standard SQL, there is an adage "null does not equal anything, even itself", which necessitates the "IS NULL" operator as opposed to "= NULL".

In standard SQL, a field with a NULL value matches an "IS NULL" expression, but does not match an "= NULL" expression. But this is not the case in CMS query syntax. Let's look at a few examples of NULL operations and how they are interpreted in standard SQL vs. CMS queries:

Expression	Standard SQL	CMS Query
si_xyz is null	True if si_xyz is null	True if object does not have an si_xyz property
si_xyz is not null	True if si_xyz has a value	True if object has an si_xyz property (even if

		blank)
`si_xyz = null`	Always false	True if object does not have an si_xyz property
`si_xyz != null`	Always false	True if object has an si_xyz property (even if blank)
`null = null`	Always false	Always true
`null != null`	Always false	Always false
`fred = fred` (assuming fred is not a column/property)	Syntax error	True
`fred = wilma` (assuming fred and wilma are not columns/properties)	Syntax error	False

The behavior of NULLs on the boolean operators apply to the following operators as well.

BETWEEN ... AND

The BETWEEN … AND operator is a shorthand operator for two separate expressions with <= and >=. For example, the following expression pairs are functionally equivalent:

```
where si_children between 5 and 10
where si_children >= 5
      and si_children <= 10

where si_owner between 'marco' and 'polo'
where si_owner >= 'marco'
      and si_owner <= 'polo'
```

Note that, as with the boolean operators, the operand to the left of BETWEEN must be a property name, and not a value. The following expression is invalid:

```
where 5 between 1 and 10
```

The order of the operands to the right of BETWEEN is important – the value on the left side of AND must be lower than the value on the right side. The following expression:

```
where si_children between 10 and 5
```
is equivalent to:

```
where si_children >= 10
      and si_children <= 5
```

which, naturally, produces no results.

IN (...), NOT IN (...)

IN and NOT IN are also shorthand operators, and they can be used in place of multiple separate AND/OR expressions. The following pairs of expressions are equivalent:

```
where si_kind in ('webi','folder','inbox')
where si_kind = 'webi'
      or si_kind = 'folder'
      or si_kind = 'inbox'

where si_id not in (0,4,23)
where not (si_id = 0
           or si_id = 4
           or si_id = 23

where si_owner in ('fred')
where si_owner = ('fred')
```

The values to the right of IN/NOT IN must be enclosed in parentheses, even if there is only one value. Also, *property names* are not allowed in IN/NOT IN – the following expression is invalid:

```
where si_owner in (si_name,si_description)
```

LIKE, NOT LIKE

The LIKE operator performs partial string comparisons – it can be used to match strings that begin with, end with, or contain a series of characters. The underline (_) matches any single character, while the percent sign (%) matches any number of characters.

To find objects with a name beginning with "report" but ending with any single character, use the following expression:

```
where si_name like 'report_'
```

To find objects whose name begins with "monthly", use:

```
where si_name like 'monthly%'
```

To find objects whose name does not contain the word "test", use:

```
where si_name not like '%test%'
```

The LIKE operator is intended to be used only with string properties. Although it can be used with numerics and dates, no wildcard substitution using _ or % takes place. For example, the following expressions are equivalent:

```
where si_id = 23
where si_id like ('23')
```

But an attempt to match all SI_ID properties that contain "456" with

```
where si_id like '%456%'
```

...does not produce any results.

As useful as it might be, it is not possible to combine LIKE with IN. To find objects with names starting with "abc", "def" or "ghi", you may be tempted to try the following:

```
where si_name like in ('abc%','def%','ghi%')
```

But this does not work. Multiple expressions are necessary to produce the desired result:

```
where si_name like 'abc%'
      or si_name like 'def%'
      or si_name like 'ghi%'
```

Square brackets ([ ]) can be used in a LIKE expression to specify one or more specific characters in a particular position in a string. For example, to find objects named "*ReportA*", "*ReportB*", or "*ReportC*" only, we can use:

```
where si_name like 'report[ABC]'
```

The bracketing matches a single character only. To match *ReportAA, ReportAB, ReportAC, ReportBA, ReportBB, ReportBC*, we have to specify two bracketed expressions:

```
where si_name like 'report[ABC][ABC]'
```

To match strings with a character other than those specified, precede the string with a carat (^). To find objects with names beginning with "*Report*" and ending with any character other than *A, B,* or *C,* use:

```
where si_name like 'report[^ABC]'
```

This finds objects named *Reportx, Report1,* or *Report@*, but not *ReportA, ReportB,* or *ReportC*. It also does **not** match *Report* or *Reportxxxx* (since we have asked for Report followed by exactly one single character that is not *A, B,* or *C*.

One crucial consideration about bracketed expressions in LIKE is that **they are case-sensitive**! Thus, you must be careful to specify upper and lower case letters if the object case is uncertain. For example, if we want to find objects named ReportA, ReportB, and ReportC, but we are uncertain about the actual case of the letters, we would have to specify each letter in both upper and lower case:

```
where si_name like 'report[AaBbCc]'
```

If we had instead tried:

```
where si_name like 'report[ABC]'
```

then we would match reports named *ReportA, ReportB,* and *ReportC,* but not *Reporta, Reportb, Reportc.*

We can exploit this behavior to do a full case-sensitive search. If we wanted to find objects named *My Year-End Report,* matching exact case, we could use:

```
where si_name like '[M][y] [Y][e][a][r]-[E][n][d] [R][e][p][o][r][t]'
```

The syntax is awkward (and painful to look at), but it works!

ANY, ALL

The ANY and ALL operators are *inspired* by standard SQL but the behavior and syntax are very different. Both operators compare the property on the left of the operator with ANY or ALL objects (respectively) in the InfoStore.

For example, the following query can be used to find the object having the highest ID in the InfoStore:

```
select *
  from ci_infoobjects
 where si_id >= all si_id
```

This returns exactly one object, that being the one with the highest ID in the CI_INFOOBJECTS table. To find the object with the highest ID across multiple tables, simply include them in the FROM clause:

```
select *
  from ci_infoobjects,ci_appobjects,ci_systemobjects
 where si_id >= all si_id
```

This only returns one object, but it is the one with the highest ID in any of the tables.

The ANY and ALL operators are not commonly used in CMS queries, as they are limited in functionality and can produce unexpected results.

NOT

The NOT operator negates a conditional expression. Quite simply, prefixing any expression with NOT inverts the true/false result of the expression. The following expression pairs are equivalent:

```
where si_kind != 'webi'
where not si_kind = 'webi'

where si_update_ts >= '2015/07/01'
where not si_update_ts < '2015/07/01'

where si_id in (4,18,23)
where not si_id not in (4,18,23)
```

The NOT operator is generally not used for simple queries (as in the examples above) since using the opposite operator (!= in place of =, for example) is generally preferable. With that said, the NOT operator can be very useful in two scenarios: inverting an existing query, and building complex queries.

Regarding the first scenario, consider the following query:

```
select *
  from ci_infoobjects
 where si_kind = 'webi'
       and (si_recurring = 1
           or si_instance = 0
           or si_schedule_status = 1)
```

This query produces a list of all WebI objects that are either recurring instances, successfully completed instances, or base reports (not an instance). Suppose you want to invert the results, and display all WebI objects that were not represented in the first query. You *could* change each expression in the query, or, more simply:

```
select *
  from ci_infoobjects
 where si_kind = 'webi'
       and not (si_recurring = 1
               or si_instance = 0
               or si_schedule_status = 1)
```

Thus, the NOT operator is generally not a necessity but can make some queries simpler to write and read.

ORDER BY

The ORDER BY clause is optional and can be used to sort the result of the query by a designated property or properties. If the ORDER BY clause is not present, then the default sort order for CMS queries is by *ascending SI_ID*.

The syntax of ORDER BY is fairly simple:

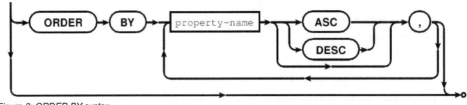

Figure 3: ORDER BY syntax

The ORDER BY clause, if provided, must contain at least one property name. Multiple property names can be given; the applied sort order is then based on the left-to-right listing of property names.

An optional ASC or DESC keyword can be specified after each property name to define the applied sort as ascending or descending (respectively). The sort order is assumed to be ascending unless DESC is specified.

Consider a simple repository containing the following objects:

SI_ID	SI_KIND	SI_NAME	SI_DESCRIPTION	SI_UPDATE_TS
100	Universe	Sales	Universe of sales transactions	2015/09/21 16:30:30
101	Universe	Employee		2014/12/08 09:01:40
102	Universe	Finance	Corporate finance data	2015/03/09 12:30:17
200	CCIS.DataConnection	TXN DM	Connection to transactional datamart	2014/06/04 10:45:21
201	CCIS.DataConnection	HR	Human resources datamart	2010/04/17 08:17:33
202	CCIS.DataConnection	Finance DM		2012/07/12 14:08:08
300	Folder	Sales	Sales universes	2013/04/23 13:00:23
301	Folder	HR		2014/02/19 11:14:21

We can use the following ORDER BY expressions to sort by descending kind, then ascending name:

```
select si_id,si_name,si_kind,si_update_ts
  from ci_appobjects
 order by kind desc,si_name
```

The output is as follows:

SI_ID	SI_KIND	SI_NAME	SI_UPDATE_TS
101	Universe	Employee	2014/12/08 09:01:40
102	Universe	Finance	2015/03/09 12:30:17
100	Universe	Sales	2015/09/21 16:30:30
301	Folder	HR	2014/02/19 11:14:21
300	Folder	Sales	2013/04/23 13:00:23
202	CCIS.DataConnection	Finance DM	2012/07/12 14:08:08
201	CCIS.DataConnection	HR	2010/04/17 08:17:33
200	CCIS.DataConnection	TXN DM	2014/06/04 10:45:21

The properties provided in ORDER BY do not need to be also provided in SELECT. If an ORDER BY expression includes a property that was not in SELECT, it is simply added to the output. For example:

```
select si_id,si_kind
  from ci_appobjects
```

```
where si_kind = 'universe'
order by si_name
```

SI_ID	SI_KIND	SI_NAME
101	Universe	Employee
102	Universe	Finance
100	Universe	Sales

If you are familiar with standard SQL, you may be tempted to specify properties in ORDER BY by position rather than name. For example:

```
order by 2 desc,1
```

This does not work in CMS query syntax – property names must be spelled out.

Chapter Review

- CMS queries are the primary mechanism for getting system metadata out of an SAP BusinessObjects system.
- The CMS Query syntax is "SQL-ish" but does not conform exactly to SQL standards.
- CMS queries can be run without programming, by using the Query Builder web application.

Quiz

1. The following are valid SQL constructs in CMS Query syntax EXCEPT:

    a) SELECT

    b) FROM

    c) GROUP BY

    d) ORDER BY

2. The following statements are valid in CMS Query syntax (select all that apply):

    a) SELECT

    b) UPDATE

    c) DELETE

    d) INSERT

3. The following aggregate functions may be used in CMS queries (select all that apply):

    a) sum

    b) count

    c) count distinct

    d) min

    e) max

4. Which of the following date conditions are valid?

    a) Where si_update_ts > '2019/01/05'

    b) WHERE si_update_ts > '2019.01.05'

    c) WHERE si_update_ts > '2019_01_05_06_30_00'

    d) WHERE si_update_ts > '2019/01'

5. True/False: This condition restricts the result to InfoObjects with a name of "fred":
   where 'fred'= si_name

6. True/False: Properties in an ORDER BY clause can be named explicitly or by position.

7. Which of the following is a valid table in CMS queries?

    a) cms_infoobjects7

    b) si_infoobjects

    c) ci_infoobjects

Answers on page 672.

Chapter 2 - Object Properties

All InfoObjects in an SAP BusinessObjects system have properties. You have seen a few of these in the previous section, such as SI_ID, SI_KIND, SI_NAME, and SI_UPDATE_TS. These properties, and a handful of others, are common and exist on all objects[10].

A number of properties are present on specific kinds of objects. For example, the SI_FILES property is present for object kinds that are associated with files in the File Repository Store (FRS), but it is not present on objects that do not have such an association. However, even for a specific kind of object, not all objects of that kind will necessarily have the same property set. The SI_SCHEDULEINFO property, for example, is present on Web Intelligence objects only if the object has scheduling options set.

Unfortunately, as of this writing, there is no published comprehensive list of all property names associated with object kids. We have compiled many of the most commonly-used properties in Appendix B.

Data Types

All object properties are of a specific data type. The most commonly used data types for properties are[11]:

- String
- Integer
- Long
- Double
- Date
- Boolean
- Byte Array
- Property Bag

---

10 Not *entirely* true, as there are some internal objects that don't have all of these core properties. But, for the objects you will typically be working with in CMS queries and with the SDK, all of these properties will be present.

11 Properties are stored internally within the SAP BusinessObjects repository and are exposed via the various SDKs in their native format. For example, a property that appears as an Integer data type in Java will appear in VBA as a Long. We will stick to the Java data types in this book when we refer to object properties.

String

Objects of the String data type contain a series of characters. Common properties of type String include SI_NAME, SI_DESCRIPTION, and SI_OWNER. Strings may contain virtually any valid ASCII character, including the newline (therefore, string properties can include multi-line text). From the SDK, string properties can be retrieved or set using a specified locale.

As mentioned in the discussion on CMS queries, string properties are stored in mixed case, but conditional expressions on **most** properties are not case sensitive.

Integer

The Integer data type represents most of the numeric properties you will encounter, but not necessarily all. If you are performing type-specific operations, be sure you know the specific data type of the numeric property[12].

As integers are 32 bit whole numbers (not floating point). They are suited to be used for sequential identifiers, such as the SI_ID property.

Long

The Long data type is only used on a few properties that are expected to hold extremely large numbers. As with Integers, Longs are also whole numbers, but 64 bits long.

Double

The Double data type is the only IEEE 754 floating-point numeric type available for object properties. As such, it is used for only the very few properties that require floating-point precision.

Date

All properties of the date data type all store both date and time, to millisecond precision. There is no support for time zones, and all dates are assumed to be in UTC.

---

12 In the Query Builder, there's nothing to indicate the data type of a particular column, other than its apparent format. When we get to Java, we will see how to determine a property's data type.

Boolean

The boolean data type contains a simple true/false value.

Byte Array

The byte array data type is not used for many properties. It contains an arbitrarily-sized array of raw binary data. Unlike the other data types, properties of the byte array data type do not currently (as of BI4) display a meaningful representation in the Query Builder (it is merely the result of a `toString()` method call).

Property Bags

Property Bags (or simply "bags") are a special type of property that contain other properties. Bags are often used in objects to contain lists of values (ex., the parent groups of users), or to collect a number of properties together that serve a common purpose. Let's look at a commonly-used property bag – the `SI_FILES` property.

The `SI_FILES` property bag is present for objects that are associated with files in the FRS. We can find one such object with the following CMS query:

```
select top 1 si_id,si_name,si_kind,si_files
  from ci_infoobjects
 where si_files is not null
```

This produces a result similar to (but likely not exactly the same as) the following:

SI_FILES *(Property Bag)*

      SI_NUM_FILES *(Integer)*
          1

      SI_FILE1 *(String)*
          aqtkbbsqn4noj3ydf.sw1ly-guid[29ae756a-b41a-4535-abcd-3b40091744955].wid

      SI_VALUE1 *(Integer)*
          55507

      SI_PATH *(String)*
          frs://Input/a_130/015/000/3970/

SI_NAME *(String)*
    Formatting Sample

SI_ID *(Integer)*
    3970

SI_KIND *(String)*
    Webi

(For clarity, we have added the data types next to the property names. They do not normally appear in Query Builder results.)

In the result above, we can see that the SI_FILES property bag contains four child properties: SI_NUM_FILES, SI_FILE1, SI_VALUE1, and SI_PATH. SI_VALUE1 contains the size, in bytes, of SI_FILE1. The other properties are self-explanatory.

Property Bags can contain zero, one, or multiple child properties. The behavior of properties in a bag is similar to properties not in a bag (that is, *root level* properties). Although our SI_FILES example above includes only String and Integer properties, bags can contain properties of any available data type – bags can (and often do) contain other bags, creating a nested property bag hierarchy.

Key point: property bags are containers; they can contain properties of any type, including other property bags.

Note that property bags can contain properties whose names are used elsewhere and have different meanings. The SI_PATH property shown above within the SI_FILES bag contains the logical path in the FRS of the object's directory. However, objects of kind *Folder* can also have an SI_PATH property, but it has a different meaning. Let's look at the properties of a sample folder:

```
select si_id,si_name,si_path
  from ci_infoobjects
 where si_kind = 'folder'
   and si_name = 'report conversion tool documents'
```

This may produce a result similar to:

```
SI_NAME (String)
        Report Conversion Tool Documents
SI_ID (Integer)
        2829
SI_PATH (String)

        SI_FOLDER_NAME1 (String)
                Report Conversion Tool
        SI_FOLDER_OBTYPE1 (Integer)
                1
        SI_FOLDER_ID1 (Integer)
                2795
        SI_NUM_FOLDERS (Integer)
                1
```

The SI_PATH property as used here has a completely different meaning (and data type) vs. when it is used as a child of SI_FILES. So, simply knowing a property's name is not sufficient to know its meaning, as the meaning may differ based on its property' parent bag.

Property Bags in WHERE Clauses

It is possible to create query conditions that reference properties within a property bag. If, for example, we wanted to identify objects that have more than one file, we can apply a condition on the SI_NUM_FILES property within the SI_FILES bag. For example:

```
select si_id,si_name,si_kind,si_files
  from ci_infoobjects
 where si_files.si_num_files > 1
```

In our WHERE condition, we use a period (.) to indicate a child property of a property bag. Any valid conditional operator can be used on child properties this way, including =, !=, IS NULL, LIKE, etc.

The syntax of conditions on property bags gives the impression of an owner-table-column relationship as in SQL, but that is not the case. In the query above, as in previous examples, the reference to SI_FILES is as a *property*, not as a *table,* and it would be incorrect to think of SI_FILES as a table.

Note that we did not need to specify SI_FILES is not null, as that is implicit with the reference to the SI_FILES property. Adding it explicitly would not change the result.

Although, as we have seen, child properties of property bags can be referenced in the WHERE clause, they cannot be referenced in the SELECT clause. It is not possible to extract only the SI_NUM_FILES property of SI_FILES with:

```
select si_files.si_num_files
  from ci_infoobjects
```

Doing so just returns empty results.

Enumerated Properties

Property bags are often used to contain lists of values – in particular, a list of IDs for other objects. Property Bags containing IDs are used in this manner when an object has a *many-to-many* or *many-to-one* relationship with other objects.

As an example, *user groups* can contain multiple *users*, and users can be a member of multiple user groups. Therefore, property bags are present on user group objects to contain the IDs of their member users. Property bags are also present on user objects to contain the IDs of the user groups that the user is a member of.

Let's look at an example of a user group's member users:

```
select si_group_members
  from ci_systemobjects
 where si_kind = 'usergroup'
     and si_name ='administrators'
```

SI_GROUP_MEMBERS *(PropertyBag)*

```
1 (Integer)
      12
2 (Integer)
      4104
3 (Integer)
      4130
4 (Integer)
      4475
5 (Integer)
      4836
SI_TOTAL (Integer)
      5
```

We can see that the SI_GROUP_MEMBERS bag contains six properties: an SI_TOTAL integer property that indicates the number of values in the bag, and five IDs representing the members of the group.

At first glance, it may appear that the properties 1 through 5 are indexes in an unnamed array, but they are in fact *property names*. So, this bag contains six enumerated properties, named 1, 2, 3, 4, 5, and SI_TOTAL.

Creating a conditional expression on SI_TOTAL is no different than with other properties. We could, for example, look for user groups with more than 10 users with the following condition:

```
where si_group_members.si_total > 10
```

But querying for specific members of that bag is tricky. If we wanted to identify any user groups that have user ID 12 ("Administrator") as their first user (the user ID occupying spot 1), we might try:

```
where si_group_members.1 = 12
```

But that produces a syntax error. Putting the bag and child property names in double quotes produces the desired result[13]:

```
where "si_group_members.1" = 12
```

Unfortunately, there's no direct way to query for the existence of a value in a property bag. Although the query above was successful at extracting user groups with Administrator as the first user, it's not possible to query for a given user ID in *any position*. In our extract of SI_GROUP_MEMBERS above, we would not be successful at finding user ID 4836 unless we were specifically looking at "SI_GROUP_MEMBERS.5".

There are two hack-ish way to deal with this. One is a brute-force method of checking for all possible positions. For example, the following condition will look for ID 4836 in

---

13 This method was discovered by accident, and may not be fully supported or exist in later releases. Use with caution.

```
SI_GROUP_MEMBERS:
```

```
where "si_group_mebers.1" = 4836
      or "si_group_mebers.2" = 4836
      or "si_group_mebers.3" = 4836
      or "si_group_mebers.4" = 4836
      or "si_group_mebers.5" = 4836
```

Obviously, this is inefficient and would require several WHERE expressions equal to the maximum number of members of SI_GROUP_MEMBERS.

The second method to find values in a property bag is with a LIKE operator:

```
where SI_GROUP_MEMBERS like '%4836%'
```

Although this works, it is risky and should be used with care. A query such as this can return unexpected data – although the query is clearly intended to find ID 4836, it could also return ID 14836, 48365, etc.

Of course, this is a common need – you may want to know which user groups include two specific users, for example. Or, which users are in Administrators but have not logged in recently. *Relationship Queries* exist for requirements such as these, and we will cover them in Chapter 4.

We will go more in-depth with SI_USER_GROUPS and other similar properties in the next section.

Special Property Bags

There are two special property bags to be aware of: SI_SCHEDULEINFO and SI_PROCESSINFO. These two bags will not appear in an iterated list of an object's properties, and can't be used directly in a WHERE statement such as where SI_SCHEDULEINFO is not null. However, they *can* be included in the SELECT clause, and individual child properties can be referenced in WHERE. For example: where SI_SCHEDULEINFO.SI_SCHEDULE_TYPE=5.

Common Properties

There are several core properties that are frequently used; familiarity with these properties is essential for working with CMS queries and SDK programs.

Unfortunately, the naming of properties does not follow a strict convention. The properties SI_CREATION_TIME, SI_UPDATE_TS, and SI_NEXTRUNTIME all contain date and time data, yet their names have different naming standards. There is inconsistent usage of underscores in place of spaces, as well. The properties SI_PARENTID and SI_PARENT_CUID are examples. These inconsistencies can make for error-prone queries, and this is not helped by the fact that the query engine does not generate an error if an incorrectly-spelled property name is used.

When we get to programming in Java, we will discuss the CePropertyID class – this class contains references to most property names and can be used to mitigate typos in queries.

Object IDs (SI_ID, SI_CUID, SI_GUID, SI_RUID)

Nearly everything in an SAP BusinessObjects system is represented by an *InfoObject*. InfoObjects include documents, folders, users, user groups, and some more abstract items such as Access Levels and Events. Each InfoObject in a system has four unique identifiers: an *ID*, *CUID*, *RUID*, and *GUID*.

You are likely familiar with IDs and CUIDs if you have spent much time developing in SAP BusinessObjects, particularly if you have worked with document linking via openDocument.jsp. These properties are used extensively in SDK programming, so it is crucial to understand when, where, and how they are used and how they differ.

Of the four identifiers, ID and CUID are used most frequently. GUID and RUID are not needed in most modern SDK programming, and they are not used in this book.

ID

The *ID* (also known as *Document ID, SI_ID, Object ID, or InfoObject ID*) is the most fundamental of the various identifiers. The ID is a sequentially-assigned integer and is fully unique within a single SAP BusinessObjects cluster. That is, no two objects of any kind will share the same ID *within the same cluster*.

The ID is used by objects to refer to each other in various relationships. A User Group, for example, will have a list of IDs that represent its member subgroups, its parent groups, and its member users.

An ID is permanently assigned in a cluster. Once assigned to an object, the ID will never be reused even if the object is deleted. It is not possible to change an object's ID.

CUID

The CUID ("*Cluster Unique Identifier*") is a generated string, usually 23 characters in length[14], and, as its name implies, is also unique within a cluster. Unlike an ID, which is unique *within* a cluster, CUIDs are also unique universally, meaning that the possibility of the same CUID being assigned to two different objects in different clusters is extremely remote[15]. For this reason, it is safe to migrate an object from one cluster to another, retain its original CUID, and not risk a collision with an existing object in the target cluster.

As with IDs, there is no supported way of modifying an object's CUID.

---

14 But not always. If you are saving CUIDs to a fixed-width field, allocate 64 characters to be safe.

15 How remote? For a 23-character CUID, using any of 64 characters (52 upper/lower case letters, 10 digits, 2 symbols), there are 64^{23} possible combinations, or 348,449,143,727,041,000,000,000,000,000,000,000,000,000.

ID vs. CUID

An important distinction between IDs and CUIDs is how they are handled when objects are migrated across clusters. When objects are migrated using any of the SAP BusinessObjects migration tools[16], only the CUID is retained. That is, an object that is migrated from a source cluster to a target receives a new ID, GUID, and RUID, but it retains the same CUID as in the source cluster[17].

In programming with the SDK, you will usually want to use the ID to refer to objects rather than CUID since operations using an integer are generally faster than those using a string. For example, you may need to use an ID to refer to an object's parent:

```
Integer parentID = infoObject.getParentID();
IinfoObject parent = infoStore.query(
    "select si_name from ci_infoobjects " +
    "where si_id = " + parentID);
```

On the other hand, if you need to save a hard-coded reference to an object (Folder, User Group, etc.) in your program, using a CUID would be preferable. This method mitigates the risk of the program not working should it and the dependent object be migrated to another cluster.

An example of this scenario would be a program that automatically adds users to a designated group using some external source such as a database. The program needs to keep a reference to the target group; storing the group's CUID with the program (ideally, in a properties files) would be preferable than using the group's ID. If the group's ID were to be used, and the program (and group) were migrated to a different cluster, the program's reference to the ID would have to be updated. This would not be the case if the group's CUID were used instead[18].

Pre-defined IDs and CUIDs

When an SAP BusinessObjects cluster is initially set up, the repository is loaded with a number of built-in objects. This includes the top-level Public Folder, Favorites Folder, the *Administrators* group, the *Administrator* user, and many other objects. These objects have predetermined IDs and CUIDs that are the same in every cluster.

The root of public folders is *always* ID 23. To refer to this folder in a CMS query, it is safe to

---

16 *Import Wizard* or *Lifecycle Management (LCM)* in XIr2/XI3; *Promotion Management* in BI4. It is important to note that the CUID is only retained when a migration tool is used to move objects across clusters. While it is possible to import a universe with Universe Design Tool, save it locally, then export it to a different cluster, doing so will result in a new CUID being assigned.

17 This is of critical importance when linking documents with openDocument.jsp, as using the CUID to reference documents rather than the ID enables the link to be used to reference the same document as it is migrated to different clusters.

18 Of course, an alternative to both ID and CUID is to reference objects by path and name. This may be an appropriate approach in some scenarios, but in general it is better to use the object's CUID since the CUID will still be valid if the object is renamed or moved to a different location.

refer to it by its ID. This simple query returns all top-level folders (children of the root folder):

```
select * from ci_infoobjects where si_parentid = 23
```

There are two helper classes in the Enterprise Java SDK that include these predetermined identifiers: `CeSecurityID` and `CeSecurityCUID`. Since, as a best practice, hardcoded identifiers should be avoided in programming, the `CeSecurityID` class can be used to mitigate the (admittedly small) risk of the Public Folder's ID being different in a future release:

```
infoStore.query("select * from ci_infoobjects " +
                "where si_parentid = " + CeSecurityID.Folder.ROOT);
```

SI_RUID and SI_GUID

These two properties are not commonly used in SDK programming. `SI_RUID` is used to uniquely identify InfoObjects in an object package. `SI_GUID` was used in earlier versions of SAP BusinessObjects but still exists in BI4. Both of these properties have the same formatting rules as `SI_CUID` (i.e., alphanumeric string, at least 23 characters),   and in fact, these three properties have the same value for most InfoObjects.

SI_NAME

The `SI_NAME` property is ubiquitous in most CMS queries, as it contains the object's name. This property is populated for all objects in the InfoStore, and it is unique (along with `SI_KIND`) within a parent. That is, a parent object cannot have two children with the same name and kind[19].

Object Type Properties

(`SI_KIND`, `SI_SPECIFIC_KIND`, `SI_OBTYPE`, `SI_PROGID`, `SI_SPECIFIC_PROGID`)

These properties all define what a particular object *is* – such as a Folder, User, Universe, etc. The most commonly-used of these is `SI_KIND`, and its values for the common object types are self-evident:

- Folder
- User
- UserGroup
- Webi

---

19 Note that this *can* happen in certain cases, such as a corruption. The SDK will prevent an attempt to create an InfoObject in a folder that already contains one with the same name and kind.

- Universe

The SI_KIND property is a shorthand version of SI_PROGID. Although you may see SI_PROGID referenced in some queries (generally from the pre-XI days), SI_KIND can be used in most applications. A sample is as follows:

SI_PROGID	SI_KIND
CrystalEnterprise.Folder	Folder
CrystalEnterprise.User	User
CrystalEnterprise.UserGroup	UserGroup
CrystalEnterprise.Webi	Webi
CrystalEnterprise.Universe	Universe

Note that most kinds fall within a specific table. All objects of kind Webi, for example, are located in the CI_INFOOBJECTS table. All User and UserGroups objects are located in CI_SYSTEMOBJECTS. However, there are exceptions. The kind *Folder* can exist in *all three* virtual tables (CI_INFOOBJECTS, CI_APPOBJECTS, CI_SYSTEMOBJECTS).

The SI_SPECIFIC_KIND and SI_SPECIFIC_PROGID properties, as their names imply, define an additional level of specificity relative to the object's type. For most object types, where the additional specificity is not required, the SI_KIND and SI_SPECIFIC_KIND properties will have the same value, as will SI_PROGID and SI_SPECIFIC_PROGID.

One example of SI_SPECIFIC_KIND is with the SI_KIND value of *Event*. When SI_KIND is *Event*, the SI_SPECIFIC_KIND is either *FileEvent*, *NotificationEvent*, *ScheduleEvent*, or *UserEvent*.

There is a quirk with objects that have an SI_SPECIFIC_KIND value different from SI_KIND. The specific kind can be used in a condition on either SI_KIND *or* SI_SPECIFIC_KIND, even though the values are different. For example, the following two queries produce the exact same result:

```
select si_id,si_kind,si_specific_kind
  from ci_systemobjects
 where si_kind = 'fileevent'
```

```
select si_id,si_kind,si_specific_kind
  from ci_systemobjects
 where si_specific_kind = 'fileevent'
```

SI_ID	8462
SI_KIND	Event
SI_SPECIFIC_KIND	FileEvent

Note that even though the SI_KIND of this object is *Event*, it was retrieved when we queried for SI_KIND='fileevent'. It appears that the query engine interprets conditions that reference SI_KIND to reference SI_SPECIFIC_KIND instead. It's possible that this may change in future versions. Therefore, we do not recommend taking advantage of the behavior, but rather always query for SI_SPECIFIC_KIND where appropriate. That is, the second example above (SI_SPECIFIC_KIND='fileevent') is what should be used. We are only mentioning this quirk here to provide the observed behavior and to address any confusion that may arise from it.

SI_OBTYPE

The SI_OBTYPE property is generally not referenced explicitly in CMS queries or with the SDK. As with SI_KIND and SI_PROGID, this property defines the *type* of object, and its values correlate with those properties. However, the SI_OBTYPE property is mandatory and is populated on *every* object in the InfoStore. There are a small number of system objects that do not have an SI_KIND or SI_PROGID but do have an SI_OBTYPE. One example of this is object ID 4, the cluster object – its SI_OBTYPE value is 13 but has no SI_KIND, SI_PROGID, or related properties.

The values of SI_OBTYPE are sequential integers, and their meanings are therefore not as readily apparent as with SI_KIND and SI_PROGID. Although the values of SI_OBTYPE correlate to SI_KIND and SI_PROGID, the correlation may not be the same in every installation of SAP BusinessObjects[20], and as such SI_OBTYPE cannot be assumed to have a consistent meaning. For example, in one installation of SAP BusinessObjects, the value of SI_OBTYPE that correlates with SI_KIND *Webi* may be 320, but in another cluster, the SI_OBTYPE value for WebI may be 323.

With that said, there is one potential use for SI_OBTYPE over SI_KIND/SI_PROGID: this property is the only one of the three that is stored in plain text in the physical CMS repository database[21]. If you have a need to perform queries on the raw CMS repository by kind, you will need to use the SI_OBTYPE property, which maps to TypeID in the physical repository.

Since the values of SI_OBTYPE are created dynamically, a CMS query is required in order to generate a mapping to SI_KIND, SI_PROGID, etc., for a particular cluster. We can use a simple query that looks for all objects with a SI_PLUGIN_OBJECT value of 1 (true):

```
select si_kind,si_obtype,si_progid,
       si_specific_kind,si_specific_progid
  from ci_systemobjects,ci_infoobjects,ci_appobjects
 where si_plugin_object = 1
 order by si_obtype
```

SI_OBTYPE	SI_KIND	SI_SPECIFIC_KIND	SI_PROGID	SI_SPECIFIC_PROGID
1	Folder	Folder	CrystalEnterprise.Folder	CrystalEnterprise.Folder
8	Shortcut	Shortcut	CrystalEnterprise.Sho	CrystalEnterprise.S

---

20 See SAP Note 1593818.

21 We will cover the structure of the physical repository in Chapter 7.

SI_OBTYPE	SI_KIND	SI_SPECIFIC_KIND	SI_PROGID	SI_SPECIFIC_PROGID
			rtcut	hortcut
16	Server	Server	CrystalEnterprise.Server	CrystalEnterprise.Server

Note that the values of SI_OBTYPE actually correlate to SI_SPECIFIC_KIND / SI_SPECIFIC_PROGID. If we restrict the above query to SI_KIND='Event", we get:

SI_OBTYPE	SI_KIND	SI_SPECIFIC_KIND	SI_PROGID	SI_SPECIFIC_PROGID
2	Event	Event	CrystalEnterprise.Event	CrystalEnterprise.Event
278	Event	FileEvent	CrystalEnterprise.Event	CrystalEnterprise.FileEvent
281	Event	UserEvent	CrystalEnterprise.Event	CrystalEnterprise.UserEvent
300	Event	ScheduleEvent	CrystalEnterprise.Event	CrystalEnterprise.ScheduleEvent

Although all four objects have a kind of *Event*, the *specific kinds* are associated with distinct values of SI_OBTYPE.

Parent Relation Properties

(SI_PARENTID, SI_PARENT_CUID, SI_PARENT_FOLDER_CUID, SI_CHILDREN)

The SI_PARENTID and SI_PARENT_CUID properties, as their names imply, identify the object's parent. Both properties always refer to the same InfoObject – the only difference between two is simply that they hold the parent object's ID and CUID, respectively.

The parent-child relationship in the InfoStore is strictly one-to-many, meaning that **every** object has one (and only one) parent. Not every object kind can have children, but those that do can have zero or more.

The only way to identify members of the parent-child relationship is with SI_PARENTID or SI_PARENT_CUID, which are properties of the child object. There is no comparable property on *parent* objects that contain all *child* IDs.

Let's illustrate this with a common activity – navigating down through public folders. To start, we query for all objects whose SI_PARENTID property is 23, the root folder):

```
select si_name,si_id
  from ci_infoobjects
 where si_parentid = 23
```

This produces a list of all top-level public folders:

SI_NAME	SI_ID
Sales Reports	3211
Finance Reports	3987
HR Reports	6243

To further navigate into the Sales Reports folder, we would perform the same action, using that folder's ID in the condition:

```
select si_name,si_id,si_cuid
  from ci_infoobjects
 where si_parentid = 3211
```

This may produce a result like:

SI_NAME	SI_ID	SI_CUID
East Division	3305	AS1oZEJAynpNjZIaZK2rc7g
Central Division	3307	AVwhi.xFgTdHmHza7wd7.7Q
Western Division	3450	AY9zJ8BgaF9OucZ2h2slcJM

...and so on.

SI_PARENTID vs. SI_PARENT_CUID

In our discussion on the usage of SI_ID vs. SI_CUID, we said that SI_ID is generally preferable since query conditions on integers, such as SI_ID, perform faster than query conditions on strings, such as SI_CUID.   That guideline applies to the usage of SI_PARENTID vs. SI_PARENT_CUID as well. But there is an additional reason to use SI_PARENTID rather than SI_PARENT_CUID – and that is that the SI_PARENTID property is the only one of the two that is indexed[22].   Query conditions on indexed properties almost always run quicker than conditions that use non-indexed properties.

With that said, there are scenarios in which referring to an object via SI_PARENT_CUID is recommended. As a general rule, we can say that when navigating through folders using IDs *retrieved in the same session*, use the object's ID and refer to it by SI_PARENTID. But if a reference to a specific object needs to be stored for use in later sessions, use the object's CUID and refer to it by SI_PARENT_CUID.

The example activity above (in which we queried for root folders) is an example of the first scenario – we are retrieving the Sales Reports folder, and immediately querying for its children by way of its ID in the child records' SI_PARENTID property. An example of the second scenario may be a program that displays the contents of a specific public folder. If we stored the folder's SI_ID property in the program, there would be a risk that the reference would become invalid if the program and folder were ever migrated to a different cluster. If we instead store the folder's SI_CUID in the program, and query for it in SI_PARENT_CUID, we

22 We will discuss indexed properties in detail in a later section.

ensure that the reference is still valid[23].

SI_PARENT_FOLDER_CUID

The SI_PARENT_FOLDER_CUID is a reference to an object's nearest ancestor that is a *Folder*. This property is most valuable when working with scheduled instances since instances do not have a folder as their parent. For all objects **do** have a folder as their parent, the SI_PARENT_FOLDER_CUID property will have the same value as SI_PARENT_CUID.

Consider the following subset of a repository:

SI_NAME	SI_KIND	SI_INSTANCE	SI_CUID	SI_PARENT_CUID	SI_PARENT_FOLDER_CUID
Sales Reports	Folder	false	BBBBB	AAAAA	AAAAA
East	Folder	false	CCCCC	BBBBB	BBBBB
Wkly Sales	WebI	false	DDDDD	CCCCC	CCCCC
Wkly Sales	WebI	true	EEEEE	DDDDD	CCCCC

Note that the last row in the table, the *Wkly Sales* report instance, is the only object whose SI_PARENT_CUID is different from its SI_PARENT_FOLDER_CUID.

This property may be useful to meet a requirement of listing all documents and document instances in a given folder. In the example repository above, we could retrieve both the *Wkly Sales* base report and instance with a single query:

```
select si_name,si_cuid,si_instance
  from ci_infoobjects
 where si_parent_folder_cuid = 'ccccc'
```

We would get a result of:

SI_NAME	SI_CUID	SI_INSTANCE
Wkly Sales	DDDDD	False
Wkly Sales	EEEEE	true

SI_CHILDREN

This property is simply a count of an object's children (that is, the count of all objects whose SI_PARENTID is equal to this object's SI_ID). This is an example of a dynamic property – the value of SI_CHILDREN is not stored in the CMS repository, but is calculated at runtime.

---

23   Of course, instead of using SI_ID or SI_CUID, the reference could be by *name*.

Timestamps

(SI_CREATION_TIME, SI_UPDATE_TS)

These two properties contain the timestamp of an object's creation and last modification, respectively. As with all system-generated timestamp properties, they contain the date and time, to millisecond precision, and are always in the UTC time zone.

The SI_CREATION_TIME property is set to the current time (in UTC) when an object is created, and this property never changes. The SI_UPDATE_TS property has the same value as in SI_CREATION_TIME upon object creation but will be updated to the current time any time the object is modified. The modification may be from a user action – such as when a Web Intelligence report is saved, but it can also be updated when certain internal events occur. For example, a User InfoObject receives a new SI_UPDATE_TS value any time the user logs in.

Scheduling Properties

Scheduling is an integral function of the SAP BusinessObjects system, and there are several roles that InfoObjects play in this activity.

We can categorize these object roles into *Non-Schedulable Objects*, *Schedulable Objects*, and *Instances*.

(See Table 2: Scheduling Properties for a matrix of the object scheduling categories and the applicable properties.)

Non-Schedulable objects simply are not capable of being scheduled. Folders, users, user groups, and universes are examples of non-schedulable objects. Objects of this type are identified by the boolean SI_IS_SCHEDULABLE property having a value of false.

Schedulable objects are of a kind that are capable of being scheduled. This would include Web Intelligence documents, Crystal Reports, Object Packages, Publications, Program Objects, and others. Schedulable objects are identified by the SI_IS_SCHEDULABLE property having a value of true.

For native object types (Web Intelligence, Crystal Reports, Publications, etc.) the value of SI_IS_SCHEDULABLE is the same for all objects of a particular kind. That is, all objects of kind *Webi* in an InfoStore have a value of true for SI_IS_SCHEDULABLE. This is the case even for Web Intelligence documents that cannot be scheduled, such as documents in an inbox. *Agnostic* documents (Excel, PDF), however, have an SI_IS_SCHEDULABLE value of true *only if they are instances* (i.e., generated from a scheduled document). Documents of this kind that have been uploaded to the CMS (and are therefore not instances), have SI_IS_SCHEDULABLE equal to false.

Instances are the result of completed schedules; *or a schedule itself*. All instances are identified by the boolean SI_INSTANCE property being true. Instances can be further categorized by status: Running, *Completed* (successful or failed), *Pending, or Paused*. Pending instances may also be classified as being a one-time run or recurring.

Running instances eventually become either a successful or failed instance (unless they are *deleted*). Currently running instances are identified by SI_SCHEDULE_STATUS = 0.

Completed Instances are either successful (in which case they have a document containing the result of the scheduled job), or failed. Failed jobs do not have a generated document, but they do have a failure reason description. Completed Instances, both successful and failed, are identified by the boolean SI_INSTANCE_OBJECT equal to true[24]. A successfully completed instance will have SI_SCHEDULE_STATUS equal to 1; failed instances will have a value of 3.

Note that it is possible for an object to have a SI_SCHEDULE_STATUS value of *1* and SI_INSTANCE_OBJECT/SI_INSTANCE both equal to *false*. This can happen if a scheduled document is opened and saved to a new folder. It is no longer an *instance*, but it retains its schedule status value. If you are querying for successful instances, it is recommended to apply a condition using "SI_INSTANCE = 1 AND SI_SCHEDULE_STATUS = 1" in order to exclude non-instances.

In BI4.2 SP05, two new schedule statuses were introduced: *Expired* and *Warning*. A recurring schedule assumes an *Expired* status if the schedule's End Date has passed. The *Warning* schedule status applies to Web Intelligence documents only, and indicates that its query (or one of its queries) hit a row limit or time limit (that is, it has a *Partial Results* warning). *Expired* is a failure – the schedule did not complete; *Warning* indicates that the report **did** complete successfully, but may have incomplete data.

Pending instances are identified with SI_SCHEDULE_STATUS equal to 8. Pending instances can be either one-time runs ("Once" or "Now"), or *recurring*.

A one-time run, naturally, is scheduled for a single generation of a report. When the instance is initially created (by a user scheduling the report in BI launch pad or CMC), a new pending instance is created in the InfoStore. When the instance begins processing at its scheduled time, its status changes to *Running*. Finally, the instance results in a status of *Success* or *Failed*. Throughout this lifecycle, the instance retains its original SI_ID, but its status and timestamps are updated as it goes.

Recurring instances, on the other hand, are processed differently. When the scheduled time for a recurring instance arrives, the instance spawns a *new* instance, essentially a copy of itself but as a one-time run. This new instance (with a new SI_ID), enters the *Running* status, and ultimately *Success* or *Failed*. Certain properties of the recurring instance itself are updated during this process, such as the SI_NEXTRUNTIME, but it remains as a recurring instance until it reaches its end date or is deleted..

A job that is in *Pending* or *Recurring* status does not automatically progress to *Running* status once its Next Run Time has passed. The following must occur (in order) because a job becomes eligible to run:

1.   The scheduled "Next Run Time" passes.

---

24   Note the difference between SI_INSTANCE (all instances) and SI_INSTANCE_OBJECT (completed instances). The ambiguity in naming can lead to confusion.

2. If the job has dependencies on any events, **all** of those events fire[25].

3. A kind-appropriate job server with sufficient processing capacity is available.

Once these criteria are met, the applicable job server initiates the processing of the job, and the job's status changes to *Running* (0).

Paused instances are inactive and do not run unless they are resumed. Paused instances are identified with a SI_SCHEDULE_STATUS of 9. As with the *Pending* status, both one-time and recurring instances can be paused.

	SI_RUNNABLE_OBJECT	SI_IS_SCHEDULABLE	SI_INSTANCE	SI_INSTANCE_OBJECT	SI_RECURRING	SI_SCHEDULE_STATUS
Non-Schedulable object	False	False	False	False	(N/A)	(N/A)
Schedulable base document	False	True	False	False	(N/A)	(N/A)
Running instance	True	True	True	False	False	0
Successful instance	False	True	True	True	True	1
Failed instance	False	True	True	True	True	3
Paused one-time schedule	True	True	True	False	False	8
Paused recurring schedule	True	True	True	False	True	8
Pending one-time schedule	True	True	True	False	False	9
Pending recurring schedule	True	True	True	False	True	9

Table 2: Scheduling Properties

Scheduling Result/Status Properties

There are several scheduling properties present at the root-level of InfoObjects (that is, not within a *property bag*). These properties relate to the object's scheduling capability, role, or result. (Most of the properties covered here were mentioned in the previous section.)

The boolean **SI_IS_SCHEDULABLE** property has a value of *true* if an object is of a kind that can be scheduled, or is a scheduled result (instance). This property is present on all objects.

The boolean **SI_INSTANCE** property is true for all objects that are instances. This includes *Pending, Recurring, Paused,* and *completed* instances. This property is present on all objects

Not to be confused with SI_INSTANCE, the SI_INSTANCE_OBJECT property is true on objects that are *completed instances* (either successful or failed). It is false for all other instance statuses, and for all objects that are not instances. This is true when SI_INSTANCE is true and SI_SCHEDULE_STATUS has a value of 1 (successful) or 3 (failed). This property is present on all objects

The boolean **SI_RUNNABLE_OBJECT** property indicates instances that are not yet completed. It

---

25 The events must fire *after* the scheduled run time in order for the run to run. That is, when the scheduled run time arrives, the job will begin waiting for the event(s). It ignores any firings of the event that occurred prior to the scheduled run time.

is `true` for instances that are *Running, Paused,* or *Pending,* and `false` on completed instances and non-instances. This is `true` when `SI_INSTANCE` is `true` and `SI_SCHEDULE_STATUS` has a value of 8 (paused) or 9 (pending). This property is present on all objects

The boolean **`SI_RECURRING`** property has a value of `true` for objects that are *Recurring instances,* and `false` for completed instances or one-time scheduled instances. This property is **only present** on instances (`SI_INSTANCE` = true).

The integer **`SI_SCHEDULE_STATUS`** property indicates the current scheduling status of an object. This property exists on all instances and will exist on non-instances in certain scenarios (such as documents in an inbox, or instances that were moved to a folder). See Table 2: Scheduling Properties for the applicable values.

The `SI_UISTATUS` property is mostly redundant with `SI_SCHEDULE_STATUS`. There are two differences between these properties:

- The value for *Pending* status is 9 in `SI_SCHEDULE_STATUS` and 12 in `SI_UISTATUS`. All other values are the same for both properties.

- The `SI_UISTATUS` property is **only** present on *instances* (`SI_INSTANCE` = *true*), while `SI_SCHEDULE_STATUS` may be present on non-instances.

There is also an `SI_UISTATUS` property in the `SI_SCHEDULEINFO` property bag, but its meaning is different.

The `SI_STARTTIME` and `SI_ENDTIME` date/time properties contain the time (in UTC) when the instance actually began processing and completed processing (respectively) on the job server.

The value of `SI_STARTTIME` may be different than the time the job was *scheduled* to begin for a number of possible reasons, including:

- All applicable job servers were at capacity, so this job had to wait for an available processing slot.

- The job had a dependency on one or more events. At the time the job was scheduled to start, it actually began waiting for the event. When the event ultimately fired, the job went into queue.

- The job was paused at the time its scheduled start time arrived; it then began processing after being un-paused.

Note that there are also `SI_STARTTIME` and `SI_ENDTIME` properties located in the `SI_SCHEDULEINFO` property bag (to be discussed later) that contains related, but different values. Be sure to reference these root-level properties rather than those in `SI_SCHEDULEINFO` if you need to obtain the time that the job actually started or completed processing.

The `SI_NEXTRUNTIME` property, which is only present on pending (one-time or recurring) instances, specifies the date and time when the next scheduled run of the job will occur. For one-time runs, this value is equal to the `SI_SCHEDULEINFO.SI_STARTTIME` property. For recurring instances, this property reflects the time of the *next* scheduled run (it is updated as the recurring schedule spawns new instances).

The SI_PROGID_MACHINE property is present on instances and non-instances that have default scheduling settings. Its value represents the SI_PROGID of the base document, regardless of the format of the scheduled instance (or default scheduling format). For example, if a Web Intelligence document is scheduled in Excel format, the SI_PROGID of the generated instance will be *CrystalEnterprise.Excel*, but the SI_PROGID_MACHINE property reflects the original document's ProgID value of *CrystalEnterprise.Webi*. This property is useful for identifying the kind of document that *generated* a particular instance, even if that instance is in a non-native format such as Excel or PDF[26].

The strangely-named but valuable **SI_NEW_JOB_ID** property is used to correlate recurring instances with the instances that they generate. If an instance is the result of a recurring schedule, then its SI_NEW_JOB_ID property is the SI_ID of the recurring instance from which it was generated. For all other instance objects, the SI_NEW_JOB_ID property is equal to their own SI_ID. Consider a subset of a repository as follows:

SI_ID	SI_INSTANCE	SI_RECURRING	SI_SCHEDULE_STATUS	SI_PARENTID	SI_NEW_JOB_ID
1001	false			987	
1732	true	false	1	1001	1732
2984	true	true	9	1001	2984
3433	true	false	1	1001	2984
8613	true	false	1	1001	2984

The first object in our repository (ID 1001) is the parent "base" document. Since it is not an instance, it does not have the SI_RECURRING, SI_SCHEDULE_STATUS, or SI_NEW_JOB_ID properties. The remaining three objects are instances of this document.

The second object (ID 1732) is a one-time scheduled instance. Its SI_SCHEDULE_STATUS property is 1, indicating success. Its SI_NEW_JOB_ID is equal to its own SI_ID (1732).

The third object (ID 2984) is a recurring instance, scheduled to run daily. Its SI_NEW_JOB_ID is also equal to its own SI_ID (2984).

The final two objects (IDs 3433 and 8613) are the two daily executions of the recurring instance (2984). Since these two instances were generated *from the recurring instance* 2984, their SI_NEW_JOB_ID property reflects that value.

Scheduling Settings

The SI_SCHEDULEINFO property bag contains properties relating to the various options that can be set for scheduling.

On *base documents* (schedulable non-instances), the contents of the SI_SCHEDULEINFO property

---

26 Unfortunately, there is no SI_KIND_MACHINE, which would be useful, but the kind can easily be determined from SI_PROGID_MACHINE.

bag are associated with the *Default Settings* panel for objects in the CMC. That is, they represent the default settings that appear in the *Schedule* panel when users create a schedule for a document. As an example, a particular WebI document may have default settings with *format* set to Excel. Whenever a user schedules this document, the format is pre-set to Excel (the user can select any other valid value before actually scheduling the instance).

For *instances*, the SI_SCHEDULEINFO property bag contains the settings that are used (pending/ paused/recurring instances), or the settings that *were* used (completed instances).

The following screenshot is of a recurring Program Object schedule, as seen in the CMC:

Instance Details: ls	
Title:	ls
Document Type:	Program
Status	Recurring
Destination:	Default
Created By:	Administrator
Creation Time:	10/6/15 7:05 AM
Next Run Time:	10/8/15 7:05 AM
Recurrence Type:	Object runs once every 1 days.
Location:	Test
Remote Instance:	No
Expiry:	10/5/25 8:50 PM

Illustration 3: Recurring instance properties in CMC

The SI_SCHEDULEINFO property bag for the above recurring instance contains the following properties[27]:

SI_APS_NAME	osboxes:6400
SI_CLEANUP	false
SI_ENDTIME	10/5/25 8:50:00 PM
SI_NAME	ls
SI_OBJID	5050
SI_OUTCOME	0
SI_PROGRESS	1
SI_RETRIES_ALLOWED	0
SI_RETRIES_ATTEMPTED	0
SI_RETRY_INTERVAL	1800
SI_RUN_ON_TEMPLATE	
SI_SCHED_NOW	false
SI_SCHEDULE_FLAGS	0

---

27 See SAP Note 1488516

SI_SCHEDULE_INTERVAL_HOURS	0
SI_SCHEDULE_INTERVAL_MINUTES	0
SI_SCHEDULE_INTERVAL_MONTHS	0
SI_SCHEDULE_INTERVAL_NDAYS	1
SI_SCHEDULE_INTERVAL_NTHDAY	0
SI_SCHEDULE_TYPE	2
SI_STARTTIME	10/6/15 7:05:00 AM
SI_SUBMITTER	Administrator
SI_SUBMITTERID	12
SI_TIMEZONE_ID	0
SI_TYPE	270
SI_UISTATUS	9

Table 3: Recurring instance properties

The scheduling options for this instance are relatively simple – it runs once per day, uses the default settings for format and destinations, and there are no calendars or events involved. There are many other properties that are present when other scheduling options are used.

All of the properties that we cover in this section are children of SI_SCHEDULEINFO, unless otherwise specified.

Start / End Times

The SI_STARTTIME property has a slightly different meaning for one-time vs. recurring instances. For one-time instances, SI_STARTTIME indicates the absolute time that the job becomes *eligible to run* (unless there are dependencies on events, in which case this is the time the job starts waiting for the events to fire).

For *recurring* schedules, the SI_STARTTIME marks the earliest date/time that the job can run, but the actual start time depends on the specific recurrence settings. Consider a report instance created on October 8, 2015, at 7:48 pm, scheduled to run on the 5th of each month, with a start date of December 1, 2015, at 4:00 am. The SI_STARTTIME of this instance would be 12/1/15 4:00 am and the first run of this instance would occur on 12/5/15 since it is the next *scheduled date after the start date.*

Note that the start *time* of a recurring instance is used as the time-of-day to start the job on the appropriate scheduled *day*. In the example above, we set a start date/time of 12/1/15 at 4:00 am. Since the job is scheduled to run on the 5th of each month, it becomes eligible to run at 4:00 am on 12/5/15, 4:00 am on 1/5/16, and so on[28].

When creating a new schedule in the CMC or BI launch pad, the default value for "Start Date/ Time" is the current system date and time. This value is stored in SI_STARTTIME, but not

---

28 This behavior also applies to reports scheduled "Every n months". If such a job was scheduled to begin on 11/15/2015 at 4:00 AM, it would run 1215/15 4:00 AM, 1/15/16 4:00 AM, etc.

displayed on the *Instance Details* page.

The SI_ENDTIME property specifies the date/time that the one-time-or recurring instance expires. For one-time executions, if the job does not start before the date/time specified in SI_ENDTIME arrives, it will fail. The error message will be "Object could not be scheduled within the specified time interval".

Recurring instances continue to run on their recurring schedule until the date/time specified in SI_ENDTIME is reached. At that moment, the recurring instance effectively disappears and no more instances are spawned from it. In BI4.2 SP05 and later, the instance not disappear but will have a status of *Expired*.

When creating a new schedule in the CMC or BI launch pad, the default value for "End Date/ Time" is the current system date and time, plus ten years. This value is stored in SI_ENDTIME, and is displayed on the *Instance Details* page as "Expiry".

When a recurring instance runs, it actually spawns a copy of itself as a one-time execution. It sets the new instance's SI_STARTTIME to be the same as the scheduled start time and set the SI_ENDTIME based on the *next scheduled runtime*. This occurs automatically, and is done to prevent multiple spawned instances from running concurrently. If a report is scheduled to run daily at 4:00 AM, then the SI_ENDTIME of the spawned job is automatically set to 4:00 AM on the following day (the start of the next scheduled run). This can cause unexpected failures if the recurrence period is very short. For example, it is possible to schedule an instance to run every minute. But if there is a delay of 60 seconds from the scheduled start of a job with this recurrence interval, the job will fail.

Recurrence Settings

The integer SI_SCHEDULE_TYPE property (not to be confused with SI_TYPE) identifies the recurrence setting of the instance. The possible values are:

0	Once
1	Hourly
2	Daily
3	Weekly
4	Monthly
5	Nth Day
6	First Monday
7	Last Day of Month
8	X Day of Nth Week of the Month
9	Calendar Template

Table 4: Schedule Type Values

Only value 0 (Once) is a one-time schedule; all others are the various recurring instance options. Note that there is no option for "Now", although it is an available option when scheduling reports. An instance scheduled to run "Now" will have an SI_SCHEDULE_TYPE of 0 ("Once"), and an SI_SCHED_NOW value of true.

Depending on the scheduling recurrence option selected, one or more additional properties will define the specific intervals to run on:

Schedule Type	Properties Used	Meaning
Once/Now	N/A	Run at the specified time only, do not recur
Hourly	SI_SCHEDULE_INTERVAL_HOURS SI_SCHEDULE_INTERVAL_MINUTES	Run every x hours plus y minutes. If SI_SCHEDULE_INTERVAL_HOURS is 1 and SI_SCHEDULE_INTERVAL_MINUTES is 30, then the job runs every 90 minutes.
Daily	SI_SCHEDULE_INTERVAL_NDAYS	Run every x days
Monthly	SI_SCHEDULE_INTERVAL_MONTHS	Run every x months
Nth Day	SI_SCHEDULE_INTERVAL_NTHDAY	Run on the nth day of every month.
Weekly	SI_RUN_ON_TEMPLATE	Run on specified days of the week
First Monday	SI_RUN_ON_TEMPLATE	Run on the first Monday of each month
Last Day of Month	SI_RUN_ON_TEMPLATE	Run on the last day of the month
X Day of Nth Week of Month	SI_RUN_ON_TEMPLATE	Run on day x of the nth week of the month
Calendar Template	SI_CALENDAR_TEMPLATE_ID	Run on every day specified in the selected calendar

Table 5: Recurrence Properties

The SI_SCHEDULE_INTERVAL... properties are all integers and specify either the number of hours/minutes/days/months between executions, or the specific day of the month to run. These properties are only applicable when the associated schedule type is selected. For example, the SI_SCHEDULE_INTERVAL_NDAYS property is ignored if the selected schedule type is anything other than *Daily*.

The *Weekly, First Monday, Last Day of Month*, and *X Day of Nth Week* recurrence options all use the SI_RUN_ON_TEMPLATE property bag. The following is an example of SI_RUN_ON_TEMPLATE when *First Monday* is the selected recurrence option:

SI_RUN_ON_TEMPLATE

```
SI_TEMPLATE_DAY1
        SI_DAYS_NTH_WEEK
              0
        SI_DAYS_OF_WEEK
              2
        SI_DATES_START_MONTH
              0
        SI_DATES_START_YEAR
              0
        SI_DATES_END_DAY
              7
        SI_DATES_END_MONTH
              0
        SI_DATES_END_YEAR
              0
        SI_DATES_START_DAY
              1
SI_NUM_TEMPLATE_DAYS
        1
```

This bag provides a very flexible methodology for setting complex recurrence settings. Strangely, the CMC and BI launch pad interfaces only allow for the selection of these pre-defined scheduling options, despite the fact that SI_RUN_ON_TEMPLATE would support the ability for users to define their own complex scheduling strategies, such as "Third Tuesday of each Quarter", or "Monday-Friday Between May and September, and Monday-Saturday Between October and December". Perhaps a future release of SAP BusinessObjects will exploit this property bag and enable user-defined scheduling strategies[29].

If an object is scheduled using the *Calendar* recurrence option, then the SI_CALENDAR_TEMPLATE_ID property will contain the ID of the associated calendar object.

Output Format Settings

The Reporting object types (Crystal Reports, Web Intelligence, Desktop Intelligence) can be scheduled to several different output types. The default behavior for all of these object types is to generate a *native copy*. For instance, a WebI document scheduled in *Web Intelligence* format will essentially be a copy of its parent WebI document, but with refreshed data. The generated WebI instance is a fully-functional WebI report, and can be modified, refreshed, exported, or copied elsewhere[30]. The same is true for Crystal Reports and Desktop Intelligence.

These objects can also be scheduled to *static* formats, such as Excel, PDF, or Text. The

---

29   The *CeScheduleType* constant associated with the SI_SCHEDULE_TYPE value of 8 is named "CALENDAR", although it displays in CMC and BI launch pad as "X Day of Nth Week". It *appears* that this value was meant to support user-defined schedules. However it is currently (as of BI4.2) only used for these three pre-defined options.

30   Document instances can never be modified and saved in-place, but they can be moved or copied to another folder.

available output formats differ by kind and are listed in Table 6: Reporting output formats.

Format	Kind	Crystal Reports	Web Intelligence	Desktop Intelligence
Crystal Report	Report	X		
Crystal Report Read Only	Report	X*		
CSV	Txt	X*	X*	
Desktop Intelligence	FullClient			X
Excel 07-2003 Data Only	Excel	X*		
Excel 97-2003	Excel	X*		X
Excel Workbook	Excel		X	
Excel Workbook Data Only	Excel	X*		
Paginated Text	Txt	X*		
PDF	PDF	X*	X	X
Plain Text	Txt	X*		
RTF	Rtf	X*		X
RTF Editable	Rtf	X*		
Tab Separated Text	Txt	X*		X
Web Intelligence	Webi		X	
Word 97-2003	Word	X*		
XML	Agnostic	X*		

Table 6: Reporting output formats[31]

Additional options included in SI_PROCESSINFO.SI_FORMAT_INFO

The selected output format is managed differently for instances vs. non-instances (base documents).   For instances, the selected output is stored in the instance's root-level SI_KIND/SI_PROGID properties.   For example, if a recurring schedule is created for a WebI report, and the output format is set to Excel, the recurring instance's SI_KIND value will be *Excel*.   Naturally, the instances that are spawned from these recurring instances (the actual

---

31 The available format options are enumerated in the SDK, in *IFullClientFormatOptions.CeFullClientFormat*, *IReportFormatOptions.CeReportFormat*, and *IWebiFormatOptions.CeWebiFormat*.

Excel documents created from the scheduling executions) will also have a SI_KIND value of *Excel*. If the default output format is selected, then the instance's SI_KIND value will match its parent's (*Webi, Report,* or *FullClient*).

For base documents, in which the output format is actually the object's default scheduling option (as opposed to being the *actual* scheduling option on instances), the output format is stored in SI_SCHEDULEINFO.SI_PROGID_SCHEDULE. As it is a PROGID property, the value of the property is in the format of CrystalEnterprise.xxx, in which xxx is one of the common values of kind (example, *CrystalEnterprise.Excel*).

A couple of examples illustrate this difference:

Example A – WebI Document With Default Output Format of PDF

SI_KIND	Webi
SI_PROGID	CrystalEnterprise.Webi
SI_PROGID_MACHINE	CrystalEnterprise.Webi
SI_INSTANCE	false
SI_SCHEDULEINFO.SI_PROGID_SCHEDULE	CrystalEnterprise.PDF

In this example, a base WebI document is set with a default output format of PDF. As it is a base document, this default setting is stored in SI_SCHEDULEINFO.SI_PROGID_SCHEDULE, but its SI_KIND remains as *Webi*.

Example B – WebI Recurring Schedule in PDF Format

SI_KIND	PDF
SI_PROGID	CrystalEnterprise.PDF
SI_PROGID_MACHINE	CrystalEnterprise.Webi
SI_INSTANCE	true
SI_RECURRING	true
SI_SCHEDULE_STATUS	9
SI_SCHEDULEINFO.SI_PROGID_SCHEDULE	(not present)

This example shows a recurring instance, in PDF format, which is a child of a WebI document. As this is an instance and not a base document, the SI_KIND and SI_PROGID properties reflect the selected output format (PDF), and the SI_PROGID_SCHEDULE property is not present. Note that the SI_PROGID_MACHINE property retains the *parent's* ProgID value.

Example C – Completed WebI instance in PDF format

SI_KIND	PDF
SI_PROGID	CrystalEnterprise.PDF
SI_PROGID_MACHINE	CrystalEnterprise.Webi
SI_INSTANCE	true
SI_RECURRING	false

SI_KIND	PDF
SI_SCHEDULE_STATUS	1
SI_SCHEDULEINFO.SI_PROGID_SCHEDULE	(not present)

Finally, here is the completed instance generated from the recurring instance in Example B. The `SI_KIND`, `SI_PROGID`, AND `SI_PROGID_MACHINE` properties have the same values as the recurring instance that produced it.

For some output formats (including most of the Crystal Reports formats), additional options can be specified beyond the broad file type that is defined in `SI_KIND`.   For example, when a Crystal Report is scheduled as *Excel*, it may be Excel 97-2003 or Excel 2010 format; and text file output may be Comma Separated (CSV), tab-delimited, or plain text. These additional settings are stored in the `SI_PROCESSINFO` property bag, in a child property bag named `SI_FORMAT_INFO`.

The contents of `SI_FORMAT_INFO` differ by the kind of output being generated. There are too many different variations of this property to cover here in their entirety, but here are a couple of examples:

Crystal Report scheduled in Excel 97-2003 format, pages 4-7 only.

SI_FORMAT	crxf_xls:9
SI_FORMAT_ENDPAGE	7
SI_FORMAT_EXPORT_ALLPAGES	false
SI_FORMAT_STARTPAGE	4
SI_USE_OPTION_IN_REPORT	true

Crystal Report scheduled to PDF format

SI_FORMAT	crxf_pdf:0
SI_FORMAT_EXPORT_ALLPAGES	true
SI_FORMAT_STARTPAGE	4

Retry Settings

The integer `SI_RETRIES_ALLOWED` and `SI_RETRY_INTERVAL` properties specify the retry strategy of instances that fail. A failed job continues to retry until it either completes successfully or the specified number of allowed retries is reached (if `SI_RETRIES_ALLOWED` is 0, then no retries are attempted). The `SI_RETRY_INTERVAL` property defines the time, in seconds, to wait after a failure before a retry is attempted. Both properties can be set when scheduling an object (the default value for `S_RETRIES_ALLOWED` is 0).

The integer `SI_RETRIES_ATTEMPTED` property is present on completed instances and indicates the actual number of retries that were attempted when the job was run. If it is 0, then either

`SI_RETRIES_ALLOWED` was 0, or the job completed successfully on its first attempt.

Destination Settings

Scheduled instances, when executed successfully, generate some form of output file. These files may be in a native format, such as Crystal Reports or Web Intelligence, or static, such as Excel, PDF, text, etc. By default, these files are stored with the scheduled instance that generated them and are only accessible via BI launch pad or the CMC (this is the "Default Enterprise Location"). However, most schedulable objects can be set to deliver the file (or files) to an additional destination.

The possible destination settings for scheduled objects are:

- Default Enterprise Location
- BI Inbox
- File system
- FTP
- SMTP (email)
- SAP StreamWork

If an option other than *Default Enterprise Location* is selected for a scheduled instance or base document, then an `SI_SCHEDULEINFO.SI_DESTINATIONS` property bag will be present, containing settings for the selected destination. This bag contains an `SI_TOTAL` integer property indicating the number of destinations, and a list of enumerated property bags for each selected destination.

Although the `SI_DESTINATIONS` bag contains enumerated properties, most schedulable objects can only support a single destination (other than the Default Enterprise Location). That is, a scheduled WebI Intelligence document can be set to distribute to the Default Enterprise Location only, or to the Default Enterprise Location and, say, Email. It is not possible to select both Email and File System as destinations for a Web Intelligence document. For this reason, the `SI_DESTINATIONS` bag will either not be present, or will contain a single enumerated child property for these kinds of objects. Publications, on the other hand, can be set to more than one destination. Publications that have multiple destinations have multiple enumerated child properties under `SI_DESTINATIONS`.

Within the enumerated destination property, the `SI_PROGID` property defines the specific destination type. This can be one of[32]:

- CrystalEnterprise.Ftp
- CrystalEnterprise.Sftp
- CrystalEnterprise.Smtp   *(Email)*
- CrystalEnterprise.Managed   *(BI Inbox)*

---

32   To list the available destinations on a system, use the following query: select si_name from ci_systemobjects where si_parentid = 29

- CrystalEnterprise.StreamWork

- CrystalEnterprise.DiskUnmanaged   *(File System)*

Let's look at an example document scheduled to an inbox:

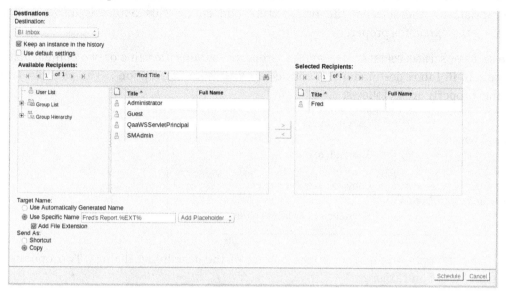

The above selections would produce a SI_SCHEDULEINFO.SI_DESTINATIONS property bag similar to the following:

```
SI_DESTINATIONS
        1
                SI_PROGID
                        CrystalEnterprise.Managed
                SI_DEST_SCHEDULEOPTIONS
                        SI_NAME
                                Fred's Report.%EXT%
                        SI_OPTIONS
                                0
                        SI_ADD_FILE_EXTENSION
                                true
                        SI_OUTPUT_FILES
                                1
                                        3597
                        SI_TOTAL
                                1
        SI_TOTAL
                1
```

The SI_DEST_SCHEDULEOPTIONS property bag contains destination options. Some of these are specific to a destination type, while others are common to all.

The SI_DEST_SCEHDULEOPTIONS.SI_NAME property specifies the name of the document to be sent to the inbox. If on the schedule options page, we had selected "*Use Automatically Generated Name*", then the SI_NAME property would be empty. However, in the example above, we have entered a name of "*Fred's Report*". By checking off "*Add File Extension*", the interface automatically adds the "%EXT% placeholder, which is replaced with a file extension appropriate for the selected file type (.xlsx, .pdf, etc.). This option is also set in the SI_ADD_FILE_EXTENSION property.

The SI_DEST_SCEHDULEOPTIONS.SI_OPTIONS property contains the value of two options that are specific to BI Inbox destinations: "Send As", and "Destination Option". The possible values for this property are as follows:

Save As option	Copy, to Inbox	0
	Shortcut, to Inbox	1
Destination Type Option	Copy, to Favorites Folder	16
	Shortcut, to Favorites Folder	17

The "*Save As*" option is present at the bottom of the scheduling dialog. Two options are available "*Copy*" and "*Shortcut*".

The "*Destination Option*", despite not being available in the scheduling interface, is actually functional. If an instance is scheduled via the SDK instead of the scheduling interface, then a value can be manually set for SI_OPTIONS. If set to 16 or 17, then the document is delivered to the recipient's favorites folder instead of the inbox.

The SI_DEST_SCEHDULEOPTIONS.SI_OUTPUT_FILES property is present for all destinations, but its meaning is different for each. For *inbox* destinations, this property contains a list of IDs of the selected recipients (users or groups). In the example above, the schedule was set to distribute to a single user, Fred, having ID 3597. If no specific recipient is selected, then this property will be empty, and the *instance owner* will implicitly be the only recipient[33].

Now let's look at a document scheduled to an email destination:

---

33 By default, the instance owner is the user who created the schedule. However, ownership of the instance can be assigned to another user (or group) via the "Schedule For" options

And the associated SI_DESTINATIONS property bag:

SI_DESTINATIONS

    1

        SI_PROGID

            CrystalEnterprise.Smtp

        SI_DEST_SCHEDULEOPTIONS

            SI_MAIL_BCC

                SI_TOTAL

                    0

            SI_SMTP_ENABLEATTACHMENTS

                true

            SI_SENDER_NAME

                sender@company.com

            SI_ADD_FILE_EXTENSION

                false

            SI_ENABLE_SSL

                false

            SI_MAIL_ADDRESSES

                1

                    fred@company.com

                SI_TOTAL

                    1

            SI_MAIL_SUBJECT

                Weekly report

            SI_MAIL_MESSAGE

                Click here to view this week's report: %SI_VIEWER_URL%

            SI_MAIL_CC

                SI_TOTAL

                    0

            SI_OUTPUT_FILES

                1

                    SI_MIME_TYPE

<pre>
                                        (empty)
                            SI_EMBED_NAME
                                        (empty)
                     SI_TOTAL
                        1
          SI_TOTAL
              1
</pre>

Since we chose the "*Automatically Generated Name*" option, there is no SI_NAME property in the SI_DEST_SCHEDULEOPTIONS bag. However, we see the properties associated with the email options – SI_SENDER_NAME, SI_MAIL_ADDRESSES, SI_CC, SI_MAIL_BCC, SI_MAIL_SUBJECT, and SI_MAIL_MESSAGE, correlating to the *from, to, cc, bcc, subject,* and *message* fields on the scheduling dialog. Note that SI_CC, SI_BCC, and SI_MAIL_ADDRESSES are property bags, since they can contain multiple addresses. Also note the SI_OUTPUT_FILES property bag, which, unlike the inbox destination, contains two (unused) email format settings.

The last destination we'll review is *File System*:

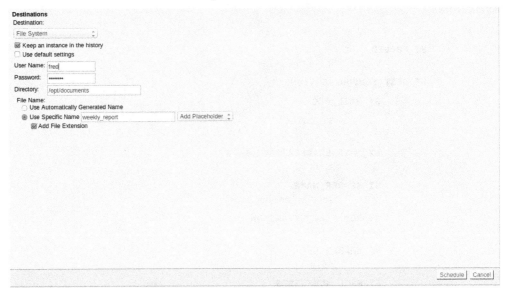

And the associated SI_DESTINATIONS property bag:

<pre>
SI_DESTINATIONS
       1
               SI_PROGID
                       CrystalEnterprise.DiskUnmanaged
               SI_DEST_SCHEDULEOPTIONS
                       (empty)
               SI_PASSWORD
                       ****
               SI_USERNAME
                       fred
               SI_ADD_FILE_EXTENSION
                       true
</pre>

```
SI_OUTPUT_FILES
        1
                    /opt/documents/weekly_report.%EXT%
        SI_TOTAL
                1
  SI_TOTAL
  1
```

The SI_PASSWORD and SI_USERNAME properties correlate with the *User Name* and *Password* fields on the scheduling dialog, but note that the password value is masked. This masking is performed by the query engine, and not in the Query Builder web application. So, although the password is stored in the CMS, it is not possible to retrieve it with a CMS query.

The SI_OUTPUT_FILES property bag for *File System* destinations, unlike the other destinations we've looked at so far, actually contains information on output files. Although it contains enumerated properties, it only holds a single file name[34].

For the examples above, we have chosen *not to* select the *"Use default settings"* option, but to enter the settings as shown. If *"Use default settings"* is selected, then, naturally, there are no settings to apply to the destination since the settings from the job server that processes the job are used. In this case, the SI_SCHEDULEOPTIONS property bag will be empty. If, for example, we chose *File System* as the destination, but checked off "Use default settings", then the instance's SI_DESTINATIONS bag would look like the following:

SI_DESTINATIONS

    1

        SI_PROGID

            CrystalEnterprise.DiskUnmanaged

        SI_DEST_SCHEDULEOPTIONS

            (empty)

    SI_TOTAL

        1

Event Settings

Scheduled objects may be set to wait for an event before running, to fire an event after running, or both. The references to these events are stored in the SI_DEPENDENCIES and SI_DEPENDANTS property bags, both located in the SI_SCHEDULEINFO bag, and both of which are property bag lists containing enumerated properties.

If a scheduled object is set to wait for one or more events, then the IDs of those events are stored in SI_DEPENDENCIES. If the object is not scheduled to wait for events, then this property will either not be present, or will only have a SI_TOTAL child property with a value of *0*.

An example of a document scheduled to wait for an event may look like:

---

34 The SAP BusinessObjects environment for this example runs on UNIX, and so the output file name is a UNIX path format. For an SAP BusinessObjects environment on Windows, a Windows-compatible file path format would be required.

SI_DEPENDENCIES

   1

       5947

   SI_TOTAL

     1

The id 5947 in this example correlates to a File Event.

The SI_DEPENDANTS property bag has a similar structure, for any events that an object is set to fire upon completion:

SI_DEPENDANTS

   1

       4181

   SI_TOTAL

     1

Server Group settings

Server Groups are collections of, well, servers. They provide a way to ensure that scheduled instances run on specified servers, or prioritizes specified servers when they run. For example, consider an SAP BusinessObjects cluster with nodes in several data center locations across the United States. The data centers may host the SAP BusinessObjects servers as well as database and file share servers. In this case, it would be suboptimal for a job server in, say, California, to process a Web Intelligence report that pulls data from a database in New York and writes its output to a file share server in that location. To alleviate this issue, we could create a Server Group that includes only the servers in New York, and then schedule our report to give preference to that Server Group. Thus, the report uses the New York servers, unless none are available. Alternatively, we could schedule the report to use **only** the New York Server Group, if we want to ensure that it does not run in any other location (in this case, the scheduled instance waits patiently until a server in the New York server group is available).

Scheduling Server Group

Set the default servers to use for scheduling this object:
- ○ Use the first available server
- ○ Give preference to servers in the selected group
  - Central Region
- ● Only use servers in the selected group
  - Central Region

☐ Run at origin site

Instances can be scheduled to:

- Use the first available server (default)

- Give preference to servers in the specified group

- Use only servers in the specified group

The settings are stored in the SI_MACHINE and SI_MACHINECHOICE properties in the SI_SCHEDULEINFO bag. If the first option is selected ("*Use the first available server*"), then either both properties will not be present, or SI_MACHINECHOICE will have a value of 0.

If the "*Give preference...*" option is selected, then SI_MACHINECHOICE will have a value of 1, and SI_MACHINE will have a reference to the specified server group object[35]:

SI_MACHINECHOICE	1
SI_MACHINE	6006

If the "*Use only servers...*" option is selected, then SI_MACHINECHOICE will have a value of 2, and SI_MACHINE will have a reference to the specified server group object:

SI_MACHINECHOICE	2
SI_MACHINE	6006

We can easily identify objects that are scheduled to use a server group:

```
select *
  from ci_infoobjects
 where si_scheduleinfo.si_machinechoice != 0
       and si_scheduleinfo.si_machine = 6005
```

Chapter Review

- All InfoObjects in an InfoStore are comprised of properties. These properties may be strings, numerics, dates, or property bags

- Property bags can contain properties themselves. One form of property bag is an enumeration – a list of integers representing the IDs of related InfoObjects.

- Many common properties exist on all InfoObjects: SI_ID, SI_CUID, SI_NAME, etc.

- A large number of properties relate to scheduling. Most of the scheduling settings are stored in two special property bags: SI_SCHEDULEINFO and SI_PROCESSINFO.

Quiz

1. Property bags can contain what number of child properties?

   a) Zero

   b) One

---

35 The server group object itself is located in the CI_SYSTEMOBJECTS table, with an SI_KIND of 'ServerGroup'.

   c) More than one

   d) Any of the above

2. True/False: property bags can be used in query conditions.

3. Which of the following IDs are unique, even across different installations of SAP BusinessObjects?

   a) `SI_ID`

   b) `SI_CUID`

   c) `SI_RUID`

   d) `SI_GUID`

4. The data type of `SI_ID` is a(n) __ while the value of `SI_CUID` is a(n) __.

   a) `Integer, String`

   b) `String, Integer`

5. The value of the __ property is generally prefixed with __.

   a) `SI_KIND / CrystalEnterprise.`

   b) `SI_PROGID / CrystalEnterprise.`

   c) `SI_KIND / BusinessObjects.`

   d) `SI_TYPE / BusinessObjects.`

6. Which property is recommended to be used when querying for children of an InfoObject?

   a) `SI_PARENT_ID`

   b) `SI_PARENTCUID`

   c) `SI_PARENT_CUID`

   d) `SI_PARENTID`

7. Which Boolean property is used to identify completed scheduled instances?

   a) `SI_SCHEDULE_STATUS`

   b) `SI_TYPE`

   c) `SI_INSTANCE`

   d) `SI_INSTANCE_OBJECT`

8. True/False: The `SI_STARTTIME` property contains the actual start time of a scheduled job, while `SI_SCHEDULEINFO.SI_STARTTIME` contains the *scheduled* start time of a job.

9. An instance that is scheduled to wait for an event has values in which property bag?

   a) `SI_EVENTS`

b) SI_DEPENDENCIES

c) SI_DEPENDANTS

Answers on page 672.

Chapter 3 - Folders

The SAP BusinessObjects InfoStore is a hierarchical folder structure. At the very top of this hierarchy is a single object representing the cluster, and having SI_ID = 4. Beneath this cluster object (that is, objects which have an SI_PARENTID value of 4) are a number of root folders. Each root folder contains specific content, such as documents, users, servers, etc. Most of these root folders, and a number of lower-level folders, have predefined object IDs or CUIDs which are the same in every installation of SAP BusinessObjects. Appendix C - Sample CMS Folder Hierarchy contains a complete folder hierarchy from a sample SAP BusinessObjects installation, including the predefined IDs and CUIDs.

> *Key point: All objects in a CMS are members of the InfoStore hierarchy; each one descends from the root cluster InfoObject, which is ID 4.*

Arguably the most well known of the folder hierarchies is *Pubic Folders*, so this is the starting point for our examination of folder hierarchies.

Public Folders

You are likely already familiar with *Public Folders* – this hierarchy contains various document types such as Web Intelligence, Crystal Reports, Programs, and others. The Public Folders InfoObject has a predefined ID 23 and a CUID of ASHnC0S_Pw5LhKFbZ.iA_j4. This object and all of its descendants are accessed via the CI_INFOOBJECTS table.

We can list the names of the children of the root Public Folder with the following query:

```
select si_name,si_id,si_kind
  from ci_infoobjects
 where si_parentid = 23
```

If we run this query on a system with a public folder structure as in Illustration 4, then we get a result similar to the following:

SI_ID	SI_NAME	SI_KIND
511	Auditing	Folder
553	System Configuration Wizard	Folder
2795	Report Conversion Tool	Folder
3968	Web Intelligence Samples	Folder
4213	Reports	Folder
4704	LCM	Folder
4707	Probes	Folder

SI_ID	SI_NAME	SI_KIND
4780	Visual Difference	Folder
4860	Platform Search Scheduling	Folder
5588	Samples	Folder

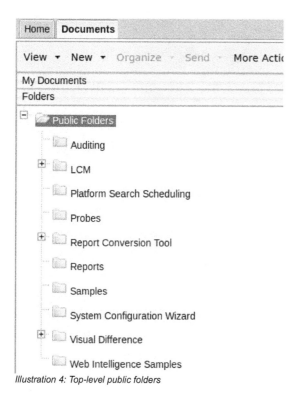

Illustration 4: Top-level public folders

Folder Navigation

A common need in SAP BusinessObjects programming is identifying the folder ancestry of an object such as a report. There are two common methods to accomplish this goal: recursive navigation and use of the SI_PATH property[36].

Consider the *Quarterly Profit* report in Illustration 5, and a need to list its folder path. We can see from the screenshot that it is in *Public Folders → Reports → Sales → Financial → Quarterly*, but we need to retrieve this information programmatically.

---

36 In the next chapter, Relationship Queries, we will cover some more efficient methods for navigating folders. But learning this more basic more of navigation is useful for understanding the structure of the folder hierarchies.

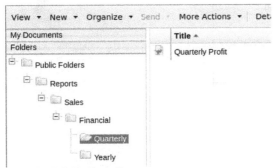

Illustration 5: Folder Navigation

Our first step is to identify the report's immediate parent. We start with the following query:

```
select si_name,si_parentid
  from ci_infoobjects
 where si_name = 'quarterly profit'
```

This produces:

SI_NAME	Quarterly Profit
SI_PARENTID	6250

Knowing that the document's parent is object 6250, we submit another query to find that object's name and its parent ID:

```
select si_name,si_parentid
  from ci_infoobjects
 where si_id = 6250
```

SI_NAME	Quarterly
SI_PARENTID	6249

We continue querying, now for the next higher folder, ID 6249:

```
select si_name,si_parentid
  from ci_infoobjects
 where si_id = 6249
```

SI_NAME	Financial
SI_PARENTID	6248

...and again, for ID 6248:

```
select si_name,si_parentid
  from ci_infoobjects
 where si_id = 6248
```

SI_NAME	Sales
SI_PARENTID	4213

So far, we have established the folder lineage of the *Quarterly Profit* report as *Sales* →

Financial → Quarterly. We continue by querying for the parent of the *Sales* folder:

```
select si_name,si_parentid
  from ci_infoobjects
 where si_id = 4213
```

SI_NAME	Reports
SI_PARENTID	0

Finally, we reach the *Reports* folder. We know we have reached a top-level public folder since this folder's parent ID is 0. We now know the full folder lineage of *Quarterly Profile: Reports → Sales → Financial → Quarterly*.

But wait – the root-level Public Folders folder is object ID 23. Why is the parent of *Reports* 0 and not 23? This appears to be a quirk and is perhaps an artifact of the old Crystal Enterprise CMS design. Although the root-level Public Folder is, in fact, object ID 23, the top-level folders in Public Folders (such as *Reports*) have an SI_PARENTID property value of 0. You may identify these top-level folders in a CMS with a condition on SI_PARENTID=23, but it is important to remember that the objects' SI_PARENTID reflects a different value[37]. Thus, when navigating upwards in the Public Folder hierarchy, reaching an object with SI_PARENTID of 0 indicates that the top of the hierarchy has been reached.

The second method for finding an object's lineage is to use the SI_PATH property on folders. We start with the same query as before, to find the *Quarterly Profit* report's parent folder:

```
select si_name,si_parentid
  from ci_infoobjects
 where si_name = 'quarterly profit'
```

SI_NAME	Quarterly Profit
SI_PARENTID	6250

Now, instead of successively submitting queries until we reach an object with SI_PARENTID of 0, we only need to retrieve the SI_PATH and SI_NAME properties of object 6250:

```
select si_name,si_path
  from ci_infoobjects
 where si_id = 6250
```

SI_NAME
      Quarterly
SI_PATH
      SI_FOLDER_ID1
            6249
      SI_FOLDER_NAME1
            Financial
      SI_FOLDER_OBTYPE1

---

37 You *could* actually query for top-level public folders with "select * from ci_infoobjects where si_parentid = 0", but it is recommended to use the "correct" parent ID of 23.

```
                    1

    SI_FOLDER_ID2
                 6248

    SI_FOLDER_NAME2
                 Sales

    SI_FOLDER_OBTYPE2
                    1

    SI_FOLDER_ID3
                 4213

    SI_FOLDER_NAME3
                 Reports

    SI_FOLDER_OBTYPE3
                    1

    SI_NUM_FOLDERS
                    3
```

The SI_PATH property bag contains a list of properties, but note that they are not standard enumerated properties. That is, we do not see a single SI_TOTAL property and a list of enumerated properties (1, 2, 3). But the behavior is the same – there is one SI_NUM_FOLDERS integer property, which contains the number of folders in the list. Each referenced ancestor folder is represented by three properties: its ID, name, and object type[38].

Perhaps unintuitively, the SI_FOLDER_NAME1, SI_FOLDER_ID1, and SI_FOLDER_OBTYPE1 properties reference the object's *immediate* parent, and then proceed *upward* from there – the last SI_FOLDER... properties (3, in this case) reference the *Reports* top-level folder[39].

Looking at the result, and starting with SI_FOLDER_NAME1, we find the *Financial* folder. This is the immediate parent of the *Quarterly* folder. Proceeding to SI_FOLDER_NAME2, we find the *Sales* folder, and then finally to SI_FOLDER_NAME3 to find the Reports folder.

From this one query for the *Quarterly* folder's SI_PATH property, we can see the complete folder lineage. (*Reports → Sales → Financial → Quarterly*). We do not need to successively run multiple queries to find each level's parent folder.

There is one limitation to using the SI_PATH property as opposed to the recursive navigation method – with SI_PATH, we only get the ID and name of each ancestral folder. If we wanted to get additional information about each folder (date created, for example), we would need to re-query the CMS for that specific object.

Navigating downward is fairly simple. Let's say we want to explore the Public Folder hierarchy beginning at the root. We would start by using the same query that we used at the beginning of this section, to retrieve the top-level public folders:

---

38 Fortunately, in the SDK, there is an accessor method that creates an array of parent folder names from the SI_PATH property. So it is generally not necessary to programmatically iterate through these properties.

39 If the hierarchy were the other way around, with the top-level folder being SI_FOLDER_NAME1, and proceeding down, then it would be possible to easily query for all descendant folders of a given folder at a given level. For example, we could identify all descendant subfolders of the top-level *Report Conversion Tool* folder with: where si_path.si_folder_name1='report conversion tool'.

```
select si_name,si_id,si_kind
  from ci_infoobjects
 where si_parentid = 23
```

SI_ID	SI_NAME	SI_KIND
511	Auditing	Folder
553	System Configuration Wizard	Folder
2795	Report Conversion Tool	Folder
3968	Web Intelligence Samples	Folder
4213	Reports	Folder
4704	LCM	Folder
4707	Probes	Folder
4780	Visual Difference	Folder
4860	Platform Search Scheduling	Folder
5588	Samples	Folder

Now we want to explore the *Reports* folder. We use the same query as the previous step, but reference ID 4213. We also add SI_CHILDREN to the query so we can know which folders contain child objects.

```
select si_name,si_id,si_kind,si_children
  from ci_infoobjects
 where si_parentid = 4213
```

SI_ID	SI_NAME	SI_KIND	SI_CHILDREN
6248	Sales	Folder	1

We continue downward, querying for the children of the *Sales* folder:

```
select si_name,si_id,si_kind,si_children
  from ci_infoobjects
 where si_parentid = 6248
```

SI_ID	SI_NAME	SI_KIND	SI_CHILDREN
6249	Financial	Folder	1

And again....

```
select si_name,si_id,si_kind,si_children
  from ci_infoobjects
 where si_parentid = 6249
```

SI_ID	SI_NAME	SI_KIND	SI_CHILDREN
6250	Quarterly	Folder	1
6277	Yearly	Folder	0

Note that the *Yearly* folder has 0 children – we know that it is empty, but the *Quarterly* folder has one child. We re-query once more, for the *Quarterly* folder:

```
select si_name,si_id,si_kind,si_children
  from ci_infoobjects
 where si_parentid = 6250
```

SI_ID	SI_NAME	SI_KIND	SI_CHILDREN
6251	Quarterly Profit	Webi	0

We know we have reached the bottom of the folder hierarchy since there are no objects with a value of SI_CHILDREN greater than 0.

Personal Folders

The hierarchy containing user's personal folders (*aka Favorites*[40]) are also located in CI_INFOOBJECTS, but stored in a different folder hierarchy, which has a root folder ID of 18. This root folder contains a subfolder for each user in the system, and this subfolder represents the users' Personal Folders.

There is one quirk in this hierarchy: the root folder (ID 18) has an SI_KIND of *Folder*, but the actual subfolders that are associated with each user have an SI_KIND of *FavoritesFolder*. Further, any folder that a user creates in the Personal Folder will have an SI_KIND of *Folder*.

To illustrate, consider a simple system containing users *Administrator*, *Guest*, and *Fred*. In his Personal Folder, Fred has a Web Intelligence report named *Returns*, and a folder named *Ad-hoc Reports (see* Illustration 6: Fred's personal folder). The Personal Folder hierarchy in this system would look like the following:

SI_NAME	SI_KIND	SI_ID
User Folders	Folder	18
Administrator	FavoritesFolder	791
Guest	FavoritesFolder	808
Fred	FavoritesaFolder	5316
Returns	Webi	10626
Ad-hoc Reports	Folder	8035

---

40 Over the years, some things in the SAP BusinessObjects architecture have assumed multiple names. In BI launch pad, a user will see "My Favorites". In CMC, these folders are collectively called "Personal Folders". Finally, the internal SI_NAME value of the folder hierarchy root is "User Folders".

Illustration 6: Fred's personal folder

If we wanted to retrieve Fred's personal folder itself, we could use the following query:

```
select *
  from ci_infoobjects
 where si_name = 'fred'
       and sI_kind = 'favoritesfolder'
```

Note that, in some cases (particularly in older versions of XI), it's possible for a user's personal folder to have a different name from the user itself. Thus, the only guaranteed way to retrieve a personal folder is to first get the SI_FAVORITES_FOLDER property from the user object:

```
select si_favorites_folder
  from ci_systemobjects
 where si_kind = 'user'
       and si_name = 'fred'
```

It is important to remember that Personal Folders and Public Folders both exist in CI_INFOOBJECTS but have different roots. If you were attempting to query for an object in public folders by name, but do not specify its ancestry, you may inadvertently retrieve an object in someone's personal folder instead[41]. Consider a need to retrieve a report named *Returns* in a public folder. From our example above, we know that Fred has a report of the same name. We attempt to retrieve the report with the following query:

```
select si_id
  from ci_infoobjects
 where si_name = 'returns'
       and si_kind = 'webi'
```

This query would return both *Returns* reports – the one in public folders as well as the one in Fred's personal folder.

To deal with this ambiguity, we can specify the folder hierarchy by ID in a query. To ensure that we retrieve only reports from public folders, we can use the special SI_ANCESTOR

---

41 Assuming you are executing the query as a user who has visibility to other users' personal folders. If not, then the query will not retrieve those objects.

75 Part One – The InfoStore

condition[42]:

```
select si_id
  from ci_infoobjects
 where si_name = 'returns'
       and si_kind = 'webi'
       and si_ancestor = 23
```

By using `SI_ANCESTOR=23`, we ensure that we only retrieve objects from public folders. Similarly, if we only wanted reports from Personal Folders, we can specify `SI_ANCESTOR=18`:

```
select si_id
  from ci_infoobjects
 where si_name = 'returns'
       and si_kind = 'webi'
       and si_ancestor = 18
```

The `SI_ANCESTOR` conditional expression can be used with any folder ID. If you need to retrieve all documents named *Returns* that are in Fred's personal folders, you could use:

```
select si_id
  from ci_infoobjects
 where si_name = 'returns'
       and si_kind = 'webi'
       and si_ancestor = 5316
```

BI Inbox

Inboxes serve a similar function to personal folders, but with a few notable differences:

- Inboxes cannot contain subfolders

- Documents in inboxes cannot be scheduled

- Documents in inboxes cannot be modified (they can, however, be moved to a different folder and modified there)

The representation of inboxes in the CMS is similar to that of personal folders. There is a root-level folder named *Inboxes* (having ID 48, CUID AVmJiqdOvoRBoU1vQCZydFE, and parent ID 4), located in the `CI_INFOOBJECTS` table. Under this folder is a folder-like object for every user in the cluster; this object is of kind *Inbox*. We can retrieve all inboxes with the following query:

```
select si_id,si_name,si_kind
  from ci_infoobjects
 where si_parentid = 48
```

---

42 The `SI_ANCESTOR` property is special in that it does not exist as a `SELECT`able object property. It can only be used in query conditions.

For our sample CMS, this produces the following:

SI_ID	787
SI_NAME	Guest
SI_KIND	Inbox

SI_ID	793
SI_NAME	Administrator
SI_KIND	Inbox

SI_ID	4107
SI_NAME	Fred
SI_KIND	Inbox

As with Personal Folders, we can query Fred's user object to ensure we reference the correct Inbox:

```
select si_inbox
  from ci_systemobjects
 where si_kind = 'user'
       and si_name = 'fred'
```

To retrieve the names and kinds of Fred's inbox documents, we simply use:

```
select si_name,si_kind
  from ci_infoobjects
 where si_parentid = 4107
```

The *Inboxes* folder hierarchy, unlike Public Folders and Personal Folders, does not contain any subfolders. Thus, the entire hierarchy consists of a maximum of three levels:

Inboxes (ID 48, kind *Folder*)

   user inboxes (kind *Inbox*)

      inbox documents (multiple kinds)

Semantic Layer Connections and Universes

As with Public and Personal Folders, universes and connections are stored in a hierarchical folder structure in which developers or administrators can add and remove folders as needed.

Both the Connections and Universes folder hierarchies are located in the CI_APPOBJECTS table.

The root folders of Connections and Universes do not have predefined object IDs, although they do have predefined *CUIDs* (the root Universe folder has CUID `AwcPjwbDdBxPoXPBOUCsKkk`, and the root Connections folder has CUID `AZVXOgKIBEdOkiXzUuybja4`). The same navigation methods can be used as in public folders, but we must look for the root folders' CUIDs instead of object IDs to identify the top of the hierarchy.

Consider the universe folders in Illustration 7. As in Public or Personal Folders, we can navigate upwards from the AR Universe. We start by retrieving its parent's CUID:

```
select si_name,si_parent_cuid
  from ci_appobjects
 where si_name = 'ar universe'
       and si_kind = 'universe'
```

Illustration 7: Sample Universe folders

This returns the CUID of the universe's parent folder, *Accounting Universes*.

SI_NAME	AR Universe
SI_PARENT_CUID	FhuamVa1EAMAHRAAAAAXId0ACAAnyavX

Since this CUID does not match the known CUID of the root Universe folder (`AwcPjwbDdBxPoXPBOUCsKkk`), we know that we are not at the root. We navigate upwards by retrieving the parent CUID of this object:

```
select si_name,si_cuid,si_parent_cuid
  from ci_appobjects
 where si_cuid = 'FhuamVa1EAMAHRAAAAAXId0ACAAnyavX'
```

SI_NAME	Accounting Universes
SI_CUID	FhuamVa1EAMAHRAAAAAXId0ACAAnyavX
SI_PARENT_CUID	FgqamVbVQAUAHRAAAACnsNwACAAnyavX

We still have not reached the root Universe folder, but now we have the name of the AR Universe's immediate parent folder: Accounting Universes. We continue to navigate upwards:

```
select si_name,si_cuid,si_parent_cuid
  from ci_appobjects
 where si_cuid = 'FhuamVa1EAMAHRAAAAAXId0ACAAnyavX'
```

SI_NAME	Accounting Universes
SI_CUID	FhuamVa1EAMAHRAAAAAXId0ACAAnyavX
SI_PARENT_CUID	FgqamVbVQAUAHRAAAACnsNwACAAnyavX

```
select si_name,si_cuid,si_parent_cuid
  from ci_appobjects
 where si_cuid = 'FgqamVbVQAUAHRAAAACnsNwACAAnyavX'
```

SI_NAME	Financial
SI_CUID	FgqamVbVQAUAHRAAAACnsNwACAAnyavX
SI_PARENT_CUID	AWcPjwbDdBxPoXPBOUCsKkk

Finally, we have reached an object whose parent CUID is AwcPjwbDdBxPoXPBOUCsKkk, so we know we have reached a top-level universe folder. We have determined the folder path of the AR Universe to be *Financial → Accounting Universes*.

As with Public and Personal Folders, we can also navigate the Universe folder hierarchy via the SI_PATH property, although its format is a little different. We'll start by getting the universe's parent folder ID:

```
select si_parentid
  from ci_appobjects
 where si_name = 'ar universe'
       and si_kind = 'universe'
```

SI_PARENTID	6285

With this ID, we can retrieve its name and SI_PATH:

```
select si_name,si_path
  from ci_appobjects
 where si_id = 6285
```

SI_NAME
      Accounting Universes

SI_PATH

       SI_FOLDER_ID1
            6284

       SI_FOLDER_OBTYPE1
            1

       SI_FOLDER_NAME1
            Financial

       SI_FOLDER_ID2
            533

       SI_FOLDER_OBTYPE2
            1

       SI_FOLDER_NAME2
            Universes

       SI_FOLDER_ID3

```
                    95
    SI_FOLDER_OBTYPE3
            1
    SI_FOLDER_NAME3
            Root Folder 95
    SI_FOLDER_ID4
            43
    SI_FOLDER_OBTYPE4
            1
    SI_FOLDER_NAME4
            Application Folder
    SI_FOLDER_ID5
            4
    SI_FOLDER_OBTYPE5
            13
    SI_FOLDER_NAME5
            osboxes:6400
    SI_NUM_FOLDERS
            5
```

With this result, we have the name of the universe's immediate parent folder ("*Accounting Universes*"), and its folder lineage. Note that, while the SI_PATH property in a Public Folder only goes as high as the top-level public folder, a *universe* folder's SI_PATH property contains the *complete* lineage, going all the way up to the cluster object (having ID 4).

We can see from the above query result that the root *Universes* folder is a couple of levels below the cluster (ID 4) (unlike the root Public Folder which is a direct child of the cluster). The hierarchy is as follows:

(Cluster) (ID 4)

   Application Folder (ID 43)

      Root Folder 95 (ID 95)

         Connections (CUID AZVXOgKIBEdOkiXzUuybja4)

         Universes (CUID AWcPjwbDdBxPoXPBOUCsKkk)

Note that the root Universes folder is a peer of the root *Connections* folder and a child of the ambiguously-named *Root Folder 95*.

The *Connections* folder, prior to BI4, was not hierarchical. That is, all universe connections were located in a single folder. This made administration difficult, as security rights had to be applied to individual connections. Fortunately, BI4 brought the ability for connections to be located in subfolders. The same root folder exists, but administrators and developers now have the ability to create subfolders and manage security on those subfolders.

The structure of the Connections folder is similar to that of the Universes folder. In Illustration 8: Connections folders, we see a sample Connections folder, including a subfolder named *Financial*. The properties of the *Financial* folder includes:

SI_NAME
    Financial

SI_PATH

    SI_FOLDER_ID1
      549

    SI_FOLDER_OBTYPE1
      1

    SI_FOLDER_NAME1
      Connections

    SI_FOLDER_ID2
      95

    SI_FOLDER_OBTYPE2
      1

    SI_FOLDER_NAME2
      Root Folder 95

    SI_FOLDER_ID3
      43

    SI_FOLDER_OBTYPE3
      1

    SI_FOLDER_NAME3
      Application Folder

    SI_FOLDER_ID4
      4

    SI_FOLDER_OBTYPE4
      13

    SI_FOLDER_NAME4
      BI4Test:6400

    SI_NUM_FOLDERS
      4

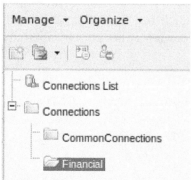

Illustration 8: Connections folders

Note that in our sample environment, we have a universes folder and a connections folder both named *Financial*. This ambiguity could cause problems if we were attempting to retrieve one of these by name alone:

```
select si_id,si_kind,si_name
```

```
from ci_appobjects
where si_name = 'financial'
```

SI_ID	SI_KIND	SI_NAME
6284	Folder	Financial
6291	Folder	Financial

What if we wanted to retrieve the *Financial connections* folder specifically? The root *Connections* folder does not have a pre-defined object ID, so we would be unable to use SI_ANCESTOR. In this case, we can use the undocumented SI_ANCESTOR_CUID property in the same fashion. From Appendix C - Sample CMS Folder Hierarchy or from CeSecurityCUID.FOLDERS.CONNECTIONS, we know that the CUID of the Connections folder is AZVXOgKIBEdOkiXzUuybja4. We can then use this in a query to find the *Financial* connections folder.

```
select si_id,si_kind,si_name
  from ci_appobjects
 where si_name = 'financial'
       and si_ancestor_cuid = 'AZVXOgKIBEdOkiXzUuybja4'
```

This returns the *Financial* folder under *Connections*:

SI_ID	SI_KIND	SI_NAME
6291	Folder	Financial

System Folders

The folders described in the past few sections are some of the more visible ones since developers and administrators interact with them in BI launch pad and CMC. There are several other folders that are not as visible but comprise a portion of the cluster hierarchy nonetheless.

Many of these folders contain specific object kinds, and these kinds can only be found in these specific folders. A good example is the *Users* folder. This folder, which is InfoObject ID 19, is a non-hierarchical folder that contains a flat list of all users in the system. So, **all** objects of kind *User* have folder 19 as their parent, and folder 19 only has objects of kind *User*.

Querying for users in the system can be done by parent ID or kind:

```
select si_name
  from ci_systemobjects
 where si_kind = 'user'
```

```
select si_name
  from ci_systemobjects
```

```
where si_parentid = 19
```

Both of these queries produce the same result. However, in part because it's much easier to remember that users have an SI_KIND value of "User" than to remember that they are in a folder with ID 19, we generally query for users using SI_KIND instead of SI_PARENTID. So you likely won't be interacting with these folders as often as, say, *Public Folders, Universes,* or *Connections.*

With that said, one of the uses of the root folders is to hold any top-level security settings. For instance, the security rights that are assigned to the top level of Users are associated with this InfoObject (ID 19). Although security rights are not visible from CMS queries, they can be retrieved when using the SDK. If there is a need to view or set top-level security rights, you will use the root folders to do so.

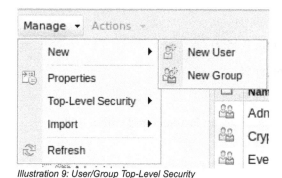

Illustration 9: User/Group Top-Level Security

Chapter Review

- The InfoStore is a hierarchical folder structure, and so all InfoObjects are children of one (and only one) folder.

- There are many top-level folders in the InfoStore, some of which are user-facing such as Public Folders, Inboxes, and Universes. Other folders are not visible even to administrators: Users, Servers, and others.

- Most of the folders that are pre-defined and present in a fresh installation of SAP BusinessObjects will have the same ID or CUID in every environment. The Public Folders folder, for example, always has an SI_ID of 23.

Quiz

1. Every user has a dedicated folder for storing their own documents. This is known as a:

    a) Personal Folder

    b) User Folder

     c) Favorites Folder

     d) All of the above

2. True/False: The SI_CHILDREN property includes an enumerated list of the IDs of the folder's children.

3. The root-level Inbox folder has an SI_ID of __ and is located in the __ table.

     a) 23 / CI_INFOOBJECTS

     b) 46 / CI_APPOBJECTS

     c) 48 / CI_INFOOBJECTS

     d) 28 / CI_APPOBJECTS

4. The parent of the root-level Universes and Connections folders is:

     a) 23 (Public Folders)

     b) 43 (Application Folder)

     c) 95 (Root Folder 95)

     d) 99 (Root Folder 99)

5. True/False: Each user group is associated with a folder.

Answers on page 672.

Chapter 4 - Relationship Queries

Nearly all objects in the InfoStore have relationships to other objects. Folders have child objects, objects have parent folders, Web Intelligence documents can have instances as well as universes, universes can have associated documents and data connections. Relationship Queries allow for the retrieval of objects based on their relationship to these other objects.

To illustrate the use of one form of relationship query, the folder hierarchy, we will use a subset of a repository:

Root Folder (*folder, ID 23)*

        Human Resources Reports (*folder, ID 3233)*

                Monthly Staff Listing (*WebI, ID 3347)*

        Sales Reports (*folder, ID 2755)*

                Monthly Sales (*WebI, ID 8744)*

                Returns (*WebI, ID 9813)*

Let's say we wanted to retrieve the contents of the *Sales Reports* folder, knowing only its name and that it is a public folder. Without the use of a relationship query, two steps would be required. First, we would need to identify the object ID of the *Sales Reports* folder:

```
select si_id
  from ci_infoobjects
 where si_parentid = 23
       and si_name = 'sales reports'
```

SI_ID	2755

With the ID of the Sales Reports folder retrieved, we can then retrieve its child objects:

```
select si_name,si_kind
  from ci_infoobjects
 where si_parentid = 2755
```

SI_KIND	SI_NAME
Folder	Monthly Sales
Webi	Returns

While this does produce the desired requirement, it is cumbersome to have to use multiple queries to obtain a single result. While this is bad enough when querying by hand in the Query Builder, performing this action in the SDK requires several discrete steps:

- Submit the initial query

- Retrieve the result

- Create a string containing the individual IDs returned

- Submit the second query, using the string from the previous step to apply a condition.

- Retrieve the second result

So, having a way to collapse two (or more) queries into one has significant benefits. Relationship Queries meet that need.

The above requirement, using a Relationship Query, can be achieved with the following single query:

```
select si_name,si_kind
  from ci_infoobjects
 where children("si_name='folder hierarchy'",
          "si_name='sales reports' and si_parentid = 23")
```

This produces the same result as our second query above but eliminates the need to perform separate queries to retrieve the WebI InfoObject IDs prior to retrieving the objects themselves.

The syntax of Relationship Queries is quite a departure from both standard SQL as well as CMS Queries. It may help to think of `children()` in the above query as a *function* that returns `true` or `false` for each row in the queried table, or like a `WHERE EXISTS` operation in standard SQL.

Although it is a single statement with a single result set, the relationship query performs two passes in order to generate the result, and it is important to think of these two passes independently. In the above example, we want to obtain objects associated with a folder meeting a specified condition (named *Sales Reports* and having parent ID 23). The CMS query engine performs the following steps to obtain that result:

1. First pass: evaluate the `children()` function, and identify all folders that meet the specified relationship criteria (`SI_NAME='sales reports' and SI_PARENTID = 23`).

2. Second pass: retrieve all objects associated with the IDs found in the previous pass (those having an `SI_PARENT_FOLDERID` property matching those found in the first pass). From the list of identified WebI objects, apply any other conditional expressions in the outer `WHERE` clause.

3. Finally, display the properties listed in the `SELECT` clause.

The text *within* the relationship function can be referred to as the *relationship query* or *inner query*; the text outside of the relationship query, including the `SELECT`, `FROM`, `ORDER BY`, and other `WHERE` conditions can be referred to as the *outer query* or *main query*.

The bold text in the example query is the **outer** or **main** query, while the underlined text is the **inner** or **relationship** query:

```
select si_name
  from ci_infoobjects
 where children("si_name='folder hierarchy'",
```

```
"si name='sales reports' and si parentid = 23")
    and si_kind = 'webi'
```

Key point: the SELECT clause has no bearing whatsoever on the behavior of the relationship condition (or any other condition, for that matter). Our sample above only SELECTed a single property (SI_NAME); you may SELECT as many, or as few, properties as appropriate when using relationship queries.

There are three components to a relationship query: the *function, type,* and *condition*. The type and condition parameters are strings enclosed in double quotes, with the strings containing valid CMS query conditional expressions. To illustrate:

```
relationship_function (
    " relationship type expression ",
    " relationship condition "
)
```

Relationship Type

```
where children("si_name='folder hierarchy'",
        "si_name='sales reports' and si_parentid = 23")
```

Since objects in a CMS can be related to each other in different ways (folders have children, user groups have users, etc.), we need to specify which *type* of relationship is to be used in our query. The *Folder Hierarchy* type is used to retrieve objects based on their ancestral folders, or to retrieve descendants of specified folders. There are other relationship types available that are used for relationships between specific kinds of objects, such as *WebI-Universe, User Group-User, Universe-Connection,* and others.

Generally, the relationship type is specified using its SI_NAME, as in the example above[43].

Although there are numerous relationship types available, there is a finite list. It is not possible to create your own relationship type by simply specifying two object kinds in the SI_NAME condition. Later in this chapter, we cover the method for listing the available relationship types.

Relationship Condition

```
where children("si_name='folder hierarchy'",
        "si_name='sales reports' and si_parentid = 23")
```

The second parameter in the children() function specifies a condition for the first pass of the query (the query that retrieves the *Sales Reports* folder). In this example, we are simply looking for folders with an SI_NAME property of "sales reports" and that are a child of folder 23 (the root folder). The **outer** query then returns all objects that are **children** of this folder.

---

43 Although it is possible to use different conditions for specifying the relationship type when creating more advanced relationship queries.

Note that we don't have to specify a condition for `SI_KIND='folder'` in the inner query. Since we are using the `children()` function with the *Folder Hierarchy* type, a condition of `SI_KIND='folder'` is implicitly applied.

The syntax of the relationship conditional expression is the same as "regular" CMS query conditional expressions and can be as complex as necessary[44]. For example, to retrieve objects that are children of folders created by Fred between May and June 2015, we would use:

```
where children("si_name='folder hierarchy'",
        "si_owner = 'fred' and si_creation_time between '2015.05.01' and
'2015.06.30' ")
```

There is one notable difference with the syntax of relationship conditions as compared to "regular" conditions: <u>relationship conditions cannot include a newline character</u>. In the example above, note that there is no newline in the condition.

Relationship Function

```
where children("si_name='folder hierarchy'",
        "si_name='sales reports' and si_parentid = 23")
```

The *relationship function* sets how the selected *relationship type* is to be used (or, put another way, in which direction the hierarchical navigation occurs). In our examples thus far, we have used the `children()` function, which, when used with the *Folder Hierarchy* type, produces *the children of the folder or folders meeting the specified condition*. To go the other way in the hierarchy, we use the `parents()` function – this retrieves the *parent folders of the specified objects*. For example, if we wanted to retrieve the parent folder names of any WebI objects with names starting with "*Monthly*", we could use:

```
select si_name
  from ci_infoobjects
 where parents("si_name='folder hierarchy'",
            "si_name like 'monthly%' and si_kind = 'webi'")
```

This query produces a list of the two folders that contain WebI reports with names starting with *Monthly*:

SI_NAME
Human Resources Reports
Sales Reports

Note that we specified an `SI_KIND='webi'` condition. Unlike our example with the `children()` function, in which an implicit `SI_KIND='folder'` condition is applied to the inner query, there is no implicit condition applied when `parents()` is used. When children() is used, we are asking the query engine for objects that are children of the specified folder, so naturally only

---

44 Including other relationship queries? Yes. Sort of. We'll cover that soon.

a folder can be specified. When `parents()` is used, we are instead asking for the *parent folder* of the specified objects; since folders can contain objects of many different kinds, we want to ensure that we specify what kinds we want to include.

There are a total of seven relationship functions available.

- `children()`
- `parents()`
- `descendants()`
- `ancestors()`
- `members()`
- `groups()`
- `connectedcomponents()`

Now that we have covered the basic structure of relationship queries, we will delve further into the different relationship types.

The Folder Hierarchy

In Chapter 3, we covered the basic folder structure and some methods for navigating up and down in the folder hierarchies. Relationship queries can be used to greatly simplify and optimize these operations.

We've already covered the basics of querying with the *Folder Hierarchy* type and the `children()` and `parents()` functions. The *Folder Hierarchy* relationship type also supports further hierarchical navigation with the `descendants()` and `ancestors()` functions. These two functions not only retrieve the direct parent or child object, but **all** descendants or ancestors. This is useful for identifying an object's full folder path, or for identifying all objects below a given folder.

The syntax of these functions is the same as what we have seen already with `parents()` and `children()`. To retrieve the complete folder path of the *Monthly Sales* WebI document, we would use the following query:

```
select si_name,si_kind
  from ci_infoobjects
 where ancestors("si_name='folder hierarchy'",
              "si_name='monthly sales' and si_kind = 'webi'")
```

This produces the following result:

SI_NAME	SI_KIND
Root Folder	Folder
Sales Reports	Folder

Note that the use of `ancestors()` simply produces a flat list of objects – there are no navigational aids in the result set to describe the folder hierarchy. We can, however, add `SI_PARENTID` and `SI_ID` to the `SELECT` clause, and use the IDs to navigate through the result. We'll also add the *Monthly Sales* object itself to the result, so that we can capture its direct parent ID.

```
select si_name,si_kind,si_id,si_parentid
  from ci_infoobjects
 where ancestors("si_name='folder hierarchy'",
                 "si_name='monthly sales' and si_kind = 'webi'")
    or (si_name='monthly sales' and si_kind='webi')
```

This produces the following result:

SI_NAME	SI_KIND	SI_ID	SI_PARENTID
Root Folder	Folder	23	4
Sales Reports	Folder	4398	23
Monthly Sales	Webi	8744	4398

We see from the result that the *Monthly Sales* object is a child of object 4398, which in turn is a child of object 23.

The `descendants()` function can be used to retrieve all descendant objects of a folder. To retrieve all descendants of the Root Folder, we can use:

```
select si_name,si_kind
  from ci_infoobjects
 where descendants("si_name='folder hierarchy'",
                   "si_id = 23")
```

SI_KIND	SI_NAME
Folder	Human Resources Reports
Webi	Monthly Staff Listing
Folder	Sales Reports
Webi	Monthly Sales
Webi	Returns

Since we did not specify a condition for `SI_KIND` in the outer query, and the Root Folder contains both Folder and WebI objects, we received a result set containing all objects under the root. If we only wanted the WebI objects, we would apply a condition to the outer query:

```
select si_name,si_kind
  from ci_infoobjects
 where descendants("si_name='folder hierarchy'",
                   "si_id = 23")
   and si_kind = 'webi'
```

SI_KIND	SI_NAME
Webi	Monthly Staff Listing
Webi	Monthly Sales
Webi	Returns

We used the Root Folder in the previous examples, but we can reference any valid folder. To retrieve all descendants of the Sales Reports folder (ID 2755), we would use:

```
select si_name,si_kind
  from ci_infoobjects
 where descendants("si_name = 'folder hierarchy'",
                   "si_name = 'sales reports'")
       and si_kind = 'webi'
```

Since the Sales Reports folder contains only direct children and no grandchildren, this query produces the same results as if we had used the `children()` function instead of `descendants()`.

Our examples above all reference the Root Folder (23) in the `CI_INFOOBJECTS` table. The same functionality can be used for the other root folders in other tables. For example, to retrieve the *universe* folder hierarchy of a universe named *Sales Reporting*, we would use:

```
select si_name,si_kind,si_parentid
  from ci_appobjects
 where ancestors("si_name = 'folder hierarchy'",
                 "si_name = 'ar universe' and si_kind='universe'")
```

On page 76, we discussed the structure of the Semantic Layer folder hierarchies and mentioned that the root Universes folder, unlike Public Folders, is two layers below the cluster object (ID 4). Thus, the above query produces ancestors above the root *Universes* folder:

SI_NAME	SI_KIND	SI_ID	SI_PARENTID
Application Folder	Folder	43	4
Root Folder 95	Folder	95	43
Universes	Folder	533	95
Accounting Universes	Folder	6285	533

The Folder Hierarchy relationship queries can technically be used with any folder, but it really only has value when used in a hierarchical folder structure, such as Public Folders, Universes, Personal Folders, etc. While it would be possible to run a relationship query on, say, the *Users* folder, there would be little value in doing as is it is non-hierarchical.

Users and User Groups

Querying for Users and User Groups is a common need in SAP BusinessObjects administration. Relationship queries can make this activity more efficient.

Users and groups have a relatively straightforward relationship:

- Users can be a member of ("belong to") zero, one, or many groups[45].

- User Groups can have zero, one, or many member users.

- A User Group can be a member of zero, one, or more other User Groups

- A User Group cannot be a member of another User Group that is also a descendant (that is, a group can not be an ancestor of a group that is its own descendant).

For this section, we use the following sample group structure:

Group Hierarchy

> Administrators

> Business

>> Exec. Management

>>> *Ephraim (user)*

>> Finance

>>> *Fred (user)*

>> Sales

>>> Northeast Region

>>>> *Nathan (user)*

>>> Southeast Region

>>>> *Sri (user)*

>>> Western Region

>>>> *Wally (user)*

> Dashboard Users

>> Exec. Management

>>> *Ephraim (user)*

>> Finance

>>> *Fred (user)*

---

45 More specifically, all User objects are a direct member of the Everyone group, and may be a member of other groups.

Everyone

> *Ephraim (user)*
>
> *Fred (user)*
>
> *Nathan (user)*
>
> *Quentin (user)*
>
> *Sri (user)*
>
> *Umit (user)*
>
> *Wally (user)*

IT

> *Isabel (user)*
>
> QA
>
> > *Fred (user)*
> >
> > *Quentin (user)*
>
> Universe Developers
>
> > *Umit (user)*

Universe Designer Users

> Universe Developers
>
> > *Umit (user)*

Let's say we want to identify all the groups that Fred is a member of. We can use the *Usergroup-User* relationship type with the `parents()` function:

```
select si_name
  from ci_systemobjects
 where parents("si_name='usergroup-user'",
               "si_name='fred'")
```

This returns the two groups that Fred is in:

SI_NAME
Everyone
Finance

Conversely, if we want to list the direct members of the Southeast Region user group, we would use the `children()` function:

```
select si_name
  from ci_systemobjects
```

```
where children("si_name='usergroup-user'",
               "si_name='southeast region'")
```

This returns the one member of the *Southeast Region* group:

SI_NAME
Sri

Note that both the `children()` and `parents()` functions return only the *direct* relatives. As with the Folder Hierarchy relationship type, we can use `ancestors()` and `descendants()` to retrieve additional levels. To retrieve all ancestor groups that Fred is in, we would use the ancestors() function:

```
select si_name
  from ci_systemobjects
 where ancestors("si_name='usergroup-user'",
                 "si_name='fred'")
```

This returns not only the two groups that Fred is a direct member of (*Everyone* and *Finance*) but all ancestral groups. The *Everyone* group has no ancestors, but the *Finance* group is a member of *Business* and *Dashboard Users*. So all of these groups appear in the result:

SI_NAME
Everyone
Finance
Business
Dashboard Users

We can use the `descendants()` function to return all descendants (direct and indirect, users and user groups) of a specified user group or groups. Let's say we want to retrieve all users that fall under the *Sales* user group. The `descendants()` function can be used in this instance:

```
select si_name
  from ci_systemobjects
 where descendants("si_name='usergroup-user'",
                   "si_name='sales'")
       and si_kind = 'user'
```

This produces:

SI_NAME
Nathan
Sri
Wally

If we want **all** descendants, including user groups, we would simply remove the SI_KIND condition:

```
select si_name
  from ci_systemobjects
 where descendants("si_name='usergroup-user'",
                   "si_name='sales'")
```

SI_NAME
Northeast Region
Southeast Region
Western Region
Nathan
Sri
Wally

As we saw in the Folder Hierarchy queries, the result of ancestors() and descendants() is only a flat list of objects. There is nothing in the above result to indicate which groups the users belong to. We can include SI_ID, SI_USERGROUPS, and SI_GROUP_MEMBERS in the result, which can then be used to determine the direct group membership.

```
select si_name,si_kind,si_id,si_group_members,si_usergroups
  from ci_systemobjects
 where descendants("si_name='usergroup-user'",
                   "si_name='sales'")
```

SI_NAME	Northeast Region	
SI_KIND	UserGroup	
SI_ID	6341	
SI_GROUP_MEMBERS	1	6344
	SI_TOTAL	1
SI_USERGROUPS	1	6333
	SI_TOTAL	1

SI_NAME	Southeast Region	
SI_KIND	UserGroup	
SI_ID	6348	
SI_GROUP_MEMBERS	1	6348
	SI_TOTAL	1
SI_USERGROUPS	1	6333
	SI_TOTAL	1

SI_NAME	Western Region

SI_KIND	UserGroup	
SI_ID	6343	
SI_GROUP_MEMBERS	1	6352
	SI_TOTAL	1
SI_USERGROUPS	1	6333
	SI_TOTAL	1

SI_NAME	Nathan	
SI_KIND	User	
SI_ID	6344	
SI_USERGROUPS	1	1
	2	6341
	SI_TOTAL	2

SI_NAME	Sri	
SI_KIND	User	
SI_ID	6348	
SI_USERGROUPS	1	1
	2	6342
	SI_TOTAL	2

SI_NAME	Wally	
SI_KIND	User	
SI_ID	6352	
SI_USERGROUPS	1	1
	2	6343
	SI_TOTAL	2

With this result, we can cross-reference the returned users and user groups. The Northeast Region group's SI_GROUP_MEMBERS property includes ID 6344. We find this ID in the result set as belonging to the *Nathan* user. Likewise, if we start with Nathan's SI_USERGROUPS property, we'll find ID 1 (the *Everyone* group), and ID 6341, for the *Northeast Region* group.

As another example of a common administration requirement, consider a need to identify users who are members of two specific, separate group hierarchies. Specifically, we want to identify any users who are direct or indirect members of the *Business* and *IT* groups. That is, users who are a member of *Business* or any descendant group, and also a member of *IT* or any descendant group. We can use the following query to achieve this need:

```
select si_name
  from ci_systemobjects
 where descendants("si_name='usergroup-user'","si_name='business'")
   and descendants("si_name='usergroup-user'","si_name='it'")
```

This returns only *Fred*, who is a member of the *Finance* group (under *Business*), and also a member of the *QA* group, which is under *IT*.

SI_NAME
Fred

We have, so far, seen the use of four relationship query functions: `parents()`, `children()`, `ancestors()`, and `descendants()`. There are two more functions that can be used with certain relationship types including *Usergroup-User*: `members()` and `groups()`.

The `groups()` function works similarly to `children()` but returns only child objects that are groups themselves. When used with *Usergroup-User*, the `groups()` function will only return **user groups** that are children of the selected group. The following two queries produce the same results:

```
select si_name
  from ci_systemobjects
 where children("si_name='usergroup-user'","si_name='it'")
       and si_kind = 'usergroup'
```

```
select si_name
  from ci_systemobjects
 where groups("si_name='usergroup-user'","si_name='it'")
```

SI_NAME
Universe Developers
QA

The `members()` function returns child objects of the selected group that are *not* groups themselves. When used with *Usergroup-User,* it returns only users. The following two queries produce the same results.

```
select si_name
  from ci_systemobjects
 where children("si_name='usergroup-user'","si_name='it'")
       and si_kind = 'user'
```

```
select si_name
  from ci_systemobjects
 where members("si_name='usergroup-user'","si_name='it'")
```

SI_NAME
Isabel

The members() and groups() functions are used for hierarchical types in which a child object may be a group capable of containing additional children, or a member which cannot have children. In addition to *Usergroup-User*, the *ServerGroup-Server* type also supports members() and groups().

The value of *UserGroup-User* relationship queries cannot be understated. With a simple group structure such as the one above, it is easy to visualize and manage all the groups and users. But in a complex environment with thousands of users and hundreds of groups, identifying users who are descendants of a particular high-level group can be an arduous process. Relationship queries can significantly reduce the amount of time and effort need to get this valuable information out of the CMS.

Documents, Universes, and Data Connections

The *Webi-Universe* relationship type is used to retrieve Web Intelligence reports associated with specific universes, and vice-versa.

Most of the relationship types, except for *Folder Hierarchy,* have names in the form of *Parent Kind-Child Kind*. Most of these are intuitive, such as the *UserGroup-User* type that we used above – the *UserGroup* kind is the parent of one or more *Users*. However, the relationship of *Webi-Universe* is not so clear, since Universes are considered to be *children* of Web Intelligence objects. As this may be unintuitive, it is essential to remember the *Parent Kind-Child Kind* format of the relationship type names.

To find the universes associated with a given Web Intelligence document, we use the children() function. For example, to identify universes associated with a report named *Pending Accounts*:

```
select si_name
  from ci_appobjects
 where children("si_name='webi-universe'",
               "si_name='Pending Accounts'")
```

This returns the one universe that is associated with the report:

SI_NAME
AR Universe

The above query introduces a subtle change in logic to what we have done so far in relationship queries. The queries we have used up until now have referenced parent and child objects *in the same table* – folders and reports in CI_INFOOBJECTS, users and user groups in CI_SYSTEMOBJECTS, etc. But the above query needs to reference child objects (universes) in CI_APPOBJECTS and parent objects (WebI reports) that live in CI_INFOOBJECTS. Our query doesn't reference CI_INFOOBJECTS *at all*. Our FROM clause references CI_APPOBJECTS only since that is the table that *contains the objects that we want to retrieve* (universes), **not** the related objects referenced in the inner query.

If we were to perform the inverse – retrieve WebI reports associated with a given universe, we would then need to reference CI_INFOOBJECTS in our FROM clause since that table contains the objects that are being retrieved:

```
select si_name
  from ci_infoobjects
 where parents("si_name='webi-universe'","si_name='AR Universe'")
```

If you are not getting expected results in a relationship query, one way to ensure that you have included the correct table is to simply include all three tables:

```
select si_name
  from ci_infoobjects,ci_appobjects,ci_systemobjects
 where parents("si_name='webi-universe'","si_name='AR Universe'")
```

This would not be a good practice for a production program but would be useful in debugging an unexpected result.

> *Key point: when using relationship queries, the FROM clause must specify the home table of the objects that are being retrieved in the final output; not the objects from the intermediate, inner query.*

One *quirk* with the *Webi-Universe* type is that the name doesn't fully represent the object kinds that can be returned. While the relationship only includes child kinds of *Universe*, it actually retrieves parent objects of the following kinds: *Webi, PDF, Excel, FullClient, CrystalReport,* and *Txt*. While this behavior offers more flexibility for querying these object kinds, it can produce unexpected results. If only WebI objects are desired, then an appropriate condition must be included:

```
select si_name
  from ci_infoobjects
 where parents("si_name='webi-universe'",
               "si_name='AR Universe'")
       and si_kind = 'webi'
```

The *Webi-Universe* relationship type explicitly includes only unv universes. To reference associations between documents and unx universes, the *Document-DSL.Universe* relationship type is used. This type's name more accurately represents the parent kinds since it includes objects of kind *Webi, PDF, Excel, CrystalReport,* and *XL.Query*.

It's important to remember that these two similar relationship types exist. It would be a simple mistake to just use *Webi-Universe* in an attempt to return universes associated with a report, only to get no results because the reports are based on unx universes, or a combination of unv and unx. To return all associated universes whether they are unv or unx, include both relationship types in the query:

```
select si_name,si_kind,si_specific_kind
  from ci_appobjects
 where children("si_name in ('webi-universe','document-dsl.universe')",
             "si_name='Customer Transaction Detail'")
```

This query would return:

SI_NAME	SI_KIND	SI_SPECIFIC_KIND
AR Universe	Universe	Universe
Transaction Universe	DSL.MetaDataFile	DSL.Universe

The relationship between Data Connections and Universes works similarly. We use the *DataConnection-Universe* type to retrieve unv universes associated with specified data connections, or vice-versa. For example, to identify any unv universes associated with a data connection named *Finance*, we would use the following query:

```
select si_kind,si_name
  from ci_appobjects
 where children("si_name='DataConnection-Universe'",
             "si_name = 'Finance'")
```

SI_NAME	SI_KIND
AR Universe	Universe
AP Universe	Universe

Relationships between **unx** universes and connections work a little differently, in part because unx universes can have multiple connections and also different *kinds* of connections. The name of the relationship type to be used is *DSL.Universe-SecuredConnections*. You may have noticed that the first difference with this type is that, unlike *DataConnection-Universe*, the universe is on the parent side of the relationship. So, to perform the same action as above (retrieve universes for specified connections), we would invert the logic by using `parents()` instead of `children()`:

```
select si_specific_kind,si_name
  from ci_appobjects
 where parents("si_name='DSL.Universe-SecuredConnections'",
             "si_name = 'Finance'")
```

SI_NAME	SI_KIND
Finance Universe.unx	DSL.MetaDataFile

Because the relationship between data connections and unv universes is parent-child, and the relationship between data connections and **unx** universes is child-parent, querying for both unv and unx universes in the same relationship query is complex. As an example, querying for all universes (unv and unx) that are associated with a specific connection named *"Finance DM"*, we would have to use two relationship expressions with an OR operator:

```
select si_name
  from ci_appobjects
 where children("si_name = 'dataconnection-universe'",
               "si_name = 'finance dm'")
     or parents("si_name='dsl.universe-securedconnections'",
                "si_name = 'finance dm'")
```

Other Relationship Types

We'll cover in the next section *why* this works, but we can list all of the available relationship types in a system with the following query:

```
select si_name
  from ci_systemobjects
 where si_parentid = 46
 order by si_name
```

The list that is generated will depend on the specific products that are installed in the cluster, but there are at least several dozen relationship types. A portion of the list returned in from out test system is as follows:

SI_NAME
ActionSet-Action
ActionUsage-Action
...
DataConnection-Universe
Document.DSLUniverse
DSL.Universe-BusinessSecurityOptions
DSL.Universe-BusinessSecurityProfile
DSL.Universe-DataSecurityOptions
DSL.Universe-DataSecurityProfile

SI_NAME
DSL.Universe-SecuredConnections
...
Folder Hierarchy
...
User-Favorites
User-Inbox
UserGroup-User
...
Webi-Universe

Relationship Type Details

In this section, we cover some of the inner workings of relationships. It is not strictly necessary to know this level of detail in order to successfully use relationship queries, but it may be helpful in understanding how they work and what to expect when using a specific relationship.

Unfortunately, there is no official reference (yet!) that lists the available relationship types and their usage, so it's necessary to dig into the CMS tables to understand what's there and how they work. Appendix D contains these details for some of the common relationship types.

As mentioned above, relationships exist in the InfoStore as objects of object 46. The properties of this object define the relationship and are used by the query engine to select the related objects. Let's look at *UserGroup-User* as an example.

```
select *
  from ci_systemobjects
 where si_parentid = 46
       and si_name = 'usergroup-user'
```

SI_CUID
        AYgTOu7lRAhDguRvZn7j2z0

SI_ID
        532

SI_NAME
        Webi-Universe

SI_PARENT_CUID
        AYYjM86wh3BFpIxkt4m0XBc

SI_PARENT_FOLDER
        46

SI_PARENTID

        46
SI_RELATION_ADD_CHILD_RIGHT
        0

SI_RELATION_ADD_PARENT_RIGHT
        0

SI_RELATION_CHILDREN_MEMBERS_PROPERTY
        SI_UNIVERSE

SI_RELATION_CONSTRAINTS_FOR_EDGE
        1

                SI_RELATION_CHILD_CLAUSE
                        SI_KIND = 'Universe'

                SI_RELATION_SELECT_USING
                        Parent

                SI_RELATION_EDGE_TYPE
                        All

        2

                SI_RELATION_PARENT_CLAUSE
                        SI_KIND   IN   ('Webi',   'PDF',   'Excel','FullClient',
                        'CrystalReport', 'Txt')

                SI_RELATION_SELECT_USING
                        Child

                SI_RELATION_EDGE_TYPE
                        All

        SI_TOTAL
                2

SI_RELATION_LINK_TYPE
        Soft

SI_RELATION_PARENTS_PROPERTY
        SI_WEBI

SI_RELATION_RELATION_IS_A_DAG
        true

SI_RELATION_RELATION_IS_A_TREE
        false

SI_RELATION_REMOVE_CHILD_RIGHT
        0

SI_RELATION_REMOVE_PARENT_RIGHT
        0

SI_RELATION_TABLE_NAME
        RELATIONS

SI_RELATION_TOUCH_CHILDREN
        false

SI_RELATIONSHIP_CONSUMERS
        1

                SI_ID
                        4754

                SI_RELATIONSHIP_DIRECTION
                        1

        2

SI_ID
4761

SI_RELATIONSHIP_DIRECTION
2

SI_TOTAL
2

SI_SUPPORTING_APPLICATIONS
1

SI_ID
525

SI_RELATIONSHIP_DIRECTION
1

SI_ML_DESCRIPTION

NL
Universes voor geselecteerde rapporten opnemen

AR
تضمين النطاقات الشاملة للتقارير المحددة

ZH_TW
...

FI
Sisällytä valittujen raporttien käyttöympäristöt

FR
Inclure les univers des rapports sélectionnés

RO
Includere universuri pentru rapoartele selectate

HU
A kijelölt jelentések univerzumainak bevonása

RU
Включить Юниверсы для выбранных отчетов

ZH_CN
...

HE
...

PL
Uwzględnij światy obiektów wybranych raportów

CS
Zahrnout universa pro vybrané sestavy

PT
Inclui universos dos relatórios selecionados

DE
Universen für ausgewählte Berichte einschließen

DA
Medtag universer for valgte rapporter

SL
Vključitev Universov za izbrana poročila

JA
...

ES
Incluir universos para informes seleccionados

```
        SK
                Zahrnúť univerzá pre vybrané zostavy
        IT
                Includi universi per i report selezionati
        TH
                ...
        EN
                Include universes for selected reports
        SOURCE
                Include universes for selected reports
        SV
                Inkludera universum för valda rapporter
        NB
                Inkluder universer for valgte rapporter
        KO
                ...
SI_TOTAL
        1
```

Although the result includes the properties common to all InfoObjects we are only showing above the ones that we're interested in. These are the SI_RELATION_ properties, in particular, SI_RELATION_CONSTRAINTS_FOR_EDGE[46], SI_RELATION_CHILDREN_MEMBERS_PROPERTY, and SI_RELATION_PARENTS_PROPERTY. These three properties are useful for finding out which kinds of objects the relationship applies to and which properties are used to join them. Let's take a closer look at SI_RELATION_CONSTRAINTS_FOR_EDGE:

```
SI_RELATION_CONSTRAINTS_FOR_EDGE
        1
                SI_RELATION_CHILD_CLAUSE
                        SI_KIND = 'Universe'
                SI_RELATION_SELECT_USING
                        Parent
                SI_RELATION_EDGE_TYPE
                        All
        2
                SI_RELATION_PARENT_CLAUSE
                        SI_KIND    IN    ('Webi',    'PDF',    'Excel','FullClient',
                        'CrystalReport', 'Txt')
                SI_RELATION_SELECT_USING
                        Child
                SI_RELATION_EDGE_TYPE
                        All
        SI_TOTAL
                2
```

The SI_RELATION_PARENT_CLAUSE tells us the WHERE condition that is applied to the parent side

---

46 "Edge" in this context is a graph theory term, not to be confused with *SAP BusinessObjects Edge*.

of the relationship query. Despite the name of the relationship being *Webi-Universe*, the relationship actually includes other kinds, specifically *PDF*, *Excel*, *FullClient*, *CyrstalReport*, and *Txt*. Consider our query from page 98 that returns documents associated with the *AR Universe* universe.

```
select si_name
  from ci_infoobjects
 where parents("si_name='webi-universe'","si_name='AR Universe'")
```

Based on what we see in the SI_RELATION_PARENT_CLAUSE property of the *Webi-Universe* relationship object, we now know that the above query will be interpreted by the CMS query engine as:

```
select si_name
  from ci_infoobjects
 where parents("si_name='webi-universe'","si_name='AR Universe'")
       and SI_KIND IN ('Webi', 'PDF', 'Excel','FullClient', 'CrystalReport', 'Txt')
```

If we were to perform a children() function with this relationship type, then the condition specified in SI_RELATION_CHILD_CLAUSE would be applied. A query to return all universes associated with a specific document such as:

```
select si_name
  from ci_appobjects
 where children("si_name='webi-universe'","si_name='Pending Accounts'")
```

...would be interpreted by the query engine as:

```
select si_name
  from ci_appobjects
 where children("si_name='webi-universe'","si_name='Pending Accounts'")
       and SI_KIND = 'Universe'
```

So, if you are uncertain as to the kinds of objects referenced by a particular relationship, the SI_RELATION_CONSTRAINTS_FOR_EDGE property will hold the answer.

The SI_RELATION_CHILDREN_MEMBERS_PROPERTY and SI_RELATION_PARENTS_PROPERTY properties indicate which properties of the parent's contain a reference to its children, and vice-versa. The SI_RELATION_CHILDREN_MEMBERS_PROPERTY of the *Webi-Universe* relationship has the value:

SI_UNIVERSE

This tells us that the parent objects (of kind Webi, PDF, etc.) contain a property named SI_UNIVERSE, which in turn contain object IDs of the related children. If we were to query for this property explicitly on a document with:

```
select si_id,si_universe
  from ci_infoobjects
 where si_name = 'returns'
       and si_kind = 'webi'
```

Then we see the SI_UNIVERSE property, which contains a reference to the associated universe:

SI_ID
    6212
SI_UNIVERSE
    1
        3965
     SI_TOTAL
        1

Similarly, the SI_RELATION_PARENTS_PROPERTY property contains the value:

SI_WEBI

Thus, the child side of the *Webi-Universe* relationship (universes) will contain a property SI_WEBI, which contains the IDs of the documents associated with the universe. If we query for this property from the universe referred to in the previous result (3965):

```
select si_id,si_webi
  from ci_appobjects
 where si_id = 3965
```

...then we receive a list of all documents associated with the universe, including ID 6212, which is the *Returns* document.

SI_WEBI
    1
        6212
    2
        6251
    3
        3970
    4
        3973
    5
        3974
    SI_TOTAL
        5
SI_ID
    3965

Nested Relationship Queries

Relationship queries are useful for retrieving valuable CMS data. But the queries we have explored so far have been fairly simple, in that they return a set of objects which have a relationship to a defined object or objects. The ability to nest relationship queries allows us to retrieve objects which have an association to objects *who have a further association with other specified objects*, and on and on. As a real-life example of where this would be useful, we can create a query to return Web Intelligence documents that are associated with universes that are associated with a specific data connection.

As a forewarning, the syntax of nested relationship queries can get a little hairy. But we believe the time invested in understanding the syntax will reap rewards when the queries are put to use.

On page 86, we defined the form of relationship queries as:

```
relationship_function (
    "relationship type expression",
    "relationship condition"
)
```

We can extend this for nested relationship queries as:

```
relationship_function (
    "relationship type expression ",
    "relationship_function (
        ' relationship type expression ',
        ' relationship condition '
    ) "
)
```

We are essentially replacing the relationship condition (which previously has been in the form of `"SI_UNIVERSE='ar universe'"`) with another complete relationship expression.

Let's start with a query that we used previously to return WebI reports associated with a given universe:

```
select si_name
  from ci_infoobjects
 where parents("si_name='webi-universe'",
               "si_name='AR Universe'")
```

We want to take this a step further, and rather than looking for reports associated with *AR Universe*, we want to identify all reports that are associated with any universes that use the *Finance Datamart* connection.

```
select si_name
  from ci_infoobjects
 where parents("si_name='webi-universe'",
               "children(
                   'si_name=' 'dataconnection-universe' '  ',
```

```
            'si_name=' 'finance datamart' '  '
        )"
    )
```

A few things to note here:

- We have added spaces between the multiple single quotes to avoid confusion with double quotes. The spacing is not necessary in actual queries (but also does not cause errors).

- Within the double-quotes (the relationship condition), we change single quotes to two single quotes and double quotes to a single quote.

- In any deeper nested conditions, two single quotes become four, etc.

- As before, everything within double quotes must be on a single line. This includes the entire nested condition. We have added newlines to the query above for readability, but they would need to be removed before execution.

As with regular relationship queries, it helps to think of the CMS engine processing the statement in multiple steps. In the case of nested queries, it starts with the innermost nested query:

```
children(
    'si_name=' 'dataconnection-universe' '  ',
    'si_name=' 'finance datamart' '  '
)
```

1. This step produces a list of *universe* objects associated with the *Finance Data* connection.

2. The list of objects found in the previous step is then passed up to the next-higher query (`parents("SI_NAME='webi-universe'",...)`. From the list of universes, this step produces a list of WebI objects associated with those universes.

3. Finally, the WebI objects from step 2 are passed to the outer query, and their names are displayed.

Let's look at another example of a nested relationship query that is used to fill a requirement that sounds simple but turns out not to be: retrieve scheduled Web Intelligence documents *associated with a specific universe*. You might try this:

```
select si_name
  from ci_infoobjects
 where si_recurring = 1
       and parents("si_name='webi-universe'","si_name='AR Universe'")
```

However, this produces no results since scheduled WebI instances do not have a populated

SI_UNIVERSES property. We instead need to evaluate the instance's *parent's* SI_UNIVERSES property to get what we need.

So, this involves two relationship "joins". One from the recurring instance that we want to its parent, then from that parent to its associated universes. We can achieve this with a nested relationship query:

```
select si_name, si_recurring          ←────────  Step 3
  from ci_infoobjects
 where si_recurring = 1                        ───  Step 2
   and children("si_name='folder hierarchy'",               ──  Step 1
                "parents('si_name=' 'webi-universe' '  ','si_name=' 'ar universe' '  ')"
      )
```

We'll walk through the execution steps as we did with the previous example, starting with the innermost nested query.

1. In the first step, the query engine identifies the parents (*WebI* objects) of universes named *AR Universe*. The list of identified WebI objects is passed to the next step.

2. The outer function (children("SI_NAME='folder hierarchy',...")) then identifies all child objects of the WebI objects from the previous step. Thus, this list includes all instances of the identified WebI objects.

3. The list of identified instances is passed to the outer query. The condition SI_RECURRING=1 is applied to this result, so the final result includes only recurring instances associated with WebI objects which are associated with the AR Universe universe.

We'll take this scenario just one step further, to illustrate a three level relationship query. Instead of looking for scheduled instances associated with a specific universe, we'll look for those associated with any universes that are in a particular universe folder ("*Accounting Universes*").

```
select si_name,si_kind,si_schedule_status
  from ci_infoobjects
 where si_recurring = 1
   and children
          ("si_name='folder hierarchy'",
           "parents('si_name=''webi-universe''',
                   'children(''si_name=''''folder hierarchy'''' '',
                            ''si_name=''''Accounting Universe'''' ''
                       )'
              )"
          )
```

Remember that the text between double-quotes cannot include line feeds. They have been added to this query only for visual clarity.

The ConnectedComponents Function

We have already covered six of the relationship functions:

- `parents()`, to retrieve the immediate parent(s) of the specified object(s)

- `children()`, to retrieve all immediate children of the specified object(s)

- `ancestors()`, to retrieve all ancestors of the specified object(s)

- `descendants()`, to retrieve all descendants of the specified object(s)

- `groups()`, to retrieve all immediate children (of the specified objects) that are groups

- `members()` to retrieve all immediate children (of the specified objects) that are members

There is one more function that we have not yet covered: `connectedcomponents()`. This function produces a list of all objects that are connected, indirectly or directly, to the specified objects, within the context of the specified relationship type or types.

Consider a simple repository that contains a single data connection and associated universe:

Connection	Universe
Finance Datamart	AR Universe

We query for the universe's connected components using the following relationship query:

```
select si_name,si_kind
  from ci_appobjects
 where connectedcomponents(
            "si_name='dataconnection-universe'",
            "si_name='ar universe' and si_kind = 'universe'")
```

This query returns:

SI_NAME	SI_KIND
Finance Datamart	CCIS.DataConnection
AR Universe	Universe

The query returns the *AR Universe* itself and the one object within the *DataConnection-Universe* relationship context that it is connected to (or *associated with*). Now let's create a new universe that is associated with the same connection. We now have:

Connection	Universe
Finance Datamart	AR Universe AP Universe

We run the same query as before:

```
select si_name,si_kind
  from ci_appobjects
 where connectedcomponents(
               "si_name='dataconnection-universe'",
               "si_name='ar universe' and si_kind = 'universe'")
```

Now we receive:

SI_NAME	SI_KIND
Finance Datamart	CCIS.DataConnection
AR Universe	Universe
AP Universe	Universe

But wait a minute. The *AR Universe* has an association with the *Finance Datamart* connection, but not with the *AP Universe*. Why did it show up? The two universes are in fact associated, indirectly, by way of the *Finance Datamart* connection. That is, the *AR Universe* is associated with the *Finance Datamart* connection, which in turn is also associated with the *AP Universe*. Querying for any member in this association returns all associated members. So, we could change our query above to query for either the *AR Universe*, the *AP Universe*, or the *Finance Datamart* connection, and receive identical results with each.

Let's add another connection and associated universe to our repository:

Connection	Universe
Finance Datamart	AR Universe AP Universe
Sales Datamart	Sales Universe

Our query from above returns the same data as it did before:

```
select si_name,si_kind
  from ci_appobjects
 where connectedcomponents(
               "si_name='dataconnection-universe'",
               "si_name='ar universe' and si_kind = 'universe'")
```

SI_NAME	SI_KIND
Finance Datamart	CCIS.DataConnection
AR Universe	Universe
AP Universe	Universe

...since neither of the new objects that we added have any association to the existing objects. However, we can now query for one of our new objects to get its connected components:

```
select si_name,si_kind
  from ci_appobjects
 where connectedcomponents(
```

```
                "si_name='dataconnection-universe'",
                "si_name='sales datamart' and si_kind = 'ccis.dataconnection'")
```

SI_NAME	SI_KIND
Sales Datamart	CCIS.DataConnection
Sales Universe	Universe

We can visualize the associations between these objects in *Illustration 10*

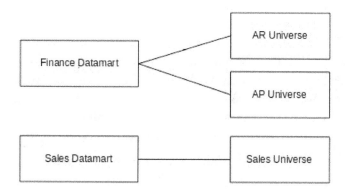

Illustration 10: Connected Components

So let's take this one step further, and add a WebI report that has two queries, one based on the *AP Universe* and the other based on the *Sales Universe*. Our repository structure now looks like Illustration 11.

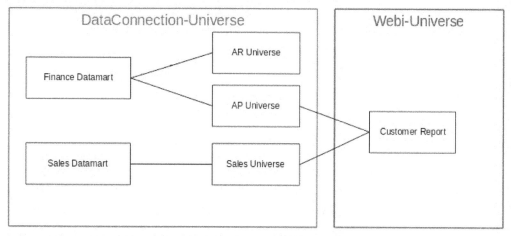

Illustration 11: Connected Components with WebI

We'll execute the same query that we have been using:

```
select si_name,si_kind
```

```
    from ci_appobjects
  where connectedcomponents(
              "si_name='dataconnection-universe'",
              "si_name='ar universe' and si_kind = 'universe'")
```

...we now get:

SI_NAME	SI_KIND
Finance Datamart	CCIS.DataConnection
AR Universe	Universe
AP Universe	Universe

So... why did the query not return the *Sales Universe* since it is connected to the *AR Universe* by way of our new *Customer Report*? The associations are only considered "connected" if they are *within the relationship context specified.* Since our query specified only the *DataConnection-Universe* relationship type, the query engine only evaluates connections between those kinds. The associations to the WebI report are not considered at all.

If we want our query to consider the associations from *Customer Report* to its associated universes, we have to include the *Webi-Universe* relationship type in our query:

```
select si_name,si_kind
  from ci_appobjects
 where connectedcomponents(
             "si_name in ('webi-universe','dataconnection-universe')",
             "si_name='ar universe' and si_kind = 'universe'")
```

Now we get:

SI_NAME	SI_KIND
Finance Datamart	CCIS.DataConnection
AR Universe	Universe
AP Universe	Universe
Sales Universe	Universe
Sales Datamart	CCIS.DataConnection

You very likely noted that we did not add CI_INFOOBJECTS to our FROM clause, and therefore we did not get the WebI document in our results. But *its associations to universes were considered when the connection path was calculated.* We can, of course, add CI_INFOOBJECTS to retrieve the complete path:

```
select si_name,si_kind
  from ci_infoobjects,ci_appobjects
 where connectedcomponents(
             "si_name in ('webi-universe','dataconnection-universe')",
```

```
"si_name='ar universe' and si_kind = 'universe'")
```

SI_NAME	SI_KIND
Finance Datamart	CCIS.DataConnection
AR Universe	Universe
AP Universe	Universe
Sales Universe	Universe
Sales Datamart	CCIS.DataConnection
Customer Report	Webi

The use of `connectedcomponents()` with hierarchical relationship types such as *Folder Hierarchy* or *UserGroup-User* is of limited use. Every object in a particular hierarchy is inherently associated with *every* other object, at least by way of the root object. So, querying for `connectedcomponents()` on any object in a hierarchy always returns **all** objects. Consider:

```
select si_name
  from ci_systemobjects
 where connectedcomponents("si_name='usergroup-user'","si_name='fred'")
```

Fred, at a minimum, is a member of the *Everyone* group, as is every other user. So, there is an association between *Fred*, the *Everyone* group, and all other users. There is also an association between all users and all user groups that have at least one member – so the query above returns all users, and all user groups with at least one member user.

The `connectedcomponents()` function is very powerful, but can easily be misused. Be sure to understand the behavior of this function if you intend to use it.

Other Relationship Type Specifications

In all of the queries above, we specified the relationship type by name, for example:

```
parents("si_name='usergroup-user'"...
```

This is the most common way to specify relationship types, but it is not the only way. Since the relationship type expression is a standard CMS query expression, any other way to identify the type (or types) can be used. Consider:

```
select si_name
  from ci_infoobjects
 where parents("si_relation_children_members_property = 'si_universe'",
       "si_name = 'ar universe'")
```

Instead of specifying the relationship type by name, we are instead using any relationship type whose parent objects reference their children with a property named SI_UNIVERSE. When we get to path queries, we will see that the query pre-processor makes use of this method of specifying relationship types.

Chapter Review

- There are many different types of relationships between InfoObjects. Some are hierarchical such as the folder and group hierarchies, while others are one-to-many and many-to-many relationships, such as *Webi-Universe* and *DataConnection-Universe*.

- Relationship queries are invaluable for the common need of retrieving objects based on their relationship to other objects. Although the syntax gets some getting used to, it is well worth the time and effort involved.

- Relationship queries require three components: 1) the relationship type, which specifies how the InfoObjects are related (ex. *Folder Hierarchy* and *Webi-Universe*), 2) the condition, which restricts the source list of InfoObjects to query, and 3) the relationship function which specifies the scope and direction of the relationship to query.

Quiz

1. Which of the following is not a valid relationship query function?

   a) `folders()`

   b) `parents()`

   c) `groups()`

   d) `children()`

   e) All of the above are valid

2. The *Folder Hierarchy* relationship type can be used to retrieve:

   a) Immediate children

   b) Immediate parents

   c) All descendants

   d) All ancestors

   e) a and b

   f) c and d

3. True/False: the *Folder Hierarchy* relationship type can only be used with folders under

Public Folders.

4. True/False: it is possible to include multiple relationship types (ex. *Webi-Universe, Document-DSL.Universe*) in a single relationship query type expression.

5. In the following relationship query, we are retrieving universes associated with the *Quarterly Report* report. What is the correct table to use in the FROM clause?

```
select si_name
  from ci_?
 where children("si_name='webi-universe'","si_name='Pending Accounts'")
```

   a) `ci_infoobject`

   b) `ci_appobjects`

   c) `ci_systemobjects`

6. What is the correct way to list all supported relationship types in a particular SAP BusinessObjects installation?

   a) `select si_name from ci_systemobjects where si_parentid = 46`

   b) `select si_name from ci_systemobjects where si_kind = 'relationship'`

   c) `select si_relation_edge_type from ci_systemobjects where si_parentid = 46`

Answers on page 672.

Chapter 5 - URI Queries

URI queries are often discussed in conjunction with *Relationship Queries* as alternative methods to query the CMS repository. While that is correct, the two methods are quite different. For one, relationship queries are simply an extension to the base "SQL-ish" CMS Query syntax. URI queries, on the other hand, are not SQL at all, but, as the name implies, in the form of a URL.

The other significant difference between relationship queries and URI queries is that the former are *native to the CMS query engine*, while the latter are not. That is, the query engine only understands the "SQL-ish" query syntax. URI queries must first be translated (by the SDK) into CMS queries, which can then be submitted to the query engine. As such, there is nothing that can be done in a URI query that cannot be accomplished with a regular CMS query.

So why use URI queries? There are a few advantages:

- The syntax of URI queries is generally more straightforward than comparable CMS queries

- URI queries are of the same format as the syntax for retrieving objects in the Raylight REST API.

- A single path query (one of the four URI query types) can produce a result that would otherwise require several separate CMS queries.

- URI queries are the only means of querying the CMS when using the Web Services SDK, as it is not possible to use the CMS SQL syntax.

The URI query syntax is one of the few parts of the overall CMS query syntax that is fairly well documented. In the *Business Intelligence Platform SDK Developer Guide*, see the *section SDK Fundamentals → Using URI Queries to retrieve objects*[47].

Also, there is an excellent introduction to Path Queries on Ted Ueda's SAP SCN Blog: https://blogs.sap.com/2009/02/20/businessobjects-enterprise-sdk-xi-3x-path-queries-and-query-builder/. Much of the information in this section, in particular, the Query Builder modifications, were drawn from Ted's very informative blog.

Enabling Query Builder to Run URI Queries

URI queries are not natively understood by the CMS query engine and must be run through a preprocessor to generate CMS query SQL. As of BI4.2, the Query Builder web application does not have this functionality built-in, so attempting to run a valid URI query in the Query Builder produces a syntax error. Fortunately, the Query Builder web application code can be

---

47   See: http://scn.sap.com/docs/DOC-27465

easily patched to support URI queries[48].

Assuming your SAP BusinessObjects system is running the default Tomcat web application server, navigate to the Tomcat home directory, then webapps\AdminTools\querybuilder. Open up query.jsp in a text editor, and search for the following line:

```
objects = iStore.query((String) session.getAttribute("sqlStmt"));
```

Delete or comment out this line, and replace it with:

```
sqlStmt = ((String) session.getAttribute("sqlStmt")).trim();
// Check to see if URI
if(java.util.regex.Pattern.matches("^\\w+://.*", sqlStmt))
{
    sqlStmt = iStore.getStatelessPageInfo(sqlStmt,
        new com.crystaldecisions.sdk.uri.PagingQueryOptions()).getPageSQL();
}
objects = iStore.query(sqlStmt);
```

We also want to display the translated CMS query SQL on the output screen, so search for the following code:

```
    <HR SIZE='1'>
<%
    //LOOP THROUGH THE COLLECTION AND DISPLAY THE OBJECT DETAILS
```

Add one line so that the code becomes:

```
    <HR SIZE='1'>
<%=sqlStmt%>
<%
    //LOOP THROUGH THE COLLECTION AND DISPLAY THE OBJECT DETAILS
```

Save query.jsp, then open up the Query Builder in your web browser. First, enter a standard CMS query, for example:

```
select si_name from ci_infoobjects where si_id = 23
```

...and execute it. We just want to make sure there are no errors in the code, and that the SQL appears at the top of the screen. If there are errors or the SQL does not appear, then the modifications were not done correctly.

Assuming the previous test was successful, we can now test the URI query functionality. Enter and execute the following query:

```
cuid://<ASHnC0S_Pw5LhKFbZ.iA_j4>
```

The output screen should look like the following:

---

48 In Chapter 5 we will cover the functionality in detail.

SAP BusinessObjects Business Intelligence platform - Query Builder

Number of InfoObject(s) returned: 1

```
SELECT TOP 1-200
SI_ID,SI_CUID,SI_NAME,SI_PARENT_CUID,SI_DESCRIPTION,SI_CREATION_TIME,SI_KIND,SI_SPECIFIC_KIND,SI_CHILDREN,SI_OWNER,SI_PATH,SI_CORPORATE_CATEGORIES_ID,SI_PERSONAL_CATEGORIES_ID,SI_F
SI_CUID, SI_PARENT_CUID FROM CI_INFOOBJECTS, CI_APPOBJECTS, CI_SYSTEMOBJECTS WHERE (SI_CUID IN ('ASHnC0S_Pw5LhKFbZ.iA_j4'))
```

Properties			
SI_DESCRIPTION			
SI_NAME	Root Folder		
SI_INSTANCE	false		
SI_ID	23		
SI_CUID	ASHnC0S_Pw5LhKFbZ.iA_j4		
SI_SPECIFIC_KIND	Folder		
SI_CREATION_TIME	9/18/15 9:42:05 AM		
SI_KIND	Folder		
SI_CHILDREN	10		
SI_PARENT_CUID	AXNWWTizCNNBrOt2AVUPfyE		
SI_OWNER	System Account		
SI_PATH	SI_FOLDER_NAME1	osboxes:6400	
	SI_FOLDER_OBTYPE1	13	
	SI_FOLDER_ID1	4	
	SI_NUM_FOLDERS	1	

Illustration 12: URI query Test

If the infamous "Not a valid query" error was displayed, but you are certain that you entered the query properly, then there was a problem with the modification in query.jsp.

*   *   *

Illustration 13 depicts the URI query Syntax diagram. There are four "protocols" that perform different querying functions. The protocol is then followed by the query text – the form of the query is different for each of the protocols, and we cover these in-depth in the following section. There are four optional parameters that may be placed after the query text. Not every protocol supports all parameters.

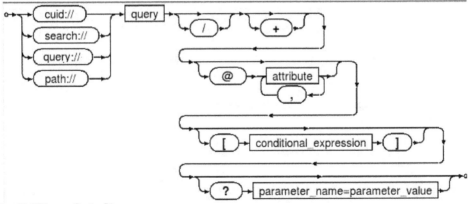

Illustration 13: URI query Syntax Diagram

As with CMS SQL queries, URI queries are mostly case-insensitive – only CUIDs/RUIDs/GUIDs in queries are case sensitive. The following queries are functionally identical:

```
cuid://<AeN4lEu0h_tAtnPEjFYxwi8>/[si_kind = 'webi']@si_name?orderby=si_name
CUID://<AeN4lEu0h_tAtnPEjFYxwi8>/[SI_KIND = 'WEBI']@SI_NAME?ORDERBY=SI_NAME
CUID://<AeN4lEu0h_tAtnPEjFYxwi8>/[SI_Kind = 'Webi']@SI_Name?OrderBy=SI_Name
```

Although URI queries look like URLs associated with the WWW, the formatting rules are not the same. Spaces and special characters **are** allowed and do not have to be escaped.

The CUID Type

The CUID URI query type allows for retrieval of objects by CUID or CUIDs. We saw an example of this query type during our test of the Query Builder modification. Here it is again:

```
cuid://<ASHnC0S_Pw5LhKFbZ.iA_j4>
```

...and the SQL that was generated from it[49]:

```
SELECT TOP 1-200
    SI_ID,SI_CUID,SI_NAME,SI_PARENT_CUID,SI_DESCRIPTION,
    SI_CREATION_TIME,SI_KIND,SI_SPECIFIC_KIND,SI_CHILDREN,
    SI_OWNER,SI_PATH,SI_CORPORATE_CATEGORIES_ID,
    SI_PERSONAL_CATEGORIES_ID,SI_FILES,SI_INSTANCE,SI_SCHEDULE_STATUS,
    SI_LAST_SUCCESSFUL_INSTANCE_ID,SI_KEYWORD, SI_CUID, SI_PARENT_CUID
FROM
    CI_INFOOBJECTS, CI_APPOBJECTS, CI_SYSTEMOBJECTS
WHERE
    (SI_CUID IN ('ASHnC0S_Pw5LhKFbZ.iA_j4'))
```

Note that we did not need to specify the table to select from (`CI_INFOOBJECTS`, `CI_SYSTEMOBJECTS`, `CI_APPOBJECTS`), as the preprocessor automatically included all three in the generated SQL.

To query for multiple CUIDs, simply separate them by commas:

```
cuid://<AS1oZEJAynpNjZIaZK2rc7g,AVwhi.xFgTdHmHza7wd7.7Q>
```

The WHERE clause in the generated SQL becomes:

```
WHERE (SI_CUID IN ('AS1oZEJAynpNjZIaZK2rc7g','AVwhi.xFgTdHmHza7wd7.7Q'))
```

Although the protocol name is "cuid", it's also possible to pass InfoObject IDs instead:

```
cuid://<23>
cuid://<23,18>
```

But it is not possible to include object IDs and CUIDs together. This produces an error:

```
cuid://<23,AWigQI18AAZJoXfRHLzWJ2c>
```

---

49 The generated SQL will not contain line feeds – we have added them here for clarity.

The Path Operators: / and +/

The CUID queries above all return the specified object (or objects). To return the *children* of the specified objects instead, append a single slash ("/") to the query. For example:

```
cuid://<ASHnC0S_Pw5LhKFbZ.iA_j4>/
```

This changes the SQL to:

```
SELECT TOP 1-200
    SI_ID,SI_CUID,SI_NAME,SI_PARENT_CUID,SI_DESCRIPTION,
    SI_CREATION_TIME,SI_KIND,SI_SPECIFIC_KIND,SI_CHILDREN,
    SI_OWNER,SI_PATH,SI_CORPORATE_CATEGORIES_ID,
    SI_PERSONAL_CATEGORIES_ID,SI_FILES,SI_INSTANCE,SI_SCHEDULE_STATUS,
    SI_LAST_SUCCESSFUL_INSTANCE_ID,SI_KEYWORD, SI_CUID, SI_PARENT_CUID
FROM
    CI_INFOOBJECTS, CI_APPOBJECTS, CI_SYSTEMOBJECTS
WHERE
    SI_PARENTID IN (23)
```

But notice something – although we specified the CUID of the root-level public folder ("ASHnC0S_Pw5LhKFbZ.iA_j4"), the generated SQL includes a condition on the root-level public folder's object ID (23) instead. What happened? This is an example of a case where the URI query pre-processor does more than simply convert from URI query syntax to SQL syntax. The pre-processor ran its own CMS query to retrieve the object ID for the CUID that we passed, then used that ID in the generated SQL.

The pre-processor is smart enough to handle multiple CUIDs. If we execute:

```
cuid://<AS1oZEJAynpNjZIaZK2rc7g,AY9zJ8BgaF9OucZ2h2slcJM>/
```

...then the generated SQL includes a WHERE clause of:

```
WHERE SI_PARENTID IN (2795,511)
```

As before, the pre-processor has done a lookup of the two CUIDs in our query, retrieved their IDs, and constructed a SQL query accordingly.

If an invalid CUID is passed to the pre-processor when the path operator is used, an error will be thrown. Note that it is the pre-processor that throws the error, and not the CMS query engine. If we attempt a query such as:

```
cuid://<fred>/
```

...then an error is displayed[50]:

```
com.crystaldecisions.sdk.exception.URIParserException$InvalidPathNode: The path node
'fred' does not exist in the repository. (FWM 03005)
```

---

50 Except in the extremely unlikely case in which your CMS has an object with a CUID of "fred".

If multiple CUIDs are included in the query, and at least one is valid, then the pre-processor generates the SQL, and the invalid CUID(s) are ignored. For example:

```
cuid://<ASHnC0S_Pw5LhKFbZ.iA_j4,fred>/
```

This produces a WHERE condition including:

```
WHERE SI_PARENTID IN (23)
```

In addition to querying for an object explicitly or for its children, we can also query for an object *and* its children. We use the +/ operator for this action:

```
cuid://<ASHnC0S_Pw5LhKFbZ.iA_j4>+/
```

This produces a condition of:

```
WHERE (SI_PARENTID IN (23) OR SI_ID IN (23))
```

...which returns object 23 (the root-level public folder) and its children.

To summarize the path operators that we've covered so far:

Operator	Meaning	Sample generated SQL
	Object only	(SI_CUID IN ('ASHnC0S_Pw5LhKFbZ.iA_j4'))
/	Object's children	SI_PARENTID IN (23)
+/	Object and children	SI_PARENTID IN (23) OR SI_ID IN (23))

The attribute operator: @

You've noticed that the CUID queries above generated a SQL statement with a pre-defined list of attributes in the SELECT clause:

```
SELECT TOP 1-200
    SI_ID,SI_CUID,SI_NAME,SI_PARENT_CUID,SI_DESCRIPTION,
    SI_CREATION_TIME,SI_KIND,SI_SPECIFIC_KIND,SI_CHILDREN,
    SI_OWNER,SI_PATH,SI_CORPORATE_CATEGORIES_ID,
    SI_PERSONAL_CATEGORIES_ID,SI_FILES,SI_INSTANCE,SI_SCHEDULE_STATUS,
    SI_LAST_SUCCESSFUL_INSTANCE_ID,SI_KEYWORD,SI_CUID,SI_PARENT_CUID
```

The CUID query can be set to return a different set of attributes, by way of the @ operator, which takes the following form:

```
protocol://query_text@property_name,property_name,property_name
```

Simply append this operator and a list of comma-separated property names to the base query. In this example, we'll request the SI_LASTLOGONTIME and SI_USERFULLNAME properties of the *Fred* user object:

```
cuid://<FoTOBlZnowIA4g4AAAA3legACAAnyavX>@si_lastlogontime,si_userfullname
```

This produces a CMS query of:

```
SELECT TOP 1-200
    si_lastlogontime, si_userfullname, SI_CUID, SI_PARENT_CUID
FROM
    CI_INFOOBJECTS, CI_APPOBJECTS, CI_SYSTEMOBJECTS
WHERE
    SI_ID IN (4104)
```

...and a result of:

SI_LASTLOGONTIME	1/15/16 5:02:04 PM
SI_CUID	FoTOBlZnowIA4g4AAAA3legACAAnyavX
SI_USERFULLNAME	Fred Frederick
SI_PARENT_CUID	AXhmigik4CBKra9ZYzR2ezE

When the @ operator is used to specify properties, the SI_CUID and SI_PARENT_CUID properties are still automatically included, but the other default properties are not. So, whenever the @ operator is used, you should specify all of the properties that should be included in the result.

Whatever is included with the @ operator is simply placed into the SELECT clause, even if the property names are invalid. For example:

```
cuid://<FoTOBlZnowIA4g4AAAA3legACAAnyavX>@si_foo
```

...is converted to:

```
SELECT TOP 1-200
    si_foo, SI_CUID, SI_PARENT_CUID
FROM
    CI_INFOOBJECTS, CI_APPOBJECTS, CI_SYSTEMOBJECTS
WHERE
    SI_ID IN (4104)
```

Instead of specific property names, we can use the static, dynamic, relationships, or * keywords (see page 5). For example, we can query for all dynamic properties of the *Fred* object with:

```
cuid://<FoTOBlZnowIA4g4AAAA3legACAAnyavX>@dynamic
```

or all properties, with:

```
cuid://<FoTOBlZnowIA4g4AAAA3legACAAnyavX>@*
```

It is possible to combine the @ operator with the / operator. To retrieve the names of the top-level public folders, we can use:

```
cuid://<ASHnC0S_Pw5LhKFbZ.iA_j4>/@si_name
```

It's worth mentioning at this point that the path operator can be easily overlooked. This can be problematic, since leaving it out (or adding it) unintentionally can produce results that are unexpected[51]. Always pay special attention to the existence of the path operator in URI queries.

The conditional operator: [ ]

Standard CMS conditional expressions can be applied to a CUID query by way of the bracket operators ([ ]). Assuming you are already familiar with the CMS query syntax, you can simply include standard conditional expressions within the brackets.

A query with a conditional operator takes the following form:

```
protocol://query_text[conditional expression]
```

For example, we can query for all objects of kind Webi in a specific folder:

```
cuid://<AeN4lEu0h_tAtnPEjFYxwi8>/[si_kind = 'webi']
```

This produces the following SQL:

```
SELECT TOP 1-200
    SI_ID,SI_CUID,SI_NAME,SI_PARENT_CUID,SI_DESCRIPTION,
    SI_CREATION_TIME,SI_KIND,SI_SPECIFIC_KIND,SI_CHILDREN,
    SI_OWNER,SI_PATH,SI_CORPORATE_CATEGORIES_ID,
    SI_PERSONAL_CATEGORIES_ID,SI_FILES,SI_INSTANCE,SI_SCHEDULE_STATUS,
    SI_LAST_SUCCESSFUL_INSTANCE_ID,SI_KEYWORD,SI_CUID,SI_PARENT_CUID
FROM
    CI_INFOOBJECTS, CI_APPOBJECTS, CI_SYSTEMOBJECTS
WHERE
    SI_PARENTID IN (3968) AND (si_kind = 'webi')
```

Anything between the brackets is simply copied into the SQL statement's WHERE condition. As such, the specified condition can be as complex as it needs to be. We can expand the previous query to include all WebI objects that are either owned by Fred or updated during or after 2015:

```
cuid://<AeN4lEu0h_tAtnPEjFYxwi8>/[si_kind = 'webi' and (si_owner = 'fred' or
si_update_ts >= '2015.01.01')]
```

The WHERE condition of the generated SQL query then includes:

```
WHERE SI_PARENTID IN (3968) AND (si_kind = 'webi' and (si_owner = 'fred' or
si_update_ts >= '2015.01.01'))
```

---

51 One of the author's favorite business intelligence axioms is that getting an error message is better than getting a result that *looks* correct, but isn't.

The parameter operator: ?

A number of different parameters can be included in the URI query to alter the querying behavior. Most of the available parameters are associated with searching and paging, which we cover in detail further on.

Parameters are specified in the following form:

```
protocol://query_text?parameter_name=parameter_value
```

The ordering of the result set can be set with the orderBy parameter. The syntax is exactly the same as the ORDER BY clause in CMS SQL queries (see page 25). To order a query by name, we would use:

```
cuid://<ASHnC0S_Pw5LhKFbZ.iA_j4>/?orderby=si_name
```

To specify reverse order, append the property name with DESC:

```
cuid://<ASHnC0S_Pw5LhKFbZ.iA_j4>/?orderby=si_name desc
```

Multiple properties can be specified with OrderBy, separated by commas:

```
cuid://<ASHnC0S_Pw5LhKFbZ.iA_j4>/?orderby=si_name desc,si_update_ts
```

Whatever is specified for OrderBy is copied into the generated SQL's ORDER BY clause. The query above produces the following SQL:

```
SELECT TOP 1-200
    SI_ID,SI_CUID,SI_NAME,SI_PARENT_CUID,SI_DESCRIPTION,
    SI_CREATION_TIME,SI_KIND,SI_SPECIFIC_KIND,SI_CHILDREN,SI_OWNER,
    SI_PATH,SI_CORPORATE_CATEGORIES_ID,SI_PERSONAL_CATEGORIES_ID,
    SI_FILES,SI_INSTANCE,SI_SCHEDULE_STATUS,
    SI_LAST_SUCCESSFUL_INSTANCE_ID,SI_KEYWORD, SI_CUID,
    SI_PARENT_CUID
FROM
    CI_INFOOBJECTS, CI_APPOBJECTS, CI_SYSTEMOBJECTS
WHERE
    SI_PARENTID IN (23)
ORDER BY
    si_name desc,si_update_ts
```

The operators that we have covered above can be combined as needed. We could, for example, create a query to retrieve the direct children of the root public folder, including the name and creation date properties, sorted by descending name, and of kind *Webi* only:

```
cuid://<ASHnC0S_Pw5LhKFbZ.iA_j4>/?orderby=si_name
desc,si_update_ts@si_name,si_creation_date[si_kind = 'webi']
```

This query is converted into the following SQL query:

```
SELECT TOP 1-200
    si_name,si_creation_date, SI_CUID, SI_PARENT_CUID
FROM
    CI_INFOOBJECTS, CI_APPOBJECTS, CI_SYSTEMOBJECTS
WHERE
    SI_PARENTID IN (23) AND (si_kind = 'webi')
ORDER BY
    si_name desc,si_update_ts
```

Effective use of CUID queries can save a lot of typing. This simple query:

```
cuid://<46>/*
```

...is a lot shorter than the comparable CMS SQL query:

```
select * from ci_systemobjects where si_parentid = 46
```

The Search Type

The `search` query type is used to retrieve objects by name or keyword. The basic form of this query type is:

```
search://{search_term search_term …}?parameter_name=parameter_value
```

The search term can be one or more strings, separated by spaces. By default, the query matches any objects whose names or keywords contain **any** of the terms. For example:

```
search://{my report}
```

...matches any object whose name or keywords contains "my" or "report". In this particular case, we want to find objects whose name contains "my report" but not "report my" or "my finance report" (although "this is my report" and "my report again" is desired). To match a string that includes any spaces, we enclose it in single quotes:

```
search://{'my report'}
```

We can combine quoted strings with unquoted strings. To search for objects with names or keywords that contain "my report" or "finance" or "annual", we would use:

```
search://{'my report' finance annual}
```

It doesn't hurt to quote strings without spaces. The following query is equivalent to the one above:

```
search://{'my report' 'finance' 'annual'}
```

The ordering of search terms has no effect. The above query could also be written as:

```
search://{annual 'my report' finance}
```

Search terms that contain special characters ({ } [ ] ? ^ < > / \ ' " ,) must be escaped by a backslash (\ ). For example, to search for an object containing the string "Fred's Report", the query would be expressed as:

```
search://{'fred\'s report'}
```

To search for an object named *Losses > $100k (Monthly)*, we would use:

```
search://{'losses \> $100k \(monthly\)'}
```

The search operation returns objects if the search term exists anywhere in the name or keywords. For example:

```
search://{abc}
```

...matches objects named *abc, abcd, xyzabc*, etc.

Wildcard characters can be specified in the search term (unless the MatchExact parameter is specified, which we'll be covering soon). To find objects with names or keywords containing the string "Fr" followed by any single character, then followed by "d", we would use:

```
search://{Fr_d}
```

See the syntax of the LIKE operator on page 22 for more detail on the wildcard characters.

You'll notice that the query does not specify the CMS table (CI_INFOOBJECTS, CI_APPOBJECTS, or CI_SYSTEMOBJECTS). As with the cuid:// query type, the query is performed on all three tables. Therefore, the query may return unexpected objects. The query:

```
search://{annual finance}
```

...might produce a result that includes folders, Web Intelligence documents, universes, users, etc., as long as their names or keywords include the specified search criteria.

Unlike the cuid:// query type, the search:// type does not support the [ ] operator for applying conditional expressions, so unfortunately it is not possible to limit a search query by object kind.

Search Parameters

The `search://` query type supports several parameters for specifying the search behavior (the `OrderBy` parameter, covered earlier, is also supported).

The search parameters all have the form:

```
parameter_name=[true | false]
```

For example, to perform a search on object names but not keywords:

```
search://{'my report'}?SearchKeywords=false
```

Multiple parameters can be combined with the & operator. We can change the above query to specify exact matches only:

```
search://{'my report'}?SearchKeywords=false&MatchExact=true
```

However, some parameters can conflict with each other. Setting both `SearchKeywords` and `SearchName` to false produces an error. Setting `MatchAllWords` and `MatchExact` to true produces no results if the search expression contains more than one term.

The available search parameters are:

SearchName

Specifies whether the search operation should consider object names (the `SI_NAME` property). If set to `false`, then only object keywords (`SI_KEYWORD`) are considered in the search (unless `SearchKeywords` is also `false`, in which case an error is generated)

The default value is **true**.

SearchKeywords

Specifies if the search operation should consider object keywords (the `SI_KEYWORD` property). If set to `false`, then only object names (`SI_NAME`) are considered in the search (unless `SearchNames` is also `false`, in which case an error is generated)

The default value is **true**.

CaseSensitive

Specifies if the search operation should match exact case. For example, the following query:

```
search://{Annual}?CaseSensitive=true
```

...matches objects named *Annual Reports* and *My Annual reports* but not *My annual reports*.

The default value is **false**.

MatchAllWords

Specifies if the search should only return objects whose name or keywords contain all of the search terms. If false, then objects that match at least one search term are returned.

Consider a report named *Monthly Financial Results*. This query:

```
search://{financial results}?MatchAllWords=true
```

...returns the report since the report name contains both of the words *financial* and *results*. This query:

```
search://{annual financial results}?MatchAllWords=true
```

...does **not** return the report since not all of the search terms exist in the report name (the report name does not contain the search term *annual*). But this query:

```
search://{annual financial}
```

...**returns** the report since *at least one* of the terms (*financial*) exists in the report name.

The default value is **false**.

FindWithoutWords

Specifies if the search operation should be negated. That is, return objects that don't match the search term.

The default value is **false**.

MatchExact

Specifies if the search operation should return objects when the search term matches the entire name or keywords. If   or unspecified, then objects are returned whose name and or keywords *contain* the search term or terms. If true, then the entire name/keyword must match at least one of the search terms.

Consider again the *Monthly Financial Results* report. This query returns it:

```
search://{'monthly financial results'}?MatchExact=true
```

...but this does not:

```
search://{'financial results'}?MatchExact=true
```

...since the search term does not match the entire name. Now consider a report simply named *Financial*. This query:

```
search://{financial results}?MatchExact=true
```

...returns the *Financial* report since the object's entire name ("Financial") matches *at least one of the search terms*.

The default value is **false**.

IncludeInstances

Specifies if object instances (those with SI_INSTANCE = true) should be included in the search result.

The default value is **true**.

The Path Type

The Path query type is arguably the most useful of the URI query types. Unlike the search://
and cuid:// types, which do a relatively simple conversion to CMS SQL, path queries can be used to combine and simplify several separate recursive queries.

> *Key point: Path queries greatly simplify the requirement to retrieve InfoObjects based on their location in a folder hierarchy.*

This works not only for public folders but for all hierarchical folders in the CMS, including universe folders, personal folders, etc.

In Chapter 4, we saw how to use Relationship Queries to retrieve objects based on their association to a parent or child, but relationship queries can get very complex when querying more than two levels in a hierarchy.

Consider the *Quarterly Profit* report in Illustration 14, and a need to retrieve it by its name and location in the folder hierarchy.

Illustration 14: The Quarterly Profit report

With a relationship query, this can be done in one step, but the query becomes very complex:

```
select
    si_name,si_id
from
    ci_infoobjects
where
  si_name = 'quarterly profit'
```

```
and
children (
  "si_name='folder hierarchy'",
  "si_name = 'quarterly'
  and children (
    'si_name=''folder hierarchy''',
    'si_name = ''financial''
    and children (
      ''si_name=''''folder hierarchy'''''',
      ''si_name=''''sales''''
      and children (
        ''''si_name=''''''''folder hierarchy'''''''' '''',
        ''''si_name = ''''''''reports''''''''
        and children (
          ''''''''si_name=''''''''''''''''folder hierarchy'''''''''''''''' '''''''',
          ''''''''si_id = 23 ''''''''
        )
        ''''
      )
      ''
    )
    '
  )
  "
)
```

Even with the added linefeeds (which aren't allowed within a relationship expression), the syntax becomes unwieldy fairly quickly. Using a path query instead is far simpler:

```
path://infoobjects/root folder/reports/sales/financial/quarterly/quarterly profit
```

The format is intuitive – simply list the folders in order beginning at the root, separated by a slash. The query can be used to retrieve specific objects, or children, of a specified object. Wildcards may also be used to retrieve objects from multiple folders.

Unlike the `cuid://` and `search://` query types, the `path://` type allows for the CMS table to be specified (`CI_INFOOBJECTS`, `CI_APPOBJECTS`, `CI_SYSTEMOBJECTS`), and in fact requires it (although a wildcard can be specified). So, all path queries **must** begin with one of the following:

- `path://infoobjects/`
- `path://appobjects/`
- `path://systemobjects/`
- `path://*/`

After the table, the path query continues with the appropriate root folder name, and down the hierarchy from there.

If the path query does not end with a slash, then the right-most object in the path itself is retrieved. To retrieve the root-level public folder:

```
path://infoobjects/root folder
```

This retrieves just one object – the root public folder (ID 23):

SI_DESCRIPTION		
SI_NAME	Root Folder	
SI_INSTANCE	false	
SI_ID	23	
SI_CUID	ASHnC0S_Pw5LhKFbZ.iA_j4	
SI_SPECIFIC_KIND	Folder	
SI_CREATION_TIME	9/18/15 9:42:05 AM	
SI_KIND	Folder	
SI_CHILDREN	10	
SI_PARENT_CUID	AXNWWTizCNNBrOt2AVUPfyE	
SI_OWNER	System Account	
SI_PATH	SI_FOLDER_NAME1	osboxes:6400
	SI_FOLDER_OBTYPE1	13
	SI_FOLDER_ID1	4
	SI_NUM_FOLDERS	1

To retrieve the top-level public folders (the children of the root folder), we append a slash to the end:

```
path://infoobjects/root folder/
```

Finally, we can use the +/ operator to retrieve the root folder **and** its children:

```
path://infoobjects/root folder+/
```

Wildcards

By default, the ending / operator retrieves all child objects. We can use wildcards to be more precise about what to return. For example, to retrieve top-level public folders beginning with the letter R, we can use a wildcard:

```
path://infoobjects/root folder/r*
```

In our sample system, the above query returns the *Reports* and *Report Conversion Tool* folders. The wildcard syntax is the same as the LIKE operator in CMS queries (see page 22, with the exception that * is used in place of %. To find top-level folders with a second character of "e", we can use:

```
path://infoobjects/root folder/_e*
```

This produces a CMS query containing the following condition:

```
WHERE SI_PARENTID IN (23) AND SI_NAME LIKE '_e%'
```

The real power of path queries comes from the ability to use wildcards for folder names. Let's return to the *reports/sales/financial/quarterly* folder from page 130, but we'll add a *Service* folder alongside *Sales*, with an identical structure, as depicted in Illustration 15:

Illustration 15: The Service folder

So the *Sales* and *Service* folders have identical content. We want to retrieve all *Quarterly Profit* reports but only if they exist in a *Quarterly* folder which is a child of a *Financial* folder. We can use the following path query to meet this need:

```
path://infoobjects/root folder/reports/*/financial/quarterly/quarterly profit
```

The * wildcard matches both the *Sales* and *Service* folders, so the query returns the *Quarterly Profit* report from both:

Reports/Sales/Financial/Quarterly

and

Reports/Service/Financial/Quarterly

The * wildcard matches only one level in a hierarchy. If we tried:

```
path://infoobjects/*/quarterly profit
```

...we would get no results since the query would be looking for objects named "Quarterly Profit" only in top-level folders. That is, the * operator would match all top-level folders, so the query looks only for children of those objects.

We could search for the report using wildcards to represent the known depth of the hierarchy. We know that Quarterly Profit is at the fifth level of the hierarchy (*Reports / Sales / Financial Quarterly / Quarterly Profit*), so we could specify a wildcard in the four parent levels:

```
path://infoobjects/root folder/*/*/*/*/quarterly profit
```

Or, we could use the ** operator, which matches all descendant objects. To find The *Quarterly Profit* report, anywhere in public folders but only if its immediate parent folder is named *Quarterly*:

```
path://infoobjects/root folder/**/quarterly/quarterly profit
```

We can also use this method to retrieve all descendants of a specified object. This query:

```
path://infoobjects/root folder/reports/sales/financial/**
```

...returns the *Quarterly* and *Yearly* folders, and the *Quarterly Profit* and *Annual Profit* reports therein. Or, to retrieve all objects in public folders:

```
path://infoobjects/root folder/**
```

InfoObjects, AppObjects, SystemObjects

Path queries can be used with all three CMS tables, but you must be careful to use the correct folder hierarchy. To list all members of a universe folder named Financial, we would use the following query:

```
path://appobjects/application folder/root folder 95/universes/financial/
```

The ancestral path of the *Universes* folder is not as straightforward as for *Public Folders*. We could achieve the same result as above by way of the ** operator, to skip over *Application Folder/Root Folder 95*:

```
path://appobjects/**/universes/financial/
```

...but this does create a slight risk of picking up an unintended result. Consider a universe structure in Illustration 16. The path query above would return the children of both the top *Financial* folder as well as the *Human Resources/Universes/Financial* folder. This may or may not be what is desired. So, when using wildcards, be aware of the potential result.

Illustration 16: Human Resources universes

Another example, from CI_SYSTEMOBJECTS:

```
path://systemobjects/users/
```

Since all users as direct children of the *Users* folder in CI_SYSTEMOBJECTS, regardless of their group membership, this query returns all users in the system.

Mixing CUID and Path Syntax

We covered the cuid:// query type earlier in this chapter, as a way to retrieve objects using their object ID or CUID. It is possible to use the path query syntax in a cuid:// query, to specify the starting point of the path navigation.

In the previous section, we saw the slightly-awkward syntax for retrieving universes:

```
path://appobjects/application folder/root folder 95/universes/financial/
```

Knowing that the Root Folder 95 object has an object ID of 95, we can specify that as the starting point of the navigation:

```
cuid://<95>/universes/financial/
```

We can use this method with any valid cuid:// query. Let's return to our *Reports* folder (see page 130. In this case, we know the CUID of the *Financial* folder ("FgFGlFb74gYAHRAAAAAXINwACAAnyavX"), which we want to use as the starting point of the path navigation[52]. To access the *Quarterly/Quarterly Profit* report in this folder, we can use a combination of cuid:// with a path expression:

```
cuid://<FgFGlFb74gYAHRAAAAAXINwACAAnyavX>/quarterly/quarterly profit
```

---

52 This would be a good strategy to use if there is the possibility of the *Financial* folder moving to a different location in Public Folders. If that were to happen, its place in the folder hierarchy would be different, but its CUID would remain the same.

Using an object ID or CUID to specify the starting point of navigation has performance benefits, too. As we'll see soon, the URI query processor needs to run its own CMS query for each level in a path expression. So, reducing the number of levels in the expression reduces the number of internal queries that must be executed.

All path expression wildcards are valid when using `cuid://`. For example, one of our wildcard examples from earlier:

```
path://infoobjects/root folder/**/quarterly/quarterly profit
```

...could be expressed as:

```
cuid://<23>/**/quarterly/quarterly profit
```

The @ and [ ] Operators With path://

The `@` (attribute) and `[ ]` (conditional) operators function the same with `path://` as they do with the `cuid://` query type. As an example, let's use one of our sample path queries from earlier in this section:

```
path://infoobjects/root folder/reports/sales/financial/**
```

This returns all descendants of the Financial folder, including two subfolders and two Web Intelligence documents. We can use the `[ ]` operator to restrict this result to just the WebI documents:

```
path://infoobjects/root folder/reports/sales/financial/**[si_kind='webi']
```

Or, retrieve only objects created after 2015:

```
path://infoobjects/root folder/reports/sales/financial/**[si_creation_time >=
'2016.01.01']
```

The `@` operator is used to specify the properties to return. If we wanted the scheduling properties of the *Quarterly Profit* report in the *Sales* folder, we would use:

```
path://infoobjects/root folder/reports/sales/financial/quarterly/quarterly
profit@si_scheduleinfo
```

Relationships

One of the most valuable uses of path queries is the ability to retrieve objects based on their relationship to other objects. We introduced relationship queries in Chapter 4; the core concepts are the same in path queries, but the syntax is much simpler.

As with the path query syntax that we've covered so far (and URI queries in general) path queries with relationships are translated into CMS SQL queries. When a path query with relationships is translated into CMS SQL, it includes the relationship query expression. As a quick example, this path query:

```
path://systemobjects/user groups/administrators/children[si_group_members]
```

produces a CMS SQL query containing the following conditional expression[53][54]:

```
WHERE
  Children("SI_RELATION_CHILDREN_PROPERTY='SI_REL_GROUP_MEMBERS'
    OR SI_RELATION_CHILDREN_ATTRIBUTE_PROPERTY
        ='SI_REL_GROUP_MEMBERS'
    OR SI_RELATION_CHILDREN_MEMBERS_PROPERTY
        ='SI_REL_GROUP_MEMBERS'
    OR SI_RELATION_CHILDREN_MEMBERS_ATTRIBUTE_PROPERTY
        ='SI_REL_GROUP_MEMBERS'
    OR SI_RELATION_CHILDREN_GROUPS_PROPERTY
        ='SI_REL_GROUP_MEMBERS'
    OR SI_RELATION_CHILDREN_GROUPS_ATTRIBUTE_PROPERTY
        ='SI_REL_GROUP_MEMBERS'", "SI_ID IN (2)")
```

Clearly, the path query with a relationship expression is much easier to read and write. When learning how to use relationship queries, it is helpful to write path queries with relationship expressions instead, if no other reason than to learn from the CMS SQL (with relationship query) that the pre-processor generates[55].

Relationship expressions in path queries take the following form:

```
path://cms_table/path/path/path/object/relationship_type[relationship_property]
```

`relationship_type` is one of the following values:

- `parents`
- `children`
- `ancestors`
- `descendants`
- `members`
- `groups`
- `connected components`[56]

---

53 As with our previous examples of relationship queries, we have added line feeds within the expression for clarity. Line feeds are not allowed within the double-quoted expressions in relationship queries.

54 Most of our examples of relationship queries used the relationship type (ex. "UserGroup-User"). Here we can see an example of specifying a relationship in a different way, by the name of the property containing the related object IDs.

55 This method is partly how the authors learned to use relationship queries. There are a few undocumented (but useful) features of relationship queries that the path query pre-processor generates.

56 When used in a relationship query, this type is `ConnectedComponents()` *(without a space)*. In a path query, it is `Connected Components`.

The `relationship_property` is the property within the *specified* objects that includes object IDs of the *related* objects.

At first glance, a path query with a relationship expression looks like a simple path query with a condition expression using the bracket operator (`[ ]`). Using our example from earlier:

```
path://systemobjects/user groups/administrators/children[si_group_members]
```

This might *appear* to be querying for an object named "children" under a folder named "administrators", while containing an awkwardly-formatted conditional expression of simply "SI_GROUP_MEMBERS". However, the pre-processor recognizes this expression as a relationship and renders it appropriately. The pre-processor looks for both of the following to be true:

- The last segment of the path ("*children*" in the example above) is one of the valid relationship types, and

- A property expression is present ("`[si_group_members]`" in the example above)

Thus, this query:

```
path://systemobjects/user groups/administrators/kids[si_group_members]
```

...would not be recognized as a path query since the last segment of the path ("*kids*") is not a relationship type. In this case, the pre-processor would attempt to query for an object named "kids" within a folder named "administrators", and apply a condition of "(SI_GROUP_MEMBERS)". Of course, this is meaningless.

Similarly, this query:

```
path://systemobjects/user groups/administrators/children
```

...would also not be recognized as a relationship expression since there is no relationship property. The pre-processor would simply look for an object named *children* within a folder named *administrators*.

Relationship expressions can not be used with parent operator (`/`), although they can be used with *wildcards*. For example, the following path query returns all *WebI* documents associated with the *eFashion* universe in the *webi universes* folder:

```
cuid://<95>/universes/webi universes/efashion/parents[si_webi]
```

...and we can use this query to return all universes in the *webi universes* folder:

```
cuid://<95>/universes/webi universes/
```

So, what if we want all WebI documents associated with all of the universes in the W*ebI*

Universes folder? We can't simply append the relationship expression to the previous query:

```
cuid://<95>/universes/webi universes/parents[si_webi]
```

...since this would actually be a request for objects associated with the *WebI Universes* folder itself, and not its children. To get the result we want, we need to use a wildcard operator:

```
cuid://<95>/universes/webi universes/*/parents[si_webi]
```

We could also use the ** operator to match all descendant objects. This query:

```
cuid://<95>/universes/**/parents[si_webi]
```

...returns all WebI objects associated with *any* unv universe.

All of the possible relationship types that we covered in Chapter 4 are available in path queries. We could retrieve all ancestors of a specified object with ancestors, for example:

```
path://systemobjects/users/fred/ancestors[si_usergroups]
```

This query retrieves all groups that *Fred* is in, all groups that those *groups* are in, and so on.

The use of relationship expressions in path queries is not as flexible as writing "raw" relationship queries in CMS SQL. For example, double relationships, such as querying for WebI objects associated with specific universe connections (by way of universes), are not possible with path queries. However, as we have seen, specifying relationships in path queries is much simpler (and less error-prone) than the raw SQL method, and is often a good alternative. There is value in understanding and using both methods.

The Query Type

The query:// URI query type supports the execution of standard CMS SQL queries within the URL syntax. When used in Query Builder or a Java SDK program, this query:// type has little use since it is just as easy to execute the "raw" SQL query without passing it through the preprocessor. That is, there's no benefit to using the query:// type in Query Builder or Java since it actually involves additional code beyond executing the raw query directly.

The syntax is simply:

```
query://{cms_sql}
```

For example:

```
query://{select * from ci_systemobjects where si_kind = 'user' and si_name = 'fred'}
```

This query type has more value in the Web Services SDK (which we are not covering in this book) since the URL syntax is the only way of executing CMS queries there.

Chapter Review

- URI queries provide an alternate, simplified method for executing CMS queries. They are formatted as URLs rather than SQL.

- There is nothing that can be done with a URI query that cannot be done with CMS SQL queries, although a single URI query can produce a result that would require several individual CMS SQL queries.

- The Query Builder application does not support URI queries out-of-the-box, but can be made to do so with a few simple changes to the web application.

- There are four query types: `cuid`, which queries for one or more specific CUIDs; `search`, which queries for InfoObjects by name or keyword; `path`, which searches for InfoObjects according to their location in the InfoStore folder hierarchy; and `query`, which performs a raw CMS SQL query.

Quiz

1. List the four URI query types

2. True/False: By default, the only text in a URI query that is case-sensitive is CUID/GUID/RUID.

3. Which operator is used to request the specified object and its children?

   a) `/*`

   b) `+/`

   c) `/`

   d) `/+`

4. Which URI query type would be most appropriate to retrieve objects with a particular keyword?

   a) `cuid`

   b) `search`

   c) `sql`

   d) `query`

  e) `path`

5. Which of the following URI queries retrieves the immediate children of the top-level *Sales* public folder?

  a) `path://infoobjects/root folder/sales/`

  b) `path:///root folder/sales/`

  c) `path://infoobjects/sales/`

  d) `path://infoobjects/sales+/`

6. True/False: Both of the following queries returns the members of the Administrators user group:

  `path://systemobjects/user groups/administrators/children[si_group_members]`

  `path://systemobjects/user groups/administrators/children`

Answers on page 672.

Chapter 6 - CMS Query Miscellany

There are a few features of the CMS Query syntax that are undocumented[57] but can be useful in specific scenarios. Take care in using any of these, as they may not be supported in all versions.

SESSION:

Every active session in an SAP BusinessObjects cluster (including those via BI launch pad, CMC, WACS, SDK, etc.) is associated with an InfoObject that is of kind *Connection*[58] and is a child of object ID 41. This object is created when the session is logged on and is deleted upon logoff. Thus, a quick way to list all currently logged-on users is with this query:

```
select si_name
  from ci_systemobjects
where si_parentid = 41
```

...or, as a URI query:

```
cuid://<41>/@si_name
```

When used in the WHERE clause, the session: placeholder holds a reference to the *Connection* instance of the current session. So, if we wanted to retrieve the *Connection* object for the currently active session (the session that the query is being executed in), we can use session:SI_ID in a conditional expression as follows:

```
select *
  from ci_systemobjects
 where si_id = session:si_id
```

Or, perhaps of even more use, we can retrieve the *User* object that owns the current session:

```
select *
  from ci_systemobjects
 where si_id = session:si_userid
```

Consider a simple web application that enables SAP BusinessObjects users to view the user groups that they are members of. We can use session:SI_USERID in a relationship query to easily retrieve this information:

```
select si_name
  from ci_systemobjects
 where parents("si_name='usergroup-user'","si_id = session:si_userid")
```

If we were to execute this query as the user *Fred*, and Fred was a member of the *Everyone*,

---

57 Technically, the entire CMS query syntax is undocumented, but these are *really* undocumented.

58 Not to be confused with *universe connections.*, which have an SI_KIND of CCIS.DataConnection.

Finance, and *QA*, the result of the above query would return those groups:

SI_NAME
Everyone
Finance
QA

IsAllowed

The `IsAllowed()` function can be used in the `WHERE` clause of a CMS query to retrieve only objects that a designated user has certain access to. There are two forms of the `IsAllowed()` function:

```
isAllowed(principalID,rightID)
IsAllowed(rightID)
```

The first form retrieves objects only if the specified *principal* has been granted the specified *right*.

The `rightID` is an integer value that represents a specific access right (ex. *View*, *Edit*, *Delete*, *Add to Folder*, etc.). There are many different kinds of access rights – some are general and apply to all objects, while others are specific to certain object kinds. Most of the general rights have predefined IDs, which are accessible via the `CeSecurityID.Right` interface (we cover this more in Chapter 18). For now, here are a few of the common rights:

Right	ID
Add Objects to Folder	1
Copy	61
Delete	22
Delete Instances	38
Edit	6
Modify Rights	8
Pause/Resume Schedule	66
Reschedule	75
Schedule	21
Schedule On Behalf Of	76
View	3
View Instances	65

So, let's say we want to identify all of the Web Intelligence documents that Fred has at least *View* access to. Our first step is getting Fred's InfoObject ID:

```
select si_id
  from ci_systemobjects
 where si_name = 'fred'
     and si_kind = 'user'
```

SI_ID	4104

Next, we need the right ID for View. From the above table, we find that it's 3. We can now create the query to get all WebI documents that Fred can see:

```
select si_name,si_id
  from ci_infoobjects
 where isallowed(4104,3)
       and si_kind = 'webi'
```

This produces a list of the six reports that Fred can view:

SI_NAME	SI_ID
Returns	6212
Quarterly Profit	6251
Annual Profit	6540
Quarterly Profit	6547
Annual Profit	6548

We can use multiple IsAllowed() functions in a query. For example, we may want to identify objects that Fred has *View* access to but not *Delete*. From the above table, we find that the *Delete* right is associated with ID 22, so we can add a NOT expression to our query as follows:

```
select si_name,si_id
  from ci_infoobjects
 where isallowed(4104,3)
       and not isallowed(4104,22)
       and si_kind = 'webi'
```

In our sample environment, this produces no results since Fred has *Delete* rights on all reports that he has *View* rights to.

Note that the IsAllowed() function evaluates *effective* rights and not just *explicit* rights. That is, Fred may have been given explicit rights to the five WebI documents, or he may be in a group that has been given permission, or the documents may be in a folder that Fred has view access to. The fact that these reports appeared in our query indicates that Fred has *View* access to them, regardless of *how* he gained that permission.

We can specify a user group as the principal instead of a user. Similar to our previous query, we want to find out which universes the *Finance* group can see. We've found that this group's ID is 6334, so we can write our query as follows:

```
select si_name
  from ci_appobjects
 where si_kind = 'universe'
       and isallowed(6334,3)
```

This produces a list of the one universe that the *Finance* group has *View* rights to:

SI_NAME	SI_ID
AR Universe	7315

It's important to keep in mind that all CMS queries only retrieve objects that the current session user has visibility to. Suppose user Wilma logs in to Query Builder and executes our query from earlier to retrieve objects that Fred has access to:

```
select si_name,si_id
  from ci_infoobjects
 where isallowed(4104,3)
       and si_kind = 'webi'
```

This query only returns objects that both Fred and Wilma have *View* access to. Alternatively, consider this query:

```
select si_name,si_id
  from ci_infoobjects
 where not isallowed(4104,3)
       and si_kind = 'webi'
```

This returns objects that Wilma has View access to, but Fred does not.

The second form of the `IsAllowed()` function takes one parameter, the right ID. This function evaluates the permission that the *current session owner* has on objects (the user that was used to log in to Query Builder). If Fred logs in to Query Builder and executes this query:

```
select si_name
  from ci_appobjects
 where si_kind = 'universe'
       and isallowed(22)
```

...it lists all universe objects for which he (Fred) has *Delete* rights. We *could* query for the View permission (right ID 3):

```
select si_name
  from ci_appobjects
 where si_kind = 'universe'
       and isallowed(3)
```

...but the `IsAllowed()` function is superfluous since any CMS query that Fred executes will only return objects that he *View* rights to. Likewise, this query

```
select si_name
  from ci_appobjects
 where si_kind = 'universe'
       and not isallowed(3)
```

...never returns any results since a CMS query will not return objects that the user does not have View rights to.

This form of the IsAllowed() function can be handy. Consider a web application that enables SAP BusinessObjects users to select reports to be scheduled. Our application displays the contents of the public folders and provides a simple interface for users to select the reports that are to be scheduled. We don't want to display reports if the user doesn't have permission to schedule (we would prefer not to display the report, rather than allow the user to select it and get an error in the next step). So, in the query to select reports for the selected folder, we add an IsAllowed(21) call:

```
select si_id,si_name,si_kind
  from ci_infoobjects
 where si_parentid = 77542
       and isallowed(21)
```

Debugging

Unlike most common SQL engines, the CMS query parser is not very helpful when debugging syntax errors. In some cases, such as with incorrect property names, no error is generated – the query simply produces no results. In other cases, such as unbalanced parentheses or incorrect table name, a simple "Not a valid query" message is generated. Knowledge of these two facts can make debugging more successful.

In the event of a "Not a valid query" error, we recommend the following debugging steps:

1. Check the FROM clause. Did you accidentally specify SI_INFOOBJECTS instead of CI_INFOOBJECTS? The FROM clause is the simplest in any query, so it is a good first place to look.

2. Check the clauses used and their ordering: the SELECT clause must be followed with the FROM clause; if a WHERE clause is specified, it must immediately follow the FROM clause. If an ORDER BY clause is specified, it must immediately follow the WHERE clause. A CMS query cannot include a GROUP BY or HAVING clause.

3. Check for mismatched parentheses and quotes.

4. Make sure there is at least one property in the SELECT clause, at least one table in the FROM clause, and at least one conditional expression if a WHERE clause is specified[59].

5. If you are using relationship queries, make sure that there are no linefeeds within the double-quoted function parameters, and that single quotes and double quotes are properly used.

6. Finally, remove the entire WHERE clause; if the error persists, then focus on the SELECT

---

59 This might seem too obvious to even bother looking for, but the authors have more than once tried to execute a query like select top 10 from ci_infoobjects

clause.

Remember that a misspelled property name will **not** cause this error. It is not worth your time validating each property name in your query in an attempt to debug the *Not a valid query* error.

In the event that the query does not produce any rows, perform the following steps:

1. Remember that the SELECT clause has no bearing on whether any rows are produced – focus on the FROM and WHERE clauses.

    Ensure that the user ID that was used to log in to Query Builder has appropriate rights to the content that you are attempting to retrieve. A good way to check is to log in to the CMC or BI launch pad with the same user ID to check if the desired objects are visible.

2. Make sure you are selecting from the right table. If you are querying for objects of kind *Webi* but are selecting from CI_APPOBJECTS, you will get no results. If you are not sure, include all three tables in FROM ("from CI_INFOOBJECTS, CI_APPOBJECTS, CI_SYSTEMOBJECTS"). If that still produces no rows, then the problem is not in the FROM clause.

3. Confirm that you are in fact receiving no rows, rather than receiving a number of empty rows. The result page of Query Builder displays the *Number of rows returned* at the top. If this is non-zero but you see no results, then it means that there were records returned but none of the properties that you specified in the SELECT clause exist on the returned objects. Refer to the next section for debugging this type of problem.

4. If the WHERE condition includes a conditional expression that references a CUID, RUID, or GUID, be sure that the CUID/RUID/GUID is in the correct case. While most object properties are not case-sensitive, these three properties are.

5. If the WHERE condition includes a conditional expression on a date/time property, make sure that the date string is formatted correctly.

If the query produces empty rows, then there is a problem with the SELECT clause:

1. Confirm that the properties in the select clause are correct. Remember that misspelled property names will not produce an error; they will just not be present in the result set.

2. For testing, use SELECT *, then identify the needed properties from the result.

Show Stats

The show stats flag can be appended to any CMS query in the Query Builder. When executed, the results page will display tracing and execution information following the query results[60]. There are several pieces of information that can be useful in debugging unexpected results or for investigating performance issues with queries.

The stats result will include the raw SQL query that would be sent to the underlying CMS database[61]. This information can be useful if particular CMS queries are taking an exceptionally long time to run – it could be that the CMS database is not optimized.

For example, we'll execute the following query:

```
select *
  from ci_infoobjects
 where si_name like '%reports'
       and si_recurrring = 1
show stats
```

The stats result includes a large number of nested properties. One of the properties is si_qry_db_predicate, which includes the CMS database query[62]:

SI_QRT_DB_PRED ICATE	SELECT CMS_InfoObjects7.ObjectID FROM CMS_InfoObjects7 WHERE ((CMS_InfoObjects7.ObjName LIKE CAST('%K1GEKOM%' AS VARBINARY(255)) OR CMS_InfoObjects7.ObjName_TR > 0) AND CMS_InfoObjects7.SI_INSTANCE_OBJECT = 0 AND CMS_InfoObjects7.SI_RUNNABLE_OBJECT = 1 AND CMS_InfoObjects7.SI_RECURRING = 1 AND CMS_InfoObjects7.SI_TABLE = 0 AND CMS_InfoObjects7.SI_HIDDEN_OBJECT = 0) ORDER BY CMS_InfoObjects7.ObjectID ASC

We can easily see the translation of our condition on si_recurring. The condition on si_name is visible and we can see that it is using the translated name value. Other conditions are implicitly added (si_hidden_object = 0), and the condition on si_table correlates to "from ci_infoobjects" in our query.

Many of the properties in the show stats result are, fortunately, self-explanatory. There are properties that contain the total query execution time, times for each step (select, where, order by), and details on the number of records retrieved from the cache vs. those retrieved from the CMS database.

CMS Query Alternatives

While the SQL-ish nature of CMS queries will be a familiar form to many SAP

---

60 Internally, the stats are produced as an InfoObject, which is then rendered to the screen by Query Builder as though it were any other kind of InfoObject.

61 We say "would be", since it is possible that the query result is cached and so no database query is actually executed.

62 See the next chapter for more information on querying the CMS repository database.

BusinessObjects administrators, this is not always the most desirable method for retrieving system metadata. There are other alternative ways to get this information without having to write and execute CMS SQL queries manually. Note, however, that knowing the CMS SQL query syntax and its associated properties is still necessary for using the Java SDK (to be covered in Part Two). But the tools described here can make many tasks much easier[63].

BI Platform Support Tool

The SAP BI Platform Support Tool (BIPST) is an application published by SAP that automates several BO administration functions. It can be used to retrieve a large amount of system metadata, including server settings and metrics, document counts by type, scheduling analysis, and more. It also includes several analysis tools that are useful for debugging system issues. See the following link for more information about the BIPST: https://wiki.scn.sap.com/wiki/display/BOBJ/SAP+BI+Platform+Support+Tool

CMS Data Access Driver

The CMS data access driver was included with BI4.2 SP03, and enables querying of the CMS via a standard SAP BusinessObjects universe. Any BI tool that can connect to a universe as a data source (WebI, Crystal, etc.) can then be used to create reports directly from the CMS. In many cases, the universe can be used as a full-on replacement for the Query Builder; all standard reporting features, including scheduling, can be used to report on CMS metadata. The driver is included with the base server installation, so no additional software has to be installed (although the middleware driver does need to be selected when the BO server software is installed). See the following link for more information: https://wiki.scn.sap.com/wiki/display/BOBJ/Unlock+the+CMS+database+with+new+data+access+driver+for+BI+4.2

Miscellaneous Useful Queries

The following is a set of CMS Queries that you may find useful:

Currently logged-in user accounts, including login time and license type (concurrent or named)

```
select si_name,si_concurrent,si_creation_time
  from ci_systemobjects
 where si_kind = 'connection'
       and si_authen_method != 'server-token'
       and si_failover_available_until is null
```

---

63 There are also third-party solutions for extracting information from the CMS; we are only focusing on SAP-provided solutions.

Recurring schedules that distribute to email

```
select *
  from ci_infoobjects
 where si_recurring = 1
       and si_scheduleinfo.si_destinations."1".si_progid = 'CrystalEnterprise.Smtp'
```

List of servers, including run state (is alive) and enabled state

```
select si_name,si_server_is_alive,si_current_disabled_state
from ci_systemobjects
where si_kind = 'server'
```

The URL for the REST API service

```
select si_access_url
  from ci_appobjects
 where si_cuid = 'AZpJlb9HDtxPjLHwEmF8xD8'
```

List of users who have either never logged in, or who have not logged in since 1/1/2017

```
select si_name,si_creation_time,si_lastlogontime
  from ci_systemobjects
 where si_kind = 'user'
       and (si_lastlogontime is null
            or si_lastlogontime < '2019-01-01')
```

Chapter Review

- The SESSION: placeholder can be used to reference the currently active session (the session that is being used to execute the CMS query).

- The IsAllowed() function is used to validate a user's or group's permissions on a particular InfoObject.

- The CMS query engine does not produce very specific error messages, and so debugging a problem in a CMS query can be difficult.

Quiz

1. The SESSION: placeholder produces an SI_ID associated with an InfoObject of what kind?

   a) SI_SESSION

   b) SI_USER

   c) SI_USER_GROUP

   d) `SI_CONNECTION`

2. The `IsAllowed()` function evaluates:

   a) Effective rights

   b) Explicit rights

   c) Neither of the above

3. True/False: The function `IsAllowed(22)` retrieves InfoObjects that the current user has permission to delete.

4. If a query produces rows that are empty, the problem is likely in which clause?

   a) `SELECT`

   b) `FROM`

   c) `WHERE`

   d) `ORDER BY`

Answers on page 672.

Chapter 7 - The Physical Repository

The CMS objects that we retrieve via CMS queries are stored in physical form in the *CMS Repository*.   The repository is a set of tables in a relational database and may be in Oracle, SQL Server, MySQL, SQL Anywhere, or a few other RDBMSs. The location of the repository is chosen during installation of the SAP BusinessObjects server software. The user performing the installation has the option of using an existing database server, in which case the appropriate logon credentials are entered. If an existing database server is not chosen, then the installer creates and configures a local database server. Depending on the version of the software, this may be MySQL or SQL Anywhere.

The repository contains metadata for all of the InfoObjects in the cluster: users, groups, documents, folders, etc. It does *not* contain files, such as .wid files for Web Intelligence documents or .unv/.unx files for universes. This content is stored in the File Repository Server; which is kept in a file system directory.

It is not generally necessary to access the physical repository directly for most administrative needs, although there are a few areas where it can be valuable (else this chapter wouldn't exist).   Using CMS queries to retrieve object data should always be preferred over the physical repository, for several reasons:

- **Security**. CMS queries inherently apply security restrictions. A CMS query executed by a user (whether in Query Builder or another program) only retrieve results that the user has at least *View* access to. If a user has access to the physical repository tables, no such security restrictions apply – that user will be able to access the metadata for every object in the system.

- **Read-only**: CMS queries are, by nature, read-only. It is not possible to execute a CMS query that modifies objects in any way. On the other hand, the physical repository can be modified with standard SQL statements. Modifying the repository in this way creates a significant risk of corrupting the entire cluster beyond repair[64].

- **Encrypted properties**: Only a handful of object properties are accessible in the repository via SQL. Most properties are stored in a single encrypted LOB field and as such can not be retrieved with SQL. However, these properties can be retrieved via CMS queries.

- **Dynamic properties**: CMS queries support the retrieval of several properties that are calculated dynamically. For example, the SI_CHILDREN property is not actually stored in the repository but is calculated when the query is executed.

- **Support**: Use of CMS queries is the standard practice for retrieving objects, and, although official documentation is scant, there are many other resources available.

---

64 In the "old days" (prior to XI), it was not uncommon to make tweaks directly in the repository. This was never an officially recommended practice but is even more so not recommended in the XI platform due to the risk of corruption.

With the above in mind, there are a few scenarios in which querying the physical repository can be useful, for example, joining with audit data or other data sources that exist in the same database as the repository.

Key point: CMS queries and repository queries have some overlapping features. Generally, however, CMS queries are the recommended way to access repository metadata.

Keep in mind that the queries we have discussed so far in this book (those executed in the Query Builder) are referred to as *CMS Queries*. The SQL queries that we are covering in this chapter that are executed against the physical repository tables are referred to as *Repository Queries*.

We present some sample SQL queries in this section that can be executed against the repository tables. Since your specific repository database may be in one of many RDBMSs, and many different types of querying tools may be used, we are not covering *how* to connect to the repository database, or how to execute the queries.

The physical repository is the ultimate source of the data that is retrieved via CMS queries. Illustration 17 shows the path that a CMS query takes when executed from a client:

1. A CMS SQL query is submitted by the client to the server machine.

2. The CMS server parses the CMS SQL.

3. The CMS server constructs one or more repository queries (in the native SQL of the RDBMS) and submits to the CMS Repository Database. Or, if the requested information exists in the system cache, then the result is returned immediately.

4. The CMS Repository Database parses the SQL statement(s), executes it, and returns the results to the CMS Server.

5. The CMS Server parses the result of the repository query result and constructs a CMS object with the appropriate properties populated.

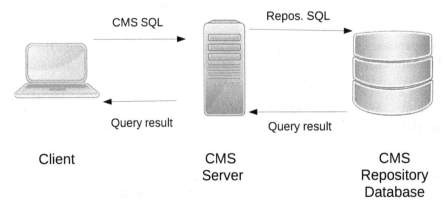

Illustration 17: CMS Query Processing

Note that the CMS Server does not merely "translate" the CMS SQL into the RDBMS' native SQL, and return a tabular result set. Rather, it constructs an InfoObject containing properties (and sub-properties, as appropriate), based on the data received from the repository. Put another way, the tabular result from the repository is used to create a property set that is returned to the client as an *IinfoObject*.

Repository Tables

The repository consists of several tables with names beginning with "CMS_". The last character of the table name indicates the major release version of the repository: 5 for XIr2, 6 for XI3, and 7 for BI4. In BI4, the repository tables are:

- CMS_InfoObjects7
- CMS_Relations7
- CMS_Aliases7
- CMS_IdNumbers7
- CMS_Sessions7
- CMS_Locks7
- CMS_VersionInfo

The first two tables above, *CMS_InfoObjects7* and *CMS_Relations7* are the primary repository tables and are covered in detail below.

CMS_InfoObjects7

CMS_InfoObjects7 is the main repository table. It contains a row for every object in the InfoStore and is keyed on the objectID column, which correlates to the SI_ID property.

Although every object in the InfoStore is associated with a row in CMS_InfoObjects7, not every *property* is accessible via the physical table. Object properties may directly map to physical columns, may be derived from physical columns, may be mapped to encrypted columns, or may be stored in a binary object. We will cover each of these categories of properties.

Directly-mapped properties

The following table lists the columns in CMS_InfoObjects7 that directly map to object properties:

Column Name	Datatype	Associated Property
ObjectID	Integer	SI_ID
ParentID	Integer	SI_PARENTID
TypeID	Integer	SI_OBTYPE
LastModifyTime	Character (32)	SI_UPDATE_TS
ScheduleStatus	Integer	SI_SCHEDULE_STATUS
SI_GUID	Character (56)	SI_CUID
SI_CUID	Character (56)	SI_CUID
SI_RUID	Character (56)	SI_RUID
SI_INSTANCE_OBJECT	Integer	SI_INSTANCE_OBJECT
SI_PLUGIN_OBJECT	Integer	SI_PLUGIN_OBJECT
SI_TABLE	Integer	SI_TABLE
SI_HIDDEN_OBJECT	Integer	SI_HIDDEN_OBJECT
SI_RECURRING	Integer	SI_RECURRING
SI_RUNNABLE_OBJECT	Integer	SI_RUNNABLE_OBJECT
SI_CRYPTOGRAPHIC_KEY	Integer	SI_CRYPTOGRAPHIC_KEY
SI_NAMEDUSER	Integer	SI_NAMEDUSER
SI_TENANT_ID	Integer	SI_TENANT_ID

Since the properties are directly mapped, a CMS query that exclusively uses the above properties can be translated slightly to be executed in the repository. For example, this CMS query:

```
select si_id,si_parentid,si_update_ts,si_cuid,si_schedule_status
  from ci_infoobjects,ci_appobjects,ci_systemobjects
 where si_instance_object = 1
```

...can be translated to the following, to be executed against the repository:

```
select objectid,parentid,lastmodifytime,si_cuid,schedulestatus
  from cms_infoobjects7
 where si_instance_object = 1
 order by objectid
```

Both of the above queries produce the same result (although, of course, the format of the repository query result depends upon the SQL query tool used).

Note that boolean property values are stored in the physical repository as 0 or 1, not as a native Boolean value.

Date columns (actually, "the" date column: LastModifyTime) are stored in the repository as character strings, in a format of YYYY MM DD HH mm ss sss. For example:

```
2015 10 02 00 43 58 740
```

This format directly corresponds to the way that date/time values are used in conditions in CMS queries, even though the Query Builder displays the values in native date/time format.

Derived columns

Some object properties are derived from other properties. The SI_INSTANCE property, for example, is derived from SI_RUNNABLE_OBJECT and SI_INSTANCE_OBJECT (see Table 2). SI_INSTANCE is true when either SI_RUNNABLE_OBJECT or SI_INSTANCE_OBJECT are true. So, a CMS query containing this condition:

```
where si_instance = 1
```

... is executed in the repository as:

```
where si_runnable_object = 1 or si_instance_object = 1
```

It would be necessary to use this same derivation if you need to retrieve the equivalent value of SI_INSTANCE via a repository query.

Calculated properties

Some properties are not stored in the repository but are calculated dynamically when a CMS query is executed. Consider this simple CMS query:

```
select si_children
  from ci_infoobjects
 where si_id = 23
```

To obtain the value of SI_CHILDREN for object ID 23 (the root public folder), the query engine needs to perform a separate query against the repository database. The logic will be similar to, but possibly not identical to, the following:

```
select parentid,count(objectid)
  from cms_infoobjects7
 where parentid = 23
 group by parentid
```

When this result is retrieved, the CMS query engine can populate the SI_CHILDREN property of object 23.

The "Properties" column

The CMS_InfoObjects7 table contains a Binary Long (or BLOB, depending on the RDBMS) column named Properties. This is an encrypted value that contains all static properties that are not otherwise stored in the table. The Properties column is in a proprietary binary format and is not readable via SQL, and so it is not possible[65] to retrieve these properties

---

65 We should say, it is *possible*, but the method is not publicly known.

other than via a CMS query.

Encoded properties

Object names which are associated with the SI_NAME property, are actually stored in two places in the physical repository. The original value of SI_NAME is located in the encrypted binary CMS_InfoObjects7.Properties column (described above). But a copy of SI_NAME is also present in the CMS_InfoObjects7.ObjName column. The value in this column is not directly readable but can be decoded with simple logic. The value is also not a true copy of the actual object name – there are derivations applied:

- Uppercase and lowercase characters are represented by the same code. For example, the value of CMS_InfoObjects7.ObjName for a report named "pPp" is "GGG"[66]. So, even if the value of ObjName were to be fully decoded, the case representation would still be lost.

- Some characters are represented by a multiple-byte code, so the length of the encoded value in ObjName can exceed the length of the original name in the SI_NAME property. The length of the ObjName column is a maximum of 255 bytes; so the ObjName column is truncated if the encoded value is longer than that amount. If this occurs, the ObjName_TR columns will have a value of 1 to indicate that ObjName contains a truncated value (or 0 otherwise).

- The encoded value is appended with an additional few characters, beginning with "!;".

Why is the object name property derived in this way? As we mentioned previously, many of the columns in CMS_InfoObjects7 are indexed, enabling fast retrieval of objects when used in a condition in a CMS query. For example, a CMS query that includes a condition on the SI_CUID property can execute quickly since the associated repository query can benefit from the index on CMS_InfoObjects7.SI_CUID. But it's not possible to create a database index on a value in the CMS_InfoObjects7.Properties column. So, consider this CMS query:

```
select si_id
  from ci_infoobjects
 where si_description = 'Quarterly report'
```

Since the SI_DESCRIPTION property exists in the CMS_InfoObjects.Properties column, and not as its own column in CMS_InfoObjects, the query engine must read in all rows from CMS_InfoObjects, then parse out the Properties column to find those objects with an SI_DESCRIPTION value of "Quarterly report".

Since SI_NAME is a very commonly-used property, it would be problematic if all CMS queries that referenced this property resulted in a full-table scan of CMS_InfoObjects7 every time. Any action in the SAP BusinessObjects interfaces that invoked a search by name could take several seconds or longer. By having a copy of the SI_NAME property as its own column in CMS_InfoObjects7, CMS queries with a condition on SI_NAME can execute much faster.

---

66 It's actually "GGG!;A". We'll cover the other characters soon.

This same logic is used for the SI_KEYWORD property; however, the associated column in CMS_InfoObjects7 has the same name (SI_KEYWORD). If the value of SI_KEYWORD is truncated, the SI_KEYWORD_TR column will have a value of 1.

We are providing two helper functions for working with the ObjName and SI_KEYWORD columns[67]. Listing 1 Contains a SQL Anywhere function named convert_name. This can be used for with CMS repositories housed in a SQL Anywhere database and can be translated for other DBMSs. The function should be passed the value of ObjName or SI_KEYWORD and returns a **partial** decode of the original value.

The convert_name function only converts characters that are letters, a space, or a period. Other characters are left unconverted. If we were to query for an object named *Year-End Reports 2015*, the result of convert_name() would be:

```
YEAR!M|Z"END REPORTS!@`|@!`|<!`|>!`|F
```

This function is not intended to be a complete solution for decoding ObjName or SI_KEYWORD, and we do not recommend its use for any real-world administration of an SAP BusinessObjects system.

With that said, the function can be handy for some ad-hoc investigation of the CMS repository. As a simple example, we can retrieve the names of top-level public folders (those that are a child of object 23):

```
select convert_name(objname)
  from cms_infoobjects7
 where parentid = 23
```

In our test environment, the above query produced:

CONVERT_NAME(OBJNAME)
AUDITING
SYSTEM CONFIGURATION WIZARD
SAMPLES
REPORTS
REPORT CONVERSION TOOL
WEB INTELLIGENCE SAMPLES
PROBES
LCM
VISUAL DIFFERENCE
PLATFORM SEARCH SCHEDULING

---

67 A more complete solution can be found at https://scn.sap.com/thread/3538583

```
CREATE OR REPLACE FUNCTION convert_name (objname CHAR(255))
RETURNS CHAR(255)
DETERMINISTIC
BEGIN
    IF (objname LIKE '%!;%') THEN
        SET objname = SUBSTR(objname,1,LOCATE(objname,'!;')-1)
    END IF;
    SET objname = REPLACE(REPLACE(objname,'!@{',' '),'!BE{','.');
    RETURN
REPLACE(REPLACE(REPLACE(REPLACE(REPLACE(REPLACE(REPLACE(REPLACE(REPLACE(REPLA
CE(REPLACE(REPLACE(REPLACE(REPLACE(REPLACE(REPLACE(REPLACE(REPLACE(REPLACE(RE
PLACE(REPLACE(REPLACE(REPLACE(objname,']','Z'),'W','X'),'U','W'),'S','V'),'Q','U'),'O
','T'),'M','S'),'K','R'),'I','Q'),'G','P'),'E','O'),'C','N'),'A','M'),'?','L'),'=','K
'),';','J'),'9','I'),'7','H'),'5','G'),'3','F'),'1','E'),'/','D'),'-','C'),'+','B'),'
)','A')
END;
```

Listing 1: The convert_name function

The SI_KIND and SI_PROGID property, commonly used in CMS queries, are not present in the CMS_InfoObjects7 table, but they can be derived from the TypeID column. Listing 2 contains another SQL Anywhere function named typeid_to_progid that can produce the value of SI_PROGID (in uppercase) for an object based on its TypeID.

```
CREATE OR REPLACE FUNCTION typeid_to_progid (i_typeid int)
RETURNS CHAR(255)
DETERMINISTIC
BEGIN
    DECLARE @v_progid CHAR(255);
    SET @v_progid = (SELECT convert_name(objname)
                        FROM cms_infoobjects7
                      WHERE typeid = i_typeid
                            AND si_plugin_object = 1);
    RETURN @v_progid;
END;
```

Listing 2: The typeid_to_progid function

As a reminder, for *most* object kinds, the value of SI_PROGID is equal to the value of SI_KIND, but prefixed with "CrystalEnterprise.", so:

SI_KIND	SI_PROGID
Folder	CrystalEnterprise.Folder
Webi	CrystalEnterprise.Webi
Inbox	CrystalEnterprise.Inbox

Note that the typeid_to_progid function works by returning the object name associated with an object having a SI_PLUGIN_OBJECT value of 1 (true) and a TypeID value equal to the value passed to the function. So, it is dependent upon the `convert_name` function in Listing 1

We can use the `typeid_to_progid` function to retrieve objects from the repository of a given kind. For example, to retrieve objects of kind *Universe*, we could use the following query:

```
select objectid,convert_name(objname)
  from cms_infoobjects7
 where typeid_to_progid(typeid) = 'CRYSTALENTERPRISE.UNIVERSE'
```

which produces:

OBJECTID	CONVERT_NAME(OBJNAME)
721	CRYSTALENTERPRISE.UNIVERSE
3386	REPORT CONVERSION TOOL AUDIT UNIVERSE
3969	EFASHION
3965	AR UNIVERSE

This query is roughly equivalent to the following **CMS** query:

```
select si_id,si_name
  from ci_appobjects,ci_infoobjects,ci_systemobjects
 where si_specific_progid = 'crystalenterprise.universe'
```

which produces:

SI_ID	SI_NAME
3386	Report Conversion Tool Audit Universe
3969	eFashion
3965	AR Universe

Note that the repository query included object 721 while the CMS query did not. Object 721 is a *PlugIn* object; plugins contain metadata about the various object kinds (it is actually this object that enables us to map Type IDs to Prog IDs). Plugin objects (identified by a `SI_PLUGIN_OBJECT` property having a value of 1) are normally filtered out of CMS queries, which is why object 721 does not appear in the results of our CMS query above. But this filtering does not occur when querying the repository direction, so 721 does appear in our **repository** query above. To produce the same result in both queries, we would have to exclude plugin objects from the repository query:

```
select objectid,convert_name(objname)
  from cms_infoobjects7
 where typeid_to_progid(typeid) = 'CRYSTALENTERPRISE.UNIVERSE'
       and si_plugin_object = 0
```

The `convert_name` and `typeid_to_progid` functions (or their equivalent implementation in other RDBMSs) can be used to get some useful information out of the repository that would be impossible with standard CMS queries, or at least would require multiple steps. Since we are querying the repository with standard SQL, we are not limited by the fairly simple implementation of SQL in CMS queries. As an example, we can use a simple query to retrieve the count of objects in the repository by ProgID:

```
select top 10 typeid_to_progid(typeid),typeid,count(*)
  from cms_infoobjects7
group by typeid
order by 2 desc
```

TYPEID_TO_PROGID(TYPEID)	TYPEID	COUNT()
CRYSTALENTERPRISE.DEPLOYMENTFILE	66	2570
CRYSTALENTERPRISE.CLIENTACTION	340	423
CRYSTALENTERPRISE.DEPENDENCYRULE	380	155
CRYSTALENTERPRISE.FOLDER	1	123
	46	80
CRYSTALENTERPRISE.PROGRAM	270	73
CRYSTALENTERPRISE.CLIENTACTIONUSAGE	348	69
CRYSTALENTERPRISE.CLIENTACTIONSET	345	56
CRYSTALENTERPRISE.SERVICE	52	41
CRYSTALENTERPRISE.USERGROUP	20	19

Notice that there is no ProgID for TypeID 46. While all objects in the CMS repository have a TypeID, not all have an associated ProgID or Kind. In the specific case above, TypeID 46 is associated with Relationship objects, which, coincidentally, are all children of object ID 46.

We'll cover some additional useful queries in the next couple of sections.

CMS_Relations7

We covered Relationship Queries in Chapter 4; the CMS_Relations7 table contains the linkages that define these relationships.

The most useful columns in this table (for us) are PARENTID, CHILDID, and RELATIONSHIPID. These are integer columns that represent the IDs of the parent and child objects (respectively), and the ID of the relationship object. The *relationship object*, as we covered in Chapter 4, defines the type of relationship that exists between the parent and child. For example, *UserGroup-User*, *Webi-Universe*, *Folder Hierarchy*, etc.

Let's look at an example to see how these relationships are represented. In our system, the *Fred* user object is ID 4104. Fred is a member of the *Everyone, Finance,* and *QA* user groups, which are associated with object IDs 1, 6334, and 6339, respectively. We execute a query against CMS_Relations7 to find records with the *Fred* object as a child in a relationship[68]:

```
select parentid,childid,relationshipid
  from cms_relations7
 where childid = 4104
```

This produces:

PARENTID	CHILDID	RELATIONSHIPID
6334	4104	547
6339	4104	547

If we execute a CMS query for ID 547, we find, not surprisingly, that it is the *Usergroup-User* relationship:

```
select si_name
  from ci_systemobjects
 where si_id = 547
```

SI_NAME	Usergroup-User

So, from the repository query, we see that the *Fred* object (ID 4104) is a child in a *Usergroup-User* relationship, with two parent groups (6334, 6339). Note that although Fred is a member of the *Everyone* group (as all users are), there is no row in CMS_Relations7 associated with this relationship. This is because the *Everyone* group is special – the CMS automatically "knows" about the *Everyone* group, so its relationships to users is not physically represented in the repository.

We'll try another example, this time looking for the Web Intelligence documents that are associated with a specific universe. Our first step is to get the ID of relationship type *Webi-Universe*, so we execute the following **CMS** query in Query Builder:

```
select si_id
  from ci_systemobjects
 where si_parentid = 46
       and si_name = 'webi-universe'
```

This produces:

SI_ID	532

68 Remember, we are querying the physical repository, not the CMS.

Now, in the **repository**, we want to look for objects on the parent side of the relationship, where the child is a given CUID (AZtmGeZqCllIugfputlCuho). In this case, we need to join the CMS_InfoObjects7 and the CMS_Relations7 tables in order to apply a condition using the CUID:

```
select parentid
  from cms_infoobjects7 i
       join cms_relations7 r
            on i.objectid = r.childid
 where i.si_cuid = 'AZtmGeZqCllIugfputlCuho'
       and r.relationshipid = 532
```

This produces the IDs of the two WebI documents associated with our selected universe:

PARENTID
3971
3972

The repository query above would be equivalent to the following CMS relationship query:

```
select si_id
  from ci_infoobjects
 where parents("si_name='webi-universe'",
               "si_cuid='AZtmGeZqCllIugfputlCuho'")
```

We can add to the value of repository-based relationship queries by using the convert_name function from page 159. To reiterate, again, the convert_name function does not do a complete conversion of object names but can be useful in some scenarios.

We'll revisit the *Usergroup-User* relationship from earlier, but now we want a list of all users in the *Administrators* group. From above, we know that the ID of the *Usergroup-User* relationship is 547, so we can build a query that retrieves the children of that relationship when the parent is *Administrators*:

```
select convert_name(cms_kid.objname)
  from cms_infoobjects7 cms_parent
       join cms_relations7 r
            on cms_parent.objectid = r.parentid
       join cms_infoobjects7 cms_kid
            on cms_kid.objectid = r.childid
 where r.relationshipid = 547
       and convert_name(cms_parent.objname) = 'ADMINISTRATORS'
```

This gives us:

CONVERT_NAME(CMS_KID.OBJNAME)

ADMINISTRATOR
ALICE

So, we know that the two members of Administrators are *Administrator* and *Alice*. This repository query is equivalent to the following CMS query:

```
select si_name
  from ci_systemobjects
 where children("si_name='usergroup-user'","si_name='administrators'")
```

Repository-based relationship queries, like their CMS-based counterparts, do not require a condition on the SI_KIND property in most cases. The *Usergroup-User* relationship only has objects of kind *UserGroup* on the parent side and only objects of kind *UserGroup* or *User* on the child side.

The use of standard SQL enables us to perform complex queries that could not be done with CMS-based relationship queries. Let's say we wanted a simple list of all universes in the system and their associated Web Intelligence documents. This would be a three-step process with CMS queries – we would first need to retrieve all universes with their SI_WEBI property, then retrieve all WebI objects with their SI_ID property, and finally, cross-reference the two lists. With a repository query, we can do this all in one step:

```
select convert_name(cms_unv.objname) as unv_name,
       convert_name(cms_webi.objname) as webi_name
  from cms_infoobjects7 cms_webi
       join cms_relations7 r
           on cms_webi.objectid = r.parentid
       join cms_infoobjects7 cms_unv
           on cms_unv.objectid = r.childid
 where r.relationshipid = 532
```

UNV_NAME	WEBI_NAME
--------	---------
AR UNIVERSE	ANNUAL PROFIT
AR UNIVERSE	QUARTERLY PROFIT
AR UNIVERSE	ANNUAL PROFIT
AR UNIVERSE	YEAR!M|Z"END REPORTS!@`|@!`|<!`|>!`|F
AR UNIVERSE	RETURNS
AR UNIVERSE	QUARTERLY PROFIT
EFASHION	INPUT CONTROLS AND VARIABLES
EFASHION	INPUT CONTROLS AND CHARTS

Repository-based relationship queries and CMS-based relationship queries each have their pros and cons. As we've just seen, performing relationship queries in the repository enables us to use complex standard SQL constructs. On the other hand, we cannot use some of the advanced functionality of CMS-based repository queries such as the ancestors() or descendants() methods. And of course, we are very limited in the properties that can be retrieved. With this in mind, we cannot say that repository vs. CMS queries are better or worse than the other – each has its own value with respect to CMS relationships.

The *Folder Hierarchy* relationship type is not represented in the `CMS_Relations7` table. However, it is not necessary in order to perform relationship queries in the repository since the relationship itself is simply based on the `ParentID` property in `CMS_InfoObjects7`.

On page 85 we used a CMS relationship query to retrieve the child objects of a folder named *Monthly Sales*:

```
select si_name,si_kind
  from ci_infoobjects
 where children("si_name='folder hierarchy'",
          "si_name='sales reports' and si_parentid = 23")
```

We can perform the same function in a relationship query with standard SQL constructs and without the need of the `CMS_Relations7` table:

```
select convert_name(cms_child.objname) as child_name,
       typeid_to_progid(cms_child.typeid),
       cms_child.objectid,
       cms_child.parentid
  from cms_infoobjects7 cms_parent
       join cms_infoobjects7 cms_child
            on cms_parent.objectid = cms_child.parentid
 where convert_name(cms_parent.objname) = 'SALES REPORTS'
       and cms_parent.parentid = 23
       and typeid_to_progid(cms_parent.typeid)
           = 'CRYSTALENTERPRISE.FOLDER'
```

Audit

Joining the repository tables with the audit tables can produce valuable information. Since the audit tables, by nature, contain historical data while the repository tables contain current state data, there may be scenarios in which it it worthwhile to join the two sources.

In order to join the CMS repository tables with the audit tables, both must be accessible from a single SQL query. Depending on the RDBMS used, the method for joining tables in different locations (be that databases, schemas, etc.) varies, and It is beyond the scope of this book to describe how this should be done – but for our examples below we are using a SQL Anywhere database that contains both the CMS and audit tables, so no cross-database querying is necessary.

It would be possible to write a whole other book on the auditing tables and methods for extracting audit data, so we are only covering the specific scenarios of joining the audit data to the CMS repository.

The primary BI4 audit table, `ADS_EVENT` contains several object references by CUID, which can be joined to `CMS_InfoObjects7.SI_CUID`:

- **User_ID:** the CUID of the user who performed the event

- **Object_ID:** the CUID of the object that the event involved

- **Object_Type_ID:** the CUID of the plugin associated with the object

- **Top_Folder_ID:** the CUID of the root folder that the object is in

- **Folder_ID:** the CUID of the object's immediate parent

Let's build up an example that ultimately joins audit with repository data. We'll start with a simple example audit query that displays the user names of those users that logged in during May 2016:

```
SELECT DISTINCT user_name
  FROM ads_event
      JOIN ads_event_type_str
          ON ads_event.event_type_id = ads_event_type_str.event_type_id
              AND ads_event_type_str.language = 'EN'
WHERE ads_event_type_str.event_type_name = 'Logon'
      AND start_time
          BETWEEN '2016-05-01 00:00:00.000'
              AND '2016-06-01 00:00:00.000'
```

This produces:

USER_NAME
Administrator
Fred
Betty

Now we want to add logic to this query to identify any users who logged in during May 2016 *but have since been deleted*. Using just the audit data, this would be a bit tricky (but not impossible) - we would have to look for an event in which the user was deleted. But by joining to the CMS repository tables, we can do it much more easily - we simply need to validate whether the user's CUID exists in the repository. If it's not there, then we know the user has been deleted. We update our query to:

```
SELECT DISTINCT user_name
  FROM ads_event
      JOIN ads_event_type_str
          ON ads_event.event_type_id = ads_event_type_str.event_type_id
              AND ads_event_type_str.language = 'EN'
WHERE ads_event_type_str.event_type_name = 'Logon'
      AND start_time
          BETWEEN '2016-05-01 00:00:00.000'
              AND '2016-06-01 00:00:00.000'
      AND user_id != '0'
      AND NOT EXISTS
          (SELECT 1
```

```
        FROM cms_infoobjects7
        WHERE ads_event.user_id = cms_infoobjects7.si_cuid)
```

This produces:

USER_NAME

Betty

From this result, we know that *Betty* logged in during May 2016, but her user ID is no longer valid.

The **AND NOT EXISTS** clause in our query only includes users whose CUIDs are **not** found in the CMS repository (`CMS_InfoObjects7`). We also had to add a condition for "`user_id != '0'`" since the audit table may include records with a valid value for `user_name` but a value of '0' in `user_id`.

For another example, we want to list the Web Intelligence documents that were refreshed in May, 2016, along with the document's last modification date. We can use the following query to perform this task:

```
SELECT ads_event.object_name,cms_infoobjects7.lastmodifytime
   FROM ads_event
        JOIN ads_event_type_str
            ON ads_event.event_type_id = ads_event_type_str.event_type_id
                AND ads_event_type_str.language = 'EN'
        LEFT JOIN cms_infoobjects7
            ON ads_event.object_id = cms_infoobjects7.si_cuid
WHERE ads_event_type_str.event_type_name = 'Refresh'
        AND start_time
            BETWEEN '2016-05-01 00:00:00.000'
                AND '2016-06-01 00:00:00.000'
```

OBJECT_NAME	LASTMODIFYTIME
-----------	--------------
Annual Profit	2016 05 03 15 50 24 275
Quarterly Profit	2015 08 17 12 35 59 263
Returns	2016 06 02 17 25 44 328

In this query, we are directly joining the primary audit table (`ADS_EVENT`) with the CMS repository (`CMS_InfoObjects7`). We are doing a `LEFT JOIN` because we still want to display records from audit event if they are not found in the CMS. This occurs if the document has been deleted.

One more example of joining the CMS repository with audit data. In this scenario, we want to identify the logins in April 2016 of users who are **currently** in the *Finance* user group regardless of what their group membership was in April. To accomplish this, we need to

know the ID of the *Usergroup-User* relationship object. From page 162, we know that the ID is
547. We'll start our query with the same foundation as one we used previously – that simply
produces users who logged in in April:

```
SELECT DISTINCT user_name
  FROM ads_event
       JOIN ads_event_type_str
           ON ads_event.event_type_id = ads_event_type_str.event_type_id
               AND ads_event_type_str.language = 'EN'
 WHERE ads_event_type_str.event_type_name = 'Logon'
       AND start_time
           BETWEEN '2016-04-01 00:00:00.000'
               AND '2016-05-01 00:00:00.000'
```

We'll create an entirely separate query on the repository tables to produce members of the
Finance user group.

```
SELECT cms_kid.si_cuid
  FROM cms_infoobjects7 cms_parent
       JOIN cms_relations7 r
           ON cms_parent.objectid = r.parentid
       JOIN cms_infoobjects7 cms_kid
           ON cms_kid.objectid = r.childid
 WHERE r.relationshipid = 547
       AND convert_name(cms_parent.objname) = 'FINANCE'
```

Finally we'll combine the two queries into one:

```
SELECT DISTINCT ads_event.user_name
  FROM ads_event
       JOIN ads_event_type_str
           ON ads_event.event_type_id = ads_event_type_str.event_type_id
               AND ads_event_type_str.language = 'EN'
       JOIN cms_infoobjects7 cms_kid
           ON ads_event.user_id = cms_kid.si_cuid
       JOIN cms_relations7 r
           ON cms_kid.objectid = r.childid
       JOIN cms_infoobjects7 cms_parent
           ON cms_parent.objectid = r.parentid
 WHERE ads_event_type_str.event_type_name = 'Logon'
       AND start_time
           BETWEEN '2016-04-01 00:00:00.000'
               AND '2016-05-01 00:00:00.000'
       AND r.relationshipid = 547
       AND convert_name(cms_parent.objname) = 'FINANCE'
```

The lines in bold represent the portion of the query related to the CMS repository; the other
lines are from the original audit query.

Chapter Review

- The InfoObject properties that are queryable via CMS queries are stored in physical form in the CMS repository, which exists in a relational database.

- Although there is human-readable data in the CMS repository, it is almost always better to use CMS queries for retrieving InfoObject metadata.

- A handful of InfoObject properties, including SI_CUID, SI_RECURRING, and SI_INSTANCE_OBJECT exist in the CMS repository. A few others exist but with different names. However, the majority of InfoObject properties are not directly queryable.

- A derivative of the SI_NAME property is present in the CMS repository. This column, called objname, is slightly encrypted, truncated, and in single case.

Quiz

1. True/False: Querying the CMS repository is safer than performing CMS queries.

2. The primary CMS repository table in BI4 (the one containing static properties) is:

    a) CI_INFOOBJECTS

    b) CI_INFOOBJECTS7

    c) CMS_INFOOBJECTS6

    d) CMS_INFOOBJECTS7

3. The SI_PARENTID InfoObject property maps to which column in the CMS repository?

    a) ParentID

    b) SI_PARENTID

    c) Something else

    d) It does not exist in the CMS repository.

4. Static properties that are not represented by their own column in the primary CMS repository table are present in:

    a) The binary CMS_InfoObjects7.Properties column

    b) As separate columns in the CMS_Properties7 table

    c) The FRS

    d) None of the above

5. The two properties that have encrypted, derived copies are SI_NAME and:

    a) SI_KEYWORD

    b) SI_OWNER

    c) `SI_DESCRIPTION`

    d) `SI_PASSWORD`

6. Which table(s) are required in order to create a query that retrieves the universes associated with a given Web Intelligence document ID?

    a) Only `CMS_InfoObjects7`

    b) Only `CMS_Relations7`

    c) `CMS_InfoObjects7` and `CMS_Relations7`

    d) `CMS_InfoObjects7` and `CMS_Relationships7`

7. Why is it recommended to use an outer join when joining `ads_event` to `CMS_InfoObjects7`?

Answers on page 672.

Part Two – The Java SDK

In Part Two, we delve into the SAP BusinessObjects BI Platform Java SDK. We begin with an overview of the various SDKs that are available and then cover the basic configuration steps necessary to begin working with the Java SDK. In Chapter 10, we create and run a basic SDK program using Eclipse. Next, we go into detail with a few of the most commonly-used interfaces: `IInfoObject`, `IInfoObjects`, and `IInfoStore`.

Chapters 14 and 15 cover Program Objects – a method for running SDK programs within the SAP BusinessObjects scheduler – and some suggestions for leveraging this feature. We cover a few specific areas that are of particular interest in SDK programming: folders, users, groups, and servers.

We complete Part Two with a discussion of managing schedules and security with the SDK.

A note on format...

In this section, we include documentation on several SDK classes and interfaces. These are **not** copies of the official SAP Javadocs. The following is a sample portion of the IFolder interface:

Package com.crystaldecisions.sdk.plugin.desktop.folder
Interface _IFolder_
extends _IContainer_, _IFolderBase_, IInfoObject

Fields

static String	FAVORITESFOLDER_KIND	FavoritesFolder
	The kind value for Favorites Folder InfoObjects	
static String	FAVORITESFOLDER_PROGID	CrystalEnterprise.FavoritesFolder
	The ProgID value for Favorites Folder InfoObjects	
static String	FOLDER_KIND	Folder
	The kind value for Folder InfoObjects	
static String	FOLDER_PROGID	CrystalEnterprise.Folder
	The ProgID value for Folder InfoObjects	

Methods

IInfoObject	add(String kind)
	Creates a new InfoObject of the specified kind, and adds it to this collection.
IInfoObjects	getChildren()
	Returns an IInfoObjects collection containing all of this object's children.
String[]	getPath()
	Retrieves the names of the folder's ancestors, as a String array.
	Associated property: SI_PATH

In the header, the underlined types identify those interfaces whose fields and methods are included in this reference. So, this block includes the methods defined in the IFolder, IContainer, and IFolderBase interfaces. While the IFolder interface does extend IInfoObject, that interface is documented elsewhere.

These are not intended to replace the official Javadocs, but to provide an in-line reference for the items being covered. We exclude methods and fields that are deprecated or identified as "internal use", except in a few instances where we believe they may be of value.

Chapter 8 - Available SDKs

There are many components in the SAP BusinessObjects Business Intelligence suite, and there are similarly a number of different SDKs. Although we are focused on the Platform SDK, it is worth knowing about some of the other libraries[69].

The official directory of the current BI4.x developer SDKs is located here: https://help.sap.com/viewer/product/JAVADOCS/1.0/en-US.

Platform

The Platform SDK (called "Enterprise SDK" prior to BI4) enables interaction with the core CMS InfoStore and its InfoObjects. This SDK provides an extensive library of classes and methods for performing many useful actions, including retrieving and modifying object properties, moving objects, creating users/groups, assigning group membership, managing security, and much more.

Most any action that can be performed in the CMC can also be done programmatically via the Platform SDK. A notable exception to this is that the Platform SDK does not support interacting with reports or universes. Although the *metadata* for these objects can be retrieved (creation time, owner ID, scheduling info, etc.), it is not possible to perform such actions as refreshing reports, listing objects used in a report, listing objects in universes, etc. These functions are supported by the Semantic Layer, Designer, Report Engine, and RESTful SDKs, mentioned below.

The Platform SDK for Java is available for all versions of SAP BusinessObjects XI and BI, from XIr2 through BI4.2[70]. This SDK is the most commonly used and most consistently documented. In fact, most references to the "SAP BusinessObjects SDK" are actually references to the Platform Java SDK.

The Platform SDK also exists for .NET, although the documentation is not as complete as for the Java SDK.

There is a subset of the Platform SDK available as a COM library which can be used in applications that support VBA, such as Microsoft Excel. Although not as complete as the Java or .NET SDKs, the COM API enables rapid development of small SAP BusinessObjects utilities in Excel. This SDK is undocumented and unsupported[71], yet it exists in all XI/BI versions to date.

The RESTful Web Services SDK was released with BI4.0 and represents an entirely new way to interact with an SAP BusinessObjects CMS. As of BI4.2, the RESTful API for BI Platform

---

69   If you're already familiar with the available SDKs, or don't care to learn more, feel free to skip this chapter.

70   The most current version, as of this writing

71   See http://scn.sap.com/thread/1470136

implements a growing portion of the functionality of the Java SDK, but this is expected to be complete in future versions.

Report Engine

The Report Engine Java and .NET SDKs enable interaction with Web Intelligence reports, and (prior to BI4.0) Desktop Intelligence. They work in conjunction with the Platform SDK – the Platform SDK is used to log in to the SAP BusinessObjects CMS and get a session token; the Report Engine SDK is then used to open and interact with reports.

The Report Engine SDKs for Java and .NET are deprecated and unsupported as of BI4.0; however, the library files still exist in the software (at least as of BI4.2). *Some* programs written for the RE SDK may still work in BI4.1 and later, but they are not guaranteed to.

The recommended method for working with reports as of BI4 is the new RESTful Web Services SDK, which provides nearly all of the functionality provided by the older SDKs.

Universe SDKs

The **Universe Design Tool COM SDK** (formerly known as the *Designer SDK*) can be used to interact with the *Universe Design Tool* programmatically and is the only SDK available for working with unv universes. To use this SDK, an installation of the *SAP BusinessObjects Client Tools*, including at least *Universe Design Tool*, is required. The UDT SDK can perform nearly all of the functionality of UDT itself, including retrieving universes from the SAP BusinessObjects server, extracting universe metadata, and making modifications to the universe.

This SDK has been in existence, mostly unchanged, since *BusinessObjects 5*.

To work with unx universes, the **BI Semantic Layer SDK** can be used. This was introduced with BI4.0 and **only** exists for Java. As with the UDT SDK, this SDK provides most of the functionality provided by the Information Design Tool.

The RESTful API introduced with BI4.0 includes the ability to retrieve universe metadata. It can provide metadata for both unv and unx universes, but it does not provide the full functionality of either the UDT or Semantic Layer SDKs. Only information about *objects* is included, while the other SDKs include joins, tables, contexts, etc. The RESTful API also does not support modifying universes at all.

The functions of the three universe SDKs can be summarized as:

Universe Design Tool SDK: exists in all versions, is a Windows COM library and enables nearly full control over unv universes.

BI Semantic Layer SDK: exists since BI4.0, is Java only, and enables nearly full control over unx universes.

<u>RESTful API</u>: exists since BI4.0, is accessible via REST calls (and is therefore platform independent), and provides summary information for both unv and unx universes.

Other SDKs

The Desktop Intelligence COM SDK, similar to the Designer COM SDK, enabled automation of the Desktop Intelligence (DeskI) application. Since DeskI is not included with the SAP BusinessObjects platform as of BI4.0, the DeskI COM SDK is also no longer available.

The Crystal Reports RAS and Viewers SDK, in Java and .NET (including extensions for Eclipse and Visual Studio, respectively), are used for interacting with and displaying Crystal Reports.

Web Services

SAP provides consumer SDKs for .NET and Java for interfacing with the BI Platform Web Services. These SDKs are not as functional as the native Platform SDKs or the RESTful API. We are not covering these SDKs in this book.

BI Automation Framework

The BI Automation Framework, part of the BI Administration Console, was introduced in BI4.2 SP05. It provides a GUI interface for performing administrative tasks that would otherwise require SDK programming. It is built around an architecture of *task templates*, *workflow templates*, and *scenarios*, which support the ability to create and execute complex, repetitive workflows. These workflows can perform a number of different actions, including refreshing reports, changing InfoObject ownership, changing the data source of Web Intelligence documents, and more.

Chapter 9 - Configuration

To compile and execute programs with the Java SDK, you need the SDK libraries (jar files). If the workstation that you are using to compile and run the programs already has the SAP BusinessObjects BI4 Client Tools installed, then the jar files are located (by default) in:

```
C:\Program Files (x86)\SAP BusinessObjects\SAP BusinessObjects Enterprise XI 4.0\java\
lib
```

The files may be referenced directly from this location, or copied to the local Eclipse project directories as needed.

If the workstation does not have the client tools installed, then the files will need to be copied from another workstation that does, or from a server that has the SAP BusinessObjects server components installed. For Windows, this is in the same location as the directory above. For UNIX, the path is:

```
<BusObj installation directory>/sap_bobj/enterprise_xi40/java/lib
```

In our test machine, running Ubuntu Linux, we copied the jar files from the server to `/home/joe/bojars`.

We'll set up a user library in Eclipse for the BI Platform SDK jars. Since there are so many of them, creating a user library allows us to add all the necessary jars to our projects quickly.

In Eclipse, go to Windows → Preferences, then to Java → Build Path → User Libraries (*see* Illustration 18, *step 1*).

Click New *(step 2)*.

Enter a name for the library: "BI4 Platform SDK" *(step 3)*.

Click OK

Click *Add External Jars... (step 4)*

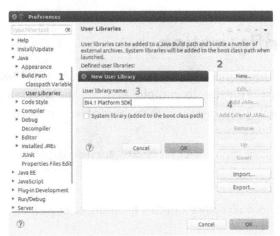

Illustration 18: Eclipse user library creation

In the dialog that appears, navigate to the directory containing the SAP BusinessObjects jar files.

Select **all** of the following jar files:

aspectjrt.jar	certjFIPS.jar	ebus405.jar
bcm.jar	cesdk.jar	freessl201.jar
biarengine.jar	cesearch.jar	log4j.jar
biplugins.jar	cesession.jar	logging.jar
ceaspect.jar	com.sap.js.passport.api.jar	pullparser.jar
cecore.jar	corbaidl.jar	SL_plugins.jar
celib.jar	ccis.jar	ssljFIPS.jar
ceplugins_core.jar	cryptojFIPS.jar	TraceLog.jar
cereports.jar	derby.jar	xpp3-1.1.3_8.jar

For BI4.2 SP04 and newer, the following are also required:

jcmFIPS.jar   cryptojce.jar

When complete, the user library should look *similar* to Illustration 19:

Illustration 19: User library created

The next step is optional but recommended. We'll associate some of the libraries that we added with the BI4 Platform SDK Javadocs to display context-sensitive help for those classes and methods.

Still in the settings for the *BI4 Platform SDK* user library, expand cesession.jar, click *Javadoc location*, then click *Edit...*:

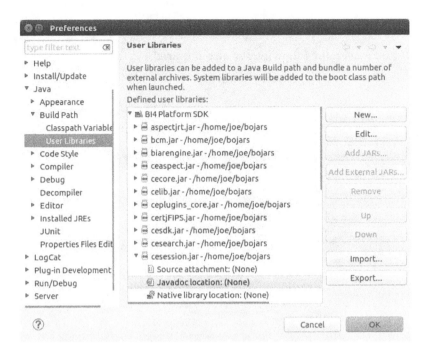

This brings up the Javadoc settings for `cesession.jar`:

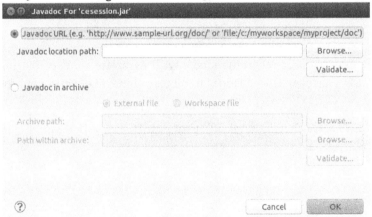

Eclipse allows for associating Javadocs by using a URL or local file. Although the BI4 Platform SDK Javadocs are online at sap.com, they are missing key files necessary for dynamic linking (at the time of this writing). So, it is necessary to download the Javadocs locally. The archives are available at http://help.sap.com, for each version. For BI4.2, the download link is at https://help.sap.com/doc/javadocs_bip_42/4.2/en-US/index.html

Download the archive for *Business Intelligence platform Java API Reference (Javadocs)*, and store it locally on your workstation. We used ~/javadocs. In the Java dialog, select *Javadoc in archive*, then type in the path or click *Browse* to navigate to it. You do not need to enter anything in the *Path within archive field*, but click the Validate button to ensure the settings are correct and the file is valid.

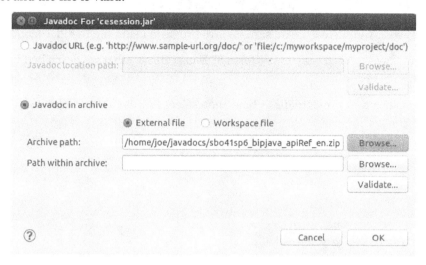

Perform the exact same steps above for the following jar files in the user library:

- ceplugins_core.jar
- cecore.jar
- biarengine.jar
- SL_plugins.jar

The Javadocs for all six jar files are included in the one archive (sbo41sp6_bipjava_apiRef_en.zip), so all six can be associated with the same file.

Click OK when done. With the user library created, we are ready to create our first SDK program.

Chapter 10 - Basic SDK Program

We'll now create a simple real-world sample Java program using the BI4 Platform SDK.

Assuming you have created the BI4 Platform SDK user library that we described in Chapter 9, we are ready to begin.

In Eclipse, create a new project: *File → New*, then select *Java Project* and hit Next.

We'll call the project *ListUsers*, but leave the other options on this page untouched (you may have a different version of the JRE listed – that's OK). Hit Next after entering the project name:

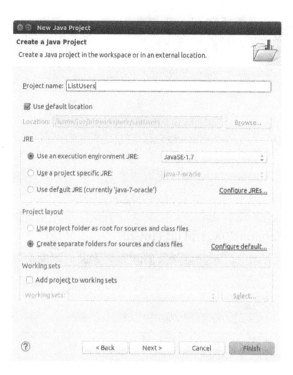

Click to the *Libraries* tab, then click *Add Library*:

Click *User Library*, and then *Next*:

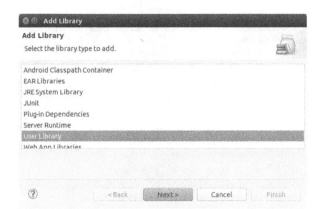

Check the box for *BI4 Platform SDK*, and hit Finish:

Finally, hit *Finish* in the New Project dialog to complete the project creation. We'll create a single class for our sample project bearing the same name ("*ListUsers*"). Either right-click on the project name and hit *New → Class*, or from the File menu click *New → Class*.

We'll use a package name *bosdkbook* and name our class *ListUsers*. Other options are left as default:

You should now have a fresh project with a stub of code in the *ListUsers* class:

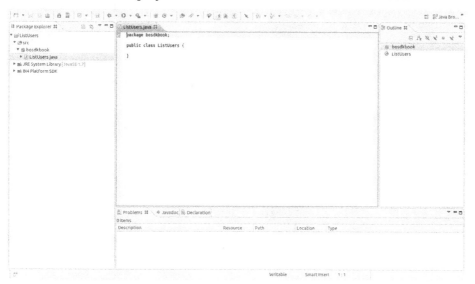

Finally, we can write some code![72] Replace the generated code stub with the code in Listing 3:

```
1  package bosdkbook;
2
3  import com.crystaldecisions.sdk.exception.SDKException;
4  import com.crystaldecisions.sdk.framework.CrystalEnterprise;
```

---

72 A reminder that all program listings are available for download at our companion site: www.bosdkbook.com.

```java
 5 import com.crystaldecisions.sdk.framework.IEnterpriseSession;

 6 import com.crystaldecisions.sdk.framework.ISessionMgr;

 7 import com.crystaldecisions.sdk.occa.infostore.IInfoObject;

 8 import com.crystaldecisions.sdk.occa.infostore.IInfoObjects;

 9 import com.crystaldecisions.sdk.occa.infostore.IInfoStore;

10

11 public class ListUsers {

12     public static void main(String[] args) throws SDKException

13     {

14         ISessionMgr sessionManager = CrystalEnterprise.getSessionMgr();

15         IEnterpriseSession session = sessionManager.logon ("administrator",
   "xxxx", "192.168.56.102", "secEnterprise");

16

17         IInfoStore infoStore = (IInfoStore) session.getService ("","InfoStore");

18

19         IInfoObjects users = infoStore.query("select si_name from
   ci_systemobjects where si_kind = 'user'");

20

21         if(users.size() == 0)

22         {

23             System.out.println("No users found!");

24             session.logoff();

25             return;

26         }

27         for(int x = 0;x < users.size(); x++)

28         {

29             IInfoObject user = (IInfoObject) users.get(x);

30             System.out.println(user.getTitle());

31         }

32         System.out.println("Done!");

33         session.logoff();

34     }

35 }
```

Listing 3: The ListUsers program

If you are using Eclipse (or another IDE), then you don't *have* to type in the import lines.

Assuming that you have correctly set the BI4 Platform SDK user library and selected it in your project, Eclipse should be able to add the imports for you – just hover over the red-underlined text and Eclipse should suggest quick fixes, with the correct import being the first item in the list (see Illustration 20. Just make sure that it is proposing the correct import (which it does in *most* cases, but still worth confirming).

Once you have gone through all of the unresolved type errors, the imports in your program should exactly match those in Listing 3, and the program should not indicate any compile errors or warnings.

```
*ListUsers.java ⊠

    package bosdkbook;


    public class ListUsers {
        public static void main(String[] args) throws SDKException
        {
            ISessionMgr sessionManager = CrystalEnterprise.getSessionMgr();
```

ISessionMgr cannot be resolved to a type

8 quick fixes available:

- Import 'ISessionMgr' (com.crystaldecisions.sdk.framework)
- Create class 'ISessionMgr'
- Create interface 'ISessionMgr'
- Change to 'IInternalSessionMgr' (com.crystaldecisions.sdk.framework.internal)
- Change to 'ISessionMgr2' (com.crystaldecisions.sdk.framework.internal)
- Create enum 'ISessionMgr'
- Add type parameter 'ISessionMgr' to 'main(String[])'
- Fix project setup...

Press 'F2' for focus

Illustration 20: Quick Fix proposal

You will need to change the logon credentials as applicable for your environment. Update line 15 with the appropriate user name, password, and CMS host (respectively):

```
IEnterpriseSession session = sessionManager.logon ("administrator", "xxxx",
"192.168.56.102", "secEnterprise");
```

*Note that we are using **secEnterprise** to specify BusinessObjects Enterprise Authentication. Although other authentication methods are possible (Windows AD, LDAP, etc.), there is additional configuration required to get those to work. We stick with Enterprise Authentication for our samples, and you will need to use an Enterprise user as well.*

Once done, save the file and run the program (*Run* → *Run*) (if prompted to select Java Application or *Applet,* choose *Java Application*). There are a few possible outcomes:

If the specified hostname is invalid or no CMS is running on the specified port, then an exception similar to the following will be thrown:

```
Exception in thread "main" Could not reach CMS '192.168.56.102'. Specify the correct
```

```
host and port and check for network issues. (FWM 20030)
```

If this error occurs, perform the following debugging steps:

- Confirm that the provided host name is valid and that it is reachable from the machine that the program is running on.

- Confirm that there is a CMS installed and running on the specified host.

- Confirm that the CMS is running on port 6400; if not, then the actual port number must be specified in the call to logon(), ex: "192.168.56.102:6401".

If the CMS is reachable, but the provided logon credentials are invalid (i.e., the user name or password is incorrect), then an exception similar to the following is thrown:

```
Exception in thread "main" com.crystaldecisions.sdk.exception.SDKServerException:
Enterprise authentication could not log you on. Please make sure your logon
information is correct. (FWB 00008)

cause:com.crystaldecisions.enterprise.ocaframework.idl.OCA.oca_abuse:
IDL:img.seagatesoftware.com/OCA/oca_abuse:3.2
detail:Enterprise authentication could not log you on. Please make sure your logon
information is correct. (FWB 00008)

The server supplied the following details: OCA_Abuse exception 10496 at
[exceptionmapper.cpp : 67]  42040 {}
    ...Enterprise authentication could not log you on. Please make sure your logon
information is correct. (FWB 00008)
```

In this case, ensure that the user name and password are valid. Note that the same message is displayed whether the user name is invalid or if the password is incorrect.

Assuming that the program actually runs, there are two more possible scenarios. If the program does not throw an exception but generates the following output:

```
No users found!
```

...then it means that the user name specified in the logon() call does not have *View* permission to any users in the system. This is not technically an error but means that the user ID that is being used to execute the script does not have sufficient permission to do so.

The last possible outcome, of course, is that the program executes as intended. On our system, the program generated the following output:

```
Guest
Administrator
SMAdmin
QaaWSServletPrincipal
Fred
Nathan
Sri
Wally
```

```
Ephraim
Quentin
Isabel
Alice
Done!
```

You should see something similar, although the actual list of users will be different. Congratulations on running your first SAP BusinessObjects SDK program!

Now, let's take a look at what the program is doing. Starting with the first line of "real" code, on line 14:

```
14      ISessionMgr sessionManager = CrystalEnterprise.getSessionMgr();
```

Here we are getting an ISsessionMgr object from CrystalEnterprise. We'll use sessionManager only once, on the following line, to perform the logon action:

```
15      IEnterpriseSession session = sessionManager.logon ("administrator",
   "xxxx", "192.168.56.102", "secEnterprise");
```

This is where the action begins – we connect to the designated CMS (192.168.56.102), and attempt to log in as *administrator*. If there is any problem with the connection/logon (ex., host not found, or invalid username/password), an exception will be thrown on this line. Otherwise, an IEnterpriseSession object is returned in session. We use this IEnterpriseSession object to interact with the CMS. Our next step is to use it to get a handle to the InfoStore, on line 17:

```
17      IInfoStore infoStore = (IInfoStore) session.getService ("","InfoStore");
```

The infoStore object is what we use to interact with the InfoStore – to retrieve InfoObjects (via CMS queries), as well as modify or create InfoObjects.

On line 19, we use the infoStore object to execute a simple CMS query:

```
19      IInfoObjects users = infoStore.query("select si_name from
   ci_systemobjects where si_kind = 'user'");
```

If the query SQL contains any syntax errors, or if the connection fails for another reason (the session has timed out, or the network connection to the server is no longer available, for example), then an SDKException is thrown. Otherwise, an IInfoObjects object is returned.

The IInfoObjects interface extends java.util.List, and represents a collection of InfoObjects. The users object, therefore, contains a collection of InfoObjects associated with the result of the passed CMS query. That is, it contains one list entry for each InfoObject (*user*, in this case) returned by the query.

If the CMS query that is passed to infoStore.query() is syntactically correct but returns no results, then the returned IinfoObjects object will be an empty list, not null.

On lines 21-25, we do a simple check for the size of the returned `users` object, then display a warning message if it is empty:

```
21      if(users.size() == 0)
22      {
23          System.out.println("No users found!");
24          session.logoff();
25          return;
26      }
```

This step isn't strictly *necessary*, but it is valuable to display the warning message rather than exit without displaying anything.

Beginning on line 27, we loop through the contents of the `users` collection. Since `IInfoObjects` is an extension of `List`, there are numerous ways to perform the loop, including using an `Iterator`. We'll use a simple `for(…;…;…)` loop for this example:

```
27      for(int x = 0;x < users.size(); x++)
28      {
29          IInfoObject user = (IInfoObject) users.get(x);
```

Although the `IInfoObjects` interface is documented to contain objects of type `IInfoObject` exclusively, its declaration is simply:

```
public interface IInfoObjects extends java.util.List
```

If it was:

```
public interface IInfoObjects extends java.util.List<IInfoObect>
```

...then it would not be necessary to cast the result of `IinfoObject.get()` to `IInfoObject`. Unless and until the BI Platform SDK fully utilizes generics, we have to perform this cast, which is what we do in line 29[73]. Here, while looping through the results of the `users` collection, we store each entry in the `user` object.

On lines 30 and 31, we complete the for loop by displaying the name (*Title*) of the `user` object:

```
30          System.out.println(user.getTitle());
31      }
```

Finally, on line 33, we close the session and exit. If we did not call `session.logoff()`, the session would still be closed when the program. However, it is good practice to close the session before exiting.

---

73 We will cover the `IInfoObject` interface in (much) more detail in the next chapter.

```
33        session.logoff();
34    }
35 }
```

*   *   *

Our sample program is elementary, but is a good illustration of the basic structure of a BI Platform SDK program:

1. Connect/log in to a CMS.

2. Execute a CMS query and retrieve a collection of InfoObjects.

3. Do something with the retrieved InfoObjects.

4. Disconnect/log off.

Of course, most programs that use the BI Platform SDK are much more complicated – interacting with users, interfacing with other applications or databases, and more. But this basic structure will be present even in the more complex applications.

Let's do one more thing before we continue. Assuming you are using Eclipse, hover your mouse cursor over ISessionMgr on line 15. Eclipse should display a popup box with the documentation for the ISessionMgr interface, as in the screenshot below. If this documentation does not appear, then the Javadoc attachments settings in your *BI4 Platform SDK* user library may need to be corrected.

```
public class ListUsers {
    public static void main(String[] args) throws SDKException
    {
        ISessionMgr sessionManager = CrystalEnterprise.getSessionMgr();
```

com.crystaldecisions.sdk.framework.ISessionMgr

This is the basic, top level client side object. This interface defines the ISessionMgr object, which includes the methods that must be called when a user attempts to access the BusinessObjects Enterprise system.

```
        return;
```

CMS Queries in Programs

In Part One, we covered the syntax of CMS queries, and we used the Query Builder to execute our examples. To execute a CMS query in an SDK program, we pass the query text to the IInfoStore.query() method. The SDK passes the query on to the CMS server, where the query engine executes the query and return any resultant InfoObjects to the SDK. Finally, the results are made available to the program as an IInfoObjects collection.

Any valid CMS query can be executed via the IInfoStore.query() method, except for URI queries, which require pre-processing. We'll cover this on page 277.

In our sample program from earlier in this chapter, we executed a simple CMS query with the `IInfoStore.query()` method:

```
19      IInfoObjects users = infoStore.query("select si_name from
   ci_systemobjects where si_kind = 'user'");
```

The query text itself is a plain ol' Java `String`, and all standard rules regarding strings apply.

As we saw when using the Query Builder, the query engine is very forgiving regarding white space and capitalization. The same behavior applies when using the `query()` method (in fact, the Query Builder application itself simply passes the entered query text to the `query()` method). We could have written the above line of code as:

```
19      IInfoObjects users = infoStore.query("select \r\n    si_name\r\n from\r\n
   ci_systemobjects\r\nwhere\r\n    si_kind = 'user'");
```

Or:

```
19      IInfoObjects users = infoStore.query(
20          "select\r\n" +
21          "   si_name\r\n" +
22          "from\r\n" +
23          "   ci_systemobjects\r\n" +
24          "where\r\n" +
25          "   si_kind = 'user'\r\n");
```

In the above query, the linefeed characters ("\r\n") are superfluous and are just an illustration of how these characters may be present in a query.

Chapter Review

- Most BI Platform SDK programs are comprised of four basic steps: connect to a CMS, execute a CMS query, do something with the InfoObjects, and logoff.

- A successful logon produces an `IEnterpriseSession` object, which enables access to the CMS. It is used to obtain an `IInfoStore` object, which is used to execute CMS queries.

Quiz

1. Which of the following objects is obtained first in a typical SDK program?

    a) `IInfoStore`

    b) `IInfoObjects`

    c) `ISessionMgr`

    d) `IEnterpriseSession`

2. If a program throws an exception containing the text "Could not reach CMS", then a possible cause is:

    a) The CMS server is not running.

    b) The user account specified in the `logon()` call does not exist.

    c) The user account exists but does not have appropriate rights.

Answers on page 673.

Chapter 11 - The IInfoObject Interface

All InfoObjects in an SAP BusinessObjects system, when retrieved via a CMS query, are represented by an IInfoObject object or one of its sub-interfaces. When a CMS query is executed via IInfoStore.query(), an IInfoObjects collection is returned which contains zero or more IInfoObject objects. This is true whether the returned InfoObjects are users, folders, Web Intelligence documents, universes, or other kinds.

Package *com.crystaldecisions.sdk.occa.infostore*
Interface IInfoObject

void	deleteNow()
	Immediately removes the object from the CMS.
String	getCUID()
	Retrieves the object's CUID (cluster unique identifier).
	Associated property: SI_CUID
String	getDescription()
String	getDescription(Locale locale)
String	getDescription(Locale locale,boolean doFallBack)
void	setDescription(String newDescription)
	Retrieves/sets the object's description. A locale may be provided to retrieve the localized (multilingual) description.
	Associated properties: SI_DESCRIPTION, SI_ML_DESCRIPTION
List<Locale>	getDescriptionLocales()
	Retrieves a list of available locales for which this object has a localized description.
	Associated property: SI_ML_DESCRIPTION
IFiles	getFiles()
IFiles	getFiles(Locale locale, IInfoObject.LocaleOption option)
	Retrieves an IFiles object, containing information about the object's files. A locale may be provided to retrieve the localized (multilingual) files.
	Associated property: SI_FILES
List<Locale>	getFileLocales()

	Retrieves a list of available locales for which this object has localized files.
	Associated property: SI_FILES
String	getGUID()
	Retrieves the object's GUID (global unique identifier).
	Associated property: SI_GUID
int	getID()
	Retrieves the object's identifier.
	Associated property: SI_ID
String	getKeyword()
	setKeyword(String keyword)
	Retrieves/sets the object's keywords.
	Associated property: SI_KEYWORD
String	getKind()
	Retrieves the object's kind.
	Associated property: SI_KIND
String	getOwner()
	Retrieves the object's owner name.
	Associated property: SI_OWNER
int	getOwnerID()
	Retrieves the SI_ID of the object's owner.
	Associated property: SI_OWNERID
IInfoObject	getParent()
	Retrieves the object's parent, as an IInfoObject.
IInfoObject	getParent(int propertySet)
	Retrieves the object's parent, as an IInfoObject. The properties to be included in the returned IInfoObject are set with the propertySet parameter. Valid values for propertySet are defined in IInfoObject.PropertySet.
String	getParentCUID()

	Retrieves the `SI_CUID` of the object's parent.
	Associated property: `SI_PARENT_CUID`
int	`getParentID()`
void	`setParentID(int parentID)`
	Retrieves/sets the ID of the object's parent. Setting this property effectively moves the object to a new parent, generally a folder.
	Associated property: `SI_PARENTID`
IProcessingInfo	`getProcessingInfo()`
	Retrieves the processing information for the object.
	Associated property: `SI_PROCESSINFO`
String	`getProgID()`
	Retrieves the object's Prog ID.
	Associated property: `SI_PROGID`
String	`getRUID()`
	Retrieves the object's RUID – a unique identifier within an object package.
	Associated property: `SI_RUID`
ISchedulingInfo	`getSchedulingInfo()`
	Retrieves the scheduling information for the object.
	Associated property: `SI_SCHEDULEINFO`
ISecurityInfo2	`getSecurityInfo2()`
	Retrieves an `ISecurityInfo2` object, containing this object's security information.
IFiles	`getSourceFiles(IInfoObject.LocaleOption option)`
	Retrieves the object's source files, using the specified locale option.
	Associated property: `SI_FILES`
String	`getSpecificKind()`
	Retrieves the object's specific kind.
	Associated property: `SI_SPECIFIC_KIND`

int	getTenantID()
void	setTenantID(int tenantID)
void	clearTenantID()

Retrieves, sets, or clears the object's tenant ID. Calling `clearTenantID()` is equivalent to `setTenantID(0)`.

Associated property: SI_TENANT_ID

String	getTitle()
String	getTitle(Locale locale)
String	getTitle(Locale locale,boolean doFallback)
void	setTitle(String newTitle)

Retrieves/sets the object's title (name). A locale may be provided to retrieve the localized (multilingual) title.

Associated property: SI_NAME

List<Locale>	getTitleLocales()

Retrieves a list of available locales for which this object has a localized name.

Associated property: SI_ML_NAME

Date	getUpdateTimeStamp()

Retrieves the timestamp of the object's most recent modification.

Associated property: SI_UPDATE_TS

boolean	isDirty()

Indicates whether any of the object's properties have been modified during this session.

boolean	isInstance()

Indicates whether the object is a scheduled instance.

Associated property: SI_INSTANCE

boolean	isMarkedAsRead()
void	setMarkedAsRead(value)

Retrieves/sets whether the object should be marked as read.

Associated property: SI_MARKED_AS_READ

boolean	isReadOnly()

	Indicates whether the object is read-only. *Associated property:* SI_INSTANCE
IProperties	properties()
	Retrieves an IProperties object containing this object's properties.
Integer[]	propertyIDs()
	Retrieves an Integer[] collection containing the IDs of the properties included in this object.
IFiles	removeFiles(Locale locale)
	Removes (and returns) the object's IFiles object associated with the specified Locale. If the object does not contain files associated with the specified Locale, then no action is taken and a null is returned. *Associated property:* SI_FILES
IFiles	removeSourceFiles()
	Removes (and returns) the object's IFiles object associated with the source locale. If the object does not contain files associated with the source locale, then no action is taken and a null is returned. *Associated property:* SI_FILES
void	retrievePropertySet(int propertySet)
	Updates this InfoObject with the properties in the specified property set from the CMS repository. The properties to be included are specified with the propertySet parameter. Valid values for propertySet are defined in IInfoObject.PropertySet.
void	save()
	Saves this object to the CMS repository.

Class/Interface 1: IInfoObject

Property Accessor Methods

The IInfoObject interface itself provides methods for working with InfoObjects of all kinds, and most of these methods are simple accessors for the InfoObjects' properties. For example, in Listing 3, we used user.getTitle() to retrieve the user's name; the getTitle() method simply returns the value of the SI_NAME property of the user InfoObject. The accessor methods for IInfoObject are listed in Table 7:

Getter method	Setter method	Data type	Property name
getCUID()	N/A	String	SI_CUID
getDescription()	setDescription()	String	SI_DESCRIPTION
getGUID()	N/A	String	SI_GUID
getID()	N/A	int	SI_ID
getKeyword()	setKeyword()	String	SI_KEYWORD
getKind()	N/A	String	SI_KIND
getOwner()	N/A	String	SI_OWNER
getOwnerID()	N/A	int	SI_OWNERID
getParentCUID()	N/A	String	SI_PARENT_CUID
getParentID()	setParentID()	int	SI_PARENTID
getProgID()	N/A	String	SI_PROGID
getRUID()	N/A	String	SI_RUID
getSpecificKind()	N/A	String	SI_SPECIFIC_KIND
getTenantID()	setTenantID(), clearTenantID()	int	SI_TENANT_ID
getTitle()	setTitle()	String	SI_NAME
getUpdateTimeStamp()	N/A	Date	SI_UPDATE_TS
isInstance()	N/A	boolean	SI_INSTANCE
isMarkedAsRead()	setMarkedAsRead()	boolean	SI_MARKED_AS_READ

Table 7: IInfoObject accessor methods

For every accessor method, there is an associated *property*. The getXxx accessor methods return the value of this property; the setXxx accessor methods set the value of this property upon being saved (we cover modifying InfoObjects in Chapter 12.

Many of the common InfoObject properties are read-only. These properties have get accessors but no associated set accessors[74]. One exception to this is SI_OWNERID – the property is actually writable, but it does not have a set accessor. The only way to modify this property is via the IInfoObject.properties() method, which we cover soon.

> *Key point: the presence of a getter method without an associated setter method is a good indication that the associated property is read-only, but this is not **always** the case.*

To retrieve property values via the getXxx() methods, the associated property names must be present in the CMS query's SELECT clause, either explicitly or via SELECT *.

If the SELECT clause does **not** contain the required property, then either a null value is returned, or an exception is thrown (depending on the particular getXxx() method).

---

74 This "safety net" is one of the advantages of using accessor methods to access InfoObject properties rather than working with the properties directly (which we will cover soon).

To illustrate this requirement, we'll make a slight change to Listing 3. Initially, we had requested the SI_NAME property in the CMS query and then displayed it with the getTitle() call:

```
19      IInfoObjects users = infoStore.query("select si_name from
   ci_systemobjects where si_kind = 'user'");

   ...

30          System.out.println(user.getTitle());
```

Let's change line 30 in the program to also display the InfoObject's owner, too:

```
30          System.out.println(user.getOwner() + "   " + user.getTitle());
```

Executing the program with this change produces the following exception:

```
Exception in thread "main"
com.crystaldecisions.sdk.exception.SDKException$PropertyNotFound: The property with ID
SI_OWNER does not exist in the object (FWM 02021)
    at
com.crystaldecisions.sdk.occa.infostore.internal.InfoObject.getOwner(InfoObject.java:3
060)
    at bosdkbook.ListUsers.main(ListUsers.java:30)
```

The getOwner() method is attempting to retrieve the SI_OWNER property from the InfoObject associated with user. But since this property was not included in the SELECT clause of the CMS query, it is not present in the result set, and so there is nothing for the getOwner() method to retrieve. To fix the problem, we need to add SI_OWNER to the CMS query (or use select *):

```
19      IInfoObjects users = infoStore.query("select si_name,si_owner from
   ci_systemobjects where si_kind = 'user'");
```

Executing the program now produces the desired result:

```
Guest   Guest
Administrator   Administrator
SMAdmin   SMAdmin
QaaWSServletPrincipal   QaaWSServletPrincipal
Administrator   Fred
Administrator   Nathan
Administrator   Sri
Administrator   Wally
Administrator   Ephraim
Administrator   Quentin
Administrator   Isabel
Administrator   Alice
Done!
```

This is an example of an accessor method (`getOwner()`) that throws an exception when the required property is not present. The behavior of other methods, such as `getDescription()` is different. Without changing the CMS query on line 19, we change line 30 to display the user's Description:

```
30              System.out.println("Name: " + user.getTitle() + "\r\nDesc: " +
     user.getDescription() + "\r\n");
```

Unlike the `getOwner()` example, we do not get an exception, but no result is generated:

```
Name: Guest
Desc:

Name: Administrator
Desc:

Name: SMAdmin
Desc:

Name: QaaWSServletPrincipal
Desc:

Name: Fred
Desc:

Name: Nathan
Desc:

Name: Sri
Desc:

Name: Wally
Desc:

Name: Ephraim
Desc:

Name: Quentin
Desc:

Name: Isabel
Desc:

Name: Alice
Desc:

Done!
```

It appears as though none of the users have a description, and the lack of any exception being thrown might reinforce that that is accurate. But it is, in fact, an incorrect result. Let's update the CMS query on line 19 to include the `SI_DESCRIPTION` property:

```
19          IInfoObjects users = infoStore.query("select si_name,si_description from
   ci_systemobjects where si_kind = 'user'");
```

Executing the program now produces a different result:

```
Name: Guest
Desc: Guest account

Name: Administrator
Desc: Administrator account

Name: SMAdmin
Desc: Solution Manager Administrator account

Name: QaaWSServletPrincipal
Desc: QaaWS User who can generate the web service definition (wsdl)

Name: Fred
Desc: Fred from Finance

Name: Nathan
Desc:

Name: Sri
Desc:

Name: Wally
Desc:

Name: Ephraim
Desc:

Name: Quentin
Desc:

Name: Isabel
Desc:

Name: Alice
Desc:

Done!
```

While there still are several users with no descriptions, we are now seeing descriptions for a few. Had we assumed that an exception-free result was accurate, we would not have seen these values. Next, we'll re-create an even more insidious problem. We'll change the CMS query on line 19 to intentionally misspell the SI_DESCRIPTION property name (we'll also restrict the result to only two users, just to shorten the result):

```
19        IInfoObjects users = infoStore.query("select si_name,ci_description from
   ci_systemobjects where si_kind = 'user' and si_name in
   ('guest','administrator')");
```

This produces:

```
Name: Guest

Desc:


Name: Administrator
Desc:


Done!
```

So, even though no exceptions were generated, and we *thought* we had included the correct property name in the CMS query, we get blanks for the description properties. At first glance, one might reasonably think that the descriptions of these InfoObjects are actually blank, when in fact they are not.

It is critical to ensure that CMS queries in programs are syntactically correct, since an incorrect script may not always generate an error or an obviously incorrect result. To help prevent against errors of this type, it is often a good idea to test CMS queries in Query Builder. If we use Query Builder to execute the query we just used:

```
select si_name,ci_description
  from ci_systemobjects
 where si_kind = 'user'
       and si_name in ('guest','administrator')
```

We get the following result:

SI_NAME	Guest

SI_NAME	Administrator

The fact that the SI_DESCRIPTION property does not appear in the result is an indication that something is wrong. Even if the property was actually blank, we should still see the property name with its blank value. A closer look at the name of the property that we requested would then reveal the actual cause of the problem.

The second requirement for accessing properties is that the property must be present in the returned InfoObjects. This requirement can result in issues that are more subtle and more difficult to debug. To illustrate, we'll start again from Listing 3, and adjust it to display the SI_FILES property for the first five InfoObjects in the CI_INFOOBJECTS table. We first change the CMS query on line 19:

```
19          IInfoObjects users = infoStore.query("select top 5 * from
   ci_infoobjects");
```

And line 30 to display the title and the size of the InfoObject's `Files` collection:

```
30              System.out.println(user.getFiles().size() + "   " + user.getTitle());
```

This produces the following exception:

```
Exception in thread "main"
com.crystaldecisions.sdk.exception.SDKException$PropertyNotFound: The property with ID
SI_FILES does not exist in the object (FWM 02021)
    at
com.crystaldecisions.sdk.occa.infostore.internal.InfoObject.getFiles_aroundBody38(Info
Object.java:1264)
    at
com.crystaldecisions.sdk.occa.infostore.internal.InfoObject.getFiles(InfoObject.java:1
)
    at
com.crystaldecisions.sdk.occa.infostore.internal.AbstractInfoObject.getFiles_aroundBod
y24(AbstractInfoObject.java:153)
    at
com.crystaldecisions.sdk.occa.infostore.internal.AbstractInfoObject.getFiles_aroundBod
y25$advice(AbstractInfoObject.java:512)
    at
com.crystaldecisions.sdk.occa.infostore.internal.AbstractInfoObject.getFiles(AbstractI
nfoObject.java:1)
    at bosdkbook.ListUsers.main(ListUsers.java:30)
```

Although we requested all properties (by way of the * wildcard), not all InfoObjects in the result set actually have the SI_FILES property. The exception tells us that a call to `getFiles()` was made on an InfoObject that does not include this property.

In this specific case, the first several InfoObjects in the CI_INFOOBJECTS table are *Folders*. Since folder InfoObjects do not contain files, these InfoObjects will not have an SI_FILES property.

The solution to this problem requires a re-examination of the purpose of the program. In this case, we want to see the number of files associated with some InfoObjects, but our query is including InfoObjects that do not have any files. If we add a condition to the query to only include objects with an SI_FILES property, we will have better luck.

Leaving line 30 as-is, we change the CMS query on line 19 to:

```
19          IInfoObjects users = infoStore.query("select top 5 * from ci_infoobjects
   where si_files is not null");
```

This produces an error-free result (albeit one of questionable value):

```
1  Formatting Sample
1  Input Controls and variables
1  Input Controls And Charts
```

```
1   Fold Unfold Sample
1   Charting Samples
Done!
```

It is not necessary to include a property name in the CMS query if the property will only be written to. If your program simply updates the description property for a bunch of InfoObjects, and you don't care about the previous description, then it is not necessary to include SI_DESCRIPTION in the SELECT clause of the query (it doesn't *hurt* to include it, of course).

There are a handful of write-only properties, most of which are associated with passwords. By nature, these properties are never read in an SDK program, and so there is no reason to include them in the SELECT clause of a CMS query. You do not need to know or care that these properties even exist.

These write-only properties are also *hidden* – even if the CMS query includes the property names explicitly or with "*", they are not displayed if you iterate through IInfoObject.properties(). Although they can be retrieved explicitly from IProperties by name, they will only display an encrypted result[75].

The Scheduling, Files, and Processing Methods

If an InfoObject is schedulable or is a scheduled instance, and if SI_SCHEDULEINFO was included in the CMS query that the InfoObject is a member of, then the getSchedulingInfo() method of IInfoObject returns an ISchedulingInfo object. This object includes information about, and enables manipulation of, the InfoObject's scheduling options.   We cover scheduling in more detail in Chapter 17.

If an InfoObject has files, and the SI_FILES property was included in the CMS query, then IInfoObject.getFiles() returns an IFiles object.   This object provides the ability to manipulate the InfoObject's files – add, remove, or read.

Some InfoObject kinds, such as Web Intelligence, Program Object, and Crystal Reports, include additional job processing/scheduling options. The IInfoObject.getProcessingInfo() method provides access to these properties. The SI_PROCESSINFO property must be included in the CMS query.

InfoObject Management Methods

The IInfoObject.deleteNow() method deletes the InfoObject from the CMS repository. This

---

75 And no, we're not going to discuss de-encrypting them.

is one of two ways to delete InfoObjects – the other being via the InfoObject's parent `IInfoObjects` collection.

The `IInfoObject.save()` method pushes any changes made to the InfoObject back to the CMS. This method commits the changes to the CMS immediately. Alternatively, all changes to InfoObjects in an `IInfoObjects` collection can be committed to the CMS together via `IInfoObjects.commit()`. We'll cover saving InfoObjects in the next chapter.

The `getCommitLevel()` and `setCommitLevel()` methods pertain to the strategy for handling multiple concurrent changes to an InfoObject.

Internal Methods

There are a number of IInfoObject methods that are documented as "internal use only" and which are only mentioned here for completeness. They are:

```
applyDelta(), getDelta(), getLockInfo(), isLockHeld(), releaseLock(), unlockNow()
```

Curiously, the following methods are also documented as "internal only", although they are simple accessor methods:

```
getOwner(), getOwnerID()
```

Security Methods

There are two methods of the `IInfoObject` interface pertaining to security access rights:

```
getSecurityInfo2()
getSecurityInfo()
```

The `getSecurityInfo2()` method returns an `ISecurityInfo2` object, which enables querying and retrieval of an InfoObject's explicit and inherited security permissions. We will cover InfoObject security in Chapter 18

Note that security rights are not stored as properties of InfoObjects, and so there are no specific properties that need to be included in a CMS query in order to call `getSecurityInfo2()`.

The `getSecurityInfo()` method was used prior to XI3 and has since been deprecated. It should not be used when working with newer versions.

The IInfoObject.properties() Method and IProperties interface

The recommended and preferred way to work with InfoObject properties is by way of the accessor methods described earlier. However, there are times when it is necessary to bypass the accessors to manipulate properties directly.

Key point: InfoObject properties can be accessed directly via the properties() method, but it is better to use accessor methods whenever possible.

Let's return to our original *ListUsers* program in Listing 3, but we will now display the timestamp that the user InfoObject was created. This value is stored in the SI_CREATION_TIME property, but unfortunately, there is no accessor method for this property in the IInfoObject interface. In order to display this property in our program, we have to take a different approach.

We first need to add the SI_CREATION_TIME property to the CMS query on line 19:

```
19        IInfoObjects users = infoStore.query("select si_name,si_creation_time
     from ci_systemobjects where si_kind = 'user'");
```

We'll then replace the for loop in lines 27-31 with the following:

```
27        for(int x = 0;x < users.size(); x++)

28        {

29            IInfoObject user = (IInfoObject) users.get(x);

30            IProperties props = user.properties();

31            IProperty creationTimeProp =
     props.getProperty(CePropertyID.SI_CREATION_TIME);

32            Date creationTime = (Date)creationTimeProp.getValue();

33            System.out.println("Name: " + user.getTitle() + "\r\nCreated: " +
     creationTime + "\r\n");

34        }
```

The complete program, with the added imports at the top, is in Listing 4

```
1 package bosdkbook;

2

3 import java.util.Date;

4

5 import com.crystaldecisions.sdk.exception.SDKException;

6 import com.crystaldecisions.sdk.framework.CrystalEnterprise;

7 import com.crystaldecisions.sdk.framework.IEnterpriseSession;
```

```java
 8 import com.crystaldecisions.sdk.framework.ISessionMgr;

 9 import com.crystaldecisions.sdk.occa.infostore.CePropertyID;

10 import com.crystaldecisions.sdk.occa.infostore.IInfoObject;

11 import com.crystaldecisions.sdk.occa.infostore.IInfoObjects;

12 import com.crystaldecisions.sdk.occa.infostore.IInfoStore;

13 import com.crystaldecisions.sdk.properties.IProperties;

14 import com.crystaldecisions.sdk.properties.IProperty;

15

16 public class ListUsers {

17     public static void main(String[] args) throws SDKException

18     {

19         ISessionMgr sessionManager = CrystalEnterprise.getSessionMgr();

20         IEnterpriseSession session = sessionManager.logon ("administrator",
   "xxxx", "192.168.56.102", "secEnterprise");

21

22         IInfoStore infoStore = (IInfoStore) session.getService ("","InfoStore");

23

24         IInfoObjects users = infoStore.query("select si_name,si_creation_time
   from ci_systemobjects where si_kind = 'user'");

25

26         if(users.size() == 0)

27         {

28             System.out.println("No users found!");

29             session.logoff();

30             return;

31         }

32         for(int x = 0;x < users.size(); x++)

33         {

34             IInfoObject user = (IInfoObject) users.get(x);

35             IProperties props = user.properties();

36             IProperty creationTimeProp =
   props.getProperty(CePropertyID.SI_CREATION_TIME);

37             Date creationTime = (Date)creationTimeProp.getValue();

38             System.out.println("Name: " + user.getTitle() + "\r\nCreated: " +
   creationTime + "\r\n");

39         }
```

```
40          System.out.println("Done!");
41          session.logoff();
42      }
43 }
```

Listing 4: The ListUsers program, with properties

In our test system, the program produced the following result:

```
Name: Guest
Created: Fri Sep 18 09:42:10 EDT 2015

Name: Administrator
Created: Fri Sep 18 09:42:11 EDT 2015

Name: SMAdmin
Created: Fri Sep 18 09:42:07 EDT 2015

Name: QaaWSServletPrincipal
Created: Fri Sep 18 10:53:51 EDT 2015

Name: Fred
Created: Sat Sep 26 12:58:04 EDT 2015

Name: Nathan
Created: Sat Feb 06 10:03:44 EST 2016

Name: Sri
Created: Sat Feb 06 10:03:55 EST 2016

Name: Wally
Created: Sat Feb 06 10:04:14 EST 2016

Name: Ephraim
Created: Sat Feb 06 10:04:54 EST 2016

Name: Quentin
Created: Sun Feb 07 10:43:53 EST 2016

Name: Isabel
Created: Mon Feb 08 15:47:29 EST 2016

Name: Alice
Created: Fri May 06 17:49:55 EDT 2016

Done!
```

Let's go through the newly-added lines. On line 35, we call `user.properties()` to get the InfoObject's root property bag, as an `IProperties` object. This `IProperties` collection is a `java.util.Map` that contains all of the InfoObject's properties. Note that the collection only includes the properties that were included in the CMS query. In addition to the standard `Map` methods, `IProperties` provides additional methods for retrieving properties from the collection.

```
35        IProperties props = user.properties();
```

On line 36, we call `props.getProperty()` to retrieve the `SI_CREATION_TIME` property from the user's properties. This method returns an `IProperty` object, which enables the manipulation of specific properties.

```
36            IProperty creationTimeProp =
    props.getProperty(CePropertyID.SI_CREATION_TIME);
```

On line 37, we retrieve the value of the `creationTimeProp` property via its `getValue()` method and store the result in `creationTime`. Since properties can be one of a number of different data types, the `getValue()` method's return type is just `Object`. We have to know which data type to cast the value to – in this case, we know that `SI_CREATION_TIME` contains a `Date`, so we cast to that type.

```
37        Date creationTime = (Date)creationTimeProp.getValue();
```

Finally, on line 38, we display the value of `creationTime`:

```
38            System.out.println("Name: " + user.getTitle() + "\r\nCreated: " +
    creationTime + "\r\n");
```

Retrieving Properties from IProperties

Each SAP BusinessObjects cluster maintains a map of property names (Strings) and their keys (Integers). This mapping includes the following properties:

Key	Name
16777219	SI_NAME
16777218	SI_ID
16777242	SI_KIND

This map includes any property names that exist in the cluster, including built-in properties such as the ones above, properties associated with plug-ins like Web Intelligence, Lumira, etc., and user-created custom properties. If you were to create a new property on an InfoObject (by calling its `properties().addProperty(…)` method), the name you give your property would be added to the cluster's property mapping, along with a system-generated ID.

InfoObjects, then, have a list of associated property keys and their InfoObject-specific values. For example, the InfoObject associated with the Everyone group contains the following properties:

Key	Name
16777219	Everyone
16777218	1
16777242	UserGroup

When retrieving from an IProperties collection, either the property's *key* or *name* can be used to specify the desired property. On line 36 of Listing 4, we referenced CePropertyID.SI_CREATION_TIME to retrieve the key of the SI_CREATION_TIME property, which is 16777241. This value is then passed to getProperty() to retrieve the property, as an IProperty object.

The CePropertyID class contains static fields for *most* of the commonly-used properties. There are too many to list here, but the Javadocs for CePropertyID contains the complete list, along with a short description of each. For BI4.2, this can be found at the following URL: https://help.sap.com/doc/javadocs_bip_42/4.2/en-US/bip/en/index.html. This page also contains definitions for most of the properties.

It is sometimes necessary to retrieve a property that is not represented as a static property field in the CePropertyID class. An example is SI_SPECIFIC_KIND, which is commonly used but is not present in CePropertyID. To retrieve this property, we can pass its name as a string directly to IProperties.getProperty(). To illustrate, we'll change line 36 from:

```
36        IProperty creationTimeProp =
   props.getProperty(CePropertyID.SI_CREATION_TIME);
```

to:

```
36        IProperty creationTimeProp = props.getProperty("si_creation_time");
```

Executing the program with these changes produces the same result as before – these are simply two different ways to retrieve the same property, by key and by name. Note that when we specify the property name as a string, it is *case insensitive*.

Using the static properties in the CePropertyID class to retrieve property IDs (vs. by name) is the recommended method for retrieving properties from an IProperties collection. For one, while retrieving a property by specifying its name in string form introduces the possibility of a misspelling, the CePropertyID properties pose no such risk. Also, when using an IDE such as Eclipse, just typing "CePropertyID." will display a popup dialog showing the available property names.

The following calls are all functionally equivalent:

```
IProperty prop = props.getProperty(CePropertyID.SI_CREATION_TIME);
IProperty prop = props.getProperty("SI_CREATION_TIME");
IProperty prop = props.getProperty("SI_Creation_Time");
IProperty prop = (IProperty)props.get(CePropertyID.SI_CREATION_TIME);
IProperty prop = (IProperty)props.get("SI_CREATION_TIME");
```

Since IProperties extends java.util.Map, it must implement the get() method. In this case, the get() method and getProperty() methods are equivalent, with the only difference being that the return type of getProperty() is IProperty. So, while you may use get() instead of getProperty(), there is little need to do so, and the result must be cast to IProperty.

The IProperty Interface

The IProperty interface contains the following fields and methods:

Package com.crystaldecisions.sdk.properties
Interface IProperty

Fields

static int	ALL	65536
	Internal use	
static int	BAG	134217728
	Property is a property bag	
static int	BINARY	4194304
	Property is a binary stream	
static int	DELETE	67108864
	Property has been marked for deletion	
static int	DIRTY	536870912
	Property value has been changed	
static int	NO_COPY	33554432
	Property should not be copied during an InfoObject copy operation	
static int	PROP_ID_LIST	2097152
	Property is a property ID list	
static int	READ_ONLY	-2147483648
	Property can not be deleted (but can be modified)	

Methods

int	getFlags()
	Retrieves the property's flags
Integer	getID()
	Retrieves the property's ID (key)
Object	getValue()
void	setValue(Object propertyValue)

	Retrieves/sets the value of the property
Boolean `isContainer()`	
	Returns `true` if the property is a property bag, and `false` otherwise

Class/Interface 2: IProperty

In the above examples, we illustrated different ways to retrieve an `IProperty` object. The `IProperty` class, as we saw on line 37, has a `getValue()` method that is used to retrieve the property's actual value. Properties may be of many different data types, including Integer, Date, String, Property Bag, etc. (see page 29 for a description of the possible datatypes). In our example, we were explicitly requesting the `SI_CREATION_TIME` property, which we know to be a `Date`, so we could safely cast the result of `getValue()` to `java.util.Date`. But what if we are unsure of the property's datatype? There is no SDK method to return the property's datatype, but the standard Java techniques of determining an object's class may be used. If we have an `IProperty` object as `prop`, we can determine its datatype with the following code:

```java
Object propValue = prop.getValue();
if(propValue instanceof String)
    System.out.println("Property is a String!");
else if(propValue instanceof Integer)
    System.out.println("Property is an Integer!");
else if(propValue instanceof Date)
    System.out.println("Property is a Date!");
else if(propValue instanceof Boolean)
    System.out.println("Property is a Boolean!");
else if(prop.isContainer())
    System.out.println("Property is a Bag!");
else
    System.out.println("Unknown data type.");
```

When we said that there were no SDK methods to determine a property's datatype, that wasn't *entirely* true. The `isContainer()` method returns `true` if the property is a *bag* (a property that contains other properties).

You may have been surprised to find that the `IProperty` interface does not include a method to return the property's *name*. While this is unfortunate, we can get the property's name using its ID and the `CePropertyID.idToName()` method. Again, assuming we have an `IProperty` object as `prop`, we can get its name with the following code:

```java
CePropertyID.idToName(prop.getID())
```

So, let's put the information above to good use and create a program that does something reasonably useful. We want to perform a function similar to Query Builder, in which we'll display all properties of an InfoObject (or multiple InfoObjects). To do this, we'll need to iterate through all of an InfoObject's properties and retrieve each one's name, datatype, and value.

The complete listing for this program is in Listing 5.

```
 1  package bosdkbook;
 2
 3  import java.util.Iterator;
 4
 5  import com.crystaldecisions.sdk.exception.SDKException;
 6  import com.crystaldecisions.sdk.framework.CrystalEnterprise;
 7  import com.crystaldecisions.sdk.framework.IEnterpriseSession;
 8  import com.crystaldecisions.sdk.framework.ISessionMgr;
 9  import com.crystaldecisions.sdk.occa.infostore.CePropertyID;
10  import com.crystaldecisions.sdk.occa.infostore.IInfoObject;
11  import com.crystaldecisions.sdk.occa.infostore.IInfoObjects;
12  import com.crystaldecisions.sdk.occa.infostore.IInfoStore;
13  import com.crystaldecisions.sdk.properties.IProperties;
14  import com.crystaldecisions.sdk.properties.IProperty;
15
16  public class ListProps {
17      public static void main(String[] args) throws SDKException
18      {
19          ISessionMgr sessionManager = CrystalEnterprise.getSessionMgr();
20          IEnterpriseSession session = sessionManager.logon ("administrator",
     "xxxx", "192.168.56.102", "secEnterprise");
21
22          IInfoStore infoStore = (IInfoStore) session.getService ("","InfoStore");
23
24          IInfoObjects ios = infoStore.query("select top 10 * from
     ci_systemobjects");
25
26          for(int x = 0;x < ios.size(); x++)
27          {
28              IInfoObject io = (IInfoObject) ios.get(x);
29              System.out.println(io.getTitle());
30              displayBag(io.properties(),"");
31              System.out.println("\n");
32          }
33          System.out.println("Done!");
```

```
34          session.logoff();

35      }

36

37      private static void displayBag(IProperties props,String indent)

38      {

39          Iterator iPropIDs = props.keySet().iterator();

40          while(iPropIDs.hasNext())

41          {

42              IProperty prop = props.getProperty(iPropIDs.next());

43              String propName = CePropertyID.idToName(prop.getID());

44              Object propValue = prop.getValue();

45

46              if(prop.isContainer())

47              {

48                  System.out.println(indent + propName + " (Bag)");

49                  displayBag((IProperties)propValue,indent + "\t");

50              }

51              else

52              {

53                  String propDatatype = propValue.getClass().getSimpleName();

54                  System.out.println(indent
                        + propName + " ("
                        + propDatatype + "): "
                        + propValue);

55              }

56          }

57      }

58  }
```

Listing 5: The ListProps program

The beginning of this program is similar to *ListUsers*. We log in, execute a CMS query, and iterate through the results. Note that in the CMS query, we are requesting all properties ("SELECT *") for the first ten InfoObjects in the CI_SYSTEMOBJECTS table.

Inside of the for loop (lines 28-31), we just display the InfoObject's title and then call displayBag(), passing it the InfoObject's root property bag (via the properties() method).

The displayBag() method is where the real work happens. On line 39, we get an Iterator for the property bag's keys. Although we know that the keys are of type Integer, the IProperties class does not specify type arguments for its implementation of `Map`. So this line displays a compiler warning for missing type parameters on `Integer iPropIDs`. This can safely be ignored, in particular because we are just passing the key vales back to `getProperty()`, and not explicitly using them as `Integers`.

On line 40, we begin our loop through the IDs of the `IProperties` collection that was passed to `displayProps()`, and on line 42 we retrieve the property into `IProperty prop`.

We retrieve the property's name on line 43, by passing the property's ID to `CePropertyID.idToName()`.

On line 44, we retrieve the property's value into `Object propValue`.

On line 46, we check to see if the property is, in fact, a property bag by calling its `isContainer()` method. If it is a bag, then we just print its name and type ("*Bag*") and recurse back into `displayProps()` increasing the indent by one tab. We can use the same `displayProps()` method because property bags are represented by an `IProperties` object, just like the InfoObjects' root property bag.

If the property is *not* a bag, then we get its datatype by calling `propValue.getClass().getSimpleName()`.

Finally, on line 54, we display the property's name, datatype, and value. Note that we are not doing any special handling to display values according to their type – since the values (other than property bags) are native Java classes such as String, Integer, Date, etc., we are depending on those classes' implementation of `toString()` to display the correct string representation. If we wanted to, say, display numeric values formatted with commas or decimals, or dates in a particular format, then we would need to cast the property value to the appropriate class and then display the value using the appropriate methods.

If we execute the above program, it will display the complete property set for the first ten objects in `CI_SYSTEMOBJECTS`. The first one (the *Everyone* group) displays the following in our test system:

```
Everyone
SI_ML_NAME (Bag)
    DE (String): Alle
    NL (String): Iedereen
    ZH_TW (String): 所有人
    SL (String): Vsi
    AR (String): كل شخص
    DA (String): Alle
    ES (String): Todos
    FI (String): Kaikki
    JA (String): Everyone
    FR (String): Tout le monde
    SK (String): Všetci
    IT (String): Tutti
    NB (String): Alle
    TH (String): ทุกคน
```

```
    RO (String): Oricine
    EN (String): Everyone
    RU (String): Bce
    HU (String): Mindenki
    ZH_CN (String): Everyone
    SV (String): Alla
    HE (String): כולם
    PL (String): Wszyscy
    PT (String): Todos
    KO (String): 모든 사람
    CS (String): Všichni
SI_MACHINES (Bag)
    SI_TOTAL (Integer): 0
SI_HAS_CHILDREN (Boolean): false
SI_USERGROUP_HAS_ENT_CHILDREN (Boolean): false
SI_SPECIFIC_PROGID (String): CrystalEnterprise.UserGroup
SI_SPECIFIC_KIND (String): UserGroup
SI_ALIASES (Bag)
    1 (Bag)
        SI_NAME (String): secEnterprise:Everyone
        SI_ID (String): secEnterprise:#1
        SI_DISABLED (Boolean): false
    SI_TOTAL (Integer): 1
SI_FRAGMENT_VERSION_MAP_PATH_TYPE (String): universal
SI_FOLLOW_INSTANCES (Boolean): false
SI_DISCUSSION_INSTANCES (Boolean): false
SI_APPLICATION_OBJECT (Boolean): false
SI_INSTANCE_OBJECT (Boolean): false
SI_GUID (String): FqsU.FUOcg0AMVwAAIDXlJYACAAnyavX
SI_INSTANCE (Boolean): false
SI_CUID (String): AWiHvq39Xe9FtwJZUWJ31h0
SI_PARENTID (Integer): 20
SI_PLUGIN_OBJECT (Boolean): false
SI_OWNERID (Integer): 10
SI_UPDATE_TS (Date): Fri Sep 18 09:43:08 EDT 2015
SI_CREATION_TIME (Date): Fri Sep 18 09:42:07 EDT 2015
SI_KIND (String): UserGroup
SI_PRINCIPAL_PROFILES (Bag)
    SI_TOTAL (Integer): 0
SI_PROGID (String): CrystalEnterprise.UserGroup
SI_PARENT_CUID (String): AW7cVzZFpgFGjOVUdCiOpfE
SI_PARENT_FOLDER_CUID (String): AW7cVzZFpgFGjOVUdCiOpfE
SI_DESCRIPTION (String): All users of this system
SI_DEFAULT_OBJECT_VERSIONINFO (Bag)
    1 (Bag)
        SI_PROPERTY_VERSION (Integer): 1
        SI_PROPERTY_NAME (String): SI_ML_NAME
    2 (Bag)
        SI_PROPERTY_VERSION (Integer): 1
        SI_PROPERTY_NAME (String): SI_ML_DESCRIPTION
    SI_TOTAL (Integer): 2
```

```
SI_DEFAULT_OBJECT_FRAGMENTS (Bag)
    SI_TOTAL (Integer): 0
SI_NAME (String): Everyone
SI_ID (Integer): 1
SI_HIDDEN_OBJECT (Boolean): false
SI_TABLE (Integer): 2
SI_OBTYPE (Integer): 20
SI_DEFAULT_OBJECT (Boolean): true
SI_FLAGS (Integer): 2070
SI_OBJECT_IS_CONTAINER (Boolean): false
SI_SYSTEM_OBJECT (Boolean): true
SI_CHILDREN (Integer): 0
SI_RUID (String): AWiHvq39Xe9FtwJZUWJ31h0
SI_REL_USERGROUPS (Bag)
    SI_TOTAL (Integer): 0
SI_RUNNABLE_OBJECT (Boolean): false
SI_OWNER (String): System Account
SI_COMPONENT (Boolean): false
SI_REL_GROUP_MEMBERS (Bag)
    SI_TOTAL (Integer): 0
SI_PARENT_FOLDER (Integer): 20
SI_GROUP_MEMBERS (Bag)
    1 (Integer): 11
    2 (Integer): 12
    3 (Integer): 502
    SI_TOTAL (Integer): 12
    4 (Integer): 3661
    5 (Integer): 4104
    6 (Integer): 6344
    7 (Integer): 6348
    8 (Integer): 6352
    9 (Integer): 6356
    10 (Integer): 6368
    11 (Integer): 6374
    12 (Integer): 6610
SI_IS_SCHEDULABLE (Boolean): false
SI_FILENAME (String): BusinessObjects_Everyone_dfo.xml
SI_PLATFORM_SEARCH_CONTAINERS (Bag)
    SI_TOTAL (Integer): 0
SI_PRINCIPAL_PUBLICATIONS (Bag)
    SI_TOTAL (Integer): 0
SI_PRINCIPALRERUN_PUBLICATIONS (Bag)
    SI_TOTAL (Integer): 0
SI_ADM_PRINCIPAL_RIGHTS (Bag)
    1 (Bag)
        SI_RIGHTS (Bag)
            1 (Bag)
                SI_VALUE (Boolean): true
                SI_ID (Integer): 3
                SI_RIGHT_TYPE (Integer): 0
                SI_OWNER_RIGHT (Boolean): true
                SI_RIGHT_SCOPE (String): descendants
```

```
                    SI_RIGHT_APPLIES_TO_KIND (String): User
            2 (Bag)
                SI_VALUE (Boolean): false
                SI_ID (Integer): 6
                SI_RIGHT_TYPE (Integer): 0
                SI_RIGHT_SCOPE (String): this
                SI_RIGHT_APPLIES_TO_KIND (String): any
            3 (Bag)
                SI_VALUE (Boolean): false
                SI_ID (Integer): 22
                SI_RIGHT_TYPE (Integer): 0
                SI_RIGHT_SCOPE (String): this
                SI_RIGHT_APPLIES_TO_KIND (String): any
            SI_TOTAL (Integer): 3
        SI_PRINCIPAL_ID (Integer): 1
    2 (Bag)
        SI_RIGHTS (Bag)
            1 (Bag)
                SI_VALUE (Boolean): false
                SI_ID (Integer): 6
                SI_RIGHT_TYPE (Integer): 0
                SI_RIGHT_SCOPE (String): this
                SI_RIGHT_APPLIES_TO_KIND (String): any
            2 (Bag)
                SI_VALUE (Boolean): false
                SI_ID (Integer): 22
                SI_RIGHT_TYPE (Integer): 0
                SI_RIGHT_SCOPE (String): this
                SI_RIGHT_APPLIES_TO_KIND (String): any
            SI_TOTAL (Integer): 2
        SI_PRINCIPAL_ID (Integer): 2
    SI_TOTAL (Integer): 2
SI_ENT_SUBGROUPS (Bag)
    SI_TOTAL (Integer): 0
SI_ENT_GROUP_MEMBERS (Bag)
    SI_TOTAL (Integer): 0
SI_ENT_USERGROUPS (Bag)
    SI_TOTAL (Integer): 0
SI_FALLBACK_LOCALE (String): en_EN
SI_CRYPTOGRAPHIC_KEY (Integer): 0
SI_SENDABLE (Boolean): false
SI_SUBSCRIBED_EVENTS (Bag)
    SI_TOTAL (Integer): 0
SI_USERGROUP_FOLDER (Bag)
    SI_TOTAL (Integer): 0
SI_ML_DESCRIPTION (Bag)
    DE (String): Alle Benutzer dieses Systems
    NL (String): Alle gebruikers van dit systeem
    ZH_TW (String): 此系統所有的使用者
    SL (String): Vsi uporabniki tega sistema
    AR (String): جميع مستخدمي هذا النظام
```

```
    DA (String): Alle brugere af dette system
    ES (String): Todos los usuarios de este sistema
    FI (String): Järjestelmän kaikki käyttäjät
    JA (String): このシステムのすべてのユーザ
    FR (String): Tous les utilisateurs de ce système
    SK (String): Všetci používatelia tohto systému.
    IT (String): Tutti gli utenti del sistema
    NB (String): Alle brukere av dette systemet
    TH (String): ผู้ใช้ทั้งหมดในระบบนี้
    RO (String): Toţi utilizatorii acestui sistem
    EN (String): All users of this system
    RU (String): Все пользователи данной системы
    HU (String): A rendszer összes felhasználója
 ZH_CN (String): 此系统的所有用户
    SV (String): Alla användare i detta system
    HE (String): כל המשתמשים ש מערכת זו
    PL (String): Wszyscy użytkownicy tego systemu
    PT (String): Todos os usuários deste sistema
    KO (String): 이 시스템의 모든 사용자
    CS (String): Všichni uživatelé tohoto systému.
SI_READ_ONLY (Boolean): false
SI_ROLES_ON_OBJECT (Bag)
    SI_TOTAL (Integer): 0
```

This result is the same content that would be generated from the Query Builder, but formatted differently, and with each property's datatype displayed.

So far in the section, we have covered how to retrieve InfoObject properties by name or ID, and how to iterate through all of an InfoObject's properties, retrieving each property's name, datatype, and value. The last topic we'll cover on `IProperty` is *flags*.

Property Flags

InfoObject properties can have zero or more flags that provide additional information about the property. The possible flags are documented in the Javadocs for `IProperty`, and as of BI4.2 are:

Name	Value	Definition
BAG	134217728	Property is a property bag
BINARY	4194304	Property is a binary stream
DELETE	67108864	Property has been marked for deletion
DIRTY	536870912	Property value has been changed
NO_COPY	33554432	Property should not be copied during an InfoObject copy operation
PROP_ID_LIST	2097152	Property is a property ID list
READ_ONLY	-2147483648	Property can not be deleted (but can be modified)

All of a property's flags are stored in a single `int` value which can be retrieved with the `IProperty.getFlags()` method. To test for the presence of a flag, use the Java bit-wise AND operator (`&`) with the `IProperty` flag constant. To check if a particular property is a property ID list, we would use the following code:

```
int flags = prop.getFlags();

if( (flags & IProperty.PROP_ID_LIST) != 0)
{
    System.out.println("Property ID List!";
}
```

Generally, you will not need to care about the actual `int` values of the flags – just use the constants in `IProperty`.

It is possible for properties to have flags with values that are not documented in the Javadocs. For example, the value 268435456 indicates that the property is a Date/Time value, and the value 8388608 indicates that the property value is encrypted.

Note that there is no `setFlags()` method in `IProperty`. Flags are either set when a property is initially created (with `IProperties.add()`), or by the SDK itself when certain operations are performed.

The `IProperty.setValue()` method, as its name implies, is used to change the value of an existing property. We will cover this in conjunction with modifying InfoObjects, in the next chapter.

IProperties shortcuts

In Listing 4, lines 35-37, we used the following code to extract the value of the `SI_CREATION_TIME` property:

```
35          IProperties props = user.properties();
36          IProperty creationTimeProp = props.getProperty(
   CePropertyID.SI_CREATION_TIME);
37          Date creationTime = (Date)creationTimeProp.getValue();
```

The `IProperties` interface provides a few shortcut methods that can be useful in scenarios like the above in which we are requesting a value from a property with a known datatype. The shortcut methods are:

Package com.crystaldecisions.sdk.properties
Interface IProperties

Shortcut methods

```
Boolean getBoolean(Object id)
```

	Retrieves the property specified by key `id` as a `Boolean`
Date	`getDate(Object id)`
	Retrieves the property specified by key `id` as a `Date`
int	`getInt(Object id)`
	Retrieves the property specified by key `id` as an `int`
long	`getLong(Object id)`
	Retrieves the property specified by key `id` as a `long`
IProperties	`getProperties(Object id)`
	Retrieves the property specified by key `id` as an `IProperties` object
IProperties	`getProperties(Object id, boolean createIfNotExist)`
	Retrieves the property specified by key `id` as an `IProperties` object, optionally creating the property if it doesn't already exist
String	`getString(Object id)`
	Retrieves the property specified by key `id` as a `String`
String	`getString(Locale locale)`
	Retrieves a `String` from this property bag, having a key which matches the specified locale.
String	`getString(Locale locale,Locale fallbackLocale,String defaultValue)`
	Retrieves a `String` from this property bag, having a key which matches the specified locale or the fallback locale. If neither locales are available in the property bag, the specified default value is returned.
void	`setProperty(Object id,boolean value)`
void	`setProperty(Object id,int value)`
void	`setProperty(Object id,long value)`
void	`setProperty(Object id,Object value)`
void	`setProperty(Object id,boolean value)`
	Sets the value of the property with key `id` to `value`.
void	`setString(Locale locale,String message)`
	Add a property to this property bag, with key `locale` and value `message`.

Class/Interface 3: IProperties

Knowing that the `SI_CREATION_TIME` property is always a `Date`, we can use the `IProperties.getDate()` method. So, we can collapse lines 36-37 into one:

```
35        IProperties props = user.properties();
```

```
36    Date creationTime = props.getDate(CePropertyID.SI_CREATION_TIME);
```

The shortcut methods are the recommended approach to retrieving property values since it eliminates the additional step of first retrieving the IProperty object then retrieving its value.

The shortcut methods expect that the specified property is of the datatype being requested, and they do not perform type conversion. For example, IProperties.getInt(…) should only be called for a property that is actually an int datatype. If we were to change line 36 above to:

```
36        int creationTime = props.getInt(CePropertyID.SI_CREATION_TIME);
```

then an exception would be generated since the SDK would be attempting to cast a Date value as an int.

The one exception to this rule is that getString() can be used with any property datatype – it returns the property's toString() result.

The IProperties.getProperties() method works the same as the other shortcuts: it is used to return the specified property, known to be a property bag, as an IProperties object. For example, if our CMS query included the SI_USERGROUPS property (which is a bag containing a list of group IDs that the user is a member of), then we could retrieve it with the following code:

```
35        IProperties props = user.properties();

36        IProperties groupIDs =
                  props.getProperties(CePropertyID.SI_USERGROUPS);
```

There is one additional shortcut that we should mention. The IInfoObject interface includes a method named propertyIDs(); this method returns an array of Integers which represent the keys of the InfoObject's root-level properties. So, the following two lines of code are functionally equivalent:

```
Integer[] propertyIDs = user.propertyIDs();

Integer[] propertyIDs = (Integer[]) user.properties().keySet().toArray();
```

Multi-Language Methods

There are a number of methods of the IInfoObject interface that support properties having multiple translations. This includes:

```
getDescriptionLocales(), getDescription(Locale locale), getDescription(Locale
locale,boolean doFallback), getFileLocales(), getFiles(Locale locale,LocaleOption
option), getSourceFiles(LocaleOption option), getTitle(Locale locale), getTitle(Locale
locale,boolean doFallBack), getTitleLocales()
```

InfoObject names and descriptions can be translated into multiple languages so that the appropriate translations are displayed if a user selects a non-default Viewing Locale in BI launch pad or CMC preferences. The Translation Management Tool (included with the BO Client Tools software) can be used to define translated names and descriptions for most user-facing content, including folders, reports, calendars, events, categories, user groups, and others. A few built-in InfoObjects have translated values defined for several languages.

If a particular InfoObject contains a translated name, that name can be retrieved with the `getTitle(Locale locale)` method, passing in the desired locale. In the following snippet, we'll retrieve the French name for the Quarterly Profit report:

```
IInfoObjects ios = infoStore.query("select * from ci_infoobjects where si_id =
5162");

IInfoObject io = (IInfoObject)ios.get(0);

System.out.println(io.getTitle(Locale.FRENCH));
```

Since we had already defined the translation for the name of this report using the Translation Management Tool, the above code prints:

```
Bénéfice Trimestriel
```

There's no guarantee that the desired translation will be present. If a request is made for a language that does not exist in the InfoObject's translations, the default name will be returned ("*Quarterly Profit*", in this case).

It's possible to check which locales are available, by using the `getTitleLocales()` method. This returns a `List` of `Locale` objects representing the available translations for this InfoObject. Note that the Translation Management Tool allows for different states of a specific translation to be set, so a translation will only be listed in `getTitleLocales()` if it is set to be in a usable state.

An InfoObject can have a single, optional *fallback locale*. If a request is made for a translation that does not exist in the InfoObject, then the fallback locale can be used. The `getTitle(Locale locale,boolean doFallback)` method is used to control whether to retrieve the fallback locale vs. the original (untranslated) name when a request is made for a translation that is not present.

We have already defined a French name for the Quarterly Profit report, and we'll also set the report's fallback locale to French. We'll also add another translation in Finnish. In Translation Management Tool, the settings look like the following:

Language	View	Translated	Visible	Fallback
Original Content Language	✓	N/A		
French (France)	✓	100% (2/2)	✓	◉
Finnish (Finland)	✓	100% (2/2)	✓	○

We'll now run our program again, but request a German translation:

```
System.out.println(io.getTitle(Locale.GERMAN));
```

Since we have specified French as the fallback locale, and there is no translation available for German, we get the French translation:

```
Bénéfice Trimestriel
```

If we wanted to get German or nothing, then we would pass a `false` for the `doFallback` parameter in the `getTItle` method:

```
System.out.println(io.getTitle(Locale.GERMAN,false));
```

Now we get:

```
null
```

Note that passing `true` for `doFallback` produces the same result as `getTitle(Locale locale)`.

In summary:
- When `getTitle()` is called: the original (untranslated) name is returned
- When `getTitle(Locale locale)`, or `getTitle(Locale locale,true)` is called...
  - ...and the requested translation is present, that translated name is returned.
  - ...and the requested translation is not present...
    - ...and a fallback locale is defined, the fallback translation is returned.
    - ...and no fallback locale is defined, the original (untranslated) name is returned.
- When `getTitle(Locale locale,false)` is called...
  - ...and the requested translation is present, that translated name is returned.
  - ...and the requested translation is not present, `null` is returned.

The above examples referred to *name*; there are equivalent methods for *description*.

Miscellaneous IInfoObject methods

The `IInfoObject.getParent()` method retrieves the InfoObject's parent, as an `IInfoObject`. Consider the following code fragment:

```
// CMS query to retrieve Web Intelligence document named "Quarterly Profit"
IInfoObjects ios = infoStore.query("select si_id from ci_infoobjects where
si_kind = 'webi' and si_name = 'quarterly profit'");

// Retrieve the one InfoObject from the IInfoObjects collection
IInfoObject io = (IInfoObject) ios.get(0);

// Call getParent(), to get the document's parent InfoObject
IInfoObject ioParent = io.getParent();

// ioParent now contains the parent of the "Quarterly Profit" report, the
// following line prints "Quarterly", which is the name of the parent object.
System.out.println(ioParent.getTitle());
```

The `getParent()` method will (internally) execute a new CMS query to retrieve the InfoObject's parent. The CMS query that it generates includes a default set of properties in the query's SELECT statement. The default property set includes the following properties:

`SI_CUID, SI_ID, SI_INSTANCE, SI_KIND, SI_NAME, SI_PARENTID, SI_PARENT_CUID`

In the above code block, the `ioParent` object would include the above properties for the *Quarterly* folder.

To retrieve an InfoObject's parent, but specify a different set of properties to be included, use the `getParent(int propertySet)` method. The value of `propertySet` should be one of the values from the `IInfoObject.PropertySet` static interface. The possible values, and the included properties, are:

Package com.crystaldecisions.sdk.occa.infostore
Interface _IInfoObject.PropertySet_

static int	DEFAULT	1
	SI_CUID, SI_ID, SI_INSTANCE, SI_KIND, SI_NAME, SI_PARENTID, SI_PARENT_CUID	
static int	STANDARD	2
	All of DEFAULT plus SI_PARENT_CUID, SI_OWNER, SI_DESCRIPTION	
static int	SCHEDULE	4
	All of STANDARD plus SI_SCHEDULEINFO	
static int	ALL	7
	All Properties (SELECT *)	

Class/Interface 4: IInfoObject.PropertySet

In our sample code block above, if we wanted to print the owner of *Quarterly Profit*'s parent, then we would need to adjust the `getParent()` call to specify either the STANDARD, SCHEDULE, or ALL value from IInfoObject.PropertySet:

```
// CMS query to retrieve Web Intelligence document named "Quarterly Profit"
```

```
IInfoObjects ios = infoStore.query("select si_id from ci_infoobjects where
si_kind = 'webi' and si_name = 'quarterly profit'");

// Retrieve the one InfoObject from the IInfoObjects collection
IInfoObject io = (IInfoObject) ios.get(0);

// Call getParent(), to get the document's parent InfoObject
IInfoObject ioParent = io.getParent(IInfoObject.PropertySet.STANDARD);

// ioParent now contains the parent of the "Quarterly Profit" report, the
// following line prints "Administrator", which is the name of the parent
// object's owner.
System.out.println(ioParent.getOwner());
```

Note that `io.getParent()` is functionally equivalent to `io.getParent(IInfoObject.PropertySet.DEFAULT)`.

A rarely needed but sometimes handy method of `IInfoObject` is `retrievePropertySet()`. This method is used to retrieve additional properties for an `IInfoObject` object already retrieved from the CMS. Consider this code fragment:

```
// CMS query to retrieve Web Intelligence document named "Quarterly Profit"
IInfoObjects ios = infoStore.query("select si_id from ci_infoobjects where
si_kind = 'webi' and si_name = 'quarterly profit'");

// Retrieve the one InfoObject from the IInfoObjects collection
IInfoObject io = (IInfoObject) ios.get(0);

// The original CMS query included only SI_ID; add all other properties to io
io.retrievePropertySet(IInfoObject.PropertySet.ALL);

// Now we can print the owner
System.out.println(io.getOwner());
```

In this sample, our CMS query included only the SI_ID property. However, later in the program, we find that we need the SI_OWNER property in order to call `io.getOwner()`. So, we call `io.retrieveProeprtySet()` to include all remaining properties to the existing `io` object before calling `getOnwer()`.

Note that the above is not a real-world scenario. If we know that we needed the SI_OWNER property in the program, we would have added that property to the initial CMS query; using `retrievePropertySet()` as we did is inefficient, as it results in multiple CMS queries being executed.

With that said, there are a couple of possible scenarios where this might be useful:

- Your program receives an `IInfoObject` object from another library, and it does not contain the necessary properties that your program requires.

- Your program retrieves a large number of InfoObjects in a CMS query, and certain actions are conditionally performed based on some criteria. An example of this scenario could be a program that pulls all InfoObjects of kind *WebI*, then for those that have a certain scheduling status, the `retrievePropertySet()` method is called to add the scheduling properties. In this way, the original CMS query does not need to include the `SI_SCHEDULEINFO` properties, but it can be retrieved later for the necessary InfoObjects.

IInfoObject Subinterfaces

The `IInfoObject` interface has many subinterfaces representing the various InfoObject *kinds*. The complete list of subinterfaces is documented in the IInfoObject Javadocs (https://help.sap.com/doc/javadocs_bip_42/4.2/en-US/bip/en/index.html). As of BI4.2, the list includes:

```
IAgnostic, IAlertingApp, IAlertNotification, IAuditEventInfo, IAuditEventInfo,
ICalendar, ICategory, IConnection, IContainer, ICryptographicKey,
ICustomMappedAttribute, ICustomRole, IDependencyRule, IDeploymentFile, IDiskUnmanaged,
IEnterpriseNode, IEvent, IExcel, IFileEvent, IFolder, IFTP, IFullClient, IHotBackup,
IHyperlink, IInbox, IInstall, ILicenseKey, ILicenseRestriction, IManaged, IManifest,
IMetricDescriptions, INotificationEvent, INotificationSchedule, IObjectPackage,
IOverload, IPDF, IPowerPoint, IProbeInfoObject, IProfile, IProgram, IPublication,
IRemoteCluster, IReplication, IReport, IRestWebService, IRTF, ISAMLServiceProvider,
IScheduleEvent, IScopeBatch, IsecEnterprise, IsecLDAP, IsecSAPR3, IsecWinAD,
IsecWinNT, IServer, IServerGroup, IService, IServiceBase, IServiceCommon,
IServiceContainer, IServiceContainerBase, ISFTP, IShortcut, ISMTP, IStreamWork,
IStreamWorkIntegration, ITenant, ITxt, IUniverse, IUser, IUserEvent, IUserGroup,
IWebi, IWebService, IWord
```

Although this list is extensive, it does not represent *every* possible kind of InfoObject (an example is the cluster object, ID 4). It is still possible to manipulate InfoObjects that don't have a kind-specific subinterface of `IInfoObject`, using the `IInfoObject` interface itself. It's only necessary to cast an `IInfoObject` to a subinterface if a method from that subinterface is needed.

Key point: since the objective of most SDK programs is to manipulate InfoObjects, the `IInfoObject` interface and its subinterfaces are ubiquitous in most programs. It is crucial to become familiar with these in order to use the SDK effectively.

The `IInfoObject` subinterfaces support properties and actions that are specific to the various InfoObject kinds. To illustrate this, let's go back to Listing 3, specifically lines 27-31:

27	`for(int x = 0;x < users.size(); x++)`
28	`{`
29	`    IInfoObject user = (IInfoObject) users.get(x);`
30	`    System.out.println(user.getTitle());`

```
31            }
```

On line 29, we are casting the contents of the `users` collection to `IInfoObject`, and then on the next line we display the result of its `getTitle()` method. This is a perfectly legitimate solution for our requirement since the `IInfoObject` interface includes all the necessary methods for what we want to do.

But what if we want to display a property that is specific to *User* InfoObjects, such as the user's full name? We could use the `properties()` method to retrieve the property directly, but there's a better way...

The `IUser` interface (a subinterface of `IInfoObject`) includes several methods specific to user InfoObjects, including `getFullName()`, which is precisely what we need. If we check the Javadocs[76] for this method, or simply hover over `getFullName()`,(*or*, check our description on page 384) we'll find the following note:

> InfoObject properties to query for:
>
> SI_USERFULLNAME

The accessor methods of most `IInfoObject` subinterfaces include notes such as the above to indicate which properties are needed by the method. The notes are not present on all accessor methods, however, but in most cases the name of the property to include is intuitive.

We'll add `SI_USERFULLNAME` to the query on line 19:

```
19        IInfoObjects users = infoStore.query("select si_name,si_userfullname from
   ci_systemobjects where si_kind = 'user'");
```

Now, on line 29, we'll change the user variable to type `IUser`, and change the cast accordingly::

```
29            IUser user = (IUser) users.get(x);
```

Eclipse *should* find and propose the correct import, which results in:

```
import com.crystaldecisions.sdk.plugin.desktop.user.IUser;
```

Finally, we change line 31 to display the user's full name in addition to the ID:

```
31            System.out.println(user.getTitle() + ": " + user.getFullName());
```

When the program is executed, it displays the user ID, and the full name if it is set for the

---

76 Many of the IInfoObject subinterfaces, such as IUser, also extend other interfaces. In addition to
    IInfoObject, IUser extends ISystemPrincipal and IUserBase. All of the User-specific methods,
    including getFullName(), are inherited from IUserBase. This inheritance strategy has no direct impact on
    your usage of these interfaces, but it does affect the layout of the Javadocs. The Javadoc page for IUser lists
    getFullName() as inherited from IUserBase – the full description of this method is on the Javadoc page for
    IUserBase.

user. In our test system, this displays:

```
Guest:
Administrator:
SMAdmin:
QaaWSServletPrincipal:
Fred: Fred Frederick
Nathan:
Sri:
Wally:
Ephraim:
Quentin:
Isabel:
Alice:
Done!
```

In this case, only the *Fred* user had a full name set.

When using the subinterfaces of IInfoObject, it is critical to ensure that the correct subinterface is used. In the example above, the CMS query included a condition to retrieve only SI_KIND of *user*, so this condition guaranteed that the IInfoObjects collection that was generated would only contain InfoObjects of kind IUser.

But what if it didn't? Let's change the CMS query on line 20 to add objects of kind *UserGroup*:

```
20        IInfoObjects users = infoStore.query("select si_name,si_userfullname from
    ci_systemobjects where si_kind in ('user','usergroup')");
```

Executing the program now results in an exception being thrown:

```
Exception in thread "main" java.lang.ClassCastException:
com.crystaldecisions.sdk.plugin.desktop.usergroup.internal.UserGroup cannot be cast to
com.crystaldecisions.sdk.plugin.desktop.user.IUser
    at bosdkbook.ListUsers.main(ListUsers.java:30)
```

The exception is pretty clear – the users collection contained an object of type UserGroup, which we attempted to cast to IUser.

Let's assume for this example what we really do want to include User Groups as well as Users in our output. If the InfoObject is a user, then we display the ID and full name, but if it a user group, we want to display the number of users in that group. We already modified our CMS query to include user groups, so we just need to add logic to distinguish between users and user groups in the result set.

The IUserGroup interface includes a method getUsers(), which returns a Set of its member users' InfoObject IDs. Checking the Javadocs for IUserGroup.getUsers() indicates that it requires the SI_GROUP_MEMBERS property, so we add that to our CMS query on line 20. Since we need to check the returned InfoObjects to determine their kind, we also add SI_KIND. Finally, for this line, we change the name of the variable from users to infoObjects since we're no longer retrieving just users:

```
20        IInfoObjects infoObjects = infoStore.query("select si_name,
si_userfullname, si_group_members, si_kind from ci_systemobjects where si_kind in
('user','usergroup')");
```

Since we renamed users to infoObjects, we also have to rename the references to this variable on line 22[77].

The entire for loop, beginning on line 28, is replaced with the following:

```
29        for(int x = 0;x < infoObjects.size(); x++)

30        {

31            IInfoObject infoObject = (IInfoObject)infoObjects.get(x);

32            if(infoObject.getKind().equals(IUser.KIND))

33            {

34                IUser user = (IUser)infoObject;

35                System.out.println("User: " + user.getTitle() + ", Full Name: " +
user. getFullName());

36            }

37            else

38            {

39                IUserGroup userGroup = (IUserGroup)infoObject;

40                System.out.println("Group: " + userGroup.getTitle() + ", member
count: " + userGroup.getUsers().size());

41            }

42        }
```

Eclipse errors on IUserGroup, on line 39, but suggests the correct import.

Line 31 is the same as before, other than renaming the variable to infoObject.

We have to determine whether infoObject is a User or UserGroup. The IInfoObject subinterfaces include static properties that define that subinterface's associated *kind* and *progid*. For example, the IUser interface has a KIND property with a value of "User".

See Interface / Kind Mapping Tables on page 663 for a list of the Kind and ProgID properties from the IInfoObject subinterfaces.

So, on line 32, we are comparing infoObject.getKind() against IUser.KIND. Note that these are both **String**s, and so we have to use getKind().equals() in order to do the comparison.

If infoObject is a User InfoObject, then we perform essentially the same function as the original listing, but first casting infoObject to IUser.

---

77 If you had renamed it on line 20 via Eclipse's rename function, it will automatically do the subsequent renaming for you.

Since our CMS query explicitly requests only kinds `User` and `UserGroup`, we know that if `infoObject` is not a `User` then it must be a `UserGroup`. So, on line 39-40, we cast `infoObject` to `IUserGroup` and print out the title and size of its `getUsers()` collection.

The complete program is in Listing 6, and on our test system it produced:

```
Group: Everyone, member count: 12
Group: Administrators, member count: 2
Group: Cryptographic Officers, member count: 1
User: Guest, Full Name:
User: Administrator, Full Name:
User: SMAdmin, Full Name:
Group: Report Conversion Tool Users, member count: 0
Group: Translators, member count: 0
Group: Universe Designer Users, member count: 0
Group: QaaWS Group Designer, member count: 0
User: QaaWSServletPrincipal, Full Name:
User: Fred, Full Name: Fred Frederick
Group: Sales, member count: 0
Group: Finance, member count: 1
Group: Exec. Management, member count: 1
Group: IT, member count: 1
Group: Business, member count: 0
Group: Universe Developers, member count: 0
Group: QA, member count: 2
Group: Dashboard Users, member count: 0
Group: Northeast Region, member count: 1
Group: Southeast Region, member count: 1
Group: Western Region, member count: 1
User: Nathan, Full Name:
User: Sri, Full Name:
User: Wally, Full Name:
User: Ephraim, Full Name:
User: Quentin, Full Name:
User: Isabel, Full Name:
User: Alice, Full Name:
Done!
```

```java
1  package bosdkbook;

2

3  import com.crystaldecisions.sdk.exception.SDKException;

4  import com.crystaldecisions.sdk.framework.CrystalEnterprise;

5  import com.crystaldecisions.sdk.framework.IEnterpriseSession;

6  import com.crystaldecisions.sdk.framework.ISessionMgr;

7  import com.crystaldecisions.sdk.occa.infostore.IInfoObject;

8  import com.crystaldecisions.sdk.occa.infostore.IInfoObjects;

9  import com.crystaldecisions.sdk.occa.infostore.IInfoStore;
```

```
10  import com.crystaldecisions.sdk.plugin.desktop.user.IUser;

11  import com.crystaldecisions.sdk.plugin.desktop.usergroup.IUserGroup;

12

13  public class ListUsersAndGroups {

14      public static void main(String[] args) throws SDKException

15      {

16          ISessionMgr sessionManager = CrystalEnterprise.getSessionMgr();

17          IEnterpriseSession session = sessionManager.logon ("administrator",
    "xxxx", "192.168.56.102", "secEnterprise");

18

19          IInfoStore infoStore = (IInfoStore) session.getService ("","InfoStore");

20

21          IInfoObjects infoObjects = infoStore.query("select si_name,
    si_userfullname, si_group_members, si_kind from ci_systemobjects where si_kind
    in ('user','usergroup')");

22

23          if(infoObjects.size() == 0)

24          {

25              System.out.println("No users or user groups found!");

26              session.logoff();

27              return;

28          }

29          for(int x = 0;x < infoObjects.size(); x++)

30          {

31              IInfoObject infoObject = (IInfoObject)infoObjects.get(x);

32              if(infoObject.getKind().equals(IUser.KIND))

33              {

34                  IUser user = (IUser)infoObject;

35                  System.out.println("User: " + user.getTitle() + ", Full Name: " +
    user. getFullName());

36              }

37              else

38              {

39                  IUserGroup userGroup = (IUserGroup)infoObject;

40                  System.out.println("Group: " + userGroup.getTitle() + ", member
    count: " + userGroup.getUsers().size());
```

```
41              }
42          }
43          System.out.println("Done!");
44          session.logoff();
45      }
46 }
```

Listing 6: The ListUsersAndGroups program

In this chapter, we introduced the basic methods of the IInfoObject interface and several subinterfaces that are associated with the various *kinds* of InfoObjects. With this knowledge, you may explore the other subinterfaces to see the functionality provided by them. In the next chapter, we introduce some (relatively) more exciting functionality.

Chapter Review

- *All* InfoObject types, such as users, folders, reports, etc., are represented in the SDK by the IInfoObject interface.

- The IInfoObject interface has a number of sub-interfaces that represent the specific InfoObject kinds. The IInfoObject interface itself contains many methods for performing actions that are common to all InfoObject kinds.

- InfoObjects consist of properties, and one of the primary uses of IInfoObject is reading and writing property values.

- Not all InfoObject properties are exposed via accessor methods; to work with properties that are not exposed in this way; it is necessary to manipulate them directly via an IProperty object.

Quiz

1. True/False: It is necessary to cast an IInfoObject object to one of its sub-interfaces to access kind-specific properties.

2. True/False: A property must be read-only if it has a get() method but no set() method.

3. What happens if a get() method is called which references a property that was not included in the CMS query?

    a) The get() returns null.

    b) An exception is thrown.

   c) The expected property value is returned.

   d) Either a) or b), depending on the specific `get()` method.

4. The save() method performs which function?

   a) Posts pending changes to the locally-cached InfoObject, to be pushed to the CMS by a later `IInfoStore.commit()` call.

   b) Immediately saves the InfoObject to the CMS.

5. In order to retrieve security information via the `getSecurityInfo2()` method, which property must be included in the CMS query's SELECT statement?

   a) `SI_SCHEDULEINFO`

   b) `SI_SECURITY`

   c) `SI_RIGHTS`

   d) None are required

6. In order to determine the data type of a property, use:

   a) `instanceof`

   b) `IProperty.getType()`

   c) `IProperty.getFlags()`

Answers on page 673.

Chapter 12 - Manipulating InfoObjects

Thus far, we have described various ways of retrieving information from an SAP BusinessObjects CMS, including CMS queries and SDK methods. While valuable on their own, much more power can be leveraged by writing back to the CMS. These methods enable the programmer to create, modify, or delete InfoObjects, in the same way that a user or administrator can perform these functions in BI launch pad or the CMC.

Of course, with great power comes great responsibility. The ability to modify or delete content via the SDK inherently creates a risk that should not be underestimated. It is possible, within a few lines of code, to screw up an entire SAP BusinessObjects cluster beyond repair[78]. But even aside from an SAP BusinessObjects Armageddon, erroneous (or even outdated) programs can create issues in a cluster that could lie undetected for a period of time, or result in a cluster that is unavailable to some users, or, the worst-case scenario of any business intelligence system: produce bad data.

Even one seemingly innocuous action can result in a corruption that requires a significant recovery effort. When a user is deleted, the following actions are performed by the CMS:

- The user object itself is deleted.

- All documents in the user's Favorites Folder and Inbox are deleted.

- All objects in public folders (including documents, universes, etc.) that are owned by the user revert to being owned by Administrator.

- Any recurring schedules owned by the user will fail and not run again.

Thus, accidentally deleting a user, or deleting the wrong user, can be a significant impact, and would likely require a restoration of both the CMS database and File Repository System to recover fully. While this risk is present even when users are deleted manually via the CMC, it is increased exponentially when performed with an SDK program.

This is not meant to discourage the reader from utilizing the SDK to its full potential, including manipulating InfoObjects when appropriate, but rather to make clear the point that these activities require an increased level of due diligence with respect to all involved procedural steps. In this chapter, we suggest several methods for performing SDK activities safely, to enable leveraging the value of the SDK while minimizing its inherent risk.

It's worth mentioning here that to manipulate an InfoObject, the user ID that the program is running as needs to have appropriate rights to that InfoObject, generally the *Edit* permission at a minimum. If you execute a program that attempts to modify an InfoObject that the user has View rights to but not Edit, an exception will be thrown when the transaction is committed. So, it's not possible to perform an action on an InfoObject with the SDK if it's not allowed via the CMC or BI launch pad.

---

78 To borrow from an age-old saying, the SDK allows the programmer to make catastrophic mistakes at an unprecedented rate of speed.

Manipulation of InfoObjects falls into three distinct operations: *creation, modification,* and *deletion.* Despite the inherent differences in these operations, they all involve the same processing steps:

1. The desired object is obtained as an `IInfoObject` instance

2. Optionally, InfoObject properties are set or changed

3. The transaction is committed

Obtaining an IInfoObject

For modification and deletion operations, the desired InfoObject (or InfoObjects) must be retrieved via a CMS query into an `IInfoObjects` collection. This action is performed in exactly the same way as the previous examples in which we used `IInfoStore.query()` to perform CMS queries. That is, there is no difference in performing CMS queries for when the intended operation is merely interrogation vs. when the InfoObject is intended to be modified or deleted.

For InfoObject *creation* operations, a new, empty IInfoObject is created via `IInfoObjects.add()`.

Properties Set or Changed

An InfoObject creation or modification operation generally requires the modification of that InfoObject's properties. This is done via setter methods or directly modifying properties via the `IInfoObject.properties()` method.

This is an optional step – changing properties is useless during delete operations for obvious reasons, but is rarely skipped during creation or modification operations.

Transaction Committed

When properties are changed in the previous step, the modification will exist only within the context of the SDK program. That is, no communication is made to the CMS server with regard to the modification until the transaction is committed. There are various methods of the `IInfoObject` and `IInfoStore` classes to perform a commit, including different methods to perform immediate commits versus batch commits.

Key point: modifying InfoObjects with setter methods (or directly modifying properties) will only affect the copy of the InfoObject in the local computer's memory. Changes are not made in the CMS until the transaction is committed.

Arguably the most common InfoObject manipulation operation is *modification,* so we start with an example of this type.

Modifying InfoObjects

For this simple example, we'll set the description for all users in the *Finance* group. We'll also take this opportunity to illustrate the use of a relationship query in an SDK program.

```
1  package bosdkbook;
2
3  import com.crystaldecisions.sdk.exception.SDKException;
4  import com.crystaldecisions.sdk.framework.CrystalEnterprise;
5  import com.crystaldecisions.sdk.framework.IEnterpriseSession;
6  import com.crystaldecisions.sdk.framework.ISessionMgr;
7  import com.crystaldecisions.sdk.occa.infostore.IInfoObject;
8  import com.crystaldecisions.sdk.occa.infostore.IInfoObjects;
9  import com.crystaldecisions.sdk.occa.infostore.IInfoStore;
10
11 public class SetFinanceUsers {
12    public static void main(String[] args) throws SDKException
13    {
14        ISessionMgr sessionManager = CrystalEnterprise.getSessionMgr();
15        IEnterpriseSession session = sessionManager.logon ("administrator",
   "xxxx", "192.168.56.102", "secEnterprise");
16
17        IInfoStore infoStore = (IInfoStore) session.getService ("","InfoStore");
18
19        IInfoObjects infoObjects = infoStore.query("select si_name,si_id from
   ci_systemobjects where children(\"si_name='usergroup-
   user'\", \"si_name='finance'\")");
20
21        for(int x = 0;x < infoObjects.size(); x++)
22        {
23            IInfoObject infoObject = (IInfoObject)infoObjects.get(x);
24            System.out.println("Setting description for user: " +
   infoObject.getTitle());
25            infoObject.setDescription("Finance User");
26            infoObject.save();
27        }
28
29        System.out.println("Done!");
```

```
30          session.logoff();

31      }

32  }
```

Listing 7: The SetFinanceUsers program

Listing 7 contains the *SetFinanceUsers* program. The structure of this program is similar to what we've seen before: on line 19, we execute a CMS query that returns the ID and name of all users that belong to the *Finance* user group. The only notable difference with this query is that we are using *Relationship Query* syntax to retrieve the users in a particular group.

Lines 21-24 are familiar, too. We are iterating through the `infoObjects` collection and retrieving an `IInfoObject` object as `infoObject`. This is the first step of InfoObject manipulation – retrieving the desired objects as `IInfoObject` instances.

On line 25, we call `infoObject.setDescription()` to set the Description property of the user. This is the second step – setting InfoObject properties.

At the end of the `for` loop is `infoObject.save()`. This is the third step of InfoObject manipulation – committing the transaction. If we had eliminated or commented this line out, no changes to the users' Descriptions would have been made.

As it is, there are two users in the Finance group in our test system, and the program above produced the following output:

```
Setting description for user: Fred
Setting description for user: Ephraim
Done!
```

Checking the CMC for the Finance group confirms that the change was completed as intended:

	Name ▲	Full Name	Type	Description
	Ephraim		User	Finance User
	Fred	Fred Frederick	User	Finance User

Since we are writing to the `SI_DESCRIPTION` property, but not reading what it was before, we don't need to include the property name in the CMS query on line 19.

The `setDescription()` method that we used above is one of the `IInfoObject` setter methods in Table 7 in Chapter 11. For the most part, properties that have an associated getter method but no setter method are read-only, or otherwise should not be written to. Example of these are the `getID()`, `getCUID()`, and `getKind()` methods. However, some other properties do not have setter methods but can be modified by way of the object that is returned by the getter method, generally a `Set` or `List`.

A good example of this is the `getGroups()` method of `IUser`, which returns a `Set`; the `Set` is a collection of `Integer` objects which represent the `SI_ID` property of the groups that the user is a member of. To add or remove a user from a group, we just need to add or remove the group's ID from that Set and commit the transaction[79] [80].

So let's do just that. We'll write a simple program that adds the *Fred* user to the *Exec. Management* group (congratulations, Fred). Before we get to modifying Fred's group membership, however, we'll just look at the contents of the getGroups() collection.

```
1  package bosdkbook;
2
3  import java.util.Set;
4
5  import com.crystaldecisions.sdk.exception.SDKException;
6  import com.crystaldecisions.sdk.framework.CrystalEnterprise;
7  import com.crystaldecisions.sdk.framework.IEnterpriseSession;
8  import com.crystaldecisions.sdk.framework.ISessionMgr;
9  import com.crystaldecisions.sdk.occa.infostore.IInfoObjects;
10 import com.crystaldecisions.sdk.occa.infostore.IInfoStore;
11 import com.crystaldecisions.sdk.plugin.desktop.user.IUser;
12
13 public class ListFredsGroups {
14     public static void main(String[] args) throws SDKException
15     {
16         ISessionMgr sessionManager = CrystalEnterprise.getSessionMgr();
17         IEnterpriseSession session = sessionManager.logon ("administrator",
   "xxxx", "192.168.56.102", "secEnterprise");
18
19         IInfoStore infoStore = (IInfoStore) session.getService ("","InfoStore");
20
21         IInfoObjects infoObjects = infoStore.query("select si_usergroups from
   ci_systemobjects where si_name = 'fred' and si_kind = 'user'");
22
23         IUser fred = (IUser)infoObjects.get(0);
24
```

---

79 User-Group management of this type is a *very* common use of the Platform SDK.

80 The IUserGroup interface has a getUsers() collection containing the IDs of the users in that group. Adding a user to a group can be done by either adding the group's ID to the user's getGroups() collection **or** by adding the user's ID to the group's getUsers() collection; both actions result in the same user-group relationship change. In order to use either method, the user ID that the program runs as must have Edit permissions on both the *user* **and** the *user group*.

```
25        Set<Integer> groupIDs = fred.getGroups();
26        for(Integer groupID : groupIDs)
27            System.out.println(groupID);
28
29        System.out.println("Done!");
30        session.logoff();
31    }
32 }
```

Listing 8: The ListFredsGroups program

Listing 8 contains the *ListFredsGroups* program. When we executed, we get the following result:

```
1
6334
Done!
```

The two integers are the IDs of the two groups that Fred is in: *Everyone* and *Finance Users*. If we had instead wanted to display the names of the groups, we would have to do additional CMS queries to retrieve those InfoObjects, but this is good enough for now.

Eclipse displays a *Type Safety* warning on line 25 since the return type of getGroups() is just Set without any type parameters. The warning can be ignored.

Now we'll do the group membership modification. In a real-world scenario, we would programmatically look up the ID of the *Exec. Management* group, but for our example, we'll just use the ID, which from the CMC we know to be 6335 (of course, this will almost certainly be a different value in your system).

We replace lines 26-27 of the program with:

```
26        groupIDs.add(6335);
27        fred.save();
```

The program will now add Fred to the *Exec. Management* group. After executing it, we check the *Fred* user in the CMC confirms that the change has been made:

Illustration 21: Fred's groups

In the previous examples, we used accessor methods to set property values. As with retrieving properties, using the built-in accessor methods is highly recommended. However, there are occasions when there are no setter methods available. A good example of this is the SI_OWNERID property – while this property is writable, and there is a getOwnerID() method of IInfoObject, there is no associated setOwnerID() method. The IInfoObject.properties() method is the solution to this problem…

Modifying Properties with IInfoObject.properties()

We discussed retrieving property values with the IInfoObject.properties() method and associated IProperties/IProperty classes in Chapter 11. The same functionality exists for creating, modifying, and deleting properties.

Directly modifying properties in this manner requires an extra measure of precaution. While the SDK disallows modifying read-only properties, it is possible to modify properties that shouldn't be modified other than by the system. Other than the example above (Owner ID), there are not many scenarios in which this is necessary. Be very careful when directly modifying properties.

For this example, we will make *Fred* the owner of all Web Intelligence documents under the *Reports* folder. Note that as of BI4, there is no support in the CMC for modifying ownership of objects, so the SDK is the only way to perform this operation.

There are two properties associated with ownership: SI_OWNER, which holds the user name (the SI_NAME property of the owner user), and SI_OWNERID, which holds the InfoObject ID of the owner user. In order to change an InfoObject's owner, we must change the SI_OWNERID value appropriately; changing the SI_OWNER property will have no effect[81].

Before we run the program to modify ownership, we'll check the current ownership status. In the CMC, we find that the *Reports* folder has an ID of 4213. Then, in Query Builder, we execute this query:

```
select si_name,si_owner
  from ci_infoobjects
 where si_ancestor = 4213
       and si_kind = 'webi'
```

---

81 The SI_OWNER property is a dynamically derived property and based on the value of SI_OWNER_ID.

This produces the following result:

SI_NAME	SI_OWNER
Quarterly Profit	Administrator
Annual Profit	Administrator
Quarterly Profit	Administrator
Annual Profit	Administrator
Year-End Reports 2015	Administrator

So, we know that we'll be changing the ownership of these five reports to *Fred*.

```
1  package bosdkbook;
2
3  import com.crystaldecisions.sdk.exception.SDKException;
4  import com.crystaldecisions.sdk.framework.CrystalEnterprise;
5  import com.crystaldecisions.sdk.framework.IEnterpriseSession;
6  import com.crystaldecisions.sdk.framework.ISessionMgr;
7  import com.crystaldecisions.sdk.occa.infostore.CePropertyID;
8  import com.crystaldecisions.sdk.occa.infostore.IInfoObject;
9  import com.crystaldecisions.sdk.occa.infostore.IInfoObjects;
10 import com.crystaldecisions.sdk.occa.infostore.IInfoStore;
11 import com.crystaldecisions.sdk.properties.IProperties;
12 import com.crystaldecisions.sdk.properties.IProperty;
13
14 public class ModifyOwnership {
15     public static void main(String[] args) throws SDKException
16     {
17         ISessionMgr sessionManager = CrystalEnterprise.getSessionMgr();
18         IEnterpriseSession session = sessionManager.logon ("administrator",
    "xxxx", "192.168.56.102", "secEnterprise");
19
20         IInfoStore infoStore = (IInfoStore) session.getService ("","InfoStore");
21
22         IInfoObjects infoObjects = infoStore.query("select
    si_name,si_owner,si_ownerid from ci_infoobjects where si_kind = 'webi' and
    si_owner != 'fred' and si_ancestor = 4213");
23
```

```
24        for(Object o : infoObjects)
25        {
26            IInfoObject infoObject = (IInfoObject)o;
27            System.out.println("Setting ownership for document: "
                                    + infoObject.getTitle());
28            IProperties props = infoObject.properties();
29            IProperty prop = props.getProperty(CePropertyID.SI_OWNERID);
30            prop.setValue(4104);
31
32            infoObject.save();
33        }
34
35        System.out.println("Done!");
36        session.logoff();
37    }
38 }
```

Listing 9: The ModifyOwnership program

Listing 9contains the *ModifyOwnership* program. When we execute this program, we receive the following output:

```
Setting ownership for document: Quarterly Profit
Setting ownership for document: Annual Profit
Setting ownership for document: Quarterly Profit
Setting ownership for document: Annual Profit
Setting ownership for document: Year-End Reports 2015
Done!
```

As expected, the program has updated the ownership for the five reports. To confirm, we'll execute the CMS query from earlier:

```
select si_name,si_owner
  from ci_infoobjects
 where si_ancestor = 4213
       and si_kind = 'webi'
```

This produces the following result:

SI_NAME	SI_OWNER
Quarterly Profit	Fred
Annual Profit	Fred
Quarterly Profit	Fred

SI_NAME	SI_OWNER
Annual Profit	Fred
Year-End Reports 2015	Fred

This confirms that our program has updated the ownership correctly.

The program is similar to Listing 4, in which we displayed the value of properties. The primary difference is that we are now *setting* the value, which we do on line 30, and then committing the change, on line 32:

```
28          IProperties props = infoObject.properties();

29          IProperty prop = props.getProperty(CePropertyID.SI_OWNERID);

30          prop.setValue(4104);

31

32          infoObject.save();
```

Note that we are passing setValue() an int, which is the correct datatype of the SI_OWNERID property. Using the correct datatype in calls to setValue() is critical, as it simply ignores unexpected datatypes. If we had instead used:

```
30          prop.setValue("Fred");
```

...then the program would complete without error, but would not apply any change.

As with getting property values, the IProperties interface has a shortcut method for setting values:

```
        void setProperty(Object id, Object value)
```

...where id is the ID or name of the desired property to set. We could re-write the above lines as:

```
28          IProperties props = infoObject.properties();

29          props.setProperty(CePropertyID.SI_OWNERID,4104);

30

31          infoObject.save();
```

Deleting InfoObjects

Deleting InfoObjects is done in a similar fashion as modifying. For this example, we implement our own version of a Recycle Bin in public folders. BI4.2 and later natively support the Recycle Bin feature, but we'll implement our own version[82]. Our process merely deletes all content in a specific public folder (named "Recycle Bin").

Listing 10 Contains the *PurgeRecycleBin* program. You'll note that the structure is similar to our previous examples in which we modified InfoObjects.

As before, on lines 20-22, we obtain the desired (doomed) InfoObjects as `IInfoObject` instances.

We are not modifying any object properties, so the second step of InfoObject manipulation is skipped.

On line 26, we commit the deletion operation with `infoObject.deleteNow()`, which completes the third step of InfoObject manipulation.

```java
1   package bosdkbook;

2

3   import com.crystaldecisions.sdk.exception.SDKException;

4   import com.crystaldecisions.sdk.framework.CrystalEnterprise;

5   import com.crystaldecisions.sdk.framework.IEnterpriseSession;

6   import com.crystaldecisions.sdk.framework.ISessionMgr;

7   import com.crystaldecisions.sdk.occa.infostore.IInfoObject;

8   import com.crystaldecisions.sdk.occa.infostore.IInfoObjects;

9   import com.crystaldecisions.sdk.occa.infostore.IInfoStore;

10

11  public class PurgeRecycleBin

12  {

13      public static void main(String[] args) throws SDKException

14      {

15          ISessionMgr sessionManager = CrystalEnterprise.getSessionMgr();

16          IEnterpriseSession session = sessionManager.logon ("administrator",
    "xxxx", "192.168.56.102", "secEnterprise");

17

18          IInfoStore infoStore = (IInfoStore) session.getService ("","InfoStore");

19

20          IInfoObjects infoObjects = infoStore.query("select si_name, si_cuid from
    ci_infoobjects where children(\"si_name='folder hierarchy'\",\"si_name =
    'recycle bin' and si_parentid = 23\")");

21
```

```
22        for(Object o : infoObjects)
23        {
24            IInfoObject infoObject = (IInfoObject)o;
25            System.out.println("Deleting: " + infoObject.getTitle());
26            infoObject.deleteNow();
27        }
28    }
29 }
```

Listing 10: The PurgeRecycleBin program

To test the program, we'll copy a couple of documents into the new *Recycle Bin* folder that we created:

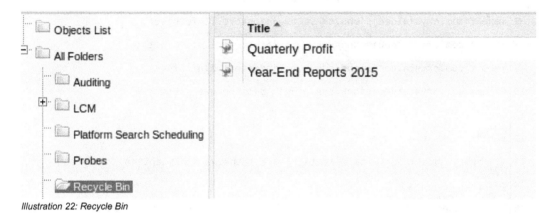

Illustration 22: Recycle Bin

When we execute the program, we get the following output:

```
Deleting: Quarterly Profit
Deleting: Year-End Reports 2015
```

Checking the *Recycle Bin* folder in the CMC confirms that it has been emptied.

Creating InfoObjects

The last form of InfoObject manipulation that we'll cover is creation.

One of the most common uses of the SDK is user and group management, including the creation of new user accounts and assignment to groups. This is also a fairly simple process, as we'll see.

Naturally, the creation of InfoObjects is a different process from modifying or deleting InfoObjects, in which case the operation first required retrieving the desired objects from the CMS via a CMS query. However, the same three steps for InfoObject manipulation apply – only the first step (obtaining an IInfoObject instance) is different.

When creating InfoObjects, we first have to create the new InfoObject via the IInfoObjects.add() method. Generally this is done with a new, empty IInfoObjects collection created via IInfoStore.newInfoObjectCollection().

For this example, we'll create a new user ID and add it to the *Finance* user group.

```
1  package bosdkbook;
2
3  import com.crystaldecisions.sdk.exception.SDKException;
4  import com.crystaldecisions.sdk.framework.CrystalEnterprise;
5  import com.crystaldecisions.sdk.framework.IEnterpriseSession;
6  import com.crystaldecisions.sdk.framework.ISessionMgr;
7  import com.crystaldecisions.sdk.occa.infostore.IInfoObject;
8  import com.crystaldecisions.sdk.occa.infostore.IInfoObjects;
9  import com.crystaldecisions.sdk.occa.infostore.IInfoStore;
10 import com.crystaldecisions.sdk.plugin.desktop.user.IUser;
11
12 public class CreateUser {
13     public static void main(String[] args) throws SDKException
14     {
15         ISessionMgr sessionManager = CrystalEnterprise.getSessionMgr();
16         IEnterpriseSession session = sessionManager.logon ("administrator",
   "xxxx", "192.168.56.102", "secEnterprise");
17
18         IInfoStore infoStore = (IInfoStore) session.getService
   ("","InfoStore");
19
20         IInfoObject financeGroup = (IInfoObject) infoStore.query("select si_id
   from ci_systemobjects where si_kind = 'usergroup' and si_name =
   'finance'").get(0);
21
22         IInfoObjects infoObjects = infoStore.newInfoObjectCollection();
23
24         IUser newUser = (IUser)infoObjects.add(IUser.KIND);
25
26         newUser.setTitle("Francine");
```

```
27          newUser.setFullName("Francine Fullworth");

28          newUser.setEmailAddress("francine@company.com");

29          newUser.setNewPassword("pAssWord");

30

31          newUser.getGroups().add(financeGroup.getID());

32

33          newUser.save();

34

35          System.out.println("Done!");

36          session.logoff();

37      }

38 }
```

Listing 11: The CreateUser program

In Listing 11 we are creating one new user, *Francine*. We will be adding Francine to the *Finance* user group, so we need to get that group's ID. We do this on line 20:

```
20          IInfoObject financeGroup = (IInfoObject) infoStore.query("select si_id
    from ci_systemobjects where si_kind = 'usergroup' and si_name =
    'finance'").get(0);
```

Note that we are being very trusting on this line, in that we are assuming that the Finance group exists. If it does not, the line will throw an exception, as we would be trying to perform a `get(0)` on an empty list.

We begin the new user creation process on line 22:

```
22          IInfoObjects infoObjects = infoStore.newInfoObjectCollection();

23

24          IUser newUser = (IUser)infoObjects.add(IUser.KIND);
```

We are not executing a CMS query, but rather creating a new, empty `IInfoObjects` collection on line 22. On line 24, we create the new user InfoObject by calling `IInfoObjects.add()`, and passing it the `SI_KIND` of the InfoObject that we want to create (*"User"*). This is the first step in InfoObject manipulation: similar to modifying and deleting, we are obtaining the newly-created InfoObject.

On lines 26-31, we set some properties as appropriate for Francine's user ID. This is the second step of InfoObject manipulation, setting properties.

On line 31, we add Francine to the *Finance* group, using the ID of the `financeGroup` object that we obtained earlier.

```
26          newUser.setTitle("Francine");

27          newUser.setFullName("Francine Fullworth");

28          newUser.setEmailAddress("francine@company.com");

29          newUser.setNewPassword("pAssWord");

30

31          newUser.getGroups().add(financeGroup.getID());
```

Finally, on line 33, we commit the transaction. At this point, the user ID is created, assigned to the *Finance* group, and available for Francine to log in with.

```
33          newUser.save();
```

In the above example, we set one common property (Title), and three IUser-specific properties. The properties that need to be set for newly-created InfoObjects vary by InfoObject kind. Some are mandatory, some optional, and others unnecessary or not allowed. We **could have** simply set the name property and not set values for the other properties. The *Francine* user ID would have been successfully created, but without a password for Francine to use to log in.

All InfoObjects have a parent InfoObject, and *most* newly-created InfoObject kinds will have a default parent. In the above example, we did not need to set the parent ID for the *Francine* user since all users are inherently assigned to the *Users* folder. The same would be true for creating user groups. Folders, on the other hand, are assigned to the root public folder (ID 23), unless assigned to a particular parent with setParentID().

The following code fragment creates a new universe folder named *Sales Universes*.

```
// Get the root-level Universes folder

        IInfoObject universeRoot = (IInfoObject) infoStore.query("select si_id from
ci_appobjects where si_cuid = '" + CeSecurityCUID.RootFolder.UNIVERSES + "'").get(0);


        IInfoObjects infoObjects = infoStore.newInfoObjectCollection();


        IInfoObject newFolder = infoObjects.add("Folder");

        newFolder.setTitle("Sales Universes");

        newFolder.setParentID(universeRoot.getID());

        newFolder.save();
```

Since there is nothing that differentiates a universe folder from a "regular" reports folder, there is nothing special that needs to be done other than to make our new folder a child (or descendant) of the root *Universes* folder.

Note that creating InfoObjects via IInfoObjects.add() only creates InfoObject metadata in the CMS repository. For users, groups, folders, and many others, this is all that needs to be done to create an InfoObject of this type. However, content, such as Web Intelligence documents, Crystal Reports, and Universes, **cannot** be created in this way. A source file (.wid, .unv, etc.) is necessary, which requires the appropriate client tool (or appropriate SDK) to create. That is, while you could create an InfoObject of kind Webi using the above methods, it would simply be a "shell" and would not function as a report.

Batch Processing

The examples so far in this chapter have used immediate commit transactions. InfoObjects are saved to the CMS one at a time via the IInfoObject.save() method for InfoObject creation and modification operations, and IInfoObject.deleteNow() for delete operations. An alternative to this is committing all InfoObjects in an IInfoObjects collection together, which is performed via the IInfoStore.commit() method.

To illustrate, we'll revisit Listing 7, in which we had set the *Description* property for all users in the *Finance* group. To adjust this program to use a batch commit, we just need to remove the infoObject.save() call on line 26 and add infoStore.commit(infoObjects) outside of the for() loop.

19	`IInfoObjects infoObjects = infoStore.query("select si_name,si_id from ci_systemobjects where children(\"si_name='usergroup-user'\", \"si_name='finance'\")");`
20	
21	`for(int x = 0;x < infoObjects.size(); x++)`
22	`{`
23	`IInfoObject infoObject = (IInfoObject)infoObjects.get(x);`
24	`System.out.println("Setting description for user: " + infoObject.getTitle());`
25	`infoObject.setDescription("Finance User");`
26	`}`
27	`InfoStore.commit(infoObjects);`
28	
29	`System.out.println("Done!");`
30	`session.logoff();`

The commit() call causes the SDK to invoke the CMS to perform any modifications made to the InfoObjects in the infoObjects collection (technically, any InfoObject in the collection that has been modified).

When this program is executed, it will perform exactly the same as the original in Listing 7.

Although there is no noticeable difference, the modification of all users was performed during the single `commit()` call on line 27, rather than individually.

The most notable difference between `IInfoObject.save()` and `IInfoStore.commit(IInfoObjects ios)` is how errors are handled. When using `IInfoObject.save()` (as the original Listing 7 does), the first occurrence of a failure will cause an exception – if unhandled, processing will stop at that point (if the exception is handled, then remaining InfoObjects can be processed). Any InfoObjects that were `save()`'d prior to the exception will already have been committed. When `commit()` is used, all of the InfoObject modifications are made together, and we can choose whether to do an *atomic* commit or a *non-atomic* commit. If an atomic commit is used, and any of the InfoObjects in the batch produce an error during the commit operation, the entire batch will fail and none of the InfoObject modifications in the batch will be committed to the CMS. If a non-atomic commit is used, and any InfoObjects produce an error, other InfoObjects in the batch will be committed to the CMS. This latter behavior (non-atomic commit) is the default for `IInfoStore.commit()`.

Let's look at an example in which we intentionally provoke a failure.

```
 1  package bosdkbook;
 2
 3  import com.crystaldecisions.sdk.exception.SDKException;
 4  import com.crystaldecisions.sdk.framework.CrystalEnterprise;
 5  import com.crystaldecisions.sdk.framework.IEnterpriseSession;
 6  import com.crystaldecisions.sdk.framework.ISessionMgr;
 7  import com.crystaldecisions.sdk.occa.infostore.IInfoObjects;
 8  import com.crystaldecisions.sdk.occa.infostore.IInfoStore;
 9  import com.crystaldecisions.sdk.plugin.desktop.user.IUser;
10
11
12  public class ProvokeError {
13      public static void main(String[] args) throws SDKException
14      {
15          ISessionMgr sessionManager = CrystalEnterprise.getSessionMgr();
16          IEnterpriseSession session = sessionManager.logon ("administrator",
     "xxxx", "192.168.56.102", "secEnterprise");
17
18          IInfoStore infoStore = (IInfoStore) session.getService ("","InfoStore");
19
20          IInfoObjects infoObjects = infoStore.query("select si_name,si_id from
```

```
     ci_systemobjects where si_name in ('fred','ephraim','sri','isabel')");
21
22          for(int x = 0;x < infoObjects.size(); x++)
23          {
24              IUser user = (IUser)infoObjects.get(x);
25              String userName = user.getTitle();
26              System.out.println("Got user: " + userName);
27
28              if(userName.equalsIgnoreCase("Fred"))
29                  user.setDescription("I am Fred");
30              else if(userName.equalsIgnoreCase("Ephraim"))
31                  user.getGroups().add(12);
32              else if(userName.equalsIgnoreCase("Isabel"))
33                  user.setTitle("Guest");
34              else if(userName.equalsIgnoreCase("Sri"))
35                  user.setDescription("I am Sri");
36          }
37
38          infoStore.commit(infoObjects);
39
40          System.out.println("Done!");
41          session.logoff();
42      }
43 }
```

Listing 12: The ProvokeError program

In Listing 12, we are modifying four user InfoObjects: *Fred, Isabel, Ephraim,* and *Sri*. The modifications that we make to *Fred* and *Sri* are successful (simply updating their *Descriptions*). The other two, however, fail: we are attempting to join Ephraim to a user group with an ID of 12 (ID 12 is a *user,* not a *user group),* and we are attempting to rename *Isabel* to *Guest,* which is the name of another user. When we execute this program, we get the following exception:

```
Exception in thread "main" com.crystaldecisions.sdk.exception.SDKBatchException: 2
exceptions occurred
Message for exception 1 : Setting the property SI_ADM_ADD_USERGROUPS_TO_USER of the
object named 'Ephraim' with id number 6356 failed because a constraint was violated.
The constraint failed for the object named 'Administrator' with id number 12 and the
object named 'Ephraim' with id number 6356 because of the following constraint: if
then SI_KIND = 'UserGroup'.
```

Message for exception 2 : Could not commit object 'Guest' because another object with
the same name and type already exists under object 'Users'. (FWB 00026)

The errors are pretty explicit, and we can understand the source of the problem. Although these two failed, the other two transactions <u>were applied successfully</u>. If we check the CMC, we will see that the descriptions for the *Fred* and *Sri* users were updated as intended in the program.

Note, however, that even with a non-atomic commit, if multiple changes are made to a one InfoObject, and one of those changes results in an error, none of the changes to **that InfoObject** are committed.

So, we can see that the default behavior of commit() is to apply the modifications for any that can be done successfully, while reporting an exception for those that failed. Sometimes this behavior (a non-atomic commit) is desirable, but not always. Fortunately, the commit() method offers some additional flexibility by way of some overloaded methods. The four ways of calling IInfoStore.commit() are:

---

void commit(IInfoObjects objects)

> Commits all changes in infoObjects to the CMS. If any individual InfoObjects fail, then those messages are reported together in a single exception. In the case of an error, any other successful InfoObject modifications in the batch will still be processed (no roll-back of the entire batch will occur).
>
> This call is equivalent to commit(infoObjects,false).

---

void commit(IInfoObjects infoObjects, boolean atomic)

> Commits all changes in infoObjects to the CMS. If any individual InfoObjects fail, then those messages are reported together in a single exception.
>
> If atomic is true, and any failures occur, then all changes are rolled back. If atomic is false, and any failures occur, then any other successful InfoObject modifications in the batch will still be processed (no roll-back of the entire batch will occur).

ICommitResult commit(IInfoObjects infoObjects, boolean atomic, CommitMode mode)

> Commits all changes in infoObjects to the CMS.
>
> If atomic is true, and any failures occur, then all changes are rolled back. If atomic is false, and any failures occur, then any other successful InfoObject modifications in the batch will still be processed (no roll-back

---

of the entire batch will occur).

If mode is equal to `CommitMode.LENIENT`, then certain missing relationships are allowed when committing; if mode is equal to `CommitMode.STRICT`, then missing relationships will cause an error.

Returns `ICommitResult`, which includes information regarding errors or warnings that occurred during the commit. No exception is thrown if there are failures.

```
ICommitResult commit(IInfoObjects infoObjects, boolean atomic, CommitMode mode,
                     java.lang.String renamePattern)
```

Commits all changes in `infoObjects` to the CMS. If any individual InfoObjects fail, then those messages are reported together in a single exception.

If `atomic` is true, and any failures occur, then all changes are rolled back. If `atomic` is false, and any failures occur, then the other InfoObjects in the batch will still be processed (no roll-back of the entire batch will occur).

If mode is equal to `CommitMode.LENIENT`, then certain missing relationships are allowed when committing; if mode is equal to `CommitMode.STRICT`, then missing relationships will cause an error.

If an object in the InfoObjects batch includes a change that results in a non-unique name in a folder, the InfoObject is renamed according to the `renamePattern` string.

Returns `ICommitResult`, which includes information regarding errors or warnings that occurred during the commit. No exception is thrown if there are failures.

Our previous example used the first syntax, which performs a non-atomic commit. If we instead wanted to perform an atomic commit, in which case the changes will only be applied if all individual operations are successful, we would use the second syntax, and pass true for the second parameter: commit(infoObjects,true).

So let's do that. We'll adjust our program to use this syntax. We'll also slightly change the descriptions that we're passing for *Fred* and *Sri*; otherwise, we can't be sure if the changes have been applied.

```
28          if(userName.equalsIgnoreCase("Fred"))
29              user.setDescription("I am still Fred");
30          else if(userName.equalsIgnoreCase("Ephraim"))
```

```
31          user.getGroups().add(12);
32       else if(userName.equalsIgnoreCase("Isabel"))
33          user.setTitle("Guest");
34       else if(userName.equalsIgnoreCase("Sri"))
35          user.setDescription("I am still Sri");
36    }
37
38    infoStore.commit(infoObjects,true);
```

We get a slightly different exception this time:

```
Exception in thread "main"
com.crystaldecisions.sdk.occa.infostore.internal.InfoStoreException: Setting the
property SI_ADM_ADD_USERGROUPS_TO_USER of the object named 'Ephraim' with id number
6356 failed because a constraint was violated. The constraint failed for the object
named 'Administrator' with id number 12 and the object named 'Ephraim' with id number
6356 because of the following constraint: if  then SI_KIND = 'UserGroup'.

cause:com.crystaldecisions.enterprise.ocaframework.idl.OCA.oca_abuse:
IDL:img.seagatesoftware.com/OCA/oca_abuse:3.2
detail:Setting the property SI_ADM_ADD_USERGROUPS_TO_USER of the object named
'Ephraim' with id number 6356 failed because a constraint was violated. The constraint
failed for the object named 'Administrator' with id number 12 and the object named
'Ephraim' with id number 6356 because of the following constraint: if  then SI_KIND =
'UserGroup'.

The server supplied the following details: Relationship constraint violated.
```

Not only is this an `InfoStoreException` rather than an `SDKBatchException`, but the exception only reported the first error that occurred – attempting to assign Ephraim to a non-existent group. The commit process stopped when it got to this error and did not apply any of the modifications. If we check the CMC now, we'll see that the descriptions for Fred and Sri are unchanged. This proves that the call to `commit()` did **not** apply any of the modifications in the `infoObjects` collection.

So far, we've covered three ways of committing transactions:

- Using `IInfoObject.save()`, which will cause the program to fail at the first instance of a failure (or skip the error if the `save()` call is wrapped in a `try/catch` block).

- Using `IInfoStore.commit(IInfoObjects infoObjects)`, which will commit all InfoObjects except those that fail.

- Using `IInfoStore.commit(IInfoObjects infoObjects,true)`, which will commit all operations unless any fail, in which case none are committed.

The decision of which method to use depends on the situation – none is inherently better or worse than the other. Consider an example in which several reports are to be moved from one folder to another. If the program uses individual `save()` operations, and one of the reports in the bunch cannot be moved for some reason, then processing will fail at that point. Any reports that were processed prior to that one will have been moved successfully, while that one report and all subsequent reports will remain in the original folder.

Alternatively, if the `IInfoObject.save()`, is wrapped in a `try/catch` block (with appropriate failure logging, of course), then processing will continue while skipping the individual reports that failed. All of the reports are moved *except* those that failed.

If, instead, the program commits all of the report moves together via `IInfoStore.commit()`, passing `true` for the `atomic` parameter, then the entire operation will fail because of the failure of the one report. The `commit()` call will throw an exception, and none of the reports are moved.

In this example, we would probably want the last option, an atomic `commit()`. If some reports were moved, but others weren't, it would likely cause confusion on the part of users. Better to let the entire operation fail, resolve the issue, and re-execute to move all of the reports at once.

A few more examples:

- A program that creates user accounts based on an input file or an external database. In this case, `IInfoObject.save()` (with `try/catch`), or a non-atomic `commit()` is likely the best option. If any of the individual user accounts fail to be created, we would still want the remaining accounts created.

- A program that archives (moves) the oldest instance of all reports in a folder. This would be a good candidate for `IInfoStore.commit(IInfoObjects ios,true)`. If these transactions were saved individually with `IInfoObject.save()`, and a failure occurred partway through, then the result would be some reports archived while others were not. If the problem was corrected and the program re-run, then the oldest instance of all reports would be archived, even the ones that were previously successful. Better to let the entire batch fail, and then re-run after the issue is resolved.

- An interactive web application that enables users to select a number of reports, then submits all to be scheduled. This choice is less obvious and would require further consideration. Would it be better to fail the entire attempt and have the user try again? Or run the ones that are successful and notify the user of the individual reports that failed?

You likely noticed that there is an overlap between the `IInfoObject.save()` and `IInfoStore.commt()` processes, so let's compare them:

IInfoObject.save() (with try/catch):

- Errors are reported as InfoObjects are saved
- Can not be used to do an atomic commit

Non-Atomic IInfoStore.commit(IInfoObjects infoObjects,false)

- All errors are reported in a single exception

- Successful modifications are applied; unsuccessful modifications are reported as failed

Atomic IInfoStore.commit(IInfoObjects infoObjects,true)

- Only first error in batch is reported in exception
- No modifications are applied in the event of a failure of any individual operation.

The third syntax of `commit()` provides additional advanced functionality. This method introduces the `CommitMode` parameter and the `ICommitResult` return type.

The `CommitMode` parameter has two possible values:

`CommitMode.STRICT`

`CommitMode.LENIENT`

The STRICT mode is used implicitly when the first two methods of `commit()` that we have used. The LENIENT mode has a very specific use: it will allow for an InfoObject to be committed even if it contains a relationship to another object that does not exist. That specific change is not made to the InfoObject, but any other changes are committed (the invalid relationship attempt is reported as a *warning*).

The `ICommitResult` object that's returned from these methods includes the status results of each InfoObject commit operation that resulted in a warning or error. Thus, commit errors do not cause the `commit()` call to throw an exception – the contents of the `ICommitResult` object need to be checked to determine if any failures or warnings occurred.

To illustrate both `ICommitResult` and `CommitMode`, we'll replace lines 22-41 with the following:

```
25          for(int x = 0;x < infoObjects.size(); x++)
26          {
27              IUser user = (IUser)infoObjects.get(x);
28              String userName = user.getTitle();
29              System.out.println("Got user: " + userName);
30
31              if(userName.equalsIgnoreCase("Fred"))
32                  user.setDescription("I am still Fred");
33              else if(userName.equalsIgnoreCase("Ephraim"))
34              {
35                  user.getGroups().add(99999);
36                  user.setDescription("I am Ephraim");
37              }
38              else if(userName.equalsIgnoreCase("Isabel"))
39                  user.setTitle("Guest");
```

```
40              else if(userName.equalsIgnoreCase("Sri"))

41                  user.setDescription("I am still Sri");

42          }

43

44      ICommitResult commitResult =
    infoStore.commit(infoObjects,false,CommitMode.LENIENT);

45      System.out.println("Errors:");

46      for(int x = 0; x<commitResult.getErrors().size();x++)

47      {

48          ICommitResultInfo resultInfo = (ICommitResultInfo)
    commitResult.getErrors().get(x);

49          System.out.println("CMS Message: " + resultInfo.getCMSMessage());

50      }

51

52      System.out.println("Warnings:");

53      for(int x = 0; x<commitResult.getWarnings().size();x++)

54      {

55          ICommitResultInfo resultInfo = (ICommitResultInfo)
    commitResult.getWarnings().get(x);

56          System.out.println("CMS Message: " + resultInfo.getCMSMessage());

57      }

58

59      System.out.println("Done!");

60      session.logoff();
```

We've made the following changes:

- We're now attempting to add Ephraim to object 99999, a non-existent InfoObject.

- We're also updating Ephraim's Description property.

- We're calling infoStore.commit(infoObjects,false,CommitMode.LENIENT).

- We display the errors and warnings in ICommitResult.

Executing the program now produces the following result:

```
Got user: Fred
Got user: Sri
Got user: Ephraim
Got user: Isabel
Errors:
CMS Message: Trying to create an object with duplicate name. Id = 6374
```

```
Warnings:
CMS Message: Objects being added to relation does not exist
Done!
```

The attempt to rename *Isabel* to *Guest* has still failed and is reported to us as "Trying to create an object with duplicate name. Id = 6374".

The attempt to add Ephraim to group 9999 produces a warning rather than an error. However, If we check the CMC, we will see that Ephraim's description has been updated. Had we used `CommitMode.STRICT`, the group assignment would have produced an error, and the description would not have been updated.

The fourth syntax of `commit()` allows for automatic renaming of objects when a name collision occurs (meaning that an InfoObject is renamed or moved into a folder, resulting in two InfoObjects in the same folder with the same name). The fourth parameter, `renamePattern`, is a `String` that defines how these InfoObjects should be renamed. The pattern must include "%1", which is replaced with the desired name, and "%2" which is replaced with an incremental value. For example, "Copy %2 of %1". We'll make this change to the commit() call in our program:

```
44        ICommitResult commitResult =
   infoStore.commit(infoObjects,false,CommitMode.LENIENT,"Copy %2 of %1");
```

We'll also add two lines to display the rename results from `ICommitResults`:

```
60        for(IRenameRecord renameResult : commitResult.getRenameResults())
61          System.out.println("Rename: " + renameResult.getOldName() + " has been
   renamed to " + renameResult.getNewName());
```

Executing the program now produces:

```
Got user: Fred
Got user: Sri
Got user: Ephraim
Got user: Isabel
Errors:
Warnings:
CMS Message: Objects being added to relation does not exist
Rename: Guest has been renamed to Copy 1 of Guest
Done!
```

If we check the CMC, we will confirm that *Isabel* has in fact been renamed to *Copy 1 of Guest*.

Batch Deletions

InfoObjects can be deleted in batch using `commit()`. In order to delete InfoObjects from the CMS, they must be deleted from the `IInfoObjects` collection that they are in. Then, the `IInfObjects` collection is committed in the same manner as above.

In Listing 10, we purged the Recycle Bin folder using immediate deletes. We can easily convert that to an atomic batch deletion with the following changes:

```
22      for(Object o : infoObjects)
23      {
24          IInfoObject infoObject = (IInfoObject)o;
25          System.out.println("Deleting: " + infoObject.getTitle());
26          infoObjects.delete(infoObject);
27      }
28      infoStore.commit(infoObjects,true);
```

When InfoObjects are deleted via `IInfoObjects.delete(IInfoObject)`, they are not immediately removed from the `IInfoObjects` collection, but rather flagged for deletion. When `IInfostore.commit()` is called, the InfoObjects are deleted from the CMS.

Since `IInfoObjects` extends `java.util.List`, it implements the `remove(int x)` method. Be careful not to confuse this with the `delete(IInfoObject infoObject)` method described above – `remove(int x)` will remove the specified object from the `IInfoObjects` collection, but will **not** cause the associated InfoObject to be deleted from the CMS. To delete InfoObjects from the CMS, you must use the `delete(IInfoObject infoObject)` method.

Miscellaneous batch processing topics:

- `IInfoStore.commit(IInfoObjects infoObjects)` can be called repeatedly for a single `IInfoObjects` collection; only those InfoObjects in the collection that are "dirty" are committed to the CMS. In fact, you may see code such as:

```
IInfoObjects infoObjects = infoStore.query("...");
for(int x = 0;x < infoObjects.size(); x++)
{
    IInfoObject io = infoObjects.get(0);
    …
    infoStore.commit(infoObjects);
}
```

  Although this code works just fine, it would be more correct to replace the `commit()` call with `io.save()`, or move the commit to outside of the `for` loop, where it will be called once for the `IInfoObjects` collection.

- A batch commit can include more than one type of operation; a single `IInfoObjects` collection could include modified InfoObjects, deleted InfoObjects, and newly-created InfoObjects.

- The three steps of InfoObject manipulation (Initiation, Property Changes, Commit) apply to batch processing as well as immediate processing. The following table includes all steps for each operation.

	Creation	Modification	Deletion
Initiation	New IInfoObject created via `IInfoObjects.add()`	Desired InfoObject(s) retrieved into `IInfoObjects` collection via `IInfoStore.query()`	
Property Changes	InfoObject properties are set/changed as needed		Flagged for deletion via `IInfoObjects.delete( IInfoObject infoObject)`
Commit (immediate)	InfoObject is saved via `IInfoObject.save()`		InfoObject is deleted via `IInfoObject.deleteNow()`
Commit (batch)	Batch mode: All InfoObjects in IInfoObjects collection committed via `IInfoStore.commit(IInfoObjects)`		

Safety

Hopefully, this chapter has expressed the power and capabilities that the Platform SDK provides. With that power comes the ability to do a significant amount of damage to a system if done carelessly. We have a few suggestions for reducing the risk of doing damage with the Platform SDK. Of course, standard software quality mechanisms should be employed, such as design reviews/code reviews, unit testing, etc. The following suggestions are specific to the Platform SDK.

Pay very close attention to any CMS queries embedded in your programs. The CMS queries define the scope of InfoObjects that may be altered by the code, so ensuring that the queries return the right result is important.

Consider possible future changes and regular activity in the system. You are tasked with creating a process to automatically purge all instances of a WebI report named *Weekly Sales Actuals* in a public folder. So you create a program to do this, which includes the following CMS query to retrieve the report:

```
select si_id from ci_infoobjects where si_name = 'weekly sales actuals'
```

This works perfectly in testing and runs successfully in production. For a while. Shortly thereafter you get a frantic call from a user wondering why all of the instances in one of her personal reports have disappeared. Of course, she had named her report *Weekly Sales Actuals*.

Use an appropriate method for identifying InfoObjects in CMS queries, to mitigate this kind of issue. There are different methods for doing this:

- Using InfoObject IDs (SI_ID) or CUIDs is the most accurate method to return a unique InfoObject, and will continue to be valid if the target InfoObjects are renamed or moved. CUIDs are also consistent when InfoObjects are migrated to a different CMS, or when the environment is upgraded to a new version.

- Certain types of InfoObjects, in particular users and user groups, are guaranteed to be unique within a CMS[83]. So, querying for SI_KIND = 'user' and SI_NAME = 'fred' will always return only one InfoObject.

- For most other kinds of InfoObjects, such as reports, universes, events, etc., querying by name and kind is not sufficient to guarantee a unique result. The query must also include a condition on the InfoObject's parent folder.

Format CMS queries in programs. Making code readable is a known contributor to quality code, and the same holds true for CMS queries. Consider the following lines:

```
String cmsQuery="select si_name,si_id,si_update_ts from
ci_infoobjects where children(\"si_name='folder
hierarchy'\",\"si_name = 'recycle bin' and si_parentid = 23\") and
(si_keyword like '%purge' or si_update_ts >= '2016-08-01')";
```

```
String cmsQuery=
    "select si_name,si_id,si_update_ts " +
    " from ci_infoobjects " +
    " where children(" +
            \"si_name='folder hierarchy'\"," +
            \"si_name='recycle bin' " +
                and si_parentid = 23\") " +
    " and (si_keyword like '%purge' " +
            or si_update_ts >= '2016-08-01')";
```

The second version is much easier to read and make changes to, if necessary.

As an alternative to coding CMS queries directly into code, you may consider moving them to a common library class or to a resource file.

Create backups whenever possible, and in particular in programs that delete InfoObjects. Creating a rolling backup directory of deleted or modified InfoObjects should not occupy a significant amount of space, even for a large environment.

Create sanity checks in the logic. Consider a program that deletes users IDs when there is no matching user name in a certain database table. If the load process of that table goes awry and the table is emptied, then the SDK program will dutifully delete all users from the SAP BusinessObjects system. A sanity check inside the program would help – if the database table contains fewer than a certain number of rows, say 1,000, then the program will not continue.

Comment out calls to save(), deleteNow(), and commit() during initial development, and instead add System.out.println() calls to indicate that the call would have been made. This

---

83 In theory, anyway. There is a small possibility that a corruption can result in two User InfoObjects having the same name. This is very rare.

will allow you to safely execute and debug the program while ensuring that no actual changes are being made.

Chapter Review

- The SDK enables a significant amount of automation in an SAP BusinessObjects environment, but this automation can be dangerous. It is critical for the programmer to aware of the possible impacts that the programs can have.

- Setting an InfoObject's properties can be done via setter methods, getter methods (for lists, sets, etc.), or `IInfoObject.properties()`. Using setters/getters is the preferred method.

- Manipulation of InfoObjects involves three steps: Obtaining an `IInfoObject`, modifying the `IInfoObject`, and committing the transactions.

- Modifying or deleting InfoObjects requires that the associated `IInfoObject` objects be obtained via a CMS query (`IInfoStore.query()`); creating a new InfoObject requires the creation of a new IInfoObject via `IInfoObjects.add()`.

- Transactions can be committed immediately for a specific InfoObject by using `IInfoObject.save()` or `IInfoObject.deleteNow()`.

- Batch processing enables more control over the handing of InfoObjects when there are failures; this is accomplished with the overloaded `IInfoStore.commit()` methods.

Quiz

1. Which access right is required in order to make a change to an InfoObject?

    a) View

    b) Edit

    c) Delete

    d) View on Demand

    e) Full Control

2. A modified InfoObject is persisted to the CMS:

    a) Immediately

    b) When `IInfoObject.save()` is called

    c) When `IInfoStore.commit()` is called

    d) None of the above

3. Which method is used to change the owner of an InfoObject?

    a) `IInfoObject.setOwner()`

    b) `IInfoObject.setOwnerID()`

    c) Manually modify the SI_OWNER property with `IInfoObject.properties()`.

    d) Manually modify the SI_OWNERID property with `IInfoObject.properties()`.

4. Which of the following InfoObject manipulation actions require a CMS query to be executed first?

    a) Modifying

    b) Deleting

    c) Creating

5. True/False: It is always necessary to assign a parent ID to an InfoObject upon creation.

6. What happens when a failure occurs during a non-atomic commit?

    a) All InfoObjects that were successfully processed prior to the failure are saved

    b) All InfoObjects other than those that failed are saved

    c) No InfoObjects are saved

Answers on page 673.

Chapter 13 - The IEnterpriseSession and IInfoStore Interfaces

We have touched on the IEnterpriseSession and IInfoStore interfaces in the past few chapters, mostly just to log in the CMS and execute queries. In this chapter, we will cover some of the additional functionality provided by these interfaces.

IEnterpriseSession

In addition to enabling access to the InfoStore, IEnterpriseSession also provides information on the system, session, and active user. Its (non-deprecated) methods are:

Package com.crystaldecisions.sdk.framework
Interface _IEnterpriseSession_

String[]	getActiveClusterMembers()
	Retrieves a list of all active nodes in the cluster.
IClusterInformation	getClusterInformation()
	Retrieves an IClusterInformation object, containing additional details about the cluster settings.
String[]	getClusterMembers()
	Retrieves a list of all nodes in the cluster.
String	getClusterName()
	Retrieves the name of the cluster.
String	getCMSName()
	Retrieves the name of the CMS that the current session is connected to.
Locale	getEffectivePreferredViewingLocale()
	Retrieves the effective preferred viewing locale for this session.
EnterpriseVersion	getEnterpriseVersionEx()
	Retrieves an EnterpriseVersion object, containing the exact version of the installed SAP BusinessObjects software. The toString() method of EnterpriseVersion returns the common dotted version number (ex. "14.2.0.0" for BI4.2).
Locale	getLocale()
void	setLocale(Locale locale)

	Retrieves/sets the locale to be used by this session.
ILogonTokenMgr	getLogonTokenMgr()
	Retrieves an ILogonTokenMgr object, which is used to create serialized logon tokens.
IPluginMgr	getPluginManager()
	Retrieves an IPluginMgr object, which is used to access the various installed plugins in the system.
ISecurityInfoMgr	getSecurityInfoMgr()
	Retrieves an ISecurityInfoMgr object, which is used to access and manage caching of security rights.
String	getSerializedSession()
	Retrieves the current session ID, as a String.
String[]	getServerNames()
	Retrieves a list of all processing servers in the cluster.
Object	getService(String serviceName)
	Retrieves a handle to a service (ex. "InfoStore").
Object	getService(String serverName,String serviceName)
	Retrieves a handle to a service (ex. "InfoStore"), hosted by the specified server. If serverName is blank, the current CMS is used.
String[]	getServiceNames(String serverName,int type)
	Retrieves a list of services hosted by a specified server. If type is 0, then all hosted services are retrieved; if 1, then only administrative services are retrieved.
String	getSessionCUID()
	Retrieves the CUID of the active session.
IProperties	getSystemInfoProperties()
	Retrieves an IProperties object, containing a list of the capabilities of the installed system.
Locale	getSystemLocale()
void	setSystemLocale(Locale locale)
	Retrieves/sets the preferred viewing locale for this session.
IUserInfo	getUserInfo()
	Retrieves an IUserInfo object, containing information about the currently active user.

boolean	isUserDefaultLocale()
void	setUserDefaultLocale()
	Retrieves/sets whether the currently active locale is the default locale.
void	logoff()
	Ends the current session.

Class/Interface 5: IEnterpriseSession

Most of the methods of IEnterpriseSession are simple accessors for system and session info, but one that we'll examine more closely is getUserInfo(). This method returns an IUserInfo object, which contains lots of useful information about the currently active user. The methods of IUserInfo are:

Package com.crystaldecisions.sdk.occa.security
Interface <u>IUserInfo</u>

void	associateWithPrincipal(ITrustedPrincipal credential)
	Associates a Trusted Authentication credential with this user.
String	getAuthenMethod()
	Retrieves the authentication method used when this session was created. Example: secEnterprise
Locale	getLocale()
void	setLocale(Locale locale)
	Retrieves/sets the user's locale.
long	getPasswordExpiry()
	Retrieves the number of days until the user's password expires. A value of 36500 indicates a non-expiring password.
void	setPassword(String oldPassword,String newPassword)
	Changes the user's password. The user's existing password must be provided in order for the password change to be successful.
int	getPersonalObjectID(String kind)
	Retrieves the InfoObject ID of the user's favorites folder, inbox, or top-level personal category. The possible values of kind are FavoritesFolder, Inbox, PersonalCategory.
String	getProfileString(String name)
void	setProfileString(String name,String value)
	Retrieves/sets a profile string by name.

String	`getProfileString(String name,boolean isRefresh)`
	Retrieves/sets a profile string by name. If `isRefresh` is true, then the profile string is retrieved directly from the CMS, and not from the local cache.
Locale	`getPreferredViewingLocale()`
void	`removePreferredViewingLocale()`
void	`setPreferredViewingLocale(Locale locale)`
	Retrieves, sets to default, or sets the user's preferred viewing locale
String	`getSecondaryCredentialEx(String name)`
void	`setSecondaryCredentialEx(String name,String value)`
	Retrieves/sets a secondary credential (ex. database credentials)
int	`getTenantID()`
	Retrieves the InfoObject ID of the tenant that the user is associated with. The value is 0 if the user is not associated with a tenant.
String	`getUserCUID()`
	Retrieves the user's CUID.
String	`getUserDesc()`
	Retrieves the user's description.
boolean	`isUserDefaultLocale()`
void	`setUserDefaultLocale()`
	Retrieves/sets whether the user uses the default locale.
int	`getUserID()`
	Retrieves the user's InfoObject ID.
String	`getUserName()`
	Retrieves the user's name.
TimeZone	`getTimeZone()`
void	`setTimeZone(TimeZone value)`
	Retrieves/sets the user's time zone.

Class/Interface 6: IUserInfo

Several of the methods in `IUserInfo` are redundant with the `IUser` interface. We will cover password methods on page 387 and profiles / secondary credentials on page 387. It's worth noting that `IUser` contains a lot more user info, but for quickly getting information about the current user, this is a better approach. This is because an `IUserInfo` object can be obtained from IEnterpriseSession with one call, whereas getting the current user's `IUser` object would necessitate a new CMS query. Once we get an `IEnterpriseSession` object, we can retrieve the current user name via:

```
session.getUserInfo().getUserName();
```

The `getPersonalObjectID()` method of `IUserInfo` returns the InfoObject ID of the active user's favorites folder, inbox, or top-level personal category[84]. The method expects a `String` value equal to the `SI_KIND` of the desired InfoObject, for example:

```
session.getUserInfo().getPersonalObjectID(IFolder.FAVORITESFOLDER_KIND);
```

In the following code snippet, we display some of the information available from `IEnterpriseSession` and `IUserInfo`:

```
IEnterpriseSession session = sessionManager.logon ("administrator", "xxxx",
"192.168.56.102", "secEnterprise");


// Display active nodes in cluster

System.out.println("Active nodes:");

for(String s : session.getActiveClusterMembers())

    System.out.println(s);


// Display all nodes in cluster

System.out.println("\nAll nodes:");

for(String s : session.getClusterMembers())

    System.out.println(s);


// Display cluster name

System.out.println("\nCluster name: " + session.getClusterName());


// Display current CMS

System.out.println("\nCMS: " + session.getCMSName());


// Display current version

System.out.println("\nBOE version: " + session.getEnterpriseVersionEx());


IUserInfo userInfo = session.getUserInfo();


// Display user name / ID
```

---

84 The `IInfoStore` interface (covered next) enables access to the actual InfoObjects, and not just the IDs.

```
System.out.println("\nUser name: " + userInfo.getUserName());


// Display authentication method:

System.out.println("Logon authentication method: " + userInfo.getAuthenMethod());


// Display password expiry

System.out.println("Days till password change: " + userInfo.getPasswordExpiry());


// Display my favorites folder ID

System.out.println("My favorites folder: " +
userInfo.getPersonalObjectID(IFolder.FAVORITESFOLDER_KIND));


// Display my inbox ID

System.out.println("My inbox: " + userInfo.getPersonalObjectID(IInbox.KIND));


// Display my personal category ID

System.out.println("My inbox: " +
userInfo.getPersonalObjectID(ICategory.PERSONALCATEGORY_KIND));
```

In our test system the above program generated the following output:

```
Active nodes:
osboxes:6400

All nodes:
osboxes:6400

Cluster name: @osboxes

CMS: osboxes:6400

BOE version: 14.2.0.0

User name: Administrator
Logon authentication method: secEnterprise
Days till password change: 36500
My favorites folder: 4568
My inbox: 4570
My inbox: 4569
```

IInfoStore

In the preceding chapters, we described the `newInfoObjectCollection()`, `query()` and `commit()` methods of `IInfoStore`; there are many other methods that this interface provides:

Package *com.crystaldecisions.sdk.occa.infostore*
Interface <u>IInfoStore</u>

InfoObjects management

void	`commit(IInfoObjects objects)`
	Commits all changes in `infoObjects` to the CMS. If any individual InfoObjects fail, then those messages are reported together in a single exception. In the case of an error, remaining InfoObjects in the batch will still be processed (no roll-back of the entire batch will occur).
	This call is equivalent to `commit(infoObjects,false)`.
void	`commit(IInfoObjects infoObjects, boolean atomic)`
	Commits all changes in `infoObjects` to the CMS. If any individual InfoObjects fail, then those messages are reported together in a single exception.
	If `atomic` is true, and any failures occur, then all changes are rolled back. If `atomic` is false, and any failures occur, then the other InfoObjects in the batch will still be processed (no roll-back of the entire batch will occur).
ICommitResult	`commit(IInfoObjects infoObjects, boolean atomic, CommitMode mode)`
	Commits all changes in `infoObjects` to the CMS. If any individual InfoObjects fail, then those messages are reported together in a single exception.
	If `atomic` is true, and any failures occur, then all changes are rolled back. If `atomic` is false, and any failures occur, then the other InfoObjects in the batch will still be processed (no roll-back of the entire batch will occur).
	If `mode` is equal to `CommitMode.LENIENT`, then certain missing relationships are allowed when committing; if mode is equal to `CommitMode.STRICT`, then missing relationships will cause an error.
	Returns `ICommitResult`, which includes information regarding errors or warnings that occurred during the commit.
ICommitResult	`commit(IInfoObjects infoObjects, boolean atomic, CommitMode mode, java.lang.String renamePattern)`

	Commits all changes in `infoObjects` to the CMS. If any individual InfoObjects fail, then those messages are reported together in a single exception. If `atomic` is true, and any failures occur, then all changes are rolled back. If `atomic` is false, and any failures occur, then the other InfoObjects in the batch will still be processed (no roll-back of the entire batch will occur). If `mode` is equal to `CommitMode.LENIENT`, then certain missing relationships are allowed when committing; if `mode` is equal to `CommitMode.STRICT`, then missing relationships will cause an error. If an object in the infoObjects batch includes a change that results in a non-unique name in a folder, the InfoObject are renamed according to the `renamePattern` string. Returns `ICommitResult`, which includes information regarding errors or warnings that occurred during the commit.
void	`deliverToInbox(IInfoObjects objects)`
	Sends a copy of each object in `objects` to the specified BI inboxes.
int	`getBatchExpiryTimeSeconds()`
void	`setBatchExpiryTimeSeconds(int batchExpiryTimeSeconds)`
	Retrieves/sets the duration (in seconds) that the commit operation can process before timing out.
IInfoObjects	`newInfoObjectCollection()`
	Creates a new, empty `IInfoObjects` collection.
IProperties	`newPropertyCollection()`
	Creates a new, empty property bag.
void	`schedule(IInfoObjects objects)`
	Create a new scheduled instance for each InfoObject in `objects`.
void	`sendTo(IInfoObjects objects)`
	Sends a copy of each object in `objects` to the specified destination.

CMS querying

ICMSQuery	`createCMSQuery(String initQuery)`
	Create a new `ICMSQuery` object using the provided CMS query SQL.
ICMSQuery	`createCMSQuery(String initQuery,boolean maintainTopN)`

	Create a new `ICMSQuery` object using the provided CMS query SQL. If `maintainTopN` is true, then any "TOP M-N" expression in the provided query will not be overridden.
`IInfoObjects`	`find(int propertySet,SearchPattern searchPattern,SortType sortType)`
	Creates and executes a CMS query that returns: • the properties identified by `propertySet`, • for the InfoObjects matching the criteria in `sarchPattern`, • ordered according to `sortType`
`IPageResult`	`getPagingQuery(String uri,PagingQueryOptions options)`
	Executes a CMS path query, returning the retrieved objects in an `IPageResult`.
`IStatelessPageInfo`	`getStatelessPageInfo(String uri,PagingQueryOptions options)`
	Converts a URI query into a standard CMS SQL query.
`IStreaminfQuery`	`getStreamingQuery(String query)`
	Executes the CMS query specified by `query`, and returns an `IStreamingQuery` object. The `IStreamingQuery` object can then be used to retrieve batches of `IInfoObjects` collections containing the result of the query.
`ICategoryPager`	`getTopCategories()`
	Creates and executes a CMS query that returns all categories. The result is returned in an `ICategoryPager` object. Note that the name of this method is misleading – it returns *all* categories.
`ICategoryPager`	`getTopCategories(int propertySet,SearchPattern searchPattern,SortType sortType)`
	Creates and executes a CMS query that returns: • the properties identified by `propertySet`, • for all categories matching the criteria in `sarchPattern`, • ordered according to `sortType` The result is returned in an `ICategoryPager` object. Note that the name of this method is misleading – it returns *all* categories.
`IFolderPager`	`getTopFolders()`

	Creates and executes a CMS query that returns all top-level public folders. The result is returned in an `IFolderPager` object.
`IFolderPager`	`getTopFolders(int propertySet,SearchPattern searchPattern,SortType sortType)`
	Creates and executes a CMS query that returns: • the properties identified by `propertySet`, • for all top-level public folders matching the criteria in `sarchPattern`, • ordered according to `sortType` The result is returned in an `IFolderPager` object.
`IInfoObjects`	`query(String query)`
	Executes the provided CMS query and returns the results in an `IInfoObjects` collection.
`IInfoObjects`	`query(ICMSQuery query)`
	Executes the CMS query generated from the settings of the provided `ICMSQuery` object, and returns the results in an `IInfoObjects` collection.
`IInfoObjects[]`	`query(String[] queries)`
	Consecutively executes a batch of CMS queries, and returns the result of each query in an array of `IInfoObjects` objects.
Session/User info	
`IFolder`	`getMyFavoritesFolder()`
	Retrieves the current user's favorites folder, as an `IFolder` object.
`IInbox`	`getMyInbox()`
	Retrieves the current user's inbox, as an `IInbox` object.
`ICategory`	`getMyPersonalCategory()`
	Retrieves the current user's top-level personal category, as an `ICategory` object.
`IPluginMgr`	`getPluginMgr()`
	Retrieves an `IPluginMgr` object, which is used to obtain information on plugins installed in the system.
`int`	`getSesstionFolderID()`
	Retrieves the InfoObject ID of this session's temporary folder.

The `schedule()`, `deliverToInbox()`, and `sendTo()` methods are covered in Chapter 17 - Scheduling.

There are three handy methods that return the current user's favorites folder, inbox, and top-level personal category: `getMyFavoritesFolder()`, `getMyInbox()`, and `getMyPersonalCategory()`. Note that the returned objects are the actual folder/category InfoObjects and not just the ID.

Advanced CMS Querying

We have used the `IInfoStore.query()` method extensively in the preceding chapters. This method is sufficient for most CMS querying needs, but there are other `IInfoStore` methods that provide additional functionality.

Most of the additional functionality of these methods pertains to paging of query results. Paging is an important consideration when working with CMS queries that can return very large result sets. What constitutes "very large" will differ based on each environment's resources and content, and so there are no hard-and-fast rules concerning when paging is necessary and the limits to use. As with the management of any other memory-intensive process, some trial-and-error may be required to nail down the most efficient and effective settings.

For CMS querying specifically, we must consider not only the number of rows that a query produces but also the number and size of the returned properties (the "width" of the query result). A query that returns only the `SI_ID` property may comfortably return 100,000 records without any negative impacts. But a query that returns all properties ("`SELECT *`") may cause performance impacts with much fewer records returned.

Streaming Queries

The `query(String query)` method returns all objects selected in the query into a single `IInfoObjects` collection. When the result includes a large number of result objects and a large number of properties (ex. `select * from CI_INFOOBJECTS`), the size of the returned `IInfoObjects` may be huge. One solution to this problem is to use a streaming query. Streaming queries allow for the results to be retrieved in batches of `IInfoObjects` objects; each batch may be processed before proceeding to the next, thereby avoiding the need to retrieve all at once.

The number of InfoObjects returned in each streaming batch is determined by the CMS based on the amount of data in the batch, and not just the number of InfoObjects. So, the number of InfoObjects per batch can be different within one query result set.

Let's look at a sample use of streaming queries:

```
1  package bosdkbook;
2
3  import com.crystaldecisions.sdk.framework.CrystalEnterprise;
4  import com.crystaldecisions.sdk.framework.IEnterpriseSession;
5  import com.crystaldecisions.sdk.framework.ISessionMgr;
6  import com.crystaldecisions.sdk.occa.infostore.IInfoObjects;
7  import com.crystaldecisions.sdk.occa.infostore.IInfoStore;
8  import com.crystaldecisions.sdk.occa.infostore.IStreamingQuery;
9
10 public class StreamingQuery
11 {
12     public static void main(String[] args) throws Exception
13     {
14         ISessionMgr sessionManager = CrystalEnterprise.getSessionMgr();
15         IEnterpriseSession session = sessionManager.logon ("administrator",
   "xxxx", "192.168.56.102", "secEnterprise");
16
17         IInfoStore infoStore = (IInfoStore) session.getService ("","InfoStore");
18
19         IStreamingQuery streamingQuery = infoStore.getStreamingQuery("select *
   from ci_infoobjects,ci_appobjects,ci_systemobjects");
20
21         while(streamingQuery.hasNext())
22         {
23             IInfoObjects ios = streamingQuery.next();
24             System.out.println(ios.size());
25         }
26         streamingQuery.close();
27     }
28 }
```

Listing 13: The StreamingQuery program

In Listing 13, we are executing a query that returns a very large result. We have not used a "TOP N" expression in the query, so the result will be no more than 1,000 objects. However, we are requesting all properties (select *), and so we expect a large result set.

When we execute *StreamingQuery*, we get the following result:

```
125
166
114
157
123
113
202
```

The numbers indicate the number of objects retrieved in each batch. In our case, the query produced seven batches, with sizes between 114 and 202 objects each. If we change the query to:

```
19        IStreamingQuery streamingQuery = infoStore.getStreamingQuery("select
   si_id from ci_infoobjects,ci_appobjects,ci_systemobjects");
```

then we get:

```
1000
```

Since we are only requesting a single property, all 1,000 objects fit within a single batch.

Compared to the other batching methods, streaming queries provide a quick, easily configurable method for processing large CMS query results.

Paging Queries & URI Queries

Another method for dealing with large result sets is *paging queries*. With paging queries, a single query produces one or more pages of results, with each page containing a limited number of InfoObjects. Unlike streaming queries, paging queries work by generating a set of standard CMS SQL statements. Each SQL statement represents a page and can be passed to `IInfoStore.query()` for execution.

Paging queries take a URI query as input (see Chapter 5), and produce standard CMS query SQL as output.

There are two methods involved in this process: `IInfoStore.getPagingQuery()`, which renders a URI query statement into one or more sub-statements, and `IInfoStore.getStatelessPageInfo()`, which translates the generated sub-statements into CMS query SQL syntax.

Let's see this in action:

```
1  package bosdkbook;
2
3  import java.util.Iterator;
```

```
4
5   import com.crystaldecisions.sdk.framework.CrystalEnterprise;
6   import com.crystaldecisions.sdk.framework.IEnterpriseSession;
7   import com.crystaldecisions.sdk.framework.ISessionMgr;
8   import com.crystaldecisions.sdk.occa.infostore.IInfoObject;
9   import com.crystaldecisions.sdk.occa.infostore.IInfoObjects;
10  import com.crystaldecisions.sdk.occa.infostore.IInfoStore;
11  import com.crystaldecisions.sdk.uri.IPageResult;
12  import com.crystaldecisions.sdk.uri.IStatelessPageInfo;
13  import com.crystaldecisions.sdk.uri.PagingQueryOptions;
14
15  public class PagingQuery
16  {
17      public static void main(String[] args) throws Exception
18      {
19          ISessionMgr sessionManager = CrystalEnterprise.getSessionMgr();
20          IEnterpriseSession session = sessionManager.logon ("administrator",
    "xxxx", "192.168.56.102", "secEnterprise");
21
22          IInfoStore infoStore = (IInfoStore) session.getService ("","InfoStore");
23
24          PagingQueryOptions pagingOptions = new PagingQueryOptions();
25
26          String urlQuery = "path://InfoObjects/**";
27          IPageResult pageResult = infoStore.getPagingQuery(urlQuery,
    pagingOptions);
28
29          Iterator<String> itPageResult = pageResult.iterator();
30          while(itPageResult.hasNext())
31          {
32              String pageQuery = itPageResult.next();
33              System.out.println("Rendered URI query: " + pageQuery + "\n");
34
35              IStatelessPageInfo page = infoStore.getStatelessPageInfo(pageQuery,
    pagingOptions);
```

```
36              System.out.println("Generated SQL query: " + page.getPageSQL() + "\
   n");
37              IInfoObjects ios = infoStore.query(page.getPageSQL());
38
39              System.out.println("Results:");
40              for(int x=0;x<Math.min(5, ios.size());x++)
41                  System.out.println(((IInfoObject)ios.get(x)).getTitle());
42
43              System.out.println("Total: " + ios.size() + "\n");
44          }
45      }
46 }
```

Listing 14: The PagingQuery program

On line 24, we create a new `PagingQueryOptions` object. We'll cover this shortly, but for now we'll use its default options.

```
24          PagingQueryOptions pagingOptions = new PagingQueryOptions();
```

On lines 26-27, we define a URI query and use it to get an `IPageResult` object:

```
26          String urlQuery = "path://InfoObjects/**";
27          IPageResult pageResult = infoStore.getPagingQuery(urlQuery,
   pagingOptions);
```

In the main `while` loop, we iterate through the contents of the `pageResult` object. The value of `pageQuery` is the original URI query with paging parameters applied, and that is displayed first:

```
Rendered URI query: path://InfoObjects/**?Page=1
```

We then pass this string to `getStatelessPageInfo()` to get the actual CMS query SQL for each page:

```
35          IStatelessPageInfo page = infoStore.getStatelessPageInfo(pageQuery,
   pagingOptions);
36          System.out.println("Generated SQL query: " + page.getPageSQL() + "\
   n");
37          IInfoObjects ios = infoStore.query(page.getPageSQL());
```

We next pass the output (`page.getPageSQL()`) on to `infoStore.query()` to execute the query and do a simple loop to print out the title property of the first five objects in the collection. Finally, we print the number of InfoObjects in the page.

The final output is:

```
Rendered URI query: path://InfoObjects/**?Page=1

Generated SQL query: SELECT TOP 1-200
SI_ID,SI_CUID,SI_NAME,SI_PARENT_CUID,SI_DESCRIPTION,SI_CREATION_TIME,SI_KIND,SI_SPECI
FIC_KIND,SI_CHILDREN,SI_OWNER,SI_PATH,SI_CORPORATE_CATEGORIES_ID,SI_PERSONAL_CATEGORI
ES_ID,SI_FILES,SI_INSTANCE,SI_SCHEDULE_STATUS,SI_LAST_SUCCESSFUL_INSTANCE_ID,SI_KEYWO
RD, SI_CUID, SI_PARENT_CUID FROM CI_INFOOBJECTS WHERE SI_ANCESTOR IN (4)

Results:
User Folders
Root Folder
Categories
Personal Categories
Inboxes
Total: 200

Rendered URI query: path://InfoObjects/**?Page=2

Generated SQL query: SELECT TOP 201-400
SI_ID,SI_CUID,SI_NAME,SI_PARENT_CUID,SI_DESCRIPTION,SI_CREATION_TIME,SI_KIND,SI_SPECI
FIC_KIND,SI_CHILDREN,SI_OWNER,SI_PATH,SI_CORPORATE_CATEGORIES_ID,SI_PERSONAL_CATEGORI
ES_ID,SI_FILES,SI_INSTANCE,SI_SCHEDULE_STATUS,SI_LAST_SUCCESSFUL_INSTANCE_ID,SI_KEYWO
RD, SI_CUID, SI_PARENT_CUID FROM CI_INFOOBJECTS WHERE SI_ANCESTOR IN (4)

Results:
ls
ls
ls
weekly
Monthly 9th
Total: 7
```

We can, of course, use any valid URI query, for example:

```
26        String urlQuery = "search://{reports}";
```

This produces a CMS query SQL statement that searches for all objects containing "reports". In our environment, this produces the following:

```
Rendered URI query: search://{reports}?Page=1

Generated SQL query: SELECT TOP 1-200
SI_CUID,SI_NAME,SI_PARENT_CUID,SI_DESCRIPTION,SI_CREATION_TIME,SI_KIND,SI_OWNER,SI_CO
RPORATE_CATEGORIES_ID,SI_PERSONAL_CATEGORIES_ID,SI_FILES,SI_INSTANCE,SI_SCHEDULE_STAT
US,SI_LAST_SUCCESSFUL_INSTANCE_ID,SI_KEYWORD, SI_CUID, SI_PARENT_CUID FROM
CI_INFOOBJECTS WHERE (((SI_NAME LIKE '%reports%') OR (SI_KEYWORD LIKE '%reports%'))
AND (SI_INSTANCE=0))

Results:
Sample reports and universes
Reports
```

```
Crystal Reports Service Processing Server
Crystal Reports Service Report Application Server
Ad-hoc Reports
Total: 6
```

Now, let's dig into PagingQueryOptions, which can alter the behavior of paging queries.

The options that can be set with PagingQueryOptions are:

- Incremental paging (*default value: false*)

- Maintain Top N (*default value: false*)

- Page size(*default value: 200*)

- Exclude temporary storage (*default value: false*)

- Include security parameters (*default value: false*)

Options can be set with either the PagingQueryOptions constructors or setter methods. Its constructors are:

Package com.crystaldecisions.sdk.uri
Class _PagingQueryOptions_

Constructors

PagingQueryOptions()

	Creates a PagingOptionsQuery object with all options set to default values.

PagingQueryOptions(int pageSize)

	Creates a PagingOptionsQuery object, setting the page size option to pageSize. All other options are left at default.

PagingQueryOptions(int pageSize,boolean isIncremental)

	Creates a PagingOptionsQuery object, setting the page size option to pageSize, and whether to use incremental paging. All other options are left at default.

PagingQueryOptions(int pageSize,int optionVals)

	Creates a PagingOptionsQuery object, setting the page size option to pageSize, and optionally setting Boolean options. All other options are left at default.

PagingQueryOptions(int pageSize,boolean isIncremental)

	Creates a PagingOptionsQuery object, setting the page size option to pageSize, and whether to use incremental paging. All other options are left at default.

PagingQueryOptions(int pageSize,int optionVals, boolean isIncremental)	
	Creates a PagingOptionsQuery object, setting the page size option to pageSize, optionally setting Boolean options, and whether to use incremental paging. All other options are left at default.

Class/Interface 8: PagingQueryOptions (constructors)

The fields and methods of PagingQueryOptions (excluding deprecated and internal-use) are:

Package com.crystaldecisions.sdk.uri
Class _PagingQueryOptions_

Fields

static int	EXCLUDE_TEMP_STORAGE	8
	Indicates whether objects in temporary storage should be excluded form query results	
static int	INCLUDE_SECURITY	4
	Indicates whether the SI_FLAGS property should be included in query results	

Methods

int	getPageSize()
void	setPageSize(int pageSize)
	Retrieves or sets the number of objects to include in each page of results. If set to 0, then no paging is performed
boolean	isIncremental()
void	setIsIncremental(boolean isIncremental
	Retrieves or sets whether incremental paging should be used.
boolean	isMaintainTopN()
void	setIsMaintainTopN(boolean maintainTopN)
	Retrieves/sets whether to maintain the original URI query's TOP M-N expression. If true, then any TOP M-N expression in the original query is retained. If false, then the expression is replaced.
boolean	isOptionSet(int option)
void	removeOption(int option)
Void	setOption(int option)

Retrieves, removes, or sets one of the binary options. The available option values are:

- `PagingQueryOptions.EXCLUDE_TEMP_STORAGE`: If set, the contents of the temporary storage folder are excluded from query results.
- `PagingQueryOptions.INCLUDE_SECURITY`: If set, the query's SELECT clause will include the SI_FLAGS property.

Class/Interface 9: PagingQueryOptions

Note that a `PagingQueryOptions` object is a mandatory parameter to both the `getPagingQuery()` and `getStatelessPageInfo()` methods. Generally, the same object are passed to both methods, as in our example above.

For paging queries, the only option in `PagingQueryOptions` that you are likely to use is *pageSize*.

The `pageSize` property defines the size of the page (the number of InfoObjects returned per call). This sets the `?Page` parameter in the URI query and the associated TOP M-N expression in the SQL query. Setting `pageSize` to 0 disables paging – only a single query is produced and no `?Page` or TOP parameters are included[85].

To illustrate `pageSize`, we'll revert our URI query back to what it was and set `pageSize` to 100:

```
24        PagingQueryOptions pagingOptions = new PagingQueryOptions(100);
25
26        String urlQuery = "path://InfoObjects/**";
```

This produces three pages, with a maximum of 100 InfoObjects each:

```
Rendered URI query: path://InfoObjects/**?Page=1


Generated SQL query: SELECT TOP 1-100
SI_ID,SI_CUID,SI_NAME,SI_PARENT_CUID,SI_DESCRIPTION,SI_CREATION_TIME,SI_KIND,SI_SPECI
FIC_KIND,SI_CHILDREN,SI_OWNER,SI_PATH,SI_CORPORATE_CATEGORIES_ID,SI_PERSONAL_CATEGORI
ES_ID,SI_FILES,SI_INSTANCE,SI_SCHEDULE_STATUS,SI_LAST_SUCCESSFUL_INSTANCE_ID,SI_KEYWO
RD, SI_CUID, SI_PARENT_CUID FROM CI_INFOOBJECTS WHERE SI_ANCESTOR IN (4)


Results:

User Folders

Root Folder

Categories

Personal Categories

Inboxes

Total: 100
```

---

85 When paging is disabled, the system-defined query limit (default of 1,000) still applies.

```
Rendered URI query: path://InfoObjects/**?Page=2


Generated SQL query: SELECT TOP 101-200
SI_ID,SI_CUID,SI_NAME,SI_PARENT_CUID,SI_DESCRIPTION,SI_CREATION_TIME,SI_KIND,SI_SPECI
FIC_KIND,SI_CHILDREN,SI_OWNER,SI_PATH,SI_CORPORATE_CATEGORIES_ID,SI_PERSONAL_CATEGORI
ES_ID,SI_FILES,SI_INSTANCE,SI_SCHEDULE_STATUS,SI_LAST_SUCCESSFUL_INSTANCE_ID,SI_KEYWO
RD, SI_CUID, SI_PARENT_CUID FROM CI_INFOOBJECTS WHERE SI_ANCESTOR IN (4)


Results:

Multi

ls

Charting Samples

Charting Samples

Charting Samples

Total: 100


Rendered URI query: path://InfoObjects/**?Page=3


Generated SQL query: SELECT TOP 201-300
SI_ID,SI_CUID,SI_NAME,SI_PARENT_CUID,SI_DESCRIPTION,SI_CREATION_TIME,SI_KIND,SI_SPECI
FIC_KIND,SI_CHILDREN,SI_OWNER,SI_PATH,SI_CORPORATE_CATEGORIES_ID,SI_PERSONAL_CATEGORI
ES_ID,SI_FILES,SI_INSTANCE,SI_SCHEDULE_STATUS,SI_LAST_SUCCESSFUL_INSTANCE_ID,SI_KEYWO
RD, SI_CUID, SI_PARENT_CUID FROM CI_INFOOBJECTS WHERE SI_ANCESTOR IN (4)


Results:

ls

ls

ls

weekly

Monthly 9th

Total: 7
```

When the `incremental` property is set to `false` (the default value), the total number of pages to retrieve is determined during the initial call to `IInfoStore.getPagingQuery()`. When set to `true`, the total page count is re-evaluated during each pass through the `IPageResult` iterator.

This is only a concern when the number of InfoObjects returned by the query can change during the execution of the program (whether by the program itself or another action). If it is a possibility, then set `incremental` to `true`, either with `PagingQueryOptions.setIncremental(true)`, or the `PagingQueryOptions` constructor. Leaving this property set to `false` can improve performance since the page count is not re-evaluated each time.

The `maintainTopN` property is only valuable in `getPagingQuery` if a URI "`query://`" query is used. In this case, and when `maintainTopN` is false (the default value), then any "`TOP M-N`" expression in the original query is replaced with the calculated values appropriate for the current page. To illustrate, we return to Listing 14 and make the following change:

```
26        String urlQuery = "query://{select top 23-47 si_id from ci_infoobjects}";
```

Since we didn't change `maintainTopN`, the default value of `false` applies, and the generated SQL ignores the "`top 23-47`" expression in the original query. The default paging calculation applies instead:

```
Rendered URI query: query://{select top 23-47 si_id from ci_infoobjects}?Page=1

Generated SQL query: SELECT TOP 1-200 si_id, SI_CUID, SI_PARENT_CUID FROM
ci_infoobjects

Results:
User Folders
Root Folder
Categories
Personal Categories
Inboxes
Total: 200

Rendered URI query: query://{select top 23-47 si_id from ci_infoobjects}?Page=2

Generated SQL query: SELECT TOP 201-400 si_id, SI_CUID, SI_PARENT_CUID FROM
ci_infoobjects

Results:
ls
ls
ls
weekly
Monthly 9th
Total: 23
```

Next, we'll run the same query but with `maintainTopN` set to `true`:

```
25        pagingOptions.setIsMaintainTopN(true);
26        String urlQuery = "query://{select top 23-47 si_id from ci_infoobjects}";
```

Now, the "`top 23-47`" expression is maintained, and no paging logic is applied:

```
Rendered URI query: query://{select top 23-47 si_id from ci_infoobjects}?Page=1

Generated SQL query: SELECT TOP 23-47 si_id, SI_CUID, SI_PARENT_CUID FROM
```

```
ci_infoobjects

Results:
Report Conversion Tool Documents
Report Conversion Tool Temporary Documents
Report Conversion Tool Audit Documents
QaaWSServletPrincipal
QaaWSServletPrincipal
Total: 25
```

The two remaining options in `PagingQueryOptions` are contained in a single `optionVals` property: `EXCLUDE_TEMP_STORAGE` and `INCLUDE_SECURITY`. These are binary `int` values and can be OR'd to set one or both at the same time:

```
pagingOptions.setOption(
        PagingQueryOptions.EXCLUDE_TEMP_STORAGE |
        PagingQueryOptions.INCLUDE_SECURITY);
```

Both options, when set, make slight changes to the generated SQL query. The `EXCLUDE_TEMP_STORAGE` option adds a condition excluding the *Temporary Storage Folder* (ID 49) from the query results. The `INCLUDE_SECURITY` option adds the `SI_FLAGS` property to the `SELEC`ted property list. Using our most recent program and setting the two options as shown above, we get:

```
Rendered URI query: query://{select top 23-47 si_id from ci_infoobjects}?Page=1

Generated SQL query: SELECT TOP 1-200 si_id, SI_CUID, SI_PARENT_CUID, SI_FLAGS FROM
ci_infoobjects WHERE NOT SI_PARENTID IN (49)

Results:
User Folders
Root Folder
Categories
Personal Categories
Inboxes
Total: 200

Rendered URI query: query://{select top 23-47 si_id from ci_infoobjects}?Page=2

Generated SQL query: SELECT TOP 201-400 si_id, SI_CUID, SI_PARENT_CUID, SI_FLAGS FROM
ci_infoobjects WHERE NOT SI_PARENTID IN (49)

Results:
ls
ls
ls
weekly
Monthly 9th
Total: 23
```

Simple URI Query Translations

So far, we've used `getPagingQuery()` to generate paged URI queries, and `getStatelessPageInfo()` to translate the generated URI queries into CMS SQL queries. The `getStatelessPageInfo()` method can be used on its own to do a simple translation of a URI query to SQL. It is called in exactly the same way, just with a user-provided URI query string rather than taking the result of `IPageResult`[86].

In fact, this is how we modified Query Builder to accept URI queries (see page 117).

The following code illustrates the use of `getStatelessPageInfo()` with a static URI query string:

```java
PagingQueryOptions pagingOptions = new PagingQueryOptions(0);


String urlQuery = "path://InfoObjects/**";

IStatelessPageInfo page = infoStore.getStatelessPageInfo(urlQuery,
pagingOptions);

System.out.println("Generated SQL query: " + page.getPageSQL() + "\n");

IInfoObjects ios = infoStore.query(page.getPageSQL());


System.out.println("Results:");

for(int x=0;x<Math.min(5, ios.size());x++)

    System.out.println(((IInfoObject)ios.get(x)).getTitle());


System.out.println("Total: " + ios.size() + "\n");
```

Note that we still have to create a `PagingQueryOptions` object since it's required for `getStatelessPageInfo()`. We're passing a 0 to its constructor to disable the paging calculation – but note that even though paging is disabled, the system-default limit of 1000 still applies (if we didn't set the page size, the generated query would include "TOP 1-200").

The result of the above is:

```
Generated SQL query: SELECT TOP 1-1000
SI_ID,SI_CUID,SI_NAME,SI_PARENT_CUID,SI_DESCRIPTION,SI_CREATION_TIME,SI_KIND,SI_SPECI
FIC_KIND,SI_CHILDREN,SI_OWNER,SI_PATH,SI_CORPORATE_CATEGORIES_ID,SI_PERSONAL_CATEGORI
ES_ID,SI_FILES,SI_INSTANCE,SI_SCHEDULE_STATUS,SI_LAST_SUCCESSFUL_INSTANCE_ID,SI_KEYWO
RD, SI_CUID, SI_PARENT_CUID FROM CI_INFOOBJECTS WHERE SI_ANCESTOR IN (4)

Results:
User Folders
Root Folder
Categories
Personal Categories
```

---

86   Of course, since we're bypassing the paging query builder, no paging logic is performed on the generated query.

```
Inboxes
Total: 223
```

Of course, we can collapse a few of these lines to make the conversion a one-liner:

```
String urlQuery = "path://InfoObjects/**";

String sqlQuery = infoStore.getStatelessPageInfo(
        urlQuery,
        new PagingQueryOptions(0)).getPageSQL();

System.out.println("Generated SQL query: " + sqlQuery + "\n");

IInfoObjects ios = infoStore.query(sqlQuery);
```

If your application requires the use of URI queries, then a simple translation to CMS SQL, without invoking the paging engine, is likely the best solution.

ICMSQuery

Yet another helper for querying the CMS is the ICMSQuery interface. It takes a standard CMS SQL query as input and provides methods for managing the paged result. Like paging queries, ICMSQuery doesn't actually produce an IInfoObjects collection – rather, it is passed back to IInfoStore.query() which executes the query and generates results. *Unlike* paging queries, ICMSQuery works with standard CMS SQL, not the URI query syntax.

The basic procedure for using ICMSQuery is:

1. Call IInfoStore.createCMSQuery(), passing in a standard CMS SQL query, and receiving an ICMSQuery object in return.

2. Optionally set options in ICMSQuery, which set the paging and caching behavior.

3. Set the current page number (usually to 0).

4. Pass the ICMSQuery object to IInfoStore.query(), receiving one page of IInfoObjects in return.

5. Optionally select the next page to retrieve, and return to step 4.

A simple example use of ICMSQuery follows:

```
1  package bosdkbook;
2
3  import com.crystaldecisions.sdk.framework.CrystalEnterprise;
4  import com.crystaldecisions.sdk.framework.IEnterpriseSession;
5  import com.crystaldecisions.sdk.framework.ISessionMgr;
6  import com.crystaldecisions.sdk.occa.infostore.ICMSQuery;
```

```
 7 | import com.crystaldecisions.sdk.occa.infostore.IInfoObject;

 8 | import com.crystaldecisions.sdk.occa.infostore.IInfoObjects;

 9 | import com.crystaldecisions.sdk.occa.infostore.IInfoStore;

10 |

11 | public class CMSQuery

12 | {

13 |     public static void main(String[] args) throws Exception

14 |     {

15 |         ISessionMgr sessionManager = CrystalEnterprise.getSessionMgr();

16 |         IEnterpriseSession session = sessionManager.logon ("administrator",
    | "xxxx", "192.168.56.102", "secEnterprise");

17 |

18 |         IInfoStore infoStore = (IInfoStore) session.getService ("","InfoStore");

19 |

20 |         ICMSQuery cmsQuery = infoStore.createCMSQuery("select si_id,si_name  from
    | ci_infoobjects where si_parentid = 23 order by si_name");

21 |

22 |         cmsQuery.setPageSize(6);

23 |         cmsQuery.setCurrentPageNumber(0);

24 |

25 |         while(cmsQuery.hasNextPage())

26 |         {

27 |             cmsQuery.nextPage();

28 |             IInfoObjects ios = infoStore.query(cmsQuery);

29 |             System.out.println("\nBatch size: " + ios.size());

30 |             for(Object o : ios)

31 |             {

32 |                 IInfoObject io = (IInfoObject)o;

33 |                 System.out.println(io.getTitle());

34 |             }

35 |         }

36 |     }

37 | }
```

Listing 15: The CMSQuery program

In this example, we're simply querying for the top-level public folders. To make the effect of paging more clear, we're setting a very small page size of 6 on line 22.

As with Paging Queries, ICMSQuery produces a paged result set, with each page containing a set maximum number of IInfoObjects. However, the method of iterating through the pages is different. While paging queries use a standard Iterator, ICMSQuery does not. Moreover, the initial pointer of ICMSQuery is page 1, requiring a call to ICMSQuery.setCurrentPageNumber(0) in order to properly iterate through all pages[87]. Thus, on line 23, we do that, then iterate through the pages beginning on line 25.

The CMS query is executed when the ICMSQuery object is passed to the overloaded IInfoStore.query() method, on line 28. From here, normal IInfoObjects processing occurs.

The usefulness of ICMSQuery comes from its support of random page access. Unlike paging queries, it is possible to retrieve pages from ICMSQuery out of order. Consider the various dialogs in BI launch pad and CMC that allow a user to navigate a page of folders, users, groups, etc. You may go forward, backward, directly to the first or last page, or to a specific page number. ICMSQuery supports all of these navigation methods.

If we wanted to iterate backwards through pages, we could do so as follows:

```
22        cmsQuery.setPageSize(6);
23
24        for(int x = cmsQuery.queryForLastPageNumber();x>0;x--)
25        {
26            cmsQuery.setCurrentPageNumber(x);
27            IInfoObjects ios = infoStore.query(cmsQuery);
28            System.out.println("\nBatch size: " + ios.size());
29            for(Object o : ios)
30            {
31                IInfoObject io = (IInfoObject)o;
32                System.out.println(io.getTitle());
33            }
34        }
```

We don't have to set the initial page number to 0 in this case since we're instead setting it to the last page (obtained via queryForLastPageNumber()).

The methods of ICSMQuery are:

Package com.crystaldecisions.sdk.occa.infostore
Interface ICMSQuery

---

87 This is a "gotcha" of ICMSQuery. It is not intuitive, and while leaving out this line does not produce any error, it does cause the first page of results to be skipped. So, it is imperative that the current page is set to 0 prior to retrieving the paged results.

int	getCurrentPageNumber()
void	setCurrentPageNumber(int pageNumber)
	Retrieves or sets the current page number. The first page is 0. Calling this method with an invalid page number does **not** produce an error.
boolean	hasNextPage()
	Returns true if there is a page after the current page (that is, does a page exist with a page number equal to the current page number plus one).
	Returns false if called immediately after the ICMSQuery is created if the query CMS produces no results or only a single page of results.
void	nextPage()
	Increments the page index. Effectively the same as calling setCurrentPageNumber() with a value equal to getCurrentPageNumber() + 1. Calling this method after the last page will **not** produce an error (that is, when getCurrentPageNumber() is greater than queryForLastPageNumber()).
int	queryForLastPageNumber()
	Retrieves the last page number in the query's result set. This method executes a CMS query to return the total number of results; for large results, this method may take a long time to complete.
	The result is calculated as the total number of objects divided by the current page size, rounded up.
int	getPageSize()
void	setPageSize(int n)
	Retrieves or sets the page size for the query. The page size represents the maximum number of objects that are retrieved in each query execution.
	The default value is 1000.
IQueryConfiguration	getQueryConfig()
void	setQueryConfig(IQueryConfiguration config)
	Retrieves or sets the cache settings for this query

Class/Interface 10: ICMSQuery

The ICMSQuery object allows for query caching settings to be defined via the IQueryConfiguration object. This is not needed for most queries, and will not be covered here.

Find

The IInfoStore.find() method is a shortcut for querying the CMS for objects by certain criteria. Like the other querying methods, the Find method doesn't do anything that can't be done with a simple CMS SQL query passed to IInfoStore.query(), it just allows for a query to be constructed without actually writing a SQL statement[88].

The find() method takes three parameters: an int defining the list of properties to return (that is, the properties to be included in the SELECT clause), a SearchPattern object defining the query criteria, and a SortType object defining the sort order of the result set.

```
IInfoObjects find(int propertySet,SearchPattern
            searchPattern,SortType sortType)
```

The value of propertySet should be one of the values from the IInfoObject.propertySet static interface. The possible values, and the included properties, are:

Package com.crystaldecisions.sdk.occa.infostore		
Interface _IInfoObject.PropertySet_		
static int	DEFAULT	1
	SI_CUID, SI_ID, SI_INSTANCE, SI_KIND, SI_NAME, SI_PARENTID, SI_PARENT_CUID	
static int	STANDARD	2
	All of DEFAULT plus SI_PARENT_CUID, SI_OWNER, SI_DESCRIPTION	
static int	SCHEDULE	4
	All of STANDARD plus SI_SCHEDULEINFO	
static int	ALL	7
	All Properties (SELECT *)	

Class/Interface 11: IInfoObject.PropertySet

The SearchPattern class is a simple POJO that contains the optional search criteria. The criteria that can be specified are:

- CUID
- ID
- Kind
- Name
- Owner
- Parent CUID

---

88 While this does mitigate the need to code SQL, you will need to understand the usage of the find() method and its supporting classes. In our opinion, using CMS SQL is easier, and so the find() method provides little additional benefit.

- Parent ID

The methods of SearchPattern to retrieve and set these options are:

Package com.crystaldecisions.sdk.occa.infostore
Class *SearchPattern*

String	getCUID()
void	setCUID(String cuid)
	Retrieves or sets the CUID (SI_CUID) to search for.
int	getID()
void	setID()
	Retrieves or sets the InfoObject ID (SI_ID) to search for.
String	getKind()
void	setKind(String kind)
	Retrieves or sets the kind (SI_KIND) to search for.
String	getName()
void	setName(String name)
	Retrieves or sets the name/title (SI_NAME) to search for.
String	getOwner()
void	setOwner(String owner)
	Retrieves or sets the object owner name (SI_OWNER) to search for.
String	getParentCUID()
void	setParentCUID(String cuid)
	Retrieves or sets the parent CUID (SI_PARENT_CUID) to search for.
int	getParentID()
void	setParentID(int parentID)
	Retrieves or sets the parent InfoObject ID (SI_PARENTID) to search for.

Class/Interface 12: SearchPattern

To specify criteria for a query, a new SearchPattern object must be created and one or more of the above setter methods called.

For example, to search for all InfoObjects named "fred", we would do the following:

```
SearchPattern searchPattern = new SearchPattern();

searchPattern.setName("fred");
```

If the searchPattern parameter in the find() call is null, or if the provided SearchPattern object has no criteria set, then no conditions are applied to the query.

The `SortType` class defines the sorting of the query. It is very limited, in that it only allows for sorting by four specific properties: CUID, name, owner name, and update timestamp.

To add a sort, first create a new `SortType` object. Then call its `addSortDimension()` method, passing an `ISortDimension` for each property to sort by. The possible values of `ISortDimension` are defined within the interface itself:

- `ISortDimension.CUID_ASC`
- `ISortDimension.CUID_DESC`
- `ISortDimension.NAME_ASC`
- `ISortDimension.NAME_DESC`
- `ISortDimension.OWNER_ASC`
- `ISortDimension.OWNER_DESC`
- `ISortDimension.UPDATE_TS_ASC`
- `ISortDimension.UPDATE_TS_DESC`

So, to have the query ordered first by descending owner name, then ascending update timestamp, we would do the following:

```
SortType sortType = new SortType();

sortType.addSortDimension(ISortDimension.OWNER_DESC);

sortType.addSortDimension(ISortDimension.UPDATE_TS_DESC);
```

`SortType` may be left blank or empty, in which case the default ordering applies (no ORDER BY clause is specified).

Now we can create a sample query using the `find()` method. We'll use `IInfoObject.PropertySet.ALL` to retrieve all properties, and use the examples above for `SearchPattern` and `SortType`.

```
1  package bosdkbook;
2
3  import com.crystaldecisions.sdk.framework.CrystalEnterprise;
4  import com.crystaldecisions.sdk.framework.IEnterpriseSession;
5  import com.crystaldecisions.sdk.framework.ISessionMgr;
6  import com.crystaldecisions.sdk.occa.infostore.IInfoObject;
7  import com.crystaldecisions.sdk.occa.infostore.IInfoObjects;
8  import com.crystaldecisions.sdk.occa.infostore.IInfoStore;
9  import com.crystaldecisions.sdk.occa.infostore.ISortDimension;
   import com.crystaldecisions.sdk.occa.infostore.SearchPattern;
   import com.crystaldecisions.sdk.occa.infostore.SortType;
10
```

```
11 | public class Find
12 | {
13 |     public static void main(String[] args) throws Exception
14 |     {
15 |         ISessionMgr sessionManager = CrystalEnterprise.getSessionMgr();
16 |         IEnterpriseSession session = sessionManager.logon ("administrator",
   | "xxxx", "192.168.56.102", "secEnterprise");
17 |
18 |         IInfoStore infoStore = (IInfoStore) session.getService ("","InfoStore");
19 |
20 |         SearchPattern searchPattern = new SearchPattern();
21 |         searchPattern.setName("fred");
22 |
23 |         SortType sortType = new SortType();
24 |         sortType.addSortDimension(ISortDimension.OWNER_DESC);
25 |         sortType.addSortDimension(ISortDimension.UPDATE_TS_DESC);
26 |
27 |         IInfoObjects ios = infoStore.find(IInfoObject.PropertySet.ALL,
   | searchPattern, sortType);
28 |
29 |         for(Object o : ios)
30 |         {
31 |             IInfoObject io = (IInfoObject)o;
32 |             System.out.println(io.getID()
   |                 + " " + io.getKind()
   |                 + " " + io.getOwner()
   |                 + " " + io.getUpdateTimeStamp());
33 |         }
34 |     }
35 | }
```

On our system, this program produces the following output:

```
4105 FavoritesFolder   Fred       Sat Jan 09 08:53:54 EST 2016
4106 PersonalCategory  Fred       Sat Jan 09 08:53:54 EST 2016
4107 Inbox      Fred        Sat Jan 09 08:53:54 EST 2016
4104 User       Administrator  Sun Dec 10 08:49:37 EST 2017
```

We *could* instead use plain CMS SQL syntax, and replace lines 20-27 with the following:

27	`        String query = "select * from`
	`ci_infoobjects,ci_appobjects,ci_systemobjects where si_name = 'fred' order by`
	`si_owner desc, si_update_ts";`
28	`        IInfoObjects ios = infoStore.query(query);`

There are four other methods related to `find()` that return the top-level public categories and top-level public folders:

ICategoryPager	`getTopCategories()`
ICategoryPager	`getTopCategories(int propertySet,SearchPattern searchPattern,SortType sortType)`
IFolderPager	`getTopFolders()`
IFolderPager	`getTopFolders(int propertySet,SearchPattern searchPattern,SortType sortType)`

The first and third methods return all of the top-level categories and top-level folders, respectively. The second and fourth methods perform the same action but allow for property set, search criteria, and sorting to be specified, using the same parameters as the `find()` method.

The methods return either `ICategoryPager` or `IFolderPager`. The two interfaces are similar, and are descendants of the now-deprecated `IPagingQueryBase` interface[89].

The methods of these two interfaces, including those inherited from `IPagingQueryBase` are:

Package com.crystaldecisions.sdk.occa.infostore
Interface *IFolderPager*
extends IPagingQueryBase

int	`getCurrPageNumber()`
void	`setCurrPageNumber(int val)`
	Retrieves or sets the current page number.
int	`getItemsPerPage()`
void	`setItemsPerPage(int lNum)`
	Retrieves or sets the number of items per page.
IFolders	`getPage()`
	Retrieves the current page of results.
int	`getPagesPerRange()`
void	`setPagesPerRange(int lNum)`

89 ICMSQuery (covered earlier) succeeds IPagingQuery for managing paged queries. Although IFolderPager and ICategoryPager are still based on the deprecated IPagingQueryBase interface, they are not deprecated themselves. Since the parent interface is deprecated, nearly all of the methods of IFolderPage and ICategoryPager are technically deprecated as well.

	Retrieves or sets the number of pages per range.
int	getRangeFirstPageNumber()
	Retrieves the first page number in the current range.
int	getRangeLastPageNumber()
	Retrieves the last page number in the current range.
boolean	hasNextPage()
	Returns true if there is a next page, false otherwise.
boolean	hasNextRange()
	Returns true if there is a next range, false otherwise.
boolean	hasPrevPage()
	Returns true if there is a previous page, false otherwise.
boolean	hasPrevRange()
	Returns true if there is a previous range, false otherwise.
void	moveToFirstPage()
	Moves to the first page.
void	moveToLastPage()
	Moves to the last page.
void	moveToNextPage()
	Moves to the next page.
void	moveToPreviousPage()
	Moves to the previous range.
void	moveToPreviousRange()
	Moves to the previous range.

Class/Interface 13: IFolderPager

Package com.crystaldecisions.sdk.occa.infostore
Interface _ICategoryPager_
*extends _IPagingQueryBase_*

int	getCurrPageNumber()
void	setCurrPageNumber(int val)
	Retrieves or sets the current page number.
int	getItemsPerPage()
void	setItemsPerPage(int lNum)

		Retrieves or sets the number of items per page.
ICategories	getPage()	
		Retrieves the current page of results.
int	getPagesPerRange()	
void	setPagesPerRange(int lNum)	
		Retrieves or sets the number of pages per range.
int	getRangeFirstPageNumber()	
		Retrieves the first page number in the current range.
int	getRangeLastPageNumber()	
		Retrieves the last page number in the current range.
boolean	hasNextPage()	
		Returns true if there is a next page, false otherwise.
boolean	hasNextRange()	
		Returns true if there is a next range, false otherwise.
boolean	hasPrevPage()	
		Returns true if there is a previous page, false otherwise.
boolean	hasPrevRange()	
		Returns true if there is a previous range, false otherwise.
void	moveToFirstPage()	
		Moves to the first page.
void	moveToLastPage()	
		Moves to the last page.
void	moveToNextPage()	
		Moves to the next page.
void	moveToPreviousPage()	
		Moves to the previous range.
void	moveToPreviousRange()	
		Moves to the previous range.

Class/Interface 14: ICategoryPager

Generally, there won't be a *huge* number of top-level folders or categories, so there is little benefit gained from the paging functions. However, this is necessary in order to navigate through the results. In the following example, we use the getTopFolders() method to retrieve all top folders.

```java
IInfoStore infoStore = (IInfoStore) session.getService ("","InfoStore");

IFolderPager pager = infoStore.getTopFolders();

for(;;)
{
    IFolders folders = pager.getPage();
    for(Object o : folders)
    {
        IFolder folder = (IFolder)o;
        System.out.println(folder.getTitle());
    }
    if(!pager.hasNextPage())
        break;
    pager.moveToNextPage();
}
```

The default page size for `IPagingQueryBase` is 1000. If we're confident that there will be fewer than this number of results, we can skip the paging logic:

```java
IInfoStore infoStore = (IInfoStore) session.getService ("","InfoStore");

IFolderPager pager = infoStore.getTopFolders();

IFolders folders = pager.getPage();
for(Object o : folders)
{
    IFolder folder = (IFolder)o;
    System.out.println(folder.getTitle());
}
```

Manual Paging

It is possible to implement paging logic without any of the helper methods described above. We can accomplish this by executing `IInfoStore.query()` in a loop that retrieves batches of results ordered by their SI_ID property.

In the following example we are retrieving all objects in CI_INFOOBJECTS, in batches of 100:

```
IInfoStore infoStore = (IInfoStore) session.getService ("","InfoStore");

Integer startID = 0;

for(;;)
{
    System.out.println("Starting batch at ID: " + startID);

    IInfoObjects ios = infoStore.query("select top 100 si_id,si_name from
ci_infoobjects where si_id > " + startID);

    if(ios.size() == 0)
        break;

    for(Object o : ios)
    {
        IInfoObject io = (IInfoObject)o;
        System.out.println(io.getTitle());
        startID = io.getID();
    }
}
```

We start out by setting startID to 0, and then executing a CMS query that retrieves the first 100 InfoObjects with an SI_ID greater than startID. We don't have to use an ORDER BY clause in the query, since CMS queries are inherently sorted by SI_ID (adding an ORDER BY for a different property would screw up the paging logic). As we loop through the returned IInfoObjects collection, we set startID to be equal to the current SI_ID; upon reaching the end of the loop, startID will contain the highest SI_ID in the batch. We can then query again for the next batch, until the query returns no results.

CMS Querying Summary

As we've seen, there are several options for performing CMS queries. The following are our recommendations for which option to choose based on the specific need.

- When the query is expected to produce a large (wide and tall) result set, paging is desired, and the number of rows per page is not critical, use *Streaming queries* (page 275). Streaming queries offer a quick, simple method for retrieving a large number of results while letting the server determine the size of each page based on its total size.

- When the query is best expressed in URI query syntax, use *Paging queries* (page 277). This translates a URI query into a CMS query and adds the appropriate paging parameters.

- If the query is in URL syntax but paging is not desired, use the `getStatelessPageInfo()` method (page 287).

- When the query is expected to produce a large number of results, and it may be necessary to retrieve pages out of order, or to change the number of items per page during processing, use `ICMSQuery` (page 288). This method provides the most control over the paging of results.

- To perform paging using only the basic `IInfoStore.query()` method, use manual paging, described on page 299.

Chapter Review

- The `IEnterpriseSession` interface is used primarily to get an `IInfoStore` object, but it also provides several methods for getting information about the system, session, and active user.

- The `IInfoStore` interface is used to access the InfoStore. All interaction with InfoObjects (creating, retrieving, modifying, deleting) is performed via the InfoStore.

- Retrieving InfoObjects from the InfoStore is a critical component of any SDK program, and the `IInfoStore` interface provides several querying methods for performing this retrieval.

Quiz

1. True/False: The current user's full name and email address can be retrieved from `IUserInfo`.

2. True/False: In order to change the current user's password with `IUserInfo.setPassword()`, the current password must be provided.

3. The `IUserInfo.getPersonalObjectID()` method can retrieve the user's...

    a) Temporary storage folder

    b) Top-level personal category

    c) Favorites folder

    d) Inbox

4. Which querying method might return a different number of rows in each batch?

    a) `ICMSQuery`

    b) Paging queries

    c) Streaming queries

    d) Manual paging

5. Which querying method uses the URI query syntax?

    a) `ICMSQuery`

    b) Paging queries

    c) Streaming queries

    d) Manual paging

Answers on page 673.

Chapter 14 - Program Objects

Program Objects provide a mechanism for scheduling the execution of certain types of scripts and programs from within the SAP BusinessObjects BI platform. As opposed to executing programs from a remote client, as we have been doing with our examples so far, Program Objects are actually executed by the SAP BusinessObjects platform itself. Thus, a Program Object can leverage the full functionality of job scheduling with the same options as scheduled reports: recurrence, events, calendars, notifications, etc.

Program Objects can be created in several formats, including Java, .NET, JavaScript, and Windows/Linux batch scripts. Java Program Objects are the most common and are our focus[90].

In addition to scheduling, Java Program Objects provide several handy features. For one, a Program Object does not have to perform a logon action, since the program is passed active IEnterpriseSession and IInfoStore objects. This eliminates the need to embed logon credentials within source code. Also, the session is associated with the user account that scheduled the instance. Thus, it is possible for different users to schedule the same Program Object and have the program execute with each users' individual security profile.

When executed from the job server, a Program Object is passed a classpath that includes the basic BI Platform SDK libraries. So it is not necessary to specify these libraries for the program's classpath (although it is possible to include additional libraries if needed). If the SAP BusinessObjects application is patched or upgraded, the Program Objects will automatically be linked to the updated BI Platform libraries – so no recompiling or re-jarring is necessary[91].

Just as Web Intelligence and Crystal Reports save instances when scheduled, Program Objects save their standard output and standard error as an instance, in a text file. A scheduled Program Object can be set for email distribution, in which case the generated output file can be included as an attachment. This is useful for regularly-scheduled maintenance programs, in that the system administrators can receive an automated email with the result of the programs.

Program Objects run only as a scheduled job and not interactively. That is, it is not possible to execute a scheduled job that interacts with a user like a Web Intelligence report can be refreshed. But they are perfectly suited to scheduled maintenance and administrative operations. A small sample of the possible uses of Program Objects includes:

- Create new user Enterprise user IDs to correspond with a third-party database, a text file, or another application.

- Perform validation of Enterprise user IDs against another source.

- Move reports past a certain age to a file system for archiving

---

90   Unless noted otherwise, any further reference to "Program Objects" are actually Java Program Objects.

91   In most cases, anyway. A change to a common method signature would require a re-compile, but this is rare.

- Purge objects from users' inboxes that are past a certain age.

- Perform regular security auditing such as validating the members of the Administrators group, checking for unexpected user access on sensitive reports, or an unexpectedly high number of recently failed schedules.

- Perform regular recertification of user access.

- Send a system status email, with information such as the number of successful and failed scheduled jobs, number of pending jobs, and server status.

There are a few things that need to be done in order to use Program Objects. We'll cover that first, and then the steps to create and execute Program Objects.

CMC Configuration

In order to run Program Objects, a couple of options need to be set in the CMC. Log in to the CMC, go the *Applications* area, then right-click on *Central Management Console* and select *Program Object Rights*.

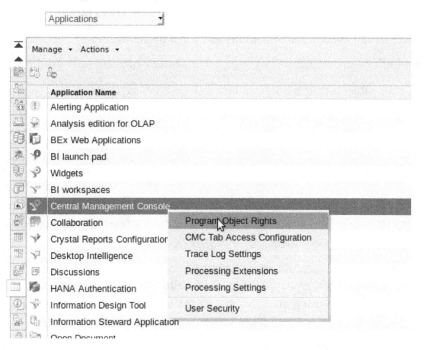

Illustration 23: Program Object Rights

There are two types of Program Objects: Java programs, and scripts/binaries. The two checkboxes at the top of the Program Object Rights page (see *Illustration 23*) allow for Java programs or scripts/binaries to be executed as Program Objects. For our purposes, we'll need the *Run Java programs* option checked off, but you will need to also check off *Run scripts/binaries* if you intend to run Program Objects of those types as well.

(We'll get back to the *Use impersonation* checkbox in a moment.)

The settings under *If credentials are not specified at schedule time* are only used for:

- Program Objects that are scripts/binaries (i.e., not Java), or

- Java programs, **only** if *Use impersonation* is checked.

In these two conditions, if *Fail job (recommended)* is selected, then operating system credentials have to be supplied for each Program Object when they are scheduled.

If *Schedule with these operating system credentials* is selected, then default operating system credentials may be supplied in the following fields. These credentials are used by the Program Objects when they are executed unless different credentials are supplied at that time in the Program Object settings.

Whether entered on this page or in Program Object settings, the credentials must be an operating system username/password that is valid on the machine that the Program Scheduling Service[92] is running on. This is true for both UNIX and Windows. For Windows, the specified account may be either a local user account or a domain account.

If *Use impersonation* is **not** checked, then Java Program Objects will **ignore** the following options. That is, Java Program Objects will always run with the same operating system credentials that the Program Scheduling Service is running as; no operating system credentials need to be supplied either in this dialog or in the Program Objects settings, and they are ignored if set.

---

92 Note that the Program Scheduling Service runs as s service on an Adaptive Job Server (AJS).

To put it another way, with *Use impersonation* **checked**, Java Program Objects and scripts/binaries will follow the same rules – operating system credentials must be supplied either on this page or in the Program Object settings. With Use impersonation **unchecked**, scripts/binaries still require operating system credentials to be entered the same way, but Java Program Objects will ignore these options and run with the same credentials as the AJS.

We suggest leaving *Use impersonation* unchecked so that no username or password will need to be supplied.

Next, make sure that there is an Adaptive Job Server (AJS) running, and that it includes the *Program Scheduling Service*. By default, BI4 will create a single AJS which includes all of the available scheduling services. However, many installations will have separate AJSes, one for each scheduling service. Either configuration is fine, as long as there is at least one AJS that has the *Program Scheduling Service*.

For more information on the Application settings and server/service configuration, see the *Business Intelligence Platform Administrator Guide*.

Application Configuration

Although it's pretty easy to modify an existing Java application to run as a Program Object, we'll start from scratch. Create a new Java application project, named *SampleProgramObject*. As before, we'll include the *BI4 Platform SDK* user library.

One crucial requirement for running Java Program Objects is that they must be compiled for compliance with the same version of Java that the SAP BusinessObjects server is running (for XI3, this is 1.5, for BI4.1 it is 1.6, and for BI4.2 it is 1.8). This does **not** mean that your workstation must have an installation of older versions of Java. You may create Program Objects for BI4.1 on a workstation that has, for example, Java 7 or 8, but the project properties must be set for compliance with 1.6.

Our test workstation has Java 7 installed. We are creating a Program Object for BI4.1, so we will need to set the compliance level to 1.6. We do this is the project properties → *Java Compiler*:

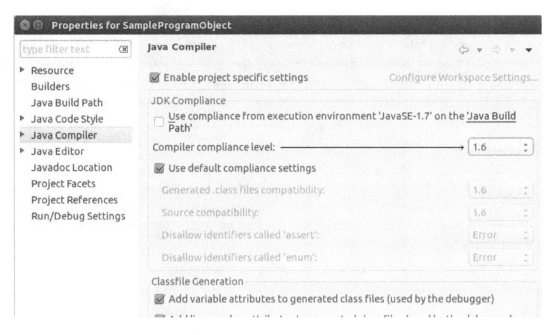

In order for a Java application to be executed as a Program Object, it must meet two requirements: it must implement the IProgramBase or IProgramBaseEx interface, and it must override the interface's run() method.

In the new project, create a new class. Name it *SampleProgramObject*, in package *bosdkbook*. We want this class to implement IProgramBaseEx, so click the *Add...* button to the right of *Interfaces:*

In the dialog that appears, enter *IProgramBaseEx*. Eclipse should match it. Click OK.

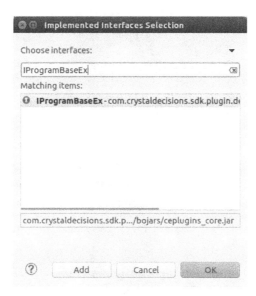

Eclipse automatically adds the necessary unimplemented methods for the interface, which in this case is one method named run(). If you are not using Eclipse, you will need to modify the class signature manually, include the appropriate imports, and add the run() method. Either way, the script so far should look like the following:

```
1  package bosdkbook;
2
3  import com.crystaldecisions.sdk.exception.SDKException;
4  import com.crystaldecisions.sdk.framework.IEnterpriseSession;
5  import com.crystaldecisions.sdk.occa.infostore.IInfoObject;
6  import com.crystaldecisions.sdk.occa.infostore.IInfoStore;
7  import com.crystaldecisions.sdk.plugin.desktop.program.IProgramBaseEx;
8
9  public class SampleProgramObject implements IProgramBaseEx {
10
11     @Override
12     public void run(IEnterpriseSession paramIEnterpriseSession,
13             IInfoStore paramIInfoStore, IInfoObject paramIInfoObject,
14             String objectID, String[] paramArrayOfString)
15             throws SDKException {
16        // TODO Auto-generated method stub
17
18     }
```

19	
20	}

The run() Method

We have chosen to implement `IProgramBaseEx` rather than `IProgramBase`. The one we've used is newer and provides more parameters to the Program Object. We recommend it for all new SDK programs, but you may see `IProgramBase` in older applications.

If you chose to use `IProgramBase` instead of `IProgramBaseEx`, then the generated `run()` method will include fewer parameters.

The `run()` method is called by the Job Server when the Program Object is executed and is the entry point into the application. Therefore, no `main()` method is required and would be ignored if it is present.

The parameters passed to the `run()` method are:

`IEnterpriseSession paramIEnterpriseSession`: This is an active, opened enterprise session object that can be used by the program. The session is created with the credentials of the user account that scheduled the Program Object instance (not necessarily the user who *created* the Program Object). The `getUserName()` method of this `paramIEnterpriseSession` object can be used to identify which account the session is associated with.

`IInfoStore paramIInfoStore`: An active `IInfoStore` object, associated with the `IEnterpriseSession` object. Any CMS queries executed using this object will reflect the security access granted to the user account who scheduled the Program Object. So, a Program Object scheduled by a user will inherit that user's security permissions on CMS objects. Two different users may schedule the same Program Object, but the CMS queries executed by it return different results due to the two users' different security access.

`IInfoObject paramIInfoObject`: This is a reference to the `IInfoObject` of the Program Object instance being executed. This can be used if the program is interested in finding out its own scheduling parameters, who scheduled it, etc. It is also used to set failure reporting for the Program Object.

`String objectID`: Similar to the above `paramIInfoObject` parameter, `objectID` contains the InfoObject ID of the Program Object instance itself.

`String[] paramArrayOfString`: This array contains any arguments that are passed to the program, as defined in the Program Object's scheduling parameters page. Arguments can be used to create multiple instances of a single program to perform operations with different input values – for example, a program may perform a purge of a specified folder, and one scheduled instance may be set up for each folder that needs to be purged, with each instance passing the program a different folder ID.

Note that run() is **not** static; it will be called on an initialized IProgramBaseEx object.

Program Body

There are few restrictions on what can be done within the body of a Program Object application. Third-party libraries may be used, and System.out may be used to generate output – this output is captured in a text file that becomes attached to the scheduled Program Object instance.

We'll use a very simplistic program to illustrate the processing of a Program Object, based on our first sample program in Listing 3 on page 185. We don't need to create an IEnterpriseSession or IInfoStore object since they are provided in the run() method, and we don't need to log the session off.

```
1  package bosdkbook;
2
3  import com.crystaldecisions.sdk.exception.SDKException;
4  import com.crystaldecisions.sdk.framework.IEnterpriseSession;
5  import com.crystaldecisions.sdk.occa.infostore.IInfoObject;
6  import com.crystaldecisions.sdk.occa.infostore.IInfoObjects;
7  import com.crystaldecisions.sdk.occa.infostore.IInfoStore;
8  import com.crystaldecisions.sdk.plugin.desktop.program.IProgramBaseEx;
9
10 public class SampleProgramObject implements IProgramBaseEx {
11
12     @Override
13     public void run(IEnterpriseSession paramIEnterpriseSession,
14             IInfoStore paramIInfoStore, IInfoObject paramIInfoObject,
15             String objectID, String[] paramArrayOfString)
16             throws SDKException {
17
18         IInfoObjects users = paramIInfoStore.query("select si_name from
   ci_systemobjects where si_kind = 'user'");
19
20         if(users.size() == 0)
21         {
22             System.out.println("No users found!");
```

```
23              return;
24          }
25          for(int x = 0;x < users.size(); x++)
26          {
27              IInfoObject user = (IInfoObject) users.get(x);
28              System.out.println(user.getTitle());
29          }
30          System.out.println("Done!");
31      }
32 }
```

Listing 16: ListUsers as program object

Listing 16 contains the combination of the ListUsers program and the Program Object stub. Since there is no `main()` method, we can't execute the program from within Eclipse, but more on this later.

Creating the Program Object

Now that we have our program written, we will package it into a jar. In Eclipse, go to *File → Export,* and select *JAR file:*

In the JAR Export dialog, select the project to export: *SampleProgramObject.*

Specify the destination of the jar file. This can be a temporary location since we'll be uploading the generated file to the CMS.

We recommend checking off *Export Java source files and resources*, to include the source (.java) files in the jar. This isn't strictly necessary, and should actually be avoided if the program contains sensitive information such as passwords. But including source files in the jar makes for an easier recovery should the original source files get deleted or lost.

We accept the default settings in the remainder of the wizard, so we can just hit *Finish* at this point.

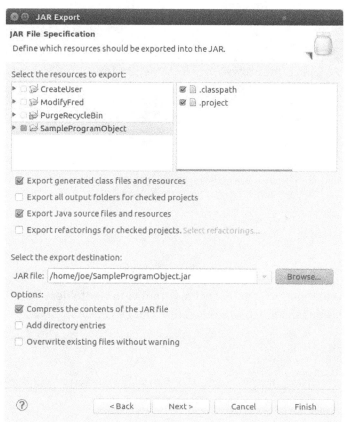

If all goes well, then nothing will happen. But you should find the generated jar file in the specified location.

Now, let's log into the CMC[93] and select a folder to contain the Program Object. Any public or personal folder will do, and it may even be a folder containing other content, such as reports. But for our purposes, we'll create a new top-level folder named *Programs*.

Right-click on the selected folder and hit *Add → Program File* (or select it from the *Manage* menu).

---

93 Program Objects can not be created in BI launchpad, only the CMC.

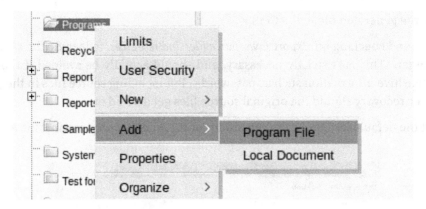

In the Program File dialog, hit Browse to select the jar file that we created above, select Java for the Program type, and hit OK to proceed.

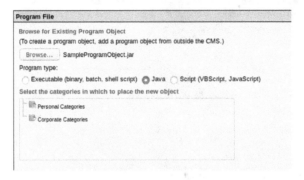

Hitting OK will create the Program Object and return to the folder listing, but the Program Object requires additional configuration before it can be executed.

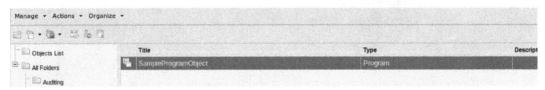

Double-click the title of the Program Object, or right-click and hit *Properties*. Once inside the properties dialog, go to *Default Settings → Program Parameters*.

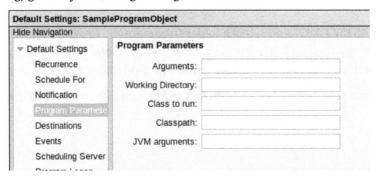

The settings on this page are important and are often the source of issues with running

Program Objects. Make sure the values entered are correct.

Arguments: This is an optional field. If populated, the value is passed to the Program Object as a String in the `paramArrayOfString` parameter.

Working Directory: Specifies the local path to be used as the current working directory when the program is executed. This should be an absolute (not relative) path and must be in the format expected by the operating system that the BOE server is running on. For example, if the BOE server is running in Windows, then the path may in the form of:

```
d:\data\programs
```

for UNIX it may be in the form of:

```
/var/programs
```

The working directory only needs to be set if the Program Object or classpath refers to relative paths rather than absolute paths. We are not doing this for the current project, so we will leave Working Directory empty (although we will make use of it later in this book).

Class to run: This is the fully-qualified name of the class to serve as the entry point for the Program Object. This **must** be the name of a class that implements `IProgramBase` or `IProgramBaseEx`, and it must include the full package path, if applicable for the class. If the class uses the default package (that is, there is no `package` specified in the program), then this should just be the class name itself. For example:

```
SampleProgramObject
```

In our sample program, we used a package named `bosdkbook`, so we will specify the class name here as:

```
bosdkbook.SampleProgramObject
```

The **Class to run** is the only parameter on this page that is required.

Classpath: When a Java Program Object is executed by the job server, it is given a classpath that includes the specified Program Object jar and several Platform SDK jars. If your Program Object depends on any additional libraries, then you may specify their location here. This is a standard classpath format with each path separated by semicolons (for Windows servers), or colons (for UNIX servers).

Individual classpath entries may be an absolute or relative form. If relative, then they are relative to the Working Directory specified above. For example, consider a UNIX file structure like the following:

```
/
/var
/var/programobjects/
/var/programobjects/lib
/var/programobjects/lib/logging.jar
/var/programobjects/lib/mail.jar
/var/programobjects/log
```

If the **Working Directory** is given as "`/var/programobjects`", then including the two jar files in the classpath can be done by setting relative paths in **Classpath**:

```
lib/logging.jar;lib/mail.jar
```

As with the Working Directory setting, the classpath must be in a form appropriate for the BOE server operating system.

For our current Program Object, we are not using any additional libraries, so we will not need to include anything in the classpath.

The **JVM arguments** parameter is optional but allows for settings to be passed to the JVM that the Program Object runs in. For example, to specify a maximum memory usage setting of 1GB for the JVM, enter the following:

```
-Xmx1024m
```

For our project, we will only need to specify the class name. So our Program Parameters look like the following:

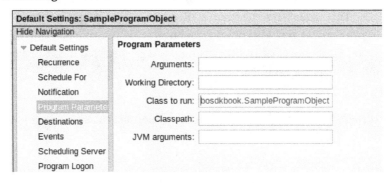

Hit Save & Close to save the default settings.

Right-click on SampleProgramObject and hit *Run Now*. Then right-click on it again and hit *History*.

This will bring you into the History view of the Program Object. You should see one entry for the instance that you created when you hit *Run Now*. If there is going to be a problem with the execution of your Program Object, now is when you'll find it. Several things can happen at this point, so we will cover some troubleshooting tips.

Program Object Troubleshooting

If the instance stays in *Pending* status for more than a few minutes, then there may be a problem. Check the following:

- Ensure that there is an Adaptive Job Server (AJS) that includes the Program Scheduling Service.

- Ensure that the AJS is running and enabled.

- The AJS may be busy processing other jobs. Check the Instance Manager, or the AJS's metrics tab to confirm.

If the instance goes into Failed status, click on the word *Failed* to get the error message. There are several possible error messages that you may see here:

```
Failed to load class: [xxx]. Reason: [java.lang.ClassNotFoundException: xxx].
```
This message indicates that the job server was not able to locate the class that was indicated by the *Class to run* parameter. There are a few possible reasons for this:

- The *Class to run* parameter does not specify the fully-qualified name of the class to execute. In our example, our fully-qualified classname is `bosdkbook.SampleProgramObject`. If we had given a *Class to run* as just `SampleProgramObject`, then this error would be displayed.

- The specified class is not present in the jar file that was uploaded to the Program Object.

- The classname is simply misspelled.

```
Program does not implement correct interface.
```
This indicates that the class was found, but it does not implement `IProgramBase` or `IProgramBaseEx`. The class signature should look like:

```
public class SampleProgramObject implements IProgramBaseEx {
```

or

```
public class SampleProgramObject implements IProgramBase {
```

```
Running programs of this type has been disabled by the administrator.
```
This indicates that the execution of Java Program Objects has not been enabled for this environment. Refer to CMC Configuration on page 304, and ensure that *Run Java programs* is enabled.

```
No operating system credentials were set for running the program.
```
If this error message is displayed for a Java Program Object, it is because the following two conditions are true:

- The *Use impersonation* option is checked off in Program Object Rights (in CMC, *Applications → Central Management Console → Program Object Rights*), and

- no operating system credentials were provided in the Program Object Rights page or in the Program Logon tab of the Program Object's scheduling options

Refer to CMC Configuration on page 304 for more information about these options. To proceed, do **one** of the following:

- Un-check *Use impersonation* in Program Object Rights, or

- provide operating system credentials on the Program Object's Program Logon tab when scheduling the Program Object, or

- on the Program Object Rights page (CMC > Applications → Central Management Console), enter default operating system credentials, and select "*Schedule with these operating system credentials*".

```
Exception caught while running program.
```

An error message that begins with this text indicates that an exception was thrown from within the program. The message should be followed by a more informative message, for example:

```
Exception caught while running program. Reason:
[com.crystaldecisions.sdk.exception.SDKServerException: Not a valid query. (FWB
00025)].
```

We will cover exception handling in more detail on page 323

Even if the Program Object has a status of *Success*, it does not guarantee that the program has successfully completed. To confirm if the program has completed successfully, we will need to look at its output. In the History view, click on either the Instance Time or the Title (just like viewing a scheduled instance of a report). Depending on your web browser, you may be prompted to download the text file, or it will be displayed immediately. Either way, the output will either contain an exception message or the successful output of the program.

If the output begins an exception similar to:

```
Exception in thread "main" java.lang.UnsupportedClassVersionError:
bosdkbook/SampleProgramObject : Unsupported major.minor version 51.0
    at java.lang.ClassLoader.defineClass1(Native Method)
```

...then it means that the program was compiled for a newer version compliance level than the JRE that is installed on the BOE server. In this specific case, the Program Object was compiled for Java 7, but we are attempting to execute it in BI4.1, which uses Java 6. See Application configuration on page 306 for more information on version compliance settings.

If you receive a `ClassNotFound` exception, then it is most likely because your program references additional libraries but they were not included in the Program Object's classpath. Set the classpath parameter on the Program Object's *Parameters* page to include the needed jar files.

Success!

If the program executes successfully, then the output file should contain the desired output of the program, a listing of all users. In our test system, the generated output is:

```
Guest
Administrator
SMAdmin
QaaWSServletPrincipal
Fred
Nathan
Sri
Wally
Ephraim
Quentin
Alice
Francine
Done!
```

Updating Program Objects

Unfortunately, the SAP BusinessObjects BI4 platform does not provide a good method for updating a Program Object's source file after it has been initially created. The two common ways of deploying a new version of a program are:

- Delete the existing Program Object and create a new one with the updated jar file.

- Hunt down the jar file in the FRS and replace it with the updated version.

Neither option is ideal. The first option, deleting and re-creating, will require re-entering all of the Program Object's parameters, and will lose any previously-scheduled instance. The second option involves modifying content in the FRS directly, which is generally not a recommended practice. It also requires that the person deploying the program has permission to write to the FRS file system. Since access to the FRS should be tightly restricted for most environments, this is also not a desirable option.

We will describe our recommended approach for management of Program Object files when we cover the Program Object Management Pattern (POMP) in the next chapter. But, for completeness, we will also fully describe the second option above.

To update the Program Object file in the FRS, we must first determine its location. The General Properties page of the Program Object's properties will contain the logical location of the file.

Illustration 24: Program Object FRS location

In Illustration 24 we see the location location of the file:

```
frs://Input/a_242/028/000/7410/SampleProgramObject-guid[0d640309-404b-466c-a9fc-
184fb896f13b1].jar
```

Note that this path is relative to the location of the FRS in the file system. From this path alone, it is impossible to locate the true physical location of the file. We need to know where the FRS is. By default, the FRS is relative to the home installation of the SAP BusinessObjects application. On Windows:

```
C:\Program Files (x86)\SAP BusinessObjects\SAP BusinessObjects Enterprise XI 4.0\
FileStore\
```

And on UNIX:

```
<Home install directory>/data/
```

So, on our Linux server, the above Program Object is actually located in:

```
/home/bi4/sap/sap_bobj/data/frsinput/a_242/028/000/7410/
```

If we look at this location, we'll see

```
$ ls -l sap_bobj/data/frsinput/a_242/028/000/7410/
```

```
-rwxrwxr-x. 1 bi4 bi4 2476 Aug 25 10:10 sampleprogramobject-guid[0d640309-404b-466c-
a9fc-184fb896f13b1].jar
```

...which is our original jar file that we uploaded via the CMC, with a GUID attached to its filename. We just need to copy the updated jar file to the FRS directory, and use the existing full name with the GUID:

```
$ cp sampleprogramobject.jar
sap_bobj/data/frsinput/a_242/028/000/7410/sampleprogramobject-guid[0d640309-404b-466c-
a9fc-184fb896f13b1].jar
```

Of course, the commands are slightly different in Windows, but the same process applies.

Program Objects, like most other CMS object types, can be migrated between environments using the Promotion Management application[94]; either directly between two environments or

---

94   Or, in versions prior to BI4, the *Import Wizard*.

via an .lcmbiar file[95]. If a Program Object is used in multiple environments, it may be updated in one environment (using the method above), then migrated to one or more other environments. In order for this to work, the Program Object must be first created in one environment, then migrated to the other environments with Promotion Management. The process would be:

1. Program Object is created in the CMC in one environment (let's say the *Development* environment).

2. A Promotion Management job is created to migrate the Program Object from the source *Development* environment to the target *Production* environment.

At this point, the Program Object exists in both the Development and Production environments. Now, to update the Program Object's jar:

1. Jar file is generated

2. Jar file in the FRS of the Development environment is overwritten with the newly-generated file.

    At this point, the updated program is functional in the Development environment.

3. A Promotion Management job is created to migrate the Program Object from the source *Development* environment to the target *Production* environment.

    Now the updated program is functional in both environments.

There are a couple of considerations when using Promotion Management to migrate Program Objects:

•   When a Program Object is initially created, the uploaded jar file is copied directly into the FRS and will retain its original name, with a GUID appended. However, if the Program Object is migrated to another environment with Promotion Management, the name of the jar file in the target environment is system-generated. So, there is no consistency between the names of the Program Object's files in the different environments. This should not be an issue when using the process described above since the manual FRS update will only be done in the source environment.

•   When a Program Object is migrated with Promotion Management, all of its default settings are migrated, including the *Working directory* and *Classpath* settings. Since it's possible that different values will need to apply in the destination environment, those values will have to be changed manually post-migraiton.

Running Program Objects in Eclipse

Often during the development of Program Objects, you'll want to test locally within Eclipse.

---

95 See the *Business Intelligence Platform Administrator Guide* for Promotion Management documentation.

However, since the Program Objects that we've created thus far do not have a `main()` method, it's not possible to execute them as a free-standing application within Eclipse. We can add a simple `main()` method to a program just for the purpose of calling it during development – it is ignored when it is executed as a Program Object by the Job Server. There are a few options for accomplishing this need:

Approach 1: We can simply add a `main()` method in the Program Object class, and use it to call the `run()` method. Going back to Listing 16, we just need to add the following code within the `SampleProgramObject` class:

```java
public static void main(String[] args) throws SDKException
{

    ISessionMgr sessionManager = CrystalEnterprise.getSessionMgr();

    IEnterpriseSession session = sessionManager.logon ("administrator", "xxxx",
"192.168.56.102", "secEnterprise");


    IInfoStore infoStore = (IInfoStore) session.getService ("","InfoStore");


    new SampleProgramObject().run(session, infoStore, null, null, args);

}
```

With this code added, we can run or debug the program in Eclipse. Note that we do have to log in via `ISessionMgr.logon()` and retrieve an `IEnterpriseSession` object since the program is not being called from the Job Server, which would pass an active session object. But, other than that, the program should run from within Eclipse as if it were being run in the Job Server.

Although this approach works, there is an inherent problem – the `main()` method, including the user ID and password used to log on, is compiled into the program and *could* be retrieved using a Java decompiler. The following approaches mitigate this risk.

Approach 2: We will use the same main() method as Approach 1, but move it into its own class.

```java
1  package bosdkbook;
2
3  import com.crystaldecisions.sdk.exception.SDKException;
4  import com.crystaldecisions.sdk.framework.CrystalEnterprise;
5  import com.crystaldecisions.sdk.framework.IEnterpriseSession;
6  import com.crystaldecisions.sdk.framework.ISessionMgr;
7  import com.crystaldecisions.sdk.occa.infostore.IInfoStore;
8
```

```
 9  public class Runner {
10      public static void main(String[] args) throws SDKException
11      {
12          ISessionMgr sessionManager = CrystalEnterprise.getSessionMgr();
13          IEnterpriseSession session = sessionManager.logon ("administrator",
    "xxxx", "192.168.56.102", "secEnterprise");
14
15          IInfoStore infoStore = (IInfoStore) session.getService ("","InfoStore");
16
17          new SampleProgramObject().run(session, infoStore, null, null, args);
18      }
19  }
```

Listing 17: Runner.java

The user ID and password are still required to be in the source code, but with this method, we can choose to exclude `Runner.class` from the compiled jar. This will allow us to use the `Runner` class to execute the Program Object while working in Eclipse but does not expose the user ID and password in the compiled jar. The one risk with this approach is that you need to ensure that `Runner.class` is not included – either when exporting manually in Eclipse or using an ant file to generate the jar.

Approach 3: The final approach that we propose is to use a separate, dedicated *project* to hold the `Runner` class. We create a brand-new project, include the *BI4 Platform SDK* user library, and move `Runner.java` into it. We also need to add a reference from the *Runner* project to the *SampleProgramObject* project. This is done in the Java Build Path → Projects tab:

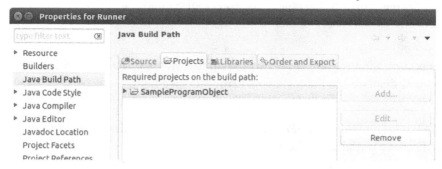

This is the most complex of the three approaches, as it requires the creation of a whole new project. But it is flexible and secure – there is no risk of accidentally including the user ID and password in the compiled Program Object jars since they are only present in the one project – *Runner*, which is not compiled as a Program Object. We can also use this same `Runner` class to execute any of the Program Objects in our Eclipse workspace. However, in that case, the *Runner* project needs to include any libraries that are used by the Program Objects, as well as references to those projects.

We recommend using Approach 2 in the real world, as we believe it offers the best balance between flexibility, security, and ease. It is also a component of the *Program Object Management Pattern*, to be described later.

Exception handling

As with any application, careful attention should be paid to how errors are handled. You, as the programmer, must decide which errors can be handled within the program (non-fatal errors), versus which errors would prevent the program from continuing execution (fatal errors). As a general rule, errors that would cause the program to be incapable of performing its primary objective would be considered fatal. Non-fatal errors are generally those that occur while iterating through a list of items, in which processing of a small number of those items are unsuccessful, while the majority are.

SDKException

Most BI Platform SDK methods, if they encounter an unrecoverable problem, will throw an exception of type SDKException (or, more specifically, one of its subclasses). If an SDKException is thrown by a method that is called in a Program Object, but not caught, it will be thrown upwards through the run() method, resulting in a fatal error. Note that the signature of run() (in both the IProgramBase and IProgramBaseEx interfaces) can throw SDKException:

```
public void run(IEnterpriseSession paramIEnterpriseSession,
        IInfoStore paramIInfoStore, IInfoObject paramIInfoObject,
        String objectID, String[] paramArrayOfString)
        throws SDKException
```

When this occurs, the Program Object will assume a status of *Failed*, and the message from the exception is displayed in the instance's Error Message field.

Let's look at an example in which we intentionally provoke such an exception in a Program Object. We'll return to the *SimpleProgramObject* program in Listing 16, and change line 18 so that the CMS query contains invalid syntax:

```
18      IInfoObjects users = paramIInfoStore.query("bleh");
```

Make the change above, then save the file, export to a jar file, and upload it to the CMC as a new Program Object. Set the classname in Program Parameters, and schedule it to run.

The Program Object instance should eventually assume a status of *Failed*. Clicking on the word *Failed* to display the instance status should then display the error message:

```
Error Message: Exception caught while running program. Reason:
```

```
[com.crystaldecisions.sdk.exception.SDKServerException: Not a valid query. (FWB
00025)].
```

The SDKServerException type referenced in the error is a subclass of SDKException; in general, the exception name itself and the description is a good indication of the cause of the problem. In this case, the *Not a valid query* message clearly indicates the cause. However, the error message in the instance status will only display the short exception message and not the full stack trace. Thus, debugging an exception in this manner may be difficult, particularly in large programs, since the location of the problem may not be obvious[96].

Additionally, since the instance is in *Failed* status, and failed instances cannot contain output files, any output generated by the program prior to the exception is lost.

For this reason, it may be desirable to use the alternate exception handling method.

In the example above, we allowed the exception from IInfoStore.query() to be thrown upwards without being caught, which resulted in a fatal exception. Alternatively, it is possible to catch and handle SDKExceptions rather than letting them result in a fatal error.

It's possible to throw your own SDKException (or one of its subclasses). This enables the program to fail with the same behavior as SDK-generated SDKExceptions. That is, they will cause the Program Object to fail and display the error message in the instance details.

There are a large number of SDKException subclasses, covering many types of problems that the SDK may encounter. It is possible to throw one of these yourself, assuming there is an exception that meets your needs (most of the SDKException subclasses have very specific purposes, so this is not always an easy task). The SDKException subclasses are also *enclosed* by SDKException; they are listed in the BI4 Platform SDK Javadocs class index prefixed with SDKException., for example:

- SDKException.AlreadyIndexing
- SDKException.AmbiguousDestinationUpdate
- SDKException.ApplicationObjectCUIDNotSet
- SDKException.AuditBatchTooLarge
- SDKException.AuditDetailUnsettableError
- SDKException.AuditFailure

To throw one of these exceptions, you will need to use the appropriate constructor, as each one is different and expects parameters that are specific to the exception type. For example, SDKException.OutOfRange can be used to indicate that a parameter value is not within an expected range. Its constructor is:

```
SDKException.OutOfRange(int invalidValue, int lowerBound, int upperBound)
```

We could throw our own OutOfRange exception by passing the appropriate parameters. As a sketch, we'll do this in our *SampleProgramObject*:

---

96 In this example, we know that the *Not a valid query* exception can only be thrown from IInfoStore.query(). Since there is only one call to this method in our program, we would know exactly where to look to begin debugging.

```
 1  package bosdkbook;
 2
 3  import com.crystaldecisions.sdk.exception.SDKException;
 4  import com.crystaldecisions.sdk.framework.IEnterpriseSession;
 5  import com.crystaldecisions.sdk.occa.infostore.IInfoObject;
 6  import com.crystaldecisions.sdk.occa.infostore.IInfoObjects;
 7  import com.crystaldecisions.sdk.occa.infostore.IInfoStore;
 8  import com.crystaldecisions.sdk.plugin.desktop.program.IProgramBaseEx;
 9
10  public class SampleProgramObject implements IProgramBaseEx {
11
12      @Override
13      public void run(IEnterpriseSession paramIEnterpriseSession,
14              IInfoStore paramIInfoStore, IInfoObject paramIInfoObject,
15              String objectID, String[] paramArrayOfString)
16              throws SDKException {
17
18          throw new SDKException.OutOfRange(10, 25, 50);
19      }
20  }
```

The parameters that we've passed to OutOfRange are simply displayed in the exception message and are not used for any other reason. If we publish this as a Program Object and schedule it, it will fail with the following error message:

```
Exception caught while running program. Reason:
[com.crystaldecisions.sdk.exception.SDKException$OutOfRange: The value 10 does not
fall within the expected 25 and 50 range (FWM 02041)].
```

Be careful when using the SDKException subclasses in this fashion. Since they are generally thrown by the SDK itself, they may cause confusion if they appear in the Program Object error message. Also, as with the example above, the messages are generally not as descriptive as would be necessary to describe the problem properly. Nor do they include the stack trace, or any output generated prior to the exception being thrown.

Unchecked Exceptions

If a Program Object generates, but doesn't handle, an unchecked exception, then it too will be thrown upwards by the `run()` method and result in a fatal error. However, unchecked exceptions <u>do not cause the scheduled Program Object instance to fail</u>. Instead, the instance will assume a status of Success, and the instance's output file will contain the exception text, including all output generated prior to the exception.

Let's look at another example. We'll use the same program as our previous example, but add the following lines above line 18:

```
18        Integer i = null;
19        i.intValue();
```

Again, save the file, create the jar, create a new Program Object, and schedule it. This time, the Program Object will report a status of *Success*. At first glance, it would appear that the program completed successfully. But if we click on the title or timestamp of the instance to retrieve the generated output file, we'll find the following:

```
Exception in thread "main" java.lang.NullPointerException: while trying to invoke the
method java.lang.Integer.intValue() of a null object loaded from local variable 'i'
    at bosdkbook.SampleProgramObject.run(SampleProgramObject.java:19)
    at
com.crystaldecisions.sdk.plugin.desktop.program.internal.ProgramWrapper.main(ProgramWr
apper.java:146)
```

It is possible to abort a Program Object by *intentionally* throwing an unchecked exception. This is generally considered to be a bad practice as unchecked exceptions are intended for situations that *should not occur*, and usually indicate a fault in the program logic rather than external data.

With that said, an unchecked exception may be thrown in a Program Object, such as:

```
throw new RuntimeException("Invalid parameter passed to program: expected 25-50 but
received 5.");
```

The advantage of this method is that we have full control over the error message. However, as with all unchecked exceptions, they do not cause the Program Object to fail. A Program Object containing the above code will report a status of *Success*, and the error message will be contained in the output file:

```
Exception in thread "main" java.lang.RuntimeException: Invalid parameter passed to
program: expected 25-50 but received 5.
    at bosdkbook.SampleProgramObject.run(SampleProgramObject.java:17)
    at
com.crystaldecisions.sdk.plugin.desktop.program.internal.ProgramWrapper.main(ProgramWr
apper.java:146)
```

To summarize, if `run()` throws any **unchecked** exceptions, they will display in the instance output, but the instance will complete successfully. If `run()` throws `SDKException` (or any of its subclasses), the instance fails and the exception message is displayed in the instance's Error Message field.

There are disadvantages to both. However, we can exert some additional control over Program Object failures with the enhanced failure reporting method.

Enhanced Failure Reporting

You may want to intentionally signal the failure of a Program Object; however, since `run()` can only throw `SDKException` and unchecked exceptions, you cannot throw your own checked exception upwards through `run()`. There is another method for signaling the failure of a Program Object, which will cause a failed Program Object to report a status of *Failed* and will allow for custom text to be displayed in the instance's error message field.

If a Program Object is going to use this method, it must first be enabled to do do. This is accomplished by setting the `SI_PROGRAM_CAN_FAIL_JOB` property to `true` in the Program Object instance that is being executed[97]. Note that this step is performed simply to *enable* the functionality; it does not actually cause the failure process to occur. Thus, it can be (and typically is) performed near the top of the Program Object program.

In order to set the `SI_PROGRAM_CAN_FAIL_JOB` property, the Program Object must implement the `IProgramBaseEx` interface rather than `IProgramBase`, since the former is the only one of the two that supplies a reference to the Program Object's `IInfoObject`. With that reference, we can set the value of the property, and save the InfoObject. The code is as follows:

```java
@Override
public void run(IEnterpriseSession paramIEnterpriseSession,
        IInfoStore paramIInfoStore, IInfoObject paramIInfoObject,
        String objectID, String[] paramArrayOfString)
        throws SDKException {


    paramIInfoObject.getProcessingInfo().properties().add(
            "SI_PROGRAM_CAN_FAIL_JOB", Boolean.TRUE, IProperty.DIRTY);
    paramIInfoObject.save();
```

If the program completes without error, then no special action is needed. Just let the program exit as usual. But to signal a failure, the following must be done:

- Print the following two lines to the beginning of standard output (using `System.out.println()`):

  ```
  PROCPROGRAM:PROGRAM_ERROR
  62009
  ```

- Print up to three lines containing the error messages. The first line is displayed in the Error Message field of the Program Object instance status; the remaining two

---

97   Reference SAP Note 1578811.

lines will only be accessible via CMS queries.

- Exit the program with `System.exit(1)`

Note that we are *not* throwing an exception from `run()`. If the Program Object is reporting a failure due to a caught exception, that exception must be caught (and **not** re-thrown) in order to use this method.

So we'll create a very simple program that does nothing but signal a failure. We'll build upon the stub above and add the code to signal the failure:

```java
1  package bosdkbook;
2
3  import com.crystaldecisions.sdk.exception.SDKException;
4  import com.crystaldecisions.sdk.framework.IEnterpriseSession;
5  import com.crystaldecisions.sdk.occa.infostore.IInfoObject;
6  import com.crystaldecisions.sdk.occa.infostore.IInfoStore;
7  import com.crystaldecisions.sdk.plugin.desktop.program.IProgramBaseEx;
8  import com.crystaldecisions.sdk.properties.IProperty;
9
10 public class SampleProgramObject implements IProgramBaseEx {
11
12     @Override
13     public void run(IEnterpriseSession paramIEnterpriseSession,
14             IInfoStore paramIInfoStore, IInfoObject paramIInfoObject,
15             String objectID, String[] paramArrayOfString)
16             throws SDKException {
17
18         paramIInfoObject.getProcessingInfo().properties().add(
19             "SI_PROGRAM_CAN_FAIL_JOB", Boolean.TRUE,
                   IProperty.DIRTY);
20         paramIInfoObject.save();
21
22         // ... Program Object body here
23
24         // Print the code to signal the failure
25         System.out.println("PROCPROGRAM:PROGRAM_ERROR");
26         System.out.println("62009");
27
```

```
28          // Print a custom error message
29          System.out.println("Whoops!");
30          System.out.println("Something happened.");
31          System.out.println("I'm giving up.");
32
33          // exit the program
34          System.exit(1);
35      }
36 }
```

When this Program Object is executed, it will fail (as expected). When we check the instance status, we'll see our "Whoops!" line as the error message:

Title:	SampleProgramObject
Document Type:	Program
Status	Failed
Destination:	Default
Created By:	Administrator
Creation Time:	9/10/16 4:14 PM
Start Time:	9/10/16 4:14 PM
End Time:	9/10/16 4:14 PM
Location:	Programs
Remote Instance:	No
Expiry:	9/10/26 4:14 PM
Error Message:	The program failed to run and supplied the following information: Whoops!

In order to see the remaining two lines, we would need to execute a CMS query:

```
select si_statusinfo
  from ci_infoobjects
 where si_schedule_status = 3
       and si_name = 'sampleprogramobject'
```

The result will include this most recent execution, with all three lines included:

SI_STATUSINFO

    SI_RESOURCEID

        62009

        SI_SUBST_STRINGS

        1

            Whoops!

        2

            Something happened.

        3

            I'm giving up.

        SI_TOTAL

3

Obviously, executing a CMS query just to get the error message of a Program Object isn't very practical, so when this method is used be sure to include as much information is appropriate on the first line of the output.

As we saw in the example above, a Program Object does not necessarily require that an exception has occurred in order to signal a failure status. But we can use this method during exception handling as well. We are, in effect, intercepting an SDKException and handling it rather than letting it be thrown by run().

We'll change our program above to intentionally cause an SDKException, which we'll then catch and handle by signaling the failure ourselves.

```java
1  package bosdkbook;
2
3  import com.crystaldecisions.sdk.exception.SDKException;
4  import com.crystaldecisions.sdk.framework.IEnterpriseSession;
5  import com.crystaldecisions.sdk.occa.infostore.IInfoObject;
6  import com.crystaldecisions.sdk.occa.infostore.IInfoObjects;
7  import com.crystaldecisions.sdk.occa.infostore.IInfoStore;
8  import com.crystaldecisions.sdk.plugin.desktop.program.IProgramBaseEx;
9  import com.crystaldecisions.sdk.properties.IProperty;
10
11 public class CaughtFail implements IProgramBaseEx {
12
13     @Override
14     public void run(IEnterpriseSession paramIEnterpriseSession,
15             IInfoStore paramIInfoStore, IInfoObject paramIInfoObject,
16             String objectID, String[] paramArrayOfString)
17             throws SDKException {
18
19         paramIInfoObject.getProcessingInfo().properties().add(
20                 "SI_PROGRAM_CAN_FAIL_JOB", Boolean.TRUE, IProperty.DIRTY);
21         paramIInfoObject.save();
22
23         try
24         {
25             IInfoObjects ios = paramIInfoStore.query("xxx");
```

```
26              }
27          catch (SDKException e)
28          {
29              // Print the code to signal the failure
30              System.out.println("PROCPROGRAM:PROGRAM_ERROR");
31              System.out.println("62009");

33              // Print the error message
34              System.out.println(e.getMessage());

36              // exit the program
37              System.exit(1);
38          }
39      }
40  }
```

Listing 18: The CaughtFail program

Listing 18 contains the CaughtFail program and begins the same as before – by setting the SI_PROGRAM_CAN_FAIL_JOB property.

On line 25, we intentionally provoke an SDKException by attempting to execute an invalid CMS query.

We catch the exception on line 27. Instead of letting the SDKException be thrown upwards, we are handling it here, by displaying the error message and exiting. On line 34, we are printing the message from the exception. Thus, the error message in the instance status will contain the exception message.

```
34              System.out.println(e.getMessage());
```

As before, compile the program into a jar, publish it as a new Program Object, and schedule it to run. It fails, and in the Error Message field we find the exception message:

Title:	CaughtFail
Document Type:	Program
Status	Failed
Destination:	Default
Created By:	Administrator
Creation Time:	9/10/16 8:44 PM
Start Time:	9/10/16 8:44 PM
End Time:	9/10/16 8:44 PM
Location:	Programs
Remote Instance:	No
Expiry:	9/10/26 8:44 PM
Error Message:	The program failed to run and supplied the following information: Not a valid query. (FWB 00025)

Illustration 25: Program object error

One requirement of this method is that the signaling code ("`PROCPROGRAM:PROGRAM_ERROR`" and "`62009`") must appear at the top of the generated output. This can be a challenge, as it means that no other text may be printed first. One way to accomplish this is to print all *other* output to a text file or logger utility (covered below) instead of `System.out` (that is, all regular output is sent to a text file or logger, but the signaling code and error message are sent to `System.out`). In this case, the program output will only be present in the log files – the scheduled instance output will be empty.

Another method is to capture all output in a `StringBuilder`. If the program fails, then the signaling code can be printed with `System.out.println()`; if not, then the contents of the `StringBuilder` is printed.

None of the options we've covered so far provide complete reporting of failures since we are only capturing the error message itself, and not any previously-generated output or the complete stack trace. However, using this alternate fatal exception handling method, along with logging (described next), enables a more complete error reporting strategy.

Logging

A good logging strategy is essential to maintaining a high level of quality in any system, especially in batch/offline systems such as Program Objects. Unfortunately, the out-of-the-box method for logging Program Object output is not very robust – all system output is captured in a text which is then associated with the Program Object's scheduled instance. It can be emailed, saved to a file, or just kept as a scheduled instance, but it does not support appending or rolling of log files.

While there are several logging solutions available, we recommend using **log4j**. In addition to being one of the most widely-used logging frameworks for Java, it also has the advantage of already being included in the classpath when Program Objects are executed by the Job Server. So, it's not necessary to reference a log4j library explicitly in a Program Object's properties. You can, of course, use any logging framework that you like, but you will need to include the appropriate libraries in the Program Object's classpath.

The log4j framework is extremely flexible, and we will only be scratching the surface here of what it can do.

Using a framework such as log4j offers several benefits:

- Log files can be placed in a centralized location

- Log files may be appended-to with each run, or a new file created each time

- Verbosity of logging can be changed by modifying one file and does not require re-deploying the Program Object.

Log4j requires a properties file[98], traditionally named `log4j.properties`. The file may be included in the Program Object's packaged jar file, or in an external location. If it is external to the jar, then it is necessary to include the file's location in the Program Object's classpath settings. We will do this later when we cover the *Program Object Management Pattern*, but for now we will include it with the project.

Let's create a new project, named PurgeRecycleBinPO. Remember to set the project's compiler compliance setting correctly (page 306).

```java
1  package bosdkbook;
2
3  import org.apache.log4j.Logger;
4
5  import com.crystaldecisions.sdk.exception.SDKException;
6  import com.crystaldecisions.sdk.framework.CrystalEnterprise;
7  import com.crystaldecisions.sdk.framework.IEnterpriseSession;
8  import com.crystaldecisions.sdk.framework.ISessionMgr;
9  import com.crystaldecisions.sdk.occa.infostore.IInfoObject;
10 import com.crystaldecisions.sdk.occa.infostore.IInfoObjects;
11 import com.crystaldecisions.sdk.occa.infostore.IInfoStore;
12 import com.crystaldecisions.sdk.plugin.desktop.program.IProgramBaseEx;
13
14 public class PurgeRecycleBinPO implements IProgramBaseEx
15 {
16     private static Logger LOGGER = Logger.getLogger(PurgeRecycleBinPO.class);
17     private IEnterpriseSession session;
18     private IInfoStore infoStore;
19
20     public static void main(String[] args) throws SDKException
```

---

98 Properties can also be set from within the program so that no properties file is needed, but we will use the file in our examples.

```
21      {
22          ISessionMgr sessionManager = CrystalEnterprise.getSessionMgr();
23          IEnterpriseSession session = sessionManager.logon ("administrator",
    "xxxx", "192.168.56.102", "secEnterprise");
24
25          IInfoStore infoStore = (IInfoStore) session.getService ("","InfoStore");
26
27          new PurgeRecycleBinPO().run(session, infoStore, null, null, args);
28      }
29
30      @Override
31      public void run(IEnterpriseSession paramIEnterpriseSession,
32              IInfoStore paramIInfoStore, IInfoObject paramIInfoObject,
33              String objectID, String[] paramArrayOfString)
34              throws SDKException
35      {
36          this.session = paramIEnterpriseSession;
37          this.infoStore = paramIInfoStore;
38
39          LOGGER.info("Starting.");
40          try
41          {
42              doPurge();
43              LOGGER.info("Done!");
44          }
45          catch (SDKException e)
46          {
47              LOGGER.fatal("Unexpected error, aborting.",e);
48          }
49      }
50
51      private void doPurge() throws SDKException
52      {
53          IInfoObjects infoObjects = infoStore.query("select si_name, si_cuid from
    ci_infoobjects where children(\"si_name='folder hierarchy'\",\"si_name = 'recycle
```

```
      bin' and si_parentid = 23\")");
54
55          LOGGER.info("Received " + infoObjects.size() + " objects to delete.");
56          for(Object o : infoObjects)
57          {
58              IInfoObject infoObject = (IInfoObject)o;
59              LOGGER.debug("Deleting: " + infoObject.getTitle());
60              try
61              {
62                  infoObject.deleteNow();
63              }
64              catch (SDKException e)
65              {
66                  LOGGER.error("Error deleting object: " + e.getMessage());
67              }
68          }
69      }
70 }
```

Listing 19: The PurgeRecycleBinPO program

Listing 19 contains the *PurgeRecycleBinPO* program, a variant of the original *PurgeRecycleBin* program from Listing 10. This program includes the necessary code to run as a Program Object, and also additional code to utilize log4j.

If you've created the BI4 Platform SDK user library as we suggested, then it will include `log4j.jar`, so no additional reference is needed to use log4j. However, there are multiple classes named `Logger` in the SDK – make sure that you are importing the correct one:

```
import org.apache.log4j.Logger;
```

On lines 20-28, we've created a `main()` function, to allow the program to be tested in Eclipse.

On lines 17-18 and 36-37, we've created and then populated class fields to hold the `IEnterpriseSession` and `IInfoStore` references that are passed to `run()`. We do this so we can reference these values within the class without having to pass them around in method parameters.

```
17      private IEnterpriseSession session;
18      private IInfoStore infoStore;
```

```
36 |        this.session = paramIEnterpriseSession;
37 |        this.infoStore = paramIInfoStore;
```

We have refactored the `run()` method to move most of the processing to a separate method, `doPurge()`. By doing so, we avoid having to wrap the entire body of the program in a `try/catch` block to handle fatal exceptions. Instead, we handle all fatal exceptions in `run()`. Specifically, on line 47, we call `LOGGER.fatal()` to capture any fatal exceptions. Note that we are also passing the `SDKException`, so that the stack trace is printed with the error message.

```
45 |        catch (SDKException e)
46 |        {
47 |            LOGGER.fatal("Unexpected error, aborting.",e);
48 |        }
```

The `doPurge()` method now performs all of the "real" processing; executing the CMS query and deleting the returned objects.

Within the main `for` loop, we wrap the `infoObject.deleteNow()` call in a `try/catch` (lines 60-67). We log any `SDKExceptions`, but do not re-throw them. Thus, any errors that occur when deleting objects will not be fatal. Also, in the `LOGGER.error()` call, we pass the error message but do **not** pass the exception itself. This will just print the error message and not the stack trace.

```
67 |            LOGGER.error("Error deleting object: " + e.getMessage());
```

Next, we need to create the log4j configuration file, `log4j.properties`. Its location in the project directory structure is important. In *Project Explorer*, right-click on the *src* directory. Select *New → Other*, then select *General → File* in the New dialog. Enter *log4j.properties* for the filename in the *New File* dialog. The dialog should look similar to the following:

Hit Finish to create the file, then double-click on it in *Project Explorer* to open it.

Enter the following text into the file:

```
log4j.rootLogger=DEBUG, console

log4j.appender.console=org.apache.log4j.ConsoleAppender
log4j.appender.console.Target=System.out
log4j.appender.console.layout=org.apache.log4j.PatternLayout
log4j.appender.console.layout.ConversionPattern=%d{yyyy-MM-dd HH:mm:ss} %-5p
%c{1}:%L - %m%n
```

Listing 20: log4j.properties for PurgeRecycleBinPO

Now we're ready to test our program. Because we added the `main()` method, we can test the program in Eclipse before deploying it as a Program Object. We just need to copy a couple of WebI reports into the Recycle Bin to give the program something to do. We do that, then execute the program, and we get the following result in the console:

```
2016-09-24 14:33:43 INFO  PurgeRecycleBinPO:39 - Starting.
2016-09-24 14:33:43 INFO  PurgeRecycleBinPO:55 - Received 3 objects to
delete.
2016-09-24 14:33:43 DEBUG PurgeRecycleBinPO:59 - Deleting: Returns
2016-09-24 14:33:43 DEBUG PurgeRecycleBinPO:59 - Deleting: Quarterly Profit
2016-09-24 14:33:43 DEBUG PurgeRecycleBinPO:59 - Deleting: Year-End Reports
2015
```

```
2016-09-24 14:33:43 INFO  PurgeRecycleBinPO:43 - Done!
```

If instead of the above, you see:

```
log4j:WARN No appenders could be found for logger
(bosdkbook.PurgeRecycleBinPO).
log4j:WARN Please initialize the log4j system properly.
```

then it means that log4j was not able to locate the `lo4j.properties` file. Double-check the location and name of the file that we created above. However, note that this message is a warning and not a fatal error. The program will continue to execute despite log4j not outputting. Since there is no output, it may appear that the program did not continue, when in fact it did but simply did not generate any output.

Next, we'll look at how errors are logged. We'll intentionally cause a syntax error in the CMS query, which will result in a fatal exception. On line 53, make the following change:

```
53 |        IInfoObjects infoObjects = infoStore.query("bleh");
```

When executed, we get the following output:

```
2016-09-24 17:07:48 INFO  PurgeRecycleBinPO:39 - Starting.
2016-09-24 17:07:48 FATAL PurgeRecycleBinPO:47 - Unexpected error, aborting.
com.crystaldecisions.sdk.exception.SDKServerException: Not a valid query.
(FWB 00025)

cause:com.crystaldecisions.enterprise.ocaframework.idl.OCA.oca_abuse:
IDL:img.seagatesoftware.com/OCA/oca_abuse:3.2
detail:Not a valid query. (FWB 00025)

The server supplied the following details: OCA_Abuse exception 7683 at
[InfoStore.cpp : 5968]  48163 {}
    ...Error generating parse tree


    at
com.crystaldecisions.sdk.exception.SDKServerException.map(SDKServerException.
java:99)
    at
com.crystaldecisions.sdk.exception.SDKException.map(SDKException.java:124)
    at
com.crystaldecisions.sdk.occa.infostore.internal.InternalInfoStore.queryHelpe
r(InternalInfoStore.java:1081)
    at
com.crystaldecisions.sdk.occa.infostore.internal.InternalInfoStore.queryHelpe
r(InternalInfoStore.java:1057)
    at
com.crystaldecisions.sdk.occa.infostore.internal.InternalInfoStore.query_arou
ndBody18(InternalInfoStore.java:926)
    at
com.crystaldecisions.sdk.occa.infostore.internal.InternalInfoStore.query(Inte
rnalInfoStore.java:1)
```

```
      at
com.crystaldecisions.sdk.occa.infostore.internal.InfoStore.query_aroundBody12
(InfoStore.java:191)
      at
com.crystaldecisions.sdk.occa.infostore.internal.InfoStore.query_aroundBody13
$advice(InfoStore.java:512)
      at
com.crystaldecisions.sdk.occa.infostore.internal.InfoStore.query(InfoStore.ja
va:1)
      at bosdkbook.PurgeRecycleBinPO.doPurge(PurgeRecycleBinPO.java:53)
      at bosdkbook.PurgeRecycleBinPO.run(PurgeRecycleBinPO.java:42)
      at bosdkbook.PurgeRecycleBinPO.main(PurgeRecycleBinPO.java:27)
Caused by: com.crystaldecisions.enterprise.ocaframework.idl.OCA.oca_abuse:
IDL:img.seagatesoftware.com/OCA/oca_abuse:3.2
      at
com.crystaldecisions.enterprise.ocaframework.idl.OCA.oca_abuseHelper.read(oca
_abuseHelper.java:106)
      at
com.crystaldecisions.enterprise.ocaframework.idl.OCA.OCAi._InfoStore_XRL4Stub
.queryEx3(_InfoStore_XRL4Stub.java:468)
      at sun.reflect.NativeMethodAccessorImpl.invoke0(Native Method)
      at
sun.reflect.NativeMethodAccessorImpl.invoke(NativeMethodAccessorImpl.java:57)
      at
sun.reflect.DelegatingMethodAccessorImpl.invoke(DelegatingMethodAccessorImpl.
java:43)
      at java.lang.reflect.Method.invoke(Method.java:606)
      at
com.crystaldecisions.enterprise.ocaframework.ManagedService.invoke(ManagedSer
vice.java:356)
      at
com.crystaldecisions.sdk.occa.infostore.internal._InfoStoreEx4Proxy.queryEx3(
_InfoStoreEx4Proxy.java:364)
      at
com.crystaldecisions.sdk.occa.infostore.internal.InternalInfoStore$XRL3WireSt
rategy.query(InternalInfoStore.java:1670)
      at
com.crystaldecisions.sdk.occa.infostore.internal.InternalInfoStore.queryHelpe
r(InternalInfoStore.java:1069)
      ... 9 more
```

We're seeing the full stack trace because we passed the original SDKException to LOGGER.error() on line 47. But, as is the case with most unexpected fatal errors, you'll want as much information as possible in order to debug.

Set the CMS query on 53 back to what it was, and we'll deploy our program as a Program Object.

Nothing special needs to be done to include the log4j.properties file – it should automatically be packaged in the jar when exported. So, create the jar, upload it as a Program Object in the CMC, and set the *Class to run* to *PurgeRecycleBinPO*. Then schedule it to run. Since we purged the recycle bin a moment ago, and we haven't added anything new, the program will take no action. But we should get valid output:

```
2016-09-24 15:50:08 INFO    PurgeRecycleBinPO:39 - Starting.
2016-09-24 15:50:08 INFO    PurgeRecycleBinPO:55 - Received 0 objects to
delete.
2016-09-24 15:50:08 INFO    PurgeRecycleBinPO:43 - Done!
```

Again, if you get the "No appenders could be found..." error, it means that the program was not able to find log4j.properties. If this happens, confirm if the file was actually included in the jar file. This can be done in a couple of different ways:

- From the command line (UNIX or Windows), with the jar utility:

  ```
  jar -tf PurgeRecycleBinPO
  ```

- From the command line (UNIX or Windows), with unzip:

  ```
  unzip -l PurgeRecycleBinPO
  ```

- With a graphical zip utility such as WinZip. You may need to rename the file to a .zip extension.

In any case, the jar file should contain the following files:

```
META-INF/MANIFEST.MF
```

```
bosdkbook/PurgeRecycleBinPO.class
```

```
log4j.properties
```

```
.project
```

```
.classpath
```

Note that the log4j.properties file is in the root of the archive, not in the *bosdkbook* directory.

So now we have successfully used log4j to create logging output to standard output. Next, we'll do something more useful – configure log4j to write the log data to a file.

We first need to choose a location for the generated log files. In our Linux workstation, we create a new directory in /var/log named bobj, then assign our user ID as the owner:

```
sudo mkdir /var/log/bobj
```

```
sudo chown joe:joe /var/log/bobj
```

This is used when we run the program in Eclipse. We also need to do the same thing on the SAP BusinessObjects server, for when we run Program Objects. We do the same as above, except that we give ownership to the service account that SAP BusinessObjects is running as ("bi4" in our case).

If on Windows, create the a folder ("*c:\bobj_logs*" for example), on the client or server machine as appropriate.

Back in Eclipse, open up log4j.properties again. We'll add a second appender using *FileAppender*. The file now contains:

```
log4j.rootLogger=DEBUG, console, file

log4j.appender.console=org.apache.log4j.ConsoleAppender
log4j.appender.console.Target=System.out
log4j.appender.console.layout=org.apache.log4j.PatternLayout
log4j.appender.console.layout.ConversionPattern=%d{yyyy-MM-dd HH:mm:ss} %-5p
%c{1}:%L - %m%n

log4j.appender.file=org.apache.log4j.FileAppender
log4j.appender.file.append=true
log4j.appender.file.file=/var/log/bobj/PurgeRecycleBinPO.log
log4j.appender.file.layout=org.apache.log4j.PatternLayout
log4j.appender.file.layout.ConversionPattern=%d{yyyy -MM-dd HH:mm:ss} %-5p
%c{1}:%L - %m%n
```

Note that we have left the existing *console* logger intact, so the generated log data will be sent to both the console and the file.

In the CMC, copy a couple of documents into the recycle bin, then run the program. The output should be the same as before (with the appropriate file names listed, of course), but if we check the log directory, we should find a new file named `PurgeRecycleBinPO.log`. The content will be the same as what was output to the console:

```
2016-09-24 16:25:29 INFO  PurgeRecycleBinPO:39 - Starting.
2016-09-24 16:25:29 INFO  PurgeRecycleBinPO:55 - Received 2 objects to
delete.
2016-09-24 16:25:29 DEBUG PurgeRecycleBinPO:59 - Deleting: Formatting' Sample
2016-09-24 16:25:29 DEBUG PurgeRecycleBinPO:59 - Deleting: Charting Samples
2016-09-24 16:25:29 INFO  PurgeRecycleBinPO:43 - Done!
```

Since we used a file *appender*, additional runs of the program will append to the file. We execute the program again, and the file now contains:

```
2016-09-24 16:25:29 INFO  PurgeRecycleBinPO:39 - Starting.
2016-09-24 16:25:29 INFO  PurgeRecycleBinPO:55 - Received 2 objects to
delete.
2016-09-24 16:25:29 DEBUG PurgeRecycleBinPO:59 - Deleting: Formatting' Sample
2016-09-24 16:25:29 DEBUG PurgeRecycleBinPO:59 - Deleting: Charting Samples
2016-09-24 16:25:29 INFO  PurgeRecycleBinPO:43 - Done!
2016-09-24 16:56:10 INFO  PurgeRecycleBinPO:39 - Starting.
2016-09-24 16:56:10 INFO  PurgeRecycleBinPO:55 - Received 0 objects to
delete.
2016-09-24 16:56:10 INFO  PurgeRecycleBinPO:43 - Done!
```

Next, package up the project in a jar as before, and upload it as a new Program Object. When executed, the output should be the same as before, but it will have generated a log file on the server.

There are many, many options in the log4j framework, making it a very flexible and robust solution for logging. If you are not already knowledgeable about it, we recommend learning more about it in order to efficiently use it with the BI4 Platform SDK.

Arguments

Arguments can be passed from a Program Object's scheduled instance as an input parameter to the program's run() method. The arguments are passed as a String array (similar to the way command line arguments are passed to a main() method). To illustrate, we'll create a simple Program Object that will purge all completed scheduled instances under a given folder:

```java
1   package bosdkbook;
2
3   import org.apache.log4j.Logger;
4
5   import com.crystaldecisions.sdk.exception.SDKException;
6   import com.crystaldecisions.sdk.framework.IEnterpriseSession;
7   import com.crystaldecisions.sdk.occa.infostore.IInfoObject;
8   import com.crystaldecisions.sdk.occa.infostore.IInfoObjects;
9   import com.crystaldecisions.sdk.occa.infostore.IInfoStore;
10  import com.crystaldecisions.sdk.plugin.desktop.program.IProgramBaseEx;
11
12  public class PurgeInstances implements IProgramBaseEx
13  {
14      @Override
15      public void run(IEnterpriseSession paramIEnterpriseSession,
16              IInfoStore paramIInfoStore, IInfoObject paramIInfoObject,
17              String objectID, String[] paramArrayOfString)
18              throws SDKException
19      {
20          String ancestor = paramArrayOfString[0];
21
22          System.out.println("Starting purge of instances from parent: " + ancestor
            );
23
24          IInfoObjects ios = paramIInfoStore.query("select si_id,si_name from
            ci_infoobjects where si_schedule_status in (1,3) and si_ancestor = " + ancestor);
```

```
25
26          for(Object o : ios)
27          {
28              IInfoObject io = (IInfoObject)o;
29              io.deleteNow();
30              IInfoObject io = (IInfoObject)o;
31          }
32      }
33 }
```

Listing 21: The PurgeInstances program

This program expects a single value as input, which is passed in as `paramArrayoOfString`. This is an array, and we only expect one value, so we extract that value on line 20. Note that we're not doing any error-checking here. In the real world, we would validate the value and possibly print a warning if there is more than one input value (or, if we expect multiple values, simply loop through each one).

The rest of the program is straightforward – we execute a CMS query to retrieve all completed instances that are descendants of the provided InfoObject ID.

Now we'll create the Program Object. In *Default Settings*, we'll provide the *Class to run* parameter, but leave *Arguments* blank for now:

Program Parameters

Arguments:	
Working Directory:	
Class to run:	bosdkbook.PurgeInstances
Classpath:	
JVM arguments:	

Next, we'll schedule the Program Object to run. We'll leave all the scheduling settings as-is except we'll add an argument on the Program Parameters tab. We'll enter 5179, which is the folder containing the instances we want to purge. Note that our CMS query retrieves all *descendants* of 5179, not just immediate children[99].

---

99   If we entered 23 for the argument, the program would dutifully delete all completed instances in public folders.

Program Parameters

Arguments:	5179
Working Directory:	
Class to run:	bosdkbook.PurgeInstances
Classpath:	
JVM arguments:	

When executed, the program will delete all completed instances under folder 5179. To perform the same operation on another folder, we just need to re-schedule the *PurgeInstaces* program and provide a different InfoObject ID for the argument.

Key point: arguments enable program objects to run dynamically – a number of scheduled instances can be created, with each one passing a different argument to the program.

Using a Build Script

Thus far, we've been using Eclipse's built-in *Export to Jar* feature to generate jar files to be used in Program Objects. While useful, there are some functions that we want to perform in jar generation that aren't supported by the *Export to Jar* user interface. In particular, we will want to exclude certain files from being included in the jar. The solution to this problem is to use an Apache Ant build script[100].

Ant is a process automation tool, designed to automate the creation of software programs, specifically Java applications. While Ant is capable of automating the entire build process, we only use it to create the jar files for our projects. Ant is incorporated within Eclipse, so we can create, maintain, and execute the build scripts natively within the Eclipse user interface.

To illustrate the use of a build script, we'll first modify our *PurgeRecycleBinPO* program to move the main() method into a Runner class. We'll then create an Ant build script to generate a jar file but without the Runner class file.

First, create the new Runner class in the bosdkbook package. Then move the main() method from PurgeRecycleBinPO.java into Runner.java[101]. Runner.java now looks like the following:

```
1  package bosdkbook;
2
3  import com.crystaldecisions.sdk.exception.SDKException;
4  import com.crystaldecisions.sdk.framework.CrystalEnterprise;
```

---

100 There are other solutions for building Java applications, such as Maven, but we will use Ant for our example.

101 Eclipse's refactoring features can help save a few clicks here. Right-click in the body of the main() method, click *Refactor → Move*, then select the Runner class.

```
 5  import com.crystaldecisions.sdk.framework.IEnterpriseSession;

 6  import com.crystaldecisions.sdk.framework.ISessionMgr;

 7  import com.crystaldecisions.sdk.occa.infostore.IInfoStore;

 8

 9  public class Runner

10  {

11

12      public static void main(String[] args) throws SDKException

13      {

14          ISessionMgr sessionManager = CrystalEnterprise.getSessionMgr();

15          IEnterpriseSession session = sessionManager.logon ("administrator",
    "xxxx", "192.168.56.102", "secEnterprise");

16

17          IInfoStore infoStore = (IInfoStore) session.getService ("","InfoStore");

18

19          new PurgeRecycleBinPO().run(session, infoStore, null, null, args);

20      }

21  }
```

Listing 22: Runner for PurgeRecycleBinPO

To confirm that this is functional, you can run or debug the program from within Runner.

Now we'll create the build script. In Project Explorer, right-click on the *PurgeRecycleBinPO* project, and hit *New → File*[102]. Call the file build.xml and hit OK. This should create a new, empty editor window for build.xml. Enter the code from Listing 23:

```
 1  <project name="buildjar" default="main">

 2      <property name="output.dir" value="/mnt/program_objects/lib"/>

 3      <basename property="project.name" file="${basedir}"/>

 4

 5      <target name="main">

 6          <jar jarfile="${output.dir}/${project.name}.jar">

 7              <fileset

 8                  dir="bin/"

 9                  includes="**/*"

10                  excludes="**/*Runner.*">
```

---

102 If you don't see File as an option, you may not have right-clicked in the right place. Make sure you're at the very top of the *PurgeRecycleBinPO* project.

11	`</fileset>`
12	`</jar>`
13	`</target>`
14	`</project>`

Listing 23: build.xml

We're not going to go through the file line-by-line, but it performs the following actions:

- Create a new jar file in the `/mnt/program_objects/lib` directory.

- The name of the file itself is taken from the name of the project, with a `.jar` extension.

- The jar file includes all files from the project's `bin/` directory...

- ...except those that match the pattern `Runner.*`.

Note that although we are hard-coding the location of the generated file, we are using the project's name for the name of the jar file. So, we can copy this `build.xml` into other projects without having to update the name.

Save the `build.xml` file but leave it open in the editor. The script may be executed in the same way as Java programs – via *Run → Run*, or (if the file is not open in the editor) by right-clicking on `build.xml` in Project Explorer and hitting *Run as → Ant Build*.

The output of Ant is displayed in the output window. A successful build appears with output similar to the following:

```
Buildfile: /home/joe/bi4workspace/PurgeRecycleBinPO/build.xml
main:
      [jar] Building jar: /mnt/program_objects/lib/PurgeRecycleBinPO.jar
BUILD SUCCESSFUL
Total time: 906 milliseconds
```

We can validate the build did what we expected if we look at the contents of the generated file:

```
$ unzip -l /mnt/program_objects/lib/PurgeRecycleBinPO.jar
Archive:  /mnt/program_objects/lib/PurgeRecycleBinPO.jar
  Length      Date    Time    Name
---------  ---------- -----    ----
        0  2016-10-08 19:32    META-INF/
      103  2016-10-08 19:31    META-INF/MANIFEST.MF
        0  2016-10-07 19:49    bosdkbook/
     3289  2016-10-08 19:31    bosdkbook/PurgeRecycleBinPO.class
      581  2016-10-05 19:15    log4j.properties
---------                      -------
     3973                      5 files
```

The jar file contains the `bosdkbook/PurgeRecycleBinPO.class` file, and `/log4j.properties,,` but does **not** contain `Runner.class`.

It is possible to call an Ant build script as part of the build process, that the script is executed automatically during a build. We do not recommend configuring this type of script to be executed during a build since the jar file would be created and deployed every time a change is made to a project file. The script can be executed with only a couple of mouse clicks, so executing it manually when needed is appropriate.

Chapter Review

- Program Objects allow for user-created programs or scripts to be run within the BOE server environment. They can be scheduled to run like any other schedulable document type.

- Java Program Objects must implement either the `IProgramBase` or `IProgramBaseEx` interface, and must implement a `run()` method. There are few other requirements for executing a Java program as a Program Object.

- Program Objects are created in the CMC. Updating an existing Program Object is not supported in the UI.

- Program Objects may fail for a variety of reasons; generally, failures are caused by incorrect entries in the Program Parameters.

- Testing a Program Object outside of BOE (ex., in Eclipse) is possible, but requires that a main() method be created to log in to the CMS and pass parameters to the run() method of `IProgramBase/IProgramBaseEx`.

- By default, exceptions thrown by BOE SDK calls in a Program Object (if uncaught) cause the scheduled instance to fail. There are many other options for managing, reporting, and throwing exceptions.

Quiz

1. Program Objects run:

   a) On a schedule

   b) Interactively

   c) Either

   d) Neither

2. The `paramIInfoObject` parameter of the `IProgramBaseEx.run()` method contains a

reference to:

a) The Program Object instance

b) The base Program Object (the parent of the scheduled instances)

c) The user who created the schedule

d) The user who created the Program Object

3. True/False: A scheduled Program Object can pass runtime parameters to the program

4. Program Objects are created in:

a) CMC only

b) BI launchpad only

c) Either

5. Which of the following program parameters are *required* for a Program Object to run?

a) Arguments

b) Working Directory

c) Class to run

d) Classpath

e) JVM arguments

6. Which of the following is *not* a likely cause of a ClassNotFoundException when a Program Object is executed?

a) The class name in the program parameters is misspelled.

b) The classpath provided in the program parameters is incorrect.

c) The program does not implement IProgramBase or IProgramBaseEx.

7. An unchecked exception that is thrown but not caught in a Program Object has the following effect:

a) The Program Object assumes a status of Failed, and the exception text is displayed in the instance's status field.

b) The Program Object succeeds and the exception text is displayed at the bottom of the instance's output file.

c) The Program Object succeeds, and no exception text is generated.

Answers on page 673.

Chapter 15 - The Program Object Management Pattern

Program Objects are quite valuable for performing regular system maintenance and administrative activities, but some inherent limitations make managing them somewhat difficult. To that end, we have compiled a number of procedures for working with Program Objects that can increase their value while making management easier and more effective. Collectively, we refer to these procedures as the *Program Object Management Pattern* (POMP)[103].

At a high level, the components of the POMP are:

- File directory structure for all Program Object files

- Publishing Program Objects to the `lib` directory

- Logging with log4j or equivalent

- Common location for third-party libraries and configuration files

- Common location for input and output files

- Using the `Runner` class

- Enhanced failure reporting with `SI_PROGRAM_CAN_FAIL_JOB`

We covered the use of the Runner class on page 322 and enhanced failure reporting on page 327. Neither of these components is strictly *required* for the POMP but is recommended for consistency.

The POMP provides several benefits for managing Program Objects, particularly in a large, complex SAP BusinessObjects environment. For one, it allows for a simpler, less error-prone method of supporting Program Objects in multiple environments than what was described on page 318. It also allows for more consistent management of third-party libraries and logging.

Directory Structure

The basis of the POMP is a directory structure that contains all files associated with the published Program Objects. In a single-machine cluster, this directory may reside on the machine itself or on a network share. In a multiple-machine cluster, the directory should be on a network share (even if the network share is hosted by one of the cluster machines).

The directory structure consists of a top-level directory named program_objects, and four subdirectories: `common`, `conf`, `lib`, `log`, and `output`[104]:

program_objects

---

103 We chose this name instead of the *Program Object Operational Pattern*, for obvious reasons....

```
└ common
└ conf
└ input
└ lib
└ log
└ output
```

- The `common` directory contains libraries (jar files) that are common to all Program Objects, and it is included in each one's classpath. For example, you may use `guava-xx.x.jar` in several Program Objects. Copying this file to the `common` directory ensures that it is available to all Program Objects when they are run.

- The `config` directory contains configuration and properties files that are read by Program Objects.

- The `input` directory contains files that are produced from some other application and used by Program Objects.

- The `lib` directory contains the jar files for each Program Object.

- The `log` directory contains the generated log files from the Program Objects.

- The `output` directory contains any output files that are generated by Program Objects, that are to be used by other applications.

At a minimum, this directory must be read/writable by the operating system account that the AJS runs as. In order to work with this directory from the client (to deploy jar files, etc.), it must also be visible to that machine and user as well.

On our BO server, we created `/opt/bobj/program_objects` and the child directory structure above. We created an NFS export for this directory to allow for access from our client. Then created a mountpoint to the server from our client, on `/mnt/program_objects`.

For Windows servers and clients, we would perform the same tasks, but in Windows syntax. If our BO server was on Windows, we would have created a local folder named `d:\program_objects`, shared it, and created the subdirectories (common, conf, etc.). From the client, we would reference this location via its UNC path, ex.: `\\bi4server\program_objects`. In any event, we need to be able to reference the `program_objects` directory from both the server machine and the client.

The following sections are dependent upon this directory structure being in place.

Publishing To the lib Directory

The SAP BusinessObjects platform does not provide a good method for updating Program Object library files (jars) once they are published. The recommended method, of manually replacing the jar files in the FRS, is undesirable for several reasons. However, we can exploit

---

104 Of course, you may choose alternate names as you see fit.

a couple of features of Program Objects to make updating them easier.

The class specified in the "Class to run" parameter of a Program Object does not necessarily need to be present in the jar file that is uploaded when the Program Object is created. The class simply must be present *somewhere* in the classpath[105]. So, we can upload a *dummy* file when creating the Program Object, put the *real* jar (the one containing the specified class) someplace else, and set the classpath to point to that "real" jar. The file that we upload when the Program Object is created can truly be a "dummy"; it is not actually used during execution.

To illustrate this procedure, we'll use the *SampleProgramObject* program from Listing 16. No changes are required in the program source code itself. So there is no need to generate a new jar, as long as you still have it available.

Step 1: Copy jar to program_objects/lib.

Our first step is to place the program's jar in `program_objects/lib`. We are copying the file from the local client to the server's `program_objects` directory; in our case, this is `/mnt/program_objects/lib`.

Step 2: Create Dummy File

Although the dummy file isn't actually used, the CMC does not let us upload a zero-byte file. But we can create a *single*-byte file[106]:

```
echo 1 > dummy.dat
```

Step 3: Create Program Object

In the CMC, we'll create a new Program Object just as we've done before. However, this time we'll select the dummy file as the file to upload:

---

105 The classpath provided to a Java Program Object includes the uploaded file, several core Platform SDK libraries, and the value passed in the Classpath parameter in the Program Object's Program Parameters properties tab (if any).

106 Since this is technically a hack, it may not work in future versions. If the CMC checks for a valid jar file, we would simply create a minimalistic Java application with an empty class, then use the generated jar when creating the Program Object.

Step 4: Set properties

The newly-created Program Object takes its name from the uploaded file, so in this case we'll have a new Program Object named *dummy*. Go to the Program Object's properties, and change its name appropriately:

Illustration 26: Program object properties

Hit *Save* before continuing. Next, in *Default Settings → Program Parameters*, we'll set the *Class to run* and *Classpath*. The *Class to run* is the same as before: `bosdkbook.SampleProgramObject`. For the Classpath, we set the location of the `SampleProgramObject.jar` file in the `program_objects/lib` directory. Note that this is done within the context of the *server*, so we use the path that is valid on that machine: `/opt/bobj/program_objects/lib/SampleProgramObject.jar`[107]:

---

107 If the BO server was Windows, this might be: `d:\program_objects\lib\SampleProgramObject.jar`.

Illustration 27: Program object parameters

We use the server's perspective of the path because we are **not** uploading the file from the client to the server as we did before, but rather telling the server *where it can find the file*. That is, all we're doing at this point is telling the server where to find `SampleProgramObject.jar`. When the Program Object is executed, the job server retrieves the specified file.

Step 5: Run

Now we'll schedule the Program Object to run. If all goes well, we'll get a *Success* message. If you instead get a *ClassNotFoundException:bosdkbook.SampleProgramObject*, then the server was not able to locate or load the jar file. Double-check:

- The `SampleProgramObject.jar` file actually contains `SampleProgramObject.class` (if you've used the same jar file as before, then this has already been confirmed)

- The *Class to run* parameter is correct

- The path specified in Classpath is valid on the server and the service account that the AJS is running as has permission to at least read the file. A good way to confirm this is to connect to the server (RDP on Windows or SSH on UNIX), log in as the service account, and attempt to read the file using the path specified in *Classpath*.

Once the above is successful, we can do what we came here to do – update a Program Object with a new version of a program.

We'll make a slight change to `SampleProgramObject.java`, just so we can confirm that the update has worked. Add a line at the beginning of the run() method, in line 18, as follows:

```
18          System.out.println("SampleProgramObject Version 2.0.");
```

Export the project to `SampleProgramObject.jar`, and replace the original one in the `program_objects/lib` directory on the BO server.

Back into the CMC, without making any changes to the Program Object, we just schedule it to run. It completes successfully, and the output begins with:

```
SampleProgramObject Version 2.0.
Guest
Administrator
SMAdmin
```

The first line reflects our recent change, and shows that our updating of the jar file was reflected in the execution of the Program Object!

From this point forward, our Program Object examples all use this method – we deploy the jar files to the `program_objects/lib` directory, and reference them from the *Classpath* parameter.

Logging with log4j

The `conf` directory is used to hold configuration files for Program Objects, while the `log` directory contains log files that are generated from Program Objects.

We'll illustrate the use of both of these directories with some changes to our *PurgeRecycleBinPO* program from Listing 19. We store the `log4j.properties` file in `conf` (rather than storing it in the Program Object's jar file) and then generate the logs to `log`.

We'll be using a single `log4j.properties` file for all Program Objects, so we'll create a new file in `/mnt/program_files/conf`[108]. We'll start with a copy of the one we created for `PurgeRecycleBinPO` (from Listing 20), and change it as follows:

```
log4j.logger.bosdkbook=DEBUG, console
log4j.logger.bosdkbook.PurgeRecycleBinPO=,PurgeRecycleBinPOAppender

log4j.appender.console=org.apache.log4j.ConsoleAppender
log4j.appender.console.Target=System.out
log4j.appender.console.layout=org.apache.log4j.PatternLayout
log4j.appender.console.layout.ConversionPattern=%d{yyyy-MM-dd HH:mm:ss} %-5p
%c{1}:%L - %m%n

log4j.appender.PurgeRecycleBinPOAppender=org.apache.log4j.FileAppender
log4j.appender.PurgeRecycleBinPOAppender.file=/opt/bobj/program_objects/log/
PurgeRecycleBinPO.log
log4j.appender.PurgeRecycleBinPOAppender.append=true
log4j.appender.PurgeRecycleBinPOAppender.layout=org.apache.log4j.PatternLayou
t
log4j.appender.PurgeRecycleBinPOAppender.layout.ConversionPattern=%d{yyyy-MM-
dd HH:mm:ss} %-5p %c{1}:%L - %m%n
```

Listing 24: /mnt/program_objects/conf/log4j.properties

We've made a couple of changes here worth noting. We left the `console` appender as-is but created a new file appender, which is program-specific (since we want to output each

---

108 This file is being created outside of the project, so use your favorite text editor to create it.

program's log to a different file).   The file appender that we're creating now is
`PurgeRecycleBinPOAppender`, and we'll add other appenders as needed as we deploy more
Program Objects.

We have set the destination of this file appender to be the `/opt/bobj/program_objects/log`
directory, with the name `PurgeRecycleBinPO.log`. Since this is executed on the server, we use
the appropriate path.

With `log4j.properties` in place, we can deploy the `PurgeRecycleBinPO` program.   We don't
actually need to make any changes to the program itself to accommodate the adjustments we
made to use the `program_objects` directory, but we **do** have to exclude the `log4j.properties`
file that is present in the project from being included in `PurgeRecycleBinPO.jar`. We want to
ensure that the program uses the `log4j.properties` file in the `program_objects/conf`
directory, rather than the one in the project. We don't actually want to *delete* the file from the
project since it would still be used if we run the program in Eclipse, so we can just exclude it
from the jar file generation.

So, we just modify the Ant build script that we created earlier (`build.xml`), to exclude
`log4j.proeprties`. Change the `excludes` property on line 10 to add `**/log4j.properties`:

```
 1  <project name="buildjar" default="main">
 2      <property name="output.dir" value="/mnt/program_objects/lib"/>
 3      <basename property="project.name" file="${basedir}"/>
 4
 5      <target name="main">
 6          <jar jarfile="${output.dir}/${project.name}.jar">
 7              <fileset
 8                  dir="bin/"
 9                  includes="**/*"
10                  excludes="**/*Runner.*,**/log4j.properties">
11              </fileset>
12          </jar>
13      </target>
14  </project>
```

Listing 25: build.xml for PurgeRecycleBinPO

Note that Ant will (intelligently) only create output files if the source files were modified
since the last build. Since we did not modify any of the source files, Ant does not rebuild the
jar when executed. You will need to either perform a "Clean", or just make a simple change
(space-backspace, Save) in `PurgeRecycleBinPO.java` to force Ant to perform a build. Watch
for the "Building jar" line in the output. If not present, then Ant did not create the jar file.

We can double-check the jar file to ensure that log4j.properties has been excluded:

```
$ unzip -l PurgeRecycleBinPO.jar
Archive:  PurgeRecycleBinPO.jar
  Length      Date    Time    Name
---------  ---------- -----   ----
        0  2016-10-09 08:53   META-INF/
      103  2016-10-09 08:53   META-INF/MANIFEST.MF
        0  2016-10-09 08:52   bosdkbook/
     3289  2016-10-09 08:52   bosdkbook/PurgeRecycleBinPO.class
---------                     -------
     3392                     4 files
```

Before we proceed, let's recap to ensure we are in sync with the contents of the `PurgeRecycleBinPO` project. The project now contains:

- The original `bosdkbook/PurgeRecycleBinPO.java` from Listing 19

- `Runner.java`, from Listing 22

- `log4j.properties`, from Listing 20

- `build.xml`, with log4j.properties excluded, from page 355

The compiled project is stored in `/mnt/program_objects/lib/PurgeRecycleBinPO.jar`.

We'll create a new Program Object for PuregeRecycleBinPO, using the method described on page 351 (create the Program Object using the `dummy.dat` file). Modify the newly-created Program Object to change the name to PurgeRecycleBinPO, then go to the *Default Settings → Program Parameters* tab.

Set the *Class to run* to `bosdkbook.PurgeRecycleBinPO`.

This example requires us to use the *Working Directory* parameter, which we'll set to `/opt/bobj/program_objects`. This allows us to include multiple paths in the classpath without having to specify the full path for each one.

Next, we'll specify the classpath. As before, we need to specify the path to the `PurgeRecycleBinPO.jar` file. Since we specified a working directory above, we only need to provide the location of the jar file *relative to that path*, which is:

`lib/PurgeRecycleBinPO.jar`

We also need to provide the location of the `log4j.properties` file in the `conf` directory. For files other than jars, we only need to specify the location of the directory containing the file, and not the file itself. So we need to add "`conf/`" to the classpath. Since our BO server is UNIX, we need to use the UNIX convention for separating classpath values, which is a colon. The full classpath parameter is now:

`lib/PurgeRecycleBinPO.jar:conf/`

If we were instead using a Windows server, the classpath would be given as:[109]

`lib\PurgeRecycleBinPO.jar;conf\`

---

109 Remember, this has nothing to do with the type of O/S on the client, but rather the BO server.

The above classpath specification, in conjunction with the working directory, would be equivalent to the following fully-qualified classpath:

```
/opt/bobj/program_objects/lib/PurgeRecycleBinPO.jar
/opt/bobj/program_objects/conf/
```

It is possible to specify an absolute path along with relative paths. If we needed to reference a jar in the classpath that is not below the working directory, we could specify its fully-qualified path. For example:

```
lib/PurgeRecycleBinPO.jar:conf/:/usr/share/java/commons-cli.jar
```

Our Program Parameters page now looks like the following:

Illustration 28: PurgeRecycleBinPO program parameters

Schedule the program to run. If all goes well, the instance will show a status of *Success*, and the contents of the output will look similar to the following:

```
2016-10-21 20:12:57 INFO  PurgeRecycleBinPO:27 - Starting PurgeRecycleBinPO
version 2.0
2016-10-21 20:12:57 INFO  PurgeRecycleBinPO:43 - Received 0 objects to
delete.
2016-10-21 20:12:57 INFO  PurgeRecycleBinPO:31 - Done!
```

We should also have a `PurgeRecycleBinPO.log` file in `/mnt/program_objects/log`. Since we set the log4j options to append to the file, it will contain the results of subsequent runs of the Program Object. For example:

```
2016-10-01 19:44:35 INFO  PurgeRecycleBinPO:39 - Starting PurgeRecycleBinPO
version 2.0
2016-10-01 19:44:35 INFO  PurgeRecycleBinPO:55 - Received 0 objects to
delete.
2016-10-01 19:44:35 INFO  PurgeRecycleBinPO:43 - Done!
2016-10-01 19:44:49 INFO  PurgeRecycleBinPO:39 - Starting PurgeRecycleBinPO
version 2.0
2016-10-01 19:44:49 INFO  PurgeRecycleBinPO:55 - Received 0 objects to
```

```
delete.
2016-10-01 19:44:49 INFO   PurgeRecycleBinPO:43 - Done!
2016-10-01 20:03:18 INFO   PurgeRecycleBinPO:39 - Starting PurgeRecycleBinPO
version 2.0
2016-10-01 20:03:18 INFO   PurgeRecycleBinPO:55 - Received 0 objects to
delete.
2016-10-01 20:03:18 INFO   PurgeRecycleBinPO:43 - Done!
2016-10-11 06:32:17 INFO   PurgeRecycleBinPO:27 - Starting PurgeRecycleBinPO
version 2.0
2016-10-11 06:32:17 INFO   PurgeRecycleBinPO:43 - Received 0 objects to
delete.
2016-10-11 06:32:17 INFO   PurgeRecycleBinPO:31 - Done!
2016-10-21 20:12:57 INFO   PurgeRecycleBinPO:27 - Starting PurgeRecycleBinPO
version 2.0
2016-10-21 20:12:57 INFO   PurgeRecycleBinPO:43 - Received 0 objects to
delete.
2016-10-21 20:12:57 INFO   PurgeRecycleBinPO:31 - Done!
```

Listing 26: program_objects/log/PurgeRecycleBinPO.log

We made several changes in the section, so there are a few opportunities for things to go wrong. Here are some suggested troubleshooting steps:

If the Program Object fails with a *ClassNotFoundException:bosdkbook.PurgeRecycleBinPO* message, then there are a few things to check:

- As before, make sure the *Class to run* in Program Parameters is correct (page 356)

- Make sure that PurgeRecycleBinPO.jar is present in /mnt/program_objects/lib, and that the jar has the correct file structure. That is, it contains `PurgeRecycleBinPO.class` in the bosdkbook directory (page 355).

- Ensure that both the *Working Directory* and *Classpath* are correct in the Program Object's *Program Parameters* page (page 357), and double-check that the correct delimiter is used in classpath (colon for UNIX servers, semicolon for Windows servers). To test, you may specify the fully-qualified path the jar file in Classpath, e.g.:

  `/opt/bobj/program_objects/lib/PurgeRecycleBinPO.jar`

- Ensure that the specified Working Directory and Classpath are valid on the SAP BusinessObjects server. In our examples, we've been using `/mnt/program_objects` on our client and `/opt/bobj/program_objects` on our server, although both paths point to the same location. Make sure you're using the server's version of the path in *Working Directory* and *Classpath*.

If the Program Object fails with this error: *The working directory '/opt/bobj/program_objects' could not be found.*, then either the directory does not exist on the server, of the user account that the CMS is running as does not have permission to access it.

If the Program Object reports a status of Success, but the output contains the following:

```
log4j:WARN No appenders could be found for logger (bosdkbook.PurgeRecycleBinPO).
log4j:WARN Please initialize the log4j system properly.
```

...then it means that the program was not able to find the `log4j.properties` file, or the file is not correct. Check the following:

- The log4j.properties file is present in `/mnt/program_objects/conf`.

- The *Working Directory* in the Program Parameters page is correct (page 357).

- The Classpath includes a reference to `conf/` (page 357)

- The log4j.properties file is correct (page 354); in particular, it includes a correct reference to `bosdkbook.PurgeRecycleBinPO`:

  ```
  log4j.logger.bosdkbook.PurgeRecycleBinPO=,PurgeRecycleBinPOAppender
  ```

*   *   *

The `conf` directory can be used for any other configuration/properties files that need to be read by Program Objects. As an example, you may want to have a Program Object that runs daily, sending emails to designated recipients with a list of schedules that had failed. The recipient list may change frequently, so it would be beneficial to put this data in a file in the `/conf` directory so it can be updated as needed without having to re-deploy the program. The following code fragment reads in the list of recipients from a file named `recipients.txt`. We would treat the `recipients.txt` file the same as `log4j.properties` above; that is, we would put it in the `src/` directory in the Eclipse project during development, but copy it to the `program_objects/conf` directory when running it as a Program Object.

```
1  BufferedReader is = new BufferedReader(
           new InputStreamReader(
               this.getClass()
                   .getClassLoader()
                   .getResourceAsStream("recipients.txt")));

2

3  String recip;

4          while ((recip = is.readLine()) != null) {

5      << do something with recipient list here >>

6  }
```

Note that we don't have to do anything with the Program Object's Program Parameters to accommodate this file. The classpath that we used in the previous example included the `conf/` directory, which allows the program to reference any file in that location.

The SyncUsers program

The *SyncUsers* example illustrates the use of all POMP components. In addition to the components described above, we will introduce the input and output directories. As their names imply, these directories are used when a Program Object needs to process files that are generated by another application, or when it needs to write files to be processed by another application. Obviously then, these directories are not used by all Program Objects but only those that have a requirement described above.

We'll illustrate the use of both the input and output directories with the *SyncUsers* program. The program would be used in a scenario in which user names in an SAP BusinessObjects system need to be synchronized with another application[110]. The other application generates a list of user names to a designated text file; the Program Object then reads this list, creating new user names as necessary. The program also removes users in the SAP BusinessObjects system if they are not present in the text file.

This program performs the following steps:

- Read the contents of a text file, which contains a list of user names.

- For each user name, check if a corresponding user name exists in the CMS.

  ○ If the user does not exist in the CMS, create it and add it to the *Synced Users* group.

  ○ If the user **does** exist, check if it is a member of the *Synced Users* group. If not, add it.

  ○ If the user exists and is a member of the *Synced Users* group, take no action.

- Go through each user in the *Synced Users* group in the CMS.

  ○ If the user's name is not present in the input file, then delete the user. Unless the user is a member of any other group, in which case it is not deleted but just removed from the *Synced Users* group.

  ○ If the user's name is present in the input file, take no action.

While this is a real-world scenario, we have simplified the program for illustration. If we were to put this program into a real production environment, we would add much more functionality such as synchronizing passwords, email addresses, and full names. We would also build in additional safety checks before deleting users.

This project includes a few of the concepts that we covered previously – including logging with log4j, and failure reporting with SI_PROGRAM_CAN_FAIL_JOB.

To begin, create a new project for the *SyncUsers* Program Object and add the SyncUsers class from Listing 28.

In order to test the program in Eclipse, we'll need the Runner class from Listing 29, and a log4j.properties file – we can re-use the one from Listing 20.

We'll need an input and output directory. Create these directories at the root of the *SyncUsers* project (*not* in the src directory).

---

110 In the real world, we would attempt to use a more out-of-the-box solution, such as leveraging LDAP groups.

In the `input` directory, create a file named `users.txt`. In this file, add the names of a few test users, for example:

```
testuser1
testuser2
testuser3
```

The project structure should look like the following:

```
SyncUsers
└ src
   └ bosdkbook
      └ Runner.java
      └ SyncUsers.java
   └ log4j.properties
└ input
   └ users.txt
└ output
```

Next, in the CMS, create a new user group named *Synced Users*[111], and we'll be ready to execute the program. But first, let's look at what the program is going to do.

As in previous examples, the `run()` method is only tasked with setting up failure reporting, calling the `doSync()` method, and performing failure reporting if necessary.

The first real task of the `doSync()` method, in lines 75-90, is to read in the contents of the `input/users.txt` file into a `Map` named `inputUsers`. The `inputUsers` map's key is the user ID in lower case, while the map value is the user ID in its original case. This allows us to do a case-insensitive lookup to the map later on.

Note that we're wrapping this file operation in a `try/finally` block but not catching any exceptions. We'll let all exceptions in `doSync()` be thrown upwards to `run()`, which results in a fatal error. Even in this case, the `finally` block is executed, ensuring that the files are closed[112].

With the file loaded into the `inputUsers` map, we then check to ensure that the list is populated (lines 92-96). If empty, we just log a message and return.

We need to get the InfoObject ID of the *Synced Users* group, so we perform a query for this in lines 101-105. If the group can't be found by name, then we throw an `Exception`, causing a fatal error.

On lines 117 and 118, we create the two output files. As above, this is wrapped in a `try/finally` block (but no `catch`).

Now we begin the real work of the program. On line 120, we start a `for` loop to iterate over the list of user names from the input file. For each user name, we execute a CMS query (line 123) to see if the user is present in the CMS.

---

111 Be aware that this program will actually be creating and deleting users.

112 If using Java 7 or newer, a `try-with-resources` block could be used to close the files instead of `finally`.

If the user does not exist (the CMS query returns no results), then we create a new user – this is done in lines 126-132. Note that we are joining the user to the *Synced Users* group (line 129), and we're printing out the created user name to the `createdusers.txt` output file.

If the user name *was* found in the CMS, then we do a second check to see if the user is present in the *Synced Users* group (line 137). If the user is not in the group, then we join it on line 140. Otherwise, we take no action with this user (as it exists in the CMS and is in the correct group).

The above-described loop is completed on line 145.

In the next phase of the program, we'll be validating the membership of users that are in the *Synced Users* group. We begin by performing a CMS query to retrieve all member users of this group (line 148-152). Note that this query will include any users that we created or updated in the previous phase. There is some redundancy here, but it won't hurt....

```
148         IInfoObjects existingUsers = infoStore.query(
149             " select si_id,si_names,si_usergroups " +
150             " from ci_systemobjects " +
151             " where children(\"si_name='usergroup-user'\"," +
152             "                \"si_name='" + syncedUserGroupName + "'\")");
```

On line 157, we start a for loop to iterate through all users in the CMS query result set. First, we check if the user name is present in the input file. Remember that the `inputUsers` map contains this list of users, and its key is the user name in lower case – so we're checking for the existence of a key in that map equal to the CMS user's name (title) in lower case:

```
160             .contains(existingUser.getTitle().toLowerCase()))
```

If the user name is not found in the `inputUsers` map, then it means the user is present in the *Synced Users* group but should not be. There are two possibilities here. If the user is **only** in the Synced Users group, then we want to delete it. Since all users are a member of the *Everyone* group, we just check to see if the user is a member of exactly two groups. If so, we delete the user (line 166). Otherwise, the user is in more than two groups, hence in a group other than *Everyone* and *Synced Users*. So in this case, we don't want to delete the user but rather remove it from *Synced Users*. We do this on line 171:

```
171             existingUser.getGroups().remove(syncUserGroup.getID());
172             existingUser.save();
```

We do not need to `commit()` the `newUsers` collection since we performed a `save()` operation after each modification and user creation. If any exception occurred in the middle of processing, this would result in some users being saved and the remaining not. In our scenario, this would be acceptable – once the problem is resolved and the program re-run, the remaining changes (whether they be additions or deletions) would be completed.

So let's do a test run of the program in Eclipse. Since this program actually does things that could be damaging to a system (specifically deleting users), it's a good idea to take some precautions before the first run. As mentioned on page 261, one option is to comment out these operations, so we'll modify line 166 accordingly:

```
166                    //existingUser.deleteNow();
```

Now (finally!) let's run the program. If all goes well, the output should be similar to the following:

```
2016-11-25 19:12:46 INFO  SyncUsers:48 - Starting SyncUsers version 1.0
2016-11-25 19:12:46 INFO  SyncUsers:99 - Read 3 records from input file.
2016-11-25 19:12:46 INFO  SyncUsers:133 - Creating new user: testuser3
2016-11-25 19:12:46 INFO  SyncUsers:133 - Creating new user: testuser1
2016-11-25 19:12:46 INFO  SyncUsers:133 - Creating new user: testuser2
2016-11-25 19:12:46 INFO  SyncUsers:161 - Read 3 existing users from CMS.
2016-11-25 19:12:46 INFO  SyncUsers:192 - Done!
```

We can see that the program created the three users that were present in the users.txt file, as we had expected. If we check the CMS, we will see these three new user accounts in the *Synced Users* group.

If instead of the above, you get the following message:

```
2016-11-25 19:18:29 INFO  SyncUsers:48 - Starting SyncUsers version 1.0
PROCPROGRAM:PROGRAM_ERROR
62009
input/users.txt (No such file or directory)
```

then there is a problem with either the input directory or the users.txt file. First, confirm that the input directory is present at the root of the project directory and that the users.txt file is present in it. If both are correct, then confirm that the project's working directory is set correctly. In Project Properties → Run/Debug Settings, there should be a single launch configuration, likely named *Runner*.   Select it and click *Edit*. On the *Arguments* tab, confirm that the Working Directory is set to Default and that the value is "$ {workspace_loc:SyncUsers}". Also, confirm that the value of inputFileName on line 30 is correct and is using the appropriate directory delimiter for the OS that you are using.

Assuming the program completed successfully, we'll do another test. Change the users.txt file to remove testuser2 and add testuser4:

```
testuser1
testuser3
testuser4
```

And run the program. The output should be similar to the following:

```
2016-11-25 19:41:24 INFO  SyncUsers:48 - Starting SyncUsers version 1.0
2016-11-25 19:41:24 INFO  SyncUsers:99 - Read 3 records from input file.
```

```
2016-11-25 19:41:24 INFO   SyncUsers:133 - Creating new user: testuser4
2016-11-25 19:41:24 INFO   SyncUsers:161 - Read 4 existing users from CMS.
2016-11-25 19:41:24 INFO   SyncUsers:173 - User: testuser2 not found in input
file.  Deleting from CMS.
2016-11-25 19:41:24 INFO   SyncUsers:192 - Done!
```

Remember that we commented out the `deleteNow()` call, so *testuser2* was not actually deleted. If we run the program again, we will get the same output (except that it won't be creating testuser4). So since we've confirmed that the program is working as expected, we can uncomment line 166 and run the program again. We'll still see the same output, but this time testuser2 will actually be deleted.

With a successful run in Eclipse, we'll now package our program to run as a Program Object. We need an Ant build file, and we can use the `build.xml` from Listing 25 on page 355. Copy this file into the root of the *SyncUsers* project. Remember that we made build.xml generic, so no modifications are required in order to use it with other projects. So, just right-click on `SyncUsers/build.xml` in the Project Explorer, and hit *Run As → Ant Build*. This should successfully create `/mnt/program_objects/lib/SyncUsers.jar`, or the equivalent path for your environment.

If the `input` and `output` directories don't already exist in the `/mnt/program_objects` directory, create them now. In the `input` directory, create a new `users.txt` file. We'll add a couple more test users to it:

```
testuser10
testuser11
testuser12
```

In order for our Program Object to log to log4j properly, we'll need to update the `log4j.properties` file in `/mnt/program_objects/conf`. The complete log4j.properties, with the new modifications in bold, are in Listing 27:

```
log4j.logger.bosdkbook=DEBUG, console
log4j.logger.bosdkbook.PurgeRecycleBinPO=,PurgeRecycleBinPOAppender
log4j.logger.bosdkbook.SyncUsers=,SyncUsersAppender

log4j.appender.console=org.apache.log4j.ConsoleAppender
log4j.appender.console.Target=System.out
log4j.appender.console.layout=org.apache.log4j.PatternLayout
log4j.appender.console.layout.ConversionPattern=%d{yyyy-MM-dd HH:mm:ss} %-5p
%c{1}:%L - %m%n

log4j.appender.PurgeRecycleBinPOAppender=org.apache.log4j.FileAppender
log4j.appender.PurgeRecycleBinPOAppender.file=/opt/bobj/program_objects/log/
PurgeRecycleBinPO.log
log4j.appender.PurgeRecycleBinPOAppender.append=true
log4j.appender.PurgeRecycleBinPOAppender.layout=org.apache.log4j.PatternLayou
t
log4j.appender.PurgeRecycleBinPOAppender.layout.ConversionPattern=%d{yyyy-MM-
dd HH:mm:ss} %-5p %c{1}:%L - %m%n
```

```
log4j.appender.SyncUsersAppender=org.apache.log4j.FileAppender
log4j.appender.SyncUsersAppender.file=/opt/bobj/program_objects/log/
SyncUsersAppender.log
log4j.appender.SyncUsersAppender.append=true
log4j.appender.SyncUsersAppender.layout=org.apache.log4j.PatternLayout
log4j.appender.SyncUsersAppender.layout.ConversionPattern=%d{yyyy-MM-dd
HH:mm:ss} %-5p %c{1}:%L - %m%n
```

Listing 27: log4j.properties updated for SyncUsers

To summarize the above few steps, we:

- Executed build.xml in Eclipse, which created `SyncUsers.jar` in `/mnt/program_objects/lib`.

- Created `/mnt/program_objects/input` and `/mnt/program_objects/output`, if they weren't already there.

- Created `users.txt` in the `/mnt/program_objects/input` directory, and added three test user names to it.

- Updated `/mnt/program_objects/conf/log4j.properties` to add settings for `SyncUsers`.

Now, in the CMC, we'll create a Program Objects for *SyncUsers*. As before, use the `dummy.dat` file when creating the new Program Object. Modify the newly-created Program Object and change its name to *SyncUsers*. Go to the *Default Settings → Program Parameters* tab, and set the values as follows:

Working Directory: `/opt/bobj/program_objects`   (or the appropriate path to the program_objects directory for your BO server)

Class to run: `bosdkbook.SyncUsers`

Classpath: `lib/SyncUsers.jar:conf/`   (for Windows server, use `lib\Syncusers.jar;conf\`)

Schedule the Program Object to run! If all goes well, the instance will be Successful, and the instance output file will be similar to the following:

```
2016-11-26 09:59:52 INFO   SyncUsers:48 - Starting SyncUsers version 1.0
2016-11-26 09:59:52 INFO   SyncUsers:99 - Read 3 records from input file.
2016-11-26 09:59:52 INFO   SyncUsers:133 - Creating new user: testuser12
2016-11-26 09:59:52 INFO   SyncUsers:133 - Creating new user: testuser11
2016-11-26 09:59:52 INFO   SyncUsers:133 - Creating new user: testuser10
2016-11-26 09:59:52 INFO   SyncUsers:161 - Read 6 existing users from CMS.
2016-11-26 09:59:52 INFO   SyncUsers:173 - User: testuser3 not found in input
file.  Deleting from CMS.
2016-11-26 09:59:52 INFO   SyncUsers:173 - User: testuser1 not found in input
file.  Deleting from CMS.
2016-11-26 09:59:52 INFO   SyncUsers:173 - User: testuser4 not found in input
file.  Deleting from CMS.
2016-11-26 09:59:52 INFO   SyncUsers:192 - Done!
```

The output indicates that the new user names that we added (testuser10, 11, 12) were created as new users. The existing users in the *Synced Users* group were deleted since they were not present in the file.

```java
1   package bosdkbook;
2
3   import java.io.BufferedReader;
4   import java.io.BufferedWriter;
5   import java.io.FileReader;
6   import java.io.FileWriter;
7   import java.io.PrintWriter;
8   import java.util.HashMap;
9   import java.util.Map;
10
11  import org.apache.log4j.Logger;
12
13  import com.crystaldecisions.sdk.exception.SDKException;
14  import com.crystaldecisions.sdk.framework.IEnterpriseSession;
15  import com.crystaldecisions.sdk.occa.infostore.IInfoObject;
16  import com.crystaldecisions.sdk.occa.infostore.IInfoObjects;
17  import com.crystaldecisions.sdk.occa.infostore.IInfoStore;
18  import com.crystaldecisions.sdk.plugin.desktop.program.IProgramBaseEx;
19  import com.crystaldecisions.sdk.plugin.desktop.user.IUser;
20  import com.crystaldecisions.sdk.properties.IProperty;
21
22  public class SyncUsers implements IProgramBaseEx
23  {
24      private IInfoStore infoStore;
25      private final static Logger LOGGER = Logger.getLogger(SyncUsers.class);
26      private final static String syncedUserGroupName="Synced Users";
27      private final static String initialPassword="P2$$w0rD";
28      private final static String createdUserLogFileName =
        "output/createdusers.txt";
29      private final static String deletedUserLogFileName =
        "output/deletedusers.txt";
30      private final static String inputFileName = "input/users.txt";
31
```

```java
32      @Override
33      public void run(IEnterpriseSession paramIEnterpriseSession,
34              IInfoStore paramIInfoStore, IInfoObject paramIInfoObject,
35              String objectID, String[] paramArrayOfString)
36              throws SDKException
37      {
38          this.infoStore = paramIInfoStore;
39
40          if(paramIInfoObject!=null)
41          {
42              paramIInfoObject.getProcessingInfo().properties().add(
43                      "SI_PROGRAM_CAN_FAIL_JOB", Boolean.TRUE,
44                      IProperty.DIRTY);
44              paramIInfoObject.save();
45          }
46
47          LOGGER.info("Starting " + this.getClass().getSimpleName() + " version
1.0");
48          try
49          {
50              doSync();
51          }
52          catch (Exception e)
53          {
54              // Print the code to signal the failure
55              System.out.println("PROCPROGRAM:PROGRAM_ERROR");
56              System.out.println("62009");
57
58              // Print the error message
59              System.out.println(e.getMessage());
60
61              // exit the program
62              System.exit(1);
63          }
64      }
```

```java
65
66      private void doSync() throws Exception
67      {
68          // inputUsers will contain the list of user IDs from the input file.
69          // The map key is the user ID in lower case; the value is the original
   ID in mixed case.
70          Map<String,String> inputUsers = new HashMap<String,String>();
71
72          // Read the input file into the inputUsers map
73          BufferedReader is = null;
74
75          try
76          {
77              is = new BufferedReader(new FileReader(inputFileName));
78
79              String inputUserLine;
80              while ((inputUserLine = is.readLine()) != null)
81              {
82                  if(!inputUserLine.trim().equals(""))
83                      inputUsers.put(inputUserLine.toLowerCase(),inputUserLine);
84              }
85          }
86          finally
87          {
88              if(is != null)
89                  is.close();
90          }
91
92          if(inputUsers.size()==0)
93          {
94              LOGGER.info("No records found in input file.  Exiting.");
95              return;
96          }
97
98          LOGGER.info("Read " + inputUsers.size() + " records from input file.");
```

369 Part Two – The Java SDK

```
99
100        // Get the "Synced Users" user group as an InfoObject, store in
     syncUserGroup
101        IInfoObjects syncUserGroups = infoStore.query("select si_id from
     ci_systemobjects where si_kind = 'usergroup' and si_name = '" +
     syncedUserGroupName + "'");
102        if(syncUserGroups.size()==0)
103        {
104            throw new Exception("Unable to locate the Synced Users group!");
105        }
106
107        IInfoObject syncUserGroup = (IInfoObject)syncUserGroups.get(0);
108
109        // Any new user IDs that we create in the CMS will be placed in the
     newUsers IInfoObjects collection
110        IInfoObjects newUsers = infoStore.newInfoObjectCollection();
111
112        PrintWriter createdUserLogWriter = null;
113        PrintWriter deletedUserLogWriter = null;
114
115        try
116        {
117            createdUserLogWriter =
                   new PrintWriter(
                       new BufferedWriter(
                           new FileWriter(createdUserLogFileName,true)));
118            deletedUserLogWriter =
                   new PrintWriter(
                       new BufferedWriter(
                           new FileWriter(deletedUserLogFileName,true)));
119
120            for(String inputUser : inputUsers.values())
121            {
122                // Check if there's an existing user in the CMS for this ID from
         the input file
123                IInfoObjects cmsUsers = infoStore.query("select
         si_id,si_name,si_usergroups from ci_systemobjects where si_kind = 'user' and
         si_name = '" + inputUser + "'");
124                    if(cmsUsers.size() == 0) // User ID does not exist in CMS
```

```
125                  {
126                      LOGGER.info("Creating new user: " + inputUser);
127                      createdUserLogWriter.println(inputUser);
128                      IUser newUser = (IUser) newUsers.add(IUser.KIND);
129                      newUser.getGroups().add(syncUserGroup.getID());
130                      newUser.setTitle(inputUser);
131                      newUser.setNewPassword(initialPassword);
132                      newUser.save();
133                  }
134              else
135              { // User ID exists in CMS; check if it's in the Synced Users
    group
136                  IUser cmsUser = (IUser)cmsUsers.get(0);
137                  if(!cmsUser.getGroups().contains(syncUserGroup.getID()))
138                  { // ID is not in Synced Users group, add it
139                      LOGGER.info("Adding existing user: " + inputUser + " to
    Synced Users group.");
140                      cmsUser.getGroups().add(syncUserGroup.getID());
141                      cmsUser.save();
142                  }
143                  // else ID exists in CMS and is in Synced Users group - no
    action
144              }
145          }
146
147          // Get a list of all user IDs in Synced User group, so we can check
    if they are in input file
148          IInfoObjects existingUsers = infoStore.query(
149              " select si_id,si_names,si_usergroups " +
150              " from ci_systemobjects " +
151              " where children(\"si_name='usergroup-user'\"," +
152              "                 \"si_name='" + syncedUserGroupName + "'\")");
153
154          LOGGER.info("Read " + existingUsers.size() + " existing users from
    CMS.");
155
```

```
156                // Go through each CMS user; check if in input file
157            for(Object o : existingUsers)
158            {
159                IUser existingUser = (IUser)o;
160                if(!inputUsers.keySet()
                        .contains(existingUser.getTitle().toLowerCase()))
161            { // CMS user not in input file.  If this user is only in two
   groups (Synced Users and Everyone), then delete the user ID
162                deletedUserLogWriter.println(existingUser.getTitle());
163                if(existingUser.getGroups().size() == 2)
164                {
165                    LOGGER.info("User: " +existingUser.getTitle() + " not
   found in input file.  Deleting from CMS.");
166                    existingUser.deleteNow();
167                }
168                else // User is in additional groups. Don't delete, but just
   remove user from Synced Users
169                {
170                    LOGGER.info("User: " + existingUser.getTitle() + " not
   found in input file.  Removing from Synced Users group.");
171                    existingUser.getGroups().remove(syncUserGroup.getID());
172                    existingUser.save();
173                }
174            }
175            }
176        }
177        finally
178        {
179            if(createdUserLogWriter!=null)
180                createdUserLogWriter.close();
181            if(deletedUserLogWriter!=null)
182                deletedUserLogWriter.close();
183        }
184        LOGGER.info("Done!");
185    }
186 }
```

Listing 28: The SyncUsers program

```
1  package bosdkbook;

2

3  import com.crystaldecisions.sdk.exception.SDKException;

4  import com.crystaldecisions.sdk.framework.CrystalEnterprise;

5  import com.crystaldecisions.sdk.framework.IEnterpriseSession;

6  import com.crystaldecisions.sdk.framework.ISessionMgr;

7  import com.crystaldecisions.sdk.occa.infostore.IInfoStore;

8

9  public class Runner

10 {

11

12     public static void main(String[] args) throws SDKException

13     {

14         ISessionMgr sessionManager = CrystalEnterprise.getSessionMgr();

15         IEnterpriseSession session = sessionManager.logon ("administrator",
   "xxxx", "192.168.56.102", "secEnterprise");

16

17         IInfoStore infoStore = (IInfoStore) session.getService ("","InfoStore");

18

19         new SyncUsers().run(session, infoStore, null, null, args);

20     }

21 }
```

Listing 29: Runner for SyncUsers

Chapter Review

- The POMP offers a consistent approach to managing Program Objects effectively and efficiently. Some of the benefits include:
    - Ease of updating Program Objects' jar files
    - Single location for third-party libraries
    - Consistent location of configuration and logging files
- Publishing a Program Object's jar file to a file share (instead of uploading it during Program Object creation) makes it easier to update the Program Object later.

- The directory structure forms the basis of the POMP; it contains program object libraries, configuration files, input/output files, and logging files.

Quiz

1. What would be the appropriate location in the POMP structure for a jar file that is used by several Program Objects?

   a) common

   b) conf

   c) lib

2. The POMP directory structure must be accessible from:

   a) The BOE server

   b) The developer's client

   c) Both

   d) Neither

3. Which POMP directory should log4j.properties be stored in?

   a) common

   b) conf

   c) lib

   d) input

   e) output

4. If the BOE server is UNIX and the developer's workstation is Windows, in which syntax should a Program Object's working directory be specified?

   a) UNIX

   b) Windows

Answers on page 673.

Chapter 16 - Working With Content

In the past few chapters, we've seen how the BI4 Platform SDK can be used to manage several different types of CMS objects, including users and groups, folders, and more. In this chapter, we'll delve further into these object types and cover additional types that you are likely to use.

Folders

In Chapter 3, we covered the properties of the various types of folders in a typical CMS. Each of these folders is represented in the infostore by the IFolder interface. The methods of IFolder are:

Package com.crystaldecisions.sdk.plugin.desktop.folder
Interface _IFolder_
extends _IContainer_, _IFolderBase_, IInfoObject

Fields

static String	FAVORITESFOLDER_KIND	FavoritesFolder
	The kind value for Favorites Folder InfoObjects	
static String	FAVORITESFOLDER_PROGID	CrystalEnterprise.FavoritesFolder
	The ProgID value for Favorites Folder InfoObjects	
static String	FOLDER_KIND	Folder
	The kind value for Folder InfoObjects	
static String	FOLDER_PROGID	CrystalEnterprise.Folder
	The ProgID value for Folder InfoObjects	

Methods

IInfoObject	add(String kind)
	Creates a new InfoObject of the specified kind, and adds it to this collection.
IInfoObjects	getChildren()
	Returns an IInfoObjects collection containing all of this object's children.
IInfoObjects	getChildren(int propertySet,SearchPattern searchPattern,SortType sortType)

	Returns an IInfoObjects collection containing all of this object's children that match the specified SearchPattern. The objects are ordered according to SortType and include the properties identified by propertySet.
IInfoObjects	getContents()
	Returns an IInfoObjects collection containing all of this object's children that are not folders themselves.
IInfoObjects	getContents(int propertySet,SearchPattern searchPattern,SortType sortType)
	Returns an IInfoObjects collection containing all of this object's children that match the specified SearchPattern, and are not folders themselves, The objects are ordered according to SortType, and include the properties identified by propertySet.
String[]	getPath()
	Retrieves the names of the folder's ancestors, as a String array. *Associated property:* SI_PATH

Class/Interface 15: IFolder

The getPath() method is used to display the full path to the folder. For example, we'll query for the *Quarterly* folder under *Sales / Financial,* and display its path:

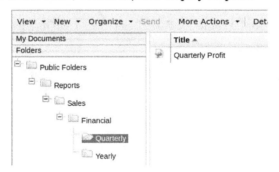

```
        IInfoObjects ios = infoStore.query("select si_path from ci_infoobjects where
si_id = 6250");


        for(Object o : ios)

        {

            IFolder sales = (IFolder)o;


            for(String p : sales.getPath())
```

```
        System.out.println(p);

    }
```

This displays:

```
Financial
Sales
Reports
```

...which are the names of *Quarterly*'s ancestors, in reverse order. That is, IFolder.getPath()
[0] always displays the name of the folder's immediate parent.

Note that while the SI_PATH property includes other information pertaining to the ancestor
folders (see page 71 for details), the getPath() method only returns the folder names. To
retrieve the IDs of the ancestors, it is necessary to retrieve the SI_PATH property values
directly:

```
        IInfoObjects ios = infoStore.query("select si_path from ci_infoobjects where
si_id = 6250");


        for(Object o : ios)

        {

            IFolder sales = (IFolder)o;


            IProperties sipath =
                sales.properties().getProperties(CePropertyID.SI_PATH);


            int folderCount = sipath.getInt("SI_NUM_FOLDERS");

            for(int x = 1;x<=folderCount;x++)

            {

                String folderName = sipath.getString("SI_FOLDER_NAME" + x);

                Integer folderID = sipath.getInt("SI_FOLDER_ID" + x);


                System.out.println(folderID + " " + folderName);

            }

        }
```

This displays the InfoObject ID along with the folder name:

```
6249 Financial
6248 Sales
4213 Reports
```

The IFolder interface provides four methods for retrieving child InfoObjects: two overloaded methods each for getChildren() and getContents(). The difference between then (as non-intuitive as it is) is that getChildren() returns all of the folder's child InfoObjects, while getContents() returns only those InfoObjects that are not folders themselves.

The two methods with no parameters retrieve an unfiltered list of InfoObjects, using the properties specified in IInfoObject.PropertySet.DEFAULT (see page 225). The other two methods allow for filtering and sorting of the result, and for a different property set to the specified. See the IInfoStore.find() method on page 292 for more information on these two parameters.

These are shortcut methods – they each perform a new CMS query to retrieve the folder's children.

Previously we worked with folders in Public Folders. For this example we'll retrieve the top-level *Universes* folder, then use IFolder.getChildren() to display its children:

```java
        IFolder folder = (IFolder) infoStore.query("select static from ci_appobjects
where si_cuid = '" + CeSecurityCUID.RootFolder.UNIVERSES + "'").get(0);


        IInfoObjects kids = folder.getChildren();


        for(Object o : kids)
        {
            IInfoObject io = (IInfoObject)o;
            System.out.println(io.getKind() + " " + io.getTitle());
        }
    }
```

This prints out the objects in the root Universes folder, which in our system are:

```
Folder Financial
Folder Human Resources
Folder Report Conversion Tool Universes
Folder webi universes
```

The IFolder.add() method is a shortcut for creating a new InfoObject with IInfoObjects.add() and then setting the new object's parent ID to this folder. In the following example, we'll create a new Hyperlink in the *Reports* folder:

```java
        IFolder folder = (IFolder) infoStore.query("select static from ci_infoobjects
where si_kind = 'folder' and si_name = 'reports' and si_parentid = 23").get(0);


        IHyperlink newLink = (IHyperlink) folder.add(IHyperlink.KIND);
```

```
    newLink.setTitle("Test link");

    newLink.setHyperlink("http://www.google.com");

    newLink.save();
```

Favorites Folders

There is a small quirk with Favorites Folders. Both Folders (SI_KIND = 'Folder') and Favorites Folders (SI_KIND = 'FavoritesFolder') are associated with the IFolder interface. For all practical purposes, there is no difference between Folders and Favorites Folders, so there is no lost functionality. But you should be aware that there is no IFavoritesFolder interface, should you go looking for one – when retrieving a Favorites Folder object via a CMS query, the returned IInfoObject should be cast to IFolder.

Categories

Categories and Folders have many similarities and differences. While both are used to organize InfoObjects in the CMS, there are a few fundamental differences that affect how they are used in SDK programming:

- *All* InfoObjects in the CMS are a child of one, and exactly one, parent folder.

  But an InfoObject can have zero, one, or several parent categories

  And only certain kinds of InfoObjects (WebI documents, Crystal Reports, etc.) can have categories assigned to them.

- Infoobjects, by default, inherit security settings assigned to their parents. An InfoObject is visible to a user if the parent folder is visible (unless its assigned rights are modified).

  But InfoObjects do not inherit any security rights from categories assigned to them. A user who has view access to a category will not see documents assigned to that category unless the user also has been granted view access to those documents as well.

- There are public ("corporate") and personal categories. A category of either type may be assigned to InfoObjects that are in either personal folders or corporate folders. That is, a personal category can be assigned to a public document, and vice-versa.

Since not all InfoObject kinds support categories, the methods to retrieve and assign categories are not present in the IInfoObject interface. The IInfoObject subinterfaces that *do* support categories extend the ICategoryContent interface. As of BI4.2, the subinterfaces that extend ICategoryContent are:

- IAgnostic

- IExcel
- IFullClient
- IHyperlink
- IObjectPackage
- IPDF
- IPowerPoint
- IProgram
- IPublication
- IReport
- IRTF
- ITxt
- IWebi
- IWord

This list represents the InfoObject kinds that can be assigned to categories. The methods of ICategoryContent that are inherited by the above interfaces are:

Package com.crystaldecisions.sdk.occa.infostore
Interface _ICategoryContent_

Set	getCorporateCategories()
	Retrieves a Set of Integers representing the InfoObject IDs of the corporate categories assigned to this InfoObject. *Associated property:* SI_CORPORATE_CATEGORIES
Set	getPersonalCategories()
	Retrieves a Set of Integers representing the InfoObject IDs of the personal categories assigned to this InfoObject. *Associated property:* SI_PERSONAL_CATEGORIES

Class/Interface 16: ICategoryContent

As we've seen, the relationship between InfoObjects and their parent folders is a simple one: every object has an SI_PARENTID property that identifies the parent, which is generally a folder. Moving an object to another folder just requires a change to the SI_PARENTID property. But assigning categories to an InfoObject involves adding or removing the category's ID from the InfoObject's SI_CORPORATE_CATEGORIES or SI_PERSONAL_CATEGORIES, as appropriate. There is no concept of *moving* an InfoObject from one category to another since an InfoObject can have multiple categories assigned.

In the following code fragment, we are querying the infostore for all categories, including corporate (SI_KIND = 'Category') and personal (SI_KIND = 'PersonalCategory'). We store the result in a Map so that we can look up the category name from its ID.

Next, we retrieve a known Web Intelligence document ("*Returns*"), and iterate through its corporate and personal categories, displaying the category name using the Map we created previously.

Finally, we assign the "Priority Reports" category to the document and save.[113]

```java
    // Query the CMS for all corporate and personal categories
    IInfoObjects ioCats = infoStore.query("select si_id,si_name from
ci_infoobjects where si_kind in('category','personalcategory'");


    // Create and load a map to hold Category ID to Name
    Map<Integer,String> cats = new HashMap<Integer,String>();
    Integer catPriority = null;
    for(Object o : ioCats)
    {
        IInfoObject io = (IInfoObject)o;
        cats.put(io.getID(),io.getTitle());
        if(io.getTitle().equalsIgnoreCase("priority reports"))
            catPriority = io.getID();
    }


    IWebi webi = (IWebi) infoStore.query("select si_corporate_categories from
ci_infoobjects where si_kind = 'webi' and si_name = 'returns'").get(0);


    // Display all corporate categories assigned to the WebI doc
    for(Object oCatID : webi.getCorporateCategories())
        System.out.println("Corporate Category: " + cats.get(oCatID));


    for(Object oCatID : webi.getPersonalCategories())
        System.out.println("Personal Category: " + cats.get(oCatID));


    // Assign the "Priority" category to the doc
    webi.getCorporateCategories().add(catPriority);
    webi.save();
```

---

113 As with many of our code samples, there is very little error-checking here. We are expecting one, and only one, WebI document named "Returns", and we expect one personal category named "Priority Reports". In the real world, we would actually confirm that these were present before continuing.

Category InfoObjects themselves are represented by the `ICategory` interface. This is similar to `IFolder` (both extend `IContainer`). And as `IFolder` represents both `Folder` and `FavoritesFolder` InfoObject kinds, the `ICategory` interface represents both `Category` and `PersonalCategory` kinds.

Package com.crystaldecisions.sdk.plugin.desktop.category
Interface _ICategory_
extends IContainer, ICategoryBase, IInfoObject

Fields

static String	CATEGORY_KIND	Category
	The kind value for Category InfoObjects	
static String	CATEGORY_PROGID	CrystalEnterprise.Category
	The ProgID value for Category InfoObjects	
static String	PERSONALCATEGORY_KIND	PersonalCategory
	The kind value for Personal Category InfoObjects	
static String	PERSONALCATEGORY_PROGID	CrystalEnterprise.PersonalCategory
	The ProgID value for Personal Category InfoObjects	

Methods

IInfoObject	add(String kind)
	Creates a new InfoObject of the specified kind, and adds it to this collection.
IInfoObjects	getChildren()
	Returns an IInfoObjects collection containing all of the objects assigned to this category.
IInfoObjects	getChildren(int propertySet,SearchPattern searchPattern,SortType sortType)
	Returns an IInfoObjects collection containing all of the objects assigned to this category., that match the specified SearchPattern. The objects are ordered according to SortType, and include the properties identified by propertySet.
IInfoObjects	getContents()
	Returns an IInfoObjects collection containing all of the objects assigned to this category, that are not categories themselves.
IInfoObjects	getContents(int propertySet,SearchPattern searchPattern,SortType sortType)

	Returns an IInfoObjects collection containing all of the objects assigned to this category, that are not categories themselves, that match the specified SearchPattern. The objects are ordered according to SortType, and include the properties identified by propertySet.
Set	getDocuments()
	Returns a collection of Integer objects representing the InfoObjects assigned to this category.
String[]	getPath()
	Retrieves the names of the category's ancestors, as a String array. *Associated property:* SI_PATH

Class/Interface 17: ICategory

Users

The IUser interface represents a user, and has the following methods:

Package com.crystaldecisions.sdk.plugin.desktop.user
Interface *IUser*
extends IInfoObject, ISystemPrincipal, IUserBase

Fields

static int	CONCURRENT	1
	Indicates that the user is associated with a concurrency license	
static int	NAMED	0
	Indicates that the user is associated with a named user license	
static String	KIND	User
	The Kind value for User InfoObjects	
static String	PROGID	CrystalEnterprise.User
	The ProgID value for User InfoObjects	

Methods

void	changePassword(String oldPassword,String newPassword)
	Changes the user's password, but only if the provided oldPassword matches the user's current password.
IAlertSubscripti ons	getAlertSubscriptions()

	Retrieves any alerts that the user is subscribed to. *Associated property:* SI_SUBSCRIBED_EVENTS
IUserAliases	getAliases()
	Retrieves an IUserAliases object, which contains information about the Enterprise or third-party aliases of the user. *Associated property:* SI_ALIASES
boolean	isAttributeBindingEnabled()
void	setAttributeBindingEnabled(boolean isEnabled)
	Retrieves or sets whether attribute binding (automatic importing of full name, email address, and other attributes) is enabled. *Associated property:* SI_ENABLE_ATTR_BINDING
int	getConnection()
set	setConnection(int newConnection)
	Retrieves or sets the user's licensing method. The possible values of newConnection are: IUserBase.CONCURRENT (1) IUserBase.NAMED (0) *Associated property:* SI_NAMEDUSER
IMappedAttribute s	getCustomMappedAttributes()
	Retrieves an IMappedAttributes collection, representing the user's attribute values. Call hasCustomMappedAttributes() first to confirm whether any attributes exist; if this method is called when no attributes exist, a new, empty IMappedAttributes collection is returned. *Associated property:* SI_CUSTOM_MAPPED_ATTRIBUTES
boolean	hasCustomMappedAttributes()
	Returns true if the user has mapped attributes, false otherwise. *Associated property:* SI_CUSTOM_MAPPED_ATTRIBUTES
String	getEmailAddress()
void	setEmailAddress(String emailAddress)

	Retrieves or sets the user's email address. The `getEmailAddress()` method throws an exception if there is no email address set for the user, or if the `SI_EMAIL_ADDRESS` property was not retrieved in the CMS query. To check for the presence of an email address without invoking an exception, use `IUser.properties().containsKey(CePropertyID.SI_EMAIL_ADDRESS)`. *Associated property:* `SI_EMAIL_ADDRESS`
Set	`getExcludedAlerts()`
	Retrieves a `Set` of `Integers` representing the InfoObject IDs of notification events that the user is excluded from receiving. *Associated property:* `SI_EXCLUDED_ALERTS`
int	`getFavoritesFolderID()`
	Retrieves the InfoObject ID of the user's favorite's folder. *Associated property:* `SI_FAVORITES_FOLDER`
String	`getFullName()`
void	`setFullName(String newFullName)`
	Retrieves or sets the user's full name. *Associated property:* `SI_USERFULLNAME`
Set	`getGroups()`
	Retrieves a `Set` of `Integers`, containing the InfoObject IDs of the user groups that this user is a member of. *Associated property:* `SI_USERGROUPS`
int	`getInboxID()`
	Retrieves the InfoObject ID of the user's inbox. *Associated property:* `SI_INBOX`
String	`getLicenseRestrictionCUID()`
void	`setLicenseRestrictionCUID(String restrictionCUID)`

	Retrieves or sets the CUID of the licensing restriction that applies to the user. The values of `restrictionCUID` are defined in:
	
	`CeSecurityCUID.LicenseRestriction.ANALYST`
	`CeSecurityCUID.LicenseRestriction.VIEWER`
	
	Associated property: `SI_USER_LICENSE_CUID`

Locale	`getLocale()`
void	`setLocale(Locale locale)` Retrieves or sets the product locale for the user. *Associated property:* `SI_DATA.SI_LOCALE`
void	`setNewPassword(String newPassword)` Changes the user's password, without validation of the current password.
boolean	`isPasswordChangeAllowed()`
void	`setasswordChangeAllowed(boolean newAllowChangePassword)` Retrieves or sets whether the user can change his or her password. *Associated property:* `SI_CHANGEPASSWORD`
boolean	`isPasswordExpiryAllowed()`
void	`setPasswordExpiryAllowed(boolean newPasswordExpiry)` Retrieves or sets whether the user's password expires. *Associated property:* `SI_PASSWORDEXPIRE`
boolean	`isPasswordToChangeAtNextLogon()`
void	`setPasswordToChangeAtNextLogon(boolean newChangePasswordAtNextLogon)` Retrieves or sets whether the user's password must be changed upon the next logon. *Associated property:* `SI_FORCE_PASSWORD_CHANGE`
int	`getPersonalCategoryID()` Retrieves the InfoObject ID of the user's personal category. *Associated property:* `SI_PERSONALCATEGORY`
Locale	`getPreferredViewingLocale()`
void	`setPreferredViewingLocale(Locale locale)`

	Retrieves or sets the preferred viewing locale for the user.
	Associated property: `SI_DATA.WIUserContentLocale`
String	`getProfileString(String name)`
void	`setProfileString(String name,String newProfile)`
void	`removeProfileString(String name)`
	Retrieves, sets, or removes the designated profile string. This includes, among other things, the user's BI launchpad preferences.
	Associated property: `SI_DATA`
IProfileValues	`getProfileValues()`
	Retrieves an `IProfileValues` collection, containing the user's profile values, which are used for creating personalized publication schedules.
	Associated property: `SI_PROFILE_VALUES, SI_PRINCIPAL_PROFILES`
IReceivedAlertNo tifications	`getReceivedAlertNotifications()`
	Retrieves an `IReceivedAlertNotifications` collection, representing the alert notifications that the user has received.
	Associated property: `SI_RECEIVED_ALERTNOTIFICATIONS`
IRecentDocuments	`getRecentDocuments(int actionType)`

	Retrieves an `IRecentDocuments` collection, representing the most recent documents that the user performed an action on.
	
	The values of `actionType` are in `IUserBase.RecentActionType`:
	`EDIT: 2`
	`SCHEDULE: 2`
	`VIEW: 1`

	Associated property: `SI_RECENT_DOCUMENTS`
void	`addSecondaryCredential(String cred,String password)`
boolean	`hasSecondaryCredential(String cred)`
void	`removeSecondaryCredential(String cred)`
	Adds, checks for the existence, of, or removes a secondary credential.
	Associated property: `SI_2ND_CREDS`

Class/Interface 18: IUser

Several of the methods of `IUser` are simple getters & setters for properties. For example, email address, full name, and connection (licensing method).

Three methods retrieve the user's favorites folder ID, inbox ID, and personal category ID (respectively): getFavoritesFolderID(), getInboxID(), and getPersonalCategoryID(). There are no setter methods since these properties are read-only.

Passwords

There are a few properties and associated methods for working with users' passwords. These **only** pertain to SAP BusinessObjects Enterprise IDs; these methods are not applicable to user accounts that do not have an enterprise alias.

There are two methods provided for changing the user's password: changePassword() and setNewPassword(). The difference between the two is that changePassword() requires the user's current password as a parameter (in addition to the new password), while setNewPassword() only requires the new password. You would use changePassword() in a case in which you are prompting the user for a password change and want to validate the user's identity (such as the password change page in BI launchpad). The setNewPassword() method would generally be used for an application used by delegated administrators to change a user's password without that validation[114].

The setNewPassword() method would also be used in a process that creates new user accounts.

The isPasswordExpiryAllowed(), isPasswordToChangeAtNextLogon(), and isPasswordChangeAllowed() methods, and their setter methods, are associated with the three password settings on the user properties panel in the CMC:

☐ Password never expires

☐ User must change password at next logon

☐ User cannot change password

Aliases

Aliases define the authentication methods and credentials for each user. Enterprise aliases are managed within the SAP BusinessObjects environment – the user name, password, and other attributes are specified when the user account is created in the CMC. Third-party aliases, such as LDAP, Windows AD, etc., are managed externally and are linked by the SAP BusinessObjects environment.

A user can have an enterprise alias, a third-party alias, or both (or multiple third-party aliases, but at most only one enterprise alias). When a user has more than one alias, he or she can log in using the credentials of any of the aliases, and see the same content. That is, if Fred has logged in with his Enterprise alias and created a report, then logs off and logs back in with his LDAP alias, he will see the report that he just created.

---

114 To use either of these two methods, the user whose credentials are being used to connect to the CMS needs to have sufficient privileges to the user account whose password is being changed.

Aliases are managed via the IUserAliases collection, retrieved from IUser.getAliases(). The IUserAliases collection contains IUserAlias objects, each one representing an associated authentication method. The methods of these two interfaces are as follows:

Package com.crystaldecisions.sdk.plugin.desktop.user
Interface *IUserAliases*
extends ISDKSet

IUserAlias	addExisting(String aliasName,String aliasId,boolean disabled)
	Map an existing authentication alias to this IUser.
IUserAlias	addNew(String aliasName,boolean disabled)
	Creates a new authentication alias for this IUser.

Class/Interface 19: IUserAliases

Package com.crystaldecisions.sdk.plugin.desktop.user
Interface *IUserAlias*

Fields

static int	ENTERPRISE	0
	Indicates that the alias uses enterprise authentication	
static int	THIRD_PARTY	1
	Indicates that the alias uses a third party authentication provider	

Methods

String	getID()
	Retrieves the ID of the alias. The format of the ID depends on the authentication type. For Enterprise aliases, the ID is "#" followed by the SI_ID of the user InfoObject. For LDAP aliases, the ID is the LDAP user's Distinguished Name (dn).
String	getName()
	Retrieves the name of the alias. As with the ID property, the format of the name depends on the authentication type.
String	getAuthentication()
	Retrieves the name of the authentication type – for example, secEnterprise and secLDAP.
String	getType()

	Retrieves the type of authentication provider. Possible values are `IUserAlias.ENTERPRISE` and `IUserAlias.THIRD_PARTY`.
boolean	`isDisabled()`
void	`setDisabled(boolean newDisabled)`
	Retrieves/sets whether the ID is enabled or disabled

Class/Interface 20: IUserAlias

Generally, when third-party authentication is used, the IDs in BO are created automatically[115]. They are also *deleted* automatically if the originating third-party account is deleted or removed from a mapped group. This can be a problem, since the contents of that user's personal folder and inbox are deleted as well. To mitigate this risk, an enterprise alias can be created for these third-party aliases. If the third-party ID is deleted or removed from a mapped group, then only the third-party alias is removed – the enterprise alias remains, and the user's contents also remain.

This is a pretty simple task with the SDK – we just have to identify user InfoObjects that do not have an Enterprise alias, and create one. To illustrate, we'll map an LDAP group and let it create some users.

One of the newly-created users is Anya – so she has only an LDAP alias:

Alias:	Authentication Type:	Enabled:	Assign Alias...	New Alias...
secLDAP:cn=anya shepherd, cn=developers, ou=users, dc=here, dc=com	LDAP	☑	Reassign Alias...	Delete Alias

```java
1  package bosdkbook;
2
3  import com.crystaldecisions.sdk.framework.CrystalEnterprise;
4  import com.crystaldecisions.sdk.framework.IEnterpriseSession;
5  import com.crystaldecisions.sdk.framework.ISessionMgr;
6  import com.crystaldecisions.sdk.occa.infostore.IInfoObjects;
7  import com.crystaldecisions.sdk.occa.infostore.IInfoStore;
8  import com.crystaldecisions.sdk.plugin.desktop.user.IUser;
9  import com.crystaldecisions.sdk.plugin.desktop.user.IUserAlias;
10
11 public class CreateAliases
12 {
13     public static void main(String[] args) throws Exception
```

---

115 One of the options for third-party authentication is whether to import all users in mapped groups immediately, or create the user ID when the user logs in for the first time.

```
14      {

15          ISessionMgr sessionManager = CrystalEnterprise.getSessionMgr();

16          IEnterpriseSession session = sessionManager.logon ("administrator",
   "xxxx", "osboxes", "secEnterprise");

17

18          IInfoStore infoStore = (IInfoStore) session.getService("", "InfoStore");

19

20          IInfoObjects users = infoStore.query("select si_name,si_aliases from
   ci_systemobjects where si_kind = 'user'");

21

22          for(Object o : users)

23          {

24              IUser user = (IUser)o;

25              boolean hasEnterpriseAlias = false;

26

27              for(IUserAlias alias : user.getAliases())

28              {

29                  if(alias.getType() == IUserAlias.ENTERPRISE)

30                      hasEnterpriseAlias = true;

31              }

32

33              if(!hasEnterpriseAlias)

34              {

35                  System.out.println("Creating new enterprise alias for user: " +
   user.getTitle());

36                  IUserAlias alias = user.getAliases().addNew("secEnterprise:" +
   user.getTitle(), false);

37                  user.save();

38              }

39          }

40      }

41 }
```

Listing 30: The CreateAliases Program

When we run the above program in our environment, we get the following output:

```
Creating new enterprise alias for user: anya
```

If we check Anya's properties in CMC, we'll see that the new Enterprise alias has been created:

Alias:	Authentication Type:	Enabled:	Assign Alias...	New Alias...
secEnterprise:anya	Enterprise	☑		Delete Alias
secLDAP:cn=anya shepherd, cn=developers, ou=users, dc=here, dc=com	LDAP	☑	Reassign Alias...	Delete Alias

Note that we did not set a password when we created the Enterprise alias. By doing so, although Anya has an enterprise alias, she will not be able to log in with "Enterprise" authentication until a password is set[116]. Our purpose in creating the Enterprise alias is just to mitigate the risk of lost content should the LDAP ID be deleted; but if we also wanted to enable Anya to log in with Enterprise credentials, we could set the password in the program.

Next, we'll remove Anya from the mapped Developers group in LDAP, then refresh LDAP users and groups in CMC → Authentication → LDAP:

┌─ On-Demand LDAP Update ───┐
│   ○ Update LDAP user groups now   │
│   ◉ Update LDAP user groups and aliases now   │
│   ○ Do not update LDAP user groups and aliases now   │
└──┘

┌─ ☐ Enable Kerberos Authentication ──┐
│   │
└──┘
Update Cancel

If we check Anya's user properties now, we'll notice the following: first, the LDAP alias is gone, and only the Enterprise alias remains:

Alias:	Authentication Type:	Enabled:	Assign Alias...	New Alias...
secEnterprise:anya	Enterprise	☑		Delete Alias

If we go to the Member Of tab of the mapped group, we can confirm that she's been removed:

	Join Group	Remove
🗋	**Title ^**	
👥	Everyone	

This, of course, is expected since she was removed from the LDAP group.

If this was a real-world scenario, and we needed to move Anya's personal reports to another user, we could do so at this point (and then fully delete her user ID if we chose to). If we had not run the program above to create her Enterprise alias, her personal folder and reports

---

116 She can, of course, log in with her LDAP password with "LDAP" authentication selected (the addition of the Enterprise alias does not affect logging in via the existing third-party credentials).

would have been deleted – we would not be able to get to them unless we were able to restore from a backup.

Enabling and disabling user accounts is done via the user aliases. Although the CMC UI implies that there is an account-level option for enabling the ID as well as individual options for each alias, this is not how the logic is implemented internally.

The "Account is disabled" option is checked off if all of the user's aliases are disabled. Checking this box disables all aliases, and unchecking it enables all aliases. In the above screenshot, we can see that Fred has two aliases: one Enterprise and one LDAP. His Enterprise ID is disabled, but since his LDAP ID is still enabled, the "Account is disabled" option is unchecked. In the SDK, there is no property at the account level to enable or disable the ID (that is, there's no property associated with the "Account is disabled" checkbox). The `IUserAlias` interface contains two methods for this: `isDisabled()` and `setDisabled()`.

We'll use the `setDisabled()` method in a program that disables all users who haven't logged in in over a year, or who have never logged in.

```java
1  package bosdkbook;

2

3  import java.text.SimpleDateFormat;

4  import java.util.Calendar;

5

6  import com.crystaldecisions.sdk.framework.CrystalEnterprise;

7  import com.crystaldecisions.sdk.framework.IEnterpriseSession;

8  import com.crystaldecisions.sdk.framework.ISessionMgr;

9  import com.crystaldecisions.sdk.occa.infostore.IInfoObjects;

10 import com.crystaldecisions.sdk.occa.infostore.IInfoStore;

11 import com.crystaldecisions.sdk.plugin.desktop.user.IUser;

12 import com.crystaldecisions.sdk.plugin.desktop.user.IUserAlias;

13

14 public class DisableInactiveUsers

15 {

16     public static void main(String[] args) throws Exception

17     {
```

```
18          ISessionMgr sessionManager = CrystalEnterprise.getSessionMgr();

19          IEnterpriseSession session = sessionManager.logon ("administrator",
   "xxxx", "osboxes", "secEnterprise");

20

21          IInfoStore infoStore = (IInfoStore) session.getService("", "InfoStore");

22

23          SimpleDateFormat sdf = new SimpleDateFormat("yyyy-MM-dd");

24          Calendar cal = Calendar.getInstance();

25          cal.add(Calendar.YEAR, -1);

26          String yearAgo = sdf.format(cal.getTime());

27

28          IInfoObjects inactiveUsers = infoStore.query("select
   si_name,si_aliases,si_lastlogontime from ci_systemobjects where si_kind = 'user'
   and (si_lastlogontime is null or si_lastlogontime <= '" + yearAgo + "') and
   si_name not in ('administrator','guest','smadmin','qaawsservletprincipal')");

29

30          for(Object o : inactiveUsers)

31          {

32              IUser inactiveUser = (IUser)o;

33              System.out.println("Disabling user: " + inactiveUser.getTitle());

34              for(IUserAlias alias : inactiveUser.getAliases())

35                  alias.setDisabled(true);

36          }

37          infoStore.commit(inactiveUsers);

38      }

39 }
```

Listing 31: The DisableInactiveUsers program

In the above listing, we first calculate the date one year ago today and format it as yyyy-MM-dd, so that it can be used in a CMS query. We then execute the query to retrieve all user accounts that either has a last logon date of over a year ago, or that do not have a last logon date. We exclude a few system accounts from this query.

On lines 34-35, we simply loop through all aliases associated with the retrieved users and disable them.

Finally, on line 37, we commit the changes that were made.

If the system's authentication options are set such that new third-party user IDs are **not** created automatically, then it is possible to create them individually in the CMC or with the SDK. To do this, we create the user ID as we normally would, but then add a new alias for the third-party ID. In the following snippet, we create a new User InfoObject for Chelsea, and then add the LDAP alias. To map the alias to LDAP, we pass "secLDAP:" followed by the full dn.

```
IInfoObjects ios = infoStore.newInfoObjectCollection();

IUser newUser = (IUser) ios.add(IUser.KIND);

newUser.setTitle("chelsea");

IUserAlias alias = newUser.getAliases().addNew("secLDAP:cn=Chelsea
Golden,cn=Developers,ou=Users,dc=here,dc=com", true);

newUser.save();
```

The same requirements for creating third-party IDs via the SDK are the same as in the CMC – the mapped user account must exist in at least one mapped group. Since Chelsea is a member of the Developers group, which we have already mapped, her ID is created successfully.

User Profiles & Database Credentials

Users' preferences can be retrieved and set with the getProfileString() and setProfileString() methods. These include preferences for CMC, BI launchpad, and the BI launchpad applications including Web Intelligence, Crystal Reports, etc.

For example, in CMC, a user may set the desired number of objects per page to 500:

CMC Preferences

Product Locale:	Use browser locale ▾
Preferred Viewing Locale:	Use browser locale ▾
Maximum number of objects per page:	500
Time Zone :	(GMT-05:00, DST) Eastern Time (US & Canada) ▾
Prompt for Unsaved Data:	Default ▾

This preference is stored in the user's profile with a name of "WCS_ADMIN_OBJSPERPAGE". We can display the current value and then change it with the following code:

```
        IUser user = (IUser) infoStore.query("select *  from ci_systemobjects where
si_kind = 'user' and si_name = 'fred'").get(0);



        // Display Fred's "objects per page" preference

        System.out.println(user.getProfileString("WCS_ADMIN_OBJSPERPAGE"));
```

```
    // Change "Objects per page" to 250
    user.setProfileString("WCS_ADMIN_OBJSPERPAGE", "250");
```

This displays the current value, and then changes it to 250:

```
500
```

A few points about profile strings:

- Profile strings are stored in the SI_DATA property bag. This property must be included in the SELECT clause of CMS queries in order to retrieve the profile strings. Attempting to get a profile string that does not exist in the profile will produce an exception.

- It's not necessary to include SI_DATA in the CMS query in order to set a profile string (but is generally a good idea).

- A profile string may be set whether or not it already exists. The above setProfileString() call would produce the same result if the profile string was not already present (although be preceding getProfileString() would have failed).

- All profile strings are stored as Strings, even if the value is numeric.

- There is no validation done by the SDK when setting a profile string. If, in the above code, we set the value to "xxx" instead of "250", the profile would still complete successfully. However, the user would receive an error when attempting to view folders in the CMC due to the invalid value.

- There are two different types of profiles that apply to users: the profile string that we are covering here, and which are associated with the getProfileString() and setProfileString() methods. There is another, unrelated method named getProfileValues(); this type of profile is used to apply dynamic filtering when scheduling publications.

The getProfileString() and setProfileString() are simple shortcut methods for accessing the SI_DATA property. The following pairs of lines are functionally identical[117]:

```
    String value;


    // Retrieve Fred's "Objects per page" preference
    value = user.getProfileString("WCS_ADMIN_OBJSPERPAGE");
    value = user.properties().getProperties("SI_DATA")
            .getString("WCS_ADMIN_OBJSPERPAGE");


    // Change "Objects per page" to 250
```

---

117 Except that the getProfileString() call throws an exception if the profile string does not exist, while the getString() call returns a null.

```
user.setProfileString("WCS_ADMIN_OBJSPERPAGE", "250");

user.properties().getProperties("SI_DATA")
        .setProperty("WCS_ADMIN_OBJSPERPAGE", "250");
```

The applications that store preferences in profile strings each do so differently. BI launchpad preferences are stored in a single JSON-formatted string named SI_IV_PREFERENCES:

SI_IV_PREFERENCES	{"catsDrawer":"default","rpp":"50","folderCUID":"","homepageCUID":"","docExplorer":"foldersDrawer","columns":"{\"RECEIVED_ON\":true,\"CREATED_ON\":false,\"DESCRIPTION\":false,\"FROM\":true,\"OBJECT_TYPE\":true,\"OBJECT_PATH\":false,\"INSTANCE_COUNT\":true,\"LAST_RUN\":false,\"OWNER\":true,\"COLLABORATION\":true}","categoryCUID":"","startPage":"docs","homePage":"default","myDocuments":"myFave","foldersDrawer":"default","vwm":"2"}

Web Intelligence preferences are stored in separate profile strings with names beginning with "DOCUMENT_":

DOCUMENT_DIViewTechno	H
DOCUMENT_WICreateTechno	I
DOCUMENT_WIDrillBar	Y
DOCUMENT_WIPromptDrillOutScope	N
DOCUMENT_WISaveAsXLSOptimized	Y
DOCUMENT_WIStartNewDrill	existing
DOCUMENT_WISyncDrillBlocks	Y
DOCUMENT_WIUCLUsage	true
DOCUMENT_WIUserContentLocale	
DOCUMENT_WIViewTechno	H

Many preferences are only present as profile strings if they are set to non-default values by the application (BI launchpad, Web Intelligence, etc.). An absence of a preference in a profile string indicates that the default value applies[118].

Only two user profile settings can be accessed explicitly with IUser methods: getLocale()/setLocale(),

and

getPreferredViewingLocale()/setPreferredViewingLocale().

Although related, the users' database account name and password are managed separately in the SDK.

---

118 And no, there is no way to retrieve the default values from a profile.

Database Credentials

☑ Enable

Account Name: `fred_db`

Password: ••••••••

Confirm: ••••••••

The account name is stored in the user's profile, in a profile string named DBUSER. This may be retrieved and set with the getProfileString() and setProfileString() methods:

```
      IUser user = (IUser) infoStore.query("select *  from ci_systemobjects where
si_kind = 'user' and si_name = 'fred'").get(0);


   // Display Fred's current database credential account name

   System.out.println(user.getProfileString("DBUSER"));


   // Change database credential account name to "fredo"

   user.setProfileString("DBUSER", "fredo");
```

The database password, however, is set via addSecondaryCredential(). There is no way to retrieve a password, only to see if one exists, via hasSecondaryCredential(). The name of the credential is DBPASS:

```
      IUser user = (IUser) infoStore.query("select *  from ci_systemobjects where
si_kind = 'user' and si_name = 'fred'").get(0);


   // Display whether a database password was already set

   System.out.println(user.hasSecondaryCredential("DBPASS"));


   // Set the database password, whether or not it was already set

   user.addSecondaryCredential("DBPASS", "Dingo");
```

To disable database credentials for a user, remove the DBUSER profile string and DBPASS credential:

```
      IUser user = (IUser) infoStore.query("select *  from ci_systemobjects where
si_kind = 'user' and si_name = 'fred'").get(0);


   // Disable database credentials

   user.removeProfileString("DBUSER");

   user.removeSecondaryCredential("DBPASS");
```

User Groups

User groups are similar to users. The methods of `IUserGroup` are:

Package com.crystaldecisions.sdk.plugin.desktop.usergroup
Interface *IUserGroup*
extends `IInfoObject`, *ISystemPrincipal*, *IUserGroupBase*

Fields

static String	KIND	UserGroup
	The kind value for UserGroup InfoObjects	
static String	PROGID	CrystalEnterprise.UserGroup
	The ProgID value for UserGroup InfoObjects	

Methods

IAlertSubscriptions	getAlertSubscriptions()
	Retrieves any alerts that the user group is subscribed to. *Associated property:* SI_SUBSCRIBED_EVENTS
IUserGroupAliases	getAliases()
	Retrieves an `IUserGroupAliases` object, which contains information about any third-party aliases assigned to the user group. *Associated property:* SI_ALIASES
Set	getParentGroups()
	Retrieves a `Set` of `Integers`, containing the InfoObject IDs of the user groups that this group is a member of. *Associated property:* SI_USERGROUPS
Set	getSubGroups()
	Retrieves a `Set` of `Integers`, containing the InfoObject IDs of the user groups that are members of this group. *Associated property:* SI_SUBGROUPS
String	getProfileString(String name)
void	setProfileString(String name,String newProfile)
void	removeProfileString(String name)

	Retrieves, sets, or removes a profile string, representing the default application options that are applied to group members. *Associated property:* SI_DATA
IProfileValues	getProfileValues()
	Retrieves an IProfileValues collection, containing the user group's profile values. *Associated property:* SI_PROFILE_VALUES, SI_PRINCIPAL_PROFILES
Set	getUsers()
	Retrieves a Set of Integers, containing the InfoObject IDs of the users that are members of this group. *Associated property:* SI_GROUP_MEMBERS

Class/Interface 21: IUserGroup

On page 238, we touched on one method to add a user to a user group. There are two ways to do this: modify the user's collection of user groups, or modify the user group's collection of members. Both methods achieve the same result.

To add a user to a user group, we just need to add the user's InfoObject ID to the user group's SI_GROUP_MEMBERS property, via the getUsers() method. In the following snippet, we are performing the same action as on page 238, but instead of adding the user group to the user, we add the user to the user group:

```
IUserGroup execMgmtGroup = (IUserGroup) infoStore.query("select si_group_members from
ci_systemobjects where si_kind = 'usergroup' and si_name = 'exec.
management'").get(0);

IUser fred = (IUser) infoStore.query("select si_id from ci_systemobjects where
si_kind = 'user' and si_name = 'fred'").get(0);


execMgmtGroup.getUsers().add(fred.getID());


execMgmtGroup.save();
```

User groups can be members of other groups. Like user – user group management, we can either add the parent user group to this children's collection of parents, or add the child user group to the parent's collection of children. In the following example, we'll perform both actions – we'll join the *Call Center* group to the *Operations* group, and we'll also add the *Customer Service* group as a child.

```
IUserGroup operationsGroup = (IUserGroup) infoStore.query("select
si_usergroups,si_parent_groups from ci_systemobjects where si_kind = 'usergroup' and
si_name = 'operations'").get(0);

IUserGroup callcenterGroup = (IUserGroup) infoStore.query("select
si_usergroups,si_parent_groups from ci_systemobjects where si_kind = 'usergroup' and
si_name = 'call center'").get(0);

IUserGroup csrGroup = (IUserGroup) infoStore.query("select
si_usergroups,si_parent_groups from ci_systemobjects where si_kind = 'usergroup' and
si_name = 'customer service'").get(0);


callcenterGroup.getParentGroups().add(operationsGroup.getID());

callcenterGroup.getSubGroups().add(csrGroup.getID());


callcenterGroup.save();
```

When we look up the groups in the CMC, we'll see that the expected structure has been created:

Like users, user groups have *aliases*, representing the authentication method supported by the group. The structure of IUserGroupAliases and IUserGroupAlias mirrors those of IUserAliases and IUserAlias. However, these interfaces contain functionality that applies to users but not user groups. Most notably, while a user can have an Enterprise alias as well as one or more third-party aliases, user groups can only have one of these. Therefore, the IUserGroupAliases collection only contains a single IUserGroupAlias object. If a new IUserGroupAlias object is added to the collection, it replaces the one that is there. For this reason, it is rare that a user group's IUserGroupAliases collection would need to be modified after its initial creation.

User groups cannot be *disabled* as users can. Calling IUserGroupAlias.setDisabled() has no effect.

Package com.crystaldecisions.sdk.plugin.desktop.usergroup
Interface _IUserGroupAliases_
extends ISDKSet

IUserGroupAlias	addExisting(String aliasName,String aliasId,boolean disabled)
	Map an existing authentication alias to this IUserGroup.
IUserGroupAlias	addNew(String aliasName,boolean disabled)
	Creates a new authentication alias for this IUserGroup.

Class/Interface 22: IUserGroupAliases

Package com.crystaldecisions.sdk.plugin.desktop.usergroup
Interface _IUserGroupAlias_

Fields

static int	ENTERPRISE	0
	Indicates that the alias uses enterprise authentication	
static int	THIRD_PARTY	1
	Indicates that the alias uses a third party authentication provider	

Methods

String	getID()
	Retrieves the ID of the alias. The format of the ID depends on the authentication type. For Enterprise aliases, the ID is "#" followed by the SI_ID of the user InfoObject. For LDAP aliases, the ID is the LDAP group's Distinguished Name (dn).
String	getName()
	Retrieves the name of the alias. This is the authentication type followed by the group name.
String	getAuthentication()
	Retrieves the name of the authentication type – for example, secEnterprise and secLDAP.
String	getType()
	Retrieves the type of authentication provider. Possible values are IUserAlias.ENTERPRISE and IUserAlias.THIRD_PARTY.
boolean	isDisabled()
void	setDisabled(boolean newDisabled)

> Retrieves/sets whether the ID is enabled or disabled

Class/Interface 23: IUserGroupAlias

Creating mapped third-party user groups via the SDK is very similar to creating mapped third-party user IDs: we create the group as normal and then add an alias for the third-party provider:

```
IInfoObjects ios = infoStore.newInfoObjectCollection();

IUserGroup newUserGroup = (IUserGroup) ios.add(IUserGroup.KIND);

newUserGroup.setTitle("Developers");

IUserGroupAlias alias =
newUserGroup.getAliases().addNew("secLDAP:cn=Developers,ou=Users,dc=here,dc=com",
true);

newUserGroup.save();
```

When a mapped group is added via the Authentication tab in the CMC, it is given a name matching the name of the mapped group (it can be renamed subsequently in the Users & Groups tab). Here we have given it a different name ("Developers") while it is being created.

Servers

Servers, such as the CMS, Adaptive Job Server, and others, can be managed by the SDK. There is a lot that can be done, and we'll only be touching on some of the more common activities.

The fields and methods of `IServer` are:

Package com.crystaldecisions.sdk.plugin.desktop.server
Interface *IServer*
*extends **IServerBase, IInfoObject***

Fields

static int	CE_SERVER_RESTART	3
	The desired state of the server is Restart	
static int	CE_SERVER_START	1
	The desired state of the server is Start	
static int	CE_SERVER_STOP	2

	The desired state of the server is Stop

Methods

boolean	isAlive()
	Returns true if the server is running.
	Associated property: SI_SERVER_IS_ALIVE

boolean	getAutoBoot()
void	setAutoBoot(boolean value)
	Retrieves/sets whether this server should start automatically when the SIA is started.
	Associated property: SI_AUTOBOOT

int	getCommunicationProtocol()
	Retrieves the communications protocol used by this server (IIOP or SSL). Valid values are in IServerBase.CeCommunicationProtocol.
	Associated property: SI_COMMUNICATION_PROTOCOL

IServiceContainer	getContainer()
	Retrieves the service container associated with this server.
	Associated property: SI_CONFIGURED_CONTAINERS

IServiceContainer	setContainer(int id)
	Sets set the service container to use, by InfoObject ID. Returns the service container as an IServerContainer object.
	Associated property: SI_CONFIGURED_CONTAINERS

String	getCurrentCommandLine()
	Retrieves the command line that was used to execute the current instance of this server.
	Associated property: SI_CURRENT_COMMAND_LINE

boolean	getCurrentDisabledState()
	Indicates whether the server is currently disabled.
	Associated property: SI_CURRENT_DISABLED_STATE

boolean	isDisabled()
void	setDisabled(boolean b)

	Retrieves/sets the desired state of the server. Note that this may differ from the *actual* state (see `getCurrentDisabledState()`). *Associated property:* `SI_DISABLED`
`int`	`getEnterpriseNodeID()`
`void`	`setEnterpriseNode(int id)`
	Retrieves/sets the ID of the node that this server is associated with. *Associated property:* `SI_ENTERPRISENODE`
`boolean`	`isExclusive()`
`void`	`setExclusive(boolean exclusive)`
	Retrieves/sets whether the server is exclusive. *Associated property:* `SI_EXCLUSIVE`
`ExpectedRunState`	`getExpectedRunState()`
`void`	`setExpectedRunState(ExpectedRunState state)`
	Retrieves/sets the desired run state of the server (started, stopped, etc.). This may differ from the actual run state (see `isAlive()`, `getState()`). *Associated property:* `SI_EXPECTED_RUN_STATE`
`Date`	`getExpectedRunStateTimestamp()`
	Retrieves the timestamp of when the server's expected run state was last changed. *Associated property:* `SI_EXPECTED_RUN_STATE_TS`
`String`	`getFriendlyName()`
`void`	`setFriendlyName(friendlyName)`
	Retrieves/sets the server's friendly name. *Associated property:* `SI_FRIENDLY_NAME`
`IConfiguredServices`	`getHostedServices()`
	Retrieves an `IConfiguredServices` collection, containing the services that are hosted on this server. *Associated property:* `SI_HOSTED_SERVICES`
`IServerMetrics`	`getMetrics()`

	Retrieves an `IServerMetrics` object, containing activity metrics for this server and its hosted services. *Associated property:* `SI_METRICS`
`String`	`getName()`
	Retrieves the server's name (this is equivalent to `IInfoObject.getTitle()`). *Associated property:* `SI_NAME`
`int`	`getPID()`
	Retrieves the server's process ID in the host operating system. *Associated property:* `SI_PID`
`boolean`	`getRequiresRestart()`
	Returns true if this server requires a restart in order for changes to take effect. *Associated property:* `SI_REQUIRES_RESTART`
`String`	`getServerAbbreviation()`
	Returns a shortened version of the server name. *Associated properties:* `SI_SERVER_ABBREVIATION, SI_KIND`
`String`	`getServerDescriptor()`
	Returns a description of the server's type. For example, "aps" for the Central Management Server. *Associated property:* `SI_SERVER_DESCRIPTOR`
`IServerDestinations`	`getServerDestinations()`
	Retrieves an `IServerDestinations` object, containing the default scheduling destinations for this server. Applies to servers with a Destination Scheduling Service only.
`String`	`getServerID()`
	Returns the fully-qualified name of this server. *Associated property:* `SI_SERVER_ID`
`String`	`getServerIOR()`

	Returns the server's unique IOR (Interoperable Object Reference).
	Associated property: `SI_SERVER_IOR`
`String`	`getServerKind()`
`void`	`setServerKind(String kind)`
	Retrieves/sets a short description of the server's kind – ex.: `eventserver, jobserver, aps`.
	Associated property: `SI_SERVER_KIND`
`String`	`getServerName()`
	Returns the name of the host that the server is running on.
	Associated property: `SI_SERVER_NAME`
`String`	`getSIAHostname()`
	Returns the name of the host that the SIA is running on.
	Associated property: `SI_SIA_HOSTNAME`
`ServerState`	`getState()`
	Retrieves a `ServerState` object, which reflects the current running state of the server (Running, Stopped, Waiting for Resources).
	Associated properties: `SI_SERVER_IS_ALIVE,` `SI_SERVER_WAITING_FOR_RESOURCES`
`IStatusInfo`	`getStatusInfo()`
	Retrieves an `IStatusInfo` object, which reflects the current running state of the server (Running, Stopped, Failed, Initializing, Running With Errors, Running With Warnings, Starting, Stopping).
	Associated properties: `SI_STATUS_INFO`

Class/Interface 24: IServer

Server State

There are three different methods to query the current run state of a server, `isAlive()`, `getStatusInfo()`, and `getState()`. The `isAlive()` method returns a boolean `true` if the server is running (alive) and `false` if it is stopped. The server is considered alive if the status is *running, initializing, running with errors,* or *running with warnings.* It is not alive if the status is *stopped, starting, stopping,* or *failed.*

The getStatusInfo() method returns an IStatusInfo object, which contains an additional level of detail concerning the server status. The IStatusInfo.getStatus() method returns an int which correlates to the status; the possible values are in the static interface IStatusInfo.Status:

Package com.crystaldecisions.sdk.plugin.desktop.server
Interface *IStatusInfo.Status*

Fields

static int[]	ALL_STATUSES	[0,1,2,3,4,5,6,7]
	Array containing all possible status values	
static int	FAILED	5
	The server failed to start	
static int	INITIALIZING	2
	The server is currently initializing	
static int	RUNNING	3
	The server is currently running	
static int	RUNNING_WITH_ERRORS	6
	The server is currently running, but with errors	
static int	RUNNING_WITH_WARNINGS	7
	The server is currently running, but with warnings	
static int	STARTING	1
	The server is currently starting	
static int	STOPPED	0
	The server is currently stopped	
static int	STOPPING	4
	The server is currently stopping	

Class/Interface 25: IStatusInfo.Status

If a server is in *Failed* status, then the IStatusInfo.getMessage() method returns the failure message.

```
1  package bosdkbook;
2
3  import java.util.Locale;
4
```

```
 5  import com.crystaldecisions.sdk.framework.CrystalEnterprise;

 6  import com.crystaldecisions.sdk.framework.IEnterpriseSession;

 7  import com.crystaldecisions.sdk.framework.ISessionMgr;

 8  import com.crystaldecisions.sdk.occa.infostore.IInfoObjects;

 9  import com.crystaldecisions.sdk.occa.infostore.IInfoStore;

10  import com.crystaldecisions.sdk.plugin.desktop.server.IServer;

11  import com.crystaldecisions.sdk.plugin.desktop.server.IStatusInfo;

12

13  public class ServerStatus

14  {

15      public static void main(String[] args) throws Exception

16      {

17          ISessionMgr sessionManager = CrystalEnterprise.getSessionMgr();

18          IEnterpriseSession session = sessionManager.logon ("administrator",
    "xxxx", "osboxes", "secEnterprise");

19

20          IInfoStore infoStore = (IInfoStore) session.getService("", "InfoStore");

21

22          IInfoObjects ios = infoStore.query("select * from ci_systemobjects where
    si_kind = 'server' order by si_name");

23

24          for(Object o : ios)

25          {

26              IServer server = (IServer)o;

27

28              System.out.print(server.getTitle() + ": " );

29

30              IStatusInfo statusInfo = server.getStatusInfo();

31              switch(statusInfo.getStatus())

32              {

33                  case IStatusInfo.Status.FAILED:

34                      System.out.println("Failed: " +
    statusInfo.getMessage(Locale.getDefault()));

35                      break;

36                  case IStatusInfo.Status.INITIALIZING:
```

```
37                    System.out.println("Initializing");
38                    break;
39               case IStatusInfo.Status.RUNNING:
40                    System.out.println("Running");
41                    break;
42               case IStatusInfo.Status.RUNNING_WITH_ERRORS:
43                    System.out.println("Running with Errors");
44                    break;
45               case IStatusInfo.Status.RUNNING_WITH_WARNINGS:
46                    System.out.println("Running with Warnings");
47                    break;
48               case IStatusInfo.Status.STARTING:
49                    System.out.println("Starting");
50                    break;
51               case IStatusInfo.Status.STOPPED:
52                    System.out.println("Stopped");
53                    break;
54               case IStatusInfo.Status.STOPPING:
55                    System.out.println("Stopping");
56                    break;
57              }
58          }
59      }
60 }
```

Listing 32: The ServerStatus program

The above listing contains the *ServerStatus* program. This displays the name and status of each server in the cluster. If the server is currently in a Failed state, then the failure message is displayed.

To purposely provoke a server failure, we changed several of the paths in the command line of the AdaptiveProcessingServer. We also set an invalid HTTPS certificate location for the WACS in order to cause a *Running with Errors* status. The output of the above program is as follows:

```
osboxes2.AdaptiveJobServer: Running
osboxes2.AdaptiveProcessingServer: Failed: This server is considered failed because
it has stopped 5 time(s) in 60 minute(s).
osboxes2.CentralManagementServer: Running
```

```
osboxes2.ConnectionServer: Stopped
osboxes2.CrystalReports2016ProcessingServer: Stopped
osboxes2.CrystalReports2016ReportApplicationServer: Stopped
osboxes2.CrystalReportsCacheServer: Stopped
osboxes2.CrystalReportsProcessingServer: Running
osboxes2.DashboardsCacheServer: Stopped
osboxes2.DashboardsProcessingServer: Stopped
osboxes2.EventServer: Stopped
osboxes2.InputFileRepository: Running
osboxes2.OutputFileRepository: Running
osboxes2.WebApplicationContainerServer: Running with Errors
osboxes2.WebIntelligenceProcessingServer: Stopped
```

The third server state method is `IServer.getState()`. It returns a `ServerState` object which displays the following status values: *Stopped, Running,* or *WaitingForResources.* The first two values correlate to the run status retrieved from `IServer.isAlive()`. The third value is only applicable to the Central Management Server.

Determining whether a server is enabled or disabled is done via `IServer.getCurrentDisabledStatus()`. This simply returns a `true` if the server is currently disabled or `false` if it is currently enabled.

To change the run state or enabled state of a server, it's necessary to set the *expected* state, then save the InfoObject (like any other property change). The SIA will then attempt to set the server to the expected state. To change the run state, we call `IServer.setExpectedRunState()`, passing it an `ExpectedState` object as a parameter. For example:

```
server.setExpectedRunState(ExpectedRunState.STOPPED);  // stop the server
```

Enabling or disabling a server is accomplished with the `IServer.setDisabled()` method, which takes a `boolean` value specifying if the server is to be disabled or not:

```
server.setDisabled(false); // enable the server
```

The expected run state of a server can be obtained with `IServer.getExpectedRunState()`. A server's expected run state will differ from the current run state while a change is in progress (that is, until the desired state is achieved). Likewise, the expected enabled state can be obtained with `IServer.isDisabled()`[119].

We can use all of the above to create a minimalist server management application. We will display the current state of all servers and allow the user to change the run state or enabled state of any server. We'll then monitor the server to check if the selected change has been made successfully.

---

119 There is an inconsistency here in the naming of the methods. The `isAlive()` method reflects the **current** run state, while the `isDisabled()` method reflects the **desired** enabled state.

```
 1 | package bosdkbook;
 2 |
 3 | import java.util.Scanner;
 4 |
 5 | import com.crystaldecisions.sdk.exception.SDKException;
 6 | import com.crystaldecisions.sdk.framework.CrystalEnterprise;
 7 | import com.crystaldecisions.sdk.framework.IEnterpriseSession;
 8 | import com.crystaldecisions.sdk.framework.ISessionMgr;
 9 | import com.crystaldecisions.sdk.occa.infostore.IInfoObjects;
10 | import com.crystaldecisions.sdk.occa.infostore.IInfoStore;
11 | import com.crystaldecisions.sdk.plugin.desktop.server.IServer;
12 | import com.crystaldecisions.sdk.plugin.desktop.server.ExpectedRunState;
13 | import com.crystaldecisions.sdk.plugin.desktop.server.IStatusInfo;
14 |
15 | public class ServerManager
16 | {
17 |     Scanner s = new Scanner(System.in);
18 |
19 |     public static void main(String[] args) throws Exception
20 |     {
21 |         new ServerManager();
22 |     }
23 |
24 |     private ServerManager()
25 |     throws SDKException, NumberFormatException, InterruptedException
26 |     {
27 |         ISessionMgr sessionManager = CrystalEnterprise.getSessionMgr();
28 |         IEnterpriseSession session = sessionManager.logon ("administrator",
   | "xxxx", "osboxes", "secEnterprise");
29 |
30 |         IInfoStore infoStore = (IInfoStore) session.getService("", "InfoStore");
31 |
32 |         boolean loop = true;
```

```
33        while(loop)

34        {

35            IInfoObjects ios = infoStore.query("select * from ci_systemobjects
   where si_kind = 'server' order by si_name");

36

37            for(int i=0;i<ios.size();i++)

38            {

39                IServer server = (IServer) ios.get(i);

40                String runState =
   getStatusDesc(server.getStatusInfo().getStatus());

41                String enabledDesc =
   getDisabledDesc(server.getCurrentDisabledState());

42                System.out.printf("%2d. %14s, %8s - %s
   %n",i+1,runState,enabledDesc,server.getTitle());

43            }

44            System.out.print("Select server to manage or 0 to exit: ");

45

46            String input = s.nextLine();

47

48            if(input.trim().equals("0"))

49                loop = false;

50            else

51                doServer((IServer) ios.get(Integer.parseInt(input)-1),
   infoStore);

52        }

53    }

54

55    private void doServer(IServer server,IInfoStore infoStore)

56    throws SDKException, InterruptedException

57    {

58        switch(server.getStatusInfo().getStatus())

59        {

60            case IStatusInfo.Status.FAILED:

61            case IStatusInfo.Status.STOPPED:

62                System.out.println("S. Start");
```

```
63              break;
64          default:
65              System.out.println("P. Stop");
66              System.out.println("R. Restart");
67              System.out.println("F. Force Stop");
68              if(server.getCurrentDisabledState())
69                  System.out.println("E. Enable");
70              else
71                  System.out.println("D. Disable");
72          }
73      System.out.println("0. Return");
74      System.out.print("Select action: ");
75
76      String input = s.nextLine();
77
78      boolean expectedDisabled = server.getCurrentDisabledState();
79
80      switch(input.trim().toUpperCase())
81      {
82          case "S":
83              server.setExpectedRunState(ExpectedRunState.RUNNING);
84              System.out.println("Attempting to start server.");
85              break;
86          case "P":
87              server.setExpectedRunState(ExpectedRunState.STOPPED);
88              System.out.println("Attempting to stop server.");
89              break;
90          case "F":
91              server.setExpectedRunState(ExpectedRunState.STOPNOW);
92              System.out.println("Attempting to force stop server.");
93              break;
94          case "R":
```

```
95              server.setExpectedRunState(ExpectedRunState.RESTART);
96              System.out.println("Attempting to restart server.");
97              break;
98          case "E":
99              server.setDisabled(false);
100             expectedDisabled = false;
101             System.out.println("Attempting to enable server.");
102             break;
103         case "D":
104             server.setDisabled(true);
105             expectedDisabled = true;
106             System.out.println("Attempting to disable server.");
107             break;
108         default:
109             return;
110     }

111

112     System.out.println("Setting server " + server.getTitle()
            + " to " + server.getExpectedRunState()
            + " / " + getDisabledDesc(expectedDisabled));
113     server.save();

114

115     boolean waiting = true;
116     while(waiting)
117     {
118         Thread.sleep(3000);
119         server = (IServer) infoStore.query("select * from ci_systemobjects
    where si_id = " + server.getID()).get(0);
120         int status = server.getStatusInfo().getStatus();
121         System.out.println("\nCurrent state: " + getStatusDesc(status) + " /
    " + getDisabledDesc(server.getCurrentDisabledState()));
122         System.out.println("Expected:  " + server.getExpectedRunState() + " /
    " + getDisabledDesc(server.isDisabled()));
123         if(status == IStatusInfo.Status.FAILED)
```

```
124                {
125                    System.out.println("Server is failed.");
126                    waiting = false;
127                }
128            if(server.getExpectedRunState() == ExpectedRunState.RUNNING
129                && (status == IStatusInfo.Status.RUNNING_WITH_ERRORS || status ==
    IStatusInfo.Status.RUNNING_WITH_WARNINGS))
130                waiting = false;
131
132            if(getStatusDesc(status)
    .equals(server.getExpectedRunState().toString())
133                    && server.getCurrentDisabledState() == server.isDisabled())
134            {
135                waiting = false;
136                System.out.println("STATUS CHANGE COMPLETE\n");
137            }
138          else
139                System.out.println("Server is not in expected state; waiting to
    check again.");
140        }
141    }
142
143    private static String getDisabledDesc(boolean isDisabled)
144    {
145        return isDisabled ? "disabled" : "enabled";
146    }
147
148    private static String getStatusDesc(int status)
149    {
150        switch(status)
151        {
152            case IStatusInfo.Status.FAILED:
153                return "Failed";
154            case IStatusInfo.Status.INITIALIZING:
```

```
155                return "Initializing";
156           case IStatusInfo.Status.RUNNING:
157                return "Running";
158           case IStatusInfo.Status.RUNNING_WITH_ERRORS:
159                return "Running WIth Errors";
160           case IStatusInfo.Status.RUNNING_WITH_WARNINGS:
161                return "Running WIth Warnings";
162           case IStatusInfo.Status.STARTING:
163                return "Starting";
164           case IStatusInfo.Status.STOPPED:
165                return "Stopped";
166           case IStatusInfo.Status.STOPPING:
167                return "Stopping";
168         }
169         return "Invalid";
170     }
171 }
```

Listing 33: The ServerManager program

The above listing is the *ServerManager* program. From lines 143 on we have two helper methods: getDisabledDesc() and getStatusDesc(), which return the text description of a server's enabled/disabled state and its current run state (respectively). We don't need a helper method for the expected run state since ExpectedRunState has a usable toString() method.

Back up to the main loop in lines 33-52, we are executing a CMS query to get the name and current state of all servers. We print out this info and ask the user for the number of the server to work with. If the user enters "0", we exit.

The doServer() method on line 55 is where the real work happens. We start by displaying another menu to the user – this menu is dynamic based on the current status of the server. If it is not running (*failed* or *stopped*), then the only possible option is to *Start* it. Otherwise, we offer to stop, restart, or force start the server. We also offer to enable or disable the server, based on its current state.

We set the appropriate run or enabled state, and save the changes on line 113. On line 116, we begin our waiting loop – we wait three seconds, then execute a CMS query to get the current state of the server. We can't simply wait until the current state matches the expected state, since in some cases that does not happen. Our first check is on line 123 – if the status is *Failed,* then we display a message accordingly and set waiting to false so that the loop won't continue. Next, we check to see if the server is in *Running With Errors* or *Running With*

Warnings status, with the expected state being *Running*. Finally, we check to see if the current run state equals the expected run state and if the current enabled state matches the expected enabled state. If so, we display a Completed message and drop out of the loop. If none of the above conditions are met, then we assume the server has not yet achieved its final state, and continue the loop.

The following is output from a run of this problem in our test environment:

```
 1.        Running, disabled - osboxes2.AdaptiveJobServer
 2.         Failed,  enabled - osboxes2.AdaptiveProcessingServer
 3.        Running,  enabled - osboxes2.CentralManagementServer
 4.        Stopped, disabled - osboxes2.ConnectionServer
 5.        Stopped, disabled - osboxes2.CrystalReports2016ProcessingServer
 6.        Stopped, disabled - osboxes2.CrystalReports2016ReportApplicationServer
 7.        Stopped, disabled - osboxes2.CrystalReportsCacheServer
 8.        Running, disabled - osboxes2.CrystalReportsProcessingServer
 9.        Stopped, disabled - osboxes2.DashboardsCacheServer
10.        Stopped, disabled - osboxes2.DashboardsProcessingServer
11.        Stopped, disabled - osboxes2.EventServer
12.        Running,  enabled - osboxes2.InputFileRepository
13.        Running,  enabled - osboxes2.OutputFileRepository
14.        Stopped, disabled - osboxes2.WebApplicationContainerServer
15.        Stopped,  enabled - osboxes2.WebIntelligenceProcessingServer
Select server to manage or 0 to exit: 1
P. Stop
R. Restart
F. Force Stop
E. Enable
0. Return
Select action: r
Attempting to restart server.
Setting server osboxes2.AdaptiveJobServer to Restart / disabled

Current state: Stopping / disabled
Expected:  Restart / disabled
Server is not in expected state; waiting to check again.

Current state: Stopping / disabled
Expected:  Restart / disabled
Server is not in expected state; waiting to check again.

Current state: Starting / disabled
Expected:  Restart / disabled
Server is not in expected state; waiting to check again.

Current state: Initializing / disabled
Expected:  Running / disabled
Server is not in expected state; waiting to check again.

Current state: Running / disabled
Expected:  Running / disabled
STATUS CHANGE COMPLETE
```

```
  1.      Running, disabled - osboxes2.AdaptiveJobServer
  2.       Failed,  enabled - osboxes2.AdaptiveProcessingServer
  3.      Running,  enabled - osboxes2.CentralManagementServer
  4.      Stopped, disabled - osboxes2.ConnectionServer
  5.      Stopped, disabled - osboxes2.CrystalReports2016ProcessingServer
  6.      Stopped, disabled - osboxes2.CrystalReports2016ReportApplicationServer
  7.      Stopped, disabled - osboxes2.CrystalReportsCacheServer
  8.      Running, disabled - osboxes2.CrystalReportsProcessingServer
  9.      Stopped, disabled - osboxes2.DashboardsCacheServer
 10.      Stopped, disabled - osboxes2.DashboardsProcessingServer
 11.      Stopped, disabled - osboxes2.EventServer
 12.      Running,  enabled - osboxes2.InputFileRepository
 13.      Running,  enabled - osboxes2.OutputFileRepository
 14.      Stopped, disabled - osboxes2.WebApplicationContainerServer
 15.      Stopped,  enabled - osboxes2.WebIntelligenceProcessingServer
Select server to manage or 0 to exit:
```

Here, we chose to manage the first server in the list – the AJS. For the action, we chose *Restart*. We can see how the restart causes the server to pass through each execution phase: *Stopping, Starting, Initializing*, before finally achieving *Running* status. Note that the server's expected run state changes during this time: it begins with *Restart* (which is what we set it to), but once the server reaches *Initializing* state, the expected state automatically changes to *Running*. We know the server is in its "final state" when both the current state and expected state are *Running*.

SAP BusinessObjects Architecture 101

Before we go further into services, it will help to cover the basic service architecture of SAP BusinessObjects BI4.

Everything in an SAP BusinessObjects environment belongs to a *Cluster*. The cluster can include installations on one or more *machines*[120]. In the InfoStore, the cluster is associated with InfoObject 4; everything else in the InfoStore is a descendant of this InfoObject.

A cluster contains one or more *Nodes*. Each node exists on one machine and belongs to one cluster. The node is created during software installation, or subsequently via the Central Configuration Manager (CCM). The node has a one-to-one association with a Server Intelligence Agent (SIA), which manages its servers. The nodes are represented in the InfoStore by InfoObjects of kind `EnterpriseNode`.

Each *node* contains one or more *servers*; these appear in the *Servers* page of the CMC. Each server is represented by InfoObjects of kind `Server`. Examples of servers include the Central Management Server (CMS), Input File Repository Server (IFRS), and the Adaptive Job Server

---

120 To clear up some ambiguity: when we refer to a *server,* it is a BO processing server such as the CMS, WebI Processing Server, etc. The UNIX or Windows server that the software is installed on is the *machine*.

(AJS). Servers are bound to one *node* (and therefore one machine and one SIA).

Each *server* hosts one or more *services*. In order for a server to do something, it must host a service of an appropriate type. An Adaptive Job Server, for example, can only process scheduled Web Intelligence jobs if it hosts a *Web Intelligence Scheduling Service*.

Services are represented in the InfoStore with InfoObjects of kind `IService`. A particular service (*Web Intelligence Scheduling Service*, for example) is represented by a single InfoObject in the InfoStore, regardless of how many servers it is hosted in.

Servers are also associated with *Service Containers*. Service Containers manage a collection of related services and form a template of sorts for servers (think of servers as an implementation of a service container template). Among other things, the service container maintains a list of the services that can be hosted by a particular server. The InfoStore contains one service container for *each kind of server* that can exist in the cluster (for example, the service container for Event Servers is named `EventServiceContainer`; the service container for Input File Store Server is named `InputFileStoreService`). Like services, there is only one InfoObject for a service container, regardless of how many servers it is associated with.

The following diagram illustrates the relationship between servers, services, and service containers. Here we have created four servers: two Event Servers and two Connection Servers. The two Event Servers each have an association with the singular `EventServiceContainer` InfoObject, as well as the three services that an Event Server can host (`EventService`, `AuditingService`, and `TraceLogService`). The `EventServiceContainer` InfoObject is also associated with the same three services. Similarly, the Connection Servers are associated with the `ConnectionServiceContainer`, and the three services that Connection Servers can host (`SSOService`, `ConnectivityService`, and the `TraceLogService`). Note that the `TraceLogService` can be hosted by both Event Servers and Connectivity Servers (as well as others).

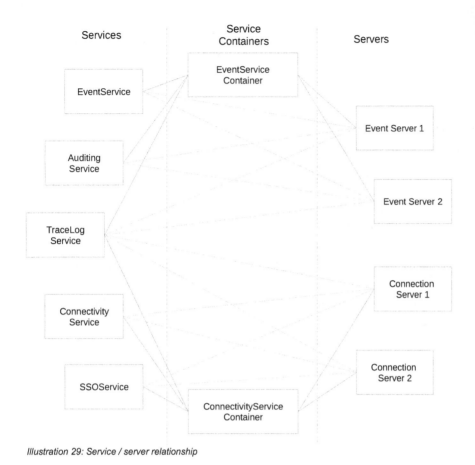

Illustration 29: Service / server relationship

There is more information about this architecture in the *Business Intelligence Platform Java SDK Developer Guide*, in the section *Server Intelligence Architecture*.

Server Metrics

Understanding the server/service architecture of BusinessObjects is necessary in order to understand how to work with server metrics. Every server in the system contains several metrics – statistics and other bits of information describing the current state of the server, past history, etc. Some of these metrics are associated with the server itself, while other metrics are associated with the services that the server hosts.

In the CMC, the server metrics are listed on the Metrics tab under the heading Common Server Metrics. For example:

Common Server Metrics

Machine Name	osboxes.localdomain
Name Server	osboxes.localdomain:6400
Registered Name	com.seagatesoftware.img.osca.aps.osboxes."osboxes.localdomain:6400"-osboxes2.cms
Operating System	Linux 3.10.0-229.11.1.el7.x86_64
CPU Type	x86_64

Metrics associated with the hosted services are also listed and will differ for each kind of server. For example, the Central Management Service in our system looks like the following:

Central Management Service Metrics

Connection to Auditing Database is Established	0
CMS Auditor	0
Auditing Database Connection Name	
Auditing Database User Name	
Auditing Database Last Updated On	Friday, December 29, 1899 7:00:00 PM EST

Retrieving the metrics for a server via the SDK is not as straightforward as it might appear. Each IServer object has an IServerMetrics container which contains the metrics, but getting the labels, formats, and structure of the metrics requires the use of *render templates* that define the structure and format of each metric.

```java
package bosdkbook;

import java.text.SimpleDateFormat;
import java.util.Calendar;
import java.util.Date;
import java.util.Iterator;
import java.util.Locale;

import com.businessobjects.sdk.plugin.desktop.common.IMetric;
import com.businessobjects.sdk.plugin.desktop.common.IMetrics;
import com.businessobjects.sdk.plugin.desktop.metricdescriptions
        .IMLDescriptions;
import com.businessobjects.sdk.plugin.desktop.metricdescriptions
        .IMetricDescriptions;
import com.businessobjects.sdk.plugin.desktop.metricdescriptions
        .IPropertyBagRenderTemplate;
import com.businessobjects.sdk.plugin.desktop.metricdescriptions
        .IPropertyRenderTemplate;
import com.businessobjects.sdk.plugin.desktop.metricdescriptions
        .ValueFormat;
import com.crystaldecisions.sdk.exception.SDKException;
```

```
17 import com.crystaldecisions.sdk.framework.CrystalEnterprise;

18 import com.crystaldecisions.sdk.framework.IEnterpriseSession;

19 import com.crystaldecisions.sdk.framework.ISessionMgr;

20 import com.crystaldecisions.sdk.occa.infostore.IInfoObjects;

21 import com.crystaldecisions.sdk.occa.infostore.IInfoStore;

22 import com.crystaldecisions.sdk.plugin.desktop.server.IServer;

23 import com.crystaldecisions.sdk.plugin.desktop.server.IServerMetrics;

24 import com.crystaldecisions.sdk.properties.IProperties;

25 import com.crystaldecisions.sdk.properties.IProperty;

26

27 public class PrintServerMetrics

28 {

29     private IMetricDescriptions mds;

30     private static final SimpleDateFormat sdf =
                   new SimpleDateFormat("MM/dd/yyyy hh:mm:ss a");

31

32     public static void main(String[] args) throws Exception

33     {

34         new ServerMetrics();

35     }

36

37     private ServerMetrics()

38     throws SDKException

39     {

40         ISessionMgr sessionManager = CrystalEnterprise.getSessionMgr();

41         IEnterpriseSession session = sessionManager.logon ("administrator",
    "xxxx", "192.168.56.102", "secEnterprise");

42

43         IInfoStore infoStore = (IInfoStore) session.getService("", "InfoStore");

44

45         // Get an IMetricDescriptions object. Used to get render templates.

46         mds = (IMetricDescriptions) infoStore.query("select * from
    ci_systemobjects where si_kind = 'metricdescriptions'").get(0);

47

48         IInfoObjects ios = infoStore.query("select * from ci_systemobjects where
    si_kind = 'server'  ");
```

```
49
50          // Iterate through each server
51          for(Object o : ios)
52          {
53              IServer server = (IServer)o;
54              IServerMetrics serverMetrics = server.getMetrics();
55
56              System.out.println("\nServer: " + server.getTitle());
57
58              // Iterate through each service that this server supports
59              @SuppressWarnings("unchecked")
60              Iterator<String> itService = serverMetrics
                        .getServiceInterfaceNames().iterator();
61              while(itService.hasNext())
62              {
63                  // Get the name and metrics for this service
64                  String serviceName = itService.next();
65                  IMetrics metrics = serverMetrics.getMetrics(serviceName);
66
67                  if(metrics.size() == 0)
68                      continue; // Don't print anything if service has no metrics
   to be displayed
69
70                  // A service may or may not have a friendly name. If not, use the
   SI_NAME value.
71                  String serviceFriendlyName =
                        mds.getServiceFriendlyName(serviceName,
                        Locale.getDefault());
72
73                  if(serviceFriendlyName==null)
74                      serviceFriendlyName = serviceName;
75
76                  System.out.println("  Service: " + serviceFriendlyName);
77
78                  // IMLDescriptions contains the render templates for the
   service's top-level metrics
```

```
79          IMLDescriptions metricDescriptions =
                mds.getMetricDescriptions(serviceName);

80

81          // Iterate through each of the service's top-level metrics

82          @SuppressWarnings("unchecked")

83          Iterator<IMetric> itMetric = metrics.iterator();

84          while(itMetric.hasNext())

85          {

86              IMetric metric = itMetric.next();

87              if(metricDescriptions == null)

88              {

89                  // If this service has no render templates, just print
    the metric name and value

90                  System.out.println("              "
                        + metric.getName()
                        + ": " + metric.getValue().toString());

91              }

92              else

93              {

94                  // Get the render template for this metric

95                  IPropertyRenderTemplate propRenderTemplate =
                        metricDescriptions
                        .getPropertyRenderTemplate(metric.getName());

96                  // If there is no render template for this metric, or if
    it's a hidden metric, then skip

97                  if(propRenderTemplate==null
                        || propRenderTemplate.getValueFormat()
                            == ValueFormat.HIDDEN)

98                      continue;

99                  // Display the metric label and value. Note that this may
    be a single value or collection

100                 printMetric(serverMetrics,
                        metric.getValue(),propRenderTemplate);

101             }

102         }

103     }

104 }

105
```

```java
106      }
107
108      void printMetric (IServerMetrics serverMetrics,Object value,
     IPropertyRenderTemplate propRenderTemplate)
109      {
110          // Get the label and format for this metric
111          String label = propRenderTemplate.getLabel(Locale.getDefault());
112          ValueFormat valueFormat = propRenderTemplate.getValueFormat();
113
114          // Print the metric's value, depending on whether it's a property bag or
     not
115          if (valueFormat == ValueFormat.PROPBAG)
116          {
117              IProperties propertyBag =
                     serverMetrics.resolveMetricString
                     (value.toString());
118              System.out.println("        " + label + ":");
119              printMetricBag(propertyBag,propRenderTemplate
                     .getRenderTemplateName(),"                    ");
120          }
121          else
122              System.out.println("        " + label + " ("
                     + propRenderTemplate.getID()
                     + "): " + formatMetricValue(value, valueFormat,
                     propRenderTemplate));
123      }
124
125
126      void printMetricBag(IProperties bag,String renderTemplateName,String indent)
127      {
128          // Get the render template for this property bag
129          IPropertyBagRenderTemplate bagRenderTemplate =
                 mds.getPropertyBagRenderTemplate(
                 renderTemplateName);
130
131          // Get the number of elements in the bag.  We first need to get the name
     of the property
132          // (ex. SI_TOTAL), then get the value of the property having that name.
```

```
133          int bagSize = bag.getInt(bagRenderTemplate.getTotalID());

134      for(int x=1;x<=bagSize;x++)

135      {

136          // Get the properties within this bag

137          IProperties ps = bag.getProperties(bagRenderTemplate
                 .getPropNamePrefix() + x);

138

139          // Iterate through the render templates within this bag. Each
    template will

140          // describe the structure of the metrics within the bag.

141          @SuppressWarnings("unchecked")

142          Iterator<IPropertyRenderTemplate> itSubTemplate =
                 bagRenderTemplate
                 .getPropertyRenderTemplates().iterator();

143          while(itSubTemplate.hasNext())

144          {

145              // Get the render template of the metric in the bag

146              IPropertyRenderTemplate subTemplate =
                     itSubTemplate.next();

147

148              // If the bag contains another bag, recurse into this method

149              if(subTemplate.getValueFormat() == ValueFormat.PROPBAG)

150              {

151                  IProperties subBag =
                         ps.getProperties(subTemplate.getID());

152                  printMetricBag(subBag,subTemplate
                         .getRenderTemplateName(),indent + "   ");

153              }

154              // Otherwise, get the metric's name and value, then format the
    value to a string

155              else

156              {

157                  String label =
                         subTemplate.getLabel(Locale.getDefault());

158                  Object subPropertyValue =
                         ps.getProperty(subTemplate.getID()).getValue();
```

```
159                String formattedMetricValue =
                        formatMetricValue(subPropertyValue,
                        subTemplate.getValueFormat(), subTemplate);

160                System.out.println(indent
                        + label
                        + ": "
                        + formattedMetricValue);

161            }

162        }

163        if(x < bagSize)

164            System.out.println(); // Don't print crlf for last entry in bag

165    }

166  }

167

168  // Inspired by: https://answers.sap.com/questions/7487062/number-of-jobs-on-
     job-servergroup.html

169  private String formatMetricValue(Object value,ValueFormat
     valueFormat,IPropertyRenderTemplate template)

170  {

171      if (valueFormat == ValueFormat.FLOAT

172          || valueFormat == ValueFormat.PERCENT

173          || valueFormat == ValueFormat.SHIFTSIZE_KB

174          || valueFormat == ValueFormat.SHIFTSIZE_MB

175          || valueFormat == ValueFormat.SHIFTSIZE_GB)

176      {

177          double val;

178          double scale = 1.0;

179

180          if(value instanceof String)

181              val = Double.parseDouble((String) value);

182          else

183              val = ((Number) value).doubleValue();

184

185          if(valueFormat == ValueFormat.PERCENT) {

186              scale = 100.0;
```

```
187              } else if(valueFormat == ValueFormat.SHIFTSIZE_KB) {
188                  scale = 1024.0;
189              } else if(valueFormat == ValueFormat.SHIFTSIZE_MB) {
190                  scale = 1024.0 * 1024.0;
191              } else if(valueFormat == ValueFormat.SHIFTSIZE_GB) {
192                  scale = 1024.0 * 1024.0 * 1024.0;
193              }
194
195              return "" + (val/scale);
196          }
197          else if(valueFormat == ValueFormat.DATETIME)
198          {
199              // A Date property can be a java.util.Date, IProperty, Float, or
        Double,
200              // convert to a Date if necessary.
201              Date date;
202              if(value instanceof IProperty)
203              {
204                  IProperty prop = (IProperty)value;
205                  date = (Date) prop.getValue();
206              }
207              else if(value instanceof Date)
208              {
209                  date = (Date)value;
210              }
211              else // Not Date or IProperty; must be a Number, in the form of
        number of days since 11/30/1899
212              {
213                  Number num = (Number)value;
214                  int days = num.intValue();
215                  double dayPortion =
                         (num.doubleValue() - days) * 86400000;
216                  Calendar cal = Calendar.getInstance();
217                  cal.set(1899, 11, 30, 0, 0, 0);
```

```
218          cal.add(Calendar.DATE, days);
219          cal.add(Calendar.MILLISECOND, (int)dayPortion);
220          date = cal.getTime();
221       }
222       if(date.getTime() == -185544796348800000L)
223          return null;
224
225       return(sdf.format(date));
226    }
227    else if(valueFormat == ValueFormat.STRING_MAP)
228    {
229       // If the value is a mapped string, look up the value using the
   string map name and property value
230       // If the string map is not found, then just return the property
   value itself
231       String mappedValue =
             mds.getMLDescription(template.getStringMapName(),
             value.toString(), Locale.getDefault());
232       if(mappedValue == null)
233          return value.toString();
234       else
235          return mappedValue;
236    }
237    else
238       return value.toString();
239  }
240 }
```

Listing 34: The PrintServerMetrics program

Listing 34 contains the *PrintServerMetrics* program, which displays the same information as the *Metrics* tabs of servers in the CMC.

The process is fairly complex, and we will not cover it line-by-line, or describe all referenced classes. But the overall process is as follows:

For each server, get a list of its hosted services (line 60-61).

For each hosted service, get its metrics (line 65), and render templates (line 79).

Iterate through each metric. Metrics, like InfoObject properties, can be a single value (string, integer, date, etc.) or a property bag. If this metric is a single value, then display its label, ID, and formatted value (line 122). If it is a property bag, then iterate through each metric therein (line 119); these sub-metrics may be property bags themselves (line 152), or single-value metrics (line 160).

In our system, the beginning of the output from this program is:

```
Server: osboxes2.EventServer
   Service: Auditing Metrics
      Current Number of Auditing Events in the Queue
(Auditing.numberOfEventsInTheQueue): 0
   Service: Common Server Metrics
      Machine Name (ISPROP_GEN_MACHINENAME): osboxes.localdomain
      Name Server (ISPROP_GEN_APSNAME): osboxes.localdomain:6400
      Registered Name (ISPROP_GEN_INFOSERVERNAME):
com.seagatesoftware.img.osca.eventserver."osboxes.localdomain"-osboxes2.EventServer
      Operating System (ISPROP_GEN_MACH_OSNAME): Linux 3.10.0-229.11.1.el7.x86_64
      CPU Type (ISPROP_GEN_MACH_PROCESSERNAME): x86_64
      CPUs (ISPROP_GEN_MACH_CUPQUANTITY): 1
```

This is displaying metrics for the *EventServer* server. First, the Auditing metrics are displayed, then the server's general metrics ("Common Server Metrics").

The following clip further on in the output is a sample of a metric containing a property bag. These are the *Connectivity Service Metrics* from the *ConnectionServer*:

```
   Service: Connectivity Service Metrics
      Data Sources:
         Network Layer: ODBC
            Database: <i>MySQL 5</i>
            Status: Failed!
            Available Connections: 0
            Jobs (CORBA): 0
            Jobs (HTTP): 0

            Database: <i>MySQL 8</i>
            Status: Failed!
            Available Connections: 0
            Jobs (CORBA): 0
```

This correlates with what we see on the Metrics tab of the ConnectionServer in the CMC, although in a different format:

Connectivity Service Metrics
Data Sources

Network Layer	Database	Status	Available Connections	Jobs (CORBA)	Jobs (HTTP)
ODBC					
	MySQL 5	Failed!	0	0	0
	MySQL 8	Failed!	0	0	0
	Oracle 11	Failed!	0	0	0

Our program is a simple list of metrics, while the CMC properly formats metric bags into tabular form.

To make our program a little more useful, we can create a method that returns the value of a selected metric.

```
1   package bosdkbook;
2
3   import java.text.SimpleDateFormat;
4   import java.util.Calendar;
5   import java.util.Date;
6   import java.util.Iterator;
7   import java.util.Locale;
8
9   import com.businessobjects.sdk.plugin.desktop.common.IMetric;
10  import com.businessobjects.sdk.plugin.desktop.common.IMetrics;
11  import com.businessobjects.sdk.plugin.desktop.metricdescriptions
                .IMLDescriptions;
12  import com.businessobjects.sdk.plugin.desktop.metricdescriptions
                .IMetricDescriptions;
13  import com.businessobjects.sdk.plugin.desktop.metricdescriptions
                .IPropertyRenderTemplate;
14  import com.businessobjects.sdk.plugin.desktop.metricdescriptions
                .ValueFormat;
15  import com.crystaldecisions.sdk.exception.SDKException;
16  import com.crystaldecisions.sdk.framework.CrystalEnterprise;
17  import com.crystaldecisions.sdk.framework.IEnterpriseSession;
18  import com.crystaldecisions.sdk.framework.ISessionMgr;
19  import com.crystaldecisions.sdk.occa.infostore.IInfoObjects;
20  import com.crystaldecisions.sdk.occa.infostore.IInfoStore;
21  import com.crystaldecisions.sdk.plugin.desktop.server.IServer;
22  import com.crystaldecisions.sdk.plugin.desktop.server.IServerMetrics;
23  import com.crystaldecisions.sdk.properties.IProperty;
24
25  public class GetServerMetrics
26  {
27      private IMetricDescriptions mds;
28      private static final SimpleDateFormat sdf =
                new SimpleDateFormat("MM/dd/yyyy hh:mm:ss a");
```

```
29
30      public static void main(String[] args) throws Exception
31      {
32          new ServerMetrics();
33      }
34
35      private ServerMetrics()
36      throws SDKException
37      {
38          ISessionMgr sessionManager = CrystalEnterprise.getSessionMgr();
39          IEnterpriseSession session = sessionManager.logon ("administrator",
    "xxxx", "192.168.56.102", "secEnterprise");
40
41          IInfoStore infoStore = (IInfoStore) session.getService("", "InfoStore");
42
43          // Get an IMetricDescriptions object. Used to get render templates.
44          mds = (IMetricDescriptions) infoStore.query("select * from
    ci_systemobjects where si_kind = 'metricdescriptions'").get(0);
45
46          IInfoObjects ios = infoStore.query("select * from ci_systemobjects where
    si_kind = 'server'  ");
47
48          // Iterate through each server
49          for(Object o : ios)
50          {
51              IServer server = (IServer)o;
52
53              System.out.println("\n" + server.getTitle() + ": ");
54              System.out.println("Auditing events: "
                    + getMetricValue(server,"Auditing Metrics",
                        "Current Number of Auditing Events in the Queue"));
55              System.out.println("PID: "
                    + getMetricValue(server,
                        "Common Server Metrics","PID"));
56          }
57      }
58
```

```
59      String getMetricValue(IServer server,String requestedServiceName,String
    requestedMetricName)

60      throws SDKException

61      {

62          IServerMetrics serverMetrics = server.getMetrics();

63

64          // Iterate through each service that this server supports

65          @SuppressWarnings("unchecked")

66          Iterator<String> itService =
                serverMetrics.getServiceInterfaceNames().iterator();

67          while(itService.hasNext())

68          {

69              // Get the name of this service

70              String serviceName = itService.next();

71

72              // A service may or may not have a friendly name. If not, use the
    SI_NAME value.

73              String serviceFriendlyName =
                    mds.getServiceFriendlyName(serviceName,
                        Locale.getDefault());

74

75              // Continue if this is not the service we're looking for

76              if(! (requestedServiceName.equals(serviceName)
                    || requestedServiceName.equals(serviceFriendlyName)))

77                  continue;

78

79              IMetrics metrics = serverMetrics.getMetrics(serviceName);

80              if(metrics == null || metrics.size() == 0)

81                  return "N/A"; // Don't print anything if service has no metrics
    to be displayed

82

83              // IMLDescriptions contains the render templates for the service's
    top-level metrics

84              IMLDescriptions metricDescriptions =
    mds.getMetricDescriptions(serviceName);

85

86              // Iterate through each of the service's top-level metrics

87              @SuppressWarnings("unchecked")
```

```
88          Iterator<IMetric> itMetric = metrics.iterator();

89          while(itMetric.hasNext())

90          {

91              IMetric metric = itMetric.next();

92

93              String metricName = metric.getName();

94              String metricLabel = ""; // will adjust below if render template
   available

95              String metricValue;

96              if(metricDescriptions == null)

97              {

98                  // If this service has no render templates, just take the
   metric's string value

99                  metricValue = metric.getValue().toString();

100             }

101             else

102             {

103                 // Get the render template for this metric

104                 IPropertyRenderTemplate propRenderTemplate =
   metricDescriptions.getPropertyRenderTemplate(metric.getName());

105

106                 // If there is no render template for this metric, or if it's
   a hidden metric, then continue

107                 if(propRenderTemplate==null)

108                     continue;

109

110                 // Get the label, value, and format

111                 MetricLabel =
                        propRenderTemplate.getLabel(Locale.getDefault());

112                 Object value = metric.getValue();

113                 ValueFormat valueFormat =
                        propRenderTemplate.getValueFormat();

114

115                 // If the metric is a bag, then just return N/A

116                 if (valueFormat == ValueFormat.PROPBAG)

117                     metricValue = "N/A";

118
```

```
119            metricValue = formatMetricValue(value,
                   valueFormat, propRenderTemplate);
120         }
121
122         // Check the metric name and label to see if it
123         // is the one we want.
124         if(requestedMetricName.equals(metricName)
              || requestedMetricName.equals(metricLabel))
125            return metricValue;
126      }
127   }
128   return ""; // metric not found
129 }
130
131 // Inspired by: https://answers.sap.com/questions/7487062/number-of-jobs-on-
job-servergroup.html
132 private String formatMetricValue(Object value,ValueFormat
valueFormat,IPropertyRenderTemplate template)
133 {
134   if (valueFormat == ValueFormat.FLOAT
135      || valueFormat == ValueFormat.PERCENT
136      || valueFormat == ValueFormat.SHIFTSIZE_KB
137      || valueFormat == ValueFormat.SHIFTSIZE_MB
138      || valueFormat == ValueFormat.SHIFTSIZE_GB)
139   {
140      double val;
141      double scale = 1.0;
142
143      if(value instanceof String)
144         val = Double.parseDouble((String) value);
145      else
146         val = ((Number) value).doubleValue();
147
148      if(valueFormat == ValueFormat.PERCENT) {
```

```
149            scale = 100.0;
150        } else if(valueFormat == ValueFormat.SHIFTSIZE_KB) {
151            scale = 1024.0;
152        } else if(valueFormat == ValueFormat.SHIFTSIZE_MB) {
153            scale = 1024.0 * 1024.0;
154        } else if(valueFormat == ValueFormat.SHIFTSIZE_GB) {
155            scale = 1024.0 * 1024.0 * 1024.0;
156        }

157
158        return "" + (val/scale);
159    }
160    else if(valueFormat == ValueFormat.DATETIME)
161    {
162        // A Date property can be a java.util.Date, IProperty, Float, or
    Double,
163        // convert to a Date if necessary.
164        Date date;
165        if(value instanceof IProperty)
166        {
167            IProperty prop = (IProperty)value;
168            date = (Date) prop.getValue();
169        }
170        else if(value instanceof Date)
171        {
172            date = (Date)value;
173        }
174        else // Not Date or IProperty; must be a Number, in the form of
    number of days since 11/30/1899
175        {
176            Number num = (Number)value;
177            int days = num.intValue();
178            double dayPortion =
                (num.doubleValue() - days) * 86400000;
179            Calendar cal = Calendar.getInstance();
```

```
180              cal.set(1899, 11, 30, 0, 0, 0);

181              cal.add(Calendar.DATE, days);

182              cal.add(Calendar.MILLISECOND, (int)dayPortion);

183              date = cal.getTime();

184          }

185          if(date.getTime() == -185544796348800000L)

186              return null;

187

188          return(sdf.format(date));

189      }

190      else if(valueFormat == ValueFormat.STRING_MAP)

191      {

192          // If the value is a mapped string, look up the value using the
     string map name and property value

193          // If the string map is not found, then just return the property
     value itself

194          String mappedValue =
             mds.getMLDescription(template.getStringMapName(),
             value.toString(), Locale.getDefault());

195          if(mappedValue == null)

196              return value.toString();

197          else

198              return mappedValue;

199      }

200      else

201          return value.toString();

202  }

203 }
```

Listing 35: The GetServerMetrics program

Listing 35 is a derivation of the previous program. Here, the getMetricValue() method searches for the specified service and metric name, and returns its value if found. We are simply iterating through the services and metrics to find the one with the desired names.

On lines 54 and 55, we are calling getMetricValue() to display the *Number of Auditing Events in the Queue* metric from the *Auditing* service, and the *PID* metric from the *Common Service* service:

```
54          System.out.println("Auditing events: "
              + getMetricValue(server,"Auditing Metrics",
                  "Current Number of Auditing Events in the Queue"));

55          System.out.println("PID: "
              + getMetricValue(server,
                  "Common Server Metrics","PID"));
```

The beginning of the program output for our system is:

```
osboxes2.EventServer:
Auditing events: 0
PID: 411

osboxes2.ConnectionServer:
Auditing events:
PID: 413

osboxes2.AdaptiveJobServer:
Auditing events: 264
PID: 4133
```

This program, or a derivation, could be useful in an application that displays the current status of the CMS. For example, we may want to display the number of active jobs in each job server, or the total memory used by all Web Intelligence servers.

Configuration Settings

Each server has global configuration settings such as command line, port, etc., as well as service-specific configuration settings. The global settings are managed via the IServer interface, described earlier. To access each hosted service's configuration, we first call IServer.getHostedServices(), which returns an IConfiguredServices container. This contains a list of IConfiguredService objects, representing the configuration settings for this hosted service. From here, we can call IConfiguredService.getConfigProps() to get a list of the settings.

```
1  package bosdkbook;
2
3  import java.util.Iterator;
4  import java.util.Locale;
5
6  import com.businessobjects.sdk.plugin.desktop.common.IConfigProperties;
7  import com.businessobjects.sdk.plugin.desktop.common.IConfigProperty;
```

```
 8  import com.businessobjects.sdk.plugin.desktop.common.IConfiguredService;

 9  import com.businessobjects.sdk.plugin.desktop.service.IService;

10  import com.crystaldecisions.sdk.exception.SDKException;

11  import com.crystaldecisions.sdk.framework.CrystalEnterprise;

12  import com.crystaldecisions.sdk.framework.IEnterpriseSession;

13  import com.crystaldecisions.sdk.framework.ISessionMgr;

14  import com.crystaldecisions.sdk.occa.infostore.IInfoObjects;

15  import com.crystaldecisions.sdk.occa.infostore.IInfoStore;

16  import com.crystaldecisions.sdk.plugin.desktop.server.IServer;

17

18  public class GetServerSettings

19  {

20      public static void main(String[] args) throws Exception

21      {

22          new GetServerSettings();

23      }

24

25      private GetServerSettings()

26      throws SDKException

27      {

28          ISessionMgr sessionManager = CrystalEnterprise.getSessionMgr();

29          IEnterpriseSession session = sessionManager.logon ("administrator",
    "xxxx", "192.168.56.102", "secEnterprise");

30

31          IInfoStore infoStore = (IInfoStore) session.getService("", "InfoStore");

32

33          IInfoObjects ios = infoStore.query("select * from ci_systemobjects where
    si_kind = 'server' and si_name like '%WebIntelligenceProcessingServer%'");

34

35          for(Object o : ios)

36          {

37              IServer server = (IServer)o;

38

39              @SuppressWarnings("unchecked")
```

```
40          Iterator<IConfiguredService> itCS =
                server.getHostedServices().iterator();

41          while(itCS.hasNext())

42          {

43              IConfiguredService cs = itCS.next();

44              System.out.println("Configuration settings for: "
                    + getServiceByID(infoStore, cs.getID())
                    .getDescription());

45

46              IConfigProperties configProps = cs.getConfigProps();

47              displayProperties(configProps,"  ");

48              System.out.println();

49          }

50      }

51  }

52

53  private void displayProperties(IConfigProperties configProps,String indent)

54  throws SDKException

55  {

56      for(String propName : configProps.getPropNames())

57      {

58          IConfigProperty configProperty =
                configProps.getProp(propName);

59          String label =
                configProperty.getDisplayName(Locale.getDefault());

60          Object propValue = configProperty.getValue();

61          if(propValue instanceof IConfigProperties)

62          {

63              System.out.println(indent + label + ":");

64              displayProperties((IConfigProperties) propValue,
                    indent + "  ");

65          }

66          else

67              System.out.println(indent + label + ": "
                    + configProperty.getValue());

68      }

69  }
```

70	
71	`    private IService getServiceByID(IInfoStore infoStore,Integer id)` `    throws SDKException`
72	`    {`
73	`        IInfoObjects ios = infoStore.query("select * from ci_systemobjects where si_id = " + id);`
74	`        if(ios.size()==0)`
75	`            return null;`
76	`        return (IService) ios.get(0);`
77	`    }`
78	`}`

Listing 36: The GetServerSettings program

Listing 36 contains the *GetServerSettings* program, an example of retrieving server configuration settings. For this example, we are only retrieving the settings for the *WebI Processing Server,* and in our system it produced the following output:

```
Configuration settings for: Web Intelligence Core Service
  Timeout Before Recycling (seconds): 1200
  Idle Document Timeout (seconds): 300
  Server polling interval (seconds): 120
  Maximum Documents per User: 5
  Maximum Documents Before Recycling: 50
  Allow Document Map Maximum Size Errors: 1
  Idle Connection Timeout (minutes): 20
  Maximum Connections: 200
  Enable Memory Analysis: 0
  Memory Lower Threshold (MB): 3500
  Memory Upper Threshold (MB): 4500
  Memory Maximum Threshold (MB): 6000
  Enable APS Service Monitoring: 1
  Retry Count on APS Service Ping Failure: 3
  APS Service Monitoring Thread Period: 300
  Enable Current Activity Logs: 0

Configuration settings for: Information Engine Service
  Enable List Of Values Cache: 1
  List Of Values Batch Size (entries): 1000
  Maximum Custom Sort Size (entries): 100
  Universe Cache Maximum Size (Universes): 20
  Maximum List Of Values Size (entries): 50000
  Maximum Parallel Queries per document: 64
  Enable Parallel Queries for Scheduling: 1

Configuration settings for: Auditing Service
  Events Per File: 500
  Auditing Temporary Directory: %DefaultAuditingDir%
```

```
    Auditing is Enabled: 1

Configuration settings for: TraceLog Service
  Log level: Unspecified

Configuration settings for: Single Sign-On Service
  Windows SSPI Configuration:
    Single Sign-On Expiry (seconds): 86400

Configuration settings for: Web Intelligence Common Service
  Cache Timeout (minutes): 4370
  Document Cache Cleanup Interval (minutes): 120
  Output Cache Directory:
  Disable Cache Sharing: 0
  Enable Document Cache: 1
  Enable Real-time Cache: 1
  Maximum Document Cache Size (KB): 1000000
  Maximum Document Cache Reduction Space (percent): 70
  Maximum Character Stream Size (MB): 15
  Binary Stream Maximum Size (MB): 50
  Images Directory:

Configuration settings for: Web Intelligence Processing Service
  Enable use of HTTP URL: 1
  Proxy value:
```

The results correlate to what's displayed on the Properties tab of the *WebIntelligenceProcessingServer* in the CMC, including:

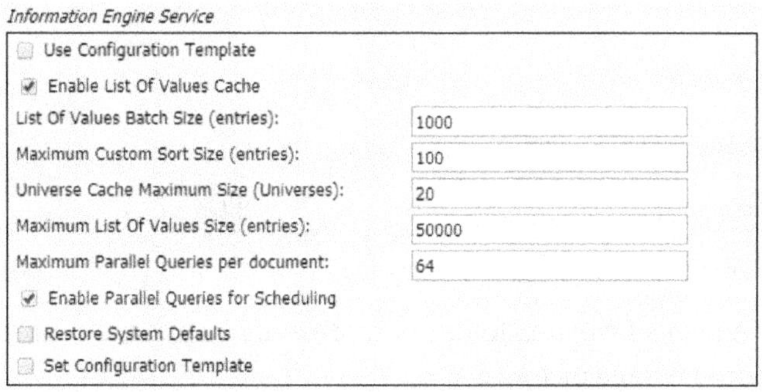

Illustration 30: Server settings

Chapter Review

- All InfoObjects are children of folders, and so there are folders for many different purposes – reports, users, servers, universes, etc.   Each of these folders is represented in the SDK by the IFolder interface.

- Categories are similar to folders in that they are a way of organizing content. However, they differ in several ways, including that an InfoObject must be in one (and only one) folder, while it may be in several categories, or none at all.

- The IUser interface contains many methods for manipulating user InfoObjects. This includes setting the password, manipulating profile strings, and managing group membership.

- The SDK can be used to manipulate servers: start/stop, enable/disable, and change settings.

- *Servers* host *services*, which define what a server can do.   The SDK exposes the configuration settings and execution metrics of servers and their hosted services.

Quiz

1. The zeroth element in the list returned from IFolder.getPath() is the folder's:

    a) Immediate parent

    b) Furthest ancestor

    c) First immediate child

    d) Self

2. Which method of IFolder is used to retrieve all of the folder's children that are also folders?

    a) getChildren()

    b) getSubFolders()

    c) getSubfolders()

    d) getContents()

3. True/False: A user's favorites folder is represented by the IFavoritesFolder interface, which is a subinterface of IFolder.

4. Security rights are inherited from an InfoObject's:

    a) Parent folder

    b) Assigned personal categories

    c) Assigned public categories

    d) Any of the above

    e) None of the above

5. To change a password, the ___ method of `IUser` requires the user's current password, while the __ method does not.

   a) `changePassword(), setPassword()`

   b) `changePassword(), setNewPassword()`

   c) `setPassword(), changePassword()`

   d) None of the above

6. The `IServer.isAlive()` method returns `true` when the server is in which of the following states?

   a) failed

   b) initializing

   c) running

   d) running with errors

   e) running with warnings

   f) starting

   g) stopped

   h) stopping

7. True/False: calling `IServer.setExpectedRunState()` immediately changes the server to the desired state.

8. A system with two Event Servers will have __ service container(s) named `EventServiceContainer`, and __ service(s) named `EventService`.

   a) 2, 2

   b) 1, 1

   c) 1, 2

   d) 2, 1

Answers on page 673.

Chapter 17 - Scheduling

The SAP BusinessObjects platform includes an advanced scheduling engine for the generation of reports and other content on a recurring basis. While the user interfaces (BI launch pad and CMC) provide adequate methods for scheduling individual documents, they are not well-suited to managing large numbers of documents[121]. There are are several third-party utilities that extend this functionality, but the SDK can also be used to manage schedules. A few examples are:

- Scheduling a large number of reports to the same destination

- Scheduling a large number of reports, using scheduling parameters from another source (that is, reading scheduling information from a file and creating the schedules accordingly)

- Identifying and re-scheduling reports that are sent to a particular email address or file share, to use a different destination.

- Automatically re-scheduling failed reports

We covered scheduling properties and actions in Part One. We'll now build upon that to manage scheduled instances with the BI4 Platform SDK. In this chapter, we will cover the creation of scheduled instances, setting default parameters, managing existing schedules, and rescheduling instances.

Creating Scheduled Instances

Scheduling objects to run via the SDK is fairly straightforward. The basic process to create a new scheduled instance is:

1. Use a CMS query to retrieve the base document as an IInfoObject.

2. Optionally set scheduling options on the retrieved IInfoObject.

3. Call the schedule() method of the retrieved IInfoObject.

We'll create a simple example program to illustrate these steps. The *CreateSched* program, in Listing 37, is a simple-as-simple-can-be program to create a new scheduled instance of a Web Intelligence report using its default scheduling parameters.

```
1  package bosdkbook;
2
3  import com.businessobjects.sdk.plugin.desktop.webi.IWebi;
```

---

121 Although *Publications* and *Object Packages* do allow for a certain amount of flexibility in this area.

```
 4  import com.crystaldecisions.sdk.exception.SDKException;

 5  import com.crystaldecisions.sdk.framework.CrystalEnterprise;

 6  import com.crystaldecisions.sdk.framework.IEnterpriseSession;

 7  import com.crystaldecisions.sdk.framework.ISessionMgr;

 8  import com.crystaldecisions.sdk.occa.infostore.IInfoObject;

 9  import com.crystaldecisions.sdk.occa.infostore.IInfoObjects;

10  import com.crystaldecisions.sdk.occa.infostore.IInfoStore;

11

12  public class CreateSched {

13

14      public static void main(String[] args) throws SDKException

15      {

16          ISessionMgr sessionManager = CrystalEnterprise.getSessionMgr();

17          IEnterpriseSession session = sessionManager.logon ("administrator",
    "xxxx", "192.168.56.102", "secEnterprise");

18

19          IInfoStore infoStore = (IInfoStore) session.getService ("","InfoStore");

20

21          IInfoObjects infoObjects = infoStore.query("select si_id from
    ci_infoobjects where si_name = 'Schedule Test' and si_kind = 'webi'");

22

23          if(infoObjects.size() > 0)

24          {

25              IWebi webi = (IWebi) infoObjects.get(0);

26              webi.schedule();

27          }

28          else

29              System.out.println("Could not find document!");

30      }

31  }
```

Listing 37: The CreateSched program

On line 21, we perform Step 1 by executing a standard CMS query. In this case, we are retrieving a Web Intelligence report named *Schedule Test*.

```
21          IInfoObjects infoObjects = infoStore.query("select si_id from
ci_infoobjects where si_name = 'Schedule Test' and si_kind = 'webi'");
```

The only consideration for CMS queries in regards to scheduling is that the query should include the `SI_SCHEDULEINFO` and `SI_RECURRING` properties[122]. While this is not technically *necessary* in order to create a schedule, these properties are required to retrieve the InfoObject's existing scheduling parameters.

The second step of the scheduling procedure is where most of the real work in scheduling objects occurs – setting the scheduling parameters. This step is optional. If any settings are *not* specified during this step, then the document's default scheduling parameters are used[123].

As a best practice, a scheduled SDK program should not depend on documents' default scheduling parameters to have expected values. Instead, all parameters should be set as appropriate in the program. If another user (or even you) were to change the default parameters of a document after a program was created, it may lead to unexpected results when the program is subsequently executed. By setting the scheduling parameters programmatically, you ensure that the correct settings are used.

As the purpose of the *CreateSched* program is to schedule the report using its default parameters, we will skip Step 2 and move right to Step 3...

The third step of scheduling documents is actually creating the new scheduled instance by calling the `schedule()` method of the base InfoObject. The new scheduled instance is then visible in the base document's History view in CMC or BI launch pad.

Since not all InfoObject kinds can be scheduled, the `schedule()` method is not included in the base `IInfoObject` interface. Schedulable kinds, such as `IWebi`, implement the `ISchedulable` interface, which provides a number of scheduling methods, including `schedule()`. So, we must cast the contents of the `infoObjects` collection to `IWebi` in order to call `schedule()`[124]:

```
25          IWebi webi = (IWebi) infoObjects.get(0);

26          webi.schedule();
```

The program generates no output (unless the document can't be found), and hopefully no errors. After executing, we find the newly-scheduled instance in the document's history:

In this case, the report was scheduled and run before we opened the history view, so it shows a status of Success. Had we opened it more quickly, the status may have still been Pending or

View ·   Organize · Send ·   More Actions ·

Instance Time *	Title	Status	Created By	Type
Dec 24, 2016 9:28 AM	Schedule Test	Success	Administrator	Web Intelligence

---

122 In the above query, we used the * wildcard, which will include the `SI_SCHEDULEINFO` property.

123 Or the instance's existing parameters, when rescheduling an instance (more on this later).

124 We could instead cast it to `ISchedulable`, which would be appropriate if the `IInfoObjects` collection included a mix of InfoObject kinds to be scheduled (WebI, Crystal Reports, etc.)

Running.

Basic Scheduling Parameters

In Chapter 2, we covered the various InfoObject properties related to scheduling. In this section, we cover how those properties are set and retrieved with the SDK.

Most scheduling parameters are set and retrieved via the ISchedulingInfo interface, which is retrieved via the IinfoObject.getSchedulingInfo() method[125]. In order to use the methods of the ISchedulingInfo interface, the CMS query that was used should include the SI_SCHEDULEINFO property. If this property was not included in the query, then the scheduling parameters may be set but not read.

The generic scheduling parameters, which are covered below, are:

- Title

- Recurrence (including start/end date and failure retries)

- Events

- Destination

- Schedule For (On behalf of)

- Server Group

- Notification

Non-generic scheduling parameters (such as output format, prompts, etc.) are covered in *Kind-Specific Scheduling Parameters*.

Title

By default, the name of a scheduled instance is the same as its parent document. This can be changed with the setTitle() method. For example:

```
25        IWebi webi = (IWebi) infoObjects.get(0);
26        webi.setTitle("My scheduled instance");
```

Unlike most of the scheduling parameters that follow, this one is not called from the ISchedulingInfo interface.

Recurrence Parameters

Recurrence parameters are stored in several separate properties. The *type* of recurrence

---

125 Note that unlike the schedule() method, the getSchedulingInfo() is applicable to IInfoObject. So, it is not necessary to cast to an IInfoObject subinterface (ex. IWebi) to call this method.

determines which of the other properties will be used to set the specific recurrence settings.

The available recurrence types can be categorized as follows:

One time: *Now, Once*

Recurring schedule: *Hourly, Daily, Monthly, Nth Day, Weekly, First Monday, Last Day of Month, X Day of Nth Week of Month*

Custom schedule: *Calendar*

The methods of `ISchedulingInfo` applicable to recurrence are:

Package *com.crystaldecisions.sdk.occa.infostore*
Interface `ISchedulingInfo`

Recurrence settings

Date	`getBeginDate()`
void	`setBeginDate(Date dtBeginDate)`
	Retrieves/sets the date that the schedule should begin.
	Associated properties: `SI_SCHEDULEINFO.SI_NEXTRUNTIME`, `SI_SCHEDULEINFO.SI_STARTTIME`
Date	`getEndDate()`
void	`setEndDate(Date dtBeginDate)`
	Retrieves/sets the date after which the schedule should cease to run.
	Associated properties: `SI_SCHEDULEINFO.SI_ENDTIME`
ICalendarRunDays	`getCalendarRunDays()`
	Retrieves an `ICalendarRunDays` collection, which is used to set granular scheduling periods (days of the week, weeks of the month, etc.) Only applicable with schedule type `CeScheduleType.CALENDAR`.
	Associated property: `SI_SCHEDULEINFO.SI_RUN_ON_TEMPLATE`
int	`getCalendarTemplate()`
void	`setCalendarTemplate(int newVal)`
	Retrieves/sets the InfoObject ID of a Calendar object which defines the days that the schedule should run. Only applicable with schedule type `CeScheduleType.CALENDAR_TEMPLATE`.
	Associated property: `SI_SCHEDULEINFO.SI_CALENDAR_TEMPLATE_ID`
int	`getIntervalHours()`

void	setIntervalHours(int newVal)
	Retrieves/sets the number of hours between executions of the schedule. Used in conjunction with intervalMinutes. Only applicable with schedule type CeScheduleType.HOURLY. *Associated property:* SI_SCHEDULEINFO.SI_SCHEDULE_INTERVAL_HOURS
int	getIntervalMinutes()
void	setIntervalMinutes(int newVal)
	Retrieves/sets the number of minutes between executions of the schedule. Used in conjunction with intervalHours. Only applicable with schedule type CeScheduleType.HOURLY. *Associated property:* SI_SCHEDULEINFO.SI_SCHEDULE_INTERVAL_MINUTES
int	getIntervalMonths()
void	setIntervalMonths(int newVal)
	Retrieves/sets the number of months between executions of the schedule. Only applicable with schedule type CeScheduleType.MONTHLY. *Associated property:* SI_SCHEDULEINFO.SI_SCHEDULE_INTERVAL_MONTHS
int	getIntervalNthDay()
void	setIntervalNthDay(int newVal)
	Retrieves/sets the day of the month when the schedule runs. Only applicable with schedule type CeScheduleType.NTH_DAY. *Associated property:* SI_SCHEDULEINFO.SI_SCHEDULE_INTERVAL_NTHDAY
int	getIntervalDays()
void	setIntervalDays(int newIntervalDays)
	Retrieves/sets the number of days between executions of the schedule. Only applicable with schedule type CeScheduleType.DAILY. *Associated property:* SI_SCHEDULEINFO.SI_SCHEDULE_INTERVAL_NDAYS
boolean	isRightNow()
void	setRightNow(boolean rightNow)

	Retrieves/sets whether the job should run immediately. If `true`, then all other recurrence settings are ignored. *Associated property:* `SI_SCHEDULEINFO.SI_SCHED_NOW`
`int`	`getType()`
`void`	`setType(int newVal)`
	Retrieves/sets the recurrence method to use (daily, monthly, etc.). Must be a value of `CeScheduleType`. *Associated property:* `SI_SCHEDULEINFO.SI_SCHEDULE_TYPE`
`TimeZone`	`getTimeZone()`
`void`	`setTimeZone(TimeZone timeZone)`
	Retrieves/sets the time zone that the schedule should run under. *Associated property:* `SI_SCHEDULEINFO.SI_TIMEZONE_ID`
`int`	`getRetriesAllowed()`
`void`	`getRetriesAllowed(int newVal)`
	Retrieves/sets the maximum number of times to retry execution in the event of a failure. *Associated property:* `SI_SCHEDULEINFO.SI_RETRIES_ALLOWED`
`int`	`getRetryInterval()`
`void`	`setRetryInterval(int newVal)`
	Retrieves/sets the number of seconds to wait after a failure before trying again. Not applicable if `retriesAllowed` is 0. *Associated property:* `SI_SCHEDULEINFO.SI_RETRY_INTERVAL`

Class/Interface 26: ISchedulingInfo

One-time Schedules

The most simple recurrence type is *Now*, which is also the default option. To schedule an instance to run *now* (that is, as soon as possible), simply call the `ISchedulingInfo.setRightNow(true)` method. No other recurrence settings need to be set when using *Now*, and all other options will be ignored if set:

```
25        IWebi webi = (IWebi) infoObjects.get(0);

26        ISchedulingInfo sched = webi.getSchedulingInfo();

27        sched.setRightNow(true);
```

```
28          webi.schedule();
```

The *Now* recurrence type is unique. All of the other types must be specified with a call to `ISchedulingInfo.setType()`. The value passed to `setType()` is an `int`, whose possible values are defined in the `CeScheduleType` interface. The values are equivalent to those of the `SI_SCHEDULE_TYPE` property (see page 51).

Similar to *Now* is *Once*. Both define a one-time schedule, but Once can be scheduled for a future time and date[126]. When scheduled to run *Once*, a *Begin Date* can be specified via `IschedulingInfo.setBeginDate()`. The Begin Date defines the absolute start date/time that the instance becomes *eligible to run*[127]. If a begin date is not specified for an instance scheduled to run Once, then the begin date defaults to the current time and date.

The following snippet schedules the document to run one time, at 3:00 am on January 17, 2017:

```
25          IWebi webi = (IWebi) infoObjects.get(0);

26          ISchedulingInfo sched = webi.getSchedulingInfo();

27          sched.setType(CeScheduleType.ONCE);

28          Calendar cal = Calendar.getInstance();

29          cal.set(2017, 0, 17, 3, 0);

30          sched.setBeginDate(cal.getTime());

31          webi.schedule();
```

An End Date is set implicitly, equal to the current date/time plus ten years. The end date can be adjusted to be a custom value via `setEndDate()`, but it cannot be a value prior to the begin date. The end date has more meaning for recurring schedule types, but can be used with *Once* schedules. When used with a *Once* schedule, an instance will fail if it has not begun execution by the time the end date has passed. Consider the following simple example:

```
25          IWebi webi = (IWebi) infoObjects.get(0);

26          ISchedulingInfo sched = webi.getSchedulingInfo();

27          sched.setType(CeScheduleType.ONCE);

28          Calendar cal = Calendar.getInstance();

29          cal.add(Calendar.MINUTE, 2);

30          sched.setEndDate(cal.getTime());

31          webi.schedule();
```

---

126 An instance can also be scheduled *Once* with a time/date in the past; this is identical to scheduling the instance for *Now*.

127 Remember that being *eligible to run* means that the instance can then be picked up and executed by a job server. The instance will start at some point *on or after* it becomes eligible to run, based on the availability of a suitable job server.

In this case, we are **not** setting a begin date, so it defaults to the current time. We **are** setting an end date, with a value of two minutes from now. If upon executing this program, there are no job servers available to run the job (that is, all job servers are busy processing other jobs, or all job servers are disabled or stopped), then the job will fail. The exact error message is **Object could not be scheduled within the specified time interval**.

By default, scheduled begin and end times are assumed to be in the local system's time zone. A different time zone can be specified with `ISchedulingInfo.setTimeZone()`, for example:

```
sched.setTimeZone(TimeZone.getTimeZone("GMT"));
```

Changing the time zone doesn't actually adjust the begin and end times that are passed with `setBeginDate()` and `setEndDate()`. Rather, it ensures that the specified dates are adjusted correctly for Daylight Saving Time. Consider a report scheduled to run at 4:00 pm, which is scheduled in EST during Daylight Saving Time. With the schedule's time zone property set to America/New_York, the schedule continues to run at 4:00 pm daily, even after Daylight Saving Time ends. If the time zone was not set correctly, then the schedule could run at a different time after Daylight Saving Time ends.

To retrieve an instance's associated time zone, simply call `ISchedulingInfo.getTimeZone();`

Recurring Schedules

Hourly

The *Hourly* recurrence type allows a document to be scheduled every x hours and y minutes. It is selected for use by calling `ISchedulingInfo.setType(CeScheduleType.HOURLY)`, and the hour and minute intervals are set with `ISchedulingInfo.setIntervalHours()` and `ISchedulingInfo.setIntervalMinutes()`.

If the hour and minute intervals are not specified, the schedule will default to an interval of one hour.

The following snippet schedules a document to run every 30 minutes:

```
25          IWebi webi = (IWebi) infoObjects.get(0);
26          ISchedulingInfo sched = webi.getSchedulingInfo();
27          sched.setRightNow(false);
28          sched.setType(CeScheduleType.HOURLY);
29          sched.setIntervalHours(0);
30          sched.setIntervalMinutes(30);
31          webi.schedule();
```

The actual interval used is the sum of the specified hour and minute intervals. The following two snippets produce an identical result:

```
sched.setIntervalHours(0);
```

```
sched.setIntervalMinutes(90);
```

```
sched.setIntervalHours(1);

sched.setIntervalMinutes(30);
```

Although the CMC and BI launch pad interfaces don't allow it, it is possible to use large values for hours and minutes. The following code:

```
sched.setIntervalHours(30);

sched.setIntervalMinutes(30);
```

... results in an instance with an interval of one day, six hours, and 90 minutes.

Note that, on line 27, we are calling setRightNow(false)*. If this is not called, the* Hourly *schedule will still be created, but attempting to reschedule the instance in the CMC does not work – the CMC instead displays a* Now *schedule. As a safety measure,* setRightNow() *should always be called, with the appropriate true or false parameter, for all schedules.*

To specify when the first occurrence of the schedule should run, you must set the begin date with ISchedulingInfo.setBeginDate(). The schedule then runs at each interval after this time. If not called explicitly, the schedule will begin immediately.

An end date may be specified, which sets the last date and time that the schedule should run. When the specified time and date arrives, the recurring instance is deleted and no further instances are generated[128]. In BI4.2 SP05 and later, the recurring instance is not deleted but assumes a status of *Expired*.

If not specified, the end date defaults to ten years from the current date and time.

The following code creates a recurring schedule that runs every ten minutes, beginning at 5:15 pm and ending at 5:30 pm on the same day.

```
IWebi webi = (IWebi) infoObjects.get(0);

ISchedulingInfo sched = webi.getSchedulingInfo();

sched.setRightNow(false);

sched.setType(CeScheduleType.HOURLY);

sched.setIntervalHours(0);

sched.setIntervalMinutes(10);

Calendar cal = new GregorianCalendar();

cal.set(2016, 11, 30, 17, 15);

sched.setBeginDate(cal.getTime());
```

---

128 More specifically, the recurring schedule is deleted after the last scheduled occurrence prior to the end date.

```
    cal.set(2016, 11, 30, 17, 30);

    sched.setEndDate(cal.getTime());

    webi.schedule();
```

The first scheduled instance begins at 5:15 pm. As long as it completes by 5:25 pm, the next instance at that time. Since the next occurrence of the schedule would be after the end time, the recurring schedule is deleted (or, in BI4.2 SP05, becomes *Expired*) as soon as the 5:25 pm instance is created.

Daily

Daily schedules function similarly to *Hourly,* except, of course, that the interval is specified in terms of full days, using the setIntervalDays() method. The following code schedules the document to run every three days, beginning at 5:15 pm on January 2, 2017:

```
    IWebi webi = (IWebi) infoObjects.get(0);

    ISchedulingInfo sched = webi.getSchedulingInfo();

    sched.setRightNow(false);

    sched.setType(CeScheduleType.DAILY);

    sched.setIntervalDays(3);

    Calendar cal = new GregorianCalendar();

    cal.set(2017, 0, 2, 17, 15);

    sched.setBeginDate(cal.getTime());

    webi.schedule();
```

If the specified begin date (of 1/2/2017 5:15 pm) is in the future, then the first instance of the schedule will start at that time (or shortly thereafter). Subsequent runs of the schedule will occur at 5:15 pm on every third day (January 5th, 8th, 11th, etc.). The start time of subsequent runs is not dependent upon when the previous run actually started, or when it ended. If, for example, the January 5th instance did not start until 5:25 pm, and completed at 5:40 pm, the January 8th instance would still have a scheduled start time of 5:15 pm.

If the specified begin date is in the **past**, then the first run of the schedule will begin immediately. The next run would then be calculated based on the xth day from the specified begin date (*not* the current date). For example, let's say the above code was executed on January 10th (at noon, for argument's sake). As soon as the program completes and the recurring instance is created, the first run of the schedule will begin execution. The start time of the *next* scheduled occurrence will then be calculated as January 11th at 5:15 pm. Effectively, a **single** immediate instance is generated (regardless of the number of intervals between the specified begin date and the current date). The recurring instance then resumes its "normal" schedule, with the next occurrence of the interval after the current date.

To illustrate:

- Program executed 1/10/2017 12:00 pm

- Specified interval: 3 days

- Begin date/time: 1/2/2017 5:15 pm

- First execution: 1/10/2017 12:00 pm

- Second execution: 1/11/2017 5:15 pm (third 3-day interval from 1/2/2017)

- Third execution: 1/14/2017 5:15 pm

The value passed to `sched.setType()` determines which interval values are used; any other interval values that are specified are ignored. If we added the following line to the above code:

```
sched.setIntervalHours(0);

sched.setIntervalMinutes(10);
```

there would be no effect; only the value of `setIntervalDays()` is recognized.

Monthly

The *Monthly* recurrence type is similar to the above; a document can be scheduled to run on the same day of the month, every x number of months. The following code generates a schedule that runs on the 15th day of every second month:

```
IWebi webi = (IWebi) infoObjects.get(0);

ISchedulingInfo sched = webi.getSchedulingInfo();

sched.setRightNow(false);

sched.setType(CeScheduleType.MONTHLY);

sched.setIntervalMonths(2);

Calendar cal = new GregorianCalendar();

cal.set(2017, 0, 15, 6, 30);

sched.setBeginDate(cal.getTime());

cal.set(2017, 7, 1, 6, 30);

sched.setEndDate(cal.getTime());

webi.schedule();
```

We've set the begin date to January 15, 2017, at 6:30 am, and the end date to August 1, 2017, at 6:30 am. Since the instance is set to run every second month, the schedule will execute on the following dates:

- January 15, 2017, 6:30 am

- March 15, 2017, 6:30 am

- May 15, 2017, 6:30 am

- July 15, 2017, 6:30 am

Nth Day

The Nth Day schedule type is similar to the previous type. The following code creates a schedule that runs on the 15th day of each month:

```java
IWebi webi = (IWebi) infoObjects.get(0);

ISchedulingInfo sched = webi.getSchedulingInfo();

sched.setRightNow(false);

sched.setType(CeScheduleType.NTH_DAY);

sched.setIntervalNthDay(15);

Calendar cal = new GregorianCalendar();

cal.set(2017, 0, 1, 6, 30);

sched.setBeginDate(cal.getTime());

cal.set(2017, 7, 1, 6, 30);

sched.setEndDate(cal.getTime());

webi.schedule();
```

As with the previous example, the first execution of this schedule is on January 15, 2017, at 6:30 am. However, this schedule runs every month on the 15th, between January and July. There is no provision for skipping months.

First Monday of Month and Last Day of Month

These two types are self-explanatory and do not require any additional parameters other than begin and end date.

The following code creates two scheduled instances – one that runs on the first Monday of each month, and one that runs on the last day of the month.

```java
IWebi webi = (IWebi) infoObjects.get(0);

ISchedulingInfo sched = webi.getSchedulingInfo();

sched.setRightNow(false);

sched.setType(CeScheduleType.FIRST_MONDAY);

Calendar cal = new GregorianCalendar();

cal.set(2017, 0, 15, 6, 30);

sched.setBeginDate(cal.getTime());

cal.set(2017, 7, 1, 6, 30);

sched.setEndDate(cal.getTime());

webi.schedule();

sched.setType(CeScheduleType.LAST_DAY);
```

```
webi.schedule();
```

We've done something new here – created two scheduled instances in the same code block, with the only difference being the scheduling type. Both scheduled instances have the same begin and end dates: January 15, 2017, at 6:30, and August 1, 2017, at 6:30 am, respectively. Each call to IInfoObject.schedule() will create a new scheduled instance.

Weekly

The *Weekly* recurrence type is a little different than the types we've covered so far. The previous types were fairly simple in terms of the parameters that needed to be specified – hour and minute for the *Hourly* type, monthly interval for the *Monthly* type, etc. For the *Weekly* scheduling type, you must specify one or more days of the week for the schedule to run. The days of the week are set by way of the ICalendarRunDays interface, retrieved via ISchedulingInfo.getCalendarRunDays().

The ICalendarRunDays interface is an implementation of java.util.List and can contain multiple templates for defining a schedule. Each template is an ICalendarDay interface instance and represents a specific scheduling "rule", such as which day of the week to run on. In order to create a *Weekly* schedule, a new ICalendarDay object is added to the ICalendarRunDays collection, for each day of the week to run on.

When we schedule a document to run weekly, the value that we pass to ISchedulingInfo.setType() is CeScheduleType.CALENDAR. Let's look at an example.

```
IWebi webi = (IWebi) infoObjects.get(0);

ISchedulingInfo sched = webi.getSchedulingInfo();

sched.setRightNow(false);

sched.setType(CeScheduleType.CALENDAR);


ICalendarRunDays runDays = sched.getCalendarRunDays();


ICalendarDay runDay = runDays.add();

runDay.setDayOfWeek(Calendar.TUESDAY);


runDay = runDays.add();

runDay.setDayOfWeek(Calendar.THURSDAY);


webi.schedule();
```

We first receive the ICalendarRunDays object into runDays.

Next, we create a new ICalendarDay object by calling runDays.add(). The add() method creates the object and adds it to the `runDays` collection. We then specify the day of the week that this `ICalendarDay` is to run on: Tuesday.

We also add a second `ICalendarDay` to the `runDays` collection, this time specifying the day as Thursday.

History Status: Schedule Test	
Title:	Schedule Test
Document Type:	Web Intelligence
Status	Recurring
Destination:	Default
Owner:	Administrator
Creation Time:	1/15/2017 9:09 AM
Next Run Time:	1/17/2017 9:09 AM
Recurrence Type:	Object will run every week on the following days:Tuesday , Thursday
Parent Object Path:	Auditing/
Remote Instance in Federated Cluster:	No
Expiry:	1/15/2027 9:09 AM
Formats:	Web Intelligence
Parameters:	

The code, when run, creates a scheduled instance that will run every Tuesday and Thursday. Since we didn't specify a begin date and time, it will run at the same time of day as when the scheduled was created (essentially, when the above program was run). In the CMC, the schedule created from the above program will look like the following:

The above is the same result had we created the schedule in the CMC, using the Weekly recurrence type and selecting Tuesday and Thursday.

If you review the values of the `CeScheduleType` interface, you will find a value for `WEEKLY`, although in the above example we used the `CALENDAR` type. The `WEEKLY` type is not used when scheduling documents in the CMC or BI launch pad but remains a valid scheduling option when using the SDK.

If a schedule is created via the SDK with a scheduling type of `CeScheduleType.WEEKLY`, then the generated schedule will run on the same day and time each week, starting on the specified begin date and time.

Consider the following code:

```
IWebi webi = (IWebi) infoObjects.get(0);

ISchedulingInfo sched = webi.getSchedulingInfo();

sched.setRightNow(false);

sched.setType(CeScheduleType.WEEKLY);

Calendar cal = new GregorianCalendar();

cal.set(2017, 0, 20, 6, 30);

sched.setBeginDate(cal.getTime());

webi.schedule();
```

This creates a schedule that runs at 6:30 am every Friday, since January 20, 2017, is a Friday. Using the WEEKLY type, it's not possible to specify multiple days per week or a weekly interval. Another caveat to using this type is that the actual recurrence type of the scheduled instance may not be obvious when looking at its properties. When we look at the properties of the instance generated by the above code, we see:

History Status: Schedule Test

Title:	Schedule Test
Document Type:	Web Intelligence
Status	Recurring
Destination:	Default
Owner:	Administrator
Creation Time:	1/15/2017 8:41 AM
Next Run Time:	1/20/2017 6:30 AM
Recurrence Type:	Object runs once each week.
Parent Object Path:	Auditing/
Remote Instance in Federated Cluster:	No
Expiry:	1/15/2027 8:41 AM
Formats:	Web Intelligence
Parameters:	

Illustration 31: Instance status

The recurrence type of "Object runs once each week", while accurate, could be misinterpreted by someone unfamiliar with nuances of scheduling via the SDK. For this reason, and the fact that weekly schedules can be created using the "Official" method (CeScheduleType.CALENDAR), we don't recommend using CeScheduleType.WEEKLY.

X Day of Nth Week, and Custom Calendars

In the previous section, we introduced the CeScheduleType.CALENDAR type, and the ICalendarRunDays and ICalendarDay interfaces. These are also used for the *X Day of Nth Week* scheduling type. This type is similar to *Weekly*, except that it allows for the scheduling to occur on a particular week of the month, such as the second Tuesday or fourth Friday.

This logic is accomplished with the setWeekNumber() method of ICalendarDay. To illustrate, we'll take one of our previous examples in which we scheduled a document to run on Tuesday, and now set it to run on the second Tuesday of the month:

```
IWebi webi = (IWebi) infoObjects.get(0);

ISchedulingInfo sched = webi.getSchedulingInfo();

sched.setRightNow(false);

sched.setType(CeScheduleType.CALENDAR);


ICalendarRunDays runDays = sched.getCalendarRunDays();
```

```
       ICalendarDay runDay = runDays.add();

       runDay.setDayOfWeek(Calendar.TUESDAY);

       runDay.setWeekNumber(2);



       webi.schedule()
```

If we look at the properties of the newly-created instance, we'll see the expected description:

Recurrence Type: Object runs every month on the Tuesday of week 2.

Note that the name setWeekNumber is slightly misleading. We are not actually specifying the *week of the month* in which to run, but rather *the nth occurrence of the specified day*. In a month beginning on Wednesday, for example, the above schedule would execute on the 14th day of the month. The 14th is the second Tuesday, although it is actually in the third (partial) week of the month). It may help to think of this method of being named setNthDayOfWeek.

The *Weekly* and *X Day of Nth Week* recurrence patterns both use the CeScheduleType.CALENDAR type. This type is actually quite powerful and provides much more scheduling capability beyond what is available in the CMC. The additional capability is leveraged by the use of other properties of the ICalendarDay interface. We've already seen the *Day of week* and *Week of month* properties of ICalendarDay. The interface includes the following:

Package com.crystaldecisions.sdk.occa.infostore
Interface _ICalendarDay_

Fields

static int	ALL	-1
	Specifies that all applicable date/time values will apply.	
static int	FINAL_WEEK	6
	Specifies that the last seven days of the month will apply.	

Methods

int	getDayOfWeek()
void	setDayOfWeek(int dayOfWeek)
	Retrieves/sets the day of the week to run. Valid values are available in java.util.Calendar (ex., java.util.Calendar.MONDAY), with Sunday having a value of 1. To run the job on every day, specify ICalendarRunDay.ALL.
int	getEndDay()
void	setEndDay(int day)

	Retrieves/sets the ending day of the month that the job will run. Valid values are 1 through 31. To run the job every day of the month, specify `ICalendarRunDay.ALL`.
int	`getEndMonth()`
void	`setEndMonth(int month)`
	Retrieves/sets the ending month of the year that the job will run. Valid values are available in `java.util.Calendar` (ex., `java.util.Calendar.MARCH`), with January being 0. To run the job every month, specify `ICalendarRunDay.ALL`.
int	`getEndYear()`
void	`setEndYear(int year)`
	Retrieves/sets the ending year that the job will run, as an absolute year value (ex. 2017). To run the job every year, specify `ICalendarRunDay.ALL`.
int	`getStartDay()`
void	`setStartDay(int day)`
	Retrieves/sets the starting day of the month that the job will run. Valid values are 1 through 31. To run the job every day of the month, specify `ICalendarRunDay.ALL`.
int	`getStartMonth()`
void	`setStartMonth(int month)`
	Retrieves/sets the starting month of the year that the job will run. Valid values are available in `java.util.Calendar` (ex., `java.util.Calendar.MARCH`), with January being 0. To run the job every month, specify `ICalendarRunDay.ALL`.
int	`getStartYear()`
void	`setStartYear(int year)`
	Retrieves/sets the starting year that the job will run, as an absolute year value (ex. 2017). To run the job every year, specify `ICalendarRunDay.ALL`.
int	`getWeekNumber()`
void	`setWeekNumber(int week)`
	Retrieves/sets the week of the month in which the job will run. Week 1 begins on the first day of the month; week 2 begins on the eighth day of the month, etc. To run the job every week, specify `ICalendarRunDay.ALL`. To run the job on the last seven days of the month, specify `ICalendarRunDay.FINAL_WEEK`.

Class/Interface 27: ICalendarDay

Thus, the possible date specifications are:

- Day of week
- Starting day of month, ending day of month
- Starting month of year, ending month of year
- Starting year, ending year
- Week of month

When an `ICalendarDay` object is created by calling `ICalendarRunDays.add()`, all of the above date specification properties are defaulted to the `ICalendarDay.ALL` constant int (value of -1), which indicates that the schedule will run on all periods. Thus, this code:

```
IWebi webi = (IWebi) infoObjects.get(0);

ISchedulingInfo sched = webi.getSchedulingInfo();

sched.setRightNow(false);

sched.setType(CeScheduleType.CALENDAR);

ICalendarRunDays runDays = sched.getCalendarRunDays();

ICalendarDay runDay = runDays.add();

webi.schedule();
```

...creates a schedule that simply runs every day. By setting the properties of `ICalendarDay` to values other than `ICalendarDay.ALL`, we can set the specific conditions for the scheduling rule. To set the schedule to run on Tuesday only, we would change the Day of week property of `runDay` accordingly:

```
sched.setType(CeScheduleType.CALENDAR);

ICalendarRunDays runDays = sched.getCalendarRunDays();

ICalendarDay runDay = runDays.add();

runDay.setDayOfWeek(Calendar.TUESDAY);

webi.schedule();
```

This, of course, is equivalent to the *Weekly* schedule type in CMC. Technically, the rule that we have defined here is:

- Run on any day of the month...
- in any week of the month
- on any month of the year...
- in any year...
- if the day of the week is Tuesday.

Now we'll extend this to an *X Day of Nth Week* schedule, by setting the *Week of month* property to 2:

```
sched.setType(CeScheduleType.CALENDAR);

ICalendarRunDays runDays = sched.getCalendarRunDays();

ICalendarDay runDay = runDays.add();

runDay.setDayOfWeek(Calendar.TUESDAY);

runDay.setWeekNumber(2);

webi.schedule();
```

Now the rule reads as:

- Run on any day of the month...

- on any month of the year...

- in any year...

- if the day is the second Tuesday of the month

We could add even more specificity to this rule, and say that we only want to run on the second Tuesday of the month, between April and September:

```
sched.setType(CeScheduleType.CALENDAR);

ICalendarRunDays runDays = sched.getCalendarRunDays();

ICalendarDay runDay = runDays.add();

runDay.setDayOfWeek(Calendar.TUESDAY);

runDay.setWeekNumber(2);

runDay.setStartMonth(Calendar.APRIL);

runDay.setEndMonth(Calendar.SEPTEMBER);

webi.schedule();
```

Now the rule reads as:

- Run on any day of the month...

- in any year...

- if the day is the second Tuesday of the month

- and the month is between April and September

In 2017, the above code would create a schedule that first runs on April 10, which is the second Tuesday of the month, then every second Tuesday thereafter until September 9. It would not run again until the second Tuesday in April 2018.

The day of month properties work the same way – a rule could be defined to run on every day between the 5th and the 20th of the month, for example.

It's possible to specify a start period without an end period, and vice-versa. If we call `setStartMonth(Calendar.APRIL)`, and do not call `setEndMonth()` (thus, leaving it set to ALL), then the schedule will run from April through the end of the year. Similarly, calling `setEndMonth(Calendar.JUNE)` and not calling `setStartMonth()` will run the job from January through June.

Note that the conditions within an instance of `ICalendarDay` are evaluated with AND logic – the rule in the above example is true if the day of the week is Tuesday **and** the week number is 2 **and** the month is greater or equal to April **and** the month is less or equal than September. If multiple `ICalendarDay` objects are present in the `ICalendarRunDays` collection, then those rules are evaluated with OR logic. We first saw an example of this in the previous section, in which we created a schedule to run on Tuesday **or** Thursday:

```
ICalendarDay runDay = runDays.add();

runDay.setDayOfWeek(Calendar.TUESDAY);


runDay = runDays.add();

runDay.setDayOfWeek(Calendar.THURSDAY);
```

Each individual `ICalendarDay` rule is evaluated independently, and, if any are true for a particular day, the schedule executes. We could alter the above logic to schedule for the first Tuesday and the second Thursday of each month:

```
ICalendarDay runDay = runDays.add();

runDay.setDayOfWeek(Calendar.TUESDAY);

runDay.setWeekNumber(1);


runDay = runDays.add();

runDay.setDayOfWeek(Calendar.THURSDAY);

runDay.setWeekNumber(2);
```

The examples above all use the `ICalendarRunDays.add()` method to create new `ICalendarDay` objects. This is actually a shortcut method, which sets all of the `ICalendarDay` properties to ALL. The longer form of this method is:

```
ICalendarDay    add(    int startDay,
                        int startMonth,
                        int startYear,
                        int endDay,
                        int endMonth,
                        int endYear,
                        int dayOfWeek,
                        int weekOfMonth)
```

This form of the `add()` method allows (and requires) all of the `ICalendarDay` properties to be defined. The following two code fragments are functionally equivalent:

```
ICalendarDay runDay = runDays.add();
runDay.setWeekNumber(1);
runDay.setDayOfWeek(Calendar.TUESDAY);
runDay.setStartMonth(Calendar.APRIL);
runDay.setEndMonth(Calendar.SEPTEMBER);
```

```
ICalendarDay runDay = runDays.add();
runDay = runDays.add(ICalendarDay.ALL,
        Calendar.APRIL,
        ICalendarDay.ALL,
        ICalendarDay.ALL,
        Calendar.SEPTEMBER,
        ICalendarDay.ALL,
        Calendar.TUESDAY,
        1);
```

Both code fragments create a schedule that runs on the first Tuesday of every month between April and September. The first form is easier to read, despite involving more method calls.

There is one significant consideration when using the `CeScheduleType.CALENDAR` type. Since it can be used to create recurrence patterns that are beyond the capabilities of what can be done in the CMC or BI launch pad, those interfaces will not properly display the properties of some SDK-generated schedules. In the most recent example above, we created a simple schedule to run on the first Tuesday and second Thursday. However, if we look at the properties of this schedule in the CMC, we'll see:

Recurrence Type: Object runs every month on the Tuesday of week 1.

The CMC *tries* to interpret the actual settings stored within the `ICalendarRunDays` collection, but it only displays what it is capable of producing itself. For this reason, we recommend using the `CALENDAR` type sparingly.

Calendar Template

The final recurrence pattern that we'll cover is *Calendar Template,* not to be confused with the `CeScheduleType.CALENDAR` type that we covered in the previous section. The Calendar Template option sets a schedule to run based on the days selected in a user-defined Calendar; the creation and maintenance of these calendars are done in the *Calendars* area of the CMC.

In order to schedule a document to use a Calendar Template, simply call `ISchedulingInfo.setCalendarTemplate()` with the InfoObject ID of the desired calendar template to use.

As with the other recurrence patterns, a begin date/time and end date/time may be specified. If not specified, they will default to the current date and time, and ten years in the future, respectively.

In the simple example below, we're scheduling a document to run on the *Quarter End* calendar template.

```java
        IInfoObjects calTemplates = infoStore.query("select si_id from
ci_systemobjects where si_kind = 'calendar' and si_name = 'quarter end'");

        if(calTemplates.size() == 0)

        {

            System.out.println("Could not find Quarter End calendar!");

            return;

        }

        IInfoObject calTemplate = (IInfoObject)calTemplates.get(0);


        IWebi webi = (IWebi) infoObjects.get(0);

        ISchedulingInfo sched = webi.getSchedulingInfo();

        sched.setRightNow(false);


        sched.setType(CeScheduleType.CALENDAR_TEMPLATE);

        sched.setCalendarTemplate(calTemplate.getID());


        webi.schedule();
```

Retry Parameters

Regardless of the recurrence pattern chosen, a schedule may be set to retry if a failure occurs. There are two applicable settings: the retry count, and the retry interval. Should a scheduled instance fail, it will try again, up to the specified number of times, waiting the specified number of seconds between each attempt.

The following code sets a schedule to retry a maximum of five times, waiting 30 seconds between each attempt: If, after five attempts, the document still fails, the instance will assume a status of *Failed*.

```java
        IWebi webi = (IWebi) infoObjects.get(0);

        ISchedulingInfo sched = webi.getSchedulingInfo();
```

```
sched.setRetriesAllowed(5);
sched.setRetryInterval(30);
webi.schedule();
```

Event Parameters

Events can be used in conjunction with recurrence settings to specify an event to wait for, or an event to fire when the schedule completes. Events must be created and maintained in the *Events* area of the CMC.

Documents may be scheduled to wait for zero, one, or more than one event. To set the events to wait for, use the `ISchedulingInfo.getDependencies()` method; this returns an `IEvents` collection, which can be used to add the InfoObject IDs of the event (or events) to wait for. The event methods of `ISchedulingInfo` are:

Package com.crystaldecisions.sdk.occa.infostore
Interface *ISchedulingInfo*

Event settings

IEvents	getDependants()
	Retrieves the collection of events that this object will fire upon completion.
	Associated property: SI_SCHEDULEINFO.SI_DEPENDANTS
IEvents	getDependencies()
	Retrieves the collection of events that this object for before running.
	Associated property: SI_SCHEDULEINFO.SI_DEPENDENCIES

Class/Interface 28: ISchedulingInfo (Event settings)

In the following example, we schedule a document to run daily while also waiting for the *Load Complete* event.

```
        IInfoObjects events = infoStore.query("select si_id from ci_systemobjects
where si_kind = 'event' and si_name = 'load complete'");

        if(events.size() == 0)

        {

            System.out.println("Could not find Load Complete event!");

            return;

        }

        IInfoObject event = (IInfoObject)events.get(0);
```

```
IWebi webi = (IWebi) infoObjects.get(0);

ISchedulingInfo sched = webi.getSchedulingInfo();

sched.setRightNow(false);

sched.setType(CeScheduleType.DAILY);


sched.getDependencies().add(event.getID());


webi.schedule();
```

The schedule that is created shows the expected properties for *Waiting for event(s)*:

Waiting for event(s):	Load Complete
Recurrence Type:	Object runs once every 1 days.

A document may be set to wait for multiple events – simply make multiple calls to getDependencies.add(), passing each event ID.

To schedule a document to fire an event upon completion, use the similarly-named getDependants().add() method. Note that while schedules can be set to **wait for** any type of event (File, Custom, or Schedule), only **schedule** events are intended to be fired by completed schedules. When scheduling documents in the CMC or BI launch pad, only schedule events may be selected to be fired on completion. However, with the SDK, it is possible to select other types of events to be fired on completion. So, it is up to the programmer to ensure that only schedule events are used when calling getDependants().add().

Schedule For Parameters

By default, when a scheduled instance is created, whether in the CMC, BI launch pad, or via an SDK program, the instance is owned by the user ID who was logged in at the time. When the schedule executes, it runs within the security context of that user.

It is possible for a user to create a schedule on behalf of another user. In this case, the instance will actually be "owned" by that other user, and the schedule will execute within that user's security context.

As an example, *Fred* schedules a Web Intelligence report but sets the Schedule For user to *Ethel*. In BI launch pad and CMC, the scheduled instance's *Created By* user will be *Ethel*. When the schedule runs, it will execute as though it were scheduled by Ethel herself. If she does not have access to the universe that the report is associated with, then the report will fail. If she does have access, and there are any universe-based security restrictions that she is subject to, then those restrictions will apply.

An instance can be run on behalf of one or more users or user groups. In this case, the scheduled job runs multiple times – once for each user. Each completed instance is owned by the applicable user.

This functionality enables a handy way to do report bursting. Consider a need to schedule a report to email to a large number of individuals. The report has row-level security applied, so all users only see their own information. Adding the user group to *Schedule For*, and setting the To address of the email destination to %SI_EMAIL_ADDRESS% accomplishes this task – the report refreshes once for each user, and each user will then get an emailed copy of the report, showing only his or her own information.

In order for this functionality to work, the user ID that is used to schedule the instances must have the appropriate security right on the IDs that are being scheduled on behalf of.

Using the Schedule For functionality in an SDK program is *slightly* more complex. We'll cover the easy stuff first.

Package com.crystaldecisions.sdk.occa.infostore
Interface _ISchedulingInfo_

"Schedule For" options

int	getScheduleOnBehalfOf()
	setScheduleOnBehalfOf()
	Retrieves/sets the InfoObject ID of a specific user that the object is scheduled on behalf of. The specified user will be the owner of the generated scheduled instance.
	Associated property: SI_OWNER
Set	getMultiPassObjects()
	Retrieves a collection of user or group InfoObject IDs that the schedule runs for. At runtime, one new instance is spawned for each individual user represented distinctly or by group membership.
	Associated property: SI_SCHEDULEINFO.SI_MULTIPASS

Class/Interface 29: ISchedulingInfo ("Schedule For" options)

To schedule an instance on behalf of **one specific user**, use the ISchedulingInfo.setScheduleOnBehalfOf() method, passing the InfoObject ID of the desired user. For example, we are running a program as *Administrator*, but we want to create a monthly schedule that will be owned by *Fred*. We know that the InfoObject ID of the *Fred* user is 4104, so we call setScheduleOnBahalfOf() accordingly:

```
    IInfoObjects infoObjects = infoStore.query("select si_id from ci_infoobjects
where si_name = 'Schedule Test' and si_kind = 'webi' and si_instance = 0");
```

```
    if(infoObjects.size() > 0)

    {

        IWebi webi = (IWebi) infoObjects.get(0);

        ISchedulingInfo sched = webi.getSchedulingInfo();


        sched.setRightNow(false);

        sched.setType(CeScheduleType.MONTHLY);

        sched.setIntervalMonths(2);

        sched.setScheduleOnBehalfOf(4104);


        webi.schedule();

    }
```

Checking the CMC after the program has executed, we see that the instance has successfully been created, as though Fred had created it himself:

Instance Time *	Title	Status	Created By	Type
Mar 2, 2017 6:31 PM	Schedule Test	Failed	Fred	Web Intelligence
Mar 2, 2017 6:31 PM	Schedule Test	Recurring	Fred	Web Intelligence

Although the user we used to run the program (*Administrator*) has access to the report, *Fred* does not. So, the first run of the schedule produced a failed instance. If we grant *Fred* the necessary rights on the right, the next scheduled instance will complete successfully.

In order to schedule on behalf of multiple users, or one or more user groups, we use the `getMultiPassObjects()` method instead of `setScheduleOnBahalfOf()`. The `getMultiPassObjects()` method returns a `Set` containing the InfoObject IDs of the users or groups to schedule for. For our next example, we again create a monthly schedule, but this time it is on behalf of the *Finance* and *Sales* user groups, which are InfoObject IDs 6334 and 6333, respectively[129].

```
    IInfoObjects infoObjects = infoStore.query("select si_id from ci_infoobjects
where si_name = 'Schedule Test' and si_kind = 'webi' and si_instance = 0");


    if(infoObjects.size() > 0)

    {

        IWebi webi = (IWebi) infoObjects.get(0);

        ISchedulingInfo sched = webi.getSchedulingInfo();
```

---

129 In the real world, you would avoid hard-coding user/group InfoObject IDs in programs, but rather look them up via the name or CUID. We are only hard-coding them here for simplicity.

```
        sched.setRightNow(false);

        sched.setType(CeScheduleType.MONTHLY);

        sched.setIntervalMonths(2);

        Set multiPassObjects = sched.getMultiPassObjects();

        multiPassObjects.add(6333);

        multiPassObjects.add(6334);


        webi.schedule();
    }
```

In the CMC, we will find the instance that was created, but note that its *Created by* user is Administrator (the user that executed the program). However, if we check the instance's *Schedule For* settings (by rescheduling the instance and going to the *Schedule For* tab), we will

see the *Finance* and *Sales* groups selected:

When the scheduled job executes, it spawns one instance for each user in the *Finance* and *Sales* groups:

	Instance Time	Title	Status	Created By
	Mar 2, 2017 6:59 PM	Schedule Test	Success	Ephraim
	Mar 2, 2017 6:59 PM	Schedule Test	Success	Francine
	Mar 2, 2017 6:59 PM	Schedule Test	Success	Wally
	Mar 2, 2017 6:59 PM	Schedule Test	Success	Srl
	Mar 2, 2017 6:59 PM	Schedule Test	Success	Fred
	Mar 2, 2017 6:58 PM	Schedule Test	Success	Nathan
	Mar 2, 2017 6:57 PM	Schedule Test	Recurring	Administrator

Each instance is independent. If Wally does not have sufficient rights to refresh the report, his instance will fail while the others complete successfully.

Now that we've covered the how-to, let's talk about the *what*. Specifically, which properties and user IDs are involved in the above scheduled instances.

There are several InfoObject properties associated with user IDs when scheduling: SI_OWNER (and its associated SI_OWNERID), SI_SUBMITTER (and its associated SI_SUBMITTERID), and SI_MULTIPASS.

In a normally-generated schedule (one without *Schedule For* settings), the owner and submitter properties both reflect the ID of the user who created the schedule, and the multipass property is empty.

When scheduled in the CMC, both the owner and submitter of **recurring** instances reflect the ID of the user who created the schedule. If *Schedule For* was used, then the multipass property contains the InfoObject IDs of the users or groups selected in *Schedule For*. When this recurring schedule executes, it spawns a one-time instance for each *Schedule For* user. Each of these one-time schedules has an owner property reflecting the *Schedule For* user, a submitter property reflecting the original user that created the recurring schedule, and an empty multipass property.

Let's illustrate this using the instances created from the last example:

Instance Time ▼	Title	Status	Created By
Mar 2, 2017 6:59 PM	Schedule Test	Success	Ephraim
Mar 2, 2017 6:59 PM	Schedule Test	Success	Francine
Mar 2, 2017 6:59 PM	Schedule Test	Success	Wally
Mar 2, 2017 6:59 PM	Schedule Test	Success	Sri
Mar 2, 2017 6:59 PM	Schedule Test	Success	Fred
Mar 2, 2017 6:58 PM	Schedule Test	Success	Nathan
Mar 2, 2017 6:57 PM	Schedule Test	Recurring	Administrator

If we were to look at the owner/submitter/multipass properties of each of these instances, we would find the following:

Status	Created by	SI_OWNER	SI_SUBMITTER	SI_MULTIPASS	
Success	Ephraim	Ephraim	Administrator	(blank)	
Success	Francine	Francine	Administrator	(blank)	
Success	Wally	Wally	Administrator	(blank)	
Success	Sri	Sri	Administrator	(blank)	
Success	Fred	Fred	Administrator	(blank)	
Success	Nathan	Nathan	Administrator	(blank)	
Recurring	Administrator	Administrator	Administrator	1 2	6333 6334

When scheduling in the CMC, we have a bit more control over the properties. Our example on page 471 in which we used `getMultiPassObjects()` to create a schedule on behalf of the *Finance* and *Sales* groups, would produce a result exactly the same as above.

However, our previous example (from page 470), in which we used `setScheduleOnBehalfOf()` to schedule on behalf of Fred, would produce a different result. The result that we saw in the CMC was:

Instance Time *	Title	Status	Created By	Type
Mar 2, 2017 6:31 PM	Schedule Test	Failed	Fred	Web Intelligence
Mar 2, 2017 6:31 PM	Schedule Test	Recurring	Fred	Web Intelligence

If we were to look at the properties of each of these instances, we would find the following:

Status	Created by	SI_OWNER	SI_SUBMITTER	SI_MULTIPASS
Failed	Fred	Fred	Administrator	(blank)
Success	Fred	Fred	Administrator	(blank)

Again, the submitter property represents the user that created the schedule (Administrator), while the owner is the user who is being scheduled on behalf of. Effectively, calling setScheduleOnBahflOf() is the same as changing the SI_OWNERID property.

So why is all this important? When creating new schedules with the SDK, it's fairly straightforward: you may use getMultiPassObjects() to schedule on behalf of one or more users or groups, or use setScheduleOnBahflOf() when scheduling on behalf of one specific user. But when working with existing instances, in particular when re-scheduling instances, a more complete understanding of the properties is necessary.

Schedule Notification Parameters

Scheduled instances can be set to deliver an email notification when the job completes. The notification may be sent when the job completes successfully or when it fails.

In the CMC, the notifications are enabled in the *Notification* tab when scheduling. It is not possible to set Notification settings in BI launch pad.

When working in the SDK, schedule notifications are managed via an INotifications interface, which is retrieved via ISchedulingInfo.getNotifications(). The getNotifications() method returns a valid INotifications object even if the object does not currently have any notifications options set. The methods of INotifications are:

Package com.crystaldecisions.sdk.occa.infostore
Interface _INotifications_

---

int	getAuditOption()
	setAuditOption(int option)
	Retrieves/sets the option for sending an audit notification.
IDestinations	getDestinationsOnFailure()
	Retrieve the collection of failure notification destinations.
IDestinations	getDestinationsOnSuccess()
	Retrieve the collection of success notification destinations.

Class/Interface 30: INotifications

The `getAuditOption()` and `setAuditOption()` methods were only applicable in BI4.0, and are not covered here[130].

The `getDestinationOnFailure()` and `getDestinationOnSuccess()` methods both return an `IDestinations` collection, which contains the applicable email destination for the notification. As mentioned in our discussion of schedule destinations, the `IDestinations` collection can contain zero or one element – if more than one elements are added to the collection, they are simply ignored.

To enable either a success or failure notification, an `IDestination` object is added to the appropriate `IDestinations` collection. The process of creating the `IDestination` object and populating the `ISMTPOptions` object (to set the email settings) is *exactly* the same as when creating a schedule to distribute to email (see Email Options on page 510).

Listing 38 contains the *CreateNotificationSched* program, which illustrates the creation of schedule notifications. Note that placeholders are supported in the email fields, although the Notifications tab in the CMC scheduling page does not indicate this fact. We make use of placeholders in the *To, Subject,* and *Message* fields[131].

In this program, we are re-using the `ISMTPOptions` object that is created on line 25, since the settings we need are mostly the same for both the Success and Failure notifications. Only the Subject line needs to be different, and therefore we modify it between the creation of the two notifications.

```
 1  package bosdkbook;

 2

 3  import com.businessobjects.sdk.plugin.desktop.webi.IWebi;

 4  import com.crystaldecisions.sdk.exception.SDKException;

 5  import com.crystaldecisions.sdk.framework.CrystalEnterprise;

 6  import com.crystaldecisions.sdk.framework.IEnterpriseSession;

 7  import com.crystaldecisions.sdk.framework.ISessionMgr;

 8  import com.crystaldecisions.sdk.occa.infostore.IDestination;

 9  import com.crystaldecisions.sdk.occa.infostore.IInfoObjects;

10  import com.crystaldecisions.sdk.occa.infostore.IInfoStore;

10  import com.crystaldecisions.sdk.occa.infostore.INotifications;

11  import com.crystaldecisions.sdk.occa.infostore.ISchedulingInfo;

12  import com.crystaldecisions.sdk.plugin.destination.smtp.ISMTP;

13  import com.crystaldecisions.sdk.plugin.destination.smtp.ISMTPOptions;
```

---

130 For a detailed explanation of why these options are not needed, see SAP Note 1950247.

131 This, of course, is true for the CMC interface as well – feel free to use placeholders there.

```
14
15  public class CreateNotificationSched {
16
17      public static void main(String[] args) throws SDKException
18      {
19          ISessionMgr sessionManager = CrystalEnterprise.getSessionMgr();
20          IEnterpriseSession session = sessionManager.logon ("administrator",
    "xxxx", "192.168.56.102", "secEnterprise");
21
22          IInfoStore infoStore = (IInfoStore) session.getService ("","InfoStore");
23
24          ISMTP smtpPlugin = (ISMTP) infoStore.query("select * from
    ci_systemobjects where si_plugin_object = 1 and si_kind = '" + ISMTP.KIND +
    "'").get(0);
25          ISMTPOptions smtpOptions = (ISMTPOptions)
    smtpPlugin.getScheduleOptions();
26
27          IInfoObjects infoObjects = infoStore.query("select * from ci_infoobjects
    where si_name = 'Schedule Test' and si_kind = 'webi' and si_instance = 0");
28
29          if(infoObjects.size() > 0)
30          {
31              IWebi webi = (IWebi) infoObjects.get(0);
32              ISchedulingInfo sched = webi.getSchedulingInfo();
33
34              // Retrieve the Notifications collection
35              INotifications notif = sched.getNotifications();
36
37              // Set the email options for a success notification
38              smtpOptions.getToAddresses()
39                  .add("%SI_USERFULLNAME% <%SI_EMAIL_ADDRESS%>");
40              smtpOptions.setSenderAddress("bo_admin@company.com");
41              smtpOptions.setSubject("%SI_NAME% report completed successfully");
42              smtpOptions.setMessage("Hello, %SI_USERFULLNAME%.\r\nThe %SI_NAME%
    report completed at %SI_STARTTIME%.");
43
44              // Create the success notification
```

```
45              IDestination successDest =
46                      notif.getDestinationsOnSuccess()
47                      .add(ISMTP.PROGID);
48
49          // Apply the SMTP options to the success notification
50          successDest.setFromPlugin(smtpPlugin);
51
52          // We re-use smtpOptions for the failure notification --
53          // we will just change the subject line.
54          smtpOptions.setSubject("%SI_NAME% report failed");
55
56          // Create the failure notification
57          IDestination failDest =
58                      notif.getDestinationsOnFailure()
59                      .add(ISMTP.PROGID);
60
61          // Apply the SMTP options to the failure notification
62          failDest.setFromPlugin(smtpPlugin);
63
64          // Schedule the document
65          webi.schedule();
66      }
67      else
68          System.out.println("Could not find document!");
69      System.out.println("Done!");
70   }
71 }
```

Listing 38: The CreateNotificationSched program

After running the program, we open the newly-created instance in the CMC to see its settings (by right-clicking and selecting *Reschedule*). The Notifications tab displays the settings that we created in our program:

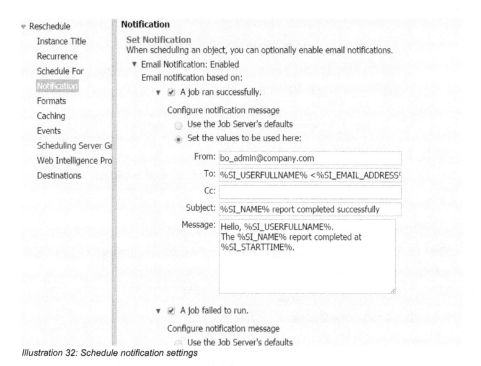

Illustration 32: Schedule notification settings

Server Group Parameters

We discussed server groups briefly on page 63. The methods of ISchedulingInfo associated with servers groups follow:

Package com.crystaldecisions.sdk.occa.infostore
Interface _ISchedulingInfo_

Server Group settings:

int	getServerGroupChoice()
void	setServerGroupChoice(int newVal)

Retrieves/sets the server group option for the scheduled instance.
newVal is an int of type ISchedulingInfo.GroupChoice

Associated property: SI_SCHEDULEINFO.SI_MACHINECHOICE

---

int	getServerGroup()
void	setServerGroup(int newVal)

Retrieves/sets the InfoObject ID of the server group to use when scheduling. Only applicable when serverGroupChoice is
ISchedulingInfo.GroupChoice.PREFERRED or
ISchedulingInfo.GroupChoice.SPECIFIED.

Associated property: SI_SCHEDULEINFO.SI_MACHINE

---

boolean	getRunOnOriginatingCluster()
void	setRunOnOriginatingCluster(boolean run)
	Retrieves/sets whether the job must run on the originating cluster. Only applicable when federation is used. *Associated property:* SI_SCHEDULEINFO.SI_SCHEDULE_REMOTELY
boolean	getRunRemotely()
	Returns true if the scheduled job is to run on a remote cluster.

Class/Interface 31: ISchedulingInfo (Server Group settings)

The sererGroupChoice property specifies whether the job should be assigned to a server group. The property is specified as an int, whose constant values are in the ISchedulingInfo.GroupChoice interface:

Package com.crystaldecisions.sdk.occa.infostore
Interface *ISchedulingInfo.GroupChoice*

static int	FIRST_AVAILABLE	0
	The job is assigned to the first available job server.	
static int	PREFERED	1
	Deprecated, for spelling correction – use PREFERRED instead. The job will give preference to the specified job server.	
static int	PREFERRED	1
	The job will give preference to the specified job server.	
static int	SPECIFIED	2
	The job will only run on the specified job server.	

Class/Interface 32: ISchedulingInfo.GroupChoice

If PREFERRED or SPECIFIED is specified for the serverGroupChoice property, then the InfoObject ID of a server group must be provided via the setServerGroup() method. The serverGroup property is ignored if FIRST_AVAILABLE is set for serverGroupChoice.

The runOnOriginatingCluster property is only applicable in an environment that uses Federation. When true, and when the job is scheduled on a federated *destination* CMS, the schedule is copied to the origin site, where it is executed. The completed instance is then returned to the destination site. The related getRunRemotely() method returns true if the job should run on a remote cluster[132].

In the following code fragment, we schedule a job to run only on the *Central Region* server

---

132 Note that these two methods aren't actually related to server groups, but we list them here since *Run at origin site* is located on the Scheduling Server Group tab.

group.

```
        IInfoStore infoStore = (IInfoStore) session.getService ("","InfoStore");


        IInfoObject sg = (IInfoObject) infoStore.query("select si_id from
ci_systemobjects where si_kind = '" + IServerGroup.KIND + "' and si_name = 'central
region'").get(0);


        IInfoObjects infoObjects = infoStore.query("select * from ci_infoobjects
where si_name = 'Schedule Test' and si_kind = 'webi' and si_instance = 0");


        if(infoObjects.size() > 0)

        {

            IWebi webi = (IWebi) infoObjects.get(0);

            ISchedulingInfo sched = webi.getSchedulingInfo();


            sched.setServerGroupChoice(ISchedulingInfo.GroupChoice.SPECIFIED);

            sched.setServerGroup(sg.getID());


            webi.schedule();

        }
```

Kind-Specific Scheduling Parameters

Each of the schedulable InfoObject kinds has its own distinct scheduling parameters. Most of the properties associated with these parameters are contained in the SI_PROCESSINFO property bag, so that property should be included in the SELECT clause of any CMS query that retrieves objects for scheduling.

We cover Web Intelligence and Crystal Report scheduling options below.

Web Intelligence

The IWebi interface includes several methods related to scheduling of Web Intelligence documents[133]. Many of these methods are associated with caching of Web Intelligence documents during scheduling; this topic is beyond the scope of this book. Refer to the Javadocs for more information.

---

133 These methods are actually inherited from interface IWebiProcessingInfo.

Package com.businessobjects.sdk.plugin.desktop.webi
Interface IWebi
extends ICategoryContent, IInfoObject, IPluginDependency, IProcessingPublicationInfo, IPublicationInfo, ISchedulable, IUniverseReference, IViewingServerGroupInfo, IWebiBase, IWebiMigration, IWebiProcessingInfo

Fields

static String	KIND	Webi
	The kind value for Web Intelligence InfoObjects	
static String	PROGID	CrystalEnterprise.Webi
	The ProgID value for Web Intelligence InfoObjects	

Processing option methods

IWebiPrompts	getPrompts()	
	Retrieves a collection of prompts associated with the document.	
boolean	hasPrompts()	
	Returns true if the document contains prompts.	
IWebiFormatOptions	getWebiFormatOptions()	
	Retrieves the output format for this scheduled instance.	
int	getViewingServerGroupChoice()	
void	setViewingServerGroupChoice(int newVal)	
	Retrieves/sets the server group option for viewing the document. newVal is an int of type ISchedulingInfo.GroupChoice	
	Associated property: SI_MACHINECHOICE	
int	getViewingServerGroup()	
void	setViewingServerGroup(int groupID)	
	Retrieves/sets the InfoObject ID of the server group to use when viewing. Only applicable when serverViewingGroupChoice is ISchedulingInfo.GroupChoice.PREFERRED or ISchedulingInfo.GroupChoice.SPECIFIED.	
	Associated property: SI_MACHINE	

Class/Interface 33: IWebi

Output Format

The getWebiFormatOptions() method returns an IWebiFormatOptions object, which is used to set the output format for a scheduled WebI report. This interface includes the following methods:

Package com.businessobjects.sdk.plugin.desktop.webi
Interface IWebiFormatOptions

int	`getFormat()`
void	`setFormat(int formatType)`
	Retrieves/sets the output format type. `formatType` is an `int` of type `IWebiFormatOptions.CeWebiFormat`.
	Associated property: `SI_FORMAT_INFO.SI_FORMAT`
Map	`getFormatOptions(int formatType)`
void	`setFormatType(int formatType,String txtQlf,String colDelim,String chSet,boolean isSepCsv)`
	Retrieves/sets the formatting options. Not used for every format type. `formatType` is an `int` of type `IWebiFormatOptions.CeWebiFormat`.

Class/Interface 34: IWebiFormatOptions

To specify an output format for a scheduled WebI document, simply call `IWebiFormatOptions.setFormat()`, passing one of the constant `int` values from `IWebiFormatOptions.CeWebiFormat`. Its values are:

Package com.businessobjects.sdk.plugin.desktop.webi
Interface IWebiFormatOptions.CeWebiFormat

static int	CSV	4
	Comma Separated Values format (CSV)	
static int	Excel	1
	Microsoft Excel format (XLSX)	
static int	MHTML	3
	Multi-part HTML format (MHTML)	
static int	PDF	2
	Portable Document Format (PDF)	
static int	TXT	5
	Plain text format (TXT)	
static int	Webi	0
	Native Web Intelligence format	

Class/Interface 35: IWebiFormatOptions.CeWebiFormat

So, so set a scheduled instance to generate output in PDF format, we could use the following code:

```
IWebi webi = (IWebi) infoObjects.get(0);

ISchedulingInfo sched = webi.getSchedulingInfo();


webi.getWebiFormatOptions().setFormat(CeWebiFormat.PDF);


webi.schedule();
```

Note that with the SDK, it is possible to schedule Web Intelligence documents to MHTML format, although this option is not available when scheduling in the CMC or BI launch pad.

In Web Intelligence, only the CSV output format supports additional format options. The following code creates a schedule in CSV format using the following options:

- Text qualifier: ' (single quote)
- Delimiter: ; (semicolon)
- Character set: CP1252
- Separate CSV per data provider: Yes

```
IWebi webi = (IWebi) infoObjects.get(0);

ISchedulingInfo sched = webi.getSchedulingInfo();


IWebiFormatOptions formatOptions = webi.getWebiFormatOptions();

formatOptions.setFormat(CeWebiFormat.CSV);

formatOptions.setFormatOptions(CeWebiFormat.CSV,
             "'",
             ";",
             "CP1252",
             true);


webi.schedule();
```

Prompts

The getPrompts() method returns an IWebiPrompts object, which is a List of IWebiPrompt objects. These may be used to view and select values for each prompt in a report. The methods of IWebiPrompt are:

Package com.businessobjects.sdk.plugin.desktop.webi
Interface _IWebiPrompt_

Fields

static String	SI_DYNAMIC	"SI_DYNAMIC"
	The name of the SI_DYNAMIC property	

Methods

List	getDataProviders()
	Retrieves a collection of IDataProvider objects representing the names and IDs of data providers associated with the prompt.
	Associated property: SI_WEBI_PROMPTS.x.SI_DATAPROVIDERS
String	getName()
	Retrieves the name (text) of the prompt.
	Associated property: SI_WEBI_PROMPTS.x.SI_NAME
List	getValueIndexes()
	Retrieves a collection of Strings representing the indexes of currently-selected prompt values.
	Associated property: SI_WEBI_PROMPTS.x.SI_INDEX
List	getValues()
	Retrieves a collection of Strings representing the currently-selected prompt values.
	Associated property: SI_WEBI_PROMPTS.SI_VALUES
List	getValuesToDisplay()
	Retrieves a collection of Strings representing the display names for the currently selected prompt values. Values will be identical to those returned by getValues() unless the prompt has display values defined.
	Associated property: SI_WEBI_PROMPTS.SI_DISPLAY_NAME
boolean	isSkipped()
void	setSkipped(int isSkipped)
	Retrieves/sets whether the prompt is to be skipped. Only applicable for optional prompts, and when no values are selected.
	Associated property: SI_DISABLED

Class/Interface 36: IWebiPrompt

There is limited support for working with prompts while scheduling in the Java SDK. While the getValues() and getValuesToDisplay() methods may be used to add and remove from the selected values list, there is no ability to add values to a prompt if it is not already represented in a scheduled instance. Nor is there support to display the available list of values (LOV) for each prompt.

Key point: while the SDK can be used to perform nearly any activity that can be done in the BI launchpad and CMC, setting prompts in a scheduled WebI report is one of the few activities that the SDK can not do.

The following snippet references an existing IWebiPrompt object, clears any existing values, and adds a new selected value ("*Nevada*"). Note that this only works if the base document has a prompt, and the default settings for the document have at least one prompt value selected.

```
IInfoStore infoStore = (IInfoStore) session.getService ("","InfoStore");


IInfoObject sg = (IInfoObject) infoStore.query("select si_id from
ci_systemobjects where si_kind = '" + IServerGroup.KIND + "' and si_name = 'central
region'").get(0);


IInfoObjects infoObjects = infoStore.query("select * from ci_infoobjects
where si_name = 'Schedule Test' and si_kind = 'webi' and si_instance = 0");


if(infoObjects.size() > 0)

{

    IWebi webi = (IWebi) infoObjects.get(0);

    ISchedulingInfo sched = webi.getSchedulingInfo();


    IWebiPrompts prompts = webi.getPrompts();

    IWebiPrompt prompt = prompts.get(0);


    prompt.getValuesToDisplay().clear();

    prompt.getValuesToDisplay().add("Nevada");

    prompt.getValues().clear();

    prompt.getValues().add("Nevada");


    webi.schedule();

}
```

Viewing Server Group

The Viewing Server Group methods determine whether or not a specific server group should be used when the generated instance is viewed. The methods work in the same way as the Scheduling Server Group methods described on page 478

Crystal Reports

The scheduling options for Crystal Reports are managed through the IReport interface[134]. There are many scheduling options, and we will only touch on a few here. The available fields and methods are:

Package com.crystaldecisions.sdk.plugin.desktop.report

Interface *IReport*

extends ICacheServerGroupInfo, ICategoryContent, IContent, IEventSource, IInfoObject, IProcessingPublicationInfo, IProcessingServerGroupInfo, IPublicationInfo, IReportBase, IReportProcessingInfo, ISchedulable, IUniverseReference, IViewingServerGroupInfo

Fields

static String	KIND	CrystalReport
	The kind value for Report InfoObjects	
static String	PROGID	CrystalEnterprise.Report
	The ProgID value for Report InfoObjects	

Processing option methods

boolean	isLogonNeeded()
void	setLogonNeeded(boolean bNeedsLogon)
	Retrieves/sets whether the database that the report connects to requires a logon.
	Associated property: SI_PROCESSINFO.DBNEEDLOGON
ISDKList	getReportLogons()
	Retrieves a collection of IReportLogon objects, representing the logon information for a database that the report connects to.
	Associated property: SI_PROCESSINFO.SI_LOGON_INFO
String	getRecordFormula()
void	setRecordFormula(String recordFormula)

---

134 The methods are extended into IReport from IReportProcessingInfo.

	Retrieves/sets the selection formula used to filter results from the database query.
	Associated property: `SI_PROCESSINFO.SI_RECORD_FORMULA`
`String`	`getGroupFormula()`
`void`	`setGroupFormula(String groupFormula)`
	Retrieves/sets the selection formula used to filter groups of records from the database query.
	Associated property: `SI_PROCESSINFO.SI_GROUP_FORMULA`
`IReportFormatOptions`	`getReportFormatOptions()`
	Retrieves an `IReportFormatOptions` object, which is used to specify the output format of the report.
	Associated property: `SI_PROCESSINFO.SI_FORMAT_INFO`
`IReportPrinterOptions`	`getReportPrinterOptions()`
	Retrieves an `IReportPrinterOptions` object, which is used to specify the printing options for the report
	Associated property: `SI_PROCESSINFO.SI_PRINTER_INFO`
`IReportProcessingExtensions`	`getProcessingSecurityExtensions()`
	Retrieves an `IReportProcessingExtensions` object, containing a collection of processing extensions for the report.
	Associated property: `SI_PROCESSINFO.SI_PROCESSING_EXTENSIONS`
`List`	`getReportParameters()`
	Retrieve a List of `IReportParameter` objects, that represent the report's parameter values.
	Associated property: `SI_PROCESSINFO.SI_PROMPTS`
`boolean`	`hasDynamicCascadePrompt()`
	Returns `true` if the report has dynamic cascading prompts; `false` if not.
	Associated property: `SI_PROCESSINFO.SI_HAS_DCP`
`List`	`getPromptGroupMembers(String groupID)`

	Retrieves a `List` of `IReportParameter` objects, representing a collection of prompts associated with the designated group. *Associated property:* `SI_PROCESSINFO.SI_PROMPTS`
`ISDKList`	`getReportAlerts()`
	Retrieves a `List` of `IReportAlert` objects, representing the report's alerts. *Associated property:* `SI_PROCESSINFO.SI_ALERT_INFO`
`List`	`getReportHyperlinks()`
	Retrieves a `List` of `IReportHyperlink` objects, representing the report's hyperlinks. *Associated property:* `SI_PROCESSINFO.SI_HYPERLINK_INFO`
`boolean`	`isRepositoryEnabled()`
`void`	`setRepositoryEnabled(boolean enabled)`
	Retrieves/sets whether the report can be updated from the repository. *Associated property:* `SI_PROCESSINFO.SI_TURNONREPOSITORY`
`boolean`	`isViewingUseLOVCustomSharingSettings()`
`void`	`setViewingUseLOVCustomSharingSettings(boolean b)`
	Returns `true` if the report is set to use custom List of Value (LOV) sharing settings; false otherwise. *Associated property:* `SI_PROCESSINFO.SI_USE_CUSTOM_LOV_SHARE_SETTINGS`
`int`	`getViewingLOVShareInterval()`
`void`	`setViewingLOVShareInterval(int newVal)`
	Retrieves/sets the number of seconds that List of Values (LOV) data can be shared. *Associated property:* `SI_PROCESSINFO.SI_LOV_SHARE_INTERVAL`
`boolean`	`isViewingUseReportSharingSettings()`
`void`	`setViewingUseReportSharingSettings(boolean b)`
	Retrieves/sets whether report-specific settings for report viewing is used. *Associated property:* `SI_PROCESSINFO.SI_SHARE_SETTINGS`
`boolean`	`isViewingShareReport()`
`void`	`setViewingShareReport(boolean b)`

	Retrieves/sets whether report sharing is being used.
	Associated property: `SI_PROCESSINFO.SI_SHARING`
int	`getViewingShareInterval()`
void	`setViewingShareInterval(int newVal)`
	Retrieves/sets the number of seconds that report data is shared.
	Associated property: `SI_PROCESSINFO.SI_SHARE_INTERVAL`
boolean	`isViewingShareHitDBOnRefresh()`
void	`setViewingShareHitDBOnRefresh(boolean hitDB)`
	Retrieves/sets whether a refresh request should retrieve data from the database.
	Associated property: `SI_PROCESSINFO.SI_RFSH_HITS_DB`
ISDKList	`getReportXMLInfo()`
	Retrieves a collection of `IReportXMLExportItem` objects, representing the report's XML info items.
	Associated property: `SI_PROCESSINFO.SI_XSLT_INFO`
int	`getReportDefaultXMLExportSelection()`
	Retrieves the index of the default XML info item..
	Associated property: `SI_PROCESSINFO.SI_XMLEXPORTFORMATTYPE`
int	`getReportSavedXMLExportSelection()`
	Retrieves the index of the saved XML info item..
	Associated property: `SI_PROCESSINFO.SI_DEFAULTITEM_INDEX`
boolean	`isSchedulingUseReportPageCountSettings()`
void	`setSchedulingUseReportPageCountSettings(boolean b)`
	Retrieves/sets whether to override the server's page count generation settings.
	Associated property: `SI_PROCESSINFO.SI_SCHEDULING_USE_REPORT_PAGE_COUNT_SETTINGS`
boolean	`isSchedulingEnableTotalPageCount()`
void	`setSchedulingEnableTotalPageCount(boolean b)`

	Retrieves/sets whether to generate and store the report's total page count. *Associated property:* SI_PROCESSINFO.SI_SCHEDULING_ENABLE_TOTAL_PAGE_COUNT
boolean	isSchedulingUseReportGenerateCacheSettings()
void	setSchedulingUseReportGenerateCacheSettings(boolean b)
	Retrieves/sets whether to override the server's page cache generation setting. *Associated property:* SI_PROCESSINFO.SI_SCHEDULING_USE_REPORT_GENERATE_CACHE_SETTINGS
int	getSchedulingNumPagesToGenerate()
void	setSchedulingNumPagesToGenerate(int numPages)
	Retrieves/sets the number of cache pages to generate. *Associated property:* SI_PROCESSINFO.SI_SCHEDULING_NUM_PAGES_TO_GENERATE
int	getTotalPageCount()
	Retrieves the total number of formatted pages in a scheduled instance. *Associated property:* SI_PROCESSINFO.SI_TOTAL_PAGE_COUNT
Locale	getFallbackLocale()
	Retrieves the locale to use if the requested locale is not found. *Associated property:* SI_FALLBACK_LOCALES

Class/Interface 37: IReport

Output Format

To set the output format of a scheduled Crystal Report, use the IReportFormatOptions interface, which is retrieved via IReport.getReportFormatOptions(). The methods of IReportFormatOptions are:

Package com.crystaldecisions.sdk.plugin.desktop.common **Interface _IReportFormatOptions_**	
int	getFormat()
	setFormat(int formatType)
	Retrieves/sets the export format type. The value of formatType must be an int of type CeReportFormat.
Object	getFormatInterface()

	Retrieves an object to set the specific format options. The class of object returned with be dependent upon the selected format type, and is one of the following:
	`ITextFormatCharacterSeparated`
	`ITextFormatTabSeparated`
	`ITextFormatPaginated`
	`ITextFormatPlain`
	`IExcelFormat`
	`IExcelDataOnlyFormat`
	`IRichTextFormat`
	`IRichTextFormatEditable`
	`IWordFormat`
	`IPDFFormat`
	`IPaginatedTextFormat`

boolean	`isUseExportOptionsInReport()`
	`setUseExportOptionsInReport(boolean value)`
	Retrieves/sets whether the report uses export options.
void	`resetFormatOptions()`
	Clears all export options.

Class/Interface 38: IReportFormatOptions

Although setting the export format is functionally similar to Web Intelligence, the implementation is quite different. We first must set the desired format type with a call to `IReportFormatOptions.setFormat()`, passing a value from `CeReportFormat`. The possible values are:

Package com.crystaldecisions.sdk.plugin.desktop.common
Interface *IReportFormatOptions.CeReportFormat*

static int	`CRYSTAL_REPORT`	0
	Native Crystal Reports format.	
static int	`EXCEL`	1
	Microsoft Excel 97-2003 format	
	Associated interface: `IExcelFormat`	
static int	`EXCEL_2007_DATA_ONLY`	16
	Microsoft 2007 (.xlsx) format, with data only	
	Associated interface: `IExcelDataOnlyFormat`	
static int	`EXCEL_DATA_ONLY`	9
	Microsoft Excel 97-2003 format, with data only	
	Associated interface: `IExcelDataOnlyFormat`	

static int	MHTML	12
	Multi-part HTML format.	

static int	NEXT_GEN_TEXT_PAGINATED	14
	Tab-separated text format	
	Associated interface: IPaginatedTextFormat	

static int	NEXT_GEN_TEXT_TAB_SEPARATED_TEXT	15
	Tab-separated paginated text format	
	Associated interface: IPaginatedTextFormat	

static int	PDF	3
	Portable Document Format (.pdf)	
	Associated interface: IPDFFormat	

static int	RPTR	17
	Crystal Reports read-only format (.rptr)	

static int	RTF	4
	Rich Text Format (.rtf)	
	Associated interface: IRichTextFormat	

static int	RTF_EDITABLE	11
	Rich Text Format (.rtf)	
	Associated interface: IRichTextFormatEditable	

static int	TEXT_CHARACTER_SEPARATED	8
	Character-separated text format	
	Associated Interfaces: ITextFormatTabSeparated, ITextFormatCharacterSeparated	

static int	TEXT_PAGINATED	6
	Paginated text format	
	Associated interface: ITextFormatPaginated	

static int	TEXT_PLAIN	5
	Plain text format	
	Associated interface: ITextFormatPlain	

static int	TEXT_TAB_SEPARATED	7
	Tab-separated text format	
static int	TEXT_TAB_SEPARATED_TEXT	10
	Tab-separated text format	
	Associated interface: ITextFormatTabSeparatedText	
static int	USER_DEFINED	1000
	User-defined format	
static int	WORD	2
	Microsoft Word format	
	Associated interface: IWordFormat	
static int	XML	13
	Extensible Markup Language format (.xml)	
	Associated interface: IXMLFormat	

Class/Interface 39: IReportFormatOptions.CeReportFormat

Let's look at an example of scheduling a Crystal Report to a specified format.

```
1   package bosdkbook;

2

3   import com.crystaldecisions.sdk.exception.SDKException;

4   import com.crystaldecisions.sdk.framework.CrystalEnterprise;

5   import com.crystaldecisions.sdk.framework.IEnterpriseSession;

6   import com.crystaldecisions.sdk.framework.ISessionMgr;

7   import com.crystaldecisions.sdk.occa.infostore.IInfoObjects;

8   import com.crystaldecisions.sdk.occa.infostore.IInfoStore;

9   import com.crystaldecisions.sdk.plugin.desktop.common.IReportFormatOptions;

9   import
    com.crystaldecisions.sdk.plugin.desktop.common.IReportFormatOptions.CeReportForma
    t;

10  import com.crystaldecisions.sdk.plugin.desktop.report.IReport;

10

11  public class CrystalToExcel {

12

13      public static void main(String[] args) throws SDKException
```

```
14      {

15          ISessionMgr sessionManager = CrystalEnterprise.getSessionMgr();

16          IEnterpriseSession session = sessionManager.logon ("administrator",
     "xxxx", "192.168.56.102", "secEnterprise");

17

18          IInfoStore infoStore = (IInfoStore) session.getService ("","InfoStore");

19

20          IInfoObjects infoObjects = infoStore.query("select * from ci_infoobjects
     where si_name = 'crystal schedule test' and si_kind = 'crystalreport' and
     si_instance = 0");

21

22          if(infoObjects.size() > 0)

23          {

24              IReport report = (IReport) infoObjects.get(0);

25              IReportFormatOptions formatOptions =
                        report.getReportFormatOptions();

26              formatOptions.setFormat(
                        CeReportFormat.TEXT_CHARACTER_SEPARATED);

27

28              report.schedule();

29          }

30          else

31              System.out.println("Could not find document!");

32          System.out.println("Done!");

33      }

34 }
```

Listing 39: The CrystalToExcel program

In Listing 39 we are scheduling a Crystal Report to export in CSV format. We simply need to call setFormat() with the appropriate constant value to set the format:

```
26              formatOptions.setFormat(
                        CeReportFormat.TEXT_CHARACTER_SEPARATED);
```

This produces a scheduled instance in Character-Separated (CSV) format.

Most, but not all of the available format types have associated interfaces that are used to set additional format-specific options. That interface is obtained from IReportFormatOptions.getFormatInterface(). In order to retrieve the correct interface, the format must have already been set with setFormat(). In Listing 39, we did **not** call getFormatInterface(), so the default CSV settings are used. If we want to change those settings, we can do so as follows:

```
 9  import
    com.crystaldecisions.sdk.plugin.desktop.common.ITextFormatCharacterSeparated;

10  import
    com.crystaldecisions.sdk.plugin.desktop.common.ITextFormatSeparated.CeExportMode;
```

```
24          if(infoObjects.size() > 0)

25          {

26              IReport report = (IReport) infoObjects.get(0);

27              IReportFormatOptions formatOptions =
                        report.getReportFormatOptions();

28              formatOptions.setFormat(
                        CeReportFormat.TEXT_CHARACTER_SEPARATED);

29              ITextFormatCharacterSeparated csvOptions =
                (ITextFormatCharacterSeparated) formatOptions.getFormatInterface();

30              formatOptions.setUseExportOptionsInReport(false);

31              csvOptions.setExportMode(CeExportMode.STANDARD_MODE);

32              csvOptions.setSeparator(";");

33              report.schedule();

34          }
```

On line 29, we retrieve the ITextFormatCharacterSeparated interface by calling getFormatInterface(). Since we have already specified the format type in the line above, we know which interface we are getting in this call.

On line 30, we must call setUseExportOptionsInReport(false) in order to override the format settings. If this is not done, then the default settings are used.

Depending on the format type, certain settings must be specified or else an error will be produced. For CSV, we have to set the export mode, which we do on line 31.

Finally, on line 32, we can set the format options. In this case, we want to change the column delimiter from the default comma to a semicolon.

When executed, the program produces a scheduled instance in CSV format, with a semicolon as the column separator.

There are many, many options for the various format types, and we will not cover them all here. Refer to the Javadocs for the various format interfaces for more information.

Destination Parameters

Scheduled documents may be set to distribute to a destination. The possible destination types include:

- The Default Enterprise Location
- BI Inbox
- Email
- FTP Server
- File Server
- SFTP Server

The first option, Default Enterprise Location, is the default destination, and the only one that has no additional possible parameters. So, most of this section pertains to the other destination types.

All management of destination settings for schedules is done via the IDestinations interface, which is retrieved via ISchedulingInfo.getDestinations(). This interface is a collection that can contain zero or more IDestination objects[135]. If the IDestinations collection of an existing schedule is empty, then the schedule is set to use the *Default Enterprise Location*. Otherwise, the instance is set to distribute to one of the other destinations.

Default Enterprise Location

The *Default Enterprise Location* type is unique in that there are no further parameters to set when this type is chosen. In fact, the simple lack of any IDestination objects in the IDestinations collection indicates that this is the selected destination.

Although this is the default destination type, it is always prudent to ensure that the desired type is selected when creating a schedule; since the document being scheduled may have default settings that are different. For the case of the *Default Enterprise Location* type, we can ensure that it is the selected type by clearing the IDestinations collection. For example:

```
IWebi webi = (IWebi) infoObjects.get(0);

ISchedulingInfo sched = webi.getSchedulingInfo();

sched.getDestinations().clear();

webi.schedule();
```

The remainder of this section is concerned with the remaining destination types; all of which have additional parameters; some common, and several type-specific.

---

135 As of BI4.2, only Publications support the ability to specify multiple destinations in a single scheduled instance. All other schedulable object types will have either an empty IDestinations (indicating the Default Enterprise Location), or it will contain a single IDestination object.

Selecting the Destination

Each destination type (other than *Default Enterprise Location*) is associated with a subinterface of `IDestinationPlugin`. They are:

- `IDiskUnmanaged` ("Unmanaged disk" is synonymous with *file system*)
- `IFTP`
- `IManaged` (BI inbox)
- `ISFTP`
- `ISMTP` (Email)
- `IStreamWork`[136]

To set the destination type for a schedule, we call `IDestinations.add()`, passing it the `SI_PROGID` value of one of the above `IDestinationPlugin` subinterfaces. Each of those interfaces has a static `PROGID` property that can be used for the call to `add()`. To set a schedule to distribute to BI inbox ("Managed Disk"), we could do the following:

```
IWebi webi = (IWebi) infoObjects.get(0);

ISchedulingInfo sched = webi.getSchedulingInfo();

sched.getDestinations().clear();

IDestination dest = sched.getDestinations().add(IManaged.PROGID);

webi.schedule();
```

The above code creates a new scheduled instance set to distribute to BI Inbox. Since we did not specify any destination parameters, the default parameters of the job server that processes the job are used. This is the same result as when checking off *Use default settings* when scheduling a document in the CMC:

The following lines list the appropriate code to add each available destination types[137]:

```
// Set destination to File System
IDestination dest = sched.getDestinations().add(IDiskUnmanaged.PROGID);


// Set destination to FTP
IDestination dest = sched.getDestinations().add(IFTP.PROGID);


// Set destination to BI Inbox
IDestination dest = sched.getDestinations().add(IManaged.PROGID);
```

---

136 The *SAP StreamWork* service was shut down in 2015, so we'll not be covering this destination type.

137 This is just an illustration of creating the various destination types and is not meant to be a runnable code fragment.

```
// Set destination to Email

IDestination dest = sched.getDestinations().add(ISMTP.PROGID);


// Set destination to SFTP

IDestination dest = sched.getDestinations().add(ISFTP.PROGID);


// Set destination to StreamWork

IDestination dest = sched.getDestinations().add(IStreamWork.PROGID);


// Set destination to Default Enterprise Location

sched.getDestinations().clear();
```

Generally, additional type-specific parameters need to be set when assigning a destination type to a schedule. We will cover those shortly.

Setting the Cleanup Option

When scheduling a document in the CMC or BI launch pad, there are two checkbox options displays for all destination types other than Default Enterprise Location. We mentioned the *Use default settings* option above. The other checkbox option is *Keep an instance in history*. When checked (which is the default), a scheduled instance is generated as a child of the scheduled document, when the schedule is executed, in addition to being sent to the selected destination. For example, if a schedule is set to distribute to Email, a successful run of the schedule will generate the email and will also create a new instance in the parent document's history. If *Keep an instance in history* is not checked, then only the email is generated – there will be no record in the scheduled document's history of the scheduled run.

To set this option when scheduling in the SDK, call IDestinations.setCleanup(). The setCleanup() method expects a Boolean value, but note that *it is the inverse of the checkbox option*. That is, to indicate that instances should be kept, call setCleanup(false); to indicate that instances should not be kept, call setCleanup(true)[138].

The following code creates a schedule that distributes to BI inbox, and **does not** keep a copy of the instance in the history:

```
IWebi webi = (IWebi) infoObjects.get(0);

ISchedulingInfo sched = webi.getSchedulingInfo();

sched.getDestinations().clear();

sched.getDestinations().setCleanup(true);

IDestination dest = sched.getDestinations().add(IManaged.PROGID);
```

---

138 The reason for this is that the *Keep an instance in the history* option used to be called *Clean up instance after scheduling* in older versions. The new wording is more clear but is the opposite of the old wording.

```
        webi.schedule();
```

Destination Type-specific Options

Setting the destination settings, for anything other than Default Enterprise Location, requires a few steps:

1. Retrieve the *destination plugin* from the CMS for the desired destination type (Email, File System, etc.), using a CMS query (this only needs to be done once per program execution). The plugin will be a subinterface of IDestinationPlugin: IDiskUnmanaged, IFTP, IManaged, ISFTP, ISMTP, or IStreamWork.

2. Retrieve the document to be scheduled, as an IInfoObject or subinterface.

3. Retrieve the *destination scheduling options* object from the IDestinationPlugin retrieved in step 1. This object will be a subinterface of IDestinationScheduleOptions, and is what's used to actually specify the destination settings. It should be cast to one of the following: IDiskUnmanagedOptions, IFTPOptions, IManagedOptions, ISFTPOptions, ISMTPOptions, or IStreamWorkOptions.

4. Set the destination settings as appropriate in the IDestinationScheduleOptions object that was obtained in the previous step.

5. With the IInfoObject object of the document to be scheduled (from Step 2), create and retrieve an IDestination object by calling getSchedulingInfo().getDestinations().add(). The parameter passed to add() is a Prog ID specifying the type of destination (Email, File System, etc.).

6. Apply the destination options (as set in Step 4) to the IDestination object by calling IDestination.setFromPlugin(), passing it the IDestinationScheduleOptions object from Step 4.

7. Set any other scheduling options as needed (recurrence, etc.).

8. Finally, schedule the document with schedule().

Let's look at a code fragment to see this process in action:

```
25      IManaged inboxPlugin = (IManaged) infoStore.query("select * from
   ci_systemobjects where si_plugin_object = 1 and si_kind = '" + IManaged.KIND +
   "'").get(0);

26

27      IInfoObjects infoObjects = infoStore.query("select si_id from
   ci_infoobjects where si_name = 'Schedule Test' and si_kind = 'webi' and
   si_instance = 0");

28

29      if(infoObjects.size() > 0)

30      {
```

```
31            IWebi webi = (IWebi) infoObjects.get(0);

32            ISchedulingInfo sched = webi.getSchedulingInfo();

33

34            IManagedOptions inboxOptions = (IManagedOptions)
                    inboxPlugin.getScheduleOptions();

35            inboxOptions.getDestinations().add(4104);

36

37            IDestination dest =
                    sched.getDestinations().add(IManaged.PROGID);

38            dest.setFromPlugin(inboxPlugin);

39            webi.schedule();

40        }
```

On line 25, we perform Step 1, in which we retrieve the Destination Plugin object. Note that this is a standard CMS query, and we are casting the result to the IManaged interface. What we are doing here is retrieving the InfoObject that represents the "Managed" destination plugin. The only thing we'll be using this object for is to obtain the scheduling parameters associated with this destination type. This step only needs to be performed once per program execution, regardless of how many documents are being scheduled.

In lines 27-32, we perform Step 2, in the same way as our previous scheduling examples.

On line 34, we perform Step 3. Using the IManaged object retrieved in Step 1, we call its getSchedulingOptions() method to get an IManagedOptions object.

Line 35 implements Step 4. Using the IManagedOptions object, we set the scheduling options for the schedule we are about to create. In this case, all we want to do is specify the inbox recipient. The IManagedOptions interface includes a method getDestinations(). This returns a java.util.Set of user IDs that will receive the document. From a separate query, we know that *Fred*'s ID is 4104, so we pass that to getDestinations().add().

On line 37, we perform Step 5: specifying the destination type of the schedule to *Managed*.

On line 38, we are copying the scheduling options from the IManagedOptions object into the schedule that is being created. More specifically, we are copying the options into the IDestination object, which is associated with the schedule. This is Step 6. We are not setting any other scheduling options, so we are skipping Step 7.

Finally, on line 39, we perform Step 8 and actually schedule the instance.

When this program is executed, a new scheduled instance is created, with its destination set to *BI Inbox* and the one recipient as *Fred*:

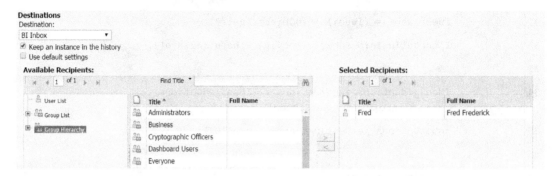

Setting the options for the various destination types all follow the same pattern as above, except that the different types have their own interfaces and available options.

Default Scheduling Options

In order for scheduled objects to run, the SAP BusinessObjects system must have an active, running job server that will process the requests. The job server must be configured to process the particular type of object being scheduled (Web Intelligence, Crystal, Program Objects, etc.). In a default installation, a single Adaptive Job Server is created, including scheduling services for all object types. However, it's common for dedicated job servers to be set up for each type (a WebI job server, Crystal job server, etc.).

Job servers can support any of the possible destination types (BI inbox, email, file system, FTP, SFTP, StreamWork), but each type must be enabled specifically. Therefore, in order to schedule a document to be distributed via email, the job server that executes the job must have the *Email* destination type enabled[139].

If a job server has a particular destination enabled, then it may also have default settings specified for that destination. For the *Email* destination type, for example, the mail server host and authentication options may be (and should be) specified. For the FTP destination type, the server host and credentials may be specified.

Documents may have default scheduling options specified, including the destination options. When a document is scheduled to run, either by the SDK or in the CMC or BI launch pad, the document's default scheduling options are used (if there are any) unless overridden. Consider a Web Intelligence document that has its default scheduling options set to deliver to *BI Inbox*, and to Fred's inbox specifically. If we were to create a new schedule for this document:

```
IWebi webi = (IWebi) infoObjects.get(0);

ISchedulingInfo sched = webi.getSchedulingInfo();
```

then we would find that `sched.getDestinations()` includes an `IDestination` object which represents the BI Inbox destination options. If we were to schedule the new instance at this

---

139 In a system with multiple job servers, it's generally recommended that all job servers that handle a particular type (Web Intelligence, for example) are configured the same way. If one job server has *Email* enabled, but another doesn't, then WebI reports scheduled to email will have inconsistent results – some will fail and some will succeed.

point, that instance would use those default settings. We could, however, override those settings – either modify the IDestination object (to specify different BI Inbox options) or delete that IDestination object from the getDestinations() collection and replace it with another – if, for example, we wanted to send the scheduled document to email instead of BI Inbox.

When a job is scheduled to a destination other than the default enterprise location, any settings not defined in the job (either set as the document's default settings or explicitly in the schedule), will revert to the job server settings. Consider an environment that includes a job server with the Email destination type enabled and all email settings populated (server, *To* address, *From* address, subject, and message). If we schedule a WebI document to email, but do not set any destination options, then the job, when run, will use all of the settings from the job server's defaults. If we schedule the document again and set the *To* address but do not touch any of the other settings, then the job, when run, will use the To address that we specified in the schedule, but will use all of the other options from the job server's defaults. It's important to keep in mind that when scheduling jobs with the SDK, it's not possible to see what the job server's default settings are – if you need this information, you would need to perform a CMS query to retrieve a job server, then interrogate its settings.

BI Inbox Options

As we saw in the example above, the IManagedOptions interface is used to set the options for BI inbox distribution. We won't cover all of the methods of this interface, but the ones of note are as follows:

Package com.crystaldecisions.sdk.plugin.destination.managed
Interface IManagedOptions
extends IDestinationScheduleOptions

int	getDestinationOption()
void	setDestinationOption(int option)
	Retrieves/sets the destination type (Favorites folder or inbox)
	Associated property: SI_OPTIONS
int	getSendOption()
void	setSendOption(int option)
	Retrieves/sets the send option (send copy or shortcut). If not set, the Job Server's default value is used.
	Associated property: SI_OPTIONS
set	getDestinations()

	Retrieve the collection of destination user IDs. If not set, the Job Server's default value is used. *Associated property:* `SI_OUTPUT_FILES`
`String`	`getTargetObjectName()`
`void`	`setTargetObjectName(String name)`
	Retrieves/sets the target's filename. *Associated property:* `SI_NAME`
`boolean`	`isAddFileExtension()`
`void`	`setAddFileExtension(boolean addFileExtension)`
	Retrieves/sets whether the type-appropriate file extension should be added to the filename. *Associated property:* `SI_ADD_FILE_EXTENSION`

Class/Interface 40: IManagedOptions

The `destinationOption` property determines whether a scheduled document is sent to the target user's BI Inbox or Favorites Folder. The "normal" schedules created in BI launch pad or CMC do not support the ability to change this option – documents can only be sent to the BI Inbox. To use this property in an SDK program, pass one of the following int values to `setDestinationOption()`:

```
IManagedOptions.CeDestinationOption.ceFavoritesFolder
IManagedOptions.CeDestinationOption.ceInbox
```

The `sendOption` property specifies what is sent to the target – either a copy of the processed document, or a shortcut to the instance in the parent document's history. The default option is to send a copy, and the possible values are:

```
IManagedOptions.CeManagedSendOption.ceCopy
IManagedOptions.CeManagedSendOption.ceShortcut
```

The `getDestinations()` method returns a `Set` of `Integers`, representing the InfoObject IDs of the recipients. The recipient IDs may be for one or more *users* or *user groups*; if user group IDs are specified, then the document is sent to the inboxes of all group members.

The `targetObjectName` and `addFileExtension` properties are common to all destination types (other than *Default Enterprise Location*). They pertain to the "Target Name" options when scheduling:

Setting `targetObjectName` to `null` or an empty string (`setTargetObjectName(null)` or `setTargetObjectName("")`) is equivalent to checking off the *Use Automatically Generated Name*

option; the file that is sent to the destination will have the same name as the scheduled instance, appended with a colon and the instance's InfoObject ID.

Calling `setTargetObjectName()` with a value that is not `null` or an empty string sets the generated filename.   The filename may include a number of placeholders, which are replaced with the appropriate value when the schedule is generated. In the CMC and BI launch pad, the listed placeholders are:

- `%SI_NAME%` *(the name of the instance)*

- `%SI_ID%` *(the InfoObject ID of the instance)*

- `%SI_OWNER%` *(the instance owner's user name)*

- `%SI_STARTTIME%` *(the date and time the scheduled job began execution)*

- `%SI_EMAIL_ADDRESS%` *(the email address of the instance owner, as set in the user's properties)*

- `%SI_USERFULLNAME%` *(the full name of the instance owner, as set in the user's properties)*

- `%EXT%` *(the file extension associated with the file type)*

So, to generate a document named "Report for: ", and appended with the recipient's full name, we could do the following:

```
setTargetObjectName("Report for: %SI_USERFULLNAME%")
```

Note that while the CMC and BI launch pad list only the above placeholders, the filename may actually include any valid InfoObject property name, for example:

- `%SI_CUID%`

- `%SI_KIND%`

- `%SI_KEYWORD%`

The `setAddFileExtension()` method determines whether the generated filename should include a file extension appropriate for the file format. Setting the value to true is equivalent to adding the ".%EXT%" placeholder to the end of the filename.

File System Options

The options for saving scheduled documents to a file system are defined in the `IDiskUnmanagedOptions` interface. Its notable methods are:

Package com.crystaldecisions.sdk.plugin.destination.diskunmanaged
Interface _IDiskUnmanagedOptions_
extends IDestinationScheduleOptions

List	getDestinationFiles()
	Retrieve the collection of destination paths/filenames.
	Associated property: SI_OUTPUT_FILES

String	getUserName()
void	setUserName(String sVal)
	Retrieves/sets the operating system user ID to use when connecting to the file system. If not set, the Job Server's default value is used. *Associated property:* SI_USERNAME
void	setPassword()
	Sets the operating system password to use when connecting to the file system. If not set, the Job Server's default value is used. *Associated property:* SI_PASSWORD
boolean	isPasswordSet()
	Returns true if a password has been set (is not null).
boolean	isPasswordNotEmpty()
	Returns true if a password has been set, **and** it is not an empty string.

Class/Interface 41: IDiskUnmanagedOptions

As with the BI Inbox destination, we first have to retrieve the IDiskUnmanaged plugin from the CMS in order to obtain an IDiskUnmanagedOptions instance:

```
    IDiskUnmanaged duPlugin = (IDiskUnmanaged) infoStore.query("select * from
ci_systemobjects where si_plugin_object = 1 and si_kind = '" + IDiskUnmanaged.KIND +
"'").get(0);

    IDiskUnmanagedOptions duOptions =
            (IDiskUnmanagedOptions) duPlugin.getScheduleOptions();
```

The getDestinationFiles() method is used to retrieve a List containing Strings, which represent the list of file paths and names to save to. For regular schedules (that is, not publications), this collection contains only a single item since schedules may only save to a single location.

If the value contains a path only (it ends with a path delimiter (/ or \)), then it is assumed to specify a directory only and not include the filename. The document is saved to that location, using the default filename (instance name appended with the instance's InfoObject ID). If the value does *not* end with a path delimiter, then it is assumed to be a complete path including the filename.

The path must be specified using the format appropriate for the operating system that the SAP BusinessObjects server is running on. For example:

Windows: d:\bi4_documents\

UNIX: /opt/bit/documents

If the path includes a filename, that filename may include any of the filename placeholders (see page 504). Placeholders may not be used in the path specification, however.

The userName and password properties are optional. If specified, then the Job Server will use those credentials to connect to the target directory when saving the file. If credentials are *not* specified, then any default credentials set in the Job Server settings are used[140]. Note that the SDK does not provide a method to retrieve a password; only to determine if one has been set (i.e., is not null), and if it has been set and is not an empty string.

The following code fragment creates a schedule that saves the generated document to the /opt/bi4/docs directory, using the user name of *fred*.

```
25        IDiskUnmanaged duPlugin = (IDiskUnmanaged) infoStore.query("select * from
   ci_systemobjects where si_plugin_object = 1 and si_kind = '" +
   IDiskUnmanaged.KIND + "'").get(0);

26

27        IInfoObjects infoObjects = infoStore.query("select si_id from
   ci_infoobjects where si_name = 'Schedule Test' and si_kind = 'webi' and
   si_instance = 0");

28

29        if(infoObjects.size() > 0)

30        {

31            IWebi webi = (IWebi) infoObjects.get(0);

32            ISchedulingInfo sched = webi.getSchedulingInfo();

33

34            IDiskUnmanagedOptions duo = (IDiskUnmanagedOptions)
   duPlugin.getScheduleOptions();

35            duo.getDestinationFiles().add("/opt/bi4/docs/");

36            duo.setUserName("fred");

37            duo.setPassword("SuperSecret");

38

39            IDestination dest =
   sched.getDestinations().add(IDiskUnmanaged.PROGID);

40            dest.setFromPlugin(duPlugin);

41            webi.schedule();

42        }
```

If the SAP BusinessObjects server was running on Windows, then line 35 might instead look like the following:

```
35            duo.getDestinationFiles().add("d:\\bi4_documents\");
```

---

140 If there are no credentials specified either in the scheduled job or in the Job Server, then the credentials that the SAP BusinessObjects server is running as will be used.

And if we wanted to set a specific filename to use:

```
35    duo.getDestinationFiles().add("d:\\bi4_documents\sample_output.wid");
```

FTP / SFTP Options

The FTP and SFTP destination types are similar, with the exception of one method. So we will cover these two together. The methods of the IFTPOptions interface are:

Package com.crystaldecisions.sdk.plugin.destination.ftp
Interface IFTPOptions
extends IDestinationScheduleOptions

void	clearServerInfo()
	Sets the following properties to null: password port serverName userName
List	getDestinationFiles()
	Retrieve the collection of destination paths/filenames. *Associated property:* SI_OUTPUT_FILES
String	getAccount()
void	setAccount(String sVal)
	Retrieves/sets the account to use when connecting to the FTP server. If not set, the Job Server's default value are used. The account name is rarely required and should be left as null unless the FTP server requires it to be specified. *Associated property:* SI_ACCOUNT
int	getPort()
void	setPort(int lVal)
	Retrieves/sets the network port to connect to on the FTP host. If not set, the Job Server's default value is used. *Associated property:* SI_PORT
String	getServerName()
void	setServerName(String sVal)

	Retrieves/sets the name of the FTP server (host) to connect to. If not set, the Job Server's default value is used.
	Associated property: SI_SERVER_NAME
String	getUserName()
void	setUserName(String sVal)
	Retrieves/sets the user name to use when connecting to the FTP host. If not set, the Job Server's default value is used.
void	setPassword()
	Sets the password to use when connecting to the FTP host. If not set, the Job Server's default value is used.
	Associated property: SI_PASSWORD
boolean	isPasswordSet()
	Returns true if a password has been set (is not null).
boolean	isPasswordNotEmpty()
	Returns true if a password has been set, **and** it is not an empty string.

Class/Interface 42: IFTPOptions

The ISFTPOptions interface includes all of the above, plus:

Package com.crystaldecisions.sdk.plugin.destination.sftp
Interface ISFTPOptions
extends IDestinationScheduleOptions

String	getFingerPrint()
void	setFingerPrint(String sVal)
	Retrieves/sets the SFTP fingerprint to use when connecting to the SFTP host.
	Associated property: SI_SFTP_FINGERPRINT

Class/Interface 43: ISFTPOptions

The port, serverName, userName, and password properties must be set for all FTP-bound schedules, either explicitly in the schedule or inherited from the job server. As with IDiskUnmanagedOptions, the password property can be set but not retrieved.

The account property is provided for compatibility with the FTP protocol but is required for very few FTP servers. It should be left blank unless specifically required.

The destinationFiles property functions the same way as in IDiskUnmanagedOptions (see page 505). If empty, the automatically-generated file name is used. Otherwise, the collection is assumed to contain a single string element, identifying the path and filename to save to.

Listing 40 Contains the *SchedFTP* program, an example of creating a schedule that distributes to an FTP destination. We are connecting to a server named *ftp.company.com*, on the default port of 21, logging in as the user *ftp_user* and password *SuperSecret*. The file that is sent is named *report.wid*, and it is uploaded to the */var/upload/* directory.

```
 1  package bosdkbook;

 2

 3  import com.businessobjects.sdk.plugin.desktop.webi.IWebi;

 4  import com.crystaldecisions.sdk.exception.SDKException;

 5  import com.crystaldecisions.sdk.framework.CrystalEnterprise;

 6  import com.crystaldecisions.sdk.framework.IEnterpriseSession;

 7  import com.crystaldecisions.sdk.framework.ISessionMgr;

 8  import com.crystaldecisions.sdk.occa.infostore.IDestination;

 9  import com.crystaldecisions.sdk.occa.infostore.IInfoObjects;

10  import com.crystaldecisions.sdk.occa.infostore.IInfoStore;

11  import com.crystaldecisions.sdk.occa.infostore.ISchedulingInfo;

12  import com.crystaldecisions.sdk.plugin.destination.ftp.IFTP;

13  import com.crystaldecisions.sdk.plugin.destination.ftp.IFTPOptions;

14

15  public class SchedFTP {

16

17      public static void main(String[] args) throws SDKException

18      {

19          ISessionMgr sessionManager = CrystalEnterprise.getSessionMgr();

20          IEnterpriseSession session = sessionManager.logon ("administrator",
    "xxxx", "192.168.56.102", "secEnterprise");

21

22          IInfoStore infoStore = (IInfoStore) session.getService ("","InfoStore");

23

24          IFTP ftpPlugin = (IFTP) infoStore.query("select * from ci_systemobjects
    where si_plugin_object = 1 and si_kind = '" + IFTP.KIND + "'").get(0);

25          IFTPOptions ftpOptions = (IFTPOptions) ftpPlugin.getScheduleOptions();

26

27          IInfoObjects infoObjects = infoStore.query("select * from ci_infoobjects
    where si_name = 'Schedule Test' and si_kind = 'webi' and si_instance = 0");
```

```
28
29          if(infoObjects.size() > 0)
30          {
31              IWebi webi = (IWebi) infoObjects.get(0);
32              ISchedulingInfo sched = webi.getSchedulingInfo();
33
34              ftpOptions.setServerName("ftp.company.com");
35              ftpOptions.setPort(21);
36              ftpOptions.setUserName("ftp_user");
37              ftpOptions.setPassword("SuperSecret");
38              ftpOptions.getDestinationFiles().add("/var/upload/report.wid");
39
40              IDestination dest = sched.getDestinations().add(IFTP.PROGID);
41              dest.setFromPlugin(ftpPlugin);
42              webi.schedule();
43          }
44          else
45              System.out.println("Could not find document!");
46
47          System.out.println("Done!");
48      }
49 }
```

Listing 40: The SchedFTP program

Email Options

As you might expect, there are many settings for email distribution. The settings are defined in the ISMTPOptions interface.

Package com.crystaldecisions.sdk.plugin.destination.smtp
Interface ISMTPOptions
extends IDestinationScheduleOptions

Mail server settings

String	getDomainName()
void	setDomainName(String sVal)

Retrieves/sets the domain name of the email server to connect to. If not set, the Job Server's default value is used.

Associated property: `SI_DOMAIN_NAME`

String	getServerName()
void	setServerName(String sVal)

Retrieves/sets the host name of the email server to connect to. If not set, the Job Server's default value is used.

Associated property: `SI_SERVER`

int	getPort()
void	setPort(int iVal)

Retrieves/sets the TCP/IP network port of the email server. If not set, the Job Server's default value is used. If the Job Server has no default value, then a value of 25 is used.

Associated property: `SI_PORT`

int	getSMTPAuthenticationType()
void	setSMTPAuthenticationType(int iVal)

Retrieves/sets the type of authentication to use when connecting to the email server. If not set, the Job Server's default value is used.
iVal must be one of:
`ISMTPOptions.CeSMTPAuthentication.LOGIN`
`ISMTPOptions.CeSMTPAuthentication.NONE`
`ISMTPOptions.CeSMTPAuthentication.PLAIN`

Associated property: `SI_AUTH_TYPE`

String	getSMTPUserName()
void	setSMTPUserName(String sVal)

Retrieves/sets the user name to use when connecting to the email server. If not set, the Job Server's default value is used. Required if the email server requires authentication.

Associated property: `SI_USERNAME`

void	setSMTPPassword()

	Sets the password to use when connecting to the email server. If not set, the Job Server's default value is used. Required if the email server requires authentication. *Associated property:* SI_PASSWORD
boolean	isSMTPPasswordSet()
	Returns true if a password has been set (is not null).
boolean	isSMTPPasswordNotEmpty()
	Returns true if a password has been set, **and** it is not an empty string.
boolean	isSslEnabled()
void	setEnableSSL(boolean bEnabled)
	Retrieves/sets whether to connect to the email server using SSL (Secure Sockets Layer). *Associated property:* SI_ENABLE_SSL

Sender address settings

String	getSenderAddress()
void	setSenderAddress(String sVal)
	Retrieves/sets the email address to use in the "From" field of the generated email. If not set, the Job Server's default value is used. *Associated property:* SI_SENDER_NAME

Recipient address settings

List	getToAddresses()
	Retrieves a collection of String objects representing the email addresses of the recipients. Calling this method when no recipients are present will create a new, empty, collection, and this will prevent the Job Server's default values from being used. So, to check if recipients have been sct, use the isToAddressesSet() method. *Associated property:* SI_MAIL_ADDRESSES
boolean	isToAddressesSet()
	Returns true if any recipients have been specified.
List	getCCAddresses()

	Retrieves a collection of String objects representing the email addresses of the Carbon Copy (CC) recipients. Calling this method when no CC recipients are present will create a new, empty, collection, and this will prevent the Job Server's default values from being used. So, to check if recipients have been set, use the `isCCAddressesSet()` method. *Associated property:* `SI_MAIL_CC`
boolean	`isCCAddressesSet()`
	Returns `true` if any CC recipients have been specified.
List	`getBCCAddresses()`
	Retrieves a collection of String objects representing the email addresses of the Blind Carbon Copy (BCC) recipients. Calling this method when no BCC recipients are present will create a new, empty, collection, and this will prevent the Job Server's default values from being used. So, to check if recipients have been set, use the `isBCCAddressesSet()` method. *Associated property:* `SI_MAIL_BCC`
boolean	`isBCCAddressesSet()`
	Returns `true` if any recipients have been specified.

Enterprise user recipient settings

Set	`getToRecipients()`
	Retrieves a collection of Integer objects representing the enterprise users or groups that will receive the email. Calling this method when no recipients are present will create a new, empty, collection, and this will prevent the Job Server's default values from being used. So, to check if recipients have been set, use the `isToRecipientsSet()` method. *Associated property:* `SI_MAIL_ADDRESSES`
boolean	`isToRecipientSet()`
	Returns `true` if any recipients have been specified.
List	`getCCRecipients()`

	Retrieves a collection of Integer objects representing the enterprise users or groups that will receive the email as Carbon Copy (CC) recipients. Calling this method when no CC recipients are present will create a new, empty, collection, and this will prevent the Job Server's default values from being used. So, to check if recipients have been set, use the `isCCRecipientsSet()` method. *Associated property:* `SI_MAIL_CC`
boolean	`isCCRecipientsSet()`
	Returns `true` if any CC recipients have been specified.
List	`getBCCRecipients()`
	Retrieves a collection of Integer objects representing the enterprise users or groups that will receive the email as Blind Carbon Copy (BCC) recipients. Calling this method when no BCC recipients are present will create a new, empty, collection, and this will prevent the Job Server's default values from being used. So, to check if recipients have been set, use the `isBCCRecipientsSet()` method. *Associated property:* `SI_MAIL_BCC`
boolean	`isBCCRecipientsSet()`
	Returns `true` if any recipients have been specified.

Other settings

String	`getSubject()`
void	`setSubject(String sVal)`
	Retrieves/sets the subject line of the email message, as a string. *Associated property:* `SI_MAIL_SUBJECT`
String	`getMessage()`
void	`setMessage(String sVal)`
	Retrieves/sets the email message body, as a string. *Associated property:* `SI_MAIL_MESSAGE`
IAttachments	`getAttachments()`
	Retrieves a collection of IAttachment objects, representing the options for sending the generated document as an attachment with the email. *Associated property:* `SI_OUTPUT_FILES`
boolean	`isAttachmentsEnabled()`

void	`setAttachmentsEnabled(boolean bEnabled)`
	Retrieves/sets whether the instance's document should be attached to the email. *Associated property:* `SI_SMTP_ENABLEATTACHMENTS`
String	`getDelimiter()`
void	`setDelimiter(String sVal)`
	Retrieves/sets the delimiter that is used to separate email addresses in the specified To/CC/BCC parameters. The default value is a semicolon (;). *Associated property:* `SI_SEPARATOR`

Class/Interface 44: ISMTPOptions

The `ISMTPOptions` interface includes more email destination parameters than what's visible when creating schedules in the CMC or BI launch pad. The mail server settings, for example, are set in the Job Servers rather than schedules; but by using the SDK, these settings can be specified for individual scheduled instances. If any of the parameters are left empty (null), then the Job Server's default values are used (which is what happens with schedules created in the CMC or BI launch pad).

In a typical environment, each Job Server has the default mail server settings (host/domain, port, etc.), and the mail *message* settings (from/to addresses, subject, body, etc.) are defined in each scheduled instance. However, it's possible to define the settings in the Job Servers and then override what's necessary when creating schedules. For example, the Job Server's email destination settings could include a default "From" address that is to be used for all schedules. When creating the individual schedules, leaving the *From* address blank will then default to the one specified in the Job Server[141].

Mail Server Settings

It's not common or recommended to specify mail server settings for individual schedules. However, if this needs to be done, the `domainName`, `serverName`, and `port` properties can be set using the applicable setter methods. If the mail server requires authentication, call `setSMTPAuthenticationType` with the appropriate value, and set the `smtpUserName` and `smtpPassword` properties accordingly. The following fragment creates a scheduled job that attempts to send an email via *mail.company.com*, on port 125, using the user name *fred* and password *freds_password*.

```
ISMTPOptions smtpOptions = (ISMTPOptions)
        smtpPlugin.getScheduleOptions();

smtpOptions.setDomainName("company.com");

smtpOptions.setServerName("mail");
```

---

141 It's possible to have multiple job servers having different default parameters. This can result in a scheduled job inheriting different scheduling parameters, based on which job server they happen to run on.

```
        smtpOptions.setPort(125);


        smtpOptions.setSMTPAuthenticationType(
                 ISMTPOptions.CeSMTPAuthentication.LOGIN);

        smtpOptions.setSMTPUserName("fred");

        smtpOptions.setSMTPPassword("freds_password");
```

Sender Settings

All email messages require a sender (or "from") address. This may be specified by passing a standard SMTP address to `setSenderAddress()`.

As with most other text parameters, the sender address may include a placeholder value. The only one that's of any real use in the sender field would be the `%SI_EMAIL_ADDRESS%` placeholder, which is replaced with the email address of the user account that owns the scheduled instance. For example, Fred schedules a report and sets the sender address to `%SI_EMAIL_ADDRESS%`. If Fred's email address (as stored in his user properties) is *fred@company.com*, then the email that is generated will have this as its *from* address.

The sender address can also include a display name as well as the address. For example, if the sender address is specified as:

Fred Frederick <fred@company.com>

...then the recipient will see both the display name and the address. Depending on the email client used, only the display name may be displayed. To set a scheduled report to use this format, the `%SI_USERULLNAME%` placeholder may be used along with `%SI_EMAIL_ADDRESS%`, like so:

```
smtpOptions.setDSenderAddress("%SI_USERFULLNAME% <%SI_EMAIL_ADDRESS%>");
```

Recipient Settings

An email message must have at least one recipient address specified in the to, cc, or bcc fields. In BI launch pad and CMC, these addresses may be specified with static SMTP email addresses, or the `%SI_EMAIL_ADDRESS%` placeholder.

The recipient address getter methods in `ISMTPOptions` return a `List` of `String` objects representing each recipient address. One or more address can be set as recipients by adding them separately to the list. For example[142]:

```
        ISMTPOptions smtpOptions = (ISMTPOptions)
                 smtpPlugin.getScheduleOptions();

        smtpOptions.getToAddresses().add("fred@company.com");

        smtpOptions.getToAddresses().add("ethel@company.com");
```

---

142 Usage of `getToAddresses().add()` in this manner produces a compiler warning since `getToAddresses()` returns a non-generic `List` (rather than `List<String>`). The warning is unavoidable but can be hidden with a `@SuppressWarnings` annotation.

It's important to note that in the CMC and BI launch pad, multiple recipients may be entered as a single string, for example:

```
fred@companycom;ethel@company.com
```

However, this format is invalid when adding recipients with the SDK; the recipients must be added to the list individually, as in the example above.

A particular characteristic of the `Address` getter methods is that a new, empty `List` will be created if they are called when there are no existing recipients specified. When this happens, any default recipients specified in the job servers are overridden. That is, by calling the getter methods, you are implicitly overriding any default values that are present in the job server, and specifying your own list. If you do not populate the list, then no recipients are specified for the scheduled instance.

As an example, let's say our job server includes a default To recipient (fred@company.com, for argument's sake). If we create a new scheduled instance and **do not** call `ISMTPOptions.getToAddresses()`, then the generated email will assume the default To address specified in the job server (fred@company.com).

However, if when creating the instance, we call `ISMTPOptions.getToAddresses()`, and do nothing with the list that's returned, the generated email will then have no To addresses specified.

Put simply, don't call `getToAddresses()` unless you intend on adding addresses to it, or you are certain that it contains values (or you really want to override the job server defaults with a blank address list).

If the document you are scheduling already has its destination set to Email[143], then the destination may already have To/CC/BCC addresses set. Since calling `getToAddresses()` overrides the job server settings, we need another method to determine if the addresses are set. We can use the `is...AddressesSet()` methods for this purpose, for example: `isToAddressesSet()`. This returns a `boolean` `true` if any To addresses have already been specified for the schedule.

The following fragment is an example of where `isToAddressesSet()` would be used prior to `getToAddresses()`.

```
        ISMTP smtpPlugin = (ISMTP) infoStore.query("select * from ci_systemobjects
where si_plugin_object = 1 and si_kind = '" + ISMTP.KIND + "'").get(0);


        IInfoObjects infoObjects = infoStore.query("select * from ci_infoobjects
where si_name = 'Schedule Test' and si_kind = 'webi' and si_instance = 0");
```

---

143 That is, if you are working with an existing `IDestination` object from the document, rather than having created a new `IDestination`.

```
if(infoObjects.size() > 0)
{
    IWebi webi = (IWebi) infoObjects.get(0);
    ISchedulingInfo sched = webi.getSchedulingInfo();


    // If sched.getDestinations() is empty, then the default
    // destination is Default Enterprise Location
    if(sched.getDestinations().size() > 0)
    {
        // Get the one (and only) destination for this schedule
        IDestination dest = (IDestination) sched.getDestinations().get(0);


        // Check the destination type
        if(dest.getName().equals(ISMTP.PROGID))
        {
            // Copy this schedule's destination settings to smtpPlugin
            dest.copyToPlugin(smtpPlugin);


            // Retrieve the SMTP Options from the plugin
            ISMTPOptions smtpOptions =
                (ISMTPOptions) smtpPlugin.getScheduleOptions();


            // Check if there is a "To" address specified
            if(smtpOptions.isToAddressesSet())
            {
                // Yes! Now we can safely retrieve it
                System.out.println(smtpOptions.getToAddresses().get(0));
            }
        }
    }
}
```

In the CMC and BI launch pad, email recipients may only be specified using email addresses in text form. However, the SDK also provides the ability to specify recipients as enterprise users or group IDs. Recipients may be specified as To, CC, or BCC using the following methods

```
getToRecipients()
```

```
getCCRecipients()
```

```
getBCCRecipients()
```

As with the `get...Addresses()` methods, there are accompanying `is...AddressesSet` methods to determine if the recipient lists are populated:

```
isToRecipientsSet()
```

```
isCCRecipientsSet()
```

```
isBCCRecipientsSet()
```

The three getter methods return a `List` containing InfoObject IDs (`SI_ID`) associated with users or groups. When a user ID is specified, then the email is sent to the email address associated with that user. When a **user group** is specified, the email is sent to the email address of all users who belong to the group.

In order for this to work as expected, the designated users must have an email address set in their user properties.

Since this method is not used by CMC or BI launch pad, a schedule created with the SDK will not show the true scheduling settings when viewed in the CMC.

Let's look at an example. Listing 41 Contains the *SchedEmailRecipient* program. This uses the `getToRecipients()` method to set the recipient list to user ID 4104, which we know to be *Fred's* InfoObject ID. When we execute this program we get a status of Success, and an email in Fred's email (the mailbox specified for Fred's email address).

```java
 1  package bosdkbook;
 2
 3  import com.businessobjects.sdk.plugin.desktop.webi.IWebi;
 4  import com.crystaldecisions.sdk.exception.SDKException;
 5  import com.crystaldecisions.sdk.framework.CrystalEnterprise;
 6  import com.crystaldecisions.sdk.framework.IEnterpriseSession;
 7  import com.crystaldecisions.sdk.framework.ISessionMgr;
 8  import com.crystaldecisions.sdk.occa.infostore.IDestination;
 9  import com.crystaldecisions.sdk.occa.infostore.IInfoObjects;
10  import com.crystaldecisions.sdk.occa.infostore.IInfoStore;
11  import com.crystaldecisions.sdk.occa.infostore.ISchedulingInfo;
12  import com.crystaldecisions.sdk.plugin.destination.smtp.ISMTP;
13  import com.crystaldecisions.sdk.plugin.destination.smtp.ISMTPOptions;
14
15  public class SchedEmailRecipient {
16
```

```
17      public static void main(String[] args) throws SDKException

18      {

19          ISessionMgr sessionManager = CrystalEnterprise.getSessionMgr();

20          IEnterpriseSession session = sessionManager.logon ("administrator",
        "xxxx", "192.168.56.102", "secEnterprise");

21

22          IInfoStore infoStore = (IInfoStore) session.getService ("","InfoStore");

23

24          ISMTP smtpPlugin = (ISMTP) infoStore.query("select * from
        ci_systemobjects where si_plugin_object = 1 and si_kind = '" + ISMTP.KIND +
        "'").get(0);

25          ISMTPOptions smtpOptions = (ISMTPOptions)
        smtpPlugin.getScheduleOptions();

26

27          IInfoObjects infoObjects = infoStore.query("select * from ci_infoobjects
        where si_name = 'Schedule Test' and si_kind = 'webi' and si_instance = 0");

28

29          if(infoObjects.size() > 0)

30          {

31              IWebi webi = (IWebi) infoObjects.get(0);

32              ISchedulingInfo sched = webi.getSchedulingInfo();

33

34              smtpOptions.getToRecipients().add(4104);

35              smtpOptions.setSubject("Email test");

36              smtpOptions.setMessage("Email test");

37

38              IDestination dest = sched.getDestinations().add(ISMTP.PROGID);

39              dest.setFromPlugin(smtpPlugin);

40              webi.schedule();

41          }

42          else

43              System.out.println("Could not find document!");

44

45          System.out.println("Done!");

46      }

47 }
```

However, if we look at the properties of the scheduled instance that was created, we find the following:

History Status: Schedule Test

Title:	Schedule Test
Document Type:	Web Intelligence
Status	Success
Destination:	Mail the instance to: "[]" with a subject of: "Email test" .
Owner:	Administrator
Creation Time:	2/20/2017 4:49 PM
Start Time:	2/20/2017 4:49 PM
End Time:	2/20/2017 4:50 PM
Duration:	27 sec

Although the email was successfully sent to Fred's address, that address does not appear in the instance status. Also, if we reschedule the instance in the CMC, the "To" address field will be blank.

So, although defining email recipients by user ID (and even more usefully, by user *group*) is possible with the SDK, we recommend using this functionality sparingly. The instances that it creates can be misunderstood since they don't accurately describe the instance's true settings.

Subject and Message Text Settings

These two properties are fairly straightforward – they are strings that contain the email subject and message text, respectively:

```
getSubject(), setSubject(), getMessage(), setMessage()
```

As with the other email properties, the subject and message can contain placeholders. The placeholders that the CMC suggests are:

- %SI_NAME% *(the name of the instance)*

- %SI_ID% *(the InfoObject ID of the instance)*

- %SI_OWNER% *(the instance owner's user name)*

- %SI_STARTTIME% *(the date and time the scheduled job began execution)*

- %SI_EMAIL_ADDRESS% *(the email address of the instance owner, as set in the user's properties)*

- %SI_USERFULLNAME% *(the full name of the instance owner, as set in the user's properties)*

- %SI_VIEWER_URL% *(a URL that opens the document instance)*

The placeholders may be intermixed with static text. The following code fragment defines a typical subject and message for a scheduled email:

```
        smtpOptions.setSubject("%SI_NAME% report is complete");

        smtpOptions.setMessage("Hello, %SI_USERFULLNAME%.\r\nThe %SI_NAME% report
completed successfully at %SI_STARTTIME%.  Click on the following link to access this
report.\r\n%SI_VIEWER_URL%");
```

The generated email would look similar to the following:

To: fred@company.com

From: fred@company.com

Date: 2/20/2017 8:08:12 pm

Subject: Sample Report report is complete

Hello, Fred.

The Sample Report report completed successfully at 2017-02-20-20-07-30. Click on the following link to access this report.

http://bi4server/BOE/OpenDocument/opendoc/openDocument.jsp?
sIDType=CUID&iDocID=FtHcVVhAfAYATRAAAAC3IUcACAAnyavX

Unlike the `Address` and `Recipient` properties, there are no special rules about checking the `Subject` and `Message` to verify if they are populated. If either of these properties is `null`, then the job server's default values are used. So, to ensure that the job server's default value for `Message` is used, use the following:

```
setMessage(null);
```

Attachment Settings

Documents that are scheduled to an email destination may optionally include the document's file as an attachment. The file format (PDF, Excel, wid, etc.) is determined by the format of the *instance*. That is, based on the selected output format on the *Formats* tab in CMC or BI launch pad.

In the SDK, email attachments are managed via the `IAttachments` interface, which is retrieved via `ISMTPOptions.getAttachments()`. Although `IAttachments` is a `List`, it only contains zero or one `IAttachment` objects.

There are three possible scenarios with respect to sending attachments with an email destination:

- No attachment is sent
- Attachment is sent with default filename
- Attachment is sent with custom filenames

In the CMC or BI launch pad, we specify that an attachment should **not** be sent by unchecking the *Add Attachment* checkbox in the destination settings page:

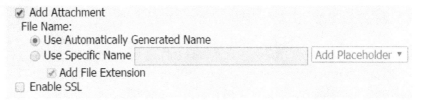

In   an   SDK   program,   this   is   specified   by   calling
`ISMTPOptions.setAttachmentsEnabled(false)`[144].

```
smtpOptions.setAttachmentsEnabled(false)
```

The second scenario, sending the attachment with the default name, is specified in the CMC by checking off *Add Attachment*, and setting the *File Name* option to *Use Automatically Generated Name*:

With the SDK, we perform this action by calling `ISMTPOptions.setAttachmentsEnabled(true)` and ensuring that the `IAttachments` collection is empty:

```
smtpOptions.setAttachmentsEnabled(true);

smtpOptions.getAttachments().clear();
```

Finally, to send an attachment with a custom file name, we use the Use Specific Name option and provide the desired name. As before, we can use any filename placeholders:

To perform this action in the SDK, we must add a new item to the `IAttachments` collection by calling its `add` method[145]. The definition of `IAttachments.add()` is:

---

144 You may have noticed that in the CMC, all of the schedule destination types (Email, BI inbox, etc.) have the same dialog for specifying the output filename. However, the SDK implementation for setting these options is different for each destination type.

145 This is the only non-inherited method of this interface.

Package com.crystaldecisions.sdk.plugin.destination.smtp
Interface IAttachments
extends `List`

IAttachment	add(String mimeType,String embedName)
	Creates a new `IAttachment` object and adds it to the collection.

Class/Interface 45: IAttachments

The `mimeType` property is not used for regular schedules and should be set to an empty string
(""). The `embedName` property should be set to the desired filename, including any
placeholders. For example:

```
smtpOptions.setAttachmentsEnabled(true);

smtpOptions.getAttachments().add("","%SI_NAME%.%EXT%");
```

Unlike most of the other email options, the attachment settings do not use the job server's
default values. Either the `attachmentsEnabled` property is `false`, in which no attachment is
sent, or it is true, and the filename is determined by the `embedName` property of the
`IAttachment` object. The only time the job server's default settings for email attachments are
used is if the *Use default settings* option is chosen (in the CMC), or no `ISMTPOptions` object is
provided to `IDestination` (in the SDK).

We've covered quite a bit of ground with the email scheduling options. Listing 42 is an
example of a typical program that creates an email schedule, in which it includes
specifications for the To/From/CC addresses, subject, message, and attachments.

```
 1  package bosdkbook;

 2

 3  import com.businessobjects.sdk.plugin.desktop.webi.IWebi;

 4  import com.crystaldecisions.sdk.exception.SDKException;

 5  import com.crystaldecisions.sdk.framework.CrystalEnterprise;

 6  import com.crystaldecisions.sdk.framework.IEnterpriseSession;

 7  import com.crystaldecisions.sdk.framework.ISessionMgr;

 8  import com.crystaldecisions.sdk.occa.infostore.IDestination;

 9  import com.crystaldecisions.sdk.occa.infostore.IInfoObjects;

10  import com.crystaldecisions.sdk.occa.infostore.IInfoStore;

11  import com.crystaldecisions.sdk.occa.infostore.ISchedulingInfo;

12  import com.crystaldecisions.sdk.plugin.destination.smtp.ISMTP;

13  import com.crystaldecisions.sdk.plugin.destination.smtp.ISMTPOptions;

14

15  public class CreateEmailSched {
```

```
16
17    public static void main(String[] args) throws SDKException
18    {
19        ISessionMgr sessionManager = CrystalEnterprise.getSessionMgr();
20        IEnterpriseSession session = sessionManager.logon ("administrator",
   "xxxx", "192.168.56.102", "secEnterprise");
21
22        IInfoStore infoStore = (IInfoStore) session.getService ("","InfoStore");
23
24        ISMTP smtpPlugin = (ISMTP) infoStore.query("select * from
   ci_systemobjects where si_plugin_object = 1 and si_kind = '" + ISMTP.KIND +
   "'").get(0);
25        ISMTPOptions smtpOptions = (ISMTPOptions)
   smtpPlugin.getScheduleOptions();
26
27        IInfoObjects infoObjects = infoStore.query("select * from ci_infoobjects
   where si_name = 'Schedule Test' and si_kind = 'webi' and si_instance = 0");
28
29        if(infoObjects.size() > 0)
30        {
31            IWebi webi = (IWebi) infoObjects.get(0);
32            ISchedulingInfo sched = webi.getSchedulingInfo();
33
34            smtpOptions.getToAddresses()
                   .add("%SI_USERFULLNAME% <%SI_EMAIL_ADDRESS%>");
35            smtpOptions.getCCAddresses().add("bo_admin@company.com");
36            smtpOptions.setSenderAddress("bo_admin@company.com");
37            smtpOptions.setSubject("%SI_NAME% report is complete");
38            smtpOptions.setMessage("Hello, %SI_USERFULLNAME%.\r\nPlease find
   attached the %SI_NAME% report.");
39
40            smtpOptions.setAttachmentsEnabled(true);
41            smtpOptions.getAttachments().add("","%SI_NAME%.%EXT%");
42
43            IDestination dest = sched.getDestinations().add(ISMTP.PROGID);
44            dest.setFromPlugin(smtpPlugin);
45            webi.schedule();
```

```
46        }

47        else

48            System.out.println("Could not find document!");

49

50        System.out.println("Done!");

51    }

52 }
```

Listing 42: The CreateEmailSched program

The schedule that this program creates is equivalent to one created in the CMC with the following options:

Illustration 33: Scheduling email settings

Scheduling in Batch

In all of our examples so far in the chapter, we have created scheduled instances by calling ISchedulable.schedule(). As an alternative to this method, it's possible to schedule a batch of InfoObjects in one go. To do this, we call IInfoStore.schedule(), passing in an IInfoObjects collection of objects to be scheduled. Generally, calling ISchedulable.schedule() on each individual object is preferable, but if you are scheduling many objects at one time this may be a better option.

As a hypothetical example, we might want to create schedules for all Web Intelligence reports in a particular folder. Using the `ISchedulable.schedule()` method, we would do this as follows:

```
20        IInfoObjects infoObjects = infoStore.query("select * from ci_infoobjects
   where si_kind = 'webi' and si_parentid = 511");

21

22        for(Object o : infoObjects)

23        {

24            IWebi webi = (IWebi)o;

25            webi.schedule();

26        }
```

We could instead use `IInfoStore.schedule()` to achieve the same result:

```
20        IInfoObjects infoObjects = infoStore.query("select * from ci_infoobjects
   where si_kind = 'webi' and si_parentid = 511");

21

22        infoStore.schedule(infoObjects);
```

Default Scheduling Options

In the CMC, default settings can be specified for all schedulable objects. These default settings are pre-filled in the *Schedule* dialog when creating a new scheduled instance and are used if the settings are not changed. Likewise, when scheduling instanced with the SDK, default settings are used if not overridden.

The process for setting the default settings for objects is identical to actually creating a schedule, with one subtle difference. Whereas we call the `schedule()` method to create a new scheduled instance, we simply call `save()` to use the specified settings as the new default settings.

For example, on page 453, we used the following code to schedule a report to run every 30 minutes:

```
25            IWebi webi = (IWebi) infoObjects.get(0);

26            ISchedulingInfo sched = webi.getSchedulingInfo();

27            sched.setRightNow(false);

28            sched.setType(CeScheduleType.HOURLY);

29            sched.setIntervalHours(0);

30            sched.setIntervalMinutes(30);
```

```
31          webi.schedule();
```

If we change the last line to:

```
31          webi.save();
```

Then, instead of creating a new instance, we would set the default recurrence for this object to be half-hourly. If we look at the Default Settings for this report in the CMC, we'll see the following:

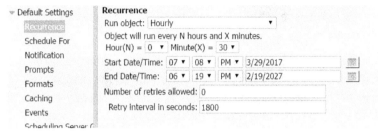

If we create a new schedule for this report in the CMC and leave the recurrence settings as-is, the newly-generated instance inherits these default recurrent settings. Likewise, if we schedule this report in the SDK, it will use the same inherited recurrence settings.

All scheduling settings, including recurrence, format, notification, etc., can be saved as default settings.

You can set the default settings and schedule the object at the same time, by first calling save() and then schedule(), for example:

```
25          IWebi webi = (IWebi) infoObjects.get(0);

26          ISchedulingInfo sched = webi.getSchedulingInfo();

27          sched.setRightNow(false);

28          sched.setType(CeScheduleType.HOURLY);

29          sched.setIntervalHours(0);

30          sched.setIntervalMinutes(30);

31          webi.save();

32          webi.schedule();
```

However, if you do this, you must call save() before schedule(). Calling schedule() first properly generates the new instance, but the original default settings are unchanged even after calling save().

Existing Instances

So far, we have discussed the creation of new scheduled instances. The SDK also enables us to manipulate existing instances, including those that are completed as well as pending or recurring.

Retrieving Instances

There are two ways to retrieve scheduled instances: with a standard CMS query, or via the ISchedulable interface.

We can use a CMS query to retrieve instances, just like any other InfoObject. W hat we are looking for will determine how the query is constructed. If, for example, we want to retrieve all child instances of a parent object, we can simply query for all objects with the parent's ID. For example, if we want to retrieve all child instances of a Web Intelligence document having ID 5927, we could use the following query:

```
select * from ci_infoobjects where si_parentid = 5927
```

Since we know that the only children a WebI object can have are instances, we don't need to further qualify this query.

If we had already retrieved the parent IInfoObject (ID 5927, in this case), then we can use one of the shortcut methods in ISchedulable to perform the query for us. The applicable methods of ISchedulable are:

Package *com.crystaldecisions.sdk.occa.infostore*
Interface *ISchedulable*

Instance retrieval methods

IInfoObjects	getInstances()
	Retrieves all child instances of this object
IInfoObjects	getInstances(int propertySet, SearchPattern searchPattern, SortType sortType)
	Retrieves all child instances that meet the specified search criteria
IInfoObject	getLatestInstance()
	Retrieves the most recent child instance of this object.
IInfoObject	getLatestInstance(int propertySet, SearchPattern searchPattern)
	Retrieves the most recent child instance that meets the specified search criteria. The returned object includes the properties specified by propertySet.

Class/Interface 46: ISchedulable

There is nothing "magical" about these methods. They are simply shortcuts to creating and executing a CMS query. The simplest of these is getInstances(), which retrieves all child instances, using the standard property set.

```
 1  package bosdkbook;

 2

 3  import com.businessobjects.sdk.plugin.desktop.webi.IWebi;

 3  import com.crystaldecisions.sdk.exception.SDKException;

 4  import com.crystaldecisions.sdk.framework.CrystalEnterprise;

 5  import com.crystaldecisions.sdk.framework.IEnterpriseSession;

 6  import com.crystaldecisions.sdk.framework.ISessionMgr;

 7  import com.crystaldecisions.sdk.occa.infostore.IInfoObjects;

 8  import com.crystaldecisions.sdk.occa.infostore.IInfoStore;

 9  import com.crystaldecisions.sdk.occa.infostore.IInfoObject;

10

11  public class RetrieveKids {

12

13      public static void main(String[] args) throws SDKException

14      {

15          ISessionMgr sessionManager = CrystalEnterprise.getSessionMgr();

16          IEnterpriseSession session = sessionManager.logon ("administrator",
    "xxxx", "192.168.56.102", "secEnterprise");

17

18          IInfoStore infoStore = (IInfoStore) session.getService ("","InfoStore");

19

20          IInfoObjects infoObjects = infoStore.query("select * from ci_infoobjects
    where si_id = 5927");

21

22          IWebi webi = (IWebi)infoObjects.get(0);

23

24          IInfoObjects kids = webi.getInstances();

25

26          for(Object o : kids)

27          {

28              IInfoObject kid = (IInfoObject)o;

29              System.out.println("Child instance " + kid.getTitle() + " completed at
    " + kid.getUpdateTimeStamp());
```

```
30            }
31      }
32 }
```

Listing 43: The RetrieveKids program

In Listing 43 we use the `getInstances()` method to retrieve child instances, then display the names and completion time of each. We *could* have manually run a CMS query instead, which would produce the same result:

```
24      IInfoObjects kids = infoStore.query("select * from ci_infoobjects where
        si_parentid = " + webi.getID());
```

Well, *almost* the same result. In the second example, we are explicitly retrieving all properties via "`select *`". The `getInstances()` method, on the other hand, retrieves the default property set, which includes only the following:

`SI_ID, SI_CUID, SI_NAME, SI_PARENTID, SI_PARENT_CUID, SI_KIND, SI_INSTANCE`

To specify a different property set to return, we can use the second form of `getInstances()`. The value for `propertySet` must be one of the constant int values from `IInfoObject.PropertySet` (see page 225 for the list of properties included in each property set). So, to retrieve all properties of the child objects, we could use:

```
24      IInfoObjects kids = webi.getInstances(PropertySet.ALL,null,null);
```

In this case, we are passing `null` to the `searchPattern` and `sortType` parameters, to indicate that we want to use the default options (no filter applied, and default sort).

The two `getLatestInstance()` methods return either the most recent child instance of the object or the most recent instance that meets the specified criteria (respectively). If there are no child instances, a `null` is returned.

Instance Properties

The `ISchedulingInfo` interface that we used extensively when creating schedules, contains several methods associated with active instances. They are:

Package com.crystaldecisions.sdk.occa.infostore
Interface *ISchedulingInfo*

Result/Status methods

String	getErrorMessage()
	Retrieves the error message for failed jobs.
	Associated property: SI_SCHEDULEINFO.SI_STATUSINFO

String	`getErrorMessage(Locale locale)`
	Retrieves the error message for failed jobs, in the specified locale.
	Associated property: `SI_SCHEDULEINFO.SI_STATUSINFO`
int	`getOutcome()`
	Retrieves the result of the scheduled job. The returned value is an `int` value of type `ISchedulingInfo.ScheduleOutcome`.
	Associated property: `SI_SCHEDULEINFO.SI_OUTCOME`
int	`getStatus()`
	Retrieves the instance's current status. The returned value is an `int` value of type `ISchedulingInfo.ScheduleOutcome`.
	Associated property: `SI_SCHEDULE_STATUS` (Note that this is a root property and not a child of the `SI_SCHEDULEINFO` bag.)

Class/Interface 47: ISchedulingInfo (Result/Status methods)

The `getStatus()` method retrieves a value that indicates the status of an instance, and is aligned with what is displayed for an instance's status in the CMC and BI launch pad (*Pending, Paused, Running, Success, Failed*). The int values are stored in `ISchedulingInfo.ScheduleStatus,` and are as follows:

Package com.crystaldecisions.sdk.occa.infostore
Interface `ISchedulingInfo.ScheduleStatus`

static int	COMPLETE	1
	The job completed successfully.	
static int	FAILURE	3
	The job failed.	
static int	PAUSED	8
	The job is currently paused.	
static int	PENDING	9
	The job is currently pending (has not reached its specified start time, is waiting for events, or waiting for an available job server.)	
static int	EXPIRED	13
	The job's specified End Time has passed.	
static int	WARNING	14

	The scheduled Web Intelligence document experienced a Partial Results warning.	
static int	RUNNING	0
	The job is currently executing.	

Class/Interface 48: ISchedulingInfo.ScheduleStatus

Note that there is no value for *Recurring*, although that is displayed as a status for recurring instances. This is because "Recurring" isn't technically a *status*. An instance is displayed with a status of *Recurring* if its SI_RECURRING property is true, and its SI_SCHEDULE_STATUS property is 9 (Pending).

If a schedule fails, the reason can be found in the getOutcome() and getErrorMessage() methods. The getOutcome() property returns an int value that identifies the failure category, while getErrorMessage() contains the text of the failure message.

The values of outcome are in ISchedulingInfo.ScheduleOutcome:

Package com.crystaldecisions.sdk.occa.infostore
Interface ISchedulingInfo.ScheduleOutcome

static int	FAIL_COMPONENT_FAILED	8
	Object Package failed due to a component scheduling failure.	
static int	FAIL_CONSTRAINTS	10
	Object failed to run because its constraints refer to missing objects. Please confirm that the server group, calendar and any dependencies are valid and that you have View rights on these objects.	
static int	FAIL_ENDTIME	5
	Object could not be scheduled within the specified time interval.	
static int	FAIL_JOBSERVER	3
	Object failed to run due to an error on the Job Server.	
static int	FAIL_JOBSERVER_CHILD	7
	Object failed to run due to an error while processing on the Job Server.	
static int	FAIL_JOBSERVER_PLUGIN	2
	The job failed due to a failure in a job server plugin.	
static int	FAIL_OBJECT_PACKAGE_FAILED	9
	Component failed to run due to an Object Package scheduling failure	
static int	FAIL_SCHEDULE	6
	Object could not be scheduled.	
static int	FAIL_SECURITY	4

	Object failed to run due to insufficient security privileges.	
static int	PENDING	0
	The job is currently pending.	
static int	SUCCESS	1
	The job completed successfully.	

Class/Interface 49: ISchedulingInfo.ScheduleOutcome

The getErrorMessage() method returns the text of the failure message. This may be either the generic description of outcome (as in the table above), or a more specific message. If, for example, a scheduled report fails due to an error received from the source database, the message returned by getErrorMessage() will include the text of the error from the database. This is the same text that is displayed in the CMC and BI launch pad for failed schedules.

We can use a combination of the SI_RECURRING property along with the getStatus() and getErrorMessage() methods to display a list of all instances in the system.

```java
        IInfoObjects infoObjects = infoStore.query("select * from ci_infoobjects
where si_instance = 1");


        for(Object o : infoObjects)
        {
            IInfoObject io = (IInfoObject)o;


            String isRecurring = (io.properties()
                    .getBoolean(CePropertyID.SI_RECURRING))
                    ? "(Recurring)"
                    : "";
            ISchedulingInfo sched = io.getSchedulingInfo();


            System.out.print(io.getTitle() + ": ");
            switch (sched.getStatus())
            {
                case ISchedulingInfo.ScheduleStatus.COMPLETE:
                    System.out.println("Completed successfully");
                    break;
                case ISchedulingInfo.ScheduleStatus.FAILURE:
                    System.out.println("Failure: " + sched.getErrorMessage());
                    break;
```

```
            case ISchedulingInfo.ScheduleStatus.RUNNING:

                System.out.println("Running");

                break;

            case ISchedulingInfo.ScheduleStatus.EXPIRED:

                System.out.println("Expired");

                break;

            case ISchedulingInfo.ScheduleStatus.WARNING:

                System.out.println("Warning");

                break;

            case ISchedulingInfo.ScheduleStatus.PENDING:

                System.out.println("Pending " + isRecurring);

                break;

            case ISchedulingInfo.ScheduleStatus.PAUSED:

                System.out.println("Paused " + isRecurring);

                break;

        }

    }
```

Executing this program in our test system produced the following output:

```
Schedule Test: Pending (Recurring)

Schedule Test: Completed successfully

Schedule Test: Completed successfully

Schedule Test: Pending

Schedule Test: Pending

Schedule Test: Pending

Schedule Test: Pending

Schedule Test: Failure: Object could not be scheduled within the specified time
interval.
```

Dates

Earlier in this chapter, we covered the `ISchedulingInfo.setBeginDate()` and `ISchedulingInfo.setEndDate()` methods, which set the earliest and latest time that the schedule can run (respectively). For existing instances, the corresponding `ISchedulingInfo.getBeginDate()` and `ISchedulingInfo.setEndDate()` methods can be used to retrieve the values of these properties.

The getEndDate() method simply returns the value that was specified when the instance was created and represents the point at which the instance will no longer run.

Likewise, the getBeginDate() method returns the value originally specified by setBeginDate() when the instance was created. However, for recurring instances that have executed at least once, getBeginDate() returns the date and time of the *next* execution.

For example, a recurring schedule is created that runs on the first of each month, with a begin date given as 8:00 a.m. on April 15, 2017. (the instance was actually created at some point prior to this date).

Immediately after this instance is created, getBeginDate() returns the value given: 8:00 a.m. on April 15, 2017. Calling getBeginDate() on this recurring instance returns the same value until it comes time for the job to execute, which is 8:00 a.m. on May 1, 2017[146]. Once this time passes, and the first monthly execution has occurred, the recurring instance will then show a *Next Run Time* of 8:00 a.m. on June 1, 2017. Calling getBeginDate() on the recurring instance returns this June 1 date. When the June 1 execution has occurred, getBeginDate() returns July 1, and so on[147].

The Begin and End dates described above represented the *scheduled* begin and end dates. Completed instances record their *actual* begin and end dates, as well. The accessor methods for these properties are in the ISchedulable interface[148]:

Package com.crystaldecisions.sdk.occa.infostore
Interface *ISchedulable*

Completion date methods

Date	getEndTime()
	Retrieves the date and time that the job completed processing
	Associated property: SI_ENDTIME
Date	getStartTime()
	Retrieves the date and time that the job began executing on the job server.
	Associated property: SI_STARTTIME

Class/Interface 50: ISchedulable

There is a quirk here, but first let's look at an example of using the above methods to display the actual start and end times of processed instances[149]:

---

146 Since we have scheduled the job to run on the first of each month.

147 Remember that we are talking about calling getBeginDate() on the *recurring* instance, not the one-time schedules that are spawned from this instance every month.

148 And, therefore, are inherited by the schedulable interfaces like IWebi and IReport.

```
        IInfoObjects infoObjects = infoStore.query("select * from ci_infoobjects
where si_name = 'schedule test' and si_instance_object = 1");


    for(Object o : infoObjects)
    {
        IInfoObject io = (IInfoObject)o;

        IWebi webi = (IWebi)o;

        System.out.println(webi.getStartTime() + "   " + webi.getEndTime());

    }
```

The quirk is that the begin and end dates are stored in the root SI_STARTTIME and SI_ENDTIME properties, but the accessor methods are located in the ISchedulable interface.   For InfoObject kinds that implement ISchedulable, such as IWebi, this is no problem – in the fragment above, we are calling IWebi.getStartTime() and IWebi.getEndTime() to get the desired property values. However, static output types, such as IExcel and IPDF, do not extend the ISchedulable interface, and therefore the getStartTime() and getEndTime() methods are not available. In order to retrieve the begin and end dates for these types, we must extract the property values directly. In the following fragment, we are retrieving the values of the SI_STARTTIME and SI_ENDTIME properties instead of calling getStartTime() and getEndTime(). Therefore we can display the properties regardless of kind.

```
        IInfoObjects infoObjects = infoStore.query("select * from ci_infoobjects
where si_name = 'schedule test' and si_instance_object = 1");


    for(Object o : infoObjects)
    {
        IInfoObject io = (IInfoObject)o;

        Date startDate = io.properties().getDate(CePropertyID.SI_STARTTIME);

        Date endDate = io.properties().getDate(CePropertyID.SI_ENDTIME);

        System.out.println(startDate + "   " + endDate);

    }
```

This produces the same result as the previous example, except that it properly displays the start and end times for instances that are in a static format.

Destination Settings

Most of the scheduling settings can be retrieved via simple accessor methods such as

---

149 Note that we are making use of the SI_INSTANCE_OBJECT property, which has a value of 1 for completed instances (successful or failed).

ISchedulingInfo.getBeginDate().   But retrieving the destination settings for existing instances is a little more involved.

As mentioned on page 496, the IDestinations collection (retrieved via ISchedulingInfo.getDestinations) will be empty if the Default Enterprise Location is selected. Otherwise, it will have a single IDestination object. To determine the specific type of destination (email, ftp, etc.), we use IDestination.getName(). The returned value is the SI_PROGID value of the destination's plug-in. The following snippet determines the type of destination for an existing scheduled instance:

```java
        IInfoObjects infoObjects = infoStore.query("select * from ci_infoobjects
where si_name = 'schedule test' and si_instance_object = 1");


    for(Object o : infoObjects)
    {

        IInfoObject io = (IInfoObject)o;

        ISchedulingInfo sched = io.getSchedulingInfo();


        if(sched.getDestinations().isEmpty())

            System.out.println("Default Enterprise Location");

        else

        {

            IDestination dest = (IDestination) sched.getDestinations().get(0);

            String pluginName = dest.getName();


            if(pluginName.equals(IDiskUnmanaged.PROGID))

                System.out.println("File system");

            else if(pluginName.equals(IFTP.PROGID ))

                System.out.println("FTP");

            else if(pluginName.equals(IManaged.PROGID ))

                System.out.println("BI Inbox");

            else if(pluginName.equals(ISMTP.PROGID ))

                System.out.println("Email");

            else if(pluginName.equals(ISFTP.PROGID ))

                System.out.println("SFTP");

            else if(pluginName.equals(IStreamWork.PROGID ))

                System.out.println("SAP Streamwork");

            else
```

```
                System.out.println("Unknown destination type");
        }
    }
```

Once the destination type is identified, its specific options can be retrieved. To do that, we need to copy its settings into an existing IDestinationScheduleOptions object. The process is a little unintuitive, but very similar to the process for setting the destination options (see *Destination Type-specific Options* starting on page 499.

The process is:

1. Retrieve the *destination plugin* from the CMS for the desired destination type (Email, File System, etc.), using a CMS query (this only needs to be done once per program execution). The plugin is a subinterface of IDestinationPlugin: IDiskUnmanaged, IFTP, IManaged, ISFTP, ISMTP, or IStreamWork.

2. Retrieve the document instance, as an IInfoObject or subinterface.

3. Retrieve the instance's IDestination object (via ISchedulingInfo.getDestinations().get(0)

4. Call IDestination.copyToPlugIn(), passing it the IDestinationPlugin retrieved in step 1.

5. Retrieve the *destination scheduling options* from the destination plugin by calling IDestinationPlugin.getScheduleOptions(), and casting the result to one of the following: IDiskUnmanagedOptions, IFTPOptions, IManagedOptions, ISFTPOptions, ISMTPOptions, or IStreamWorkOptions.

6. Retrieve the scheduling options from the object retrieved in Step 5.

The following code fragment is an example of retrieving destination scheduling options:

```
24      IInfoStore infoStore = (IInfoStore) session.getService ("","InfoStore");

25

26      IDiskUnmanaged diskUnmanagedPlugin = (IDiskUnmanaged)
   infoStore.query("select * from ci_systemobjects where si_plugin_object = 1 and
   si_kind = '" + IDiskUnmanaged.KIND + "'").get(0);

27

28      IInfoObjects infoObjects = infoStore.query("select * from ci_infoobjects
   where si_instance = 1");

29

30      for(Object o : infoObjects)

31      {

32          IInfoObject io = (IInfoObject)o;

33          ISchedulingInfo sched = io.getSchedulingInfo();
```

```
34
35              if(!sched.getDestinations().isEmpty())
36              {
37                  IDestination dest =
                        (IDestination)sched.getDestinations().get(0);
38                  String pluginName = dest.getName();
39                  if(pluginName.equals(IDiskUnmanaged.PROGID))
40                  {
41                      dest.copyToPlugin(diskUnmanagedPlugin);
42                      IDiskUnmanagedOptions managedOptions =
                            (IDiskUnmanagedOptions) diskUnmanagedPlugin
                            .getScheduleOptions();
43                      System.out.println(
                            managedOptions.getDestinationFiles().get(0));
44                  }
45              }
46          }
```

On line 26, we perform the first step, by retrieving the *Unmanaged Disk* plugin object from the CMS. Note that this is identical to what we did when creating schedules.

```
26          IDiskUnmanaged diskUnmanagedPlugin = (IDiskUnmanaged)
    infoStore.query("select * from ci_systemobjects where si_plugin_object = 1 and
    si_kind = '" + IDiskUnmanaged.KIND + "'").get(0);
```

Next, we retrieve the desired document instances on lines 28-33.

We perform the third step of the process on lines 35-37, in which we first check for the existence of an IDestination object in the IDestinations collection, then retrieve it if present.

If the retrieved IDestination object is *unmanaged disk* (identified by comparing its title property to the static IDiskUnmanaged.PROGID constant), then we proceed.

On line 41, we perform step 4: calling IDestination.copyToPlugin, which copies the instance's destination settings to the diskUnmanagedPlugin object we created earlier.

We retrieve the scheduling options from diskUnmanagedPlugin on line 42, which is the fifth step of the process.

Finally, on line 43, we perform the last step, in which we simply print out the output path stored in the disk unmanaged settings.

Retrieving All Settings

A real-world administrative need is the retrieval of scheduling settings for a number of instances. Although the Instance Manager in CMC can list pending and completed schedules, it does not display all of the settings for each schedule. With the SDK methods described in this chapter, we've seen how to access all of this informative data.

Listing 44 contains the *RetrieveSched* program. There is nothing really new here, just a compilation of some of the methods described previously for retrieving the scheduling settings.

In lines 39-70, we create lookup maps for all calendar templates, events, destination plug-ins, users, and groups. Each map is keyed on either the object's InfoObject ID or its name, depending on how it is looked up.

On line 73, we retrieve an `IInfoObjects` collection of all instances:

```
73        IInfoObjects infoObjects = infoStore.query("select * from ci_infoobjects
     where si_instance = 1");
```

Then, in the "big loop" starting on line 75, we display the scheduling settings for all of the retrieved `IInfoObjects`. The following settings are displayed:

- Name
- Owner
- Recurrence
- Status (including error message if failed)
- Destinations
- Events

In our test system, the program generated a large list of all scheduled instances. A sample of one of the returned instances follows:

```
Instance name: Schedule Test
Owner: Administrator
Recurrence: Every 0 hours and 15 minutes
Status: Success
Destination: BI Inbox
    Fred
Events to wait for:
Events to fire on completion:
```

Although it presents valuable information, the program is not very useful in its current state as it simply displays the returned data to the screen. Also, it displays results for all instances, which is likely to be a very large list of mostly repeating results. However, this would be a good foundation for a web application that displays the results in a more user-friendly manner and allows for the filtering of results by status, name, etc.

```java
1  package bosdkbook;
2
3  import java.util.HashMap;
4  import java.util.Iterator;
5  import java.util.List;
6  import java.util.Map;
7
8  import com.crystaldecisions.sdk.exception.SDKException;
9  import com.crystaldecisions.sdk.framework.CrystalEnterprise;
10 import com.crystaldecisions.sdk.framework.IEnterpriseSession;
11 import com.crystaldecisions.sdk.framework.ISessionMgr;
12 import com.crystaldecisions.sdk.occa.infostore.CeScheduleType;
13 import com.crystaldecisions.sdk.occa.infostore.IDestination;
14 import com.crystaldecisions.sdk.occa.infostore.IDestinationPlugin;
15 import com.crystaldecisions.sdk.occa.infostore.IInfoObject;
16 import com.crystaldecisions.sdk.occa.infostore.IInfoObjects;
17 import com.crystaldecisions.sdk.occa.infostore.IInfoStore;
18 import com.crystaldecisions.sdk.occa.infostore.ISchedulingInfo;
19 import com.crystaldecisions.sdk.plugin.destination.diskunmanaged
        .IDiskUnmanaged;
20 import com.crystaldecisions.sdk.plugin.destination.diskunmanaged
        .IDiskUnmanagedOptions;
21 import com.crystaldecisions.sdk.plugin.destination.ftp.IFTP;
22 import com.crystaldecisions.sdk.plugin.destination.ftp.IFTPOptions;
23 import com.crystaldecisions.sdk.plugin.destination.managed.IManaged;
24 import com.crystaldecisions.sdk.plugin.destination.managed.IManagedOptions;
25 import com.crystaldecisions.sdk.plugin.destination.sftp.ISFTP;
26 import com.crystaldecisions.sdk.plugin.destination.smtp.ISMTP;
27 import com.crystaldecisions.sdk.plugin.destination.smtp.ISMTPOptions;
28 import com.crystaldecisions.sdk.plugin.destination.streamwork.IStreamWork;
29
30 public class RetrieveSched {
31
```

```java
32      public static void main(String[] args) throws SDKException
33      {
34          ISessionMgr sessionManager = CrystalEnterprise.getSessionMgr();
35          IEnterpriseSession session = sessionManager.logon ("administrator",
    "xxxx", "192.168.56.102", "secEnterprise");
36
37          IInfoStore infoStore = (IInfoStore) session.getService ("","InfoStore");
38
39          // Retrieve a list of all calendar templates in the infostore
40          IInfoObjects ioCalendars = infoStore.query("select * from
    ci_systemobjects where si_kind = 'calendar'");
41          Map<Integer,String> calendarMap= new HashMap<Integer,String>();
42
43          // Load the ioCalendars map with calendar templates, keyed by ID
44          for(Object o : ioCalendars)
45              calendarMap.put(((IInfoObject)o).getID(),
                        ((IInfoObject)o).getTitle());
46
47          // Retrieve a list of all events in the infostore
48          IInfoObjects ioEvents = infoStore.query("select * from ci_systemobjects
    where si_kind = 'event'");
49          Map<Integer,String> eventMap= new HashMap<Integer,String>();
50
51          // Load the ioEvents map with events, keyed by ID
52          for(Object o : ioEvents)
53              eventMap.put(((IInfoObject)o).getID(),
                        ((IInfoObject)o).getTitle());
54
55          // Retrieve a list of all plugins in the infostore (we filter for only
    the Destination plugins below)
56          IInfoObjects ioDesintationPlugins = infoStore.query("select * from
    ci_systemobjects where si_plugin_object = 1");
57          Map<String,IDestinationPlugin> destinationPluginMap = new
    HashMap<String,IDestinationPlugin>();
58
59          // Load the ioDesitnationPlugins map with IDestinationPlugin objects,
    keyed by plugin name
60          for(Object o : ioDesintationPlugins)
```

```
61              if(o instanceof IDestinationPlugin)

62                  destinationPluginMap.put((((IInfoObject)o).getTitle(),
                                (IDestinationPlugin)o);

63

64      // Retrieve a list of all users and user groups in the infostore

65         IInfoObjects ioUsersGroups = infoStore.query("select si_id,si_name from
    ci_systemobjects where si_kind in ('user','usergroup')");

66         Map<Integer,String> usersGroupsMap = new HashMap<Integer,String>();

67

68      // Load the ioUsersGroups map, keyed by ID

69      for(Object o : ioUsersGroups)

70          usersGroupsMap.put((((IInfoObject)o).getID(),
                        ((IInfoObject)o).getTitle());

71

72      // Retrieve a list of all instances in the infostore

73         IInfoObjects infoObjects = infoStore.query("select * from ci_infoobjects
    where si_instance = 1");

74

75      for(Object o : infoObjects)

76      {

77          IInfoObject io = (IInfoObject)o;

78          ISchedulingInfo sched = io.getSchedulingInfo();

79

80          System.out.println("Instance name: " + io.getTitle());

81          System.out.println("Owner: " + io.getOwner());

82

83          displayRecurrence(calendarMap, sched);

84

85          displayStatus(io, sched);

86

87          displayDestination(destinationPluginMap, usersGroupsMap, sched);

88

89          System.out.println("Events to wait for:");

90          for(Object oe : sched.getDependencies())

91          {

92              System.out.println("    " + eventMap.get(oe));
```

```
93                    }
94
95              System.out.println("Events to fire on completion:");
96              for(Object oe : sched.getDependants())
97              {
98                  System.out.println("     " + eventMap.get(oe));
99              }
100
101             System.out.println("------------------------\n");
102         }
103     }
104
105     // DIsplay the status of the instance.  If failed, include the error message
106     private static void displayStatus(IInfoObject io, ISchedulingInfo sched)
107     throws SDKException
108     {
109         switch(sched.getStatus())
110         {
111             case ISchedulingInfo.ScheduleStatus.COMPLETE:
112                 System.out.println("Status: Success");
113                 break;
114             case ISchedulingInfo.ScheduleStatus.PAUSED:
115                 System.out.println("Status: Paused");
116                 break;
117             case ISchedulingInfo.ScheduleStatus.PENDING:
118                 System.out.println("Status: Pending");
119                 break;
120             case ISchedulingInfo.ScheduleStatus.RUNNING:
121                 System.out.println("Status: Running");
122                 break;
123             case ISchedulingInfo.ScheduleStatus.EXPIRED:
124                 System.out.println("Status: Expired");
125                 break;
126             case ISchedulingInfo.ScheduleStatus.Warning:
```

```
127             System.out.println("Status: Warning");
128                 break;
129           case ISchedulingInfo.ScheduleStatus.FAILURE:
130             System.out.println("Status: Failure\n     " +
     sched.getErrorMessage());
131                 break;
132           default:
133             System.out.println("Unknown status value: " + sched.getStatus());
134       }
135    }
136
137    // Display the recurrence settings for the instance
138    private static void displayRecurrence(Map<Integer, String> calendarMap,
            ISchedulingInfo sched)
139    {
140        if(sched.isRightNow())
141           System.out.println("Recurrence: Run Now");
142        else
143           switch (sched.getType())
144           {
145               case CeScheduleType.ONCE:
146                   System.out.println("Recurrence: Once");
147                   break;
148               case CeScheduleType.DAILY:
149                   System.out.println("Recurrence: Every " +
     sched.getIntervalDays() + " days");
150                   break;
151               case CeScheduleType.MONTHLY:
152                   System.out.println("Recurrence: Every " +
     sched.getIntervalMonths() + " months");
153                   break;
154               case CeScheduleType.HOURLY:
155                   System.out.println("Recurrence: Every " +
     sched.getIntervalHours() + " hours and " + sched.getIntervalMinutes() + "
     minutes");
156                   break;
157               case CeScheduleType.FIRST_MONDAY:
```

```
158              System.out.println("Recurrence: First Monday of each month");
159                  break;
160              case CeScheduleType.LAST_DAY:
161                  System.out.println("Recurrence: Last day of each month");
162                  break;
163              case CeScheduleType.NTH_DAY:
164                  System.out.println("Recurrence: Day " +
     sched.getIntervalNthDay() + " of each month");
165                  break;
166              case CeScheduleType.CALENDAR_TEMPLATE:
167                  System.out.println("Recurrence: Calendar template: " +
     calendarMap.get(sched.getCalendarTemplate())));
168                  break;
169              case CeScheduleType.CALENDAR:
170                  System.out.println("Recurrence: Custom calendar");
171                  break;
172              default:
173                  System.out.println("Recurrence: Unknown value");
174          }
175      }
176
177      // Display the destination settings of the instance
178      private static void displayDestination(Map<String, IDestinationPlugin>
             destinationPluginMap,
179          Map<Integer, String> usersGroupsMap, ISchedulingInfo sched)
180      throws SDKException
181      {
182          System.out.print("Destination: ");
183          if(sched.getDestinations().isEmpty())
184              System.out.println("Default Enterprise Location");
185          else
186          {
187              IDestination dest = (IDestination) sched.getDestinations().get(0);
188              String pluginName = dest.getName();
189
```

```
190        IDestinationPlugin plugin = destinationPluginMap.get(pluginName);
191
192        dest.copyToPlugin(plugin);
193
194        if(pluginName.equals(IDiskUnmanaged.PROGID))
195        {
196            System.out.println("File system");
197            if(dest.isSystemDefaultOptionsUsed())
198            {
199                System.out.println("    (job server defaults)");
200            }
201            else
202            {
203                IDiskUnmanagedOptions diskUnmanagedOptions =
204                    (IDiskUnmanagedOptions)plugin.getScheduleOptions();
205                String path = (String)
                       diskUnmanagedOptions
                       .getDestinationFiles()
                       .get(0);
206                String userName = diskUnmanagedOptions.getUserName();
207                if(userName == null)
208                    userName = "(job server default)";
209                String password = diskUnmanagedOptions.isPasswordSet()
210                        ? "xxxx"
211                        : "(job server default";
212                System.out.println("    Path: " + path);
213                System.out.println("    User: " + userName);
214                System.out.println("    Password: " + password);
215            }
216        }
217        else if(pluginName.equals(IFTP.PROGID ))
218        {
219            System.out.println("FTP");
220            if(dest.isSystemDefaultOptionsUsed())
221            {
```

```java
222              System.out.println("   (job server defaults)");
223            }
224        else
225        {
226              IFTPOptions ftpOptions =
227                  (IFTPOptions) plugin.getScheduleOptions();
228              String host = ftpOptions.getServerName();
229              String path = (String)
                      ftpOptions.getDestinationFiles().get(0);
230              String userName = ftpOptions.getUserName();
231              if(userName == null)
232                  userName = "(job server default)";
233              String password = ftpOptions.isPasswordSet()
234                      ? "xxxx"
235                      : "(job server default";
236              System.out.println("   Host: " + host);
237              System.out.println("   Path: " + path);
238              System.out.println("   User: " + userName);
239              System.out.println("   Password: " + password);
240          }
241        }
242        else if(pluginName.equals(IManaged.PROGID ))
243        {
244          System.out.println("BI Inbox");
245          if(dest.isSystemDefaultOptionsUsed())
246          {
247              System.out.println("   (job server defaults)");
248          }
249          else
250          {
251              IManagedOptions managedOptions =
252                  (IManagedOptions) plugin.getScheduleOptions();
253              for(Iterator<Integer> i =
                      managedOptions.getDestinations().iterator();
                      i.hasNext();)
```

```
254                        {
255                            System.out.println("   " +
                                   usersGroupsMap.get(i.next()));
256                        }
257                    }
258                }
259            else if(pluginName.equals(ISMTP.PROGID ))
260            {
261                System.out.println("Email");
262                if(dest.isSystemDefaultOptionsUsed())
263                {
264                    System.out.println("   (job server defaults)");
265                }
266                else
267                {
268                    ISMTPOptions smtpOptions =
269                            (ISMTPOptions) plugin.getScheduleOptions();
270                    String toAddresses = formatAddresses(
271                            smtpOptions.isToAddressesSet(),
272                            smtpOptions.getToAddresses());
273                    String ccAddresses = formatAddresses(
274                            smtpOptions.isCCAddressesSet(),
275                            smtpOptions.getCCAddresses());
276                    String bccAddresses = formatAddresses(
277                            smtpOptions.isBCCAddressesSet(),
278                            smtpOptions.getBCCAddresses());
279                    System.out.println("Server: " +
                               smtpOptions.getServerName());
280                    System.out.println("Sender: " +
                               smtpOptions.getSenderAddress());
281                    System.out.println("To: " + toAddresses);
282                    System.out.println("Cc: " + ccAddresses);
283                    System.out.println("Bcc: " + bccAddresses);
284                    System.out.println("Subject: " + smtpOptions.getSubject());
285                    System.out.println("Message: " + smtpOptions.getMessage());
```

```
286                    }
287                }
288            else if(pluginName.equals(ISFTP.PROGID ))
289                System.out.println("SFTP");
290            else if(pluginName.equals(IStreamWork.PROGID ))
291                System.out.println("SAP Streamwork");
292            else
293                System.out.println("Unknown destination type");
294        }
295    }
296
297
298    // Format a list of email addresses into a semicolon-delimited String
299    private static String formatAddresses(boolean isSet,
           List<String> addresses)
300    {
301        if(!isSet)
302            return "(job server default)";
303        StringBuilder sb = new StringBuilder();
304        for(String address : addresses)
305        {
306            if(sb.length()!=0)
307                sb.append(";");
308            sb.append(address);
309        }
310        return sb.toString();
311    }
312 }
```

Listing 44: The RetrieveSched program

Rescheduling

In the CMC and BI launch pad, all scheduled instances may be rescheduled, regardless of status. Rescheduling is simply the act of creating a new scheduled instance using the same settings as the original instance. Rescheduling can be done with the SDK, too. The method for doing this very similar to creating schedules initially:

1. Retrieve the original instance as an `IInfoObject`.

2. Optionally change the scheduling settings.

3. Call `ISchedulable.schedule()` or `IInfoStore.schedule()`.

In the following code fragment, we are rescheduling the most recent instance of a WebI report having ID 7090:

```
        IInfoObjects ios = infoStore.query("select top 1 si_update_ts from
ci_infoobjects where si_parentid = 7090 order by si_id desc");


    if(ios.size() > 0)

    {

        ISchedulable io = (ISchedulable) ios.get(0);

        io.schedule();

    }
```

This creates a new scheduled instance, using the exact same scheduling options that were used for the original schedule. Of course, we could instead use the `IInfoStore.schedule()` method, and saved a couple of lines:

```
        IInfoObjects ios = infoStore.query("select top 1 si_update_ts from
ci_infoobjects where si_parentid = 7090 order by si_id desc");


    infoStore.schedule(ios);
```

There are a couple of considerations when rescheduling instances. One is that the instance's original recurrence and event settings are used, unless changed. Consider a report that is scheduled to run daily and wait for an event named *Data Load Complete*. This report fails one day due to a source database problem, and once the issue is resolved, we use the SDK to reschedule the report using one of the methods above. Since the original scheduled instance was set to wait for an event, the rescheduled instance will, too. We wanted the rescheduled report to run immediately, but it will instead wait until the event fires again before it runs[150].

In order to achieve the desired result of the rescheduled report running immediately, we need to change the recurrence and event settings when rescheduling. To clear the dependency on any events, we need to call `ISchedulingInfo.getDependencies().clear()`. Also, to ensure that the new instance runs immediately, we should call `ISchedulingInfo.setRightNow(true)`[151]. Our code now looks like the following:

---

150 This isn't unique to the SDK – if we were to reschedule this InfoObject in the CMC, the same thing would happen (we would have to remove the Events in order for it to run immediately).

```
        IInfoObjects ios = infoStore.query("select top 1 si_update_ts from
ci_infoobjects where si_parentid = 7090 order by si_id desc");


        if(ios.size() > 0)

        {

              ISchedulable io = (ISchedulable) ios.get(0);

              ISchedulingInfo sched = io.getSchedulingInfo();

              sched.setRightNow(true);

              sched.getDependencies().clear();

              io.schedule();

        }
```

The other consideration to keep in mind when rescheduling is the owner of the instance. By default, when an instance is created, it is owned by the user that performed the action. This is true for newly-created instances as well as those that are reschedules of other instances.

Consider the following: In the CMC, Ethel creates a new one-time schedule of a report. The schedule, naturally, is owned by *Ethel*. Once the schedule has completed, Fred executes an SDK program (similar to the above) that reschedules Ethel's instance. The program that Fred executes logs in to the CMS with his credentials, and so the instance that is created is owned by Fred.

This *may* not present a problem. If, however, the original schedule that Ethel created was set to distribute to *BI Inbox*, with default settings, then the completed instance is sent to Ethel's own inbox. The rescheduled instance, however, is sent to Fred's inbox, as he is the owner of the instance. Also, if Fred and Ethel have different security permissions on the report, or the report's data source user row-level security, then Fred's rescheduled instance may produce different data that Ethel's.

Let's consider another, more real-world example. On one particular day, a database outage results in the failure of hundreds of Web Intelligence reports. It would be fairly easy to create an SDK program to reschedule all the failed reports to run again. But if the reports were scheduled by several different people, the rescheduled reports may not produce the correct data, or be sent to the correct recipients. In this case, we need to ensure that the rescheduled instances are owned by the same user as the instances they are being rescheduled from.

Fortunately, this is easy to do. We simply need to call ISchedulingInfo.setScheduleOnBehalfOf(), and pass it the original user's InfoObject ID, which can be retrieved from IInfoObject.getOwnerID().

---

151 This isn't strictly necessary when rescheduling a failed one-time instance, or an instance created from a recurring schedule. But it ensures that the new instance will run immediately if the instance being rescheduled is a recurring instance.

In the following code fragment, we are retrieving all failed instances that ran during a specified time period, then creating a new scheduled instance for each one. The rescheduled instance assumes the same owner as the instance it was rescheduled from.

```
        IInfoObjects ios = infoStore.query("select * from ci_infoobjects where
si_schedule_status = 3 and si_update_ts between '2017.05.28 00.00.00' and '2017.05.29
00.00.00'");


    for(Object o : ios)

    {

        IInfoObject io = (IInfoObject) o;

        ISchedulingInfo sched = io.getSchedulingInfo();

        sched.setRightNow(true);

        sched.getDependencies().clear();

        sched.setScheduleOnBehalfOf(io.getOwnerID());

        ISchedulable is = (ISchedulable) io;

        is.schedule();

    }
```

In order for this to work, the user account that executes the program must have permission to schedule reports on behalf of the owner of the original (failed) instance. If not, then the rescheduled instance will fail due to insufficient permissions.

Let's make one more tweak the code above. In our scenario, we're rescheduling a bunch of reports that failed due to a source database problem. We don't want to leave failed instances lying around that have been successfully rescheduled, as it might confuse anyone looking at the reports' history. So, once the instance is rescheduled, we can delete it. We simply call `IInfoObject.deleteNow()` once have `schedule()` has been called:

```
        IInfoObjects ios = infoStore.query("select * from ci_infoobjects where
si_schedule_status = 3 and si_update_ts between '2017.05.28 00.00.00' and '2017.05.29
00.00.00'");


        for(Object o : ios)

        {

            IInfoObject io = (IInfoObject) o;

            ISchedulingInfo sched = io.getSchedulingInfo();

            sched.setRightNow(true);

            sched.getDependencies().clear();

            sched.setScheduleOnBehalfOf(io.getOwnerID());

            ISchedulable is = (ISchedulable) io;
```

```
        is.schedule();

        io.deleteNow();

    }
```

Now, the original failed instances are removed and replaced with new one-time instances.

Changing Existing Instances

If a recurring or pending instance needs to be changed, there are two ways to do it:

- Reschedule the instance and delete the original one

- Modify the instance and save

Prior to XI3, saving changes to instances was not possible, and so only the first option was available[152]. For this reason, many code examples in which instances are modified will actually use the reschedule/delete method. However, it is now possible to simply made the desired changes to an instance and save it.

For example, we have a large number of reports scheduled to run every hour, which we want to change to every two hours.

---

152 In fact, as of BI4.2, the CMC and BI launch pad interfaces do not support changing recurring or pending instances, only "rescheduling" and optionally deleting the rescheduled instance.

We can accomplish this by simply making the desired modification to the identified instances, and saving:

```
        IInfoObjects ios = infoStore.query("select * from ci_infoobjects where
si_recurring = 1  and si_scheduleinfo.si_schedule_interval_hours = 1");


    for(Object o : ios)

    {

        IInfoObject io = (IInfoObject) o;

        ISchedulingInfo sched = io.getSchedulingInfo();

        sched.setIntervalHours(2);

        System.out.println("Changing schedule for: " + io.getTitle());

        io.save();

    }
```

If you really want to use the reschedule method to make changes to pending/recurring instances, then the method is similar to our prior rescheduling examples:

```
        IInfoObjects ios = infoStore.query("select * from ci_infoobjects where
si_recurring = 1  and si_scheduleinfo.si_schedule_interval_hours = 1");


    for(Object o : ios)

    {

        IInfoObject io = (IInfoObject) o;

        ISchedulingInfo sched = io.getSchedulingInfo();

        sched.setIntervalHours(2);

        System.out.println("Changing schedule for: " + io.getTitle());

        ((ISchedulable)io).schedule();

        io.deleteNow();

    }
```

However, the same caveat applies regarding ownership of rescheduled instances: they are owned by the user account that executed the program, and not the original owner of the instance. To retain the original ownership, we need to call `setScheduleOnBehalfOf()`:

```
        IInfoObjects ios = infoStore.query("select * from ci_infoobjects where
si_recurring = 1  and si_scheduleinfo.si_schedule_interval_hours = 1");


        for(Object o : ios)
        {
            IInfoObject io = (IInfoObject) o;
            ISchedulingInfo sched = io.getSchedulingInfo();
            sched.setIntervalHours(2);
            System.out.println("Changing schedule for: " + io.getTitle());
            sched.setScheduleOnBehalfOf(io.getOwnerID());
            ((ISchedulable)io).schedule();
            io.deleteNow();
        }
```

Sending Documents

Documents can be distributed immediately to destinations, similar to scheduling (but without being refreshed). In BI launch pad, this is accomplished via the *Send* menu button, and in CMC via the *Organize* → *Send* menu. The same destinations that are available for scheduling are also available for sending: BI Inbox, FTP, SFTP, Email, and File Location.

The process for sending is very similar to the steps described for scheduling beginning on page 499:

1. Retrieve the *destination plugin* from the CMS for the desired destination type (Email, File System, etc.), using a CMS query (this only needs to be done once per program execution). The plugin will be a subinterface of `IDestinationPlugin`: either `IDiskUnmanaged`, `IFTP`, `IManaged`, `ISFTP`, `ISMTP`, or `IStreamWork`.

2. Retrieve the document to be sent, as an `IInfoObject` or subinterface.

3. Retrieve the *destination scheduling options* object from the `IDestinationPlugin` retrieved in Step 1. This object will be a subinterface of `IDestinationScheduleOptions`, and is what's used to actually specify the destination settings. It should be cast to one of the following: `IDiskUnmanagedOptions`, `IFTPOptions`, `IManagedOptions`, `ISFTPOptions`, `ISMTPOptions`, or `IStreamWorkOptions`.

4. Set the destination settings as appropriate in the `IDestinationScheduleOptions` object that was obtained in the previous step.

5. With the IInfoObject object of the document to be sent (from Step 2), retrieve an IDestination object by casting the IInfoObject to ISendale and calling ISendable.getSendToDestination().

6. Apply the destination options (as set in Step 4) to the IDestination object by calling IDestination.setFromPlugin(), passing it the IDestinationScheduleOptions object from Step 4.

7. Finally, send the document by calling IInfoStore.sendTo(), passing in the IInfoObjects collection containing the document to be sent.

The following code fragment all the WebI documents in folder 5155 to Fred's inbox (which we have already looked up and found to be ID 4104).

```
25    IManaged inboxPlugin = (IManaged) infoStore.query("select * from
      ci_systemobjects where si_plugin_object = 1 and si_kind = '" + IManaged.KIND +
      "'").get(0);

26

27    IInfoObjects ios = infoStore.query("select * from ci_infoobjects where
      si_parentid = 5155 and si_kind = 'webi'");

28

29    for(Object o : infoObjects)

30    {

31        IInfoObject io = (IInfoObject)o;

32        ISendable sendable = (ISendable)infoObjects.get(0);

33        IDestination dest = sendable.getSendToDestination();

34

35        IManagedOptions inboxOptions = (IManagedOptions)
      inboxPlugin.getScheduleOptions();

36        inboxOptions.getDestinations().add(4104);

37

38        dest.setFromPlugin(inboxPlugin);

39    }

40

41    infoStore.sendTo(infoObjects);
```

Sending to other destination types (email, FTP, etc.) is done in exactly the same way, using the appropriate plugin and scheduling options interfaces.

There is another way to send documents to BI inboxes, using the getDeliverToInboxPrincipals() method of ISendable in conjunction with the deliverToInboxes() method of IInfoStore. This has the benefit of not requiring a separate query to retrieve the inbox plugin, but it does require that the InfoObjects to be sent are first copied to new InfoObjects.

The following fragment performs the same action as the previous one, but using `deliverToInbox()`:

```
25        IInfoObjects infoObjects = infoStore.query("select * from ci_infoobjects
   where si_parentid = 5155 and si_kind = 'webi'");

26        IInfoObjects newIOs = infoStore.newInfoObjectCollection();

27

28        for(Object o : infoObjects)

29        {

30            IInfoObject io = (IInfoObject)o;

31            IInfoObject newIO = newIOs.copy(io,
                    IInfoObjects.CopyModes.COPY_NEW_OBJECT_NEW_FILES);

32            ISendable sendable = (ISendable)newIO;

33            sendable.getDeliverToInboxPrincipals().add(4104);

34        }

35        infoStore.deliverToInbox(newIOs);
```

On line 31, we are copying each report `IInfoObject` to the new `IInfoObjects` collection, `newIOs`. Note that we are casting this new object to `ISendable` before adding in the destination inbox ID (4104).

A couple of additional notes regarding the difference between scheduling and sending:

- When scheduling, the destinations may be left blank. This indicates that the destination is the *Default Enterprise Location* (a historical instance) and the document will not be distributed to any other destination. When sending, however, an empty destination will result in no action – no document is sent.

- Casting `IInfoObject` to `ISendable` is different than casting to `ISchedulable`. While the `IInfoObject` subinterfaces (ex. `IWebI`) extend `ISchedulable`, they do not extend `ISendable`. So, while it is possible to see which InfoObject kinds are schedulable (by looking at "All Known Subinterfaces" in the Javadocs), the same is not true for `ISendable` – there is no direct way to determine which InfoObject kinds are sendable. In general (at least from what we've seen), all InfoObject kinds that are *schedulable* are also *sendable*. So, we can assume that if an `IInfoObject` subinterface extends `ISchedulable`, then its associated concrete classes will implement `ISendable`. That is, since `IWebi` extends `ISchedulable`, we can assume that it can be cast to `ISendable`.

- If a scheduled instance fails, the instance will assume a status of *Failed* and be visible in the parent document's history. If there is a failure when **sending** a document, however, the failure will appear in the Temporary Storage folder.

Chapter Review

- Scheduling of reports is a powerful feature of SAP BusinessObjects; using the SDK to assist with the management of schedules adds even more value.

- Scheduling documents involves three steps: 1) retrieve the InfoObject to be scheduled, 2) optionally set scheduling parameters, and 3) submit the InfoObject for scheduling.

- There is a large number of optional scheduling parameters; most of these are set via the `ISchedulingInfo` interface.

- Schedules can be created to run on a number of different recurrence patterns, including daily, hourly, monthly, etc., as well as on a custom calendar. The default scheduling option is Now, which is set with `ISchedulingInfo.setRightNow()`; other recurrence patterns are set with `ISchedulingInfo.setType()`.

- The schedulable document kinds (Web Intelligence, Crystal Reports, etc.) each have their own unique scheduling options for such things as output format, parameters, and caching.

- Documents can be set to distribute to destinations including email, file server, FTP, SFTP, and BI inbox. The SDK can be used to set all of the options associated with these destinations, although the process for doing so requires a few steps.

- Existing scheduled instances of any status can be rescheduled; a new pending instance is created while the old one is retained. The newly-scheduled instance can have the same settings as the original schedule, or they can be modified as needed.

- In addition to being scheduled, documents can be sent directly to destinations.

Quiz

1. An InfoObject is scheduled by calling:

   a) `IInfoObject.schedule()`

   b) `ISchedulable.schedule()`

   c) `ISchedulingInfo.schedule()`

   d) `IInfoStore.schedule()`

2. Which of the following is **not** a scheduling parameter?

   a) Title

   b) Recurrence

   c) Start Time

   d) Priority

    e) Destination

    f) Server Group

3. True/False: The value passed to `ISchedulingInfo.setIntervalMinutes()` **must** be less than 60.

4. To schedule a report to run multiple times with the security contexts of several users, which method should be used?

    a) `ISchedulingInfo.setScheduleOnBehalfOf()`

    b) `ISchedulingInfo.setMultiPassObjects()`

    c) Either

    d) Neither

5. The SDK call that performs the same action as checking off the "Keep an instance in history" option in the scheduling dialog is:

    a) `IDestinations.setKeepInHistory(true)`

    b) `IDestinations.setKeepInHistory(false)`

    c) `IDestinations.setCleanup(true)`

    d) `IDestinations.setCleanup(false)`

6. Which of the following is not a valid value of `ISchedulingInfo.ScheduleStatus`?

    a) `COMPLETE`

    b) `FAILURE`

    c) `RECURRING`

    d) `PAUSED`

7. Which of the following scheduling attributes are **not** retained when rescheduling an existing instance?

    a) Recurrence

    b) Destination format

    c) Events

    d) Title

    e) Owner

Answers on page 673.

Chapter 18 - Security

The SAP BusinessObjects platform has a robust, mature security model, capable of supporting a large number of independent user groups, each with differing needs for access to content and functional usage. Through the use of inheritance, built-in access levels, custom access levels, and advanced rights, it is possible to easily implement a security model of significant flexibility.

Although the CMC provides a user-friendly system for managing security, it is sometimes necessary to perform security tasks that exceed its capability. As a simple example, you may want to identify all objects for which a particular user has explicitly-assigned rights. Or, to comply with regulatory requirements, you may need to identify all individual user IDs that have implicit or explicit access to a particular report. Although the CMC can assist with these examples, the SDK can do them much more efficiently, particularly when similar demands arise on a regular basis.

A few security-related points to get out of the way upfront:

- A sound understanding of the BI Platform security concepts is critical to using the SDK to query or (especially) modify security. Two good resources are the *Administrator's Guide* and *BI Platform Security for Mere Mortals* (http://www.forumtopics.com/busobj/viewtopic.php?t=229912).

- To reiterate what was mentioned earlier regarding modifying content in the CMS, doing so with security can potentially result in a "bricked" SAP BusinessObjects system that is completely unusable. *Make sure you know what you are doing before you modify security with the SDK.*

- Unlike everything we've covered so far regarding InfoObjects, security rights are not implemented in InfoObject properties. You won't see security rights listed anywhere in the results of a CMS query, so it is not possible to use a simple CMS query to list the rights applied to an object.

- Security is implemented with attributes on InfoObjects, which define the principals and roles/rights that are assigned. We mention this only because security in pre-XI BusinessObjects was the inverse – users and groups had attributes that defined the objects that they had been granted access to.

And some terms:

- A *principal* refers to a user or user group for which security rights have been assigned.

- A *role* refers to a predefined access level (*View, View on Demand, Schedule, Full Control*) or a custom access level. Strangely, in the SDK, the term "Custom Role" is used to describe both predefined and custom roles. *Role, Security Role,* and *Access Level* are synonymous.

- A *right* is a discrete access permission, such as *View objects, Schedule to destinations,* and many more. Roles contain groups of assigned rights.

- *Explicit* rights and roles are assigned to a specific principal on a specific InfoObject. *Inherited* rights and roles apply to an InfoObject but explicitly assigned to an ancestral InfoObject or the principal's ancestral user group. The *effective* rights that a principal has on an InfoObject are calculated based on the explicit rights and roles that the principal has, combined with any inherited rights and roles.

- There is a difference between **assigning** a right and **granting** a right. When we refer to *assigning* a right for a principal on an InfoObject, that right may be either *granted* or *denied*. *Roles*, on the other hand, are simply assigned or not assigned.

Managing Security

To manage security for an InfoObject, we first need to retrieve it as an `IInfoObject` object. Once retrieved, we can retrieve an `ISecurityInfo2` object via `IInfoObject.getSecurityInfo2()`[153]. All security is managed through this `ISecurityInfo2` object.

Although security is not applied via InfoObject properties, it is still necessary to perform a CMS query just like the previous examples in this book. The CMS query must return at least one property in order to be valid syntax (`SI_ID`, usually), but of course, other properties may be included in the query if needed for other operations in the program.

The following code is the beginning of the *GetSec* program. At this point, its only purpose is to access the `ISecurityInfo2` object for a root-level public folder named *Reports*.

```
 1  package bosdkbook;
 2
 3  import com.crystaldecisions.sdk.framework.CrystalEnterprise;
 4  import com.crystaldecisions.sdk.framework.IEnterpriseSession;
 5  import com.crystaldecisions.sdk.framework.ISessionMgr;
 6  import com.crystaldecisions.sdk.occa.infostore.IInfoObject;
 7  import com.crystaldecisions.sdk.occa.infostore.IInfoObjects;
 8  import com.crystaldecisions.sdk.occa.infostore.IInfoStore;
 9  import com.crystaldecisions.sdk.occa.infostore.ISecurityInfo2;
10
11  public class GetSec {
12
```

---

153 Yes, there is an `ISecurityInfo` interface and `IInfoObject.getSecurityInfo()` method. These are present only for compatibility with XIr2 and are now deprecated.

```
13      public static void main(String[] args) throws Exception

14    {

15        ISessionMgr sessionManager = CrystalEnterprise.getSessionMgr();

16        IEnterpriseSession session = sessionManager.logon ("administrator",
   "xxxx", "192.168.56.102", "secEnterprise");

17

18        IInfoStore infoStore = (IInfoStore) session.getService ("","InfoStore");

19

20        IInfoObjects ios = infoStore.query("select si_id from ci_infoobjects
   where si_parentid = 23 and si_name = 'reports'");

21

22        for(Object o : ios)

23        {

24            IInfoObject io = (IInfoObject) o;

25            ISecurityInfo2 sec = io.getSecurityInfo2();

26        }

27    }

28 }
```

Listing 45: The GetSec program

The ISecurityInfo2 interface includes methods that enable access to roles, rights, and instance limits (whether effective or explicitly-assigned).

There are several different ways to access the assigned security rights, as there are different scenarios in which this information would be used. In general, the scenarios and associated methods are:

To determine if the current user or another user has a specific effective right for a specific InfoObject. For example, to know if the current user has permission to delete a specific InfoObject.	Use the checkRight()/checkRights() methods.
To obtain a list of all security rights that a user or group has for an InfoObject (whether inherited or explicitly-assigned)... or, to know from which ancestral source a principal inherited a specific right... or, to know which roles a principal has inherited an InfoObject	For all principals who have effective rights on this InfoObject from parent folders, use getEffectivePrincipals(). To get this information for a specific user or group, use getAnyPrincipal().

To obtain a list of principals who have explicitly-assigned roles or rights…	Use getExplicitPrincipals().
or, to assign roles or advanced rights to a principal.	

There are many deprecated methods in ISecurityInfo2 as of BI4 due to some of the security enhancements in that version. We are not covering those. The remaining methods are:

Package com.crystaldecisions.sdk.occa.infostore
Interface *ISecurityInfo2*

boolean	checkRight(RightDescriptor right, boolean useCache)
	Returns true if the current user has been granted the specified right for this InfoObject, or false if not.
boolean	checkRight(RightDescriptor right, int principal, boolean useCache)
	Returns true if the specified principal has been granted the specified right for this InfoObject, or false if not.
boolean[]	checkRights(RightDescriptor[] right, boolean useCache)
	Returns an array of booleans indicating whether the current user has been granted the specified rights for this InfoObject.
boolean[]	checkRights(RightDescriptor[] right, int principal, boolean useCache)
	Returns an array of booleans indicating whether the specified principal has been granted the specified rights for this InfoObject.
IEffectivePrincipal	getAnyPrincipal(int principal)
	Retrieves the effective rights that the specified principal has been assigned for this InfoObject.
IEffectivePrincipals	getEffectivePrincipals()
	Retrieves a collection of IEffectivePrincipal objects, representing all principals that have effective (explicit or inherited) rights for this InfoObject.
IExplicitPrincipals	getExplicitPrincipals()
	Retrieves a collection of IExplicitPrincipal objects, representing the principals (users or groups) that have explicitly-assigned rights for this InfoObject.
IPluginBasedRightIDs	getKnownRightsByPlugin()

	Retrieves a collection of the rights and limits that are applicable for this kind of InfoObject.
`IRoleID[]`	`getKnownRoles()`
	Retrieves a collection of IRoleID objects representing the available roles (predefined and custom access levels) in the system.
`IExplicitPrincip als`	`newExplicitPrincipals()`
	Creates a new, empty `IExplicitPrincipals` collection.

Class/Interface 51: ISecurityInfo2

We will first cover the `checkRight`/`checkRights` methods, then explicit security, effective security, and finally instance limits.

Checking rights

The four `checkRight`/`checkRights` methods in `ISecurityInfo2` are used to evaluate a principal's effective security access to *this* InfoObject (that is, the `IInfoObject` to which this `ISecurityInfo2` object is associated with).   All four of these methods require a `RightDescriptor` parameter.   `RightDescriptor` is a simple class that is used to specifically identify a right.   We'll cover it in more detail shortly

The first form of `checkRight` returns `true` or `false`, signifying whether the current user has the specified right to this InfoObject.   We can add lines to our *GetSec* program to display whether the current user has *Delete* permission:

```
26          RightDescriptor rightDesc = new
                RightDescriptor(CeSecurityID.Right.DELETE,"",false);

27          System.out.println(sec.checkRight(rightDesc, true));
```

Here, we are creating a new `RightDescriptor` object which identifies the right we want to evaluate.   Since we are logging in as *Administrator,* this always returns true.   If we log in as a different user (Fred, for example), we will get a `true` or `false` depending on Fred's permissions on the *Reports* folder.

The second parameter in `checkRight` is a `boolean` that specifies whether or not to use the rights cache.   Unlike most of the calls in the `IInfoObject` interface, querying an InfoObject's security requires a network call to the CMS.   Thus, caching the result of security queries can improve program execution time by reducing the number of network calls that need to be made.   However, using the cache introduces the possible risk of receiving stale information. This is rarely a concern, except in scenarios where it is likely that an InfoObject's security rights could be modified at the exact same time that the SDK program is running.   So we recommend passing `true` for `useCache`, unless it is critical that the most current security right is retrieved.

The second form of `checkRight` is similar to the first and is used to query the security rights for a specified principal. The principal can be a user or user group and is specified with the principal's InfoObject ID. Knowing that *Fred*'s ID is 4104, we can use this form of `checkRight` to check if Fred has been granted the *Delete* right[154].

```
26          RightDescriptor rightDesc = new
                RightDescriptor(CeSecurityID.Right.DELETE,"",false);

27          System.out.println(sec.checkRight(rightDesc, 4104, true));
```

The `checkRight` methods all evaluate the *effective* rights granted to a principal. That is, all explicitly-assigned roles and advanced rights are considered, as well as inherited roles and advanced rights. Simply put, `checkRight` returns an indicator that tells whether or not the principal has the specified permission, regardless of where the right may have been inherited from.

To illustrate, we'll assign the *View* access level to the *Finance* user group for the *Reports* folder. In the CMC, the security for *Reports* looks like the following:

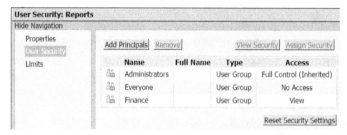

Objects in the Reports folder inherit the same security assignment (unless overridden). If we look at the security for the *Sales* subfolder, we'll see that rights have been inherited from *Reports*:

Since Fred is a member of the *Finance* group, he inherits the View access level. We can test this by changing the CMS query in *GetSec* to return the *Sales* folder:

```
20      IInfoObjects ios = infoStore.query("select si_id from ci_infoobjects
        where si_name = 'sales'");

21
```

---

154 The result of this call is the same as calling the first form of `checkRights()` when executed as *Fred*.

```
22          for(Object o : ios)
23          {
24              IInfoObject io = (IInfoObject) o;
25              ISecurityInfo2 sec = io.getSecurityInfo2();
26              RightDescriptor rightDesc = new
                    RightDescriptor(CeSecurityID.Right.VIEW,"",false);
27              System.out.println(sec.checkRight(rightDesc, 4104, true));
28          }
29      }
```

This displays true since Fred has inherited this right. If we change line 26 to evaluate whether Fred has the *Edit* right...

```
26                  RightDescriptor(CeSecurityID.Right.EDIT,"",false);
```

...then we will get a result of false since *Fred* has only been granted the *View* access level.

The two checkRights methods perform the same function as checkRight but allow for multiple rights to be queried in a single call. This can improve runtime since only a single network call to the CMS needs to be made. The return value of these two methods is an array of boolean values; the order of the values in the array is aligned with the original order of the RightDescriptor[] array that was passed in.

In the following example, we use checkRights to evaluate Fred's *View, Edit,* and *Delete* permissions.

```
20          IInfoObjects ios = infoStore.query("select si_id from ci_infoobjects
    where si_name = 'sales'");
21
22          for(Object o : ios)
23          {
24              IInfoObject io = (IInfoObject) o;
25              ISecurityInfo2 sec = io.getSecurityInfo2();
26              RightDescriptor viewRight = new
                    RightDescriptor(CeSecurityID.Right.VIEW,"",false);
27              RightDescriptor editRight = new
                    RightDescriptor(CeSecurityID.Right.EDIT,"",false);
28              RightDescriptor deleteRight = new
                    RightDescriptor(CeSecurityID.Right.DELETE,"",false);
29              RightDescriptor rights[] = new
                    RightDescriptor[] {viewRight,editRight,deleteRight};
30              boolean result[] = sec.checkRights(rights, 4104,false);
```

31	`        System.`*`out`*`.println("Has View right: " + result[0]);`
32	`        System.`*`out`*`.println("Has Edit right: " + result[1]);`
33	`        System.`*`out`*`.println("Has Delete right: " + result[2]);`
34	`    }`
35	`}`

Since Fred has *View* right to the Sales folder, but not *Edit* or *Delete*, the result that is displayed is:

```
Has View right: true
Has Edit right: false
Has Delete right: false
```

The RightDescriptor Class

In the examples above, we used the `RightDescriptor` class to specifically identify the security right to be evaluated. This specificity is needed because the same security right ID (an integer) may have different meanings depending on the type of plugin (kind) it is applied to. Also, a right may apply to the InfoObject itself, its children, or both. Finally, a right may be granted such that it only applies to InfoObjects that the principal owns.

The `RightDescriptor` class has the following constructors[155]:

Package com.crystaldecisions.sdk.occa.infostore
Class *RightDescriptor*
extends RightIDDescriptor

Constructors

`RightDescriptor(int rightID, java.lang.Object kind, boolean isOwner)`

> Creates a `RightDescriptor` using the security right ID, the security right's parent plugin, and the owner flag. See the next constructor for field definitions.
>
> This is equivalent to calling the second form of the constructor with "this" for `scope` and "Any" for `applicableObjectType`.

`RightDescriptor(int rightID, java.lang.Object kind, boolean isOwner, java.lang.String scope, java.lang.Object applicableObjectType)`

---

155 There are others, but they have been deprecated since BI4 and are not covered here.

Creates a `RightDescriptor` using the security right ID, the security right's parent plugin, the owner flag, the scope (parent, children, or both), and the InfoObject kind to which the right applies.

- `rightID` is an `int`. The values of **system** rights are in `CeSecurityID.Right`.
- `kind` is an `Object`. It may be an `Integer` identifying the plugin's type ID (e.g., its `SI_OBTYPE`), or a `String` containing the plugin's *kind* (e.g., its `SI_KIND`). For system rights, pass either an `Integer` 0 or an empty string (""").
- `isOwner` is a `boolean`. It determines whether the assignment applies only to objects that the user owns.
- `scope` is a `String`. The possible values are in `CeSecurityOptions.RightScope`.
- `applicableObjectType` is an `Object`. It may be an `Integer` identifying the plugin's type ID (e.g., its `SI_OBTYPE`) or a `String` containing the plugin's *kind* (e.g., its `SI_KIND`). To apply to all kinds, pass an `Integer` 0 or `CeSecurityOptions.ANY_OBJTYPE` (which is the constant string "Any")

```
RightDescriptor(RightDescriptor right)
```

Creates a copy of an existing `RightDescriptor` object.

Class/Interface 52: RightDescriptor

The `kind` parameter indicates the source of the specified `rightID`. The source may be either the system (for general rights) or a plugin such as Web Intelligence. The system rights may be applied to InfoObjects of any kind, and includes the commonly-used rights such as *View*, *Edit*, *Delete*, *Schedule*, etc. Since these rights are owned by the system, they do not have a parent kind. When referencing these rights in a `RightDescriptor` constructor, we pass an empty string ("") or a zero for `kind`:

```
new RightDescriptor(CeSecurityID.Right.EDIT,"",false);
```

In addition to these system rights, many InfoObject kinds have their own set of available security rights. For example, for Web Intelligence, we can assign rights to *Edit Query*, *Refresh the report's data*, *Save as PDF*, and more.

Unfortunately, there's currently no constant values class for kind-specific rights like `CeSecurityID.Right` for system rights, so obtaining the integer right ID for a particular security right is not as straightforward. You will need to either iterate through all rights in a plugin or check the rights of an existing InfoObject to identify the ID.

The following code can be used to list the kind-specific rights for a particular plugin (*WebI* in this case):

```
20          IInfoObject plugin = (IInfoObject) infoStore.query("select si_id from
     ci_systemobjects where si_plugin_object = 1 and si_kind = 'webi'").get(0);

21          IPluginBasedRightIDs pluginRights =
                plugin.getSecurityInfo2().getKnownRightsByPlugin();

22

23          Map<String,Set<IRightID>> pluginRightMap =
                pluginRights.getPluginRights();

24

25          Set<IRightID> webiRights = pluginRightMap.get(IWebi.PROGID);

26

27          for(IRightID webiRight : webiRights)

28          {

29              if(!webiRight.getRightPluginKind().equals(IWebi.KIND))

30                  continue;

31              System.out.println(webiRight.getBaseID() + " " +
                    webiRight.getDescription(Locale.getDefault()));

32          }
```

This lists the kind-specific rights for WebI, along with the right IDs:

```
3 Refresh the report's data
3 Refresh the report's data (owner right)
5 Edit Query
5 Edit Query (owner right)
6 Refresh List of Values
6 Refresh List of Values (owner right)
7 Use Lists of Values
7 Use Lists of Values (owner right)
8 View SQL
8 View SQL (owner right)
9 Save as Excel or Text
9 Save as Excel or Text (owner right)
10 Save as PDF
10 Save as PDF (owner right)
11 Save as CSV
11 Save as CSV (owner right)
60 Export the report's data
60 Export the report's data (owner right)
```

To perform this query for different kinds, just change the *IWebi* references on lines 20, 25, and 29.

With this result, we find that the ID of the *Edit Query* right is 5^{156}. To check if a user has been

---

156 Although kind-specific right IDs are not defined in any SDK constant class, they are consistent across individual installations (at least as of BI4). So, Webi's *Edit Query* right always has an ID of 5.

granted the *Edit Query* right, we would create the following `RightDescriptor`:

```
new RightDescriptor(5,IWebi.KIND,false);
```

The applicableObjectType Parameter

While the `kind` parameter identifies the source (parent) of a specific right, the `applicableObjectType` parameter defines which InfoObject kinds the right applies to. Generally, applied system rights apply to all InfoObject kinds – if a principal is granted the *View* right for a folder, then the principal can see the folder itself and all of its children, regardless of kind. However, it is possible to grant that *View* right (or any other system right) for only specific kinds. We could, for example, grant the *View* right only for Folders and Web Intelligence documents. By doing so, the principal will not see objects of any other kind (Crystal Reports, Hyperlinks, etc.). In the CMC, these rights are assigned to specific kinds via the *Content* category and the *General rights for...* panel:

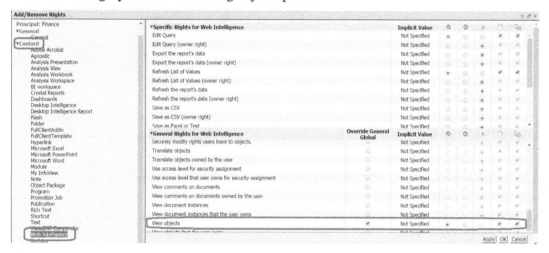

We can also explicitly deny rights in the same way. In the following example, we have granted the *View* right for *Web Intelligence* but denied it for *Crystal Reports*:

To check whether a right has been granted for a specific kind, pass its kind name in the `applicableObjectType` parameter. The following constructor creates a `RighDescriptor` object that specifically references the *View* right for Web Intelligence objects:

```
new RightDescriptor(CeSecurityID.Right.VIEW,
    0,
    false,
    CeSecurityOptions.RightScope.CURRENT_OBJECT,
    IWebi.KIND);
```

We can then use this to check if Fred has *View* rights for *WebI* and *Crystal* objects in the *Sales* folder:

```
20        IInfoObjects ios = infoStore.query("select si_id from ci_infoobjects
          where si_name = 'sales'");

21

22        for(Object o : ios)

23        {

24            IInfoObject io = (IInfoObject) o;

25            ISecurityInfo2 sec = io.getSecurityInfo2();

26

27            RightDescriptor webiRight = new
                  RightDescriptor(CeSecurityID.Right.VIEW,
                      0,
                      false,
                      CeSecurityOptions.RightScope.CURRENT_OBJECT,
                      IWebi.KIND);

28            RightDescriptor webiRight = new
                  RightDescriptor(CeSecurityID.Right.VIEW,
                      0,
                      false,
                      CeSecurityOptions.RightScope.CURRENT_OBJECT,
                      IReport.KIND);

29

30            System.out.println("View Webi: " + sec.checkRight(webiRight,
              4104,true));

31            System.out.println("View Crystal: " + sec.checkRight(crRight,
              4104,true));

32        }

33    }
```

Since we had granted the *View* right for *WebI* but not *Crystal*, the output of the above is:

```
View Webi: true
View Crystal: false
```

If we change the security settings to remove the kind-specific assignments and instead just grant the general View right:

...then the above program produces:

```
View Webi: true
View Crystal: true
```

...which is correct since the assigned security is granting the View permissions for all InfoObject kinds.

Use the constant value `CeSecurityOptions.ANY_OBJTYPE` in the `applicableObjectType` parameter to evaluate general-level assigned rights. Since we just assigned the View right at the general level, the following code displays `true`:

```
27          RightDescriptor genRight = new
                RightDescriptor(CeSecurityID.Right.VIEW,
                    0,
                    false,
                    CeSecurityOptions.RightScope.CURRENT_OBJECT,
                    CeSecurityOptions.ANY_OBJTYPE);

28          System.out.println("View All: " + sec.checkRight(genRight,
     4104,true));
```

In summary, to check if a right has been granted at the general level, either use the first (short) form of the `RightDescriptor` constructor or use the second form with `CeSecurityOptions.ANY_OBJTYPE`. To check if a right has been granted for a particular kind, use the second form and specify the kind name for `applicableObjectType`.

If a type-specific right is specified via the `kind` parameter, the same kind does not **need** to be specified in the `applicableObjectType` parameter. For example, we'll grant WebI's *Edit Query* right for the Reports folder:

Collection	Type	Right Name	Status	Apply To
General	General	View objects	⊘	🗎
Content	Web Intelligence	Edit Query	⊘	🗎

We can then check for this right with the following:

```
27          RightDescriptor editQueryRight = new
                RightDescriptor(5,
                    IWebi.KIND,
                    false,
                    CeSecurityOptions.RightScope.CURRENT_OBJECT,
                    CeSecurityOptions.ANY_OBJTYPE);

28          System.out.println(sec.checkRight(editQueryRight,4104,true));
```

Here, we are saying that the parent of the indicated right (5) is WebI. However, the right may be applied to any InfoObject kind.

Incidentally, the documented way to specify "any InfoObject kind" in the `applicableObjectType` parameter is the `CeSecurityOptions.ANY_OBJTYPE` constant. However, all of the following values are synonymous:

- `CeSecurityOptions.ANY_OBJTYPE`

- null

- 0

- ""

- "Any"

Of course, using the documented method is recommended, but we mention this here in case you come across the other values.

The isOwner Parameter

The `isOwner` property in `RightDescriptor` is only needed when assigning rights to an object, not when checking rights with `checkRights`. So, this property may be set to `false` when using `checkRights`.

Scope

By default, a security right applies to the object to which it is assigned, as well as the object's descendants. It is possible, however, to assign a right that only applies to the object **or** to its descendants.

An example of a requirement for this feature may be a folder that contains a large number of subfolders, each of which has different security requirements. We want **everyone** to be able to see the *Reports* folder, but each of its subfolders has different security requirements. To meet this need, we can grant the *View* right to the *Everyone* group for the *Reports* folder, and set its scope to "object only". By doing so, all users will see the Reports folder, but not anything under it. In order to see subfolders, users would need to be in a group that has been granted that permission to that subfolder.

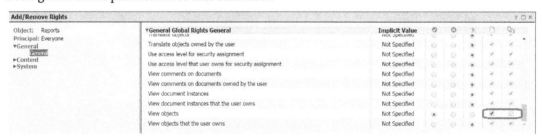

In almost all cases in which you'll be using `checkRight`, you will want to evaluate the effective permission that the principal has **on this InfoObject**. To do so, set the scope parameter to the `CeSecurityOptions.RightScope.CURRENT_OBJECT` constant value. To instead evaluate whether the permission has been propagated to the InfoObject's children, pass the `DESCENDANTS` constant value. The following code separately evaluates whether the user has *View* permission to the current object and its children.

```
27        RightDescriptor selfRight = new
              RightDescriptor(CeSecurityID.Right.VIEW,
                 0,
```

```
                        false,
                        CeSecurityOptions.RightScope.CURRENT_OBJECT,
                        CeSecurityOptions.ANY_OBJTYPE);
28              RightDescriptor childRight = new
                    RightDescriptor(CeSecurityID.Right.VIEW,
                        0,
                        false,
                        CeSecurityOptions.RightScope.DESCENDANTS,
                        CeSecurityOptions.ANY_OBJTYPE);
29              System.out.println("This: " + sec.checkRight(selfRight,4104,true));
30              System.out.println("Children: " +
        sec.checkRight( childRight,4104,true));
```

This displays the following output:

```
This: true
Children: false
```

Note that the fact that rights have been propagated to child objects does not guarantee that the principal effectively has those rights on the child objects. It's possible that the principal could have been explicitly denied the right on a child object.

Explicit Security

Security roles, advanced rights, and instance limits are assigned explicitly to a specific principal for a specific InfoObject. Using the IExplicitPrincipal interface, we can retrieve and set the explicit rights and instance limits.

The ISecurityInfo2.getExplicitPrincipals() method returns an IExplicitPrincipals collection, which contains a list of IExplicitPrincipal objects. Each IExplicitPrincipal object represents a principal that has explicit roles, rights, or instance limits for this InfoObject[157]. The IExplicitPrincipals collection only correlates to principals that have *explicit* rights to the InfoObject. If a principal only has *inherited* rights, then it will not be present in IExplicitPrincipals (although it is represented in I**Effective**Principals (covered later)).

In the following screenshot, the Administrators and Everyone groups have inherited security roles from the parent of the *Service* folder, and the *Finance* group has been explicitly assigned the *View On Demand* role.

---

157 That is, the InfoObject that the ISecurityInfo2 object was retrieved from.

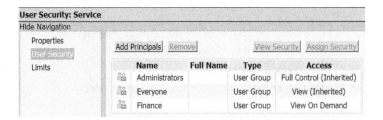

This code retrieves the explicit principals for the Service folder:

```
20      IInfoObjects ios = infoStore.query("select si_id from ci_infoobjects
   where si_name = 'service'");

21

22      for(Object o : ios)

23      {

24          IInfoObject io = (IInfoObject) o;

25          ISecurityInfo2 sec = io.getSecurityInfo2();

26

27          Iterator<IExplicitPrincipal> iPrinc =
                 sec.getExplicitPrincipals().iterator();

28

29          while(iPrinc.hasNext())

30          {

31              IExplicitPrincipal princ = iPrinc.next();

32              System.out.println(princ.getName());

33          }

34      }

35  }
```

Since there is only one principal with explicit security assignments, we get:

```
Finance
```

The IExplicitPrincipals interface enables us to retrieve, add, or remove principals that have explicit security, as well as manage security inheritance for the InfoObject. Its methods are:

Package com.crystaldecisions.sdk.occa.infostore
Interface _IExplicitPrincipals_
extends _IPrincipalsBase_

IExplicitPrincip al	add(int id)

	Creates a new `IExplicitPrincipal` object for the designated user/group. If the principal is already present in the collection, then the existing object is returned.
`IExplicitPrincip al`	`get(int id)`
	Retrieves an existing principal from `IExplicitPrincipals`.
`boolean`	`isGlobalInheritFolders()`
`void`	`setGlobalInheritFolders()`
	Retrieves/sets whether security for this InfoObject can be inherited from its parent.
`Iterator`	`iterator()`
	Retrieves an `iterator` that may be used to access all `IExplicitPrincipal` objects in the collection.
`void`	`remove(int id)`
	Removes the designated principal's explicitly-assigned roles, rights, or instance limits.
`int`	`size()`
	Retrieves the number of `IExplicitPrincipal` objects in the collection.

Class/Interface 53: IExplicitPrincipals

Although `IExplicitPrincipals` appears at first glance to be a standard `Collection`, it is not. The only way to access its members are with the `get()` method, which takes a principal ID as a parameter, and the `iterator()` method (as used above).

If we know that a particular user or user group is present in the collection, then we can retrieve it with its InfoObject ID. If we wanted to retrieve the principal for the *Finance* group, and knowing that its ID is 5947, we could use:

```
ISecurityInfo2 sec = io.getSecurityInfo2();


IExplicitPrincipal princ =
    sec.getExplicitPrincipals().get(5947);


System.out.println(princ.getName());
```

The `add(int id)` method is used when explicit security needs to be set for a principal that does not already have it. We will use this in the following sections when we add security roles and rights.

The `remove(int id)` method removes a principal from the collection, effectively removing the principal's explicitly-assigned roles, rights, and instance limits. Note that this does not necessarily cause the revocation of access for the principal – if the principal is also inheriting rights from its parent, then those effective rights will still be applicable. This method has the same function as the "Remove" button in the User Security dialog:

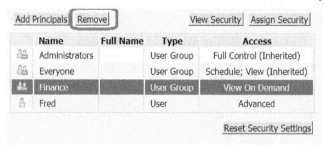

The `globalInheritFolders` property defines whether the InfoObject can inherit security from its parent folder. This property is not currently exposed in the CMC, so it may only be set via the SDK. For this reason, we do not recommend changing its value as it could be confusing for anyone examining the InfoObject in the CMC. However, it may be useful in some scenarios. Calling `setGlobalInheritFolders(false)` prevents the InfoObject from inheriting security from its parents – only principals with explicitly-assigned security will have any access to the InfoObject. Calling `setGlobalInheritFolders(true)` on the same InfoObject will again allow inherited rights to be applied. This property should not be confused with the *"Inherit From Parent..."* options, described below.

The `IExplicitPrincipal` interface is used to manage security for a principal. It has the following methods:

Package com.crystaldecisions.sdk.occa.infostore
Interface *IExplicitPrincipal*
extends IPrincipalBase

int	`getID()`
	Returns the principal's InfoObject ID.
`IExplicitLimits`	`getLimits()`
	Returns an `IExplicitLimits` object, which contains `IExplicitLimit` objects representing instance limits that apply to this principal for this InfoObject.
String	`getName()`
	Returns the principal's name.
`IExplicitRights`	`getRights()`
	Returns an `IExplicitRights` object, which contains `IExplicitRight` objects representing advanced rights that are applicable to this principal for this InfoObject. This does **not** include rights that are applied by way of a *role*.

IExplicitRoles	getRoles()
	Returns an IExplicitRoles object, which contains IExplicitRole objects representing any roles (access levels) that are applicable to this principal for this InfoObject.
boolean	isInheritFolders()
void	setInheritFolders()
	Retrieves/sets whether the principal should inherit security from the InfoObject's parent folder.
boolean	isInheritGroups()
void	setInheritGroups()
	Retrieves/sets whether the principal should inherit security from its parent user group(s).

Class/Interface 54: IExplicitPrincipal

We will cover instance limits, including the getLimits() method and associated IEffectiveLimits interface, later in this chapter.

The getID() and getName() methods return the ID and name (respectively) of the user or user group that is the security principal.

The four isInherit..()/setInherit...() methods are associated with the *Inherit From Parent Folder* and *Inherit From Parent Group* checkboxes on the Assign Security tab:

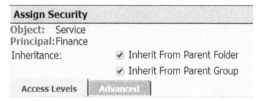

Explicit Roles

A principal may be assigned zero, one, or more pre-defined or custom security roles. The assigned roles can be managed with the IExplicitRoles interface, which is retrieved via IExplicitPrincipal.getRoles(). Its methods are:

Package com.crystaldecisions.sdk.occa.infostore
Interface *IExplicitRoles*

IExplicitRole	add(int id)
	Adds the designated security role to the principal. If the role has already been assigned to the principal, then the existing IExplicitRole is returned, and no other action is taken.
IExplicitRole	get(int id)

	Retrieves the designated security role as an `IExplicitRole`. Returns `null` if the designated role has not been assigned to the principal.
Iterator	`iterator()`
	Retrieves an `iterator` that may be used to access all `IExplicitRole` objects in the collection.
void	`remove(int id)`
	Removes the designated security role from the principal.
int	`size()`
	Retrieves the number of `IExplicitRole` objects in the collection.

Class/Interface 55: IExplicitRoles

The `IExplicitRole` interface contains only two methods:

Package com.crystaldecisions.sdk.occa.infostore **Interface _IExplicitRole_**	
int	`getID()`
	Retrieves the InfoObject ID of the security role.
String	`getTitle()`
	Retrieves the name of the security role.

Class/Interface 56: IExplicitRole

For this example, we'll work with the *Reports* root-level public folder. We'll start by resetting its security settings to default:

Next, we'll use the SDK to assign the *View* role to the *Finance* group.

```
20        IInfoObjects ios = infoStore.query("select si_id from ci_infoobjects
   where si_name = 'reports'");

21

22        ICustomRole roleView = (ICustomRole) infoStore.query("select si_id from
   ci_systemobjects where si_cuid = '" + CeSecurityCUID.Role.VIEW + "'").get(0);

23

24        IUserGroup finance = (IUserGroup) infoStore.query("select si_id from
   ci_systemobjects where si_kind = 'usergroup' and si_name = 'finance'").get(0);

25
```

```
26        for(Object o : ios)

27        {

28            IInfoObject io = (IInfoObject) o;

29            ISecurityInfo2 sec = io.getSecurityInfo2();

30

31            IExplicitPrincipal princ =
                 sec.getExplicitPrincipals().add(finance.getID());

32

33            princ.getRoles().add(roleView.getID());

33

34            io.save();

35        }

36    }
```

On line 22, we're retrieving the *View* security role via a CMS query and using the CeSecurityCUID.Role.VIEW constant to do so. Unfortunately, only the CUID is predefined and not the InfoObject ID, else we would not even need the CMS query.

On line 13, we create an IExplicitPrincipal object for the finance group, using its InfoObject ID. Note that if the Finance group was already present as a principal, this call would just return the associated IExplicitPrincipal object. That is, it does not create a new IExplicitPrincipal unless necessary, and so it is safe to call add() instead of get() if you are not sure whether the principal is already present.

On line 33, the *View* role is added to the *Finance* principal, using the InfoObject ID. As with IExplicitPrincipal, it is safe to call add() using a role id that is already present.

Finally, on line 34, we save the InfoObject. As with modifications to InfoObject properties, it is necessary to commit security changes in order for them to be applied in the CMS.

The program produces no output. However, once it completes we see that the *Finance* group has been added as a principal to the *Reports* folder, and been assigned the *View* role.

Add Principals	Remove		View Security	Assign Security

	Name	Full Name	Type	Access
	Administrators		User Group	Full Control (Inherited)
	Everyone		User Group	No Access
	Finance		User Group	View

Reset Security Settings

Key point: security roles are InfoObjects and therefore can be retrieved from the CMS using CMS queries. A security role's InfoObject ID is used to assign a role to an InfoObject.

Adding custom roles is only slightly more involved. For our example, we'll create a custom role named View Object Only, which only includes the right to view objects for the current object (and not subobjects).

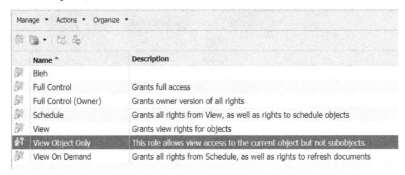

To add this role to Finance, we only need to change the CMS query that was used to retrieve the *View* role InfoObject. As we're now retrieving a custom role, there is no predefined CUID and we therefore have to retrieve it by name and kind. We change line 22 to:

```
22      ICustomRole roleView = (ICustomRole) infoStore.query("select si_id from
   ci_systemobjects where si_name = 'view object only' and si_kind = '" +
   ICustomRole.KIND + "'").get(0);
```

We're not doing any error-checking here, so the program will throw an exception if anything is wrong with the query. Assuming there isn't, the program will complete successfully and we'll see that the *View Object Only* Role has been added to the *Finance* group:

Of course, roles can just as easily be removed from a principal by changing `add()` to `remove()`:

```
33      princ.getRoles().remove(roleView.getID());
```

If the role has not been assigned to the principal, then no action is taken.

We can use the `IExplicitRoles` and `IExplicitRole` interfaces to display the roles currently assigned to a principal:

```
20      IInfoObjects ios = infoStore.query("select si_id from ci_infoobjects
   where si_name = 'reports'");
```

```
21
22          IUserGroup finance = (IUserGroup) infoStore.query("select si_id from
   ci_systemobjects where si_kind = 'usergroup' and si_name = 'finance'").get(0);
23
24          for(Object o : ios)
25          {
26              IInfoObject io = (IInfoObject) o;
27              ISecurityInfo2 sec = io.getSecurityInfo2();
28
29              IExplicitPrincipal princ =
                    sec.getExplicitPrincipals().add(finance.getID());
30
31              if(princ != null)
32              {
33                  IExplicitRoles roles = princ.getRoles();
34                  Iterator<IExplicitRole> itRole = roles.iterator();
35
36                  while(itRole.hasNext())
37                  {
38                      IExplicitRole role = itRole.next();
39                      System.out.println(role.getID() + " " + role.getTitle());
40                  }
41              }
42          }
43      }
```

In our system, this produces:

```
31749 View Object Only
554 View
```

...which represents the IDs and names of the security roles assigned to the *Finance* group.

Here we are iterating through the IExplicitRoles collection to retrieve each IExplicitRole object, then calling its getID() and getTitle() methods.

Explicit Rights

Managing explicit advanced rights is similar to managing explicit roles, if somewhat more

complex.   Rights are managed via the `IExplicitRights` interface, retrieved via
`IExplicitPrincipal.getRights()`. Its methods are:

Package com.crystaldecisions.sdk.occa.infostore
Interface *IExplicitRights*

`IExplicitRight`	`add(RightDescriptor right)`
	Adds the designated advanced right to the principal. If the right has already been assigned to the principal, then the existing `IExplicitRight` is returned, and no other action is taken.
`IExplicitRight`	`get(RightDescriptor right)`
	Retrieves the designated advanced right as an `IExplicitRight`. Returns `null` if the designated right has not been assigned to the principal.
`Iterator`	`iterator()`
	Retrieves an `iterator` that may be used to access all `IExplicitRight` objects in the collection.
`void`	`remove(RightDescriptor right)`
	Removes the designated right from the principal.
`int`	`size()`
	Retrieves the number of `IExplicitRight` objects in the collection.

Class/Interface 57: IExplicitRights

The methods are similar to that of `IExplicitRole`, except that it relates to rights via a
`RightDescriptor` object. We covered `RightDescriptor` earlier with respect to its usage with
`checkRight()/checkRights()`. It serves a similar purpose here, except that it is used for both
assigning as well as retrieving rights.

*Key point: the contents of `IExplicitRights` only relate to advanced rights assigned to an
InfoObject via the Advanced tab of the Assign Security dialog, and not rights granted via a
security role. If a principal has been assigned a security role (ex. View On Demand) but does not
have any additional advanced rights assigned, then the `IExplicitRights` collection will be
empty.*

Assigning Advanced Rights

Assigning an advanced right for a principal on an InfoObject is a two-step process:

1. Assign the right to the principal using `IExplicitRights.add()`

2. Optionally grant the right

For step 1, we need to create a `RightDescriptor` object that identifies the specific right that is
to be assigned. The `RightDescriptor` object is created in much the same way as previously

described (beginning on page 569). The `add()` call returns an `IExplicitRight` object, representing the newly-assigned right, which can then be used to grant the right if desired[158].

To prepare for the following examples, we'll again reset the security settings on the *Reports* folder.

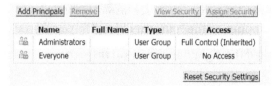

Next, using the same `RightDescriptor` that we used on page 575 we'll grant the *View (object only)* right to the *Finance* group:

```
20        IInfoObjects ios = infoStore.query("select si_id from ci_infoobjects
     where si_name = 'reports'");

21

22        IUserGroup finance = (IUserGroup) infoStore.query("select si_id from
     ci_systemobjects where si_kind = 'usergroup' and si_name = 'finance'").get(0);

23

24      for(Object o : ios)

25      {

26          IInfoObject io = (IInfoObject) o;

27          ISecurityInfo2 sec = io.getSecurityInfo2();

28

29          IExplicitPrincipal princ =
                sec.getExplicitPrincipals().add(finance.getID());

30

31          if(princ != null)

32          {

33              RightDescriptor rightDesc = new
                    RightDescriptor(CeSecurityID.Right.VIEW,
                        0,
                        false,
                        CeSecurityOptions.RightScope.CURRENT_OBJECT,
                        CeSecurityOptions.ANY_OBJTYPE);

34

35              IExplicitRights explicitRights = princ.getRights();

36              explicitRights.add(rightDesc);

37          }
```

---

158 Remember that an **assigned** right is not necessarily a **granted** right.

38	io.save();
39	}
40	}

On line 33, we created the `selfRight RightDescriptor` object, using the *View* pre-defined right ID, and specified it to be applied to the "current object".

Then, on line 36, we applied the right defined in `selfRight` to the principal's explicit rights.

On line 38, we saved the InfoObject.

When complete, the *User Security* tab shows that the Finance group has been added as a principal:

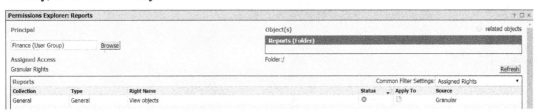

And the Advanced view shows that the View objects right has been assigned (denied, actually) to the current object:

Permissions Explorer: Reports						? □ ×
Principal			Object(s)			related objects
Finance (User Group)	Browse		Reports (Folder)			
Assigned Access			Folder:/			
Granular Rights						Refresh
Reports				Common Filter Settings: Assigned Rights		▼
Collection	Type	Right Name		Status	Apply To	Source
General	General	View objects		⊘	▯	Granular

We can see that the right was assigned as *Denied*, which is the default status. To instead assign it as *Granted*, we must first retrieve an `IExplicitRight` object from the `IExplicitRights.add()` call, then call its `setGranted()` method[159]. Replace line 36 with the following:

36	IExplicitRight viewRight = explicitRights.add(rightDesc);
37	viewRight.setGranted(true);

After executing the program, we'll see that the right has been granted:

---

159 We'll cover `IExplicitRight` later in this chapter. For applying rights, it's only used for granting a right, as described here.

Note that we used most of the existing code, including the add() call on line 36, even though the right was already assigned. The add() call replaces an existing right.

Object / Subobject Rights

In our most recent example, we granted the *View object* right, which was applied to *Object* only and not *Subobjects*. It's not very obvious in the above screenshot, but more so if we look at the Add/Remove Rights panel:

While it would seem appropriate that the Object / Subobject setting would be a property of an explicit right, that is not the case. Rather, they are actually independent explicit rights. In order to assign the right to both Object and Subobjects, it needs to be added to IExplicitRights twice. So for our next example, we'll assign the *View instances* right, and apply it to both Object and Subobjects.

```
20        IInfoObjects ios = infoStore.query("select si_id from ci_infoobjects
   where si_name = 'reports'");

21

22        IUserGroup finance = (IUserGroup) infoStore.query("select si_id from
   ci_systemobjects where si_kind = 'usergroup' and si_name = 'finance'").get(0);

23

24     for(Object o : ios)

25     {

26         IInfoObject io = (IInfoObject) o;

27         ISecurityInfo2 sec = io.getSecurityInfo2();

28

29         IExplicitPrincipal princ =
              sec.getExplicitPrincipals().add(finance.getID());

30

31         if(princ != null)

32         {

33             IExplicitRights explicitRights = princ.getRights();
```

```
34
35                  RightDescriptor rightDescSelf = new
                        RightDescriptor(CeSecurityID.Right.VIEW_INSTANCE,
                            0,
                            false,
                            CeSecurityOptions.RightScope.CURRENT_OBJECT,
                            CeSecurityOptions.ANY_OBJTYPE);
36
37                  IExplicitRight viewRightSelf =
                        explicitRights.add(rightDescSelf);
38                  viewRightSelf.setGranted(true);
39
40                  RightDescriptor rightDescSubs = new
                        RightDescriptor(CeSecurityID.Right.VIEW_INSTANCE,
                            0,
                            false,
                            CeSecurityOptions.RightScope.DESCENDANTS,
                            CeSecurityOptions.ANY_OBJTYPE);
41
42                  IExplicitRight viewRightSubs =
                        explicitRights.add(rightDescSubs);
43                  viewRightSubs.setGranted(true);
44              }
45          io.save();
46          }
47      }
```

In lines 35-38, we're doing the same as before, except that we're now using the VIEW_INSTANCE
constant.

In lines 40-43, the same right is assigned, but using the DESCENDANTS constant for the scope
parameter in RightDescriptor.

Once executed, the *View instances* right has been assigned, and applied to both *Objects* and
Subobjects:

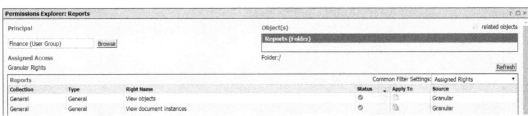

Since Object and Subobject rights are assigned separately, it would *appear* that it should be possible to grant access to one while denying the other. For example, in the program above, we might assume that we could pass `false` to `setGranted` on line 43, thereby denying the *View instance* right to the folder's children while granting it to the folder itself. However, this does not work. Although the program completes without erroring, the desired result is not be achieved. When assigning rights to Object and Subobject, it is necessary to either grant both or deny both.

Kind-specific and Kind-applied Rights

The `applicableObjectType` parameter in `RightDescriptor` can be used to assign rights for specific InfoObject kinds. For example, we replace lines 35 and 40 above with the following, which grants the *Edit* right for Crystal Reports objects only:

```
35          RightDescriptor rightDescSelf = new
                    RightDescriptor(CeSecurityID.Right.EDIT,
                        0,
                        false,
                        CeSecurityOptions.RightScope.CURRENT_OBJECT,
                        IReport.KIND);


40          RightDescriptor rightDescSubs = new
                    RightDescriptor(CeSecurityID.Right.EDIT,
                        0,
                        false,
                        CeSecurityOptions.RightScope.DESCENDANTS,
                        IReport.KIND));
```

This produces the expected result in the CMC:

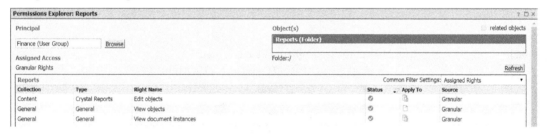

The `kind` parameter of the `RightDescriptor` class defines the source (parent) of the specific right ID. We can use this when assigning explicit rights, too. On page 571, we listed the rights that are owned by *WebI*, and gave an example of a `RightDescriptor` constructor that uses them. We'll use a similar constructor to assign the *View SQL* right to the *Reports* folder. We'll again replace lines 35 and 40 in our program with the following:

```
35          RightDescriptor rightDescSelf = new
                    RightDescriptor(8,
                        IWebi.KIND,
                        false,
                        CeSecurityOptions.RightScope.CURRENT_OBJECT,
```

```
                              CeSecurityOptions.ANY_OBJTYPE);


40          RightDescriptor rightDescSubs = new
                    RightDescriptor(8,
                        IWebi.KIND,
                        false,
                        CeSecurityOptions.RightScope.DESCENDANTS,
                        CeSecurityOptions.ANY_OBJTYPE);
```

After execution, we'll see the *View SQL* right granted:

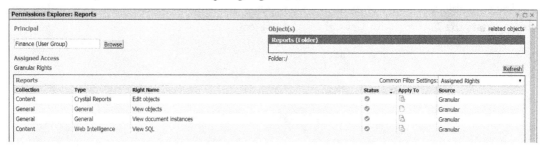

Finally, the `isOwner` parameter can be used to specify that the right is to be applied to the object owner only. Again we'll replace lines 35 and 40, and set the `isOwner` parameter to true. We'll do this for the system *Delete objects* right.

```
35          RightDescriptor rightDescSelf = new
                    RightDescriptor(CeSecurityID.Right.DELETE,
                        0,
                        true,
                        CeSecurityOptions.RightScope.CURRENT_OBJECT,
                        CeSecurityOptions.ANY_OBJTYPE);



40          RightDescriptor rightDescSubs = new
                    RightDescriptor(CeSecurityID.Right.DELETE,
                        0,
                        true,
                        CeSecurityOptions.RightScope.DESCENDANTS,
                        CeSecurityOptions.ANY_OBJTYPE);
```

and we'll see that the *Delete objects that the user owns* right has been granted:

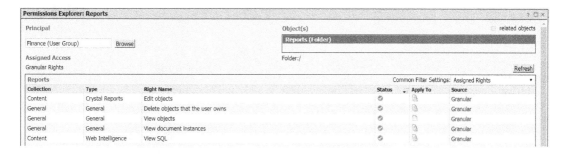

Retrieving Explicit Rights

The `IExplicitRights` interface may be used to retrieve existing explicit rights for a principal, either iteratively or specifically. To prepare for the code samples, we'll reset security on the *Reports* folder and then set the advanced rights as follows for *Fred*:

In General Rights:

- *Add objects to the folder*: Granted, object only

- *Delete objects*: Denied, object and subobjects

- *Edit objects that the user owns*: Granted, object and subobjects

- *View objects*: Granted, object and subobjects

In Content → Web Intelligence:

- *Edit Query*: Granted, object and subobjects

- *Delete objects*: Granted (overriding general global), object and subobjects

When done, Fred's permission on the Reports folder looks like the following:

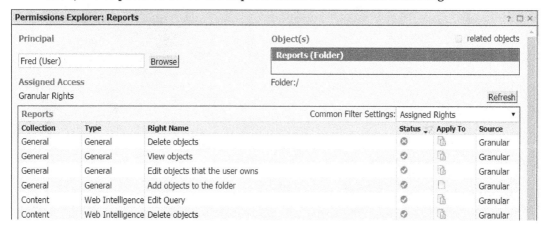

Now, we'll retrieve this explicit security with the SDK.

```
1 package bosdkbook;
2
3 import java.util.Iterator;
```

```
 4 import java.util.Locale;

 5

 6 import com.crystaldecisions.sdk.framework.CrystalEnterprise;

 7 import com.crystaldecisions.sdk.framework.IEnterpriseSession;

 8 import com.crystaldecisions.sdk.framework.ISessionMgr;

 9 import com.crystaldecisions.sdk.occa.infostore.IExplicitPrincipal;

10 import com.crystaldecisions.sdk.occa.infostore.IExplicitRight;

11 import com.crystaldecisions.sdk.occa.infostore.IInfoObject;

12 import com.crystaldecisions.sdk.occa.infostore.IInfoObjects;

13 import com.crystaldecisions.sdk.occa.infostore.IInfoStore;

14 import com.crystaldecisions.sdk.occa.infostore.ISecurityInfo2;

15

16 public class DisplayRights

17 {

18     public static void main(String[] args) throws Exception

19     {

20         ISessionMgr sessionManager = CrystalEnterprise.getSessionMgr();

21         IEnterpriseSession session = sessionManager.logon ("administrator",
   "xxxx", "192.168.56.102", "secEnterprise");

22

23         IInfoStore infoStore = (IInfoStore) session.getService ("","InfoStore");

24

25         IInfoObjects ios = infoStore.query("select si_id from ci_infoobjects
   where si_parentid = 23 and si_name = 'reports'");

26

27         for(Object o : ios)

28         {

29             IInfoObject io = (IInfoObject) o;

30             ISecurityInfo2 sec = io.getSecurityInfo2();

31

32             Iterator<IExplicitPrincipal> iPrinc =
                sec.getExplicitPrincipals().iterator();

33

34             while(iPrinc.hasNext())

35             {
```

```
36              IExplicitPrincipal princ = iPrinc.next();

37

38              System.out.println("Principal: " + princ.getName());

39

40              System.out.println(
                    "Source Kind\tApplies\tGranted\tScope\tDescription");

41

42              Iterator<IExplicitRight> itRight = princ.getRights().iterator();

43              while(itRight.hasNext())

44              {

45                  IExplicitRight right = itRight.next();

46

47                      String sourceKind = right.getRightPluginKind();

48                  if(sourceKind.equals(""))

49                      sourceKind="General";

50

51              String out = right.getRightPluginKind() + "\t"

52                  + right.getApplicableKind() + "\t"

53                  + (right.isGranted() ? "Granted\t" : "Denied\t")

54                  + right.getScope() + "\t"

55                  + right.getDescription(Locale.getDefault());

56

57                  System.out.println(out);

58              }

59          }

60      }

61  }

62 }
```

Listing 46: The DisplayRights program

Listing 46 contains the *DisplayRights* program, which we'll use to display the explicit rights assigned to the *Reports* folder. We've formatted and sorted the output for readability:

```
Principal: Fred
```

Source Kind	Applies	Granted	Scope	Description
General	Any	Denied	this	Delete objects
General	Any	Denied	descendants	Delete objects
General	Any	Granted	this	View objects
General	Any	Granted	descendants	View objects
General	Any	Granted	this	Edit objects that the user owns
General	Any	Granted	descendants	Edit objects that the user owns
General	Any	Granted	this	Add objects to the folder
Webi	Any	Granted	this	Edit Query
Webi	Any	Granted	descendants	Edit Query
General	CrystalEnterprise.Webi	Granted	this	Delete objects
General	CrystalEnterprise.Webi	Granted	descendants	Delete objects

One of the first things you may have noticed is that most of the rights appear twice – once with a scope of "this" and one of "descendants". As mentioned on page 575, the rights for Object and Subobjects are actually implemented as two separate right assignments. Apart from Scope, the output of this program aligns neatly with the screenshot of the Permissions Explorer above.

There is one quirk that should be kept in mind when retrieving right descriptions. When retrieving rights other than system rights, it is necessary to call IExplicitRight.isGranted() prior to calling IExplicitRight.getDescription(). If this is not done, then the correct description will not be returned. To illustrate, we'll modify the *DisplayRights* program to return the description prior to the grant:

47	`String out = sourceKind + "\t"`
48	`+ right.getApplicableKind() + "\t"`
49	`+ right.getDescription(Locale.getDefault())`
50	`+ right.getScope() + "\t"`
51	`+ (right.isGranted() ? "Granted\t" : "Denied\t");`

With this change, the output is now:

Principal:	Fred			

Source Kind	Applies	Granted	Scope	Description
General	Any	Denied	this	Delete objects
General	Any	Denied	descendants	Delete objects
General	Any	Granted	this	View objects
General	Any	Granted	descendants	View objects
General	Any	Granted	this	Edit objects that the user owns
General	Any	Granted	descendants	Edit objects that the user owns
General	Any	Granted	this	Add objects to the folder
Webi	Any	Granted	this	**Unknown right**
Webi	Any	Granted	descendants	**Unknown right**
General	CrystalEnterprise.Webi	Granted	this	Delete objects
General	CrystalEnterprise.Webi	Granted	descendants	Delete objects

The two rights associated with *WebI* appear as *Unknown right* instead of *Edit Query*.

The IExplicitRight Class

The IExplicitRight class isn't used much when assigning rights to a principal (just for granting a right, as shown on page 587), but is used more when retrieving rights. Its methods are:

Package com.crystaldecisions.sdk.occa.infostore
Interface _IExplicitRight_
extends IRightBase, IRightIDBase

String	getApplicableKind()
	Returns the name of the plugin (kind) that this right applies to. This is equivalent to the applicableObjectType property in RightDescriptor, when the kind name is used.
int	getApplicableType()
	Returns the InfoObject ID of the plugin that this right applies to. This is equivalent to the applicableObjectType property in RightDescriptor, when the plugin ID is used.
int	getBaseID()
	Returns the base ID of the right.

String	getDescription(Locale locale)
	Returns the description of this right in the specified locale. For example: "View document instances". For rights other than system rights, it is necessary to call isGranted() prior to getDescription().
RightDescriptor	getRightDescriptor()
	Returns a RightDescriptor object applicable to this right.
String	getRightPluginKind()
	Returns null if the right is a system right, or the plugin kind name if the right is sourced from a plugin. This is equivalent to the kind parameter in RightDescriptor when the kind name is used.
int	getRightPluginType()
	Returns 0 if the right is a system right, or the plugin ID if the right is sourced from a plugin. This is equivalent to the kind parameter in RightDescriptor when the plugin ID is used.
String	getScope()
	Returns the scope of this right. The possible values are in CeSecurityOptions.RightScope, and are either "this" or "descendants". This is equivalent to the scope parameter in RightDescriptor.
boolean	isGranted()
void	setGranted(boolean granted)
	Retrieves/sets whether the right is granted or denied. The value is true if the right is granted and false if denied.
boolean	isOwner()
	Returns true if the grant applies only when the user is the owner of the InfoObject.
boolean	isSpecified()
	Returns true if the right is explicitly or effectively assigned (may be granted or denied), and false if the right is unassigned (i.e., "Not Specified").

Class/Interface 58: IExplicitRight

The getDescription(locale) method returns the description text of the right, in the specified locale (if available). This is the same text that is displayed in the various security dialogs. For example, *"Delete objects"*, *"Replicate content"*, *"View objects"*, etc.

The getRightDescriptor() method returns a RightDescriptor object containing the properties associated with the right (ID, parent kind, applicable kind, scope, and owner). However, it is not necessary to retrieve the RightDescriptor object in order to access the specific properties of the right, as there are shortcut methods in IExplicitRight for that purpose. Unfortunately, however, the property names are not the same. The following table maps the property names in RightDescriptor to the associated accessor methods in IExplicitRight:

RightDescriptor property	IExplicitRight method
applicableObjectType	getApplicableKind() getApplicableType()
id	getBaseID()
isOwner	isOwner()
kind	getRightPluginKind() getRightPluginType()
scope	getScope()

Thus, the following pairs of statements produce the same results:

```
IExplicitRight explicitRight = ...;


// Retrieve applicable kind

System.out.println(explicitRight
    .getRightDescriptor().applicableObjectType);

System.out.println(explicitRight.getApplicableKind());


// Retrieve base ID of right

System.out.println(explicitRight.getRightDescriptor().id);

System.out.println(explicitRight.getBaseID());


// Retrieve owner flag

System.out.println(explicitRight.getRightDescriptor().isOwner);

System.out.println(explicitRight.isOwner());


// Retrieve parent kind

System.out.println(explicitRight.getRightDescriptor().kind);

System.out.println(explicitRight.getRightPluginKind());


// Retrieve scope

System.out.println(explicitRight.getRightDescriptor().scope);
```

```
System.out.println(explicitRight.getScope());
```

When a `RightDescriptor` class is created, either an InfoObject ID or kind name may be used for the `applicableObjectKind` and `kind` properties. However, the RightDescriptor class retrieved from `IExplicitRight` only contains the kind **names** in these properties. To retrieve the IDs (which is infrequently needed in most SDK programs), use the `getApplicableType()` and `getRightPluginType()` methods.

Retrieving Effective Security

Managing effective security is very similar to managing explicit security, with the exception that effective security classes include methods for retrieving inherited rights, yet do not allow for the manipulation of rights.

The corresponding classes are:

Explicit Security	Effective Security
IExplicitPrincipal	IEffectivePrincipal
IExplicitPrincipals	IEffectivePrincipals
IExplicitRight	IEffectiveRight
IExplicitRights	IEffectiveRights
IExplicitRole	IEffectiveRole
IExplicitRoles	IEffectiveRoles

As with explicit security, effective security originates with a security *principal*. The `getAnyPrincipal()` and `setEffectiveRights()` methods of `ISecurityInfo2` are used to retrieve the security roles, advanced rights, and instance limits that are explicitly assigned to principals **or** inherited from the InfoObject's parent. They are similar to `checkRight`/`checkRights` in that they reflect the *effective* rights that principals have for an InfoObject.

The `getEffectivePrincipals()` method returns an `IEffectivePrincipals` collection, which contains a collection of `IEffectivePrincipal` objects. Each `IEffectivePrincipal` object in this collection represents a principal that has either been granted explicit rights to this InfoObject or who has inherited rights from this InfoObject's parent. The list of `IEffectivePrincipal` objects correlates to the display of principals in the User Security view in the CMC. In the following example, for the *Service* folder,, the *Administrators* and *Everyone* groups are inheriting the *Full Control* and *View* roles (respectively), and the *Finance* group has been explicitly granted the *View On Demand* role:

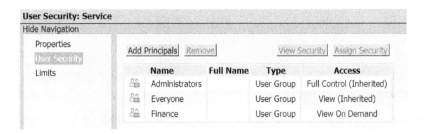

We'll examine the IEffectivePrincipals collection for the Service folder and we'll find that it contains an object for each of these three principals:

```
20        IInfoObjects ios = infoStore.query("select si_id from ci_infoobjects
   where si_name = 'service'");

21

22     for(Object o : ios)

23     {

24         IInfoObject io = (IInfoObject) o;

25         ISecurityInfo2 sec = io.getSecurityInfo2();

26

27         Iterator<IEffectivePrincipal> iPrinc =
               sec.getEffectivePrincipals().iterator();

28

29         while(iPrinc.hasNext())

30         {

31             IEffectivePrincipal princ = iPrinc.next();

32             System.out.println(princ.getName());

33         }

34     }

35 }
```

The above snippet produces:

```
Everyone
Administrators
Finance
```

This code is very similar to our earlier example for retrieving explicit principals, on page 577.

A couple of notes about IEffectivePrincipals before we go much further:

- As seen in the example above, it will contain IEffectivePrincipal objects representing principals that either have explicit or inherited rights/roles/limits.

- Only a single IEffectivePrincipal object will be present in the IEffectivePrincipals collection regardless of how many different ways it has been assigned rights. That is, even if a principal has been assigned explicit roles, explicit rights, and also has inherited roles and rights, it will only be associated with a single IEffectivePrincipal object. (Effective rights, by definition, include both inherited and explicitly-assigned rights).

We use the IEffectivePrincipal object to determine which roles (access levels), rights, or instance limits have been applied to the principal for an InfoObject. The methods of IEffectivePrincipal are as follows:

Package com.crystaldecisions.sdk.occa.infostore
Interface IEffectivePrincipal
extends IPrincipalBase

int	getID()
	Returns the principal's InfoObject ID.
IEffectiveLimits	getLimits()
	Returns an IEffectiveLimits object, which contains IEffectiveLimit objects representing instance limits that are applicable to this principal for this InfoObject.
String	getName()
	Returns the principal's name.
IEffectiveRights	getRights()
	Returns an IEffectiveRights object, which contains IEffectiveRight objects representing advanced rights that are applicable to this principal for this InfoObject.
IEffectiveRoles	getRoles()
	Returns an IEffectiveRoles object, which contains IEffectiveRole objects representing any roles (access levels) that are applicable to this principal for this InfoObject.
boolean	isAdvanced()
	Returns true if the principal has any effective advanced rights (rights that are not assigned by way of a role).
boolean	isInherited()
	Returns true if **all** of the principal's effective rights are inherited. That is, the principal has no explicitly-assigned rights.
boolean	isInheritFolders()

	Returns `true` if the principal can inherit rights from the InfoObject's parent.
`boolean`	`isInheritGroups()`
	Returns `true` if the principal can inherit rights from its parent groups.

Class/Interface 59: IEffectivePrincipal

Effective security is inherently read-only, and so there are no methods of the `IEffectivePrincipal` interface that can be used to modify security. Modifying security in the SDK is done via the `IExplicitPrincipal` interface, covered earlier.

The `isInheritFolders()` and `isInheritGroups()` methods are associated with the *Inherit From Parent Folder* and *Inherit From Parent Group* checkboxes on the Assign Security tab. They return the same values as the associated methods in `IExplicitPrincipal` (see page 580), although in the `IEffectivePrincipal` interface there are no **setter** methods for these properties.

The `getID()` and `getName()` methods return the InfoObject ID and name (respectively) of the user or user group that is the security principal.

Effective Roles

A principal may have been assigned a role explicitly for an object, and roles may also be inherited from its parent group or the InfoObject's parent folder. The `getRoles()` method of `IEffectivePrincipal` returns an `IEffectiveRoles` object that references any roles that the principal has been assigned for this InfoObject.

To illustrate, we'll use the *Reports* and *Service* folders, and set up security as follows:

Reports

- Administrators – Full Control (Inherited from Root)
- Everyone – View

Service

- Administrators – Full Control (inherited from Root)
- Everyone – View (inherited from Reports), Schedule
- Finance – View on Demand

In the CMC, the security for the *Service* subfolder looks like:

The *Everyone* group inherited the *View* role from *Reports*, and we have added the *Schedule* role. The *Finance* group did not inherit any roles from *Reports*, but we have granted the *View on Demand* role. We'll use the getRoles() method in the following snippet to display the roles associated with each principal.

```
20        IInfoObjects ios = infoStore.query("select si_id from ci_infoobjects
   where si_name = 'service'");

21

22        for(Object o : ios)

23        {

24            IInfoObject io = (IInfoObject) o;

25            ISecurityInfo2 sec = io.getSecurityInfo2();

26

27            Iterator<IEffectivePrincipal> iPrinc =
                 sec.getEffectivePrincipals().iterator();

28

29            while(iPrinc.hasNext())

30            {

31                IEffectivePrincipal princ = iPrinc.next();

32                IEffectiveRoles roles = princ.getRoles();

33                Iterator<IEffectiveRole> itRole = roles.iterator();

34

35                while(itRole.hasNext())

36                {

37                    IEffectiveRole role = itRole.next();

38                    System.out.println(princ.getName()
                         + ": " + role.getTitle()
                         + (role.isInherited()
                             ? " (inherited)"
                             : " (explicit)"));

39                }

40            }

41        }

42    }
```

Like the IEffectivePrincipals object, the only way to iterate through the members of IEffectiveRoles is with its iterator() method.

On line 37, we retrieve the IEffectiveRole object, and then on line 38, we print the principal's name, the name of the role, and whether the role has been inherited or explicitly assigned.

The result that we get is consistent with the security roles that we assigned:

```
Everyone: Schedule (explicit)
Everyone: View (inherited)
Administrators: Full Control (inherited)
Finance: View On Demand (explicit)
```

The `IEffectiveRole` interface has only four methods. They are:

Package com.crystaldecisions.sdk.occa.infostore
Interface *IEffectiveRole*__

int	getID()
	Returns the role's ID.
List	getSources()
	Returns a List of `IRoleSource` objects, representing the ancestral principals/InfoObjects from which this role assignment is inherited from.
String	getTitle()
	Returns the role's name.
boolean	isInherited()
	Returns `true` if this role assignment is inherited from the principal's parent group or the InfoObject's parent folder.

Class/Interface 60: IEffectiveRole

We used `getTitle()` and `isInherited()` in our the code above. We'll add to the program to illustrate the `getSources()` method. In the *View Security* dialog in the CMC, clicking in the Source column displays the principal and object from which the access has been assigned and which is inherited by the current object. For example, the below view is of the *Administrators* principal on the *Service* folder:

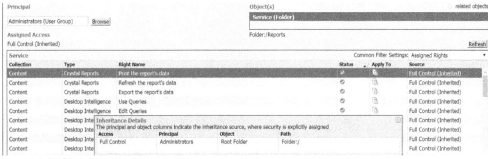

Illustration 34: Displaying access rights source

The *Inheritance Details* box shows that the Full Control role is being inherited from an explicit role assignment on the *Root Folder* for the *Administrators* group.

This same information is available via the `getSources()` method of `IEffectiveRole`. This method returns a List of `IRoleSource` objects, which identify where the role was originally assigned. The `IRoleSource` interface includes three methods:

Package com.crystaldecisions.sdk.occa.infostore
Interface _IRoleSource_

int	getObjectID()
	Returns the id of the InfoObject upon which the role was explicitly assigned.
int	getPrincipalID()
	Returns the id of the user or user group for which the role was explicitly assigned.
boolean	isInherited()
	Returns `true` if this role assignment is inherited from the principal's parent group or the InfoObject's parent folder.

Class/Interface 61: IRoleSource

We'll expand our previous program to display the origins of the role assignments:

```
20        IInfoObjects ios = infoStore.query("select si_id from ci_infoobjects
   where si_name = 'service'");

21

22        for(Object o : ios)

23        {

24            IInfoObject io = (IInfoObject) o;

25            ISecurityInfo2 sec = io.getSecurityInfo2();

26

27            Iterator<IEffectivePrincipal> iPrinc =
                 sec.getEffectivePrincipals().iterator();

28

29            while(iPrinc.hasNext())

30            {

31                IEffectivePrincipal princ = iPrinc.next();

32                IEffectiveRoles roles = princ.getRoles();

33                Iterator<IEffectiveRole> itRole = roles.iterator();

34

35                while(itRole.hasNext())

36                {
```

```
37              IEffectiveRole role = itRole.next();
38              System.out.println(princ.getName()
                        + ": " + role.getTitle());
39
40              List<IRoleSource> roleSources = role.getSources();
41              for(IRoleSource roleSource : roleSources)
42                  if(roleSource.isInherited())
43                  {
44                      System.out.println("  Inherited from: "
                    + getNameFromID(infoStore, roleSource.getPrincipalID())
                    + " / "
                    + getNameFromID(infoStore, roleSource.getObjectID())));
45                  }
46                  else
47                      System.out.println("  Explicit");
48              }
49          }
50      }
51  }
52
53  private static String getNameFromID(IInfoStore infoStore,Integer id)
54  throws SDKException
55  {
56      IInfoObjects ios = infoStore.query("select si_name from
    ci_systemobjects,ci_infoobjects,ci_appobjects where si_id = " + id);
57      if(ios.size() == 0)
58          return "";
59      return ((IInfoObject)ios.get(0)).getTitle();
60  }
```

The program produces:

```
Everyone: Schedule
  Explicit
Everyone: View
  Inherited from: Everyone / Reports
Administrators: Full Control
  Inherited from: Administrators / Root Folder
Finance: View On Demand
  Explicit
```

We can see that the *Everyone* group has inherited the *View* role from the *Reports* folder, and the *Administrators* group has inherited the *Full Control* role from *Root Folder*.

In lines 41-47, we are iterating through the `IRoleSource` collection returned from `getSources()`. For each `IRoleSource`, we display the originating principal and InfoObject, but only if the access was inherited. If the access was explicitly assigned, the `IRoleSource` object would contain a reference to the current principal and InfoObject, as that is the source of the role assignment. We are just choosing not to display it, since we are only interested in access that is inherited.

Unfortunately, there are no methods in `IRoleSource` to return the **name** of the source object or principal, so we need to get it ourselves with a CMS query. The `getNameFromID()` method in lines 53-60 performs this function.

Note that security rights in a role may override security rights in another role. The built-in roles only contain grants (no denials), so there is no risk of this type of overriding with the built-in roles (all grants are combined, but none are overridden). But consider a scenario in which a principal inherits both the *View* role and a custom role that denies the *View document instances* right. It would be incorrect to assume that the *View* role provides the *View document instances* right, since in this case it is overridden by the custom role. So, while it is appropriate to use the `getRoles()` method to identify which roles a principal is inheriting, it is necessary to evaluate the specific rights that are inherited if the objective is to confirm that a specific right has been granted. That is, if you need to ensure that the principal has the *View document instances* right, you should evaluate that specific right (with `getRight()` or `getEffectiveRights()`), rather than just checking for the presence of a role.

Similar to `IExplicitRoles`/`IExplicitRole`, it is possible to retrieve an `IEffectiveRole` object from the `IEffectiveRoles` collection by calling the `get()` method with the InfoObject ID of the role. This is useful for quickly confirming whether or not a particular role has been assigned to a principal.

To do so, we need to obtain the ID of the role. Once obtained, we can use it to retrieve an `IEffectiveRole` from `IEffectiveRoles`.

```
    ICustomRole fullControl = (ICustomRole) infoStore.query("select si_id from
ci_systemobjects where si_cuid = '" + CeSecurityCUID.Role.FULL_CONTROL + "'").get(0);



    ...



    IEffectiveRoles roles = princ.getRoles();

    IEffectiveRole effRole = roles.get(fullControl.getID());



    if(effRole != null)

        System.out.println("Has Full Control");
```

The getRights() method of IEffectivePrincipal returns an IEffectiveRights collection that contains IEffectiveRight objects, representing the individual rights that the principal has either inherited or that have been explicitly assigned. That is, the rights referenced by IEffectiveRight aligns with the list of rights that are displayed in the "View Security" dialog when the "Assigned Rights" filter is displayed.

IEffectiveRights and IEffectiveRight are similar in structure and function to IExplicitRights and IExplicitRight. However, they differ in one important aspect: while IExplicitRights includes only advanced rights that have been explicitly assigned (not including rights assigned via a role), IEffectiveRights includes all effective rights that a principal has on an InfoObject, regardless of their source.

The rights may come from any of the following sources:

- An explicitly-assigned role

- A role inherited from the principal's parent group

- A role inherited from the InfoObject's parent folder

- A role inherited from a parent group *and* a parent folder

- An explicitly-assigned advanced right

- An advanced right inherited from the principal's parent group

- An advanced right inherited from the InfoObject's parent folder

- An advanced right inherited from a parent group *and* a parent folder

The contents of IEffectiveRight consider all sources of a right and present the final calculated result. So, a particular right (ex. *View document instances*) is only referenced once in an IEffectiveRights collection, regardless of how many different sources may include it.

Note that the checkRight()/checkRights() methods described earlier also consider effective rights – if checkRight() returns true for a particular right and principal, then IEffectiveRights will also reflect that the right as granted.

The IEffectiveRight interface has several methods (as with IEffectiveRole, all methods are read-only). They are[160]:

Package com.crystaldecisions.sdk.occa.infostore
Interface *IEffectiveRight*
extends IRIghtBase

String	getApplicableKind()
	Returns the name of the plugin (kind) that this right applies to. This is equivalent to the applicableKind property in RightDescriptor, when the kind name is used.
int	getApplicableType()

---

160 Deprecated methods are excluded from this list.

	Returns the InfoObject ID of the plugin that this right applies to. This is equivalent to the `applicableKind` property in `RightDescriptor`, when the plugin ID is used.
int	`getBaseID()`
	Returns the base ID of the right.
String	`getDescription(Locale locale)`
	Returns the description of this right in the specified locale. For example: "View document instances".
List	`getImplicitSources()`
	Returns a List of `IRightSource` objects reflecting the sources that the principal would have inherited a grant from, had it not been granted explicitly on this object. If this is `null`, then the right is **only** granted explicitly and would not otherwise be inherited.
RightDescriptor	`getRightDescriptor()`
	Returns a `RightDescriptor` object applicable to this right.
String	`getRightPluginKind()`
	Returns `null` if the right is a system right, or the plugin kind name if the right is sourced from a plugin. This is equivalent to the `kind` parameter in `RightDescriptor` when the kind name is used.
int	`getRightPluginType()`
	Returns `0` if the right is a system right, or the plugin ID if the right is sourced from a plugin. This is equivalent to the `kind` parameter in `RightDescriptor` when the plugin ID is used.
String	`getScope()`
	Returns the scope of this right. The possible values are in `CeSecurityOptions.RightScope`, and are either "this" or "descendants". This is equivalent to the `scope` parameter in `RightDescriptor`.
List	`getSources()`
	Returns a List of `IRightSource` objects, representing the ancestral principals/InfoObjects from which this right assignment is inherited from.
boolean	`isGranted()`
	Returns `true` if the right is granted, and `false` if it is denied. This represents the final calculated assignment, considering any explicitly-assigned and inherited rights.
boolean	`isImplicitGranted()`

	Returns `true` if the principal would have inherited a grant for this right, had it not been granted explicitly on this object.
boolean	`isInherited()`
	Returns `true` if the right is inherited from a parent folder or parent group.
boolean	`isOwner()`
	Returns `true` if the grant applies only when the user is the owner of the InfoObject.
boolean	`isSpecified()`
	Returns `true` if the right is explicitly or effectively assigned (may be granted or denied), and `false` if the right is unassigned (i.e., "Not Specified").

Class/Interface 62: IEffectiveRight

Most of the methods in `IEffectiveRight` are equivalent to `IExplicitRight`, covered earlier[161]. The `IEffectiveRight` interface does not include `setGranted()` since effective rights can not be granted, but it does include four additional methods relating to inheritance: `getImplicitSources()`, `getSources()`, `isImplicitGranted()`, and `isInherited()`.

We'll again use the Service folder for our examples. The security had previously been configured as:

Reports

- Administrators – Full Control (Inherited from Root)

- Everyone – View

Service

- Administrators – Full Control (inherited from Root)

- Everyone – View (inherited from Reports), Schedule

- Finance – View on Demand

To have some additional rights to play with, we'll explicitly grant the "*Delete Objects*" right to the Finance group, on the Service folder,.

---

161 All of the common methods between `IEffectiveRight` and `IExplicitRight` are inherited from the `IRightBase` and `IRightIDBase` interfaces.

And on the **Reports** folder, we'll explicitly **deny** the *Edit objects* right for the *Everyone* group.

To list the effective rights on the Service folder, we'll use the *DisplayRights* program from Listing 46. We'll change all occurrences of "Explicit" to "Effective", and change the CMS query to pull the *Service* folder instead of *Reports*.

```java
1  package bosdkbook;
2
3  import java.util.Iterator;
4  import java.util.Locale;
5
6  import com.crystaldecisions.sdk.framework.CrystalEnterprise;
7  import com.crystaldecisions.sdk.framework.IEnterpriseSession;
8  import com.crystaldecisions.sdk.framework.ISessionMgr;
9  import com.crystaldecisions.sdk.occa.infostore.IEffectivePrincipal;
10 import com.crystaldecisions.sdk.occa.infostore.IEffectiveRight;
11 import com.crystaldecisions.sdk.occa.infostore.IInfoObject;
12 import com.crystaldecisions.sdk.occa.infostore.IInfoObjects;
13 import com.crystaldecisions.sdk.occa.infostore.IInfoStore;
14 import com.crystaldecisions.sdk.occa.infostore.ISecurityInfo2;
15
16 public class DisplayRights
17 {
18     public static void main(String[] args) throws Exception
19     {
20         ISessionMgr sessionManager = CrystalEnterprise.getSessionMgr();
```

```
21        IEnterpriseSession session = sessionManager.logon ("administrator",
   "xxxx", "192.168.56.102", "secEnterprise");

22

23        IInfoStore infoStore = (IInfoStore) session.getService ("","InfoStore");

24

25        IInfoObjects ios = infoStore.query("select si_id from ci_infoobjects
   where si_name = 'reports'");

26

27      for(Object o : ios)

28      {

29          IInfoObject io = (IInfoObject) o;

30          ISecurityInfo2 sec = io.getSecurityInfo2();

31

32          Iterator<IEffectivePrincipal> iPrinc =
                sec.getEffectivePrincipals().iterator();

33

34          while(iPrinc.hasNext())

35          {

36              IEffectivePrincipal princ = iPrinc.next();

37

38              System.out.println("Principal: " + princ.getName());

39

40              System.out.println(
                   "Source Kind\tApplies\tGranted\tScope\tDescription");

41

42              Iterator<IEffectiveRight> itRight = princ.getRights().iterator();

43              while(itRight.hasNext())

44              {

45                  IEffectiveRight right = itRight.next();

46

47                      String sourceKind = right.getRightPluginKind();

48                      if(sourceKind.equals(""))

49                          sourceKind="General";

50

51                  String out = sourceKind + "\t"
```

```
52                        + right.getApplicableKind() + "\t"
53                        + (right.isGranted() ? "Granted\t" : "Denied\t")
54                        + right.getScope() + "\t"
55                        + right.getDescription(Locale.getDefault());
56
57              System.out.println(out);
58          }
59        }
60      }
61    }
62 }
```

Listing 47: DisplayRights - Effective rights

The result of the program includes over 300 rights in total since all effective rights, including those granted via an access level, are displayed:

Principal: Everyone				
Source Kind	Applies	Granted	Scope	Description
busobjReporter	Any	Granted	descendants	Desktop Intelligence Report Interaction
busobjReporter	Any	Granted	this	Desktop Intelligence Report Interaction
busobjReporter	Any	Granted	descendants	Drill Through
busobjReporter	Any	Granted	this	Drill Through
busobjReporter	Any	Granted	descendants	Edit Scope of Analysis
busobjReporter	Any	Granted	this	Edit Scope of Analysis
busobjReporter	Any	Granted	descendants	Print Documents
busobjReporter	Any	Granted	this	Print Documents
busobjReporter	Any	Granted	descendants	Retrieve Documents
busobjReporter	Any	Granted	this	Retrieve Documents
busobjReporter	Any	Granted	descendants	Run VBA Code
busobjReporter	Any	Granted	this	Run VBA Code
busobjReporter	Any	Granted	descendants	Save Desktop Intelligence Documents
busobjReporter	Any	Granted	this	Save Desktop Intelligence Documents
busobjReporter	Any	Granted	descendants	Send Documents to Inbox
busobjReporter	Any	Granted	this	Send Documents to Inbox
busobjReporter	Any	Granted	descendants	Send Documents to Mail
busobjReporter	Any	Granted	this	Send Documents to Mail
busobjReporter	Any	Granted	descendants	Send Documents to Repository

busobjReporter	Any	Granted	this	Send Documents to Repository
busobjReporter	Any	Granted	descendants	Work in Drill Mode
busobjReporter	Any	Granted	this	Work in Drill Mode
busobjReporter	Any	Granted	descendants	Work in Slice-and-Dice Mode
busobjReporter	Any	Granted	this	Work in Slice-and-Dice Mode
CrystalReport	Any	Granted	descendants	Export the report's data
CrystalReport	Any	Granted	this	Export the report's data
CrystalReport	Any	Granted	descendants	Print the report's data
CrystalReport	Any	Granted	this	Print the report's data
FullClient	Any	Granted	descendants	Export the report's data
FullClient	Any	Granted	this	Export the report's data
FullClient	Any	Granted	descendants	Refresh List of Values
FullClient	Any	Granted	this	Refresh List of Values
FullClient	Any	Granted	descendants	Use Lists of Values
FullClient	Any	Granted	this	Use Lists of Values
Note	Any	Granted	descendants	Allow discussion threads
Note	Any	Granted	this	Allow discussion threads
SharedQuery	Any	Granted	descendants	Create and edit queries based on the universe
SharedQuery	Any	Granted	this	Create and edit queries based on the universe
SharedQuery	Any	Granted	descendants	Data access
SharedQuery	Any	Granted	this	Data access
Webi	Any	Granted	descendants	Export the report's data
Webi	Any	Granted	this	Export the report's data
Webi	Any	Granted	descendants	Refresh List of Values
Webi	Any	Granted	this	Refresh List of Values
Webi	Any	Granted	descendants	Save as CSV
Webi	Any	Granted	this	Save as CSV
Webi	Any	Granted	descendants	Save as Excel or Text
Webi	Any	Granted	this	Save as Excel or Text
Webi	Any	Granted	descendants	Save as PDF
Webi	Any	Granted	this	Save as PDF
Webi	Any	Granted	descendants	Use Lists of Values
Webi	Any	Granted	this	Use Lists of Values
General	Any	Granted	descendants	Comment on documents
General	Any	Granted	this	Comment on documents
General	Any	Granted	descendants	Copy objects to another folder
General	Any	Granted	this	Copy objects to another folder
General	Any	Granted	descendants	Define server groups to process

				jobs
General	Any	Granted	this	Define server groups to process jobs
General	Any	Granted	descendants	Delete instances that the user owns
General	Any	Granted	this	Delete instances that the user owns
General	Any	Denied	descendants	Edit objects
General	Any	Denied	this	Edit objects
General	Any	Granted	descendants	Edit objects that the user owns
General	Any	Granted	this	Edit objects that the user owns
General	Any	Granted	descendants	Pause and Resume document instances
General	Any	Granted	this	Pause and Resume document instances
General	Any	Granted	descendants	Reschedule instances
General	Any	Granted	this	Reschedule instances
General	Any	Granted	descendants	Schedule document to run
General	Any	Granted	this	Schedule document to run
General	Any	Granted	descendants	Schedule to destinations
General	Any	Granted	this	Schedule to destinations
General	Any	Granted	descendants	View comments on documents
General	Any	Granted	this	View comments on documents
General	Any	Granted	descendants	View document instances
General	Any	Granted	this	View document instances
General	Any	Granted	descendants	View objects
General	Any	Granted	this	View objects
Principal: Administrators				
Source Kind	Applies	Granted	Scope	Description
busobjReporter	Any	Granted	descendants	Always Regenerate SQL
busobjReporter	Any	Granted	this	Always Regenerate SQL
busobjReporter	Any	Granted	descendants	Copy to Clipboard
busobjReporter	Any	Granted	this	Copy to Clipboard
busobjReporter	Any	Granted	descendants	Create And Edit Connections
busobjReporter	Any	Granted	this	Create And Edit Connections
busobjReporter	Any	Granted	descendants	Create Desktop Intelligence Documents
busobjReporter	Any	Granted	this	Create Desktop Intelligence Documents
busobjReporter	Any	Granted	descendants	Create Templates
busobjReporter	Any	Granted	this	Create Templates
busobjReporter	Any	Granted	descendants	Data Provider Manipulation
busobjReporter	Any	Granted	this	Data Provider Manipulation

busobjReporter	Any	Granted	descendants	Desktop Intelligence Document Interaction
busobjReporter	Any	Granted	this	Desktop Intelligence Document Interaction
busobjReporter	Any	Granted	descendants	Desktop Intelligence Report Interaction
busobjReporter	Any	Granted	this	Desktop Intelligence Report Interaction
busobjReporter	Any	Granted	descendants	Drill Through
busobjReporter	Any	Granted	this	Drill Through
busobjReporter	Any	Granted	descendants	Edit Euro Converter Rate
busobjReporter	Any	Granted	this	Edit Euro Converter Rate
busobjReporter	Any	Granted	descendants	Edit Free-hand SQL
busobjReporter	Any	Granted	this	Edit Free-hand SQL
busobjReporter	Any	Granted	descendants	Edit List of Values
busobjReporter	Any	Granted	this	Edit List of Values
busobjReporter	Any	Granted	descendants	Edit Personal Data Files
busobjReporter	Any	Granted	this	Edit Personal Data Files
busobjReporter	Any	Granted	descendants	Edit Queries
busobjReporter	Any	Granted	this	Edit Queries
busobjReporter	Any	Granted	descendants	Edit Query SQL
busobjReporter	Any	Granted	this	Edit Query SQL
busobjReporter	Any	Granted	descendants	Edit Scope of Analysis
busobjReporter	Any	Granted	this	Edit Scope of Analysis
busobjReporter	Any	Granted	descendants	Edit Stored Procedures
busobjReporter	Any	Granted	this	Edit Stored Procedures
busobjReporter	Any	Granted	descendants	Edit VBA Code
busobjReporter	Any	Granted	this	Edit VBA Code
busobjReporter	Any	Granted	descendants	Euro Converter
busobjReporter	Any	Granted	this	Euro Converter
busobjReporter	Any	Granted	descendants	Install Add-Ins
busobjReporter	Any	Granted	this	Install Add-Ins
busobjReporter	Any	Granted	descendants	Manage All Corporate Categories
busobjReporter	Any	Granted	this	Manage All Corporate Categories
busobjReporter	Any	Granted	descendants	Manage My Corporate Categories
busobjReporter	Any	Granted	this	Manage My Corporate Categories
busobjReporter	Any	Granted	descendants	Print Documents
busobjReporter	Any	Granted	this	Print Documents
busobjReporter	Any	Granted	descendants	Refresh Desktop Intelligence Document
busobjReporter	Any	Granted	this	Refresh Desktop Intelligence Document

busobjReporter	Any	Granted	descendants	Refresh Document List and Categories
busobjReporter	Any	Granted	this	Refresh Document List and Categories
busobjReporter	Any	Granted	descendants	Refresh List of Values
busobjReporter	Any	Granted	this	Refresh List of Values
busobjReporter	Any	Granted	descendants	Retrieve Documents
busobjReporter	Any	Granted	this	Retrieve Documents
busobjReporter	Any	Granted	descendants	Run VBA Code
busobjReporter	Any	Granted	this	Run VBA Code
busobjReporter	Any	Granted	descendants	Save Desktop Intelligence Documents
busobjReporter	Any	Granted	this	Save Desktop Intelligence Documents
busobjReporter	Any	Granted	descendants	Save documents for all users
busobjReporter	Any	Granted	this	Save documents for all users
busobjReporter	Any	Granted	descendants	Send Documents to Inbox
busobjReporter	Any	Granted	this	Send Documents to Inbox
busobjReporter	Any	Granted	descendants	Send Documents to Mail
busobjReporter	Any	Granted	this	Send Documents to Mail
busobjReporter	Any	Granted	descendants	Send Documents to Repository
busobjReporter	Any	Granted	this	Send Documents to Repository
busobjReporter	Any	Granted	descendants	Use Free-hand SQL
busobjReporter	Any	Granted	this	Use Free-hand SQL
busobjReporter	Any	Granted	descendants	Use List of Values
busobjReporter	Any	Granted	this	Use List of Values
busobjReporter	Any	Granted	descendants	Use other SQL requests than Select
busobjReporter	Any	Granted	this	Use other SQL requests than Select
busobjReporter	Any	Granted	descendants	Use Personal Data Files
busobjReporter	Any	Granted	this	Use Personal Data Files
busobjReporter	Any	Granted	descendants	Use Queries
busobjReporter	Any	Granted	this	Use Queries
busobjReporter	Any	Granted	descendants	Use Stored Procedures
busobjReporter	Any	Granted	this	Use Stored Procedures
busobjReporter	Any	Granted	descendants	Use Templates
busobjReporter	Any	Granted	this	Use Templates
busobjReporter	Any	Granted	descendants	Use User Objects
busobjReporter	Any	Granted	this	Use User Objects
busobjReporter	Any	Granted	descendants	View SQL
busobjReporter	Any	Granted	this	View SQL
busobjReporter	Any	Granted	descendants	Work in Drill Mode
busobjReporter	Any	Granted	this	Work in Drill Mode

busobjReporter	Any	Granted	descendants	Work in Slice-and-Dice Mode
busobjReporter	Any	Granted	this	Work in Slice-and-Dice Mode
CrystalReport	Any	Granted	descendants	Export the report's data
CrystalReport	Any	Granted	this	Export the report's data
CrystalReport	Any	Granted	descendants	Print the report's data
CrystalReport	Any	Granted	this	Print the report's data
CrystalReport	Any	Granted	descendants	Refresh the report's data
CrystalReport	Any	Granted	this	Refresh the report's data
FullClient	Any	Granted	descendants	Download files associated with the object
FullClient	Any	Granted	this	Download files associated with the object
FullClient	Any	Granted	descendants	Export the report's data
FullClient	Any	Granted	this	Export the report's data
FullClient	Any	Granted	descendants	Refresh List of Values
FullClient	Any	Granted	this	Refresh List of Values
FullClient	Any	Granted	descendants	Refresh the report's data
FullClient	Any	Granted	this	Refresh the report's data
FullClient	Any	Granted	descendants	Use Lists of Values
FullClient	Any	Granted	this	Use Lists of Values
FullClient	Any	Granted	descendants	View SQL
FullClient	Any	Granted	this	View SQL
FullClientAddin	Any	Granted	descendants	Download files associated with the object
FullClientAddin	Any	Granted	this	Download files associated with the object
FullClientTemplate	Any	Granted	descendants	Download files associated with the object
FullClientTemplate	Any	Granted	this	Download files associated with the object
Note	Any	Granted	descendants	Allow discussion threads
Note	Any	Granted	this	Allow discussion threads
SharedQuery	Any	Granted	descendants	Assign security profiles
SharedQuery	Any	Granted	this	Assign security profiles
SharedQuery	Any	Granted	descendants	Create and edit queries based on the universe
SharedQuery	Any	Granted	this	Create and edit queries based on the universe
SharedQuery	Any	Granted	descendants	Data access
SharedQuery	Any	Granted	this	Data access
SharedQuery	Any	Granted	descendants	Edit security profiles
SharedQuery	Any	Granted	this	Edit security profiles

SharedQuery	Any	Granted	descendants	Retrieve Shared Query
SharedQuery	Any	Granted	this	Retrieve Shared Query
Webi	Any	Granted	descendants	Edit Query
Webi	Any	Granted	this	Edit Query
Webi	Any	Granted	descendants	Export the report's data
Webi	Any	Granted	this	Export the report's data
Webi	Any	Granted	descendants	Refresh List of Values
Webi	Any	Granted	this	Refresh List of Values
Webi	Any	Granted	descendants	Refresh the report's data
Webi	Any	Granted	this	Refresh the report's data
Webi	Any	Granted	descendants	Save as CSV
Webi	Any	Granted	this	Save as CSV
Webi	Any	Granted	descendants	Save as Excel or Text
Webi	Any	Granted	this	Save as Excel or Text
Webi	Any	Granted	descendants	Save as PDF
Webi	Any	Granted	this	Save as PDF
Webi	Any	Granted	descendants	Use Lists of Values
Webi	Any	Granted	this	Use Lists of Values
Webi	Any	Granted	descendants	View SQL
Webi	Any	Granted	this	View SQL
General	Any	Granted	descendants	Add objects to the folder
General	Any	Granted	this	Add objects to the folder
General	Any	Granted	descendants	Comment on documents
General	Any	Granted	this	Comment on documents
General	Any	Granted	descendants	Copy objects to another folder
General	Any	Granted	this	Copy objects to another folder
General	Any	Granted	descendants	Define server groups to process jobs
General	Any	Granted	this	Define server groups to process jobs
General	Any	Granted	descendants	Delete instances
General	Any	Granted	this	Delete instances
General	Any	Granted	descendants	Delete objects
General	Any	Granted	this	Delete objects
General	Any	Granted	descendants	Download files associated with the object
General	Any	Granted	this	Download files associated with the object
General	Any	Granted	descendants	Edit objects
General	Any	Granted	this	Edit objects
General	Any	Granted	descendants	Modify the rights users have to

				objects
General	Any	Granted	this	Modify the rights users have to objects
General	Any	Granted	descendants	Pause and Resume document instances
General	Any	Granted	this	Pause and Resume document instances
General	Any	Granted	descendants	Replicate content
General	Any	Granted	this	Replicate content
General	Any	Granted	descendants	Reschedule instances
General	Any	Granted	this	Reschedule instances
General	Any	Granted	descendants	Schedule document to run
General	Any	Granted	this	Schedule document to run
General	Any	Granted	descendants	Schedule on behalf of other users
General	Any	Granted	this	Schedule on behalf of other users
General	Any	Granted	descendants	Schedule to destinations
General	Any	Granted	this	Schedule to destinations
General	Any	Granted	descendants	Securely modify right inheritance settings
General	Any	Granted	this	Securely modify right inheritance settings
General	Any	Granted	descendants	Securely modify rights users have to objects.
General	Any	Granted	this	Securely modify rights users have to objects.
General	Any	Granted	descendants	Translate objects
General	Any	Granted	this	Translate objects
General	Any	Granted	descendants	Use access level for security assignment
General	Any	Granted	this	Use access level for security assignment
General	Any	Granted	descendants	View comments on documents
General	Any	Granted	this	View comments on documents
General	Any	Granted	descendants	View document instances
General	Any	Granted	this	View document instances
General	Any	Granted	descendants	View objects
General	Any	Granted	this	View objects
Principal: Finance				
Source Kind	Applies	Granted	Scope	Description
busobjReporter	Any	Granted	descendants	Refresh Desktop Intelligence Document
busobjReporter	Any	Granted	this	Refresh Desktop Intelligence Document
CrystalReport	Any	Granted	descendants	Export the report's data

CrystalReport	Any	Granted	this	Export the report's data
CrystalReport	Any	Granted	descendants	Print the report's data
CrystalReport	Any	Granted	this	Print the report's data
CrystalReport	Any	Granted	descendants	Refresh the report's data
CrystalReport	Any	Granted	this	Refresh the report's data
FullClient	Any	Granted	descendants	Export the report's data
FullClient	Any	Granted	this	Export the report's data
FullClient	Any	Granted	descendants	Refresh List of Values
FullClient	Any	Granted	this	Refresh List of Values
FullClient	Any	Granted	descendants	Refresh the report's data
FullClient	Any	Granted	this	Refresh the report's data
FullClient	Any	Granted	descendants	Use Lists of Values
FullClient	Any	Granted	this	Use Lists of Values
Note	Any	Granted	descendants	Allow discussion threads
Note	Any	Granted	this	Allow discussion threads
SharedQuery	Any	Granted	descendants	Create and edit queries based on the universe
SharedQuery	Any	Granted	this	Create and edit queries based on the universe
SharedQuery	Any	Granted	descendants	Data access
SharedQuery	Any	Granted	this	Data access
Webi	Any	Granted	descendants	Export the report's data
Webi	Any	Granted	this	Export the report's data
Webi	Any	Granted	descendants	Refresh List of Values
Webi	Any	Granted	this	Refresh List of Values
Webi	Any	Granted	descendants	Refresh the report's data
Webi	Any	Granted	this	Refresh the report's data
Webi	Any	Granted	descendants	Save as CSV
Webi	Any	Granted	this	Save as CSV
Webi	Any	Granted	descendants	Save as Excel or Text
Webi	Any	Granted	this	Save as Excel or Text
Webi	Any	Granted	descendants	Save as PDF
Webi	Any	Granted	this	Save as PDF
Webi	Any	Granted	descendants	Use Lists of Values
Webi	Any	Granted	this	Use Lists of Values
General	Any	Granted	descendants	Comment on documents
General	Any	Granted	this	Comment on documents
General	Any	Granted	descendants	Copy objects to another folder
General	Any	Granted	this	Copy objects to another folder
General	Any	Granted	descendants	Define server groups to process

				jobs
General	Any	Granted	this	Define server groups to process jobs
General	Any	Granted	descendants	Delete instances that the user owns
General	Any	Granted	this	Delete instances that the user owns
General	Any	Granted	descendants	Delete objects that the user owns
General	Any	Granted	this	Delete objects that the user owns
General	Any	Granted	descendants	Edit objects that the user owns
General	Any	Granted	this	Edit objects that the user owns
General	Any	Granted	descendants	Pause and Resume document instances
General	Any	Granted	this	Pause and Resume document instances
General	Any	Granted	descendants	Reschedule instances
General	Any	Granted	this	Reschedule instances
General	Any	Granted	descendants	Schedule document to run
General	Any	Granted	this	Schedule document to run
General	Any	Granted	descendants	Schedule to destinations
General	Any	Granted	this	Schedule to destinations
General	Any	Granted	descendants	View comments on documents
General	Any	Granted	this	View comments on documents
General	Any	Granted	descendants	View document instances
General	Any	Granted	this	View document instances
General	Any	Granted	descendants	View objects
General	Any	Granted	this	View objects

Effective Right Inheritance

As with effective roles, we can retrieve the source of effective rights, via the `IEffectiveRight.getSources()` method. This returns a `List` of `IRightSource` objects, each representing the object/principal from which the grant was assigned.

The `IRightSource` interface contains the following methods:

Package com.crystaldecisions.sdk.occa.infostore
Interface *IRightSource*

String	getApplicableKind()
	Returns the name of the plugin (kind) that this right applies to.
int	getObjectID()
	Returns the id of the InfoObject upon which the role was explicitly assigned.
int	getPrincipalID()

	Returns the id of the principal (group or user) from which the security right is inherited.
String	getScope()
	Returns the scope of this right. The possible values are in CeSecurityOptions.RightScope, and are either "this" or "descendants".
int	getSourceRole()
	Returns the id of the security role from which the right assignment is inherited. If the right assignment is an advanced right (i.e., not from a security role), then the value is 0.
boolean	isFromRole()
	Returns true if the right assignment originates from a security role, or false otherwise. When true, getSourceRole() returns 0.
boolean	isInherited()
	Returns true if this role assignment is inherited from the principal's parent group or the InfoObject's parent folder.

Class/Interface 63: IRightSource

To illustrate the retrieval of effective right sources, we'll modify the *DisplayRights* program from Listing 47. We'll add in the logic to display right sources, and we'll only display advanced rights that are inherited but *not* inherited from roles (otherwise, the output would be hundreds of lines long).

```
1  package bosdkbook;
2
3  import java.util.Iterator;
4  import java.util.Locale;
5
6  import com.crystaldecisions.sdk.exception.SDKException;
7  import com.crystaldecisions.sdk.framework.CrystalEnterprise;
8  import com.crystaldecisions.sdk.framework.IEnterpriseSession;
9  import com.crystaldecisions.sdk.framework.ISessionMgr;
10 import com.crystaldecisions.sdk.occa.infostore.IEffectivePrincipal;
11 import com.crystaldecisions.sdk.occa.infostore.IEffectiveRight;
12 import com.crystaldecisions.sdk.occa.infostore.IInfoObject;
13 import com.crystaldecisions.sdk.occa.infostore.IInfoObjects;
14 import com.crystaldecisions.sdk.occa.infostore.IInfoStore;
15 import com.crystaldecisions.sdk.occa.infostore.IRightSource;
```

```
16   import com.crystaldecisions.sdk.occa.infostore.ISecurityInfo2;

17

18   public class DisplayRights

19   {

20       public static void main(String[] args) throws Exception

21       {

22           ISessionMgr sessionManager = CrystalEnterprise.getSessionMgr();

23           IEnterpriseSession session = sessionManager.logon ("administrator",
     "xxxx", "192.168.56.102", "secEnterprise");

24

25           IInfoStore infoStore = (IInfoStore) session.getService ("","InfoStore");

26

27           IInfoObjects ios = infoStore.query("select si_id from ci_infoobjects
     where si_name = 'service'");

28

29           for(Object o : ios)

30           {

31               IInfoObject io = (IInfoObject) o;

32               ISecurityInfo2 sec = io.getSecurityInfo2();

33

34               Iterator<IEffectivePrincipal> iPrinc =
                     sec.getEffectivePrincipals().iterator();

35

36               while(iPrinc.hasNext())

37               {

38                   IEffectivePrincipal princ = iPrinc.next();

39

40                   System.out.println("Principal: " + princ.getName());

41

42                   Iterator<IEffectiveRight> itRight =
                         princ.getRights().iterator();

43

44                   while(itRight.hasNext())

45                   {

46                       IEffectiveRight right = itRight.next();

47
```

```
48                    for(Object o2 : right.getSources())
49                       {
50                          IRightSource source = (IRightSource)o2;
51                          if(source.isInherited() && !source.isFromRole())
52                             {
53                                String sourceKind = right.getRightPluginKind();
54                                if(sourceKind.equals(""))
55                                   sourceKind="General";
56
57                                String out = "Source kind: "
                                        + right.getRightPluginKind() + "\n"
58                                        + "Applies to: "
                                        + right.getApplicableKind() + "\n"
59                                        + "Scope: " + right.getScope() + "\n"
60                                        + "Description: "
                                        + right.getDescription(Locale.getDefault())
                                        + "\n"
61                                        + "Inherited from object: "
                                        + getNameFromID(infoStore,source.getObjectID())
                                        + "\n"
62                                        + "Inherited from principal: "
                                        + getNameFromID(infoStore,
                                             source.getPrincipalID()) + "\n"
63                                        + "Assignment: "
                                        + (right.isGranted() ? "Granted\n" : "Denied\n");
64
65                                System.out.println(out);
66                             }
67                       }
68                    }
69                 }
70          }
71    }
72
73    private static String getNameFromID(IInfoStore infoStore,Integer id)
74    throws SDKException
75    {
```

```
76        IInfoObjects ios = infoStore.query("select si_name from
   ci_systemobjects,ci_infoobjects,ci_appobjects where si_id = " + id);

77        if(ios.size() == 0)

78            return "";

79        return ((IInfoObject)ios.get(0)).getTitle();

80    }

81 }
```

Listing 48: DisplayRights with source

This produces the following result:

```
Principal: Everyone
Source kind: General
Applies to: Any
Scope: this
Description: Edit objects
Inherited from object: Reports
Inherited from principal: Everyone
Assignment: Denied

Source kind: General
Applies to: Any
Scope: descendants
Description: Edit objects
Inherited from object: Reports
Inherited from principal: Everyone
Assignment: Denied

Principal: Administrators
Principal: Finance
```

This tells us that for the *Everyone* group, the *Edit objects* right has been inherited from the *Reports* folder. The right was Denied, and it applied to both the object itself and descendants. The *Administrators* and *Finance* groups, while they are principals on the *Source* folder, are not inheriting any advanced rights, so nothing is displayed.

RightDescriptor Revisited

A `RightDescriptor` object may be retrieved from `IEffectiveRight`, similar to the corresponding method in `IExplicitRight`. One potential use of the `RightDescriptor` object would be to copy all **effective** rights for a principal/InfoObject to **explicit** rights, as in the following snippet:

```
20        IInfoObjects ios = infoStore.query("select si_id from ci_infoobjects
   where si_name = 'service'");

21

22        for(Object o : ios)
```

```
23              {

24                  IInfoObject io = (IInfoObject) o;

25                  ISecurityInfo2 sec = io.getSecurityInfo2();

26

27                  Iterator<IEffectivePrincipal> iPrinc =
                        sec.getEffectivePrincipals().iterator();

28

29              while(iPrinc.hasNext())

30              {

31                  IEffectivePrincipal princ = iPrinc.next();

32

33                  IExplicitPrincipal exPrinc =
                            sec.getExplicitPrincipals().get(princ.getID());

34              if(exPrinc==null)

35                  exPrinc = sec.getExplicitPrincipals().add(princ.getID());

36

37                  IEffectiveRights effectiveRights = princ.getRights();

38                  Iterator<IEffectiveRight> iEffectiveRight =
                            effectiveRights.iterator();

39

40              while(iEffectiveRight.hasNext())

41              {

42                  IEffectiveRight effectiveRight = iEffectiveRight.next();

43

44                  IExplicitRight newRight =
        exPrinc.getRights().add(effectiveRight.getRightDescriptor());

45                  newRight.setGranted(effectiveRight.isGranted());

46              }
```

By doing this, all rights that a principal has for an InfoObject, whether they are explicit-assigned advanced rights, assigned via a role, or inherited from a parent group or parent InfoObject, will now be explicitly assigned. This might be useful if a particular InfoObject needs to be moved to a new parent folder, but retain all security rights that are assigned in the current folder.

Chapter Review

- The security model in SAP BusinessObjects is very flexible and powerful. Using the SDK to manage security can improve efficiency and reduce the time spent on administrative tasks.

- Access Levels (roles) and rights can be explicitly assigned to a principal for an InfoObject, or they can be inherited from an ancestral folder or user group.

- Explicitly-assigned roles and rights are managed via the `IExplicitPrincipals` collection; effective rights can be retrieved (but not assigned) via the `IEffectivePrincipals` collection.

- The `IEffectiveRights` collection (retrieved from `IEffectivePrincipal`) contains the actual calculated collection of rights that apply to an InfoObject for a principal. This considers all of the possible ways that a principal can be assigned access (explicit rights & roles, rights/roles inherited from the parent InfoObject, rights/roles inherited from the principal's parent groups).

- The `RightDescriptor` class is used to identify a specific right since the same right (ex. "View objects") may be applied in different ways. This class is used to assign rights as well as retrieve existing rights.

Quiz

1. What is the appropriate method to use to determine if Fred has permission to delete the *Quarterly Reports* folder?

    a) `ISecurityInfo2.checkRight()`

    b) `ISecurityInfo2.getEffectivePrincipals()`

    c) `ISecurityInfo2.getAnyPrincipal()`

    d) `ISecurityInfo2.getExplicitPrincipals()`

2. What is the appropriate method to use to get a listing of all of the rights that Fred has on the *Quarterly Reports* folder?

    a) `ISecurityInfo2.checkRight()`

    b) `ISecurityInfo2.getEffectivePrincipals()`

    c) `ISecurityInfo2.getAnyPrincipal()`

    d) `ISecurityInfo2.getExplicitPrincipals()`

3. True/False: Fred is a member of the *Finance* user group, and that group has been assigned the Full Control role on the *Reports* folder. Fred's InfoObject ID is present in the collection retrieved from a call to the *Reports* folder's `ISecurityInfo2.getExplicitPrincipals()`.

4. Roles and rights can be assigned to principals via:

    a) `IEffectivePrincipals`

    b) `IExplicitPrincipals`

    c) Both

    d) Neither

5. True/False: Rights can be either granted, denied, or unassigned. Roles can only be assigned or unassigned.

6. To grant a right on an InfoObject and also its children:

    a) Assign two rights, one each for `CURRENT_OBJECT` and `DESCENDANTS`.

    b) Call `IExplicitRight.setScope(CeSecurityOptions.RightScope.BOTH)`

7. In the `RightDescriptor` class, the __ property specifies the source of a right, while the __ property specifies what kinds of InfoObjects the right applies to.

    a) `kind, applicableObjectType`

    b) `applicableObjectType, kind`

    c) Neither

Answers on page 674.

Appendices

Appendix A - CMS Query Syntax Diagram

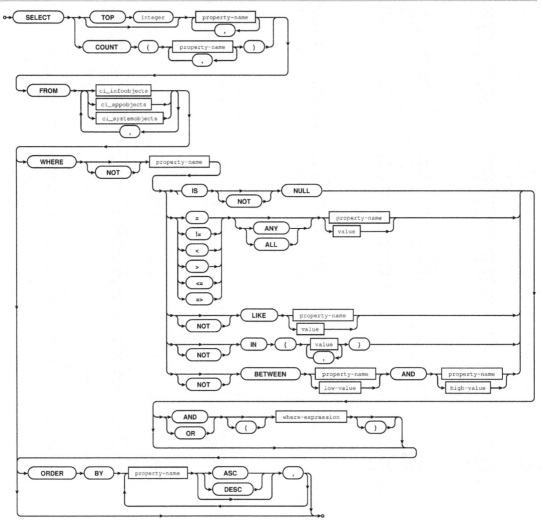

Appendix B - Property Reference

The following is a reference of some of the InfoObject properties that are commonly used in CMS queries and SDK programming.

Common Properties

SI_AGGREGATE_COUNT			
Definition:	The number of objects that meet the criteria of the CMS query. Only returned in queries that include a COUNT() function.		
Data type:	Integer		
Getter:	N/A	Setter:	N/A
Physical column:	N/A	Indexed:	No
Present on:	N/A	See:	Page 7

SI_ANCESTOR			
Definition:	A special property that can only be used in the WHERE condition of a CMS query. It restricts the query results to only those objects that are descendants of the specified InfoObject ID.		
Data type:	Integer		
Getter:	N/A	Setter:	N/A
Physical column:	N/A	Indexed:	No
Present on:	N/A	See:	Page 74

SI_ANCESTOR_CUID			
Definition:	A special property that can only be used in the WHERE condition of a CMS query. It restricts the query results to only those objects that are descendants of the specified InfoObject CUID.		
Data type:	String		
Getter:	N/A	Setter:	N/A
Physical column:	N/A	Indexed:	No
Present on:	N/A	See:	Page 81

SI_CHILDREN		
Definition:	The number of child objects that this InfoObject has	
Data type:	Integer	
Getter:	N/A	*Setter:* N/A (read only)
Physical column:	N/A	*Indexed:* No
Present on:	All InfoObjects	*See:* Page 43

SI_CREATION_TIME		
Definition:	The date and time that this InfoObject was initially created	
Data type:	Date/Time	
Getter:	`IInfoObject` `.getUpdateTimeStamp()`	*Setter:* N/A (read only)
Physical column:	`LastModifyTime`	*Indexed:* Yes
Present on:	All InfoObjects	*See:* Page 44

SI_CORPORATE_CATEGORIES		
Definition:	Property bag containing a list of IDs of corporate categories that this InfoObject is associated with	
Data type:	Bag	

Getter:	`ICategoryContent`
	`.getCorporateCategories`
	`()`
		Setter: N/A

Physical column:	N/A	*Indexed:* No
Present on:	InfoObject kinds that support categories	*See:* Page 378

SI_CUID		
Definition:	The InfoObject's cluster-unique identifier, as a string. The SI_CUID is between 23 and 64 characters (most are 23). It is unique within a cluster, and can safely be assumed to be universally unique. The value is retained if the InfoObject is migrated to another cluster.	
Data type:	String	
Getter:	`IInfoObject` `.getCUID()`	*Setter:* N/A (read only)
Physical column:	`SI_CUID`	*Indexed:* Yes
Present on:	All InfoObjects	*See:* Page 36

SI_EMAIL_ADDRESS

Definition:	The user's email address			
Data type:	String			
Getter:	IUser .getEmailAddress()		*Setter:*	IUser .setEmailAddress(String emailAddress)
Physical column:	N/A		*Indexed:*	No
Present on:	User InfoObjects (si_kind = 'user')		*See:*	Page 384

SI_DSL_UNIVERSE

Definition:	Property bag containing InfoObject IDs of the unx universes associated with this Web Intelligence document			
Data type:	Bag			
Getter:	IWebi .getDSLUniverses()		*Setter:*	N/A (read only)
Physical column:	N/A		*Indexed:*	No
Present on:	Web Intelligence InfoObjects (si_kind = 'webi')		*See:*	N/A

SI_FAVORITES_FOLDER

Definition:	The InfoObject ID of the user's Favorites Folder			
Data type:	Integer			
Getter:	IUser .getFavoritesFolderID()		*Setter:*	N/A (read only)
Physical column:	N/A		*Indexed:*	No
Present on:	User InfoObjects (si_kind = 'user')		*See:*	Page 74

SI_FILES

Definition:	Contains references to an InfoObject's physical files in the FRS. Included in this bag are the logical location (path) within the FRS, and the name and size of each file.			
Data type:	Bag			
Getter:	IInfoObject .getFiles()		*Setter:*	N/A
Physical column:	N/A		*Indexed:*	No
Present on:	InfoObjects with associated files		*See:*	Page 31

SI_GROUP_MEMBERS			
Definition:	Bag containing the InfoObject IDs of the members of this group; this may include both users and user groups		
Data type:	Bag		
Getters:	IUserGroup .getSubGroups() IUserGroup .getUsers()	*Setter:*	N/A (add or remove elements from the returned Set).
Physical column:	N/A	*Indexed:*	No
Present on:	User Group InfoObjects (si_kind = 'usergroup')	*See:*	Page 33

SI_ID			
Definition:	The object's unique identifier, as an integer. The SI_ID property is assigned incrementally within a cluster, and is unique within a cluster but not between clusters. An InfoObject's SI_ID property is not retained if the InfoObject is migrated to another cluster.		
Data type:	Integer		
Getter:	IInfoObject.getID()	*Setter:*	N/A (read only)
Physical column:	OBJECTID	*Indexed:*	Yes
Present on:	All InfoObjects	*See:*	Page 36

SI_INSTANCE			
Definition:	Indicates if the InfoObject is a scheduled instance (1 = true)		
Data type:	Integer		
Getter:	IInfoObject .isInstance()	*Setter:*	N/A (read only)
Physical column:	N/A	*Indexed:*	No
Present on:	All InfoObjects	*See:*	Page 45

SI_INSTANCE_OBJECT			
Definition:	Indicates if the InfoObject is a completed (successful or failed) scheduled instance (1 = true)		
Data type:	Integer		
Getter:	N/A	*Setter:*	N/A (read only)
Physical column:	SI_INSTANCE_OBJECT	*Indexed:*	Yes
Present on:	All InfoObjects	*See:*	Page 45

SI_INBOX			
Definition:	The InfoObject ID of the user's inbox		
Data type:	Integer		
Getter:	IUser .getInboxID()	*Setter:*	N/A (read only)
Physical column:	N/A	*Indexed:*	No
Present on:	User InfoObjects (si_kind = 'user')	*See:*	Page 76

SI_IS_SCHEDULABLE			
Definition:	Indicates if this InfoObject is capable of being scheduled (1 = true)		
Data type:	Integer		
Getter:	N/A	*Setter:*	N/A (read only)
Physical column:	N/A	*Indexed:*	No
Present on:	All InfoObjects	*See:*	Page 44

SI_KIND			
Definition:	String identifying what the InfoObject *is*, for example: Folder, User, UserGroup, Server, etc. This is a short version of SI_PROGID.		
Data type:	String		
Getter:	IInfoObject .getKind()	*Setter:*	N/A (read only)
Physical column:	N/A	*Indexed:*	No
Present on:	All InfoObjects (excluding some system objects)	*See:*	Page 39

SI_NAME			
Definition:	The InfoObject's name, as a string.		
Data type:	String		
Getter:	IInfoObject.getTitle()	*Setter:*	IInfoObject .setTitle(String newTitle)
Physical column:	OBJNAME (encrypted)	*Indexed:*	Yes
Present on:	All InfoObjects	*See:*	Page 38

SI_NAMEDUSER			
Definition:	Indicates the user's assigned licensing mode: named user or concurrent		
Data type:	Integer		

Getter:	`IUser`
	`.getConnection()`
		Setter:	`IUser`
			`.getConnection(int`
			`newConnection)`

Physical column:	SI_NAMEDUSER	*Indexed:*	Yes
Present on:	User InfoObjects (si_kind = 'user')	*See:*	Page 383

SI_OBTYPE			
Definition:	Integer value identifying the type of InfoObject. This value maps to `SI_KIND` and `SI_PROGID`, but is not guaranteed to be consistent across different installations of SAP BusinessObjects.		
Data type:	Integer		
Getter:	N/A	*Setter:*	N/A (read only)
Physical column:	TypeID	*Indexed:*	Yes
Present on:	All InfoObjects	*See:*	Page 40

SI_OWNER			
Definition:	The name of the user who owns the InfoObject.		
Data type:	String		
Getter:	`IInfoObject` `.getOwner()`	*Setter:*	N/A (read only)
Physical column:	N/A	*Indexed:*	No
Present on:	All InfoObjects	*See:*	Page 241

SI_OWNERID			
Definition:	The `SI_ID` of the user who owns this InfoObject		
Data type:	Integer		
Getter:	`IInfoObject` `.getOwnerID()`	*Setter:*	N/A
Physical column:	N/A	*Indexed:*	No
Present on:	All InfoObjects	*See:*	Page 241

SI_PATH			
Definition:	Bag containing the names and InfoObject IDs of this folder's ancestors		
Data type:	Bag		
Getter:	`IFolder.getPath()`	*Setter:*	N/A
Physical column:	N/A	*Indexed:*	No
Present on:	Folder InfoObjects (si_kind = 'folder')	*See:*	Page 71

SI_PARENT_CUID			
Definition:	The `SI_CUID` value of the InfoObject's parent		
Data type:	String		
Getter:	`IInfoObject` `.getParentCUID()`	*Setter:*	N/A
Physical column:	N/A	*Indexed:*	No
Present on:	All InfoObjects	*See:*	Page 41

SI_PARENT_FOLDER_CUID			
Definition:	The `SI_CUID` value of the InfoObject's nearest ancestor that is a Folder.		
Data type:	String		
Getter:	N/A	*Setter:*	N/A (read only)
Physical column:	N/A	*Indexed:*	No
Present on:	All InfoObjects	*See:*	Page 43

SI_PARENTID			
Definition:	The SI_ID value of the InfoObject's parent		
Data type:	Integer		
Getter:	`IInfoObject` `.getParentID()`	*Setter:*	`IInfoObject` `.setParentID(int parentID)`
Physical column:	`ParentID`	*Indexed*	Yes
Present on:	All InfoObjects	*See:*	Page 41

SI_PERSONAL_CATEGORIES			
Definition:	Property bag containing a list of IDs of personal categories that this InfoObject is associated with		
Data type:	Bag		
Getter:	ICategoryContent .getPersonalCategories( )	*Setter:*	N/A
Physical column:	N/A	*Indexed:*	No
Present on:	InfoObject kinds that support categories	*See:*	Page 378

SI_PROGID			
Definition:	String identifying what the InfoObject *is*, for example: CrystalEnterprise.Folder. This is a long version of SI_KIND.		
Data type:	String		
Getter:	IInfoObject .getProgID()	*Setter:*	N/A (read only)
Physical column:	N/A	*Indexed:*	No
Present on:	All InfoObjects (excluding some system objects)	*See:*	Page 39

SI_PROGRAM_CAN_FAIL_JOB			
Definition:	Indicates whether the Program Object can signal a failure, causing the scheduled instance to fail (1 = true)		
Data type:	Integer		
Getter:	N/A	*Indexed:*	N/A
Physical column:	N/A	*Indexed:*	No
Present on:	Program Objects	*See:*	Page 327

SI_RUNNABLE_OBJECT			
Definition:	Indicates whether the instance is not yet completed. The value is true for instances that are running, paused, or pending (1 = true).		
Data type:	Integer		
Getter:	N/A	*Indexed:*	N/A
Physical column:	N/A	*Indexed:*	No
Present on:	All InfoObjects	*See:*	Page 46

SI_SPECIFIC_KIND

Definition:	String that provides additional specificity of the InfoObject's `SI_KIND` value. Only applicable for certain object kinds.		
Data type:	String		
Getter:	`IInfoObject` `.getSpecificKind()`	*Setter:*	N/A (read only)
Physical column:	N/A	*Indexed:*	No
Present on:	All InfoObjects (excluding some system objects)	*See:*	Page 39

SI_SPECIFIC_PROGID

Definition:	String that provides additional specificity of the InfoObject's `SI_PROGID` value. Only applicable for certain ProgIDs.		
Data type:	String		
Getter:	`IInfoObject` `.getSpecificProgID()`	*Setter:*	N/A (read only)
Physical column:	N/A	*Indexed:*	No
Present on:	All InfoObjects (excluding some system objects)	*See:*	Page 39

SI_TABLE

Definition:	Indicates which logical table this InfoObject is in: 0 = CI_INFOOBJECTS, 1 = CI_APPOBJECTS, 2 = CI_SYSTEMOBJECTS		
Data type:	Integer		
Getter:	N/A	*Setter:*	N/A (read only)
Physical column:	SI_TABLE	*Indexed:*	Yes
Present on:	All InfoObjects		

SI_UNIVERSE

Definition:	Property bag containing InfoObject IDs of the unv universes associated with this Web Intelligence document		
Data type:	Bag		
Getter:	`IWebi` `.getUniverses()`	*Setter:*	N/A (read only)
Physical column:	N/A	*Indexed:*	No
Present on:	Web Intelligence InfoObjects (si_kind = 'webi')	*See:*	N/A

SI_UPDATE_TS			
Definition:	The timestamp of the most recent modification (or creation) of this InfoObject		
Data type:	Date/Time		
Getter:	`IInfoObject` `.getUpdateTimeStamp()`	Setter:	N/A (read only)
Physical column:	`LastModifyTime`	Indexed:	Yes
Present on:	All InfoObjects	See:	Page 44

SI_USERFULLNAME			
Definition:	The user's full name		
Data type:	String		

Getter:	`IUser`
	`.getFullName()`
		Setter:	`IUser`
			`.setFullName(String`
			`newFullName)`

Physical column:	N/A	Indexed:	No
Present on:	All InfoObjects	See:	Page 384

Scheduling Properties

SI_ENDTIME			
Definition:	The date/time that the scheduled instance completed execution. This property is in the root property bag, not to be confused with `SI_SCHEDULEINFO.SI_ENDTIME`.		
Data type:	Date/Time		
Getter:	`ISchedulable` `.getEndTime()`	Setter:	N/A
Physical column:	N/A	Indexed:	No
Present on:	Instances	See:	Page 47

SI_NEW_JOB_ID			
Definition:	For completed recurring instances, this property contains the `SI_ID` of the recurring instance from which this instance was created.		
Data type:	Integer		
Getter:	N/A	Setter:	N/A
Physical column:	N/A	Indexed:	No
Present on:	Instances	See:	Page 48

SI_NEXTRUNTIME

Definition:	The date and time of the next scheduled run of this instance. For one-time runs, this equals `SI_SCHEDULEINFO.SI_STARTTIME`. For recurring instances, it is the date and time of the next run.		
Data type:	Date/Time		
Getter:	`ISchedulingInfo` `.getBeginDate()`	*Setter:*	N/A
Physical column:	N/A	*Indexed:*	No
Present on:	Instances	*See:*	Page 47

SI_PROGID_MACHINE

Definition:	Contains the `SI_PROGID` value of the document that this instance was created from		
Data type:	String		
Getter:	N/A	*Setter:*	N/A
Physical column:	N/A	*Indexed:*	No
Present on:	Instances	*See:*	Page 48

SI_SCHEDULEINFO.SI_CALENDAR_TEMPLATE_ID

Definition:	The InfoObject ID of the Calendar that defines the days that the schedule runs on		
Data type:	Integer		

Getter:	`ISchedulingInfo`
	`.getCalendarTemplate()`
		Setter:	`ISchedulingInfo`
			`.setCalendarTemplate(int`
			`newVal)`

Physical column:	N/A	*Indexed:*	No
Present on:	Instances	*See:*	Page 53

SI_SCHEDULEINFO.SI_DEPENDANTS

Definition:	Bag containing InfoObject IDs of events that are to be fired when this schedule completes		
Data type:	Bag		
Getter:	`ISchedulingInfo` `.getDependants()`	*Setter:*	N/A
Physical column:	N/A	*Indexed:*	No
Present on:	Instances	*See:*	Page 62

SI_SCHEDULEINFO.SI_DEPENDENCIES			
Definition:	Bag containing InfoObject IDs of events that this schedule waits for		
Data type:	Bag		
Getter:	`ISchedulingInfo` `.getDependencies()`	*Setter:*	N/A
Physical column:	N/A	*Indexed:*	No
Present on:	Instances	*See:*	Page 62

SI_SCHEDULEINFO.SI_DESTINATIONS			
Definition:	Property bag containing information regarding the destinations of this schedule		
Data type:	Bag		
Getter:	`ISchedulingInfo` `.getDestinations()`	*Setter:*	N/A
Physical column:	N/A	*Indexed:*	No
Present on:	Instances	*See:*	Page 57

SI_SCHEDULEINFO.SI_ENDTIME			
Definition:	The date/time that this instance expires. This property is in the `SI_SCHEDULEINFO` property bag, not to be confused with `SI_ENDTIME` in the root property bag.		
Data type:	Date/Time		
Getter:	`ISchedulingInfo` `.getEndDate()`	*Setter:*	`ISchedulingInfo` `.setEndDate(Date dtBeginDate)`
Physical column:	N/A	*Indexed:*	No
Present on:	Instances	*See:*	Page 50

SI_SCHEDULEINFO.SI_MACHINE			
Definition:	The InfoObject ID of the server group that this instance is scheduled to use		
Data type:	Integer		
Getter:	`ISchedulingInfo` `.getServerGroup()`	*Setter:*	`ISchedulingInfo` `.setServerGroup(int newVal)`
Physical column:	N/A	*Indexed:*	No
Present on:	Instances	*See:*	Page 64

SI_SCHEDULEINFO.SI_MACHINECHOICE			
Definition:	Indicates whether a server group is to be used when this schedule runs		
Data type:	Integer		
Getter:	ISchedulingInfo .getServerGroupChoice()	*Setter:*	ISchedulingInfo .setServerGroupChoice(int newVal)
Physical column:	N/A	*Indexed:*	No
Present on:	Instances	*See:*	Page 64

SI_SCHEDULEINFO.SI_MULTIPASS			
Definition:	Property bag containing the InfoObject IDs of the users or groups whose credentials are used when the schedule runs. This is defined via the *Schedule For* feature.		
Data type:	Bag		
Getter:	ISchedulingInfo .getMultiPassObjects()	*Setter:*	N/A
Physical column:	N/A	*Indexed:*	No
Present on:	Instances	*See:*	Page 472

SI_SCHEDULEINFO.SI_RETRIES_ALLOWED			
Definition:	The number of times that the instance attempts to retry after a failure		
Data type:	Integer		
Getter:	ISchedulingInfo .getRetriesAllowed()	*Setter:*	ISchedulingInfo .setRetriesAllowed(int newVal)
Physical column:	N/A	*Indexed:*	No
Present on:	Instances	*See:*	Page 56

SI_SCHEDULEINFO.SI_RETRIES_ATTEMPTED			
Definition:	The number of times the schedule was retried after an initial failure		
Data type:	Integer		
Getter:	N/A	*Setter:*	N/A
Physical column:	N/A	*Indexed:*	No
Present on:	Completed instances	*See:*	Page 56

SI_SCHEDULEINFO.SI_RETRY_INTERVAL			
Definition:	The number of seconds between retry attempts		
Data type:	Integer		
Getter:	ISchedulingInfo .getRetryInterval()	Setter:	ISchedulingInfo .setRetrieyInterval(int newVal)
Physical column:	N/A	Indexed:	No
Present on:	Completed instances	See:	Page 56

SI_SCHEDULEINFO.SI_RUN_ON_TEMPLATE			
Definition:	Property bag containing custom calendar templates		
Data type:	Bag		
Getter:	ISchedulingInfo .getCalendarRunDays()	Setter:	N/A
Physical column:	N/A	Indexed:	No
Present on:	Instances	See:	Page 52

SI_SCHEDULEINFO.SI_SCHED_NOW			
Definition:	Indicates whether the schedule is set to run now (1 = true)		
Data type:	Integer		
Getter:	ISchedulingInfo .isRightNow()	Setter:	ISchedulingInfo .setRightNow(boolean rightNow)
Physical column:	N/A	Indexed:	No
Present on:	Instances	See:	Page 52

SI_SCHEDULEINFO.SI_SCHEDULE_INTERVAL_HOURS			
Definition:	The number of hours between scheduled runs, when the *Hourly* recurrence type is used. This is used in conjunction with SI_SCHEDULE_INTERVAL_MINUTES.		
Data type:	Integer		
Getter:	ISchedulingInfo .getIntervalHours()	Setter:	ISchedulingInfo .setIntervalHours(int newVal)
Physical column:	N/A	Indexed:	No
Present on:	Instances	See:	Page 52

SI_SCHEDULEINFO.SI_SCHEDULE_INTERVAL_MINUTES			
Definition:	The number of minutes between scheduled runs, when the *Hourly* recurrence type is used. This is used in conjunction with SI_SCHEDULE_INTERVAL_HOURS.		
Data type:	Integer		

Getter:	`ISchedulingInfo`
	`.getIntervalMinutes()`
		Setter:	`ISchedulingInfo`
			`.setIntervalMinutes(int`
			`newVal)`

Physical column:	N/A	*Indexed:*	No
Present on:	Instances	*See:*	Page 52

SI_SCHEDULEINFO.SI_SCHEDULE_INTERVAL_MONTHS			
Definition:	The number of months between scheduled runs, when the *Monthly* recurrence type is used		
Data type:	Integer		

Getter:	`ISchedulingInfo`
	`.getIntervalMonths()`
		Setter:	`ISchedulingInfo`
			`.setIntervalMonths(int`
			`newVal)`

Physical column:	N/A	*Indexed:*	No
Present on:	Instances	*See:*	Page 52

SI_SCHEDULEINFO.SI_SCHEDULE_INTERVAL_NDAYS			
Definition:	The number of days between scheduled runs, when the *Daily* recurrence type is used		
Data type:	Integer		

Getter:	`ISchedulingInfo`
	`.getIntervalDays()`
		Setter:	`ISchedulingInfo`
			`.setIntervalDays(int`
			`newIntervalDays)`

Physical column:	N/A	*Indexed:*	No
Present on:	Instances	*See:*	Page 52

SI_SCHEDULEINFO.SI_SCHEDULE_INTERVAL_NTHDAY			
Definition:	The day of the month the schedule runs when the "Nth Day" recurrence type is used		
Data type:	Integer		

Getter:	`ISchedulingInfo`
	`.getIntervalNthDay()`
		Setter:	`ISchedulingInfo`
			`.setIntervalNthDay(int`
			`newVal)`

Physical column:	N/A	*Indexed:*	No
Present on:	Instances	*See:*	Page 52

SI_SCHEDULEINFO.SI_STARTTIME		
Definition:	The date/time that this instance is scheduled to start. This property is in the SI_SCHEDULEINFO property bag, not to be confused with SI_STARTTIME in the root property bag.	
Data type:	Date/Time	
Getter:	ISchedulingInfo .getBeginDate()	_Setter:_ ISchedulingInfo .setBeginDate(Date dtEndDate)
Physical column:	N/A	_Indexed:_ No
Present on:	Instances	_See:_ Page 50

SI_RECURRING		
Definition:	Indicates whether the InfoObject is a recurring scheduled instance (1 = true)	
Data type:	Integer	
Getter:	N/A	_Setter:_ N/A (read only)
Physical column:	SI_RECURRING	_Indexed:_ Yes
Present on:	Instances only	_See:_ Page 47

SI_SCHEDULE_STATUS		
Definition:	The scheduling status of the InfoObject	
Data type:	Integer	
Getter:	ISchedulingInfo .getStatus()	_Setter:_ N/A (read only)
Physical column:	ScheduleStatus	_Indexed:_ Yes
Present on:	Instances only	_See:_ Page 45

SI_SCHEDULE_TYPE		
Definition:	The recurrence type that the schedule runs on, for example: Daily, Hourly, Monthly, etc. Values are defined in CeScheduleType.	
Data type:	Integer	
Getter:	ISchedulingInfo .getType()	_Setter:_ ISchedulingInfo .setType(int type)
Physical column:	N/A	_Indexed:_ No
Present on:	Instances only	_See:_ Page 51

SI_STARTTIME			
Definition:	The date/time that the scheduled instance began execution. This property is in the root property bag, not to be confused with `SI_SCHEDULEINFO.SI_STARTTIME`.		
Data type:	Date/Time		
Getter:	`ISchedulingInfo .getDependencies()`	*Setter:*	N/A
Physical column:	N/A	*Indexed:*	No
Present on:	Instances	*See:*	Page 47

SI_SUBMITTER			
Definition:	The name of the user who scheduled this instance		
Data type:	String		
Getter:	N/A	*Setter:*	N/A
Physical column:	N/A	*Indexed:*	No
Present on:	Instances only	*See:*	Page 472

SI_SUBMITTERID			
Definition:	The InfoObject ID of the user who scheduled this instance		
Data type:	Integer		
Getter:	N/A	*Setter:*	N/A
Physical column:	N/A	*Indexed:*	No
Present on:	Instances only	*See:*	Page 472

Appendix C - Sample CMS Folder Hierarchy

The following tables contain the folder hierarchies from a sample BI4 system. Only objects of kind *Folder* are included, and not folder-like objects such as *FavoritesFolder* or *Inbox*. Objects in bold are root-level folders. Object IDs or CUIDs are provided for those that are pre-defined and are the same in every system. It is possible (likely) that there are other folders with IDs and CUIDs that are the same in every system. However, only those that are actually *documented* as predefined are listed here.

The folders that exist in a particular installation of SAP BusinessObjects are based on several factors, including the products that are installed and the features that are enabled (and, of course, the folders that are created in CMS or BI launch pad). Therefore, a different installation may have a different structure than the following.

CI_INFOOBJECTS

SI_NAME	SI_ID	SI_CUID
Categories	45	AaIf8uqN5AZAn7jke7q8ffw
Inboxes	48	AVmJiqdOvoRBoU1vQCZydFE
Internal Storage Folder		
Personal Categories	47	ATI2BcB9RGBFuBi5s1TwL7k
Root Folder	23	ASHnC0S_Pw5LhKFbZ.iA_j4
Auditing		
LCM		
Promotion Jobs		
Platform Search Scheduling		
Probes		
Report Conversion Tool		
Report Conversion Tool Documents		
Report Conversion Tool Audit Documents		
Report Conversion Tool Temporary Documents		
Samples		
System Configuration Wizard		
Visual Difference		
VisualDiff Comparator		
Web Intelligence Sample		
Temporary Storage	49	AcUD83fMJzRDqb5l9u92aAA
User Folders	18	AWigQI18AAZJoXfRHLzWJ2c

CI_APPOBJECTS

SI_NAME	SI_ID	SI_CUID
Application Folder		AdoctK9h1sBHp3I6uG0Sh7M
Administrative Tools		
BIVariants Folder		
Client Actions		AR1Zth00HO5Bp8N4HfboAYg
Permission_CMC_TabAccess_Configuration		
CrystalEnterprise.SolutionKits		
__SAPSEC_PUBLIC_INFO__		
Platform Search Root		
Data Search Data Access Providers		
Platform Search Content Extractors		
Platform Search Content Stores		
Platform Search Content Surrogates		
Platform Search Delta Index Folder		
Platform Search Index Engines		
Platform Search Queues		
Platform Search Search Agents		
Platform Search Service Session Objects		
Platform Search Special Queues		
Promotion Management Settings		
Promotion Override		
CCIS.DataConnection		
CommonConnection		
CrystalReport		
MetaData.DataConnection		
QaaWS		
Promotion Override Scans		
History		
QaaWS Folder		AcTDjF_lm8dElXVCUgHI2Ps
Root Folder 95	95	AXvZXmnw0m5FlCfZzIxMzBI
Connections		AZVXOgKIBEdOkiXzUuybja4
CommonConnections		AeREkNubrwVLhCTVNuIcrk8
Projects		
SecurityProfiles		

SI_NAME	SI_ID	SI_CUID
Universes		AWcPjwbDdBxPoXPBOUCsKkk
Report Conversion Tool Universes		
webi universes		
Root Folder 97	97	Ae2vMmNGW.JGhGacJCbvzno
Root Folder 98	98	Af70yrP9E5NPjrwxzuyZoaU
Dynamic Cascading Prompts		Aef.3x0HXzRAqt.urpVdmiI
Root Folder 99	99	AWItAeqx.FpBgqTpFH8LqwE
VisualDiff		
VMS Folder		

CI_SYSTEMOBJECTS

SI_NAME	SI_ID	SI_CUID
Alert Notifications		
Calendars	22	
Cryptographic Keys	65	ARtaDNN5dJNMhN84nfkyscc
Custom Dynamic Properties		
Custom Roles	57	AQxIJpjkbaRBrhcMvtnHAT4
Dependency Rules		
Deployment Files		
Events	21	
Crystal Reports Events		
Custom Events		
System Events		
Event Folder		
Indexes		
License Keys	24	
License Restrictions		
Logon Sessions	41	
Plugins	25	
Admin Plugins	28	
Auth Plugins	26	
Desktop Plugins	27	
Destination Plugins	29	

SI_NAME	SI_ID	SI_CUID
Meta Plugins		
Profiles	50	AR7QX6oTAqpLn1M6b8hsYjM
Relationships		
Remote Connections		AVwSekNrtFxGqJ6Jp2rLwrI
Replication Lists		ASOr8wap3MJOgdWV5HLcZ1M
SAML Service Providers		
SecurityTokens	58	Ad5.8vflzphPiTJaXLjj5Qg
Server Intelligence	62	
Enterprise Nodes	59	
Installs	53	AfU5Q80d399NiOBp7v1TdQk
Server Groups	17	
Server Intelligence Resources	63	
Servers	16	
Service Categories	61	AflTiDQu6zBCsSHzVHFAnQY
Service Containers	55	AUqIth9qbA9AmPDPV1crYCU
Services	52	AYHAA_QSVttBrtqoWXCsDso
System Resources		AXixtdKpAlJOhiL1A.BviEA
Tenants		AcyEtdI_1RxKp5AHSjavFCU
Tokens		
User Groups	20	AW7cVzZFpgFGjOVUdCiOpfE
Users	19	AXhmigik4CBKra9ZYzR2ezE

The following table contains folders that have predefined IDs, CUIDs, or both. The IDs/CUIDs are defined in two Java classes, `com.crystaldecisions.sdk.occa.infostore.CeSecurityID.Folder` and `com.crystaldecisions.sdk.occa.infostore.CeSecurityCUID.RootFolder` (respectively). The table below contains the specific (`static final`) properties within these tables and their values.

How to use this table: the folder with name *Root Folder* below is the parent of all Public Folders. Its predefined object ID property is named ROOT, and its value (23) can be retrieved with the property `com.crystaldecisions.sdk.occa.infostore.CeSecurityID.Folder.ROOT`. Similarly, its predefined CUID property is named FOLDERS, and can be retrieved via `com.crystaldecisions.sdk.occa.infostore.CeSecurityCUID.FOLDERS`.

Folder Name	ID Property / Value	CUID Property / Value
Application Folder		APPLICATIONS AdoctK9h1sBHp3I6uG0Sh7M

Folder Name	ID Property / Value	CUID Property / Value
Client Actions		CLIENTACTIONS AR1Zth00HO5Bp8N4HfboAYg
QaaWS Folder		QAAWS AcTDjF_lm8dElXVCUgHI2Ps
Root Folder 95	SEMANTIC_LAYERS 95	SEMANTIC_LAYERS AXvZXmnw0m5FlCfZzIxMzBI
Connections		CONNECTIONS AZVXOgKIBEdOkiXzUuybja4
CommonConnections		COMMON_CONNECTIONS AeREkNubrwVLhCTVNuIcrk8
Universes		UNIVERSES AWcPjwbDdBxPoXPBOUCsKkk
Root Folder 97	97	COLLABORATIONS Ae2vMmNGW.JGhGacJCbvzno
Root Folder 98	98	REPOSITORIES Af70yrP9E5NPjrwxzuyZoaU
Dynamic Cascading Prompts		LOVS Aef.3x0HXzRAqt.urpVdmiI
Root Folder 99	APPLICATIONS 99	APPLICATION_CONFIGS AWItAeqx.FpBgqTpFH8LqwE
Calendars	CALENDARS 22	
Categories	CORPORATE_CATEGORIES 45	CATEGORIES AaIf8uqN5AZAn7jke7q8ffw
Cryptographic Keys	CRYPTOGRAPHIC_KEYS 65	CRYPTOGRAPHIC_KEYS ARtaDNN5dJNMhN84nfkyscc
Custom Roles	CUSTOMROLES 57	CUSTOMROLES AQxIJpjkbaRBrhcMvtnHAT4
Events	EVENTS 21	
Inboxes	INBOXES 48	INBOXES AVmJiqdOvoRBoU1vQCZydFE
License Keys	LICENSES 24	
Logon Sessions	CONNECTIONS 41	
Personal Categories	PERSONAL_CATEGORIES 47	PERSONAL_CATEGORIES ATI2BcB9RGBFuBi5s1TwL7k
Plugins	PLUGINS 25	
Admin Plugins	ADMININSTRATION_PLUGINS 28	
Auth Plugins	AUTHENTICATION_PLUGINS 26	

Folder Name	ID Property / Value	CUID Property / Value
Desktop Plugins	DESKTOP_PLUGINS 27	
Destination Plugins	DESTINATION_PLUGINS 29	
Profiles	PROFILES 50	PROFILES AR7QX6oTAqpLn1M6b8hsYjM
Remote Connections		REMOTECLUSTERS AVwSekNrtFxGqJ6Jp2rLwrI
Replication Lists		MANIFESTS ASOr8wap3MJOgdWV5HLcZ1M
Root Folder	ROOT 23	FOLDERS ASHnC0S_Pw5LhKFbZ.iA_j4
SecurityTokens	SECURITYTOKENS 58	SECURITYTOKENS Ad5.8vflzphPiTJaXLjj5Qg
Server Intelligence	SERVERINTELLIGENCE 62	
Enterprise Nodes	ENTERPRISENODES 59	
Installs	INSTALLS 53	INSTALLS AfU5Q8Od399NiOBp7v1TdQk
Server Groups	SERVER_GROUPS 17	
Server Intelligence Resources	SERVERINTELLIGENCE_RESOU RCES 63	
Servers	SERVERS 16	
Service Categories	SERVICECATEGORIES 61	SERVICECATEGORIES AflTiDQu6zBCsSHzVHFAnQY
Service Containers	SERVICECONTAINERS 55	SERVICECONTAINERS AUqIth9qbA9AmPDPV1crYCU
Services	SERVICES 52	SERVICES AYHAA_QSVttBrtqoWXCsDso
System Resources		CUSTOM_MAPPED_ATTRIBUTES AXixtdKpAlJOhiL1A.BviEA
Temporary Storage	TEMPORARY_STORAGE_FOLDER S 49	TEMPORARY_STORAGE_FOLDERS AcUD83fMJzRDqb5l9u92aAA
Tenants		TENANTS AcyEtdI_1RxKp5AHSjavFCU
Tokens		
User Folders	FAVORITE_FOLDERS 18	FAVOURITE_FOLDERS AWigQI18AAZJoXfRHLzWJ2c
User Groups	USER_GROUPS 20	USER_GROUPS AW7cVzZFpgFGjOVUdCiOpfE

Folder Name	ID Property / Value	CUID Property / Value
Users	USERS 19	USERS AXhmigik4CBKra9ZYzR2ezE

Appendix D - Relationship Types

The following table contains details for the most commonly-used relationship types. For each type, the implicit condition and relationship property is provided for both parent and child (where applicable).

The *Referring* property for the parent reflects the property of the parent object that contains a reference to the children. In the first block below (*CrystalReport-BusinessView*), the SI_BUSINESSVIEWS property is present on *Crystal Report* objects and contains a list of the associated *Business Views*.

CrystalReport-BusinessView	
Parent	
Condition:	SI_KIND IN ('CrystalReport', 'MetaData.MetaDataRepositoryInfo')
Referring property:	SI_BUSINESSVIEWS
Child	
Condition:	SI_KIND = 'MetaData.BusinessView'
Referring property:	SI_REPORTS

CustomRole-Object	Include access levels set on selected objects
Parent	
Condition:	SI_KIND = 'CustomRole'
Referring property:	
Child	
Condition:	
Referring property:	SI_ROLES_ON_OBJECT

DataConnection-Universe	Include connections used by selected universes
Parent	
Condition:	SI_KIND = 'CCIS.DataConnection'
Referring property:	SI_CONNUNIVERSE
Child	
Condition:	SI_KIND = 'Universe'
Referring property:	SI_DATACONNECTION

Document-DSL.Universe	
Parent	
Condition:	SI_KIND IN ('Webi', 'PDF', 'Excel', 'CrystalReport', 'XL.Query')
Referring property:	SI_DSL_UNIVERSE
Child	
Condition:	SI_SPECIFIC_KIND = 'DSL.Universe'
Referring property:	SI_SL_DOCUMENTS

Document-Excel	
Parent	
Condition:	SI_KIND IN ('Webi')
Referring property:	SI_EXCEL_OF_DOCUMENT
Child	
Condition:	SI_SPECIFIC_KIND = 'Excel'
Referring property:	SI_DOCUMENTS_OF_EXCEL

Document-Txt	
Parent	
Condition:	SI_KIND IN ('Webi')
Referring property:	SI_TXT_OF_DOCUMENT
Child	
Condition:	SI_SPECIFIC_KIND IN ('Txt', 'Excel')
Referring property:	SI_DOCUMENTS_OF_TXT

DSL.Universe-SecuredConnections	
Parent	
Condition:	`SI_SPECIFIC_KIND = 'DSL.Universe'`
Referring property:	`SI_SL_UNIVERSE_TO_CONNECTIONS`
Child	
Condition:	`SI_KIND in ('MetaData.DataConnection','CCIS.DataConnection','CommonConnection','DataFederator.DataSource')`
Referring property:	

RelationalConnection-CrystalReport	
Parent	
Condition:	`SI_KIND = 'CrystalReport'`
Referring property:	`SI_RELATIONAL_CONNECTION`
Child	
Condition:	`SI_KIND = 'CCIS.DataConnection'`
Referring property:	`SI_REPORT`

ServerGroup-Server	
Parent	
Condition:	`SI_KIND = 'ServerGroup'`
Referring property:	`SI_SERVERS`
Child	
Condition (Member):	`SI_KIND = 'Server'`
Condition (Group):	`SI_KIND = 'ServerGroup'`
Referring property:	`SI_SERVERGROUPS`

Service-Server	
Parent	
Condition:	SI_KIND = 'Service'
Referring property:	SI_SERVICE_HOSTS
Child	
Condition:	SI_KIND = 'Server'
Referring property:	SI_HOSTED_SERVICES

Universe(Core)-DSL.Universe	
Parent	
Condition:	SI_SPECIFIC_KIND = 'DSL.Universe'
Referring property:	SI_DSL_DERIVEDUNIVERSE
Child	
Condition:	SI_SPECIFIC_KIND = 'DSL.Universe'
Referring property:	SI_DSL_COREUNIVERSE

User-Favorites	Include personal folders for selected users
Parent	
Condition:	SI_KIND = 'User'
Referring property:	SI_FAVORITES_FOLDER
Child	
Condition:	SI_KIND = 'FavoritesFolder'
Referring property:	SI_FAVORITES_USER

User-Inbox	Include inboxes for selected users
Parent	
Condition:	SI_KIND = 'User'
Referring property:	SI_INBOX
Child	
Condition:	SI_KIND = 'Inbox'
Referring property:	SI_INBOX_USER

User-PersonalCategory	Include personal categories for selected users
Parent	
Condition:	SI_KIND = 'User'
Referring property:	SI_PERSONALCATEGORY
Child	
Condition:	SI_KIND = 'PersonalCategory'
Referring property:	SI_PERSONALCATEGORY_USER

User-RecycleBin	
Parent	
Condition:	SI_KIND = 'User'
Referring property:	SI_RECYCLEBIN_FOLDER
Child	
Condition:	SI_KIND = 'Folder' AND SI_PARENT_CUID='AQbJ_w80vzFKoHvId1bZRIQ'
Referring property:	SI_RECYCLEBIN_USER

UserGroup-User	Include members of selected user groups
Parent	
Condition:	SI_KIND = 'UserGroup'
Referring property:	SI_REL_GROUP_MEMBERS
Child	
Condition (Member):	SI_KIND = 'User'
Condition (Group):	SI_KIND = 'UserGroup'
Referring property:	SI_REL_USERGROUPS

Webi-Universe		Include universes for selected reports
Parent		
Condition:		SI_KIND IN ('Webi', 'PDF', 'Excel','FullClient', 'CrystalReport', 'Txt', 'Rtf', 'Word', 'Agnostic')
Referring property:		SI_UNIVERSE
Child		
Condition:		SI_KIND = 'Universe'
Referring property:		SI_WEBI

WebiFHSQL-DataConnection		
Parent		
Condition:		SI_KIND = 'Webi'
Referring property:		SI_FHSQL_RELATIONAL_CONNECTION
Child		
Condition:		SI_KIND = 'CCIS.DataConnection'
Referring property:		SI_FHSQL_WEBI_DOCUMENT

List of all relationship types:

ActionSet-Action	DFS.ConnectorConfiguration
ActionUsage-Action	DefaultObject-Application
AlertNotification-User	Document-BIVariant
Application-Action	Document-DSL.Universe
Application-DependencyRule	Document-Excel
Application-Relationship	Document-Follower
Category-Document	Document-PersistenceQuery
CommonConnection-AOPresentation	Document-Txt
CommonConnection-AOWorkbook	Document-UnFollower
CommonConnection-Document	Document.discussion
CommonConnection-MDAnalysis	Documents-SharedElements
CommonConnection-pQuery	DSL.DataSecurityProfile-SecuredConnections
Container-ActionUsage	DSL.SecurityProfile-Principal
CrystalReport-BusinessView	DSL.Universe-BusinessSecurityOptions
CustomRole-Object	DSL.Universe-BusinessSecurityProfile
DataConnection-Universe	DSL.Universe-DataSecurityOptions
DataFederator.DataSource-	DSL.Universe-DataSecurityProfile

```
DSL.Universe-SecuredConnections            Server-MON.ManagedEntityStatus

EnterpriseData-Flash                       ServerGroup-MON.ManagedEntityStatus

EnterpriseNode-MON.ManagedEntityStatus     ServerGroup-Server

EnterpriseNode-Server                      Service-Server

Event-AlertNotification                    Service-ServiceContainer

Event-Principal                            Service-ServiceDep

Event-Principal-Exclusion                  ServiceCategory-MON.ManagedEntityStatus

EventSource-AlertNotification              ServiceCategory-Service

EventSource-Event                          ServiceContainer-Server

Folder Hierarchy                           ServiceUsedBy-Service

Folder-MON.ManagedEntityStatus             Sets-DSL.Universe

InfoObject-Shortcuts                       SharedElement-DataSource

Install-EnterpriseNode                     TaskTemplate-Scenario

Install-Service                            TaskTemplate-WorkflowTemplate

Install-ServiceContainer                   Tenant-ServerGroup

Landscape-Scenario                         Universe-UserGroup

Lock                                       Universe(Core)-DSL.Universe

Manifest-ReplicableObject                  Universe(Core)-Universe

MON.ManagedEntityStatus-MON.MonitoringEventUpgradeManagementTool-LogicalGroup

MON.ManagedEntityStatus-MON.Subscription   UpgradeManagementTool-Plugin

PlatformSearchContainer-                   User-BIVariant
PlatformSearchObject
                                           User-CommonConnection
Plugin-Action
                                           User-Favorites
Profile-Principal
                                           User-FavouriteMEStatus
Publication-ExcludedPrincipal
                                           User-Inbox
Publication-FC
                                           User-MON.ManagedEntityStatus
Publication-Principal
                                           User-MON.Subscription
Publication-PrincipalReRun
                                           User-PersonalCategory
Publication-Profile
                                           User-RecycleBin
PublicationArtifacts-SourceDoc
                                           User-VisualDiffComparator
PublicationScopeBatch-Artifact
                                           UserGroup-Folder
PublicationScopeBatchDoc-Artifact
                                           UserGroup-User
QAAWS-WEBI
                                           Webi-Universe
ReferringDoc-SharedDoc
                                           WebiFHSQL-DataConnection
RelationalConnection-CrystalReport
                                           XL.XcelsiusEnterprise-DataSource
Relationship-Application
                                           XL.XcelsiusEnterprise-XL.Query
RemoteCluster-ConflictingObjects
```

Appendix E - Interface / Kind Mapping Tables

Interface / Kind / Specific Kind Mapping Table

The following table lists, for each IInfoObject subinterface, its associated *Kind* and *Specific Kind* property values.

The properties are **static** properties of the interfaces. To retrieve the kind value of the IAdminTool interface, use:

IAdminTool.KIND

Interface	KIND	SPECIFIC_KIND
IAdminTool	AdminTool	–
IAgnostic	Agnostic	–
IAlertingApp	AlertingApp	–
IAlertNotification	AlertNotification	–
IAuditEventInfo	AuditEventInfo2	–
ICalendar	Calendar	–
ICategory**	**	–
IConnection	Connection	–
ICryptographicKey	CryptographicKey	–
ICustomMappedAttribute	CustomMappedAttribute	–
ICustomRole	CustomRole	–
IDeploymentFile	DeploymentFile	–
IDiskUnmanaged	DiskUnmanaged	–
IEnterpriseNode	EnterpriseNode	–
IEvent	Event	–
IExcel	Excel	–
IFileEvent	Event	FileEvent
IFolder**	**	–
IFTP	Ftp	–
IHotBackup	HotBackup	–
IHyperlink	Hyperlink	–
IInbox	Inbox	–
IInstall	Install	–
ILicenseKey	LicenseKey	–
IManaged	Managed	–

Interface	KIND	SPECIFIC_KIND
IManifest	Manifest	-
IMetricDescriptions	MetricDescriptions	-
INotificationEvent	Event	NotificationEvent
INotificationSchedule*	NotificationSchedule*	NotificationSchedule*
IObjectPackage	ObjectPackage	-
IOverload	Overload	-
IPDF	Pdf	-
IPowerPoint	Powerpoint	-
IProfile	Profile	-
IProgramPlugin	Program	-
IPublication	Publication	-
IRemoteCluster	RemoteCluster	-
IReplication	Replication	-
IReport	CrystalReport	-
IRestWebService	RestWebService	-
IRTF	Rtf	-
ISAMLServiceProvider	SAMLServiceProvider	-
IScheduleEvent	Event	ScheduleEvent
IScopeBatch	ScopeBatch	-
IsecEnterprise	secEnterprise	-
IsecLDAP	secLDAP	-
IsecSAPR3	secSAPR3	-
IsecWinAD	-	-
IServer	Server	-
IServerGroup	ServerGroup	-
IService	Service	-
IServiceContainer	ServiceContainer	-
ISFTP	Sftp	-
IShortcut	Shortcut	-
ISMTP	Smtp	-
IStreamWork	StreamWork	-
IStreamWorkIntegration	StreamWorkIntegration	-
ITenant	Tenant	-
ITxt	Txt	
IUser	User	-
IUserEvent	Event	UserEvent

Interface	KIND	SPECIFIC_KIND
IUserGroup	UserGroup	-

*The INotificationSchedule interface includes a SPECIFIC_KIND property but no KIND property, even though it is not a "specific kind" of another interface.

The IFolder and ICategory interfaces are special since IFolder is associated with **two different InfoObject kinds: *Folder* and *FavoritesFolder*, and, similarly, ICategory is associated with *Category* and *PersonalCategory*. These two interfaces do not have KIND/PROGID properties, but instead have the following values:

In IFolder:

Property name	Property value
FOLDER_KIND	Folder
FOLDER_PROGID	CrystalEnterprise.Folder
FAVORITESFOLDER_KIND	FavoritesFolder
FAVORITESFOLDER_PROGID	CrystalEnterprise.FavoritesFolder

In ICategory:

Property name	Property value
CATEGORY_KIND	Category
CATEGORY_PROGID	CrystalEnterprise.Category
PERSONALCATEGORY_KIND:	PersonalCategory
PERSONALCATEGORY_PROGID:	CrystalEnterprise.PersonalCategory

Note that these are static values that are used for retrieving the SI_KIND/SI_SPECIFIC_KIND strings associated with an IInfoObject subinterface, and do not necessarily reflect that actual value associated with an instance of IInfoObject. That is, if an IFolder object is extracted from an IInfoObjects collection, its FOLDER_KIND value is static and will therefore always be "Folder", even if the IFolder is actually a Favorites Folder. In this case, calling getKind() returns *FavoritesFolder*.

Prior to BI4, the static values for *Kind* and *ProgID* were stored in two classes, CeKind and CeProgID (respectively), rather than in each IInfoObject subinterface. They did not provide an association between the Kind/ProgID values and IInfoObject subinterfaces, but were rather just a list of the available Kind and ProgID names. The CeKind / CeProgID classes are deprecated in BI4, but are still present in the SDK and are commonly seen in legacy SDK programs.

The following tables list the properties of the deprecated CeKind and CeProgID classes, the property values, and the associated property names in BI4. Note that many of the CeKind and CeProgID properties are not represented in the BI4 IInfoObject subinterfaces as KIND or PROGID. This is because some kinds no longer exist in BI4, and also not all kinds have a dedicated IInfoObject subinterface.

These tables can be used to identify the IInfoObject subinterface associated with a particular kind or progid from CeKind / CeProgID.

CeKind Mapping Table

CeKind Property Name	Property Value	BI4 Property Name
AFDASHBOARDPAGE	AFDashboardPage	—
AGNOSTIC	Agnostic	IAgnostic.KIND
ANALYSIS	Analysis	—
ANALYTIC	Analytic	—
APPFOUNDATION	AppFoundation	—
AUDITEVENTINFO	AuditEventInfo	—
AUDITEVENTINFO2	AuditEventInfo2	IAuditEventInfo.KIND
CALENDAR	Calendar	ICalendar.KIND
CATEGORY	Category	ICategory.CATEGORY_KIND
CLIENTACTION	ClientAction	—
CLIENTACTIONSET	ClientActionSet	—
CLIENTACTIONUSAGE	ClientActionUsage	—
CMC	CMC	—
COMMONCONNECTION	CommonConnection	—
CONNECTION	Connection	IConnection.KIND
CRYSTAL_REPORT	CrystalReport	IReport.KIND
CUSTOMROLE	CustomRole	ICustomRole.KIND
DATACONNECTION	MetaData.DataConnection	—
DELTASTORE	DeltaStore	—
DESIGNER	Designer	—
DESTINATION	Destination	—
DISCUSSIONS	Discussions	—
DISKUNMANAGED	DiskUnmanaged	IDiskUnmanaged.KIND
DSWSAPPCONF	DSWSAppConf	—
ENCYCLOPEDIA	Encyclopedia	—
ENTERPRISENODE	EnterpriseNode	IEnterpriseNode.KIND
EVENT	Event	IEvent.KIND
EXCEL	Excel	IExcel.KIND
FAVORITESF	FavoritesFolder	IFolder.FAVORITESFOLDER_KIND
FEDERATION	Federation	—
FLASH	Flash	—

CeKind Property Name	Property Value	BI4 Property Name
FOLDER	Folder	IFolder.FOLDER_KIND
FTP	Ftp	IFTP.KIND
FullClient	FullClient	-
FullClientAddin	FullClientAddin	-
FullClientTemplate	FullClientTemplate	-
HYPERLINK	Hyperlink	IHyperlink.KIND
INBOX	Inbox	IInbox.KIND
INFOVIEW	InfoView	-
INSTALL	Install	IInstall.KIND
LICENSEKEY	LicenseKey	ILicenseKey.KIND
MANAGED_DEST	Managed	IManaged.KIND
MANIFEST	Manifest	IManifest.KIND
MDANALYSIS	MDAnalysis	-
MESSAGE	Message	-
MYINFOVIEW	MyInfoView	-
OBJECTPACKAGE	ObjectPackage	IObjectPackage.KIND
OVERLOAD	Overload	IOverload.KIND
PDF	Pdf	IPDF.KIND
PERSONALCAT	PersonalCategory	ICategory.PERSONALCATEGORY_KIND
POWERPOINT	Powerpoint	IPowerPoint.KIND
PROFILE	Profile	IProfile.KIND
PROGRAM	Program	IProgramPlugin.KIND
PUBLICATION	Publication	IPublication.KIND
QAAWS	QaaWS	-
REMOTECLUSTER	RemoteCluster	IRemoteCluster.KIND
REPLICATION	Replication	IReplication.KIND
REPORTCONVTOOL	ReportConvTool	-
RTF	Rtf	IRTF.KIND
SAMLASSERTION	SAMLAssertion	-
SCOPEBATCH	ScopeBatch	IScopeBatch.KIND
SEC_ENTERPRISE	secEnterprise	IsecEnterprise.KIND
SEC_LDAP	secLDAP	IsecLDAP.KIND
SEC_WINAD	secWinAD	-
SEC_WINDOWSNT	secWindowsNT	-
SERVER	Server	IServer.KIND
SERVERGROUP	ServerGroup	IServerGroup.KIND

CeKind Property Name	Property Value	BI4 Property Name
SERVICE	Service	IService.KIND
SERVICECATEGORY	ServiceCategory	–
SERVICECONTAINER	ServiceContainer	IServiceContainer.KIND
SESSIONTOKEN	SessionToken	–
SFTP	Sftp	ISFTP.KIND
SHORTCUT	Shortcut	IShortcut.KIND
SMTP	Smtp	ISMTP.KIND
STRATEGY_BUILDER	StrategyBuilder	–
TEXT	Txt	ITxt.KIND
UNIVERSE	Universe	–
USER	User	IUser.KIND
USERGROUP	UserGroup	IUserGroup.KIND
WEBI	Webi	IWebi.KIND
WEBINTELLIGENCE	WebIntelligence	–
WORD	Word	IWord.KIND
WSCONVERSATIONCONFIG	WSConversationConfig	–
WSSAMLTOKENISSUERCONFIG	WSSAMLTokenIssuerConfig	–
WSSCTTOKENISSUERCONFIG	WSSCTTokenIssuerConfig	–
WSSECURITYCONFIG	WSSecurityConfig	–
WSSERVICECONFIG	WSServiceConfig	–
WSSTSDISPATCHCONFIG	WSSTSDispatchConfig	–
X509KEYBINDING	X509KeyBinding	–
XCELSIUS	Xcelsius	–
XCELSIUSDMTEMPLATE	XCelsiusDMTemplate	–

CeProgID Mapping Table

CeProgID Property Name	Property Value	BI4 Property Name
AFDASHBOARDPAGE	CrystalEnterprise.AFDashboardPage	–
AGNOSTIC	CrystalEnterprise.Agnostic	IAgnostic.PROGID
ANALYSIS	CrystalEnterprise.Analysis	–
ANALYTIC	CrystalEnterprise.Analytic	–
APPFOUNDATION	CrystalEnterprise.AppFoundation	–
AUDITEVENTINFO	CrystalEnterprise.AuditEventInfo	–

CeProgID Property Name	Property Value	BI4 Property Name
AUDITEVENTINFO2	CrystalEnterprise.AuditEventInfo2	IAuditEventInfo.PROGID
CALENDAR	CrystalEnterprise.Calendar	ICalendar.PROGID
CATEGORY	CrystalEnterprise.Category	ICategory.CATEGORY_PROGID
CLIENTACTION	CrystalEnterprise.ClientAction	-
CLIENTACTIONSET	CrystalEnterprise.ClientActionSet	-
CLIENTACTIONUSAGE	CrystalEnterprise.ClientActionUsage	-
COMMONCONNECTION	CrystalEnterprise.CommonConnection	-
CONNECTION	CrystalEnterprise.Connection	IConnection.PROGID
CUSTOMROLE	CrystalEnterprise.CustomRole	ICustomRole.PROGID
DATACONNECTION	CrystalEnterprise.MetaData.DataConnection	-
DELTASTORE	CrystalEnterprise.DeltaStore	-
DESIGNER	CrystalEnterprise.Designer	-
DESTINATION	CrystalEnterprise.Destination	-
DISKUNMANAGED	CrystalEnterprise.DiskUnmanaged	IDiskUnmanaged.PROGID
DSWSAPPCONF	CrystalEnterprise.DSWSAppConf	-
ENCYCLOPEDIA	CrystalEnterprise.Encyclopedia	-
ENTERPRISENODE	CrystalEnterprise.EnterpriseNode	IEnterpriseNode.PROGID
EPORTFOLIO	CrystalEnterprise.ePortfolio	-
EVENT	CrystalEnterprise.Event	IEvent.PROGID
EXCEL	CrystalEnterprise.Excel	IExcel.PROGID
FAVORITESF	CrystalEnterprise.FavoritesFolder	IFolder.FAVORITESFOLDER_PROGID
FEDERATION	CrystalEnterprise.Federation	-
FLASH	CrystalEnterprise.Flash	-
FOLDER	CrystalEnterprise.Folder	IFolder.FOLDER_PROGID
FTP	CrystalEnterprise.Ftp	IFTP.PROGID
FullClient	CrystalEnterprise.FullClient	-
FullClientAddin	CrystalEnterprise.FullClientAddin	-
FullClientTemplate	CrystalEnterprise.FullClientTemplate	-
HYPERLINK	CrystalEnterprise.Hyperlink	IHyperlink.PROGID
INBOX	CrystalEnterprise.Inbox	IInbox.PROGID
INFOVIEW	CrystalEnterprise.InfoView	-
INSTALL	CrystalEnterprise.Install	IInstall.PROGID
JAVASCHEDULING	CrystalEnterprise.JavaScheduling	-

CeProgID Property Name	Property Value	BI4 Property Name
LICENSEKEY	CrystalEnterprise.LicenseKey	ILicenseKey.PROGID
MANAGED_DEST	CrystalEnterprise.Managed	IManaged.PROGID
MANIFEST	CrystalEnterprise.Manifest	IManifest.PROGID
MDANALYSIS	CrystalEnterprise.MDAnalysis	–
MESSAGE	CrystalEnterprise.Message	–
MYINFOVIEW	CrystalEnterprise.MyInfoView	–
OBJECTPACKAGE	CrystalEnterprise.ObjectPackage	IObjectPackage.PROGID
OVERLOAD	CrystalEnterprise.Overload	–
PDF	CrystalEnterprise.Pdf	IPDF.PROGID
PERSONALCAT	CrystalEnterprise.PersonalCategory	ICategory.PERSONALCATEGORY_ PROGID
POWERPOINT	CrystalEnterprise.Powerpoint	IPowerPoint.PROGID
PRINT	CrystalEnterprise.print	–
PROFILE	CrystalEnterprise.Profile	IProfile.PROGID
PROGRAM	CrystalEnterprise.Program	IProgramPlugin.PROGID
PUBLICATION	CrystalEnterprise.Publication	IPublication.PROGID
QAAWS	CrystalEnterprise.QaaWS	–
REMOTECLUSTER	CrystalEnterprise.RemoteCluster	IRemoteCluster.PROGID
REPLICATION	CrystalEnterprise.Replication	IReplication.PROGID
REPORT	CrystalEnterprise.Report	IReport.PROGID
REPORTCONVTOOL	CrystalEnterprise.ReportConvTool	–
RTF	CrystalEnterprise.Rtf	IRTF.PROGID
SAMLASSERTION	CrystalEnterprise.SAMLAssertion	–
SB_SEC_INTELLIGENCE_ MANAGEMENT	CrystalEnterprise.SBIntelligenceMa nagement	–
SB_SEC_PERFORMANCE_M ANAGEMENT	CrystalEnterprise.SBPerformanceMan agement	–
SB_SEC_STRATEGY_BUIL DER	CrystalEnterprise.SBStrategyBuilde r	–
SCOPEBATCH	CrystalEnterprise.ScopeBatch	IScopeBatch.PROGID
SEC_ENTERPRISE	secEnterprise	IsecEnterprise.PROGID
SEC_LDAP	secLDAP	IsecLDAP.PROGID
SEC_WINAD	secWinAD	IsecWinAD.PROGID
SERVER	CrystalEnterprise.Server	IServer.PROGID
SERVERGROUP	CrystalEnterprise.ServerGroup	IServerGroup.PROGID
SERVICE	CrystalEnterprise.Service	IService.PROGID
SERVICECATEGORY	CrystalEnterprise.ServiceCategory	–

CeProgID Property Name	Property Value	BI4 Property Name
SERVICECONTAINER	CrystalEnterprise.ServiceContainer	IServiceContainer.PROGID
SESSIONTOKEN	CrystalEnterprise.SessionToken	-
SFTP	CrystalEnterprise.Sftp	ISFTP.PROGID
SHORTCUT	CrystalEnterprise.Shortcut	IShortcut.PROGID
SMTP	CrystalEnterprise.Smtp	ISMTP.PROGID
STRATEGY_BUILDER	CrystalEnterprise.StrategyBuilder	-
TEXT	CrystalEnterprise.Txt	ITxt.PROGID
UNIVERSE	CrystalEnterprise.Universe	-
USER	CrystalEnterprise.User	IUser.PROGID
USERGROUP	CrystalEnterprise.UserGroup	IUserGroup.PROGID
WEBI	CrystalEnterprise.Webi	IWebi.PROGID
WEBI_SEC_ADMINISTRATION	CrystalEnterprise.WebiAdministration	-
WEBI_SEC_ANALYSIS	CrystalEnterprise.WebiAnalysis	-
WEBI_SEC_INFO_VIEW	CrystalEnterprise.WebiInfoView	-
WEBI_SEC_PUBLICATIONS	CrystalEnterprise.WebiPublications	-
WEBI_SEC_QUERY_WEB_PANEL	CrystalEnterprise.WebiQueryWebPanel	-
WEBINTELLIGENCE	CrystalEnterprise.WebIntelligence	-
WORD	CrystalEnterprise.Word	IWord.PROGID
WSCONVERSATIONCONFIG	CrystalEnterprise.WSConversationConfig	-
WSSAMLTOKENISSUERCONFIG	CrystalEnterprise.WSSAMLTokenIssuerConfig	-
WSSCTTOKENISSUERCONFIG	CrystalEnterprise.WSSCTTokenIssuerConfig	-
WSSECURITYCONFIG	CrystalEnterprise.WSSecurityConfig	-
WSSERVICECONFIG	CrystalEnterprise.WSServiceConfig	-
WSSTSDISPATCHCONFIG	CrystalEnterprise.WSSTSDispatchConfig	-
X509KEYBINDING	CrystalEnterprise.X509KeyBinding	-
XCELSIUS	CrystalEnterprise.Xcelsius	-

Appendix F - Quiz Answers

Chapter 1

1. c
2. a
3. b
4. a,b,c
5. False
6. False
7. c

Chapter 2

1. d
2. True
3. b
4. a
5. b
6. d
7. d
8. True
9. b

Chapter 3

1. d
2. False
3. c
4. c
5. False

Chapter 4

1. a

2. f
3. False
4. True
5. b
6. c

Chapter 5

1. cuid, search, path, query
2. True
3. b
4. b
5. a
6. False

Chapter 6

1. d
2. a
3. True
4. a

Chapter 7

1. False
2. d
3. a
4. a
5. a
6. c

7. If an InfoObject has been deleted from the CMS, it will not be present in the CMS repository, but may still have data in audit. The outer join ensures that all audit data is returned, even if the InfoObject was deleted.

Chapter 10

1. c
2. a

Chapter 11

1. False
2. False (in general this is true but not in every case)
3. d
4. b
5. d
6. a

Chapter 12

1. b
2. b and c
3. d
4. a and b
5. False
6. b

Chapter 13

1. False
2. True
3. b, c, d
4. c

5. b

Chapter 14

1. a
2. a
3. True
4. a
5. c
6. c
7. b

Chapter 15

1. a
2. b
3. b
4. a

Chapter 16

1. a
2. d
3. False
4. a
5. b
6. b, c, d, e
7. False
8. b

Chapter 17

1. b or d
2. d
3. False
4. b

5. d   2. c

6. c   3. False

7. e   4. b

                                   5. True

Chapter 18   6. a

1. a   7. a

Acknowledgments

Ken Burke, for first suggesting a book on BusinessObjects

Document created with LibreOffice

Railroad diagram generator: http://wiki.tcl.tk/21708

Cover image: Beaver Dam Mountains, by Chris M Morris: https://flic.kr/p/dDV6RY licensed under CC BY 2.0 (https://creativecommons.org/licenses/by/2.0/)

Index

W

Class/Interface References

Program Listings

www.ingramcontent.com/pod-product-compliance
Lightning Source LLC
Chambersburg PA
CBHW060633060326
40690CB00020B/4387